SOCIOLOGY
Third Edition

David B. Brinkerhoff
Lynn K. White
University of Nebraska-Lincoln

WEST PUBLISHING COMPANY
St. Paul   New York   Los Angeles   San Francisco

COPY EDITOR: Nancy Palmer Jones
ILLUSTRATIONS: John and Jean Foster
COMPOSITION: Parkwood Composition Service
COVER ART: painting by Ted Katz

Library of Congress Cataloging-in-Publication Data

Brinkerhoff, David B.
    Sociology / David B. Brinkerhoff, Lynn K. White.--3rd ed.
        p.   cm.
    Includes bibliographical references and index.
    ISBN 0-314-74128-3
    1. Sociology.   I. White, Lynn K.   II. Title.
    HM51.B8535   1991
    301--dc20

90-43805

∞ CIP

Acknowledgments

Table 13.2 and quotations on page 352. Greenblat, C. S., "The salience of sexuality in the early years of marriage," JMF May 1983. Copyright © 1983 by the National Council on Family Relations, 1910 West County Road B Suite 147, St. Paul, Minnesota 55113. Reprinted by permission.

Page 615. Population Crisis Committee. Reprinted with permission.

Figures 20.1 and 20.2. Reprinted from "The nature of cities" by Chauncy D. Harris and Edward L. Ullman in volume no. 242 of The Annals of the American Association of Political and Social Science. Copyright © 1945. All rights reserved. Permission also granted from C. D. Harris.

Figure 16.1. Graph adapted from Graham T. T. Molitor. 1981. The Futurist. With permission from Public Policy Forecasting, 9208 Wooden Bridge Road, Potomac, Maryland 20854.

Photocredits

2 Arthur Grace, Stock, Boston; 5 Comstock; 6 Brown Brothers; 7 Brown Brothers; 9 (top) The Bettmann Archive, 9 (bottom) Brown Brothers; 10 Mike Maple, Woodfin Camp & Associates; 11 (top) The Bettmann Archive; 11 (bottom) Ed Kashi; 12 The Granger Collection; 14 Bob Daemmrich, Stock, Boston; 16 Donald Dietz, Stock, Boston; 19 Ed Kashi; 23 Comstock; 26 Rick Smolan, Stock, Boston; 30 Sipa; 32 Ed Kashi; 35 Owen Franken, Stock, Boston; 41 Ed Kashi; 43 Phil Huber, Black Star; 46 Ed Kashi; 48 A/P Worldwide Photos; 51 Cartoon reprinted by special permission of North American Syndicate; 54 James Kamp, Black Star; 56 Rick Geenbaum, from the Norma Bradley Allen Collection; 58 (left) Charles D. Winters, Stock, Boston; 58 (right) Martin Rogers, Stock, Boston; 62 Victor Englebert, Black Star; 63 "The Far Side" cartoon by Gary Larson is reprinted by permission of Chronicle Features, San Francisco, CA; 65 (left) Martha Cooper, Peter Arnold, Inc.; 65 (right) EKM-Nepenthe; 66 Ed Kashi; 72 Peter Turnley, Black Star; 77 Barbara Barnes, Photo Researchers; 78 WestLaw; 79 J. P. Laffont, Sygma; 82 John Hendrickson; 83 Judy Canty, Stock, Boston; 84 (top, left) Bob Daemmrich, Stock, Boston; 84 (top, right) Fredrick D. Bodin, Stock, Boston; 84 (middle) Martin Rogers, Stock, Boston; 84 (bottom) Joel Sohm/Chromosohm, Stock, Boston; 85 (left) David Cross; 85 (right) John Hendrickson; 86 (top) Susan Leavines, Photo Researchers; 86 (bottom) Grace, Green Peace; 87 David Cross; 88 John Running, Stock, Boston; 91 Ed Kashi; 93 Bob Daemmrich, Stock, Boston; 94 Liane Enkelis, Stock, Boston; 95 Rhoda Sidney, Stock,

(Continued following index)

Contents in Brief

■

UNIT FIVE

Contents

SOCIOLOGY
Third Edition

■

UNIT TWO

CONFORMITY AND NONCONFORMITY   139

■

UNIT THREE

DIFFERENTIATION AND INEQUALITY   219

■

UNIT FIVE

CHANGE   517

FOCUS ON: THE
CALAMITOUS CENTURY
524

Preface

The most stimulating aspect of the discipline of sociology is that it directly confronts the major issues affecting our individual lives and public policy. Sociology is not an ivory tower discipline, but one that grapples with the real problems of everyday life—personal issues such as getting a job, getting married (and staying that way), and the payoff of a college education; public issues such as homelessness, gun control, and the ghetto poor. Every chapter in *Sociology*, third edition has an "ah ha—so that's how that works!" dimension that provides readers new insights about familiar issues. For example, the student will be stimulated to consider his or her own employment prospects, divorce prospects, or voting behavior as well as considering larger issues such as the war on drugs and the rationing of health care.

The third edition of *Sociology* is a balanced and thoroughly contemporary text. It is designed to present sociology in a format that students and teachers will find enjoyable and useful. The result is an attractive and stimulating book, written in a warm personal style, that addresses issues of contemporary society in a direct way. Building from a foundation of clear, straightforward prose, *Sociology* is designed to be an effective tool for student learning.

This book covers all of the basics in the discipline and will be an excellent foundation for advanced work in the field. For those students who go on to take further courses as well as for the much larger group of non-majors, we have two goals: 1) to develop an accurate understanding of American society—for example, to understand contemporary racism and inequality; 2) to develop a sociological imagination with which to analyze the role of social structure in contemporary issues such as homelessness, alcoholism, and school failure. We hope that long after students have forgotten the distinction between mores and folkways, they will be able to apply the sociological perspective to thinking about the critical issues of their times.

The third edition of *Sociology* retains the pedagogical features that made the first two editions a success: Each chapter starts with a personal application and concludes with a public policy application; there is one boxed insert per chapter; clearly identified concepts, concept summaries, and chapter summaries aid students in mastering the material.

The twenty-two chapters of *Sociology*, third edition cover all the standard areas of the discipline, plus many new and exciting theories and topics. These include topical issues such as homelessness, the war against drugs, the unique disadvantages of African American men, gun control, the environmental movement, and immigration reform. They also include exciting new sociological developments such as the debate over the "truly disadvantaged," the "new structuralism" in our discipline, and the growing body of research on the political economy of the world system. Throughout this edition, there is greater emphasis on the global dimensions of contemporary issues.

The third edition of *Sociology* has been revised to reflect changes in the discipline and in the world. The resulting text is contemporary, sociological, and very accessible to the undergraduate student. In addition, we believe our excellent ancillary package will make an important addition to the introductory course.

MAJOR CHANGES IN THE THIRD EDITION

The easiest part of a revision is providing the latest data and research findings. We have carefully reviewed all of the major journals and many specialty journals to reflect new findings. In addition, of course, we have haunted the library and called government offices to make certain that the book reflects the very latest available data. In addition to these basic steps in the revision process, the third edition of *Sociology* reflects three major changes: more explicit theory, a new chapter on medicine, and photoessays.

MORE EXPLICIT THEORY

During the last several years, there have been two changes in the theoretical underpinnings of our discipline. First, the discipline has become more structural, and this change in the discipline is reflected in the third edition. Second, recent work makes it increasingly clear that a latent structural-functionalism has been built into many of our basic frameworks. In order to make the theoretical underpinnings of our concepts clearer, this edition takes a more self-conscious approach to theory in every chapter, including, for example, both a structural-functional and a conflict analysis of culture in Chapter 3.

NEW CHAPTER ON SOCIOLOGY OF MEDICINE

Chapter 18 in the third edition tackles the broad subject of sociology of medicine. It begins with a symbolic interaction approach to health and sickness and moves on to a consideration of social epidemiology, medical professions, and the medical/industrial complex. This is a high-interest chapter that covers issues such as who is responsible for good health, whether the fitness movement can be a form of "blaming the victim," and issues related to paying for and rationing health care.

PHOTO ESSAYS ON ENVIRONMENT, SPORT, AND INFORMATION TECHNOLOGY

The discipline of sociology expands every year, but our academic terms do not. In order to include high-interest material that cannot be allocated chapter-length treatment, we have included three six-page photo essays. The outstanding photographs and shorter written material will introduce students to the range of sociological concerns in these three areas.

PLAN OF THE BOOK

Sociology is designed to give a comprehensive, contemporary view of the discipline in a format that students will enjoy reading and be able to master. The following features are designed to meet these goals.

PROLOGUES

Each chapter begins with a short prologue that makes a direct appeal to the student's personal experience. All prologues are in a "Have You Ever . . ." format that encourages students to consider how material covered in the chapter applies to their own experiences.

APPLICATION TO SOCIAL ISSUES

The last section of each chapter, Issues in Social Policy, brings the student full circle to a concern with another application, this time on the societal level. Public issues added in the third edition include the war against drugs (Chapter 8), homelessness (Chapter 7), the truly disadvantaged (Chapter 9), gun control (Chapter 16), and rationing health care (Chapter 18).

FOCUSES

One boxed insert is used in each chapter to introduce provocative and interesting issues. Because we believe that the practice of social research can be provocative and interesting, some of these cover measurement and research issues, for example a study of gift giving (Chapter 5) and cohort versus age effects in the measurement of self-concept (Chapter 12). Others add historical and cross-cultural breadth by covering such issues as the kibbutz (Chapter 9) and a historical perspective on women of color (Chapter 11).

CHAPTER SUMMARIES

A short point-by-point summary lists the chief points made in each chapter. This will aid the beginning student in studying the text and discriminating central from the supporting points.

CONCEPT LEARNING AIDS

Learning new concepts is vital to developing a new perspective. In *Sociology*, this learning is facilitated in three ways. When new concepts first appear in the text, they are bold-faced and complete definitions are set out clearly in the margin. Whenever a group of related concepts are introduced (for example, power, coercion, and authority), a concept summary is included in a text figure to summarize the definitions, give examples, and clarify differences. Finally, a glossary appears at the end of the book for handy reference.

SUPPLEMENTAL MATERIALS

Four kinds of supplemental materials have been developed to ease the tasks of learning and teaching from *Sociology*: a large, revised test bank, a unique instructor's manual, a student study guide, and a new student-research software package that will enable students to participate in sociological research.

TEST BANK

A revised test bank includes 100 multiple choice and ten essay questions for each chapter. Approximately half of these questions are new, reflecting both new material and new approaches to the retained material. The test bank is available in hard copy and as Westest II on microcomputer diskettes for IBM and IBM-compatible, Macintosh, and Apple computers.

INSTRUCTOR'S RESOURCE MANUAL

The authors have revised their unique instructor's manual to include an even wider variety of teaching aids. As in previous editions, the instructor's manual provides innovative and absorbing classroom activities—for the instructor with 350 students as well as the instructor with 35. Each chapter provides at least one fully-developed class exercise. Copy-ready versions of these exercises are included in a separate packet so that instructors can easily prepare handouts and instruction sheets.

New to this edition are several fully-developed lectures, covering such topics as social networks and educational tracking, an annotated guide to video tapes available from West Publishing, suggestions about how the "Your Research" student software may be most effectively used, and transparencies for major tables and figures for classroom use.

The Instructor's Manual continues to offer instructor-oriented chapter outlines, multiple suggestions for classroom discussions and activities, and a questionnaire that may be used to collect sociological data from students. Many of the questions on this instrument are identical to those discussed in the text. We have found the comparison of class data to national data an invaluable aid for engaging student interest and for teaching about the merits and pitfalls of survey research. Suggested uses for the questionnaire are presented in the Instructor's Resource Manual on a chapter-by-chapter basis.

STUDENT STUDY GUIDE

The Student Study Guide, written by Charles O'Connor (Bemidji State University) and Charles M. Mulford (Iowa State University), will be invaluable in helping students master the material. The study guide contains an outline of each chapter, practice questions in matching, completion, multiple-choice, and essay form. A computerized form of the study guide, prepared for both IBM-compatible and Macintosh machines, is available for use by students with personal computers as well as by departments that provide micro labs for their undergraduates.

SOFTWARE

Kenneth Kinze (Louisiana State University at Shreveport) has developed an exciting software package that allows students direct participation in sociological research. The Your Research package includes software for IBM-compatible computers and a student workbook. The package allows students to play with four data sets, one from the General Social Surveys and three aggregate-level data sets. The Adults Data Set includes 25 variables on 504 adults interviewed by the GSS in 1988. It includes questions about gender roles, church attendance, and community satisfaction. The Cultures Data Set includes 59 variables on 186 primitive or traditional cultures; it provides an outstanding opportunity to bring a cross-cultural perspective into the introductory sociology course. The Nations Data Set provides contemporary information on 23 variables for 129 nations, and the State Data Set provides 46 variables for the contemporary United States. These data sets can be manipulated by students on their home PCs or used in a micro lab.

The student workbook provides student instructions and worksheets for one analysis project for each major content area. For example, the "Social Control: Violent Crime for States" exercise takes students through an analysis of the correlates of violent crime rates in the United States. For the instructor who enjoys playing with data and working with student research projects, however, the user-friendly software and the multiple data sets provide nearly endless possibilities.

ACKNOWLEDGMENTS

In the third as in the earlier editions of *Sociology*, we have accumulated many debts. We are especially grateful for the goodnatured and generous advice of our colleagues at the University of Nebraska-Lincoln. Special thanks go to Robert Benford, Jay Corzine, Jennifer Lehmann, Helen Moore, Suzanne Ortega, Wayne Osgood, Keith Parker, John Shafer, Susan Welch, Hugh Whitt, and Al Williams. They were always willing to share their expert knowledge and to comment and advise on our own forays into their substantive areas. We thank all of them for their encouragement and support. We also wish to thank Dean John Peters and Associate Dean Steven Hilliard of the College of Arts and Sciences, whose strong championship of undergraduate education supported our commitment to writing this text.

Special thanks go to the people at West Publishing. Our editor, Clyde Perlee, was generous with encouragement and advice and we benefited greatly from his knowledge of what makes a college textbook usable. Our production editor, Janine Wilson, played an invaluable role in turning our material into an attractive finished product. Her production skill, good sense, patience, and good-humor contributed a great deal to the quality of the final product and to the mental health of the authors. The visual appeal of the book is the result of her contributions and those of her assistant, Lee Anne Storey. We thank Bill Stryker for once again providing an attractive design for the book. Our copyeditor, Nancy Palmer Jones, not only saved us from technical gaffes and inconsistencies, but performed an especially valuable service in screening the manuscript for difficult or problematic examples and wording. Her questions contributed not only to clearer writing, but also to clearer thinking about sociological ideas and their implications. At all levels, the people at West have been a delight to work with—ready to make our book the best possible, but always leaving the substance and direction of the book in our hands.

Once again we wish to extend our thanks to those people who reviewed the manuscript for the first two editions of our text. Their thoughtful comments and suggestions were an enormous help.

First Edition

Paul J. Baker
Illinois State University

Carolie Coffey
Cabrillo College, California

Paul Colomy
University of Akron, Ohio

David A. Edwards
San Antonio College, Texas

William Egelman
Iona College, New York

Constance Elsberg
Northern Virginia Community College

Daniel E. Ferritor
University of Arkansas

Charles E. Garrison
East Carolina University, North Carolina

James R. George
Kutztown State College, Pennsylvania

Rose Hall
Diablo Valley College, California

Michael G. Horton
Pensacola Junior College, Florida

Sidney J. Kaplan
University of Toledo, Ohio

James A. Kithens
North Texas State University

Mary N. Legg
Valencia Community College, Florida

Joseph J. Leon
California State Polytechnic University, Pomona

J. Robert Lilly
Northern Kentucky University

Richard L. Loper
Seminole Community College, Florida

Carol May
Illinois Central College

Rodney C. Metzger
Lane Community College, Oregon

Vera L. Milam
Northeastern Illinois University

James S. Munro
Macomb College, Michigan

Lynn D. Nelson
Virginia Commonwealth University

J. Christopher O'Brien
Northern Virginia Community College

Robert L. Petty
San Diego Mesa College, California

Will Rushton
Del Mar College, Texas

Rita P. Sakitt
Suffolk Community College, New York

Barbara Stenross
University of North Carolina

Ida Harper Simpson
Duke University, North Carolina

James B. Skellenger
Kent State University, Ohio

James Steele
James Madison University, Virginia

Steven L. Vassar
Mankato State University, Minnesota

Jane B. Wedemeyer
Santa Fe Community College, Florida

Thomas J. Yacovone
Los Angeles Valley College, California

David L. Zierath
University of Wisconsin

Second Edition

William C. Jenné
Oregon State University

Florence Karlstrom
Northern Arizona University

John M. Smith, Jr.
Agusta College, Georgia

Phillip R. Kunz
Brigham Young University

Ed Crenshaw
University of Oklahoma

Robert Benford
University of Nebraska

Mike Robinson
Elizabethtown Community College, Kentucky

Christopher Ezell
Vincennes University, Indiana

Cornelius C. Hughes
University Southern Colorado

Joseph Falmeier
South Dakota State University

John P. Rehn
Gustavus Adolphus College, St. Peter, Minnesota

Ruth A. Pigott
Kearney State College, Kearney, Nebraska

Martin Scheffer
Boise State University, Idaho

During the course of writing this revision, we have benefited from the advice of many sociologists from across the country. Special thanks go to Laura Eells (The Wichita State University), Suzanne Ortega (University of Nebraska-Lincoln), and Charles O'Connor (Bemidji State University) for their ideas, constructive criticism, and thoughtful reviews. Emil Vajda (Northern Michigan University) provided especially valuable suggestions on the population chapter.

John K. Cochran
Wichita State University, Kansas

Lynda Dodgen
North Harris County College, Texas

Christopher Ezell
Vincennes University, Indiana

Charles E. Garrison
East Carolina University, North Carolina

Harold C. Guy
Prince George Community College, Maryland

William Kelly
University of Texas

Phillip R. Kunz
Brigham Young University, Utah

Diane Kayongo-Male
South Dakota State University

Adrian Rapp
North Harris County College, Texas

Ricky L. Slavings
Radford University, Virginia

SOCIOLOGY
Third Edition

INTRODUCTION

CHAPTER 1
THE STUDY OF
SOCIETY

CHAPTER 2
DOING
SOCIOLOGY

CHAPTER 3
CULTURE

CHAPTER 4
SOCIAL
STRUCTURES AND
INSTITUTIONS

CHAPTER 5
GROUPS,
NETWORKS, AND
ORGANIZATIONS

1

THE STUDY OF SOCIETY

PROLOGUE

$\mathbf{H}$AVE YOU EVER . . .

Known anyone who committed suicide? When we hear about such a tragedy, we usually suppose that some unique, personal misery lay behind it, such as a terminal illness, rejection by friends and family, or mental illness. The decision to take one's own life is an intensely personal affair, and to understand any single suicide would require intimate knowledge about the individual.

We can also learn some important things about suicide, however, by looking at common patterns. There are about 31,000 suicides in the United States each year. Although each one is unique, there are some recurrent patterns in the likelihood of committing suicide. For example, approximately four times more men than women kill themselves; among the elderly, men are eight times more likely to kill themselves than women. The persistence of such patterns suggests that an understanding of suicide must go beyond looking at individual troubles to an examination of the ways that age and sex affect our lives—and our deaths.

Sociology is a field that examines how society—its patterns of inequality, values, and opportunities—affects individual lives. If you are interested in why men are more apt to commit suicide than women, why African Americans get less education than white Americans, why children are more apt than the elderly to be poor, and if you are not content to explain these things through unique personality traits in the individuals involved, then sociology can help provide the answers. In this book, we will provide a framework for understanding the recurrent patterns that shape our lives and our society.

3

■

WHAT IS SOCIOLOGY?

Each of us engages in the study of society simply by observing the world around us. We may wonder, for example, why girls are underrepresented in high school calculus classes and why, more than 125 years after the end of slavery, African Americans are still disadvantaged in U.S. society. We may have more personal concerns, too, such as whether a college education is really necessary to get ahead.

Sociology is a discipline that tries to place individual experiences—such as taking math, going to school, and getting ahead—in a larger social context. The unique perspective of sociology is perhaps best understood if we compare it with its sister discipline, psychology.

Both psychology and sociology are interested in human behavior. Both focus on the question of why people do what they do. Psychology, however, focuses more on causes occurring within the individual and sociology focuses more on causes that spring from society. For example, a psychologist who wants to know why some people get ahead and others don't will look at individual factors such as intelligence and motivation. A sociologist, on the other hand, will look at opportunity structures and social class systems.

Sociology is the systematic study of human social interaction.

Sociology is a social science whose unique province is the systematic study of social structures and how they affect human behavior. It shares with psychology and other social sciences an emphasis on the scientific method as the best way to gain knowledge. In other words, as sociologists, we rely on critical and systematic examination of the evidence, and we try to be objective observers. This scientific approach is what distinguishes the social sciences from journalism and other fields that comment on the human condition.

A **social structure** is a recurrent pattern of relationships.

What distinguishes sociology from other social sciences is its focus on social structures. We will treat social structure more elaborately in Chapter 4, but we define **social structures** as recurrent patterns of social behavior. Education is a social structure that provides widely-shared patterns of behavior for students and teachers. The behavior of women and men in our society is also socially structured: Patterns exist that provide models for how women and men are expected to act. Learning to recognize social structures and how they affect our lives is central to the development of the "sociological imagination"

THE SOCIOLOGICAL IMAGINATION

The **sociological imagination** is the ability to see the intimate realities of our own lives in the context of common social structures; it is the ability to see personal troubles as public issues.

The ability to see personal experience in the context of social structures has been called the **sociological imagination** (Mills 1959, 15). Sociologist C. Wright Mills suggests that the sociological imagination is developed when we can place such personal troubles as poverty, divorce, or loss of faith into a larger social context, when we can see them as common public issues. He suggests that many of the things we experience as individuals are really beyond our control. They have to do with society as a whole, its historical development, and the way it is organized. In 1959, Mills gave us some examples of the differences between a personal trouble and a public issue:

This homeless person is obviously experiencing dire personal problems: no food, no home, no shelter, no money, no medical care. Unfortunately, there are somewhere between 300,000 and 3 million others who share the same circumstances— roughly for the same reasons. Although individual homeless people may have personal inadequacies, the extent of homelessness reflects the shortage of housing and jobs in contemporary America. Learning to see personal experiences and tragedies as part of larger patterns of social problems is a vital element of the sociological imagination.

When, in a city of 100,000, only one man is unemployed, that is his personal trouble, and for its relief we properly look to the character of the man, his skills, and his immediate opportunities. But when in a nation of 50 million employees, 15 million men are unemployed, that is an issue, and we may not hope to find its solution within the range of opportunities open to any one individual. The very structure of opportunities has collapsed. Both the correct statement of the problem and the range of possible solutions require us to consider the economic and political institutions of the society, and not merely the personal situation and character of a scatter of individuals. . . .

Consider marriage. Inside a marriage a man and a woman may experience personal troubles, but when the divorce rate during the first four years of marriage is 250 out of every 1,000 attempts, this is an indication of a structural issue having to do with the institutions of marriage and the family and other institutions that bear on them (Mills 1959, 9).

In everyday life, we do not define personal experiences in these terms. We frequently do not consider the impact of history and social structures on our own experiences. If a child becomes a drug addict, parents tend to blame themselves; if spouses divorce, their friends usually focus on their personality problems; if you flunk out of school, everyone will be likely to blame you personally. To develop the sociological imagination is to understand how outcomes such as these are, in part, a product of society and not fully within the control of the individual. Many people flunk out of school, for example, not because they are stupid or lazy but because they come from a social class that does not give them the financial or psychological support that they need. These students may be working 25 hours a week in addition to going to school; they are going to school despite their family's indifference. On the other hand, there are students for whom it would be difficult to fail: Their parents provide tuition, living expenses, a personal computer, encouragement, and moral support. As we will discuss in more detail in Chapter 14, parents' social class is one of the best predictors of who will fail and who will graduate. Success or failure is thus not entirely an individual matter; it is socially structured.

Sociological imagination, the ability to see our own lives and those of others in the context of social structure, is central to sociology. Once you develop this imagination, you will be less likely to explain others' behavior through their personality and will increasingly look to the social structures that surround them. You will also recognize that the solutions to many social problems lie not in changing individuals but in changing social structures. Although poverty, divorce, illegitimacy, and racism are experienced as intensely personal hardships, they are unlikely to be reduced effectively through massive personal therapy. To solve these and many other social problems, we need to change social structure. Sociological imagination offers a new way to look at—and a new way to search for solutions to—the common troubles and dilemmas that face individuals. This concern with understanding and solving social problems has been central to sociology since its beginning 150 years ago.

■ THE EMERGENCE OF SOCIOLOGY

Sociology emerged as a field of inquiry during the 19th century. Between 1800 and 1900, the industrial revolution transformed society. Within a few generations, traditional rural societies were replaced by industrialized urban societies. The rapidity and scope of the change resulted in substantial social disorganization. Millions struggled desperately to make the adjustment from rural peasantry to urban working class.

The picture of urban life during these years—in London, Chicago, or Hamburg—was one of disorganization, poverty, and dynamic and exciting change. The turmoil and tragedy were the inspiration for much of the intellectual effort of the 19th century: Charles Dickens's novels, Jane Addams's reform work, Karl Marx's revolutionary theory. It also inspired the scientific study of society. These were the years in which science was a new enterprise and nothing seemed too much to hope for. After the discovery of electricity and the invention of the telegraph and the X-ray, who was to say that science could not discover how to turn stones into gold or how to eliminate poverty or war? Many hoped that the tools of science could help in understanding and controlling a rapidly changing society.

The first scholars to attempt a scientific study of society were not themselves sociologists. They were philosophers, economists, and preachers. A brief review of their work gives a flavor of the issues and concerns that dominated sociology in the 19th century and that, to a significant extent, continue to be central concerns today.

THE FOUNDERS: COMTE, MARX, DURKHEIM, AND WEBER

Auguste Comte (1798–1857).   The first major figure to be concerned with the science of society was the French philosopher Auguste Comte. He coined the term *sociology* in 1839 and is generally considered the founder of this field.

Auguste Comte, 1798–1857

Comte was among the first to suggest that the scientific method could be applied to social events (Konig 1968). The philosophy of **positivism,** which he developed, suggests that the social world can be studied with the same scientific accuracy and assurance as the natural world. Once the laws of social behavior were learned, he believed, scientists could accurately predict and even control events. Although thoughtful people wonder whether we will ever be able to predict human behavior with the same kind of accuracy that we can predict the behavior of molecules, the scientific method remains central to sociology.

Another of Comte's lasting contributions was his recognition that an understanding of society requires a concern for both the sources of order and continuity and the sources of change. Comte called these divisions the theory of statics and the theory of dynamics. Although sociologists no longer use his terms, Comte's basic divisions of sociology continue under the labels *social structure* (statics) and *social process* (dynamics).

Karl Marx (1818–1883).   A philosopher, economist, and social activist, Karl Marx was born in Germany to middle-class parents. Marx received his doctorate in philosophy at the age of 23, but because of his radical views he was unable to obtain a university appointment and spent most of his adult life in exile and poverty (Rubel 1968).

Marx was repulsed by the poverty and inequality that characterized the 19th century. Unlike other scholars of his day, he was unwilling to see poverty as either a natural or a God-given condition of the human species. Instead, he viewed poverty and inequality as man-made conditions fostered by private property and capitalism. As a result, he devoted his intellectual efforts to understanding—and eliminating—capitalism. Many of Marx's ideas are of more interest to political scientists and economists than to sociologists, but he left two enduring legacies to sociology: the theories of economic determinism and the dialectic.

ECONOMIC DETERMINISM.   Marx began his analysis of society by assuming that the most basic task of any human society is providing food and shelter to sustain itself. Marx argued that the ways in which society does this— its modes of production—provide the foundations on which all other social and political arrangements are built. Thus, he believed that family, law, and religion all develop after and adapt to the economic structure; in short, they are determined by economic relationships. This idea is called **economic determinism.**

A good illustration of economic determinism is the influence of economic conditions on marriage choices. In traditional agricultural societies, young people often remain economically dependent upon their parents until well into adulthood because the only economic resource, land, is controlled by the older generation. In order to support themselves now and in the future, they must remain in their parents' good graces; this means they cannot marry without their parents' approval. In societies where young people can earn a living without their parents' help, however, they can marry when they please and whomever they please. Marx would argue that this shift in mate selection practices is the result of changing economic relationships. Because Marx saw all human relations as stemming

Positivism is the belief that the social world can be studied with the same scientific accuracy and assurance as the natural world.

Economic determinism means that economic relationships provide the foundation on which all other social and political arrangements are built.

Karl Marx, 1818–1883

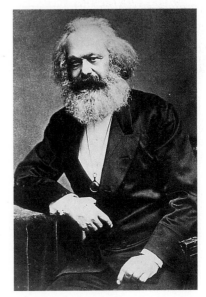

ultimately from the economic system, he suggested that the major goal of a social scientist is to understand economic relationships: Who owns what, and how does this pattern of ownership affect human relationships?

THE DIALECTIC.   Marx's other major contribution was a theory of social change. Many 19th-century scholars applied Darwin's theories of biological evolution to society; they believed that social change was the result of a natural process of adaptation. Marx, however, argued that the basis of change was conflict, not adaptation. He argued that conflicts between opposing economic interests lead to change.

Marx's thinking on conflict was influenced by the German philosopher Georg Hegel, who suggested that for every idea (thesis), a counter-idea (antithesis) develops to challenge it. As a result of conflict between the two ideas, a new idea (synthesis) is produced. This process of change is called the **dialectic** (see Figure 1.1).

Marx's contribution was to apply this model of ideological change to change in economic and material systems. Within capitalism, Marx suggested that the capitalist class was the thesis and the working class was the antithesis. He predicted that conflicts between them would lead to a new economic system, a new synthesis that would be socialism. Indeed, in his role as social activist, Marx hoped to encourage conflict and ignite the revolution that would bring about the desired change. The workers, he declared, "have nothing to lose but their chains" (Marx and Engels [1848] 1965).

Although few sociologists are revolutionaries, many accept Marx's ideas on the importance of economic relationships and economic conflicts. Much more controversial is Marx's argument that the social scientist should also be a social activist, a person who not only tries to understand social relationships but also tries to change them.

Émile Durkheim (1858–1917).

Like Marx, Durkheim was born into a middle-class family. While Marx was starving as an exile in England, however, Durkheim spent most of his career occupying a prestigious professorship at the Sorbonne. Far from rejecting society, Durkheim embraced it, and much of his outstanding scholarly energy was devoted to understanding the stability of society and the importance of social participation for individual happiness. Whereas the lasting legacy of Marx is a theory that looks for the conflict-laden and changing aspects of social practices, the lasting legacy of Durkheim is a theory that examines the positive contributions of social patterns. Together they allow us to see both order and change.

Durkheim's major works are still considered essential reading in sociology. These include his studies of suicide, education, divorce, crime, and social change. Two lasting legacies are his ideas about the relationship between individuals and society and the development of a method for social science.

One of Durkheim's major concerns was the balance between social regulation and personal freedom. He argued that community standards of morality, which he called the collective conscience, not only confine our behavior but also give us a sense of belonging and integration. For example,

---

Dialectic philosophy views change as a product of contradictions and conflict between the parts of society.

■
FIGURE 1.1
THE DIALECTIC

The dialectic model of change suggests that change occurs through conflict and resolution rather than through evolution.

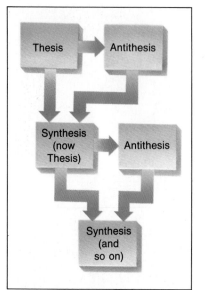

many people complain about having to dress up; they complain about having to shave their faces or their legs, having to wear a tie or pantyhose. "What's wrong with my jeans?" At the same time, most of us feel a sense of satisfaction when we appear in public in our best clothes. We know that we will be considered attractive and successful. Although we may complain about having to meet what appear to be arbitrary standards, we often feel a sense of satisfaction in being able to meet those standards successfully. In Durkheim's words, "institutions may impose themselves upon us, but we cling to them; they compel us, and we love them" (Durkheim [1895] 1938, 3). This beneficial regulation, however, must not rob the individual of all freedom of choice.

In his classic study, *Suicide,* Durkheim identified two types of suicide that stem from an imbalance between social regulation and personal freedom. Fatalistic suicide occurs when society overregulates and allows too little freedom, when our behavior is so confined by social institutions that we cannot exercise our independence ([1897] 1951, 276). Durkheim gave as an example of fatalistic suicide the very young husband who feels overburdened by the demands of work, household, and family. Anomic suicide, on the other hand, occurs when there is too much freedom and too little regulation, when society's influence does not check individual passions ([1897] 1951, 258). Durkheim said that this kind of suicide is most likely to occur in times of rapid social change. When established ways of doing things have lost their meaning, but no clear alternatives have developed, individuals feel lost. The high suicide rate of Native Americans (approximately twice that of Caucasian Americans) is generally attributed to the weakening of traditional social regulation.

Durkheim was among the first to stress the importance of using reliable statistics to examine theories of social life. Each of his works illustrates his ideal social scientist: an objective observer who only wants the facts. As sociology became an established discipline, this ideal of objective observation replaced Marx's social activism as the standard model for social science.

Emile Durkheim, 1858–1917

Max Weber, 1864–1920

Max Weber (1864–1920).   A German economist, historian, and philosopher, Max Weber (Veh-ber) provided the theoretical base for half a dozen areas of sociological inquiry. He wrote on religion, bureaucracy, method, and politics. In all these areas, his work is still valuable and insightful; it is covered in detail in later chapters. Three of Weber's more general contributions were an emphasis on the subjective meanings of social actions, on social as opposed to material causes, and on the need for objectivity in studying social issues.

Weber believed that knowing patterns of behavior was less important than knowing the meanings people attach to behavior. For example, Weber would argue that it is relatively meaningless to compile statistics such as two-thirds of all marriages contracted today may end in divorce compared to only 10 percent in 1890 (Martin and Bumpass 1989). More critical, he would argue, is understanding how the meaning of divorce has changed in the past hundred years. Weber's emphasis on the subjective meanings of human actions has been the foundation of scholarly work on topics as varied as religion and immigration.

Baptism is a religious ritual common to most Christian faiths. We can study what baptism means in Christian theology, we can compile statistics on the percentage of the population that has been baptized, or we can follow Weber's emphasis on subjective meanings by asking what it means to the individuals who take part in it. The typical Presbyterian baptism in which an infant's head is sprinkled with a few drops of water during a formal service is quite different in symbolic meaning from this woman's baptism by immersion.

Weber trained as an economist, and much of his work concerned the interplay of things material and things social. He rejected Marx's idea that economic factors were the determinants of all other social relationships. In a classic study, *The Protestant Ethic and the Spirit of Capitalism*, Weber tried to show how social and religious values may be the foundation of economic systems. This argument is developed more fully in Chapter 17, but its major thesis is that the religious values of early Protestantism (self-discipline, thrift, and individualism) were the foundation for capitalism.

One of Weber's more influential ideas was his declaration that sociology must be **value free.** Weber argued that sociology should be concerned with establishing what is and not what ought to be. Weber's dictum is at the heart of the scientific approach that is generally advocated by modern sociologists. Thus, although one may study poverty or racial inequality because of a sense of moral outrage, such feelings must be set aside to achieve an objective grasp of the facts. This position of neutrality is directly contradictory to the Marxian emphasis on social activism, and sociologists who adhere to Marxist principles generally reject the notion of value-free sociology. Most modern sociologists, however, try to be value free in their scholarly work.

Value-free sociology concerns itself with establishing what is, not what ought to be.

SOCIOLOGY IN THE UNITED STATES

Sociology in the United States developed somewhat differently than in Europe. Although U.S. sociology has the same intellectual roots as European sociology, it has some distinctive characteristics. Three features that have characterized U.S. sociology from its beginning are a concern with social problems, a reforming rather than a radical approach to these problems, and an emphasis on the scientific method.

One reason that U.S. sociology developed differently from European sociology is that our social problems differ. Slavery, the Civil War, and high immigration rates, for example, made racism and racial and ethnic inequality a much more salient issue in the United States. One of the first sociologists to study these issues was W. E. B. Du Bois. Du Bois, who received his doctorate in 1895 from Harvard University, devoted his career to developing empirical data about African Americans and to using those data to combat racism.

The first sociology course in the United States was taught at Yale University in 1876. By 1910, most colleges and universities in the United States offered sociology courses, although separate departments were slower to develop. Most of the courses were offered jointly with other departments, most often with economics but frequently with history, political science, philosophy, or general social science departments.

By 1960, almost all colleges and universities had departments of sociology, and by 1990, 120 offered doctorate programs. The popularity of higher-degree sociology programs is greater in the United States than in any other country in the world. This is partly because sociology in the United States has always been oriented toward the practical as well as the theoretical. The focus has consistently been on finding solutions to social issues and problems, with the result that U.S. sociologists not only teach sociology but also work in government and industry.

W. E. B. Du Bois, 1868–1963

This group of people is staging a counter-demonstration to challenge a gathering of white supremacists at the "Aryan Woodstock" festival. Although sociologists are interested in routine matters such as courtship, voting, and church attendance, it is also fair to say that, whenever crowds form, sociologists want to be involved. Sociology has always had a social problems orientation, and sociologists are keenly interested in contemporary social problems. In the U.S. today these issues include racism, inequality, divorce, drug abuse, and environmental destruction.

Jane Addams, a Founding Mother

When sociology emerged as a discipline in the late 19th century, it was particularly hospitable to women. The boundaries of the early field were ill defined, and people from diverse points of view were welcomed. Some came from philosophy, some from economics, and some from natural science. Almost all, however, shared an abiding interest in social issues.

During this period, several prominent women activists claimed the title of sociologist. The early women sociologists differed from their male counterparts in their dedication to direct social action. A vivid example of this difference can be seen in the life and work of Jane Addams, founder of Hull House, recipient of the 1931 Nobel Peace Prize, and one of the first members of the American Sociological Society.

Hull House was a settlement house founded by Addams in 1889 in Chicago. Its group-living quarters (commune) provided lodging and a meeting ground for a variety of intellectuals and for Chicago's poor and oppressed. The purpose of assembling this very mixed group of residents was to fuse the personal and the professional by eliminating what these activists perceived to be a false distinction between thought and action. Addams and the other women who lived at Hull House fought for social equality, for women's rights, for child labor laws, for juvenile courts—and they fought in the trenches rather than from the campus.

By all criteria, Addams was a sociologist. She published in the *American Journal of Sociology;* she belonged to and was active in the American Sociological Society. Nevertheless, she refused to ally herself directly with the academic profession of so-

Jane Addams

ciology and refused offers of a faculty position in the Department of Sociology at Chicago because she disapproved of the direction in which she saw the field of sociology going. Although she was ahead of most of her generation in relying on quantitative data, she was not interested in pursuing abstract knowl-

edge for its own sake. She wanted to use data to document the need for social action. In this she was remarkably effective: Her organization pushed through legislation on safer working conditions, a better juvenile justice system, better public sanitation, and services for the poor.

■

Her organization pushed through legislation on safer working conditions, a better juvenile justice system, better public sanitation, and services for the poor.

As sociology became more established, its practice retreated from the streets into university hallways. The new generation of sociology professors was embarrassed by activists such as Addams, and the golden era of women as leaders in the field ended in 1918. Why 1918? Because this was the year that the United States entered World War I. The pacifism of Addams and other women sociologists was the last straw, the straw that convinced the academic establishment that outspoken social activism was incompatible with academic respectability.

SOURCE: Deegan, Mary Jo. 1987. Jane Addams and the Men of the Chicago School, 1892–1918. New Brunswick, NJ: Transaction.

■

CURRENT PERSPECTIVES IN SOCIOLOGY

As this brief review of the history of sociological thought has demonstrated, there are many ways of approaching the study of social structure and human behavior. The ideas of Marx, Weber, Durkheim, and others have given rise to dozens of theories about how our lives are shaped by social structure. In this section, we summarize the ideas that underlie the three dominant perspectives in sociology today: structural functionalism, conflict theory, and symbolic interactionism.

STRUCTURAL-FUNCTIONAL THEORY

Structural-functional theory addresses the question of social organization and how it is maintained. This theoretical perspective has its roots in natural science and the analogy between society and an organism. In the analysis of a living organism, the scientist's task is to identify the various parts (structures) and determine how they work (function). In the study of society, a sociologist with this perspective tries to identify the structures of society and how they function—hence the name *structural functionalism.*

Structural-functional theory addresses the question of social organization and how it is maintained; it is also known as consensus theory.

Assumptions Underlying Structural Functionalism. In the sense that any study of society must begin with an identification of the parts of society and how they work, structural functionalism is basic to all perspectives. Scholars who use this perspective, however, are distinguished from other social analysts by their reliance on three major assumptions.

1. *Stability.* The chief evaluative criterion for any social pattern is whether it contributes to the maintenance of society.
2. *Harmony.* As the parts of an organism work together for the good of the whole, so the parts of society are also characterized by harmony.
3. *Evolution.* Change occurs through evolution—the adaptation of social structures to new needs and demands and the elimination of unnecessary or outmoded structures.

Because it emphasizes harmony and adaptation, structural functionalism is sometimes called *consensus theory.*

Structural-Functional Analysis. A structural-functional analysis asks two basic questions: What is the nature of this social structure (what patterns exist)? What are the consequences of this social structure (does it promote stability and harmony)? In this analysis, positive consequences are called **functions** and negative consequences are called **dysfunctions**. A distinction is also drawn between **manifest** (recognized and intended) consequences and **latent** (unrecognized and unintended) consequences.

The basic strategy of looking for structures and their manifest and latent functions and dysfunctions is common to nearly all sociological analysis. Scholars from widely different theoretical perspectives use this framework for examining society. What sets structural-functional theorists apart from

Functions are consequences of social structures that have positive effects on the stability of society.

Dysfunctions are consequences of social structures that have negative effects on the stability of society.

Manifest functions or dysfunctions are consequences of social structures that are intended and recognized.

Latent functions or dysfunctions are consequences of social structures that are neither intended nor recognized.

Structural-functional theory focuses on the benfits that social structures provide for individuals and society. They argue that the regularity and routine provided by such social structures as the family and government are as necessary as the regulations governing a school crossing. Theorists from this school often have a tendency to focus on the advantages rather than the disadvantages of particular social structures.

others who use this language are their assumptions about harmony and stability.

In 1989, the state of Virginia passed a law that made teenage driving privileges dependent on school enrollment: If you drop out of high school, you lose your driver's license. Since then, many other states have passed or considered the same legislation. What are the consequences of this new social structure? The manifest function (intended positive outcome) is to encourage students to stay in school. The manifest dysfunction is to make it harder for youths to hold jobs, thus raising the unemployment rate for high school dropouts. A latent dysfunction may be that youths who are coerced into staying in school will be disruptive elements in the classroom. Another latent outcome is more difficult to classify: The new policy will have little or no effect on inner-city youth, few of whom drive or have cars. This class bias is a latent (unintended) outcome. Is it a function or a dysfunction? This is a difficult question to answer from a neutral point of view, and it is here that the assumptions behind structural-functional theory guide the analysis. Following the assumption that the major criterion for judging a social structure is whether it contributes to the maintenance of society, structural-functional analysis has tended to call structures that preserve the status quo "functions" and those that challenge the status quo "dysfunctions." Because the class bias in this law contributes to the continuity of established patterns, the class bias would be judged a latent *function* (see Figure 1.2).

As this example suggests, a social pattern that contributes to the maintenance of society may benefit some groups more than others. A pattern may be functional—that is, help maintain the status quo—without being either desirable or equitable.

■

FIGURE 1.2
A STRUCTURAL-FUNCTIONAL ANALYSIS OF LAWS LINKING ADOLESCENT DRIVING PRIVILEGES TO SCHOOL ATTENDANCE

Structural-functional analysis examines the intended and unintended consequences of social structures. It also assesses whether the consequences are positive (functional) or negative (dysfunctional). There is no moral dimension to the assessment that an outcome is positive; it merely means that the outcome contributes to the stability of society.

	Manifest	Latent
Function	Encourages youths to stay in school	Encourages schooling more for middle-class than lower-class youth (class bias)
Dysfunction	Raises unemployment rate for high school dropouts	Increases disruption in classroom

Evaluation of Structural Functionalism. Structural-functional theory tends to produce a static and conservative analysis of social systems (Turner 1982). This tendency is not a requirement for functional analysis, but it is commonplace. For example, an enumeration of the ways in which the education system contributes to the maintenance of inequality (an argument outlined in Chapter 14) is not the same thing as saying that maintaining inequality is a good thing. The distinction is a fine one, however, and in general structural functionalism tends to be a more attractive perspective for those who want to preserve the status quo than for those who want to challenge it.

CONFLICT THEORY

If structural-functional theory sees the world in terms of consensus and stability, then it can be said that conflict theory sees the world in terms of conflict and change. Conflict theorists contend that a full understanding of society requires a critical examination of the competition and conflict in society, especially of the processes by which some people are winners and others losers. As a result, **conflict theory** addresses the points of stress and conflict in society and the ways in which they contribute to social change.

Conflict theory addresses the points of stress and conflict in society and the ways in which they contribute to social change.

Assumptions Underlying Conflict Theory. Conflict theory is derived from Marx's ideas. The following are three primary assumptions of modern conflict theory:

1. *Competition.* Competition over scarce resources (money, leisure, sexual partners, and so on) is at the heart of all social relationships. Competition rather than consensus is characteristic of human relationships.
2. *Structured inequality.* Inequalities in power and reward are built into all social structures. Individuals and groups that benefit from any particular structure strive to see it maintained.

Conflict theory takes a critical look at the social patterns that are part of social routine. Why, for example, are these poorly-paid garment workers in Miami all women and mostly Latino? Who benefits from low wages for women and immigrants and what social structures serve to maintain this centuries old pattern?

3. *Revolution.* Change occurs as a result of conflict between competing interests rather than through adaptation. It is often abrupt and revolutionary rather than evolutionary.

Conflict Analysis.   Like structural functionalists, conflict theorists are interested in social structures. The two questions they ask, however, are different. Conflict theorists ask: Who benefits from these social structures? How do those who benefit maintain their advantage?

A conflict analysis of modern education, for example, notes that the highest graduation rates, the best grades, and the highest monetary returns per year of education go to students from advantaged backgrounds. The answer to the question "Who benefits?" is that educational benefits go to the children of those who are already well off. Conflict theorists go on to ask how this situation developed and how it is maintained. Their answers (developed more extensively in Chapter 14) focus on questions such as how educational resources (texts, teachers, school buildings) are allocated by neighborhood and whether the curriculum is designed for one kind of child (white middle class) rather than other kinds. They also look for ways in which this system benefits the powerful—for example, by creating a class of nongraduates who can be hired cheaply.

Evaluation of Conflict Theory.   Thirty years ago, sociology was dominated by structural-functional theory, but conflict theory has grown increasingly popular. It allows us to ask many of the same questions as structural-functional theory (what is the social structure? what are its outcomes?), but it also encourages us to take a more critical look at outcomes: functional for whom? Together the two perspectives provide a balanced view, allowing us to analyze the sources of both conflict and harmony, order and change.

Conflict theory tends to produce a critical picture of society, and the emphasis on social activism and social criticism that is at the heart of conflict theory tends to attract scholars who would like to change society. In general, conflict theorists place less emphasis than other sociologists on the importance of value-free sociology.

SYMBOLIC INTERACTION THEORY

Both structural-functional and conflict theories focus on social structures and the relationships between them. What about the relationship between individuals and social structures? Sociologists who focus on the ways that individuals relate to and are affected by social structures generally use symbolic interaction theory. **Symbolic interaction theory** addresses the subjective meanings of human acts and the processes through which we come to develop and share these subjective meanings. The name of this theory comes from the fact that it studies the *symbolic* (or subjective) meaning of human *interaction*.

> **Symbolic interaction theory** addresses the subjective meanings of human acts and the processes through which people come to develop and communicate shared meanings.

Assumptions Underlying Symbolic Interaction Theory. When symbolic interactionists study human behavior, they begin with three major premises (Blumer 1969):

1. *Symbolic meanings are important.* Any behavior, gesture, or word can have multiple interpretations (can symbolize many things). In order to understand human behavior, we must learn what it means to the participants.
2. *Meanings grow out of relationships.* When relationships change, so do meanings.
3. *Meanings are negotiated.* We do not uncritically accept others' meanings. Each of us plays an active role in negotiating the meaning that things will have for us.

Symbolic Interaction Analysis. These premises direct symbolic interactionists to the study of how individuals are shaped by relationships and social structures. For example, symbolic interactionists would be interested in how growing up in a large as opposed to a small family or in a working-class as opposed to an upper-class family affects individual attitudes and behaviors.

Symbolic interactionists are also interested in the active role of the individual in modifying and negotiating his or her way through these relationships. Why do two children raised in the same family turn out differently? The answer lies in part in the fact that each child experiences subtly different relationships and situations; the meanings the youngest child derives from the family experience may be different from those the oldest child derives.

Most generally, symbolic interaction is concerned with how individuals are shaped by relationships. This question leads first to a concern with childhood and the initial steps we take to learn and interpret our social worlds. It is also concerned with later relationships with lovers, employers, and teachers.

CONCEPT SUMMARY
Major Theoretical Perspectives in Sociology

	STRUCTURAL FUNCTIONALISM	CONFLICT THEORY	SYMBOLIC INTERACTIONISM
Nature of society	Interrelated social structures that fit together to form an integrated whole	Competing interests, each seeking to secure its own ends	Interacting individuals and groups
Basis of interaction	Consensus and shared values	Constraint, power, and competition	Shared symbolic meanings
Major question	What are social structures? Do they contribute to social stability?	Who benefits? How are these benefits maintained?	How do social structures relate to individual subjective experiences?
Level of analysis	Social structure	Social structure	Interpersonal interaction

Evaluation of Symbolic Interaction Theory.   The value of symbolic interaction is that it focuses attention on the personal relationships and encounters that are so important in our everyday lives. By showing how the relationships dictated by the larger social structure affect our subjective worlds, symbolic interactionists give us a more complete picture of these social structures.

Neither symbolic interactionism nor the conflict and structural-functional theories are complete in themselves. Symbolic interactionism focuses on individual relationships, and the other two theories focus largely on society. Together, however, they provide a valuable set of tools for understanding the relationship between the individual and society.

INTERCHANGEABLE LENSES

As this brief review of major theoretical perspectives illustrates, a variety of theoretical perspectives is used in the field of sociology. These perspectives can be regarded as interchangeable lenses through which to view society. Just as a telephoto lens is not always superior to a wide-angle lens, one sociological theory will not always be superior to another.

Occasionally, the same subject can be viewed through any of these perspectives. For example, one can examine prostitution through the theoretical lens of structural-functional, conflict, or symbolic interaction theory. Following are three snapshots of female prostitution using these perspectives.

The Functions of Prostitution.   The functional analysis of female prostitution begins by examining its social structure. It identifies the recurrent patterns of relationships among pimps, prostitutes, and customers. Then it examines the consequences of this social structure. In 1961, Kingsley Davis listed the following outcomes of prostitution:

This photograph was taken at the Mustang Ranch, a legal brothel in Nevada. Whether legal or illegal, prostitution is certainly a patterned form of behavior, occuring in nearly every culture and every epoch of history. Sociologists analyze prostitution using a variety of perspectives. Symbolic interaction would emphasize the social setting where hookers do business, the gestures and vocabulary used to communicate symbolic meanings. The conflict perspective would focus on prostitution as an economic relationship created because of differential access to legitimate rewards. A structural functional perspective would emphasize that prostitution is a voluntary exchange that benefits both prostitutes and society.

- It provides a sexual outlet for men who cannot compete on the marriage market—the physically or mentally handicapped or the very poor.
- It provides a sexual outlet for men who are away from home a lot, such as salesmen and sailors.
- It provides a sexual outlet for the kinky.

Provision of these services is the manifest or intended function of prostitution. Davis goes on to note that, by providing these services, prostitution has the latent function of protecting the institution of marriage from malcontents who, for one reason or another, have not developed a satisfactory sexual relationship in marriage. Prostitution is the safety valve that makes it possible to restrict respectable sexual relationships (and hence childbearing and childrearing) to marital relationships while still allowing for the variability of human sexual appetites.

Prostitution: Marketing a Scarce Resource.   Conflict theorists analyze prostitution as part of the larger problem of unequal allocation of scarce resources. Women, they argue, have not had equal access to economic opportunity. In some societies, they are forbidden to own property; in others, they suffer substantial discrimination in opportunities to work and earn. When denied the opportunity to support themselves, women have had to rely on economic support from men. They get this support by exchanging a scarce resource: sexual availability. To a Marxist, it makes little difference whether a woman barters her sexual availability by the job (prostitution) or by contract (marriage); the underlying cause is the same.

Although most analyses of prostitution focus on adult women, the conflict perspective helps explain the growing problem of prostitution among runaway and homeless boys and girls. The young people have few realistic opportunities to support themselves by regular jobs: many are not old enough to work legally and, in any case, a minimum wage would be inadequate to enable them to support themselves. Their young bodies are their most marketable resource.

Prostitution: Learning the Trade.   Symbolic interactionists who examine prostitution will take an entirely different perspective. They will want to know how prostitutes learn the trade and how they manage their self-concept so that they continue to think positively of themselves in spite of engaging in a socially disapproved profession. One such study was done by Barbara Heyl, who intensively interviewed a middle-aged woman who had spent her career first as a prostitute and then as a madam and trainer of prostitutes. Heyl found that much of the training in the prostitute's role consists of business training, not sex. They learn how to hustle—how to get the maximum amount of money for the minimum amount of work. In speaking of what her training produces, the madam says she is turning out professional hustlers, not whores. She is proud of her work. She says, "They find that I am teaching them how to make money, to dress tastefully, to converse and be poised with men, to be knowledgeable about good hygiene, to have good working habits, such as punctuality, which will help them whether they stay in the rackets or not, and to have self-respect" (Heyl 1979, 105).

Summary.   As these examples illustrate, many topics can be fruitfully studied with any of these three theoretical perspectives. Just as a photographer with only one lens can shoot almost any subject, the sociologist with only one perspective will not be unduly limited in what to examine. One will generally get better pictures, however, by selecting the theoretical perspective that is best suited to the particular subject. In general, structural functionalism and conflict theory are well suited to the study of social structures, or **macrosociology.** Symbolic interactionism is well suited to the study of the relationship between individual meanings and social structures, or **microsociology.**

Macrosociology focuses on social structures and organizations and the relationships between them.

Microsociology focuses on interactions among individuals.

◼

SOCIOLOGISTS: WHAT DO THEY DO?

In this chapter, we have tried to give an overview of sociological perspectives so that you can get some idea of what sociology is. Another way of looking at the discipline is by looking at what sociologists do.

COLLEGE AND UNIVERSITY TEACHING

Nearly three-quarters of the members of the American Sociological Association teach sociology at the college or university level. They teach approximately 60,000 sociology classes every year, which works out to close to 2 million students annually (Gans 1989). The effect that these teachers have on their students is one of the major paths through which sociology affects society.

Although teachers' goals vary, most sociology courses have two objectives: to give students a better understanding of their own society—for example, its crime rates, inequality, school systems, and population; and to help students see the degree to which individual experience is shaped by larger social structures—that is, to develop the sociological imagination.

Although one course isn't likely to change the way you view the world, studies show that social science majors do learn to view the world differently than others do. One recent study asked college students and the public to rate the importance of various causes of poverty and unemployment (Guimond, Begin, and Palmer 1989). The authors found that although many students and much of the public tended to blame individuals ("poor people spend foolishly," "poor people do not try hard enough"), social science majors were much more likely to blame the system ("jobs are inadequately paid," "the economic situation is unfavorable"). Teaching students to take this broader perspective is one of the most important things that sociologists do.

RESEARCH

Research (described in more detail in Chapter 2) is the other major activity of professional sociologists. It engages nearly all of the sociologists who work for government, industry, or nonprofit organizations, as well as many sociology professors. Much of this research is *basic sociology*, which has no immediate practical application and is motivated simply by a desire to describe or explain some aspect of human social behavior more fully. Even basic research, however, often has implications for social policy. For example, Lenore Weitzman's research on the consequences of no-fault divorce, as discussed in Chapter 13, played a key role in establishing a new federal law enforcing child-support payments ("Weitzman's Research" 1985).

In addition to the pure research motivated by scholarly curiosity, an increasing proportion of sociologists are engaged in *applied sociology*, seeking to provide immediate practical answers to problems of government, industry, or individuals. The proportion of sociologists who are engaged in applied work has more than doubled in the last decade, from 9 percent in 1976 to more than 20 percent today. This increase is evident in government, business, and nonprofit organizations.

Working in Government.   A long tradition of sociological work in government has to do with measuring and forecasting population trends. This work is vital for decisions about where to put roads and schools and when to stop building schools and start building nursing homes. In addition, sociologists have been employed to design and evaluate public policies in a wide variety of areas. In World War II, sociologists designed policies to increase the morale and fighting efficiency of the armed forces. During the so-called war on poverty in the 1960s, sociologists helped plan and evaluate programs to reduce the inheritance of poverty.

Sociologists work in nearly every branch of government. Sociologist William Darrow, for example, is employed by the Centers for Disease Control (CDC). His assignment is to examine social relationships related to the transmission of AIDS, to understand how intravenous drug users share needles and how AIDS is transmitted along chains of sexual partners. While the physicians and biologists of CDC examine the medical aspects of AIDS, Darrow works at understanding the social aspects. In speaking of his choice of work, Darrow (cited in Howery 1983) says:

John F. Kennedy had just become president and I thought I heard him asking me what I could do for my country. Rather than accepting a decent job as a management trainee for Bauer and Black, I chose to work with the Sharks and the Jets on the West Side of Manhattan for $4,490 a year. *West Side Story* is ancient history, but I am still trying to figure out how diseases spread in communities, and how chains of disease transmission can be broken.

Working in Business.   Sociologists are employed by General Motors and Pillsbury, as well as by advertisers and management consultants. Part of their work concerns internal affairs (bureaucratic structures and labor relations), but much of it has to do with market research. Business and industry employ sociologists so that they can use their knowledge of society to predict which way consumer demand is likely to jump. For example, the sharp increase in single-person households has important implications for life insurance companies, for food packagers, and for the construction industry. To stay profitable, companies need to be able to predict and plan for these kinds of changes. Another area of extensive involvement for sociologists is the preparation of environmental impact statements, in which they assess the impact of, say, a coal slurry operation on the social and economic fabric of a proposed site.

Working in Nonprofit Organizations.   Nonprofit organizations range from hospitals and clinics to social-activist organizations and private think tanks; sociologists are employed in all of them. Sociologists at Planned Parenthood, for example, are interested in determining the causes and consequences of teenage sexual behavior, with evaluating communication strategies that can be used to prevent teenage pregnancy, and with devising effective strategies to pursue some of that organization's more controversial goals, such as the preservation of legal access to abortion on demand.

The training that sociologists receive has a strong research orientation and is very different form the therapy-oriented training received by social workers. Nevertheless, a thorough understanding of the ways that social structures impinge on individuals can be useful in helping individuals cope with personal troubles. Consequently, some sociologists also do marriage counseling, family counseling, and rehabilitation counseling.

Sociology in the Public Service.   Although most sociologists are committed to a value-free approach to their work as scholars, many are equally committed to changing society for the better. As a result, sociologists have served on a wide variety of public commissions and in public offices in order to effect social change. Examples include Daniel Patrick Moynihan, U.S. senator from New York, Professor Ilene Nagel from the University of Indiana, who serves on the federal commission to establish uniform criminal sentencing, and Katrina Johnson, who heads a federal task force to uncover the reasons for the high risk of heart disease in minority Americans.

Perhaps the clearest example of sociology in the public service is the award of the 1982 Nobel Peace Prize to Swedish sociologist Alva Myrdal for her unflagging efforts to increase awareness of the dangers of nuclear armaments. Value-free scholarship does not mean value-free citizenship.

ISSUES IN SOCIAL POLICY

Sociology's Role

Every chapter of this text will end with an "Issues in Social Policy" section that links chapter material to an issue that is currently a matter of public debate. In Chapter 9, for example, we show how sociological research relates to public programs designed to reduce inequality, while in Chapter 19, we consider what sociological analysis can tell us about policies concerning illegal immigration.

Some of the issues that concern sociologists are relatively philosophical and of more concern to scholars than to the public. To a great extent, though, sociologists are interested in the same topics that interest the public. We are interested in why some people get ahead and others don't, in the ways in which age and sex structure our lives, in drug abuse and drug policy, and in divorce, to name just a few.

Sociology has had a social-problems orientation since its beginning over a hundred years ago, and even today most sociologists are drawn into the field by a concern with specific social problems. A recent study of sociologists belonging to the American Sociological Association found that their major research and teaching interests were health; jobs and the organization of work; differences between men and women; poverty; family relationships; and aging ("Future Organizational Trends" 1989, 1). These are the very same topics that come up again and again as the areas of concern to the average American. This strong overlap between sociological and public concerns means that sociology is not an "ivory-tower" discipline that exists independent of society and the average citizen. Instead, sociology grapples with the issues of today's women, men, and children.

SOCIOLOGY'S UNIQUE CONTRIBUTION TO PUBLIC POLICY DEBATES

Public policy is generally formulated in legislatures, boardrooms, and oval offices. In the United States, this means that it is usually formed by

This picture of President Bush and some of the leaders of Congress accurately portrays the kinds of people who usually make social policy decisions in our society: middle-aged, native-born, Ivy-League educated, European-American males. One of the goals of sociology is to represent the life experiences and opinions of the other 99 percent of the population. Sociologists feel a special obligation to understand the disadvantaged and disenfranchised.

white men from upper-middle-class or elite backgrounds and that, while it reflects their understanding of the public interest, it also reflects their own backgrounds and political agendas.

In this setting, sociologists have two chief contributions to make. First, sociologists try to be objective. They try to gather and assess evidence independent of political agendas. Second, sociologists study ordinary people. Although there are many research strategies in sociology, most sociological research relies on talking to and observing average citizens. In doing so, it has a special concern with representing the unheard and the disadvantaged. Thus, sociological research is an important mechanism through which the concerns of ordinary men and women are represented in the public arena (Gans 1989).

SUMMARY

1. While its sister discipline, psychology, focuses on individual-level factors that affect human behavior, sociology focuses on how social structures affect behavior. Learning to understand how individual behavior is affected by social structures is the process of developing the "sociological imagination."

2. Sociology is a social *science*. This means it relies on critical and systematic examination of the evidence before reaching any conclusions and that it approaches each research question from a position of neutrality. This is called value-free sociology.

3. The rapid social change that followed the industrial revolution was an important inspiration for the development of sociology. Problems caused by disorganization and rapid change stimulated the demand for accurate information about social processes. This social-problems orientation remains an important thread in sociology today.

4. Comte is regarded as the founder of sociology. Two Germans, Karl Marx and Max Weber, and a Frenchman, Émile Durkheim, were important early theorists. Sociology was established in the U.S. in the last quarter of the 19th century. U.S. sociology is distinguished from its European counterpart in its concern with social problems, its reforming rather than radical approach to these problems, and its emphasis on the scientific method.

5. There are three major theoretical perspectives for approaching the study of social structures and human behavior in sociology: structural-functional theory, conflict theory, and symbolic interaction theory. The three can be seen as alternate lenses through which to view society, each having value as a tool for understanding how social structures shape human behavior.

6. Structural-functionalism has its roots in evolutionary theory. It identifies social structures and analyzes their consequences for social harmony and the maintenance of society. Identification of manifest and latent functions and dysfunctions is part of its analytic framework.

7. Modern conflict theory is derived from Karl Marx's ideas. It analyzes social structures by asking who benefits and how are these benefits maintained. It assumes that competition is more important than consensus and that change occurs as a result of conflict and revolution rather than through evolution.

8. Symbolic interaction theory examines how individuals relate to and are affected by social structures. It asks how social structures affect individual subjective experiences. While structural functionalism and conflict theory study macrosociology, symbolic interactionism is a form of microsociology: It focuses on individual relationships.

9. Most sociologists teach and do research in academic settings. A growing minority are employed in government and business, where they do applied research. Regardless of the setting, sociological theory and research have implications for social policy.

SUGGESTED READINGS

The American Journal of Sociology. Chicago: University of Chicago Press. Published regularly for nearly 100 years, this oldest U.S. sociology journal is also one of the most accessible to non-specialists. A glance through any issue will acquaint you with the variety of issues of concern to contemporary sociologists.

Bart, Pauline, and Frankel, Linda. 1986. The Student Sociologist's Handbook. (4th ed.) New York: Random House. Information on sociological perspectives, research materials, and sociological writing for the beginning student.

Berger, Peter L. 1963. Invitation to Sociology: A Humanistic Perspective. Garden City, N.Y.: Doubleday Anchor. A delightful, well-written introduction to what sociology is and how it differs from other social sciences. Blends a serious exploration of basic sociological understandings with scenes from everyday life—encounters that are easy to relate to and that make sociology both interesting and relevant.

Mills, C. Wright. 1959. The Sociological Imagination. New York: Oxford University Press. A penetrating account of how the study of sociology expands understanding of common experiences.

Nock, Steven L. and Kingston, Paul. 1990. The Sociology of Public Issues. Belmont, Calif: Wadsworth. A breezy introduction to the variety of public issues that can be examined with a sociological imagination, including drug testing, blacks in sports management, and anti-drunk driving crusades.

Riis, Jacob A. 1971. How the Other Half Lives. New York: Dover Publishers. A photo essay and narrative of conditions in New York City in the second half of the 19th century. Riis, a police reporter turned social reformer, documents through pictures and statistics the deplorable conditions in New York that accompanied industrialization and that eventually spawned the development of modern sociology.

DOING SOCIOLOGY

Have you ever . . .

Heard those advertisements that start with a statement such as "Nine out of 10 doctors surveyed recommended brand X?" Most Americans have listened to so many far-fetched commercials that they are pretty cynical about such claims. Even without training in proper research techniques, many will wonder exactly how these doctors were identified and exactly what questions they were asked. Were these doctors evaluating free samples, or what?

In the case of chewing gum or brands of aspirin, the credibility of the research isn't terribly critical. We don't really care very much whether the study design is biased in favor of one brand name or the other. There are many urgent contemporary issues, however, that demand our best efforts. For example, as many as 15 percent of babies being born in urban hospitals suffer some damage because their mothers used crack cocaine during pregnancy. What programs will be the most successful in reducing crack use among young women?

Building effective programs to address problems such as crack babies, highschool dropouts, and divorce requires reliable evidence from representative samples. We cannot afford to waste either our time or our money on programs built on a foundation of shoddy evidence. In this chapter, we cover the research strategies generally used by sociologists to provide high quality data. One chapter won't prepare you to do research, but we hope it will make you a better consumer of research, more aware of its potential strengths and weaknesses.

THE SCIENTIFIC PERSPECTIVE
Defining Science

A BRIEF PRIMER ON SOCIOLOGICAL RESEARCH
The Research Process
Some General Principles of Research
Evaluation: How Good Is Sociological Research?

THREE STRATEGIES FOR GATHERING DATA
The Experiment
The Survey
Participant Observation
Alternative Strategies

EXAMPLES OF SOCIOLOGICAL RESEARCH
The Survey: Adolescent Sexuality and Pregnancy
Participant Observation: Tally's Corner
The Experiment: Does Anybody Give A Damn?

THE ETHICS OF SOCIAL RESEARCH
Ethical Principles
Ethical Issues in Practice

THE SCIENTIFIC PERSPECTIVE

The things that sociologists study—for example, deviance, marital happiness, and poverty—have probably interested you for a long time. You may have developed your own opinions about why some people have good marriages and some have bad marriages or why some people use cocaine and others do not. Sociology is an academic discipline that uses the procedures of science to examine common sense explanations of human social behavior. Science is not divorced from common sense but is an extension of it.

DEFINING SCIENCE

The ultimate aim of science is to understand the world better. Science directs us to find this understanding by observing and measuring what actually happens. This is not the only means of acquiring knowledge. Some people get their perceptions form the Bible or the Koran or the Book of Mormon. Others get their answers from their mothers or their husbands or their girlfriends. When you ask such people, "But how do you know that that is true?" their answer is simple. They say "My mother told me" or "I read it in *Reader's Digest*."

Science is a way of knowing based on empirical evidence.

Science differs from these other ways of knowing in that it requires an *objective* and *critical* approach to *empirical* evidence. What does this mean?

An *objective approach* requires that we evaluate evidence fairly and without personal bias. The evidence should be considered objectively, without regard to the race, class, or sex of the investigator, without regard to how the results will affect our careers or personal profit, without regard to how well the results match our personal preferences. For example, a sociologist investigating the effects of daycare programs is expected to be open to the possibility that such programs have negative effects even if his or her own children are at a daycare center while the sociologist is at work.

The *critical approach* means that we take a skeptical attitude toward all new research findings. Science is slow to accept new findings, and all research results are critically examined to see if they meet technical standards. Generally, results are accepted only after they have been **replicated**—that is, only when other researchers have repeated the study and gotten the same results.

Replication is repeating empirical studies with another investigator or a different sample to see if the same results occur.

Empirical refers to evidence that can be confirmed by the human senses. Science requires the use of evidence that we can see, hear, smell, or feel. This means we do not accept public opinion or divine revelation as a source of factual knowledge.

A simple example shows how the scientific perspective works. Suppose we undertake a scientific investigation of the saying, "An apple a day keeps the doctor away." Before we accept this statement, we need empirical evidence: We need a study that documents apple intake by a representative sample of individuals. Then, we need their health records. Even if the empirical evidence shows that frequent apple eaters go to the doctor less, we will need to be critical. Apple eating is probably part of a generally healthy life-style; it may be that exercise, a low-fat diet, and other aspects of a healthy life-style are responsible for the apple eaters' good health. If this is true, then these people would be healthier than others even if they ate no fruit at all. Finally, even if I own stock in an apple orchard, I must assess the information objectively.

The scientific perspective does not guarantee that we will arrive at the truth. It is, however, the best means that our society offers for seeking and validating new knowledge. By giving us a method for systematically evaluating evidence, science gradually helps us weed out wrong conclusions and identify correct ones. Within the field of sociology, the use of the scientific perspective allows us to examine highly charged issues—such as divorce, welfare, and drug use—and produce answers that stand up to critical evaluation by objective observers.

A BRIEF PRIMER ON SOCIOLOGICAL RESEARCH

The procedures used in sociological research are covered in classes on research methods, statistics, and theory construction. At this point, we want to introduce a few ideas that you must understand if you are to be an educated consumer of the research results you will read later in this book. We begin by looking at the general research process and then review three concepts central to research: variables, operational definitions, and sampling.

THE RESEARCH PROCESS

The research process has two goals: description and explanation. In sociology we want to describe human social behavior, answering such questions as "What is the divorce rate?" or "Who are the unemployed?" After we know what is going on, we hope to be able to explain it. (What causes divorce? What causes unemployment?) There are four steps to achieving these goals.

Step One: Gathering Data.   The first step in the research process begins with collecting data. We may rely on the census to get information about people's income or unemployment or on the police to provide information about crime rates. It is important to recognize that neither of these sources provides unbiased data: People can and do give false information on census forms, and the police obviously don't have a complete and unbiased record about crime. Collecting accurate data is a difficult task that may never be complete.

Step Two: Finding Patterns.   The second step in the research process is to find patterns in the data. If we study unemployment, for example, we will find that black Americans are more than twice as likely as white Americans to experience unemployment (U.S. Department of Labor 1990). This generalization notes a **correlation,** an empirical relationship between two variables—in this case, between race and unemployment.

Correlation occurs when there is an empirical relationship between two variables.

In the course of daily routine, each of us provides huge quantities of data that are used for sociological research. When we marry, die, divorce, register for school or the draft, go to jail, or file taxes, we provide information that can be used to build an empirical picture of American society. In addition to the data provided on these routine occasions, every ten years the government conducts a monumental survey research project in the form of the decennial Census. Because the Census includes 250 million people, it provides data on small populations—such as Native Americans or middle-aged bachelors—that are not available from sample surveys.

Theory is an interrelated set of assumptions that explains observed patterns.

Step Three: Generating Theories.   After finding a pattern, we need to explain it. *Why* are black Americans more likely to experience unemployment? Explanations are usually embodied in a **theory,** an interrelated set of assumptions that explains observed patterns. Theory always goes beyond the facts at hand; it includes untested assumptions that explain the empirical evidence.

For example, one might theorize that the reason black Americans face more unemployment than whites is because many of today's black adults grew up in a time when the racial difference in educational opportunity was much greater than it is now. This simple explanation goes beyond the facts at hand to include some assumptions about how education is related to race and unemployment. Although the theory rests on an empirical generalization, the theory itself is not empirical; it is . . . well, theoretical.

It should be noted that many theories may be compatible with a given empirical generalization. We have proposed that education explains the correlation between race and unemployment. An alternate theory might argue that the correlation arises because of discrimination. Because there are often many plausible explanations for any correlation, theory development is not the end of the research process. We must go on to test the assumptions of the theory by gathering new data.

Step Four: Testing Hypotheses.   To test theories, we deduce **hypotheses**—statements about empirical relationships that we expect to observe if our theory is correct. From the theory linking higher black unemployment to educational deficits, for example, we can deduce the hypothesis that blacks and whites of equal education will experience equal unemployment. To test this hypothesis, we need more data, this time about education and its relationship to race and unemployment.

A recent study by Daniel Lichter (1989) tests a closely-related hypothesis. Lichter (1989) asked whether educational deficits explained why black men experienced greater employment hardship than white men in the rural South. He found the hypothesis was not supported: even if educational levels were equal, the odds that black men would experience employment hardship were 52 percent higher than for white men.

Lichter's finding is a new correlation and can be the basis for a revised theory. This new theory will again be subject to empirical test, and the process begins again. As this example illustrates, the process of science can be viewed as a continuously turning wheel that moves us from data to theory and from theory to data. In the language of science, the process of moving from data to theory is called **induction,** and the process of moving from theory to data is called **deduction.** These two processes and their interrelationships are illustrated in Figure 2.1.

SOME GENERAL PRINCIPLES OF RESEARCH

Variables.   Human behavior is complex. In order to narrow the scope of inquiry to a manageable size, we focus on variables rather than on people. **Variables** are measured characteristics that vary from one individual or group to the next (Babbie 1986).

For example, Lichter's study focused on three variables: race, education, and employment hardship. The individuals included in his study were, of course, complex and interesting human beings, but Lichter was interested

Hypotheses are statements about relationships that we expect to find if our theory is correct.

Induction is the process of moving from data to theory by devising theories that account for empirically observed patterns.

Deduction is the process of moving from theory to data by testing hypotheses drawn from theory.

Variables are measured characteristics that vary from one individual or group to the next.

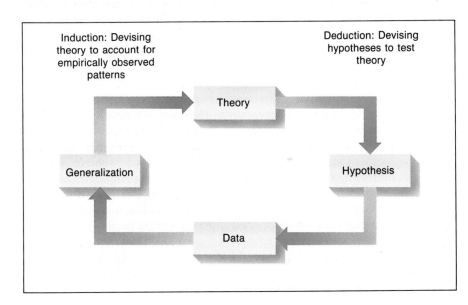

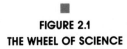

FIGURE 2.1
THE WHEEL OF SCIENCE

The process of science can be viewed as a continuously turning wheel that moves us from data to theory and back again.

SOURCE: Adapted from Wallace, Walter. 1969. *Sociological Theory.* Chicago: Aldine.

Despite many changes in the last 50 years, the rural South continues to be the poorest area of the country and black Americans in the rural South continue to be systematically disadvantaged relative to both their urban counterparts and to rural whites. In 1989, Daniel Lichter concluded that this disadvantage cannot be explained by deficits in education, experience, or training.

The **independent variable** is the variable that does the causing in cause-and-effect relationships.

The **dependent variable** is the effect in cause-and-effect relationships. It is dependent on the actions of the independent variable.

Operational definitions describe the exact procedures by which a variable is measured.

only in their scores on these three variables. Variables, rather than the individuals themselves, are the focus of sociological study.

When we hypothesize a cause-and-effect relationship between two variables, the cause is called the **independent variable** and the effect is called the **dependent variable.** In Lichter's hypothesis, for example, education was the independent variable and employment hardship the dependent variable; that is, he hypothesized that employment hardship depended on education.

Operational Definitions.   The research process requires exact specification of how variables will be measured. How will we decide whether an individual is experiencing employment hardship? The exact procedures by which a variable is measured are called **operational definitions.** Reaching general agreement about these definitions often poses a problem. For example, Lichter's procedure coded a man as experiencing employment hardship if (a) he was unemployed, *or* (b) he was working part time but would rather be working full time, *or* (c) his wages were below a specified level. Obviously, a researcher who just used unemployment might get different results. Likewise, a researcher who asked people, "Do you feel that you face an employment hardship?" might identify an entirely different set of people. Consumers of research should always check carefully to see what operational definitions are being used when they evaluate study results.

Sampling.   It would be time consuming, expensive, and probably nearly impossible to get information on race, education, and employment hardship for all adults. It is also unnecessary. The process of **sampling,** taking a systematic selection of representative cases from a larger population, allows us to get accurate empirical data at a fraction of the cost that it would take to examine all possible cases.

A **sample** is a systematic selection of representative cases from the larger population.

Sampling involves two processes: getting a list of the population you want to study and then selecting a representative subset or sample from the list. Selecting from the list is easy: Choosing a relatively large number by a random procedure generally assures that the sample will be unbiased. The more difficult task is getting a list. A central principle of sampling is that a sample is only representative of the list from which it is drawn. If we draw a list of people from the telephone directory, then our sample can only be said to describe households listed in the directory; it will omit those with unlisted numbers, those with no telephones, and those who have moved since the directory was issued. The best surveys begin with a list of all the households or telephone numbers in the target region. Lichter's study of employment hardship used a federal survey that drew a sample of 60,000 households from a master list of all the households in the United States. Obviously, data from such a study should be taken much more seriously than results from a study of, say, 400 people listed in the Bemidji, Minnesota telephone directory.

EVALUATION: HOW GOOD IS SOCIOLOGICAL RESEARCH?

In the remaining 20 chapters of this book, we report the results of hundreds, even thousands, of different research studies. All of these studies appeared in professional journals, where they received a rigorous screening process that is designed to be both objective and critical. A brief review of this process should raise your confidence in what you are about to read.

At the conclusion of a research project, the researcher writes up the study results, being very specific about operational definitions and sampling strategy, and sends it off to a professional journal. The journal replaces the researcher's name with a number and sends it out for a blind review—that is, the reviewers don't know who did the research and the researcher doesn't know who the reviewers are. This blind review reduces the likelihood that research will be accepted because it is written by somebody famous or because it is written by somebody who might give the reviewer a job. At the top journals, *90 percent of all research reports are rejected as not meeting adequate standards.* They are rejected because they have small, unrepresentative samples or because their operational definitions are inadequate. As a result of this process, the research reports that do make it into the professional journals tend to be of very high quality and meet the highest scientific standards.

This means that the results reported in this text have survived pretty critical and objective evaluations. Nevertheless, the scientific perspective requires that all research consumers apply their own critical intelligence to evaluating the merits of claims about knowledge. As you read the results in the next 20 chapters, you should critically evaluate issues such as operational definitions and sample size.

■
THREE STRATEGIES FOR GATHERING DATA

The theories and findings reported in this book have used a variety of research strategies. Three of the more general strategies are outlined here: experiments, survey research, and participant observation. In this section, we review each method and illustrate its advantages and disadvantages by showing how it would approach the test of a common hypothesis, that marijuana use reduces grades in school. In the following section, we describe three published research projects using each method in order to give a more complete and realistic illustration of these data-gathering strategies. Finally, we conclude the chapter with a section on research ethics.

THE EXPERIMENT

The **experiment** is a method in which the researcher manipulates independent variables to test theories of cause and effect.

An **experimental group** is the group in an experiment that experiences the independent variable. Results for this group are compared with those for the control group.

A **control group** is the group in an experiment that does not receive the independent variable.

The **experiment** is a research method in which the researcher manipulates the independent variable to test theories of cause and effect. Sometimes experiments are conducted in carefully controlled conditions in laboratories, but often they take place in normal classrooms and work environments. In the classic experiment, a group that experiences the independent variable, an **experimental group,** is compared with a **control group** that does not. If the groups are equal on everything else, a comparison between them will show whether experience with the independent variable is associated with unique change in the dependent variable.

An experiment designed to assess whether marijuana use affected grades, for example, would need to compare an experimental group that smoked marijuana with a control group that did not. A hypothetical experiment might begin by observing student grades for several weeks until students' normal performance levels had been established. Then the class would be randomly divided into two groups. If the initial pool is large enough, we can assume that the two groups are probably equal on nearly everything. For example, we can assume that both groups probably contain an equal mix of good and poor students, of lazy and ambitious students. The control group might be requested to abstain from marijuana use for five weeks and the experimental group might be requested to smoke marijuana three times a week during the same period. At the end of the five weeks, we would compare the grades of the two groups. Both groups might have experienced a drop in grades because of normal factors such as fatigue, burnout, and overwork. The existence of the control group, however, allows us to determine whether marijuana use causes a reduction in grades over and above that which normally occurs.

Experiments are excellent devices for testing hypotheses about cause and effect. They have three drawbacks, however. First, experiments are often unethical because they expose subjects to the possibility of harm. It should be obvious, for example, that the hypothetical experiment described here would be wildly unethical: Encouraging students to smoke marijuana might damage student grades, introduce students to bad habits, or otherwise injure them. A more extreme example is the question of whether people who were abused as children are more likely to abuse their own children. We could not set up an experiment in which one of two randomly assigned groups of children was beaten and the other not. Because of such ethical issues, many areas of sociological interest cannot be studied with the experimental method.

A second drawback to experiments is that subjects often behave differently when they are under scientific observation than they would in their normal environment. For example, although marijuana use might normally have the effect of lowering student grades, the participants in our study might find the research so interesting that their grades actually improved. In this case, the subjects' knowledge that they are participating in an experiment affects their response to the independent variable. This response is called the **guinea-pig effect.** In sociology, it is often called the Hawthorne effect because it was first documented in a research project in the Hawthorne Electric plant.

The **guinea-pig effect** occurs when subjects' knowledge that they are participating in an experiment affects their response to the independent variable.

A final drawback to the experiment is especially relevant to laboratory experiments such as that described later in this chapter. When researchers try to set up social situations in laboratories, they often must omit many of the factors that would influence the same behavior in a real-life situation. The result is often a highly artificial social situation. Like the guinea-pig effect, this artificiality has the effect of reducing our confidence that the same results that appear in the experiment can be generalized to the more complex conditions of the real world.

Because of these disadvantages and because of ethical limitations, relatively little sociological research uses the controlled experiment. The areas in which it has been most useful are the study of small-group interaction and the simulation of situations that seldom occur in real life.

The research method that you choose will depend upon your research question. If you want to know whether this pleasant-looking couple goes to church or votes, survey research will be entirely appropriate. They probably will be quite cooperative and reasonably honest. Even people such as this, however, cannot be depended on to give you accurate answers to questions about family violence or drug abuse. Although survey research is our best all-around strategy for gathering data, it does have its limitations.

THE SURVEY

Survey research is a method that involves asking a relatively large number of people the same set of standardized questions.

Incidence is the frequency with which an attitude or behavior occurs.

Trends are changes in phenomena over time.

Differentials are differences in the incidence of a phenomenon across subcategories of the population.

A **cross-sectional design** uses a sample (or cross section) of the population at a single point in time.

Control variables are measures of the background factors that may be confounding the true relationship between our study variables.

The **panel design** follows a sample over a period of time.

In **survey research,** the investigator asks a relatively large number of people the same set of standardized questions. These questions may be asked in a personal interview, over the telephone, or in a paper-and-pencil format. This technique is the one most commonly used to gather sociological data. Because it asks the same questions of a large number of people, it is an ideal method for furnishing evidence on **incidence** (the frequency of phenomena in the population), **trends** (changes in the phenomena over time), and **differentials** (differences among population subgroups on the phenomena). For example, survey data on marijuana use may allow us to say such things as: Thirty percent of the undergraduates at Midwestern State smoke marijuana (incidence); the proportion using marijuana has gone down in the last 10 years (trend); and the proportion using marijuana is higher for males than females (differential). Because survey research can easily be used with large, national samples, it is an excellent source of descriptive data. It is also very versatile: It can be used to study attitudes, behavior, and values.

Most surveys use what is called a **cross-sectional design;** they take a sample (or cross section) of the population at a single point in time. Thus, in our study of marijuana use, we would take a sample of students, expecting to find that some of them smoke marijuana and some do not. We could then compare these two groups to see which gets the best grades.

If we were to do this, we might find a correlation between marijuana use and grades (see Focus on Research in this chapter). The difficulty with the cross-sectional design is that we cannot reach any firm conclusions about cause and effect. We cannot tell whether marijuana use causes bad grades or whether bad grades lead to marijuana use. A more striking problem is that we cannot be sure there is a cause-and-effect relationship at all. Since the smokers and nonsmokers were not randomly assigned to the two categories, the two groups differ on many other variables besides smoking. For example, the smokers may have less conventional families, come from worse neighborhoods, or be less religious. It could be that one of these factors is causing the poor grades and that smoking behavior is just coincidental.

To try to rule out as many of these alternate explanations as possible, we introduce **control variables**—measures of the background factors that may be confounding the true relationship between our study variables. For example, to control for the possibility that social class is the real cause of poor grades, we can restrict our analysis to middle-class students. Even if we were to add controls for race, sex, religion, and family life, however, we could not feel certain that the two groups were equivalent. A skeptic would still have grounds for asserting that students who chose to smoke were different than those who did not.

One strategy that survey researchers use to improve the strength of their conclusions is to employ a **panel design,** which follows a sample over a period of time. During this period of time, some sample members will experience the independent variable, and we can observe how they differ before and after this experience from those who have no contact with the independent variable. To use this design for examining the effect of marijuana use on grades would require selecting a sample of, say, 10-to-16-

year-olds and interviewing them at several points over the next few years. This design would not alter the fact that some people choose to smoke and others do not, but it would let us look at the same people before and after their decision. It would allow us to see whether students' grades actually fell after they started to smoke marijuana or whether they were always poor students. A study that actually used this design followed a group of 700 Colorado youngsters for four years; the investigators concluded that a poor attitude toward school generally preceded marijuana use (Jessor and Jessor 1977). The major disadvantage of this design is that it is expensive and time consuming. The study described here, for example, took five years from design to final analysis.

Another important drawback of survey research is that respondents may misrepresent the truth. Prejudiced people may tell you that they are unprejudiced, and only a small fraction of those who abuse their children are likely to admit it. This misrepresentation is known as **social-desirability bias**—the tendency for people to color the truth so that they appear to be nicer, richer, and generally more desirable than they really are. The consequences of this bias vary in seriousness depending on the research aim and topic. Obviously, it is a greater problem for such sensitive topics as drug use and prejudice.

Survey research is designed to get standard answers to standard questions. It is not the best strategy for studying deviant or undesirable behaviors or for getting at ideas and feelings that cannot easily be reduced to questionnaire form. An additional drawback of survey research is that it is a method designed to study individuals rather than contexts. Thus, it focuses on the individual smoker or nonsmoker rather than the setting and relationships in which smoking takes place. For these kinds of answers we must turn to participant observation.

PARTICIPANT OBSERVATION

Under the label **participant observation** we classify a variety of research strategies—participating, interviewing, observing—that examine the context and meanings of human behavior. Instead of sending forth an army of interviewers, participant observers go out into the field themselves to see firsthand what is going on. These strategies are used most often by sociologists interested in symbolic interaction theory—that is, researchers who want to understand subjective meanings and personal relationships. The goals of this research method are to discover patterns of interaction and to find the meaning of the patterns for the individuals involved.

The three major tasks involved in participant observation are interviewing, participating, and observing. A researcher goes to the scene of the action, where she may interview people informally in the normal course of conversation, participate in whatever they are doing, and observe the activities of other participants. Not every participant observation study includes all three dimensions equally. A participant observer studying drug use on campus, for example, would not need to get stoned every night. She would, however, probably do long, informal interviews with both users and nonusers, attend student parties and activities, and attempt to get a feel for how marijuana use fits in with certain student subcultures.

Social-desirability bias is the tendency of people to color the truth so that they sound nicer, richer, and more desirable than they really are.

Participant observation includes a variety of research strategies—participating, interviewing, observing—that examine the context and meanings of human behavior.

FOCUS ON MEASUREMENT

Survey Research—Interpreting the Results

The most common research method used in sociology today is survey research. Many of the findings reported in later chapters rely on survey data. Here we present some guidelines for interpreting and evaluating these results.

The Problem

In the spring of 1990, to gather data for a class exercise, we conducted a survey among our introductory sociology students. In this exercise, we wanted to examine the hypothesis that marijuana use was related to student grades. Social class was included as a control variable. This simple research project therefore required information on three variables: marijuana use, social class, and grades.

The actual questions and instructions are reproduced in Figure 2.2. Notice that the instructions encourage students to answer but give them the option of refusing. It would be unethical to require students to give personal information as part of a class assignment.

The Frequency or Percentage Table. The simplest way to present data is in a frequency, or percentage, table, which summarizes data about a single variable. (Frequencies are often converted to percentages so they will be easier to interpret.) Table 2.1 is a percentage table for marijuana use. It shows that 536 students, or 69 percent of the total sample of 771, reported that they had never used marijuana when they were high school seniors.

FIGURE 2.2
A SAMPLE SURVEY OF COLLEGE STUDENTS

To the student:

The results of this questionnaire are intended for instructional use only. Your participation is entirely voluntary, and you may decline to fill out the questionnaire. If, for any reason, you object to a particular question, leave that question out and go on. Because the questionnaire is to be entirely anonymous, we ask that you refrain from putting your name or student identification number on the questionnaire. Thank you for your cooperation.

1. During your last year of high school, what was your grade point average?
   ( )A or A+
   ( )B or B+
   ((C or C+
   ( )D or lower
2. Did you ever use marijuana during your senior year in high school?
   ( )No
   ( )Yes
3. If you were asked to use one of four names for your parents' social class, which would you say they belong in?
   ( )Upper class
   ( )Middle class
   ( )Working class
   ( )Lower class

TABLE 2.1
FREQUENCY OF MARIJUANA USE AMONG 771 INTRODUCTORY SOCIOLOGY STUDENTS AT A MIDWESTERN STATE UNIVERSITY, JANUARY 1990

"Did you ever use marijuana during your senior year in high school?"

	Number	Percent
No	536	69%
Yes	235	31
TOTAL	771	100%

Cross-Tabulations. To examine the general hypothesis that marijuana use results in lower grades, we need to compare the grades of users and nonusers. Table 2.2 presents this comparison. Because we are looking at two variables simultaneously, we refer to this as a cross-tabulation. A few important guidelines should be followed in reading such a table.

1. Read the headings carefully. A good table will tell you something about the origin and size of the sample as well as the operational definitions used in measuring the variables.

2. Figure out how the percentages are calculated. The usual convention is to percentage within categories of the independent variable. Thus, Table 2.2 tells you that 40 percent of those who did not use marijuana in high school got A's, 48 percent got B's, and 12 percent got C's or lower.

3. Compare the percentages across categories of the independent variable. The critical information in this table is given in the percentages across the rows: that 40 percent of those who did not smoke marijuana got A's compared to only 19 percent among those who did smoke marijuana. Note that 12 percent of the nonusers and 25 percent of the users got C's or below in high school.

4. Interpret the results. Before going on, study the table. Do marijuana users get lower grades?

Controls. Table 2.2 shows a relationship between marijuana use and high school grade point average: Students who used marijuana were less likely to get A's. This is not necessarily evidence of a causal relationship. One plausible rival explanation is that both smoking behavior and grades are determined by the student's social class. To test this hypothesis, we introduce a control for social class.

TABLE 2.2
CROSS-TABULATION OF HIGH SCHOOL GRADES BY USE OF MARIJUANA IN HIGH SCHOOL, 771 INTRODUCTORY SOCIOLOGY STUDENTS AT A MIDWESTERN STATE UNIVERSITY, 1990

	USED MARIJUANA IN HIGH SCHOOL	
High School Grades	No	Yes
A or A+	40%	19%
B or B+	48	56
C+ or below	12	25
Total	100%	100%
Number	536	235

TABLE 2.3
RELATIONSHIP BETWEEN HIGH SCHOOL GRADES AND MARIJUANA USE CONTROLLING SOCIAL CLASS IDENTIFICATION AMONG 771 INTRODUCTORY SOCIOLOGY STUDENTS AT A MIDWESTERN STATE UNIVERSITY, 1990

	SOCIAL CLASS IDENTIFICATION			
	Lower or Working Class		Middle or Upper Class	
	Used Marijuana		Used Marijuana	
High School Grades	No	Yes	No	Yes
A or A+	41%	16%	40%	20%
B or B+	46	56	48	55
C+ or less	13	29	12	25
Total	100%	100%	100%	100%
Number	142	45	391	187

Table 2.3 shows the relationship between grades and marijuana use for two subgroups: those who identified themselves as lower or working class and those who identified themselves as middle or upper class. The results show that social class background has little effect on the relationship between marijuana use and grades. Among those from the lower and working class, 41 percent of the nonsmokers got A's compared to 16 percent of the smokers; among students who identified with the middle or upper class, nonsmokers were also twice as likely to get A's as nonsmokers (40 versus 20 percent). The difference between smokers and nonsmokers is a little stronger in the first group of students, but it is clear that marijuana smoking is strongly correlated with grades in both groups.

Interpretation

This simple study demonstrates a strong and consistent correlation between grades and marijuana use: People who report smoking marijuana in high school also report getting lower grades. It also tells us that this relationship exists regardless of social class. These results are suggestive but not compelling. The critical research consumer would point out at least four problems with these results.

1. *Sample:* This sample of midwestern college students is not very rep-

resentative. The results would be more compelling if they included noncollege students or college students from other regions.

2. *Operational definition:* Do we really expect one joint to ruin a student's grades? A better study would measure extent of marijuana use to distinguish between the one-time smoker and the regular user.

3. *Causal order:* Because this study is cross-sectional, we cannot tell whether poor grades preceded or followed marijuana use—or whether both are the result of some other variable.

4. *Control variables:* This illustration used only one control variable. A better study would control sex, religion, family background, city size, and other variables.

There are few perfect studies, and cross-sectional survey research is open to multiple criticisms. It is nevertheless an invaluable tool for establishing frequencies and correlations. Although we might quibble about *why* the correlation between marijuana use and grades exists, the data in Tables 2.2 and 2.3 provide pretty compelling evidence that the relationship exists.

The data produced by participant observation are often based on small numbers of individuals who have not been selected according to random-sampling techniques. The data tend to be unsystematic and the samples not very representative; however, we do know a great deal about the few individuals involved. This detail is often useful for generating ideas that can then be examined more systematically with other techniques. In this regard, participant observation may be viewed as a form of initial exploration of a research topic.

In some situations, however, participant observation is the only reasonable way to approach a subject. This is especially likely when we are examining undesirable behavior, real behavior rather than attitudes, or uncooperative populations. In the first instance, social-desirability bias makes it difficult to get good information about undesirable behavior. Thus, what we know about running a brothel (Heyl 1979) or the homeless (Snow and Anderson 1987) rests largely on the reports of participant observers. This style of research produces fewer distortions than would have occurred if a middle-class survey researcher dropped by to ask the participants about their activities.

In the second case, participant observation is well suited to studies of behavior—what people do rather than what they say they do. Behaviors are sometimes misrepresented in surveys simply because people are unaware of their actions or don't remember them very well. For example, individuals may believe they are not prejudiced, yet observational research will demonstrate that these same people systematically choose not to sit next to persons of another race on the bus or in public places. Sometimes actions speak louder than words.

In the third case, we know that survey research works best with people who are predisposed to cooperate with authorities and who are relatively literate. Where either one or both of these conditions is not met, survey research may not be possible. For this reason there is little survey research on prison populations, juvenile gangs, preschoolers, or rioters. Participant observation is often the only means to gather data on these populations.

A major disadvantage of participant observation is that the observations and generalizations rely on the interpretation of one investigator. Since

What is going on here? Survey research is not going to give you the answer. Not only is there no time to select a sample and draw up a questionnaire, this fellow doesn't appear to be a cooperative respondent. When we want to study social process or when we want to study deviant and uncooperative populations, participant research is usually our best research strategy. In this case—a confrontation between white supremacists, the police, and counter demonstrators at the "Aryan Woodstock" festival—a researcher would need to be on the scene for as long as possible and then track down participants later to discuss their behavior and motivations.

researchers are not robots, it seems likely that their findings reflect some of their own world view. This is a greater problem with participant observation than with survey or experimental work, but all social science suffers to some extent from the phenomenon. The answer to this dilemma is replication—redoing the same study with another investigator to see if the same results occur.

ALTERNATIVE STRATEGIES

The bulk of sociological research uses these three strategies. There are, however, a dozen or more other imaginative and useful ways of doing research, many of them involving analysis of social artifacts rather than people. For example, a study of women's magazines of the 19th century illustrates changing attitudes toward spinsterhood during that period (Hickok 1981). A study of children's portraits over the centuries has shown how our ideas of childhood have changed (Aries 1962). Studies of court records and government statistics have demonstrated frequencies, trends, and differentials in many areas of sociological interest.

EXAMPLES OF SOCIOLOGICAL RESEARCH

In this section, we present detailed descriptions of three published pieces of research that use the research strategies we have described. These case studies illustrate how research designs are actually implemented and show some of the dilemmas faced by those working within each research tradition.

■

CONCEPT SUMMARY
Research Methods

CONTROLLED EXPERIMENTS

Procedure   Dividing subjects into two equivalent groups, applying the independent variable to one group only, and observing the differences between the two groups on the dependent variable

Advantages   Excellent for analysis of cause-and-effect relationships; can simulate events and behaviors that do not occur outside the laboratory in any regular way

Disadvantages Based on small, nonrepresentative samples examined under highly artificial circumstances; unclear that people would behave the same way outside the laboratory; unethical to experiment in many areas

SURVEY RESEARCH

Procedure   Asking the same set of standard questions of a relatively large, systematically selected sample

Advantages   Very versatile—can study anything that we can ask about; can be done with large, random samples so that results represent many people; good for incidence, trends, and differentials

Disadvantages Shallow—does not get at depth and shades of meaning; affected by social-desirability bias; better for studying people than situations

PARTICIPANT OBSERVATION

Procedure   Observing people's behavior in its normal context; experiencing others' social settings as a participant; in-depth interviewing

Advantages   Seeing behavior in context; getting at meanings associated with behavior; seeing what people do rather than what they say they do

Disadvantages Limited to small, nonrepresentative samples; dependent on interpretation of single investigator

THE SURVEY:
ADOLESCENT SEXUAL ACTIVITY AND PREGNANCY

Rates of sexual activity among teenagers are of concern to both the public and sociologists, largely for the same reason: Sexual activity is the prelude to pregnancy. Why do sociologists care about pregnancy and childbearing? One reason is that the women who bear children while young and unmarried, and their children as well, get a poor start in life. On the average, both mothers and children have lower educational attainment, lower incomes, and less stable family lives (Furstenberg, Brooks-Gunn, and Morgan 1987).

Because early pregnancy and childbearing can have serious consequences, sociologists have been interested in documenting trends in adolescent sexual activity. More important, we want to understand the circumstances under which sexually active adolescents are likely to get pregnant
and bear children. One of the most recent studies of these issues was
carried out by Carol Aneshensel, Eve Fielder, and Rosina Becerra (1989)
from the University of California, Los Angeles.

Because of financial limitations, their sample had to be limited to Los
Angeles County. Obviously, there is no list of the names of all the young
women in Los Angeles County. The researchers did, however, have a list
of all the blocks in the county. Their solution was to sample in two stages.
First, they took a sample of all the blocks in Los Angeles, and then they
sent fieldworkers to walk around the selected blocks and list all the households. This produced a list of 18,397 occupied housing units. Second,
interviewers were sent to knock on each door to ask whether a Mexican-
American or Anglo (White, non-Hispanic) female aged 13 to 19 lived in
the household. (Black females were omitted because they had already been
studied in several previous projects.) This procedure identified 1,124 respondents, of whom 91 percent agreed to be interviewed. This is an un-
usually high response rate; some survey research projects have response
rates of only 50 percent. Nevertheless, even a loss of 9 percent can be a
problem. The 9 percent who refused or were never at home are probably
not a random sample of the population of young women. If the nonres-
pondents had higher rates of sexual activity, for example, then the survey
would underestimate the actual amount of sexual activity among young
women.

Sampling and interviewing of this sort are very expensive. Despite the
fact that interviews were restricted to the Los Angeles area, this study cost
$100,000, approximately $100 for each young woman interviewed. The
expense is one of the drawbacks of good survey research.

The researchers wanted to use a standard set of questions that all respondents would understand and respond to. In order to find out what
terms would communicate best with their target population, they began
their project by doing 50 long, informal interviews with young women
from these same ethnic backgrounds. (This is an example of using the less
formal techniques of participant observation as preparation for survey research.) On the basis of these interviews, they developed a set of standard
questions that were phrased in terms the young women would easily
understand. For example, they asked, "Sometimes people refer to sexual
intercourse as 'doing sex,' 'having sex,' 'making love,' or 'going all the way.'
Have you ever had sexual intercourse?"

Table 2.4 presents some of their results. In terms of overall frequency,
50 percent of the young women reported that they had had sexual intercourse by the age of 18. Differentials by ethnic groups showed that Mexican-
American women were less likely than Anglo women to be sexually active:
Forty-two percent of the Mexican-American women reported sexual intercourse by the age of 18 compared to 66 percent of the Anglo women.

More important than sexual intercourse, however, is pregnancy. One
of the critical findings of this research is that sexual activity was much
more risky for the Mexican-American women. Because they were much

*Approximately one million teenage
women get pregnant every year in the
United States. Over the course of
adolescence, this works out to a one-
in-three chance of getting pregnant
between 13 and 19. Although
adolescent pregnancy isn't necessarily
a social problem, most such
pregnancies are unwanted and pose
health and social risks. This kind of
issue is relatively easy to study using
survey research, and in the last decade
we have amassed a growing body of
empirical research that documents
incidence, trends, and differentials in
adolescent pregnancy. Research shows
that growing up in a single-parent
family is one of the best predictors of
adolescent pregnancy.*

■
TABLE 2.4

SEXUAL ACTIVITY, PREGNANCY, AND CHILDBEARING IN A SAMPLE OF 1,023 ADOLESCENT WOMEN FROM LOS ANGELES COUNTY, 1988

	Mexican American	*Non-Hispanic White*
Percent Ever Had Intercourse		
By Age 18	42%	66%
Percent of Sexually Active		
Who Ever Used Contraception	48	81
Percent of Sexually Active		
Ever Pregnant	50	26
Percent of Ever Pregnant Who		
Bore a Child	66	38
Number of Cases	706	317

SOURCE: Adapted from Aneshensel, Fielder, and Becerra 1989.

less likely to use contraception than their Anglo counterparts, 50 percent of the sexually active Mexican-American teens had been pregnant at least once, compared to only 26 percent of the Anglo teens. Because they were also much less likely to have an abortion, a full 33 percent of the sexually active Mexican-American women had actually had a child compared to only 10 percent of the Anglos.

For both groups, the best predictor of whether a sexually active teen would get pregnant was whether she came from a broken home. Regardless of ethnicity, young women who did not live with both their natural parents were more likely to be sexually active, less likely to use contraception, and more likely to get pregnant. Because nearly half of today's children will experience broken homes (Bumpass 1984), these results suggest that the incidence of teenage pregnancy is likely to increase. The authors conclude that "although the prevention or delay of sexual intercourse may be a desirable intervention goal, the prevention of pregnancy among the sexually active is the most pressing intervention priority" (Aneshensel, Fielder, and Becerra 1989, 75).

PARTICIPANT OBSERVATION TALLY'S CORNER

One of the best participant observation studies is described in the book *Tally's Corner*, a classic study of street-corner men in an urban slum (Liebow 1967). It offers a clear example of the strengths of this methodology; it also provides insight into a world that is unfamiliar to most Americans.

In spite of urban renewal, Head Start, and open-housing laws, urban slums in the United States have become poorer, blacker, and more despairing with every year. At one point in their development, they were just poor inner-city neighborhoods, but over the 45 years since World War II they have become the source of a hereditary class of the socially dispossessed. Little is known about the people who live in urban ghettos. Survey researchers are afraid to enter the neighborhoods, much less the tenement building themselves. The U.S. Census which spends billions of dollars trying to reach each citizen, misses 20 percent of the young men in central cities. Many do not have telephones or are so transient they are hard to reach. If someone from a survey research center does reach them to ask, "How do you feel about your economic prospects: Would you say they're staying the same, getting better, or getting worse?," a large proportion will decline to participate in such a personally meaningless and possibly threatening exercise.

What we know about the people who live in ghettos comes largely from the portion of the ghetto population that is in contact with authorities. Thus, we know something about schoolchildren (their scores on standardized exams, their reading levels, their nutrition), about mothers on welfare, and about men who get picked up by the police. These people are not a representative sample of the people who live in ghettos. Overriding the question of sampling is the question of whether information given involuntarily in welfare offices and police stations is truthful and open.

Obviously, people who live in inner-city neighborhoods grow up, pair up, have children, support themselves, and belong to families and to networks of friends. They do not act randomly; their behavior is hedged around and directed by the social structures of their community. A major question for social science research is what these structures are and what they mean to the individuals involved.

Elliot Liebow, author of *Tally's Corner*, wrote his doctoral dissertation as part of a larger research project that was designed to look at childrearing practices among lower-class families. For the reasons already given, survey research with questionnaires and paper-and-pencil tests were out of the question. More important, Liebow wanted to get an insider's view, a description of lower-class people and their lives in their terms and from their viewpoint. Because something was already known about lower-class women and children, Liebow chose to concentrate on the adult males.

Liebow chose a corner in Washington, D.C., and hung out there off and on for a year. He makes no pretense that this is a representative corner or that the men he came to know were representative of the men in Washington's slums. What he intends to do is offer a well-rounded picture of 15 to 20 men that enables us to see the social structure through their eyes. What does life look like in terms of their education, their economic opportunities, their environment?

Liebow is white and has many more years of schooling than the men he was studying. He presented himself at the corner wearing T-shirts and khaki pants, prepared to use bad grammar and bad language. He came, as did the real participants, just to hang out, to see "what's happening." He did not carry a tape recorder, take notes, or ask questions. He just made small talk with the regulars. After each observation period was finished, however, he returned to his office and made detailed notes on what he had observed. These field notes became his written record. When he came to write up his conclusions at the end of his year on the corner, the field notes enabled him to remember who had said what and what had actually happened.

The men on the corner knew that Liebow was there as part of his job, but since he took pains not to act, dress, or talk like a social scientist, he felt he was soon accepted by them—although always aware of his separateness from them because of his color. He was eventually invited to their homes, went out drinking with them, and was asked to come to court with

Frequently, sociologists are more interested in knowing about people than people are interested in being known about. Refusal to cooperate is especially likely among the unsuccessful, the disadvantaged, and the alienated. Thus, what we know about such people is likely to come from coerced data collection in prisons, welfare offices, and emergency room clinics. Elliot Liebow's participant observation study of Tally's Corner *was designed to balance such coerced data with a picture of what everyday life is like for streetcorner men.*

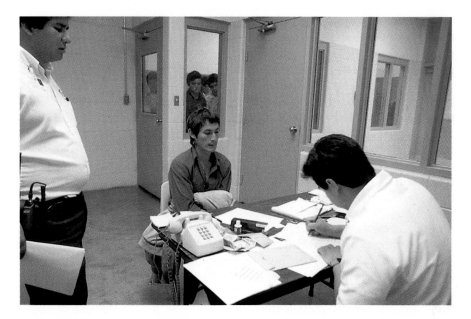

them on occasion to provide support or advice when they had brushes with the law or the authorities. From this year's experience he came to see the differences between their public performance (the kinds of stories people tell about themselves to people they meet for the first time—and to survey researchers) and their real situations.

Some of Liebow's most insightful findings cover the relationship of these men to work. Although there are excuses of health and layoffs, Liebow concludes that "getting a job, keeping a job, and doing well at it [are] clearly of low priority" (Liebow 1967, 34). Does this make failure a matter of irresponsibility or a lower-class value that rejects conventional success? Liebow tells us the life stories of several men, all of whom are failures, who know they are failures—and who cannot see that taking and keeping a job will keep them from being failures. No matter how many years of school they may have had, they are largely illiterate and unskilled. The jobs they can get (janitor, dishwasher, day laborer at construction sites) are dead-end jobs with low wages. The only people who can hold such jobs and maintain their self-esteem are students who are taking the jobs only temporarily on their way to better things. A 35-year-old man who washes dishes is a failure, in his own eyes and those of society. In short, he can get from the job neither enough money to support himself and his family nor self-esteem and self-respect. How does this affect the rest of his life?

> He carries this failure home where his family life is undergoing a parallel deterioration. His wife's adult male models also failed as husbands and fathers and she expects no less from him. . . . (Nevertheless, she has hoped against hope that he would be a good provider and take on a role of "man of the house.") When he fails, it enlarges his failure in both of their eyes.
>
> Increasingly he turns to the street corner where a shadowy system of values constructed out of public fictions serves to accommodate just such men as he, permitting them to be men once again provided they do not look too closely at one another's credentials (pp. 212–213).

These shadow values include the theory of manly flaws, an assertion that one is too much of a man to fulfill the expected man's role: that one's sexual urges are too strong for one to remain faithful, that one's independence is too strong for one to submit to authority on the job, and so on. In short, these men claim to have the characteristics accorded to manhood in our society in such great quantity that they are precluded from playing that social role successfully. The men did not blame the system— or they didn't in Washington, D.C., in 1962—and they were unable to acknowledge their own faults because of a need for some sense of self-worth. They created an explanation for their failure that required neither social activism nor self-hate, a twilight world of values that paralleled their twilight place in the economic structure.

The 15 to 20 men whom Liebow studied intensively may not have been representative of all poor black men in Washington, D.C., in 1962; the street corner may not have been representative of all black urban neighborhoods. It is sufficient, however, that these processes were at work among these people in this neighborhood. The study told us much that was new in a way that made it possible for many readers to grasp the subjective meaning of employment hardship for the first time. This rich and valuable information could have been provided only through participant observation. (In Chapter 10 we will consider whether things have changed in the 30 years since this study was completed.)

THE EXPERIMENT: DOES ANYBODY GIVE A DAMN?

In the spring of 1962, a young woman returned from her job as manager of a bar and parked her red Fiat in a parking lot a hundred feet from the doorway of her apartment building in Queens, New York. It was after 3 A.M., and the neighborhood was quiet. As she was locking her car, she became nervously aware of a man lurking nearby, and she headed for the police call box a short distance away. Before she could get there, the man attacked and stabbed her. The woman screamed, "Oh, my God, he stabbed me! Please help me! Please help me!" One of her neighbors threw open a window and hollered down, "Let that girl alone!" This caused the assailant to move off down the street. Nobody came to help, and the woman struggled to her feet. The lights went off again in the neighboring apartments, and the woman tried to get to the door of her apartment building. The assailant returned and stabbed her again. This time she shrieked, "I'm dying! I'm dying!" Windows were thrown up and lights turned on, but no one did anything. Apparently frightened off by the lights, the assailant got in his car and drove away. The woman managed to pull herself into the doorway of her apartment building but couldn't get up the steps. She lay there for perhaps 15 to 20 minutes before her assailant returned again and stabbed her a third time, this time fatally (Rosenthal 1964).

Twenty minutes after Kitty Genovese died, the police received a call from one of her neighbors. He had waited until after the final attack and then called a friend to ask what he should do. Finally, he went to a neighboring apartment and got another tenant to make the call to the police. He didn't want to get involved. All in all, 38 of her neighbors watched the assailant take 35 minutes to kill Kitty Genovese on the street. None of them tried to rescue her; aside from the man who shouted from his window, no

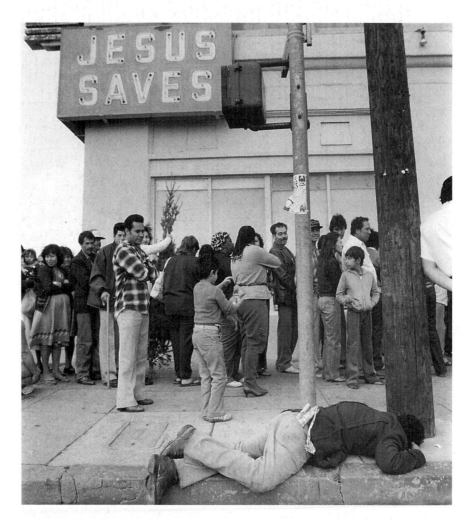

This crowd is waiting at the Soul Clinic Mission in downtown Los Angeles for the promised distribution of free Christmas trees. In the process of receiving help themselves, these passersby are nearly oblivious to the man lying along the curb. Is he drunk? Is he sick? No one makes an attempt to find out. Studies of bystanders generally suggest that when other bystanders are present, responsibility for helping becomes more diffuse and any single bystander is less likely to offer help.

one tried to interfere; none of them even lifted the telephone to call the police to come and rescue her. Several of them went back to bed.

The incident stirred the entire nation. What are we coming to? was a prevailing question. Has our society become so callous that we care nothing about our fellow human beings? Many of the initial reactions focused personally on those 38 witnesses. What was wrong with them? More careful consideration suggested that the problem did not lie with those 38 individuals. One person's refusal to act could be interpreted as a personal problem—stupidity, indecisiveness, depravity, insensitivity. For 38 persons to behave in the same way suggests that there was something about the social structure that invited noninterference. After much soul searching about apathy and insensitivity, a group of scholars finally started to investigate what is now called the bystander effect: Under what circumstances will people intervene to help a stranger?

The question is approached with experimental research rather than with participant observation or survey research. We forgo participant observation for the reason that such events, luckily, do not normally occur in any predictable way. Furthermore, a field researcher who stumbled on such a situation could not ethically stand by and examine the reactions of bystanders rather than offer help. We forgo survey research because few people would tell you that they would ignore a plea for help, that they wouldn't even make an anonymous telephone call to the police. Thus, the study is done in the laboratory, where an emergency can be simulated and where the effects of circumstances surrounding the emergency can be carefully manipulated and the likelihood of offering assistance can be gauged.

The findings reported here are drawn from the work of sociologists Shalom Schwartz and Avi Gottlieb (1980). The previous research on the bystander effect led Schwartz and Gottlieb to hypothesize that two major factors worked to inhibit a helping response:

1. *Diffusion of responsibility among potential helpers.* Where bystanders are aware that other witnesses are on the scene who also ought to do something, they are less likely to feel they personally have a responsibility to help.

Hypothesis: Bystanders who know that there are other bystanders will be less likely to help than will those who believe they are alone.

2. *Fear of what others will think.* Even among strangers, we want people to think well of us. Nobody wants to be seen as the kind of clod who would fail to help somebody in trouble.

Hypothesis: Bystanders who believe their presence is unknown will be less likely to help than will bystanders who are known to be on the scene.

The subjects in the experiment were 127 undergraduates who were recruited to take part in an experiment allegedly on extrasensory perception (ESP). The experiments were carried out at night in an isolated wing of the social science building. As subjects arrived separately, they were conducted past an open doorway in which they could see a man sitting at a console. Each subject was then escorted into a separate cubicle, where a video monitor showed the front view of, apparently, the same man. The subjects were told that the man was going to exchange ESP messages with a third party and that their task was to intercept the messages if possible. The experimenter said that she herself was going to leave the area so that her presence could not interfere with the transmissions but that if a subject wanted her, she could be called from the telephone in the corner of the cubicle.

After the experimenter left, each subject watched the man for 7.5 minutes. The subject then saw on the screen a large, roughly dressed man entering the transmitter's room, grabbing a calculator from the desk, and throwing the other man against the wall, hitting him in the stomach, and, after he had fallen to the ground, kicking him several times. The stranger left 35 seconds after having grabbed the calculator. The research question is whether the subjects' responses to the crisis are predictable by the research hypotheses.

To test their hypotheses, Schwartz and Gottlieb randomly divided the student subjects into two groups. This random assignment means that other relevant factors—such as kindness, courage, and intelligence—should be equal in both groups. Then the two groups were exposed to two different sets of circumstances that roughly simulated the conditions in the hypotheses:

■ **Group 1.** Students believed they were the lone bystander and that the victim/transmitter knew of their presence. This condition was hypothesized to produce the maximum response since the student would believe that he or she was the only one who could help and would further believe that the victim would expect this help.
■ **Group 2.** Students believed there were other bystanders in the experimental area who could help and that the victim/transmitter was ignorant of their presence. This condition was hypothesized to produce the minimum response since the student might count on someone else offering help and would further believe that the victim would not be expecting help.

The results showed that 89 percent of the subjects made some attempt to provide help within the first five minutes. This was true regardless of the experimental conditions. The speed with which they tried to help, however, was significantly related to experimental conditions. Results show that people in Group 1 were nearly twice as likely as those in Group 2 (75 versus 40 percent) to provide immediate aid. Being a lone and known bystander does increase the likelihood of coming to someone's aid. Further manipulations showed that either one of these conditions by itself is sufficient to encourage a helping response: Both lone and known bystanders are highly likely to come to a victim's aid. It is the situation created for Group 2, where a bystander is neither known or alone, that permits the minimum helping response.

The results from the Schwartz and Gottlieb experiment help us understand why 38 of Kitty Genovese's neighbors watched her die without making any effort to help her. Her situation matched the condition of Group 2: Other bystanders were present, and the presence of each individual bystander was unknown to the victim or other observers. It is worth noting that the man who eventually had the police called had been caught looking out his window by another neighbor; in short, he was a known bystander. This experiment is an excellent example of how the laboratory can simulate situations that seldom occur in real life and that suffer from bias and unreliability in personal reporting.

THE ETHICS OF SOCIAL RESEARCH

During the early 1970s, several scandalous cases of unethical medical and biological research came to public attention. One of them was a medical study designed to measure the extent to which the side effects of birth control pills are psychological rather than physical. The physicians involved in the study reasoned that if the effects were psychological, they would

occur among women who thought they were taking the pill, whether they were or not. To test this hypothesis, they recruited a group of women who were interested in contraception and gave half of them real birth control pills and half of them sugar pills. All of the women thought they were taking the real pill. The results showed that the side effects were more pronounced among the group taking the real pill, thus substantiating a physical cause. Of course, one particular side effect—pregnancy—was much more pronounced among the women taking the sugar pill.

The physicians involved in this study were unconcerned about the effect an unwanted pregnancy might have on their subjects; their only concern was learning about the side effects. When asked why they didn't explain the experiment to the subjects, the physician in charge said, "If you think you could explain [this experiment] to these women, you haven't met Mrs. Gomez from the West Side" (cited in Seaman 1972).

A similar lack of concern is evident in a study sponsored by the U.S. Public Health Service between 1932 and 1972. In the so-called Tuskegee study, more than 400 black men who had syphilis were misled about the nature of their illness and deliberately left untreated so that the doctors could observe what happened to untreated syphilis (Jones 1981). It is probably no accident that in both of these experiments the subjects were members of minority groups.

These scandalous cases of unethical research resulted in immediate demands for increased ethical training for scientists and more supervision of research ethics. The federal government instituted new requirements that all federally funded studies using human subjects had to demonstrate that the subjects would not come to any physical, psychological, or social harm through participation in a study. Most universities and professional associations followed this pattern and established strict codes of ethics and committees designed to review research proposals that involve human subjects.

Compared to medical and biological research, sociological research raises few ethical issues. Assuming that investigators follow a few general guidelines, people who participate in sociological research—who answer questions, have their behavior observed, or participate in sociological experiments—are not likely to be harmed by the research.

ETHICAL PRINCIPLES

The American Sociological Association's (1988) code of ethics includes the following principles for dealing with human subjects:

1. "Individuals, families, households, kin and friendship groups that are subjects of research are entitled to rights of biographical anonymity." This means that research reports should not be written in such a way that readers can identify the individual(s) whose behavior or attitudes are being described.

2. "Sociologists should take culturally appropriate steps to secure informed consent and to avoid invasions of privacy. Special actions may be necessary where the individuals studied are illiterate, of very low social status, and/or unfamiliar with social research." This means that subjects must understand fully the proposed research and must freely and voluntarily agree to participate.

3. "The process of conducting sociological research must not expose subjects to substantial risk of personal harm." Personal harm is interpreted broadly to include social embarrassment, possible legal penalties (for example, for admitting to drug use), job loss, and mental trauma, as well as physical harm.

4. When research subjects are promised that their behavior or replies will be anonymous or confidential, the researcher must take every possible step to make certain that such confidences are kept and that the respondent's name cannot be linked by others to his or her information.

ETHICAL ISSUES IN PRACTICE

To a significant extent, the ethical issues raised in sociological research depend on the type of research design used. We will review briefly the major ethical issues associated with experiments, survey research, and participant observation.

Ethical Issues in Sociological Experiments.   In spite of the fact that experimental work in other fields was the cause of the ethical furor, ethics is only a minor issue in sociological experiments. The major issue that arises in experimental research is that deception is almost always involved. Although the subjects do agree to take part, they are seldom told what the purpose is; to do so would reduce the validity of their response. Whether they were trying to help or confound the experimenter, they would be responding to something other than the experimental stimulus.

Experimenters are usually careful to debrief their subjects after the experiment, explaining the real purpose and answering any questions, and the deception is not usually important or challenging. Special criticism, however, has been directed at experiments such as the Schwartz and Gottlieb one reported in this chapter. Such experiments expose the subjects to a stressful situation and, for those who don't help, to a painful self-knowledge. This is not what the subjects bargained for when they volunteered for an experiment on ESP.

Ethical Issues in Survey Research.   Survey research raises the fewest ethical questions. If I call you on the telephone, all you have to do is decline to be interviewed. I cannot interview you without your consent. Also, any time you object to a question, you can either refuse to answer it or hang up on me. At one point, there was some concern that survey research might expose people to the risk of substantial harm by putting ideas into their heads. For example, my asking you whether you have been thinking about divorce might cause you to think about it for the first time. There is no evidence that respondents are as suggestible as this, however, and most people enjoy talking about themselves as part of survey research.

Ethical Issues in Participant Observation.   Some of the most serious ethical issues in sociological research concern participant observation, which is often a disguised form of research. To avoid social-desirability bias or the guinea-pig effect, researchers often try to disguise their purpose so that people will act naturally. This means, of course, that they do not ask the subjects if they are willing to be studied.

This issue has raised serious ethical questions. A classic example of the problem is Laud Humphrey's (1970) study of homosexual encounters in public bathrooms. In this study, Humphreys presented himself in the bathrooms as a "watch queen," a person who likes to watch others' sexual encounters but doesn't want to take part. Did he violate the right to privacy of his research subjects or expose them to the risk of substantial harm?

The answers are unclear. The consensus is that people do not have a right to privacy regarding their actions in public places. People who choose to have sexual encounters in public bathrooms have given up their right to privacy. They are, however, entitled to biographical anonymity; that is, their names and any biographical details that would give their identity away must be protected. Also, when "the subject's responses, if known, would place them at risk of criminal or civil liability or . . . when the research deals with sensitive aspects of a subject's own behavior, such as illegal behavior, drug use, sexual behavior, or use of alcohol," assurance of the researcher's ability and willingness to protect confidentiality must be given to a human-subjects review committee.

Studying The War on Drugs

From the scientist's point of view, the major dilemma with sociological research is that it is so hard to *prove* anything. Year after year, for example, our student surveys show us that the students who use marijuana get lower grades than students who don't. The same results are found in big, national surveys. Because cross-sectional survey research leaves so many questions unanswered, however, few sociological researchers would feel comfortable appearing as an expert witness, say at a congressional hearing, and arguing that their evidence supported antidrug legislation as a means to improve student performance.

This caution in accepting conclusions is good scientific principle. It poses a dilemma, however, in social policy. At the beginning of this chapter, we made reference to "crack babies." These infants are born sick; many suffer permanent developmental disorders because their mothers took crack while pregnant. Crack use became an epidemic virtually overnight; between 1983 and 1989, the percentage of babies affected by their mothers' drug abuse rose from 2 to 20 percent in many inner-city hospitals. Policy makers desperately need solutions, and they need them now. Mayors, social workers, and program administrators want to know what they can do to reduce crack use, especially among young women. Should they build more prisons, more drug treatment programs, more schools, or what? These administrators are impatient with the slow pace of sociological research. Speaking of academic caution and the need for replication and skepticism, one observer says that caution "is OK if you're coming up with the 15th interpretation of '*Moby Dick*,' but not when you're dealing with something like this" ("Counting Trees" 1989,29).

Thus, research on social policy issues walks a tightrope between scientific standards and social demand. Sometimes, as with crack babies, a social problem develops too quickly for painstaking re-

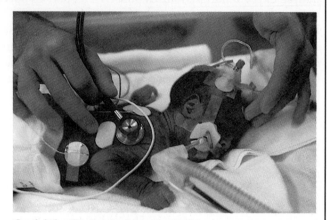

Crack baby, Ft. Lauderdale, FL, 1990.

search designs; other times, the social problem rises to the top of the political agenda before enough research has been done. The "war on poverty" of the 1960s was one such example; the new "war on drugs" is another. All of a sudden, the government is prepared to spend billions of dollars on a social problem. All of a sudden, researchers who had been having trouble getting $20,000 to fund a study of treatment alternatives will be asked how best to spend $20 million.

The social researcher often finds himself or herself caught between political realities and scientific standards. The researcher who goes out on a limb and recommends a program without having adequate evidence is likely to be severely criticized if it doesn't work; the researcher who refuses to make a suggestion on the basis of having inadequate evidence will be ridiculed for being a pointy-headed, ivory-tower intellectual.

The actual war on drugs will be discussed in more detail in Chapter 8. At this point, it is enough to say that most sociologists who study drug use suggest that schools are more effective than prisons and that legitimate opportunities to be successful are more important than the number of police officers on the street.

SUMMARY

1. Science is not a specific set of procedures, but rather a way of approaching data and theory. It is objective, critical, and empirical.

2. The four steps in the research process are gathering data, finding generalizations, forming theories, and testing hypotheses. These steps form a continuous loop, called the "wheel of science." The movement from data to theory to data is called induction, and the movement from theory through hypothesis testing is deduction.

3. Scientific research focuses on variables rather than on whole individuals. When these variables are hypothesized to have a cause-and-effect relationship, the cause is called the independent variable and the effect is called the dependent variable.

4. Operational definitions specify the precise procedures through which research concepts are measured. They seldom tap the full meaning of the words we use in our theories and hypotheses.

5. Sampling is critical to social research because there is so much variability between one research subject and the next. Systematic procedures must be used to ensure that a sample is drawn from a comprehensive list of the members of a population, chosen by random procedures, and of adequate size to provide reliable data.

6. Scientific research is subjected to rigorous evaluation before it appears in scholarly journals. The blind-review process encourages critical and objective evaluations of research findings.

7. The experiment is a method designed to test cause-and-effect hypotheses deduced from theory. Although it is the best method for this purpose, it has the disadvantage of using unrepresentative samples in highly artificial conditions. It is most often used for small-group research and for simulation of situations not often found in real life.

8. Survey research is a method that asks a large number of people a set of standard questions. It is good at describing incidence, trends, and differentials for random samples, but it is not as good at describing the contexts of human behavior.

9. Participant observation is a method in which a small number of individuals who are not randomly chosen are observed or interviewed in depth. The strength of this method is the detail it provides about the contexts of human behavior and its subjective meanings; its weaknesses are lack of generalizability and of verification by independent observers.

10. Sociological research is unlikely to cause substantial harm to subjects or respondents. Nevertheless, the ethics code of sociology requires that subject identities be carefully guarded.

SUGGESTED READINGS

Babbie, Earl R. 1989. The Practice of Social Research. (5th ed.) Belmont, Calif.: Wadsworth. A textbook for undergraduates that covers the major research techniques used in sociology. Coverage is up to date, thorough, and readable.

Golden, M. Patricia. 1976. The Research Experience. Itasca, Ill.: Peacock Publishers. An excellent collection of research articles that discuss a variety of strategies. The unique part of this collection is the inclusion of a special report by each author on the problems and considerations that led to the particular research design.

Jones, James H. 1981. Bad Blood: The Tuskegee Syphilis Experiment. New York: Free Press. Covers the long history of the Tuskegee experiment noted in this chapter, including lessons about ethics, experimentation, and race relations in the United States.

Liebow, Elliot. 1967. Tally's Corner. Boston: Little, Brown. A classic study that provides an excellent introduction to the richness of participant observation studies.

Lofland, John, and Lofland, Lyn. 1984. Analyzing Social Settings. (2d ed.) Belmont, Calif.: Wadsworth. In case you think participant observation is a matter of just hanging around, the Loflands' text on doing fieldwork will set you straight and give you direction.

CULTURE

Quilt by Fannie Shaw, "Prosperity is Just Around the Corner" 1932

Have you ever . . .

Looked at a contemporary sculpture or painting and thought to yourself, "This is art?"

Mark Twain once said that one person's truth is another's bunkum, but in fact there is remarkable consensus in society as to what is good and desirable. Certainly the holdings in the Dallas Museum of Art tend to be very much the same sorts of things that appear in the Boston Museum of Fine Arts or London's National Gallery.

Just as art critics and museum curators demonstrate a remarkable agreement about what is beautiful, we find great consensus among the public about what is good. On matters ranging from how we should rear our children to what toys we should buy them, we tend to agree on common standards. For example, one year, every child seems to want a Cabbage Patch doll; a few years later, Nintendo games are the favorites.

The processes through which children come to share common definitions of what they want are not all that different from the processes through which art critics decide what is beautiful. For all of us, our ideas about what is desirable are social products, they are the outcome of economic forces, learning, and relationships with others.

Social science cannot tell you whether a particular sculpture is good art or bad art or whether a Nintendo game is really a good thing. What we can do is to document the toys, art, and ideas about good and bad that develop in a culture and show how they relate to the social structures of society—how they fit in with the family system, religion, and class structure.

INTRODUCTION TO CULTURE

Culture is the total way of life shared by members of a society. It includes not only language, values, and symbolic meanings but also technology and material objects.

In Chapter 1 we said that sociology is concerned with analyzing the contexts of human behavior and how these contexts affect our behavior. Our neighborhood, our family, and our social class provide part of that context, but the broadest context of all is our culture. **Culture** is the total way of life shared by members of a society.

Culture resides essentially in nontangible forms such as language, values, and symbolic meanings, but it also includes technology and material objects. A common image is that culture is a "tool kit" that provides us with the equipment necessary to deal with the common problems of everyday life (Swidler 1986). Consider how culture provides patterned responses to eating. We share a common set of tools and technologies in the form of refrigerators, ovens, toasters, microwaves, and coffeepots. And, as the advertisers suggest, we share similar feelings of psychological release and satisfaction when, after a hard day of working or playing, we take a break with a cup of coffee or a cold beer. The beverages we choose and the meanings attached to them are part of our culture.

Culture can be roughly divided into two categories: material and nonmaterial. *Nonmaterial culture* consists of language, values, rules, knowledge, and meanings shared by the members of a society. *Material culture* includes the physical objects that a society produces—tools, streets, sculptures, and toys, to name a few. These material objects depend on the nonmaterial culture for meaning. For example, Barbie dolls and figurines of fertility goddesses share many common physical features; their meaning depends on nonmaterial culture.

In this Peruvian picture, a traditional medicine man uses herbs and religious ritual to cure illness. In sharp contrast, the techniques of modern science are being used by a team of specialists in Zaire. Despite the obvious differences among cultures, a close look shows a great many underlying similarities. Although some rely on prayer and others on antibiotics, all cultures provide some routine set of mechanisms for dealing with illness and injury.

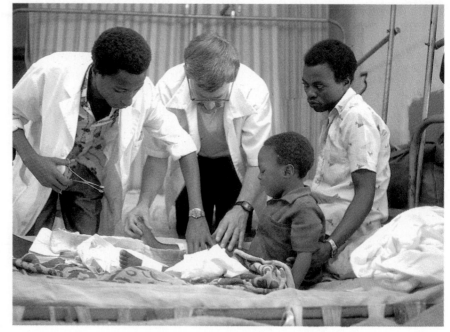

THEORETICAL PERSPECTIVES ON CULTURE

Within sociology, there are two approaches to the study of culture (Wuthnow and Witten 1988). The first approach treats culture as the underlying basis of interaction. It accepts culture as a given and is more interested in how culture shapes us than in how culture itself is shaped. Scholars from this approach have concentrated on illustrating how norms, values, and language guide our behavior. The second approach focuses on culture as a social product. It asks why particular aspects of culture develop. These scholars would be interested, for example, in why the content of commercial television is so different from the content of public television. How does the economic structure of television affect its products? How does the way arts are funded in the United States affect what art gets accepted by the public? Generally, the first perspective on culture is characteristic of structural-functional theory, while conflict theorists are more interested in the determinants of culture. Since both the content of culture and the determinants of culture are of interest to us, we will use both perspectives.

BASES OF HUMAN BEHAVIOR: CULTURE AND BIOLOGY

Why do people behave as they do? What determines human behavior? To answer these questions, we must be able to explain both the varieties and the similarities in human behavior. Generally, we will argue that biological factors help explain what is common to humankind across societies, but culture explains why people and societies differ from one another.

CULTURAL PERSPECTIVE

Regardless of whether they are structural functionalists or conflict theorists, sociologists share some common orientations toward culture: Culture is *problem solving*, culture is *relative*, and culture is a *social product*.

Culture Is Problem Solving. Regardless of whether people live in tropical forests or in the crowded cities of New York, London, or Tokyo, they confront some common problems. They all must eat, they all need shelter from the elements (and often each other), and they all need to raise children to take their place and continue their way of life. Although these problems are universal, the solutions are highly varied. For example, responsibility for childrearing may be assigned to the mother's brother, as is done in the Trobiand Islands; to the natural mother and father, as is done in the United States; or to communal nurseries, as is done in the Israeli kibbutz.

Whenever people face a recurrent problem, cultural patterns will have evolved to provide a ready-made answer. This does not mean that the answer provided is the best answer or the only answer or the fairest answer, merely that culture provides a standard pattern for dealing with this common dilemma. One of the issues that divides conflict and functional theorists is how these answers develop. Functionalists argue that the solutions we use today have evolved over generations of trial and error and that they have survived because they work, because they help us meet basic needs. A conflict theorist would add that these solutions work better for some people than others. Conflict theorists argue that elites manipulate culture in order to rationalize and maintain solutions that work to their advantage. Scholars from both perspectives agree that culture provides ready-made answers for most of the recurrent situations that we face in daily life; they disagree in their answer to the question "Who benefits?" from a particular solution.

Culture Is Relative.   The solutions that each culture devises may be startlingly different. Among the Wodaabe of Niger, for example, mothers are not allowed to speak directly to their first- or second-born children and, except for nursing, are not even allowed to touch them. The babies' grandmothers and aunts, however, lavish affection and attention on them (Beckwith 1983). The effect of this pattern of childrearing is to emphasize loyalties and affections throughout the entire kin group rather than just to one's own children or spouse. This practice helps ensure that each new entrant will be loyal to the group as a whole. Is it a good or a bad practice? That is a question we can answer only by seeing how it fits in with the rest of the Wodaabe culture. Does it help the people meet recurrent problems and maintain a stable society? If so, then it works; it is functional. The idea that each cultural trait should be evaluated in the context of its own culture is called **cultural relativity.** A corollary of cultural relatively is that no practice is universally good or universally bad; goodness and badness are relative, not absolute.

This type of evaluation is sometimes a difficult intellectual feat. For example, no matter how objective we try to be, most of us believe that infanticide, human sacrifice, and cannibalism are absolutely and universally wrong. Such an attitude reflects **ethnocentrism**—the tendency to use the norms and values of our own culture as standards against which to judge the practices of others.

Ethnocentrism usually means that we see our way as the right way and everybody else's way as the wrong way. When American missionaries came to the South Sea Islands, they found that many things were done differently in Polynesian culture. The missionaries, however, were unable to view Polynesian folkways as simply different. If they were not like American practices, then they must be wrong and were probably wicked. As a result, the missionaries taught the islanders that the only acceptable way (the American way) to have sexual intercourse was in a face-to-face position with the man on top, the now-famous "missionary position." They taught the Polynesians that women must cover their breasts, that they should have clocks and come on time to appointments, and a variety of other Americanisms that the missionaries accepted as morally right behavior.

Ethnocentrism is often a barrier to interaction of people from different cultures, leading to much confusion and misinterpretation. It is not, however, altogether bad. In the sense that it is pride in our own culture and confidence in our own way of life, ethnocentrism is essential for social integration. In other words, we learn to follow the ways of our culture

Cultural relativity requires that each cultural trait be evaluated in the context of its own culture.

Ethnocentrism is the tendency to view the norms and values of our own culture as standards against which to judge the practices of other cultures.

because we believe that they are the right ways; if we did not share that belief, there would be little conformity in society. Ethnocentrism, then, is a natural and even desirable product of growing up in a culture. An undesirable consequence, however, is that we simultaneously discredit or diminish the value of other ways of thinking and feeling.

Culture Is a Social Product.   A final assumption sociologists make about culture is that culture is a social, not a biological, product. The immense cultural diversity that characterizes human societies is not the product of isolated gene pools, but of cultural evolution.

Some aspects of culture are produced deliberately. Shakespeare picked up paper and pen in order to write *Hamlet*; some advertising executive worked to invent Spuds Mackenzie. Governments, bankers, and home owners deliberately commission the designing of homes, offices, and public buildings, and people buy publishing empires so that they can spread their own version of the truth. Other aspects of culture—such as our culture's ideas about right and wrong, its dress patterns, and its language—develop gradually out of social interaction. But all of these aspects of culture are human products; none of them is instinctive. People *learn* culture and, as they use it, they modify it and change it.

Culture depends on a unique human attribute: the capacity for language. Only after language is invented can pieces of practical knowledge (such as "don't use electricity in the bathtub") or ideas (such as "God exists") be transmitted from one generation to the next. Inventions, discoveries, and forms of social organization are socially bestowed and intentionally passed on so that each new generation potentially elaborates on and modifies the accumulated knowledge of the previous generations. In short, culture is cummulative only because of language.

Because of language, human beings are not limited to the slow process of genetic evolution in adapting to their circumstances. Cultural evolution is a uniquely human way for a species to adapt to its environment. Whereas biological evolution may require literally hundreds of generations to adapt the organism fully to new circumstances, cultural evolution allows the changes to be made within a short period of time. In this sense, cultural evolution is an extension of biological evolution, one that speeds up the processes of change and adjustment to new circumstances in the environment (van den Berghe 1978).

BIOLOGICAL PERSPECTIVE

As the continued popularity of *National Geographic* attests, the wide diversity of human cultures is a continuous source of fascination. Costumes, eating habits, and living arrangements vary dramatically. It is tempting to focus on the exotic variety of human behavior and to conclude that there are no limits to what humankind can devise. A closer look, however, suggests that there are some basic similarities in cultures around the world— the universal existence of the family, religion, aggression, and warfare. When we focus on these universals, then cultural explanations are likely to be supplemented with biological explanations.

Sociobiology is the study of the biological basis of all forms of human behavior.

Within the past two decades sociology has witnessed renewed interest in the role of evolution and biology in human behavior. A relatively new field, **sociobiology,** is the study of the biological basis of all forms of human behavior (E. O. Wilson 1978). Sociobiology makes the assumption that humans and all other life forms developed through evolution and natural selection. According to this perspective, change in a species occurs primarily through one mechanism: Some individuals are more successful at reproduction than others. As the offspring of successful reproducers grow in number relative to those of the less successful reproducers, the species comes to be characterized by the traits that mark successful reproducers.

Who are the successful reproducers? They are those who have more children and raise more of them until they are old enough to reproduce themselves (Daly and Wilson 1983). Among the characteristics of human society that are thought to be related to these reproductive strategies are altruism and male/female differences in mating behavior, parenting, and aggression. For example, sociobiologists suggest that parents who are willing to make sacrifices for their children, occasionally even giving their life for them, are more successful reproducers; by ensuring their children's survival, they increase the likelihood that their own genes will contribute to succeeding generations. Thus, sociobiologists argue that we have evolved biological predispositions toward altruism (an unselfish concern for others), *but only insofar as our own kin are concerned.*

Sociobiology provides an interesting theory about how the human species has evolved over 10,000 years. Most of the scholars who study the effect of biology on human behavior, however, are concerned with more contemporary questions such as "How do hormones, genes, and chromosomes affect human behavior?" Joint work by biologists and social sci-

In trying to uncover what may be the common nature of our species, social scientists have emphasized the search for cultural universals. They have reasoned that if the same pattern is evident in all societies, it may have a biological or genetic basis. Dominance is one such universal pattern; another is mothering. In all societies, caring for children is an important role of women.

entists is helping us to understand how biological and social factors work together to determine human behavior.

This approach is nicely illustrated in a recent set of studies by Udry, who asks how the biological changes that accompany puberty interact with social structures to determine adolescent sexuality. Using blood and urine analyses to determine hormone levels, Udry finds that boys and girls with higher levels of testosterone report higher levels of sexual behavior and sexual interest. He also finds that strict family supervision, especially having a father in the home, can override the effect of hormonal change among girls (Udry 1988). This suggests that social *and* biological factors play a role in adolescent sexuality.

We are at the same time animals and social products. It is a false dichotomy to ask whether culture or biology determines behavior; instead, our behavior represents an intersection between the two. One leading sociologist has argued, for example, that "ignorance of biological processes may doom efforts" to create equality between women and men or to decrease the burden that child care poses for women (Rossi 1984, 11). Only by recognizing and taking into account the joint effects of culture and biology can we have the complete picture of the determinants of human behavior.

THE FAR SIDE   By GARY LARSON

"And now, Randy, by use of song, the male sparrow will stake out his territory . . . an instinct common in the lower animals."

THE CARRIERS OF CULTURE

In the following sections, we review three vital aspects of nonmaterial culture—language, values, and norms—and show how they shape both societies and individuals.

LANGUAGE

The essence of culture is the sharing of meanings among members of a society. The chief mechanism for this sharing is a common language. Language is the ability to communicate in symbols—orally or in writing.

What does *communicate with symbols* mean? It means that when you see the combinations of circles and lines that appear on your textbook page as the word *orally*, you are able to understand that it means "speaking aloud." On a different level, it means that the noise we use to symbolize "dog" brings to your mind a four-legged domestic canine. Almost all communication is done through symbols. Even the meanings of physical gestures such as touching or pointing are learned as part of culture.

Scholars of sociolinguistics (the relationship of language to society) point out that language has three distinct relationships to culture: Language embodies culture, language is a framework for culture, and language is a symbol of culture (Fishman 1985a, 1985b).

Language Embodies Culture.   Language is the carrier of culture; it embodies the values and meanings of a society as well as its rituals, ceremonies, stories, and prayers. Until you share the language of a culture, you cannot participate in it (Fishman 1985b).

A corollary is that loss of language may mean loss of a culture. Currently, many Native American languages have fewer than 40 speakers, most of whom are more than 50 years old. When these people die, they will take their language with them, and important aspects of those Native American cultures will be lost. This vital link between language and culture is why many Jewish parents in the United States send their children to Hebrew school on Saturdays. This is why U.S. law requires that people must be able to speak English before they can be naturalized as American citizens. To participate fully in Jewish culture requires some knowledge of Hebrew; to participate in American culture requires some knowledge of English.

Language as a Framework.   Language gives us capabilities, but it also shapes and confines us. The **linguistic relativity hypothesis** associated with Whorf (1956) argues that the grammar, structure, and categories embodied in each language affect how its speakers see reality and that, therefore, reality *is* different for speakers of, say, English and Lakota (Sioux). The argument is that our thinking and perceptions are in some ways fashioned by our linguistic capacities (Fishman 1985b).

We can see the shaping qualities of language in the development of written language. Literacy allows us to communicate with those whom we cannot see; it takes communication out of the face-to-face context and makes it impersonal (Cicourel 1985). This means that literate individuals have the capacity to experience the world beyond themselves in a way not open to the nonliterate. Written language thus expands and changes the world we experience. Writing also encourages a different mode of thinking, an analytic approach in which the written word can be set down, modified, and studied in a way that oral communication cannot. The bureaucratic form of organization and the development of science would both be impossible without written language.

Because language shapes how we perceive reality, one way to change perceptions is to change the words we use. For example, in the last few years, a growing number of black leaders have begun to use "African American" instead of "black." This shift in language usage symbolizes a distinction based on cultural heritage (African) rather than on race (color). It moves us away from thinking about physical differences to thinking about cultural differences. Obviously, this shift has important implications for understanding the causes of current racial inequalities and for framing policy responses. Because most of the research reported in this text is based on respondents identifying themselves by race (black or white), however, we generally use the racial labels in reporting research results.

Language as a Symbol.   A common language is often the most obvious outward sign that people share a common culture. This is true of national cultures such as French and Italian and subcultures such as youth. A distinctive language symbolizes a group's separation from others while it simultaneously symbolizes unity within the group of speakers (Cobarrubias 1983). For this reason, groups seeking to mobilize their members often insist on their own distinct language.

Linguistic relativity hypothesis argues that the grammar, structure, and categories embodied in each language affect how its speakers see reality.

VALUES

After language, the most central and distinguishing aspect of culture is **values,** shared ideas about desirable goals. Values are typically couched in terms of whether a thing is good or bad, desirable or undesirable (Williams 1970, 27). For example, many Americans believe that a happy marriage is desirable. In this case and many others, values may be very general. They do not, for example, specify what a happy marriage consists of.

Some cultures value tenderness, others toughness; some value cooperation, others competition. Nevertheless, because all human populations face common dilemmas, certain values tend to be universal. For example, nearly every culture values stability and security, a strong family, and good health. There are, however, dramatic differences in the guidelines that cultures offer for pursuing these goals. In societies like ours, an individual may try to ensure security by putting money in the bank or investing in an education. In many traditional societies, security is maximized by having a large number of relatives. In societies such as that of the Kwakiutl of the Pacific Northwest, security is achieved, not by saving your wealth, but by giving it away. The reasoning is that all of the people who accept your goods are now under an obligation to you. If you should ever need help, you would feel free to call on them and they would feel obliged to help. Thus, although many cultures place a value on establishing security against uncertainty and old age, the specific guidelines for reaching this goal vary. The guidelines are called norms.

NORMS

Shared rules of conduct are **norms.** They specify what people *ought* to or *ought not* to do. The list of things we ought to do sometimes seems endless. We begin the day with an "I'm awfully tired, but I ought to get up," and

Values are shared ideas about desirable goals.

Norms are shared rules of conduct that specify how people ought to think and act.

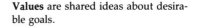

Values are shared sentiments about what is good and worthy. Because values rest on sentiments rather than on evidence, it is difficult to resolve conflicts between them. Is God a man of war? Are nuclear weapons good or bad? Value conflicts such as these cannot be resolved by scientific evidence. When sociologists study values they do not address issues of right or wrong, but instead consider issues such as "What effect does this value have on behavior?" or "What factors cause people to embrace this value?"

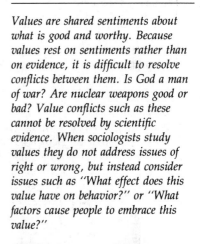

many of us end the day with "This is an awfully good show, but I ought to go to bed." In between, we ought to brush our teeth, eat our vegetables, work hard, love our neighbors, and on and on. The list is so extensive that we may occasionally feel that we have too many obligations and too few choices. Of course, some things are optional and allow us to make choices, but the whole idea of culture is that it provides a blueprint for living, a pattern to follow.

Norms vary enormously in their importance both to individuals and to society. Some, such as fashions, are powerful while they last but are not central to society's values. Others, such as those supporting monogamy and democracy, are central to our culture. Generally, we distinguish between two kinds of norms: folkways and mores.

Folkways.   The word **folkways** describes norms that are simply the customary, normal, habitual ways a group does things. Folkways is a broad concept that covers relatively permanent traditions (such as fireworks on the Fourth of July) as well as short-lived fads and fashions (such as wearing Ray-Bans or not tying your hightop tennis shoes).

A key feature of all folkways is that there is no strong feeling of right or wrong attached to them. They are simply the way people usually do things. For example, if you choose to have hamburgers for breakfast and oatmeal for dinner, you will be violating American folkways. If you sleep on the floor or dye your hair purple, you will also be deviating from the usual pattern. If you violate folkways, you may be regarded as eccentric, weird, or crazy, but you will not be regarded as immoral or criminal.

Mores.   Some norms are associated with strong feelings of right and wrong. These norms are called **mores** (more-ays). Whereas eating oatmeal for dinner may only cause you to be considered crazy (or lazy), there are some things you can do that will really offend your neighbors. If you eat your dog or spend your last dollar on liquor when your child needs shoes, you will be violating mores. At this point, your friends and neighbors may decide that they have to do something about you. They may turn you in to the police or to a child protection association; they may cut off all interaction with you or even chase you out of the neighborhood. Not all violations of mores result in legal punishment, but all result in such informal reprisals as ostracism, shunning, or reprimand. These punishments, formal and informal, reduce the likelihood that people will violate mores.

Laws.   Rules that are enforced and sanctioned by the authority of government are **laws.** Very often the important mores of society become laws and are enforced by agencies of the government. If the laws cease to be supported by norms and values, they are either stricken from the record or become dead-letter laws, no longer considered important enough to enforce. Not all laws, of course, are supported by public sentiment; in fact, many have come into existence as the result of lobbying by powerful interest groups. Laws regulating marijuana use in the United States, for example, owe their origins to lobbying by the liquor industry. Similarly, laws requiring the wearing of seat belts are not a response to social norms. In these cases, laws are trying to create norms rather than respond to them.

Folkways are norms that are customary, normal, habitual ways a group does things.

Mores are norms associated with fairly strong ideas of right or wrong; they carry a moral connotation.

Laws are rules that are enforced and sanctioned by the authority of government. They may or may not be norms.

This Tennessee barber shop provides explicit written instruction about appropriate language. For the most part, the norms that govern daily life are not as clear as this. Nevertheless, most of us pick up a pretty good understanding of these and other norms by observing how others behave and watching others' reactions to our behavior. Negative sanctions such as stares of surprise or consternation, grimaces of distaste, and shrugs of distain will tell us we have crossed a sensitive line and violated a norm.

CONCEPT SUMMARY
Values, Norms, and Laws

CONCEPT	DEFINITION	EXAMPLE FROM MARRIAGE	RELATIONSHIP TO VALUES
Values	Shared ideas about desirable goals	It is desirable that marriage include physical love between wife and husband.	
Norms	Shared rules of conduct	Have sexual intercourse regularly with each other, but not with anyone else.	Generally accepted means to achieve value
Folkways	Norms that are customary or usual	Share a bedroom and a bed; kids sleep in a different room.	Optional but usual means to achieve value
Mores	Norms with strong feelings of right and wrong	Thou shalt not commit adultery.	Morally required means to achieve value
Laws	Formal standards of conduct, enforced by public agencies	Illegal for husband to rape wife; sexual relations must be voluntary.	Legally required means; may or not be supported by norms

---

SOCIAL CONTROL

From our earliest childhood we are taught to observe norms, first within our families and later within peer groups, at school, and in the larger society. After a period of time, following the norms becomes so habitual that we can hardly imagine living any other way—they are so much a part of our lives that we may not even be aware of them as constraints. We do not think, "I ought to brush my teeth or else my friends and family will shun me"; instead we think, "It would be disgusting not to brush my teeth, and I'll hate myself if I don't brush them." For thousands of generations, no human considered it disgusting to go around with unbrushed teeth. For most Americans, however, brushing their teeth is so much a part of their feeling about themselves, about who they are and the kind of person they are, that they would disgust themselves by not observing the norm.

Through indoctrination, learning, and experience, many of society's norms come to seem so natural that we cannot imagine acting differently. No society relies completely on this voluntary compliance, however, and all encourage conformity by the use of **sanctions**—rewards for conformity and punishments for noncomformity. Some sanctions are formal, in the sense that the legal codes identify specific penalties, fines, and punishments that are to be meted out to individuals found guilty of violating formal laws. Formal sanctions are also built into most large organizations to control absenteeism and productivity. Some of the most effective sanctions, however, are informal. Such positive sanctions as affection, approval, and inclusion encourage normative behavior, whereas such negative sanctions as a cold shoulder, disapproval, and exclusion discourage norm violations.

Sanctions are rewards for conformity and punishments for nonconformity.

Despite these sanctions, norms are not always a good guide to what people actually do, and it is important to distinguish between normative behavior (what we should do) and actual behavior. For example, our own society has powerful mores supporting marital fidelity. Yet research has shown that nearly half of all married men and women in our society have committed adultery (Thompson 1983). In this instance, culture expresses expectations that differ significantly from actual behavior. This does not mean the norm is unimportant. Even norms that a large minority, even a majority, fail to live up to are still important guides to behavior. The discrepancy between actual behavior and normative behavior—termed deviance—is a major area of sociological research and inquiry (see Chapter 8).

SUBCULTURES AND COUNTERCULTURES

Subcultures are groups that share in the overall culture of society but also maintain a distinctive set of values, norms, life-styles, and even language.

Countercultures are groups having values, interests, beliefs, and life-styles that are opposed to those of the larger culture.

Sharing a culture does not mean there is complete homogeneity. When segments of society face substantially different kinds of social environments, subcultures grow up to help them adapt to these unique problems. **Subcultures** share in the overall culture of society, but also maintain a distinctive set of values, norms, life-styles, and even language. Examples of American subcultures are ethnic and religious subcultures, regional subcultures, and the youth subculture.

Countercultures are groups that have values, interests, beliefs, and life-styles that conflict with those of the larger culture. This theme of conflict can be observed for groups as varied as hippies, punkers, delinquent gangs, revolutionary Marxists, and such religious sects as the Moonies, the Hare Krishnas, and even the early Christians. Countercultures reflect radical revisions in and rejection of taken-for-granted ways of life (Berger 1981).

SOCIETY

A **society** is the population that shares the same territory and is bound together by economic and political ties.

Culture is a way of life. In some places, it cuts across national boundaries and takes in people who live in two, three, or four nations. In other places, two distinct cultures (English and French in Canada) may coexist within a single national boundary. For this reason, we distinguish between cultures and societies. A **society** is the population that shares the same territory and is bound together by economic and political ties. Often the members share a common culture, but not always.

CULTURAL VARIATION AND CHANGE

Culture provides solutions to common and not-so-common problems. The solutions devised by societies are immensely variable. Part of this variation can be explained by unique environmental conditions. Other conditions that produce diversity include isolation, technology, diffusion, and dominant cultural themes. Each of these conditions affects the elaboration of culture and the development of society.

Hard Times in Inis Beag

Inis Beag, a remote two-square-mile island settled during the seventeenth-century by a group of Irish emigrants escaping political conflict, provides a unique example of how factors such as isolation, physical environment, dominant cultural themes, and unique historical events affect the evolution of culture. Isolation in particular severely restricted contact with outsiders, enabling the islanders to retain their culture relatively unchanged until the middle of this century. This report is based on field work in the 1950s.

Inis Beag is an island of rock located off the coast of Ireland. Because of the absence of any deep-water ports, the islanders were virtually cut off from shipping and trade with outsiders. Any exchange required shipping vessels to anchor off the coast, where canoes were used to transport both limited trade goods and visitors to and from the island.

■

This culture has been branded the most sexually repressed in history.

Much of the island's farmland is found on the northeastern side, where stone fences mark off hundreds of plots used for simple subsistence agriculture. Over the years, the soil of these plots has been deepened and enriched by the addition of seaweed, sand, and human wastes. A relatively simple subsistence technology consisting of

digging sticks, spades, and scythes persisted for centuries. The island lacked electricity and running water, and its only vehicles were donkey-drawn carts. As with most peasant communities, the standard of living was low, the family was of central importance, and the birthrate was high (the average couple had seven children). Unlike other folk societies, however, Inis Beag had a low death-rate and a low illiteracy rate.

There were approximately 350 residents, making up 59 families located in four villages on the island. The people's lives were highly influenced by the very small physical size of their island and by the difficulty of supporting themselves. They shared this dilemma with much of the rest of Ireland, but with greater urgency; their small island placed clear boundaries on growth. The plots were already so small (an average of 12 acres per family) that any further subdivision would make them too small to support a family. The Irish solution, one shared by Inis Beag, was to pass all of the family's land to one son. This solution had its costs. In the first place, only the chosen son was able to support a family of his own—and he could not do this until his parents passed their land on to him. Because life expectancy had increased, this often did not occur until the son reached middle age. His sisters and brothers faced an even less desirable situation. They usually had a choice of staying home and working as free labor for their parents or their brother or emigrating to the Irish mainland or the United States. Of course, some of the girls managed to

snag a middle-aged bachelor as he came into his inheritance.

As a result of this situation, the average person who remained on Inis Beag married many years after reaching sexual maturity; many never married at all. The average age at marriage was 36 for men and 25 for women. Unlike the contemporary United States, being single on Inis Beag meant total abstinence from sexual activity. To squash sexual desires thoroughly, the entire culture was geared to depress sexual thoughts and opportunities. This culture has been branded the most sexually repressed in history.

Almost from infancy, girls and boys were raised separately. They did not play together or pray together; they were separated at home, church, and school. Courtship was practically nonexistent; most marriages were arranged, primarily on the basis of economic considerations.

These normative practices were reinforced by a strong sense of modesty. Anything to do with the body was regarded as shameful; such things as pregnancy, urination, and defecation could not be spoken of in public. (In fact, although human wastes were an essential element of their agricultural technique, islanders would not admit that they used them.) Both men and women on Inis Beag found nudity offensive, and the body was always fully covered. As a result, the people never bathed, contenting themselves with washing only their hands, face, and feet. Even sexual intercourse took place with the couple as fully clothed as possible. Intercourse was viewed as physically unhealthy, to be engaged in only for the purpose of procreation. Although sexual relations are regarded as a woman's duty (as opposed to pleasure) in many societies, Inis Beag may be the only culture in the world where sex has also been defined as a man's duty. As a result, intercourse was an infrequent, speedy, and secretive act.

Sexual repression on Inis Beag stemmed from a combination of circumstances—a harsh environment, a limited land supply, and a religion that stressed the overwhelming fear of damnation. This particular form of Catholicism was at one time common to much of Ireland. Although it had been supplanted on the mainland, the isolation of Inis Beag allowed it to persist as a dominant

cultural theme. Beginning with the introduction of television in 1963, however, the people of Inis Beag have been drawn increasingly into contemporary western culture.

SOURCE: Messenger 1969.

Note: Inis Beag is not the real name of this island. The name has been changed to provide biographic immunity for the community and the people who live there.

ENVIRONMENT

Why are the French different from the Australian aborigines, the Finns different from the Navajo? Although it is just possible that they have different genetic makeups, a far more obvious difference is their physical environments. Hot or cold climates, fertile or sandy soils, dense or sparse vegetation, the presence of animals, rainfall, and fuels—all are environmental conditions to which people must adapt.

The physical and natural environment of an area sets the stage for the cultural adaptations of a society. For example, the monsoons that annually cross India, Pakistan, and Indochina are vital to the agricultural economy of these countries and their cultures reflect the importance of the monsoons to their survival. In India, the chief of the Vedic gods is Indra, the god of rain. As the people wait for the monsoons to arrive, they do so with considerable anxiety and religious ceremony. Modern adaptations to the same phenomenon include government planning agencies, disaster relief organizations, and agricultural extension agents.

American culture has been shaped by its physical environment in innumerable ways. The mobility, independence, and thirst for change that characterized 19th century America may justly be traced to the existence of an open frontier. Transplanting English culture to a rich and largely empty environment caused changes in the original culture. Change continues. Our environment is not as uncrowded as it used to be, and the apartment house and condominium are replacing the single-family home on its quarter-acre lot. Acid rain, ozone holes, polluted streams and lakes, beaches awash in garbage, and overcrowded landfills are only a few of the signs that our old ways of adapting to the environment need revision.

ISOLATION

When cultural patterns evolve as adaptations to the physical environment of an area, the absence of contact with other societies tends to perpetuate the patterns. Many of the geographically isolated societies located along the headwaters of the Amazon, in the back country of Australia, in the interior of Africa, and in the dense forests of Malaysia have been cut off from the rest of the world until just recently. The cultural patterns of these societies have evolved over centuries as distinct adaptations to conditions unique to their environment.

Isolation can be socially as well as geographically imposed. In modern Western societies, specific groups wishing to escape the influences of the dominant culture have intentionally isolated themselves. The Hutterites, Amish, 19th-century Mormons, and, more recently, Jonesville cultists are examples of religious sects that have used geographical isolation as a means of preserving the stability of their subcultures.

An important factor that increases isolation is ethnocentrism. Because we believe that our ways are the right ways, we may erect a symbolic wall between our culture and others'. Our negative judgments become a barrier to contact and to borrowing or adapting cultural characteristics from others. In this case, ethnocentrism is the cultural equivalent to geographic isolation, cutting one society off from the influence of others.

TECHNOLOGY

Cultural variation also results from the technological position of a society. This particular cause of cultural variation is stressed by Marxists. Marx argued that the mode of economic production—the technology and resources used in production—determined all of the other social structures in society. Thus, Marxists emphasize that differences in level of technology and in physical resources may be among the most important causes of diversity. They may also be among the most potent causes of change.

Consider, for example, the development of the cotton gin. Before the invention of the cotton gin, cotton—and slavery—was confined to a narrow belt along the East Coast. The state of Georgia experimented with a new kind of cotton and found that it grew well inland, but it could not be processed with existing equipment. Thus, although large amounts of cotton were grown, only a small percentage was ever processed and brought to market. Lured by a commission from the state of Georgia, Eli Whitney in 1793 invented the cotton gin, a machine designed to mill the new cotton. As a result, cotton—and slavery—spread through out the Deep South. King Cotton and the spread and profitability of slavery owed much to the technological advances of the industrial revolution (Wright 1978).

DIFFUSION

As noted earlier, the processes of cultural evolution are much more rapid than are the processes of biological evolution. In part, this is because learning is accelerated by diffusion, the spread of cultural traits when one culture comes into contact with another. Where the conditions of isolation preclude contact, as on Inis Beag, a culture continues on its own course, unaltered and uncontaminated by others. Inis Beag, however, is unusual in this regard. Since the middle of the 18th century, industrialization and colonialism have extended Western culture to many previously isolated societies, producing rapid cultural change through contact and diffusion.

Modern technology enables diffusion to take place much more rapidly than before. Ideas can sweep the world within days and be introduced into the remotest villages within weeks and months. A fervor of democracy, for example, swept the world in 1989. The year began with the student protests in Tienanmen Square in Beijing and ended with the fall of the Berlin Wall and the toppling of communist governments in Eastern Europe. Many of those seeking freedom and democracy relied on the ideals and symbols of the French and American revolutions of 200 years ago; the

The "Goddess of Liberty" that symbolized the pro-democracy demonstrations in Tienanmen Square in Beijing in Spring 1989 bears a striking resemblance to our own Statue of Liberty. Both the ideals of democracy, its symbols, and even the constitutional forms that have been developed to embody it have been diffused throughout the world. The rapidity of global diffusion means that ideas, fashions, and technologies are spread rapidly throughout the world. Nevertheless, economic and political realities may distort or repel ideas that are not congenial to established patterns.

Statue of Liberty lent her symbolic support to the ill-fated democracy demonstrations at Tienanmen Square.

The speed of contemporary diffusion means more rapid change in all areas of life, and it also means growing international similarity. In Moscow, Beijing, Nairobi, and Boston, business leaders are wearing the same kinds of suits and young people are listening to the same kinds of music. A recent article in a Soviet sociology journal, for example, analyzes the ill effects of "khard-roka and khevi-metallu" on Soviet youth (Sarkitov 1987). On a more serious level, it means that AIDS and nuclear weapons technology are also widespread.

DOMINANT CULTURAL THEMES

Cultural patterns generally contain dominant cultural themes that further contribute to variations among cultures. These themes give a distinct character and direction to a culture; they also create, in part, a closed system. New ideas, values, and inventions are usually accepted only when they fit into the existing culture or represent changes that can be absorbed without too greatly distorting existing patterns. The Native American hunter, for example, was pleased to adopt the rifle as an aid to the established tradition, or cultural theme, of hunting. Western types of housing and legal customs regarding land ownership, however, were rejected because they were alien to a nomadic and communal way of life.

Weber was one of the first sociologists to stress the importance of cultural themes as a determinant of cultural variability. He suggested that cultures tend to select and reinterpret the new ideas that are meaningful to them. If they can find no point of correspondence between the new ideas and their usual ones, then the new ideas are abandoned (Gerth and Mills [1946] 1970, 63).

AMERICAN CULTURE

American culture is a unique blend of complex elements. It is a product of the United States' environment, its immigrants, its technology, and its place in history. It closely resembles the cultures of two close cousins, Australia and Canada, with which it shares vital characteristics. All three are new countries settled by diverse groups of immigrants yet dominated by English culture, all three had uncrowded spaces and a sense of frontier, and all three now offer high levels of industrialization and wealth. Yet American culture is distinguishable from the cultures of these first cousins as well as from those of more distant relatives in Europe, with which the United States shares a general Western culture.

AMERICAN NORMS AND VALUES

In 1970, one analyst of American values concluded that the following values were of central significance in understanding American culture (Williams 1970):

■ *Work:* Work is a good thing in itself, over and above the need to earn a living.
■ *Achievement:* To strive to better yourself and get ahead is a good thing; being contented with your present lot is considered rather lazy.
■ *Morality:* Americans wish to be thought a just, egalitarian, and generous nation. Following moral principles is seen as more desirable than acting in your own interest.

To a significant extent these values continue to guide Americans. There are signs, however, that the relative importance of these older values has dropped.

Changing Values.   As the United States has changed to a wealthy, urban, industrialized society, some values have shifted in priority. The results of a 1989 survey of American values are presented in Figure 3.1. They show that having a good family life is ranked number one, closely followed by a good self-image, good health, and a feeling of accomplishment. There is wide consensus across America that these are worthwhile goals. Old and young, women and men, Easterners and Westerners all put these values at the head of their list.

These survey results and other indicators suggest that there have been three major changes in American values: A growing emphasis on self-fulfillment, a reduced emphasis on work, and greater emphasis on consumerism.

■
FIGURE 3.1.
AMERICAN VALUES IN 1989

SOURCE: The Gallup Reports, March/April 1989, 36.

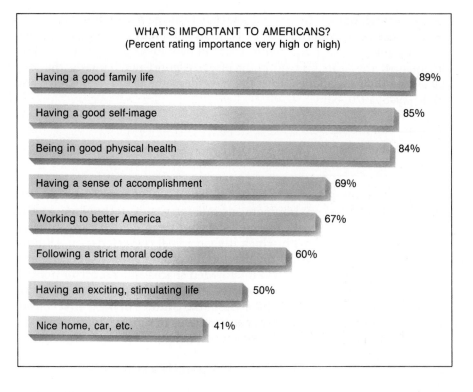

WHAT'S IMPORTANT TO AMERICANS?
(Percent rating importance very high or high)

Having a good family life — 89%
Having a good self-image — 85%
Being in good physical health — 84%
Having a sense of accomplishment — 69%
Working to better America — 67%
Following a strict moral code — 60%
Having an exciting, stimulating life — 50%
Nice home, car, etc. — 41%

SELF-FULFILLMENT.   Increasingly, it is considered desirable, even obligatory, to identify and develop one's personal potential (Glassner 1989). Evidence for this value shift is found in the explosion of the fitness industry, higher education, and self-help groups. There is concern that it might also be reflected in the high rate of divorce: Individuals are less willing to sacrifice their personal achievements for their children or family. This value is not new to American culture—it is the value that drove Daniel Boone and countless frontier explorers to abandon their families to see what was on the other side of the mountain—but it may recently have become more important to a larger share of the population.

REDUCED EMPHASIS ON WORK.   Americans still take pride in being hard-working, but there are many signs of increased emphasis on a balance between work and leisure. The average American worker retires as soon as it is financially feasible, often at age 55 or 60 instead of 65 or 70; time off and long vacations are often more important benefits than higher wages. Complementing this decline in time at work is a growing emphasis on leading a full life through active leisure.

CONSUMERISM.   Although Americans have always been distinguished by the wealth of their material goods, many observers believe that acquiring material possessions is growing in importance. For example, studies of college freshmen show continuing declines in support of values related to social concern and helping others, but sharp increases in commitment to earning a very great deal of money (Astin 1989). Both the United States government and individual consumers are criticized for letting their debts mount and their savings slide as they pursue the goal of "more, *now*."

Observers from many points on the ideological spectrum have been critical of changing American values (Bellah and Associates 1985). They worry that the growing emphasis on consumerism and self-fulfillment may mean a reduced willingness to support families and communities and to help the less fortunate, and they suggest that changes in American values may be an important reason why the U.S. is falling behind other industrialized nations in its productivity.

Signs of Continuity.   Recent decades have witnessed a sharp change in many of the norms guiding American life. Premarital sex, childless marriages, working mothers, interracial marriages—many of the things that were considered plainly wrong two decades ago are increasingly being accepted by the American public.

It would be incorrect, however, to assume a massive change in American norms and values. American norms now allow a wider variation in the means people use to achieve the value of a happy family life, but the value itself hasn't changed. Some people may court success by selling dope, others by becoming stockbrokers; some may seek self-fulfillment through drugs, others through prayer. Across, America, however, there remains broad consensus that achievement, belief in God, and a strong family are good things.

AMERICAN SUBCULTURES AND COUNTERCULTURES

In spite of general agreement on dominant cultural values, a great deal of cultural diversity exists in the United States. People who live in the rural South *are* different from people who live in Los Angeles, and the rich do speak, dress, and live differently than the poor. Some of this diversity will be covered in greater detail in subsequent chapters on deviance, race and ethnicity, social class, education, religion, and so on.

Subcultures.   There are hundreds and perhaps thousands of subcultures in the United States. These subcultures generally share major American values, but they are distinguished by their own vocabularies and folkways. Nearly every major occupational group can be regarded as a subculture, and there have been scholarly studies of the subcultures of coal miners, police officers, musicians, correctional officers, and physicians. Body-builders have their own subculture, as do jocks, professors, and model railroaders. In addition, of course, are subcultures built around shared religious or ethic identity.

Among the most prominent subcultures are those based on region. The stereotypes we hold about people from the Midwest, California, or the South reflect beliefs about regional subcultures. We expect people living in these different parts of the country to have some distinctive values, norms, speech-patterns, and life-styles. To some extent, these expectations are correct. For example, empirical studies show that people who live in the South *are* more likely to be frequent church attenders, have strong religious affiliations, and hold traditional attitudes (Hurlbert 1989). Compared to Americans from other regions, they are more likely to own guns and to approve of using violence to settle interpersonal quarrels (Huff-Corzine, Corzine, and Moore 1986). Also, they have a distinctive speech pattern that serves as a symbol of their group membership. These differences and many others reflect a unique cultural legacy that makes them, while a part of the larger American culture, distinct.

From hoe-downs to bar mitzvahs, opening nights to Monday night football, American subcultures share rituals and ceremonies that unite them with others of their kind and separate them, if only marginally, from others. Whenever people share unique circumstances, they will develop unique vocabularies and folkways to deal with them.

American Countercultures.   Compared to 20 or 25 years ago, there are relatively few well-publicized countercultures active in the United States today. The countercultures of the past generation—the Moonies, hippies, and radical and revolutionary political factions—have largely passed from the public stage. Two exceptions are punk and white supremacists.

Punk is a recent form of counterculture that deliberately attempts to "offend, shock, and attack" mainstream society by dress, music, and behavior (Baron 1989). Some punks are just part-timers, who dye their hair purple and listen to death rock, but nevertheless manage to go to school or hold a job. True punks, however, angrily reject all contact with straight society. They refuse to work or take organized charity; they live angry and sometimes hungry lives on the streets. Asked about the kind of music he liked, one punk said "I like hard core a lot. I don't like idiotic stuff though like Venom and stuff. I like lyrics that actually say something and music that makes you want to beat somebody up" (Baron 1989, 30).

A less public but more dangerous counterculture consists of the white supremacists. There are several distinct organizations of white supremacists, ranging from the American Nazi Party and the Aryan Nation through small bands of armed extremists. All are characterized by extreme racism, antisemitism, patriarchy, and patriotism. Although they typically believe that they are reestablishing traditional American values, their enthusiasm for killing all Jews, and blacks, and communists and for driving women back into the kitchen appall most Americans. As a result, most Americans see them not as a harmless variation of American culture (a subculture) but as a threat to American culture (a counterculture).

Elite Culture/Popular Culture

Social scientists always make a point of saying that culture refers to the norms and values of society as a whole, not to elite culture, as in art, opera, and symphony. Yet culture is influenced by social class, and, like everything else, the norms and values of the upper classes tend to be perceived as superior to the norms and values of the lower classes (Blau 1986). If we prefer Monday night football to *Swan Lake*, Hank Williams, Jr. to Bach, we recognize that these preferences have lower status.

Because of this variety in tastes, sociologists make a distinction between elite culture (the culture of the educated upper classes) and popular culture

White supremacist groups such as the Ku Klux Klan (KKK) are examples of American countercultures. Although they usually present themselves as returning to traditional values, literally and figuratively wrapping themselves in the American flag, such groups want revolutionary changes in American society: they want to kill or deport Jews, African Americans, and communists; they want women out of politics and the labor force. Because such groups challenge the values of the larger culture, they are seen as not just different, but as dangerous and threatening.

(what the rest of us like) (Gans 1974). Both cultures express the values and aesthetics of their distinct constituencies. Sociologists who study popular culture focus on such cultural forms as murder mysteries, gothic romances, quilts, television programming, and sports. This focus on the material and nonmaterial culture of ordinary women and men helps us understand both the solidarities and the divisions in society (Mukerji and Schudson 1986). Popular culture may not be high status, but, as Mick Jagger said, "I know it's only rock and roll, but I like it."

THE PRODUCTION OF AMERICAN CULTURE

In the United States, the production of popular culture is driven by market forces. Commercial value and market size determine what goes on television or radio, into movie theaters, and onto store shelves. Elite culture also requires financial backing, but it is less dependent on mass appeal. Elite culture generally relies on funding from wealthy patrons and from governments. City, county, state, and federal governments subsidize galleries, museums, public television, and theaters; they also give direct grants to individual artists, writers, dancers, and playwrights.

In 1989, a major controversy arose over federal funding for the arts when a government-sponsored exhibition included a photograph entitled "Piss Christ," showing a crucifix floating in a jar of urine; another picture in the same exhibition showed children in erotic poses. A large portion of the public would probably find the pictures blasphemous, in poor taste, offensive, and definitely not art. In response to the controversy, Congress agreed to bar federal funds from any art deemed to be obscene or to denigrate a religion, race, ethnic background, age group, or handicap ("Funds to Be Denied" 1989). Critics of the new legislation argue that this is censorship and that the government should not be in the business of deter-

"Lifting Flag" by Alice Dalton Brown

mining cultural expression. By a significant margin, the public agrees. A Gallup poll shows that by a 58 to 22 percent margin, the public thinks the government should stay out of deciding what is art; the public goes farther, however, and by a 47 to 35 percent margin, prefers that the government get out of arts funding altogether ("When Taxes Pay" 1989).

Arts funding is only the tip of the iceberg. In 1989, the combined expenditures of federal, state, and local governments were well over $1.5 trillion. Whether this was spent on education, highways, missiles, or health care affects American culture. Similarly, government laws, from taxes to civil rights, affect our culture. In the "Issues in Social Policy" section, we address recent governmental attempts to control culture by legislating language use.

Should the U.S. Have an Official Language?

Language is the primary carrier of culture. For ethnic subcultures it is especially important as a symbol of shared ties. This shared language is essential to maintaining such aspects of culture as religion, ceremonies, and art. Some students of language would argue that attempts to substitute the dominant group's language for the subgroup's language are equivalent to attempting to eliminate the subgroup's culture.

In the United States, this is an especially controversial issue and one that is currently being debated in Congress and in statehouses across the country (Guy 1989). The issue can be stated simply: Should we or should we not pass the English Language Amendment (ELA) to the Constitution? The amendment, proposed in both houses of the U.S. Congress every year since 1982, reads:

Maintaining the language of one's cultural heritage is a vital means of maintaining common group identity. While it creates solidarity within the group, however, it simultaneously erects a barrier against outsiders. Many non-Hispanic Americans feel like foreigners in their own country when they go into Hispanic communities. Although most Hispanic Americans shift to English as their mother tongue by the third generation, the growth of large Spanish-speaking communities may reduce the speed of this transition.

The English language shall be the official language of the United States.

Some people are startled to find out that English is not already the official language of the United States. When our constitution was created in the 18th century, the Founding Fathers considered and rejected an official language stipulation, believing that forced linguistic conformity was antidemocratic. Subsequently, the courts have consistently interpreted the Constitution to support the right to speak the language of your choice, based on the freedom of speech and freedom of religion amendments to the Constitution. In recent years, the right has been given additional support by the Civil Rights Act, which states that equal protection of the law shall not be denied on the basis of race or national origin.

In the early 1980's, U.S. policy moved toward greater recognition of the *right* to speak the language of your choice. It was this movement, supported by the courts, that made ELA an issue. Current rights for non-English speakers are supported by the courts in four situations (Keller 1983): the voting booth (ballots must be printed in a second language if more than 5 percent of the voters in an area speak a single non-English language and are not literate in English); the courtroom (the right to be tried in your own language); the classroom (if a sizable minority of students cannot get equal opportunity in education because of a language barrier, instruction must be offered in their language at least on a transitional basis, usually interpreted as the first three grades); and the radio (broadcasts must be available in an alternate language if many residents of a community are non-English speakers). In addition, many stage governments, especially California and New Mexico, give non-English speakers additional rights, such as rights to government services in their language.

ISSUES IN SOCIAL POLICY continued

The alternate language that is causing most of the concern is Spanish. The issue is not particular to Spanish or the current wave of Mexican immigrants, however. Other linguistic groups that have recently settled in large numbers in particular communities, such as Koreans in the Los Angeles area, have also felt the pressures imposed by local ELA-type enactments. The situation is similar to that in the early part of this century when many people were concerned about floods of European immigrants whom some felt to be too slow in learning English.

Supporters of the ELA claim that it will help unify the United States and eliminate what they believe to be the false signal sent by bilingual education, that you can make it in America without learning English. Opponents argue that the ELA is a "sure path to divisiveness and discord" (Guy 1989, 52) and that it violates the basic rights of individuals. They propose an amendment that would recognize the right "to preserve, foster, and promote their respective historical, linguistic,

and culture origins. . . . No person shall be denied the equal protection of the laws because of culture or language."

So far, Congress has not voted on the ELA. It has been on several state agendas: California, Florida, Arizona, and Colorado have passed an ELA; New Mexico and Texas rejected it; and Nebraska repealed an ELA that had been on its books since 1920.

The ELA appears to have more symbolic than practical import. For example, Illinois passed an ELA in 1969, but still requires that agencies having contacts with large numbers of non-English speakers be prepared to serve them in their own language. This does not mean that the ELA is unimportant. Its symbolic message—that we reject Spanish language and Spanish culture—is an important one. Many feel that the ELA is thinly-disguised racism and that the U.S. should retain the policy of linguistic tolerance that saw it through its first 200 years (Ambrose 1989).

SUMMARY

1. Culture includes all of the material and nonmaterial products of society. It can be conceived of as a tool kit that provides us with the ideas and technology to deal with the common problems of everyday life.
2. Generally, structural functionalists take culture as a given and ask how it affects us; conflict theorists ask about the social forces that produce culture.
3. Culture is problem solving, relative, and a human creation. Language is a unique human attribute that makes culture uniquely human.
4. A relatively new field, sociobiology, urges us to recognize that human behavior may be shaped by biology and evolution as well as by culture. Human behaviors linked to successful reproduction, such as mate selection and parenting, are especially likely to be genetically encoded.

5. Language, or symbolic communication, is a central component of culture. Language embodies culture, serves as a framework for perceiving the world, and symbolizes common bonds.
6. Norms (mores and folkways) specify appropriate behavior for reaching socially valued goals. Laws may or may not be norms. Although most of us behave as expected because we accept our society's norms as right, sanctions encourage conformity.
7. The cultures of large and complex societies are not homogeneous. Subcultures with distinct life-styles and folkways develop to meet unique regional, class, and ethnic needs. Occasionally, countercultures develop to challenge the dominant culture.

8. The most important factors accounting for cultural variation are the natural environment, isolation from other cultures, technological level, diffusion, and dominant cultural themes.

9. Americans say that they value the family, good health, a good self-image, and a sense of accomplishment. Three changes in American values over the last generation are more emphasis on self-fulfillment, a reduced emphasis on work, and greater emphasis on consumerism.

10. U.S. culture is far from homogeneous; in addition to the split between popular culture and elite culture, there are many regional, racial and ethnic, and age subcultures. Among contemporary American countercultures are punks and white supremacists.

■

SUGGESTED READINGS

Bell, Robert W., and Bell, Nancy (eds.). 1989. Sociobiology and the Social Sciences. Lubbock, Tex.: Texas Tech Press. A collection of essays applying the sociobiological perspective to topics such as family violence, sexual attraction, and single parenting.

Bellah, Robert N., and Associates. 1985. Habits of the Heart: Individualism and Commitment in American Life. Berkeley: University of California Press. A critical look at contemporary American values. The authors argue that an emphasis on individual fulfillment at the expense of commitment is damaging to society and to personal integration.

Kephart, William M. 1987. Extraordinary Groups: The Sociology of Unconventional Life-Styles. (3d ed.) New York: St. Martin's Press. A fascinating tour of some of the most interesting subcultures and countercultures in the United States, both past and present: the Amish, gypsies, Shakers, and Hutterites. Painless sociology— the application of basic concepts and theory to truly extraordinary groups.

Messenger, John C. 1969. Inis Beag: Isle of Ireland. New York: Holt, Rinehart and Winston. A report of Messenger's fieldwork over a period of years among the Inis Beag islanders. Illuminates the joys and perils of fieldwork as well as the culture and life-styles of the people of Inis Beag.

Williams, Robin W., Jr. 1970. American Society. (3rd ed). New York: Knopf. A classic analysis of American culture, society, and institutions, especially the dominant values operating in society after World War II.

Yinger, Milton J. 1982. Countercultures: The Promise and the Peril of a World Turned Upside Down. New York: Free Press. An examination of various social groups characterized by values and norms that are contradictory to the dominant values and norms of society.

■ PHOTO ESSAY: **Environmental Damage: A Cultural Product?**

Across the entire industrialized world, acid rain is destroying healthy forests and leaving behind the ugly skeletons of chemical death. This dying forest in Mitchell, North Carolina is the result of failure to enact strong clean air acts and to enforce the legislation we already have on the books. Ultimately, it is a product of our unwillingness to pay the costs of higher prices and more regulation.

A glance at the news or at the world around you will tell you that our physical environment is in trouble. Among the most urgent problems are health hazards and environmental damage caused by toxic waste and pollution; the disappearance of species and wilderness areas in the face of development; and the overuse of nonrenewable resources. How did we get in this condition—perhaps more importantly, how do we get out of it?

Although many people blame our environmental troubles on somebody else—those who illegally dump toxic waste, build nuclear reactors, or run their oil tankers aground—the truth is that many of the causes of our environmental problems are built into our culture and social structures. Each of us, by participating in the American way of life, contributes to environmental damage. Among the many aspects of the American life-style that contribute to environmental damage are expansive lawns that demand heavy watering; lack of carpooling and excessive numbers of lone motorists driving to work every day; the use of polystyrene; driving cars, motorboats, motorcycles, and snowmobiles for recreation; disposable diapers, microwave dishes, paper plates and towels; and the vast amount of garbage (approximately 35 pounds per person) that the average American generates each week.

Wait a minute, you say. How else can I get to school besides driving? There is no mass transit in my city, and I live too far away to bicycle to school. You might also note that it is very difficult *not* to generate a lot of garbage when compact disks, for example, are sold in huge packages. Even if you want to recycle, it is virtually impossible to buy many grocery products in glass jars. Also, many communities are not set up to accept recyclables.

These defenses are legitimate. They make the critical point that environmental damage is not generally the result of personal character flaws, but a product of our culture and social structure. Environmentally destructive practices and values are built into our social structures and the solution is not completely within the scope of individual action. Certainly, you should recycle and cut down on waste, but individual action alone cannot get at the source of the problem. The sociological imagination suggests that the answer lies in changing our cultural values and social structures that encourage environmentally destructive lifestyles. We suggest that changes in two areas are especially im-

■ PHOTO ESSAY: **Environmental Damage: A Cultural Product?**

■

Very high levels of consumption and waste are part of the American way of life. We buy an awfully lot of things (gadgets, food, electronic equipment, and so on) that we don't really need; many of these purchases end up in the garbage or stuffed in the back of closets. Although individual shoppers can afford to pay for their purchases, the manufacture and disposal of these wasteful and wasted goods imposes burdens on our environment.

■

What is the connection between a dead cormorant and rush hour traffic? High demands for oil have encouraged the development of fragile lands and vastly multiplied the number of oil tankers plying the world's estuaries and waterways. Oil spills are directly related to our routine commuting practices.

portant: values, and political and economic structures.

Values: What Use is a Spotted Owl?

In the United States today, there are two competing sets of environmentally relevant values. The most common set may be called *utility ethics*. From this perspective, the environment is of concern only insofar as it affects human needs. If spotted owls get in our way, we are free to exterminate them. What good are spotted owls, anyway? On the other hand, this ethic suggests that we do need to be concerned about toxic waste and acid rain because they affect the health and economy of human societies. This perspective is the basis for much of our current environmental policy. Although the utility ethic encourages policies such as the Clean Air Act, it is willing to tolerate a few lost species, a little toxic waste, and some dirty air in exchange for jobs and prosperity. Current thinking suggests that the original 1977 Clean Air Act was too tolerant of dirty air and it seems likely that the 1990 Congress will enact tougher pollution controls on factories, automobiles, and electric power plants.

At the other end of the continuum is a set of values that is sometimes called the *biocentric ethic*. This perspective emphasizes the wholeness of nature, in which humankind is only one part—of equal, but not greater, importance as the spotted owl. This perspective flatly denies that the Earth exists merely as a resource for human beings. It argues that it is our duty to preserve nature—not because we need it, but because it is intrinsically worthwhile and we have no right to put our needs above those of other species.

Many people find something to agree with in both of these

Which is more important—jobs or owls? This question directly confronts the contradiction between utility ethics and bioethics. An environmentalist subscribing to bioethics would place the survival of an owl species before jobs (though not necessarily before human lives).

■ PHOTO ESSAY: Environmental Damage: A Cultural Product?

■

Even those people who would happily trade the spotted owl for a more profitable logging industry become environmentalists when faced with toxic waste. Toxic waste challenges the survival of our species. Reducing toxic waste and pollution is a top priority if the natural world is going to be able to continue to support human society.

ethics. Environmental ethics can be understood as the result of choices we make among six values: the values of development, preservation, protecting humankind, protecting nature, securing the present, and guaranteeing the future (Seligman 1989). Each of us would probably endorse all six values; the question is one of emphasis and balance. Generally, the utility ethic—which dominates Western culture—emphasizes development over preservation, protecting humankind over nature, and securing the present over guaranteeing the future. Because our culture also values preservation, nature, and the future, however, our culture contains the seeds for a more biocentric ethic.

Recent studies suggest that a change in values is taking place. A large majority of Americans believe the environmental problem is serious, and they are willing to make changes to address the problem. They are demanding safe waste disposal sites, recycling their own garbage, and are willing to pay higher prices to protect the environment. How many people, however, are willing to pay $1.50 for a can of tuna that is dolphin-safe when they can get an apparently identical product for 50 cents? The product wouldn't be on the market unless producers believe that a substantial minority are willing to buy it, but the number of people who will actually volunteer to pay extra for it may still be small.

Value change takes place in response to changes in the physical and social environment. We can hurry this value change along by deliberately changing the political and economic environment in which people make decisions.

Economic and Political Structures: The Tragedy of the Commons.

Who owns the water and the air and the whooping crane? The answer is everybody—and that

■

This tuna has been caught in a driftnet, a fishing practice that also kills dolphins. Stores now offer environmentalists a chance to put their money where their mouth is by paying 3–4 times as much for tuna caught by alternate means.

is part of the problem. In a classic article titled "The Tragedy of the Commons," Garrett Hardin (1968) pointed out that a resource held in common is very likely to be abused. Each person's share is so small and diffuse that is doesn't seem worthwhile defending it. Your share of the national forests, for example, is .000000004 (1 divided by 250 million). If a timber company comes in and clear-cuts a forest, you are unlikely to hire a lawyer to defend your tiny share. If a specific tree was your individual property, however, you might camp out there to defend it. Because resources are owned in common, no specific individual has a vested interest in taking care of them. You can bet that if a private individual had patent or copyright permission on a species, it wouldn't be disappearing.

In contemporary nations—capitalist and socialist—the state is the guardian of the environment. In almost all nations, however, the state has been a slum landlord rather than a careful investor, and so far has done little to protect and preserve its property. Instead, the public guardian has allowed people and corporations to pollute the environment and eliminate habitats without asking for payment for the damages.

One strategy to reduce the environmental problem is to make individual polluters pay the state the full cost of their environmental damage: for example, putting a $2-per-gallon tax on gasoline to pay for the cleanup costs of dirty air. Another example is charging $10 for a single polystyrene cup because its manufacture releases pollutants into the air and, because Styrofoam may take more than 100 years to decompose, its disposal contributes to filling up our landfills. Faced with the full cost of life-style or production choices, many of us probably will make different choices.

A different strategy is to rely on the coercive power of government to legislate the care of its (our) property—the environment. Such laws might regulate industrial pollution, restrict the kinds of product packaging we can use, limit the size or use of our cars, and make recycling mandatory.

Summary

Clearly, choosing an economic strategy will change our lives by making many things far more expensive than they are now. The political strategy will change our lives by imposing far more regulation. Ultimately, protecting the environment will require changes in our culture—changes in our values, lifestyles, forms of recreation, and our freedom to use the commons. Available evidence, from surveys and from the grocery shelves, suggests that a growing number of Americans are willing to make these changes.

The jobs these protesters are so cavalier about are not their own jobs, but somebody else's. Protecting the environment is not a simple case of good versus evil, but a complex problem that involves competition among regions and social classes.

4

SOCIAL STRUCTURES AND INSTITUTIONS

Have you ever . . .

Tried to play a simple game and instead spent all your time haggling over the rules? If you have watched children playing or can remember when you were a child, you can probably cite instances where a simple game, such as baseball, degenerated into arguments about the rules. For example, does it count if someone throws the ball and you're not ready? Do you lose your place in line if you have to go in to eat? Who gets to go first? Is it fair if the bigger kids get to play? Do you have to let boys (or girls) play?

As we grow older, we find that the rules have already been established for many of the games we will play; the players have been identified and norms have been set up to guide their behavior. For example, most of us understand that in the marriage game the rules limit us to one spouse at a time, no sexual contacts outside the marriage, and a financial and emotional obligation to our spouse. Similarly, the rules of the education game describe who can play and how the players should behave. At work, in bridge groups, even in bars, shared norms evolve, and newcomers must learn them if they are to fit into the group.

These patterned ways of behaving are referred to as social structure. In this chapter, we explore the concept of social structure and show how it helps us understand our own behavior and our society.

SOCIAL STRUCTURE:
THE CONCEPTUAL FRAMEWORK

A **social structure** is a recurrent pattern of relationships.

Formally, **social structures** are recurrent patterns of relationships. Social structures can be found at all levels in society. Friendships, football games, and corporations all fall into patterns that are repeated day after day or game after game. Some of these patterns are reinforced by formal rules or laws, but many are maintained by force of custom.

The patterns in our lives are both constraining and enabling (Giddens 1984). If you would like to be free to work on your own schedule, then you will find the nine-to-five, Monday-to-Friday work pattern a constraint. On the other hand, preset patterns provide convenient and comfortable ways to handle many of the routine aspects of daily life. They help us get through cross-town traffic, find dating partners or spouses, and raise our children.

The analysis of these patterns or social structures revolves around three concepts: status, role, and institution. In this section we introduce this conceptual framework, and in the remainder of the book, we will apply this framework to recurrent patterns from deviance to college graduation.

STATUS

A **status** is a specialized position within a group.

An **achieved status** is optional, one that a person can obtain in a lifetime.

An **ascribed status** is fixed by birth and inheritance and is unalterable in a person's lifetime.

The basic building block of society is the **status**—a specialized position in a group. Sociologists who want to study the status structure of society include two types of statuses: achieved and ascribed. An **achieved status** is an optional position that a person can obtain in a lifetime. Being a father or president of the PTA is an achieved status. An **ascribed status** is a position fixed by birth and inheritance; it is unalterable in a person's lifetime. Sex and race are examples of ascribed statuses.

The range of statuses available in a society and the distribution of people and rewards among these statuses set the stage for further relationships (Blau 1974). Sociologists who take this approach to analyzing social structures are typically concerned with four issues (Blau 1987; Blau and Schwartz 1984).

1. *Identification.* What statuses are available in a society? Does this society, for example, have a distinct status of physician or teacher or ex-convict? What ascribed statuses—for example, what racial or ethnic categories— does this society recognize?
2. *Distribution.* What is the distribution of people among these statuses? Does 90 percent of the population hold the status "farmer," or, as in the contemporary United States, are only 3 percent farmers? The relative size of each status shapes the opportunities open to people who occupy these statuses.
3. *Consequences.* How different are the rewards and resources for people who occupy one status rather than another? Does it matter whether one is a physician or a farmer, male or female, married or single?
4. *Combinations.* What combinations of statuses are possible? Can one be a female and a physician, or is this combination impossible or unlikely?

Spring Hill, Tennessee is a small community of 1000 people. Although its schools and police department are racially integrated, at least some of its churches—as evidenced by this 1989 photograph—are not. In a community that includes approximately seven times more whites than blacks, such racial segregation is not random; it is socially structured behavior. Sociologists want to understand the processes that encourage and support recurrent patterns of behavior such as racial segregation.

Understanding the processes that make some combinations of statuses more likely than others is a central concern for sociology. For example, why did the physician status traditionally overlap with the statuses of white and male?

A Case Study: The Social Structure of Race.   If we analyze the major achieved and ascribed statuses in our society along these four dimensions, we develop an understanding of how our lives are patterned by status membership. To illustrate this approach, we apply it to racial status and ask how holding one particular racial status—being African American— affects patterned relationships in the United States.

IDENTIFICATION.   How many racial statuses are there in the United States? The 1990 census asked us to sort ourselves into one of five racial categories: white, black, Native American, Asian, or other. Although the labels may change, the same question appears on many of the other forms you fill out as well as on almost every social survey. The apparent consensus on which statuses are important and the nearly universal degree of concern over our racial status tell us a great deal about how race affects our relationships. It is interesting, for example, that the government is barred from asking about our religious status but appears to show almost an insatiable concern about which of these five racial statuses we occupy.

DISTRIBUTION.   The numerical distribution of the population among statuses may either encourage or discourage certain patterns of behavior. In 1980, for example, the census identified 2 million black residents in New York City, but only seven black residents of Worland, Wyoming. This means that in New York City, black residents may choose to restrict almost all of their associations to others of the same race: There are black neighborhoods, schools, doctors, grocery stores, and so on. In Worland, this is not possible. In New York City, there are four whites for every black; in Worland the ratio is 1,000 to one. This means that a quarter of all whites in New York *could* marry or be best friends with a black person; in Worland, it is impossible for more than a few whites to be linked closely with a black resident. To the extent that the numerical distribution of people among statuses restricts (or encourages) their interactions, we say that their behavior is socially structured. (The effect of sex ratios in schools or on army bases is another example of how the relative numbers of people in various statuses can structure interactions.)

CONSEQUENCES.   On nearly every measure that one might choose, there is a substantial inequality in rewards and resources between blacks and whites in the United States. Black unemployment is twice that of whites; the percent living below the poverty level is three time higher; the infant mortality rate is twice as high; the likelihood of being murdered is six times higher. These facts demonstrate that substantial disadvantage is attached to holding the status "black" in American society. Obviously, racial status is consequential and has an enormous influence on the structure of daily experiences.

COMBINATIONS.   Forty years ago, racial statuses overlapped considerably with educational and occupational statuses. Being black meant having much less education and very different kinds of jobs than whites. Today, knowing a person's racial status is not such an accurate guide to his or her other statuses. Nevertheless, 30 percent of all maids in the United States but only 4 percent of all physicians are black (U.S. Bureau of the Census 1989a, 388–89). Understanding the processes through which this continued overlap of racial, political, and economic statuses is maintained is the focus of Chapter 10.

ROLES

The status structure of a society provides the broad outlines for interaction. These broad outlines are filled in by **roles,** sets of norms that specify the rights and obligations of each status. Roles provide the normative dimension of social structure; they define how people who occupy specific statuses *ought* to act and feel toward one another.

A **role** is a set of norms specifying the rights and obligations associated with a status.

The relationship between statuses and roles can be nicely illustrated through a theatrical metaphor: The set of statuses within a group is equivalent to the cast of characters, and roles are equivalent to the scripts that define how the characters are expected to relate to one another. Generally, there is much more variability in roles than in statuses. For example, whether we analyze kindergartens, high schools, or universities, there are two primary statuses: teachers and students. The roles attached to these statuses, however, vary dramatically from one type of school to the next.

This language from the theater helps to make a vital point about the relationships between status and role: People *occupy* statuses, but they *play* roles. This distinction is helpful when we analyze how structures work in practice—and sometimes why they don't work. A man may occupy the status of teacher, but he may play the role associated with it very poorly.

Factors Affecting Role Performance.

Social structure is a concept designed to account for the patterns that appear in human behavior. Taken to extremes, it suggests a machine-like conformity in which we play the parts we are assigned. Within the general pattern, however, there are many variations. Not everyone who occupies the status "teacher" will play the role the same way. Some of these variations in role behavior are socially structured; others are due to individual actors negotiating their own roles. In this section, we cover four structural factors that affect role performance: compatibility of roles, adequate role definitions, existence of appropriate sanctions, and availability of resources.

COMPATIBILITY OF ROLES.   Sometimes people fail to fulfill role requirements despite their best intentions. This failure is particularly likely when people are faced with incompatible demands owing to multiple or complex roles. Sociologists distinguish between two types of incompatible role demands: When these incompatible role demands develop within a single status, we refer to **role strain;** when they develop because of multiple statuses, we refer to **role conflict.**

Some of the clearest examples of role strain, or incompatible role demands within a single status, occur in the family. For example, parents' responsibilities include supporting their children economically and emotionally, teaching them, and disciplining them. Many parents face role

Football games offer a graphic metaphor of social structure. The 11 people on the team occupy 11 different statuses, each with a relatively unique role. Quarterbacks have one role to play and tight ends have another. Less formally, the family includes three major statuses: dad, mom, and the kids. In both kinds of social structure, however, success depends on all status occupants playing the roles attached to their position.

Role strain is caused by incompatible role demands within a single status.

Role conflict is caused by incompatibility between the roles of two or more statuses held by an individual.

Despite widely shared standards of behavior, people deviate in major or minor ways. Sometimes this is because they don't understand the rules. In other cases, it is because, with the best will in the world, they simply cannot do it all. Giving chidren emotional support, helping them with their school work, getting dinner on the table, and perhaps talking to his broker are obviously giving this man a case of role overload. In this case, it is likely that his meal, his math advice, and his financial strategems may not meet expected standards.

strains when their provider role interferes with their role of being there when their children need them. The simultaneous demand to provide loving support and discipline can also be a source of strain.

When role incompatibility occurs between the demands of two or more statuses (role conflict), people also find it difficult or impossible to meet all of their role expectations. College students, for example, who try to combine school with work or marriage, or both, often discover that the role demands of one status interfere with the expectations of another. Not surprisingly, a spouse may expect a little attention in the evening, whereas the student role obliges one to stay at the library or lock oneself up in the bedroom to read. An employer is likely to demand overtime at Christmas, which is when a student needs time off to prepare for final exams. In circumstances such as these, it becomes almost inevitable that a person will fail to meet some role obligations. Even with the best will in the world, the person is likely to be regarded as a disappointment by his or her teachers, employer, or spouse.

ADEQUACY OF ROLE DEFINITIONS.   We cannot expect people to fulfill expectations that we haven't made clear. Thus, one prerequisite for good role performance is clear communication about role requirements. New college students, for example, are often confused about what is expected of them. Instructors frequently open class with the statement that no attendance will be taken and that it is entirely up to the student whether to attend class; a significant portion of each freshman class makes the mistake of thinking that this means that attendance is unimportant. In cases such as this, the likelihood of good role performance can be markedly improved by advance training and by clearly spelling out the expectations associated with each role.

APPROPRIATE SANCTIONS.   People must be motivated to meet their role obligations by a system of sanctions. When there is little reward for proper role performance, people become more lax about meeting expectations. For example, if you have ever had a teacher who waited two months to return a major paper and then returned it, apparently unread, with an "OK" on the last page, you know how the absence of rewards can drastically reduce your motivation to put out your best effort. As students, parents, teachers, and employees, we are more likely to fulfill our role obligations if successful performance is adequately rewarded and poor performance results in unpleasant consequences.

AVAILABILITY OF RESOURCES. Adequate role performance generally requires some basic resources and opportunities. A college student cannot be successful if he or she cannot afford to buy the books, has no time to study, or cannot understand the language the professors use or the examples they give. A parent cannot meet the obligation to support his or her children if there are no jobs or if his or her skills have been outdated and are no longer in demand.

When there is no realistic opportunity to live up to one's normative obligations, then role expectations will be seen as irrelevant or impossible. A case study at the end of this chapter gives a detailed example of role failure among the Ojibwa Indians of Canada, a failure that can be traced directly to such a lack of opportunity. In the case of the Ojibwa and many other Native American peoples, it is no longer possible to carry out their traditional roles.

The Negotiated Order. Although there is general consensus across American society on how parents ought to behave toward each other and their children, probably no two families are alike. An important reason for this is that the norms of any social structure are never complete. For example, although the norms associated with family roles provide the broad

Occupational statuses are often more clearly defined than our other statuses. This officer's behavior is guided by formal regulations that prescribe how he should dress, drive, speak, and act. Even in this extreme case, however, his behavior is not completely guided by formal role prescriptions. Dozens of times throughout each shift, he will face ambiguous situations that require independent decisions. Although shared social structure produces patterned regularities in the ways officers behave, there is also considerable diversity.

Institutions are enduring and complex social structures that meet basic human needs.

■

In most societies, elder care is built into the family institution, and family statuses—especially that of daughter—include obligations to care for parents. Although Social Security and Medicaid have lifted the economic burden of elder support from children, most of the infirm elderly in the United States rely on their children for many direct services. Because these obligations have been institutionalized—built into statuses and roles and supported by norms and values—this help is generally forthcoming.

outlines for acceptable behavior, they leave a lot of details unresolved. Being honest and standing by your family are both norms, but what do you do when telling the truth gets your brother in trouble? What do you do when something comes up that the script doesn't cover? Say, your mother wants to get a divorce and move in with you? Although social structures give us a great deal of guidance about appropriate behavior, no role is fully scripted. Even with the most well-defined role, there are many occasions in everyday life when we must improvise and negotiate. This means that there will be variability in the ways people play their parts. This source of social heterogeneity is covered in more detail in Chapter 7.

INSTITUTIONS

Social structures vary in their scope and importance. Some, such as those that pattern baseball games, have limited application. Baseball commissioners could change all the rules tomorrow and most of us wouldn't care. Other social structures, however, have the power to shape the basic fabric of our lives. We call these social structures **institutions.**

An institution is an enduring and complex social structure that meets basic human needs. Its primary features are that it endures for generations, that it includes a complex set of statuses, roles, norms and values, and that it addresses a basic human need. Embedded in the statuses and roles of the family institution, for example, are enduring patterns for dating and courtship, for childrearing, and for care of the elderly.

Institutions provide routine patterns for dealing with predictable problems of social life. Because these problems tend to be similar across societies, we find that every society tends to have the same types of institutions.

The Basic Institutions.   Five basic institutions are found in every society:

- The family, to care for dependents and rear children
- The economy, to produce and distribute goods
- Government, to provide community coordination and defense
- Education, to train new generations
- Religion, to supply answers about the unknown or unknowable.

These institutions are basic in the sense that every society provides *some* set of enduring social arrangements designed to meet these important social needs. The arrangements may vary from one society to the next, sometimes dramatically. Government institutions may be monarchies or democracies or dictatorships. But a stable social structure that has the responsibility for meeting these needs is common to all societies.

In simple societies, all of these important social needs—political, economic, educational, and religious—are met through one major social institution: the family or kinship group (Adams 1971). Social relationships based on kinship obligations organize production, reproduction, education, and defense.

As societies grow larger and more complex, the kinship structure is less able to furnish solutions to all the recurrent problems. As a result, some activities gradually are transferred to more specialized social structures

The Mormon Challenge

In the early part of the 19th century several religious groups in the United States attempted to establish social structures that were radically different from the existing institutional structures. Among the more successful of these groups were the Mormons, a religious group that began in New York in 1830 and migrated to the Utah Territory in the decade before the Civil War. The almost complete absence of any other settlers in the Utah Territory plus the large and growing number of Mormons (150,000 by 1880) allowed for the full flowering of Mormon institutions.

The Mormons challenged three traditional American institutions: the family, the economy, and the separation of church and state. First, the Mormons endorsed the practice of polygyny, a form of plural marriage in which men are allowed to have more than one wife. It is estimated that approximately 10 percent of Mormon men had more than one wife. Of these, most had two or three wives, although one church leader, Brigham Young, had 27 (Young 1954). Second, the Mormons practiced a collective form of economic organization called the United Order. Under church sponsorship, cooperative economic enterprises were established throughout Mormon communities: retail stores, various factories and mills, banking and finance. Patronizing Mormon businesses was considered a sign of religious loyalty. The communal economic system challenged the value of free enterprise and made it virtually impossible for outsiders to compete. Third, the religious and economic integration of church members was supplemented by political integration through the People's Party, a political party directed by church leaders. Thus, the Mormons formed an integrated unit in Utah; religious leaders were also political and economic leaders.

Throughout the second half of the 19th century, the economic and political power of the Mormon church grew rapidly. The church came to dominate the Utah Territory, and non-Mormons were not welcome there. As the church grew, so did its opposition. Much of the opposition was directed at plural marriage, but in retrospect it seems clear that economic and political competition were also important.

■

The Mormons challenged three traditional American institutions: the family, the economy, and the separation of church and state.

The practice of polygyny in the 19th century allowed some well-to-do Mormon men to have several wives. This patriarch, Joseph F. Smith, appears to have had at least four wives and dozens of children. The practice of polygyny flourished for approximately 40 years but was finally abandoned by the church in 1890.

Shortly after the Civil War, a series of federal laws prohibiting some of the Mormon practices was passed. The Edmunds Act of 1882 provided heavy penalties for plural marriages, including the loss of voting rights and of the right to hold office. Although officially aimed at preventing plural marriages, the law had the effect of removing Mormon leaders from political office and destroying the political power of the Mormon leadership in the Utah Territory. In 1886, the Edmunds-Tucker Act reinforced the penalties for polygyny and prohibited the Mormon church from holding property.

Initially, Mormons evaded the consequences of these laws. Plural marriages were performed by the church, not in the civil courts, and the corporate holdings of the church were transferred to individual church leaders. Continued pressure from federal and territorial officials, however, eventually drove many church leaders into hiding or jail. During this period, considerable church property was confiscated, undermining the communal economic organization of Mormon communities.

By 1890, the Mormon church surrendered. The president of the church issued a manifesto that officially ended the practice of plural marriages (and the church's challenge to the institution of monogamous marriage). The People's Party was dissolved, and the collective economic efforts of the church were substantially reduced. In exchange, convicted polygynists were granted amnesty and some church property was returned. In 1896, the Utah Territory was granted statehood, bringing to a close one of the most radical challenges to the basic institutions of 19th-century American society.

Today, the Mormon church remains a central institution in the state of Utah. Over 75 percent of the population of Utah belongs to the Mormon church, and the church continues to dominate the political and economic life of the state. The entire congressional delegation from Utah (two senators and three representatives) is Mormon, as are the governor and much of the state legislature (Barone and Ujifusa 1989). The Mormon church holds extensive property in Utah and elsewhere and is believed to be the richest church in the United States on the basis of holdings per member (Kephart 1983). And although the Mormon church officially opposes polygyny, splinter groups have broken away from the church in order to maintain the practice. Because it is illegal, there is no official count of how many people practice polygyny in Utah today. One plural wife, however, suggests that there are more practicing polygynists in Utah today than there were a century ago (Kephart 1983, 271).

Although the Mormon church continues to prosper, its challenge to conventional institutions was unsuccessful. A conflict theorist would attribute this failure to the greater power of non-Mormons, who were able to destroy social structures that challenged and excluded them. A structural-functional theorist would argue that Mormonism's unique institutions failed because they were not adaptable to a territory that was growing rapidly and increasing its involvement with the larger world. Which perspective makes the most sense to you?

outside the family. The economy, education, religion, and government become fully developed institutionalized structures that exist separately from the family. (The institutions of the contemporary United States are the subjects of Chapters 13 to 18.)

As the social and physical environment of a society changes and the technology for dealing with that environment expands, the problems that individuals have to face change. Thus, institutional structures are not static; new structures emerge to cope with new problems. Among the more recent social structures to be institutionalized in Western society are medicine, science, sports, the military, law, and the criminal justice system. Each of these areas can be viewed as an enduring social structure, complete with interrelated statuses and a unique set of norms and values.

Institutional Interdependence.   Each institution of society can be analyzed as an independent social structure, but none really stands alone. Instead, institutions are interdependent; each affects the others and is affected by them.

In a stable society, the norms and values embodied in the roles of one institution will usually be compatible with those in other institutions. For example, a society that stresses male dominance and rule by seniority in the family will also stress the same norms in its religious, economic, and political systems. In this case, interdependence reinforces norms and values and adds to social stability.

Sometimes, however, interdependence is an important mechanism for social change. Because each institution affects and is affected by the others, a change in one tends to lead to changes in the others. Changes in the economy lead to changes in the family; changes in religion lead to changes in government. For example, when the number of years of school completed becomes more important than one's hereditary position in determining occupation, then hereditary positions will be endangered in government, the family, and religion.

Whether studying change or continuity, the notion of institutional interdependence leads us beyond looking at one institution at a time. To understand any single institution fully, we must understand the other institutions with which it is interdependent.

Institutions: Agents of Stability or Oppression? Sociologists use two major theoretical frameworks to approach the study of institutions: structural functionalism and conflict theory. The first focuses on the part that institutions play in creating social and personal stability; the second focuses on the role of institutions in legitimizing inequality (Eisenstadt 1985).

A STRUCTURAL-FUNCTIONAL VIEW OF INSTITUTIONS. Institutions provide ready-made patterns to meet most recurrent social problems. These ready-made patterns regulate human behavior and are the basis for social order. Because we share the same patterns, social life tends to be stable and predictable.

According to structural-functional theorists, institutions have "evolved" to help individuals and societies survive. This emphasis on evolution implies a neutral, natural process. Just as our natural characteristics (such as

Institutions are interdependent. Religion and politics do mix; so do religion and education and family and economics. Generally, this means that institutions share common values and support one another. Each of the institutions represented in this picture, the state and the church, has traditionally been headed by an older white man—a similarity that symbolizes the degree to which they rest on common standards. Their similarities go beyond this. Both church and state are vast bureaucracies and ideas such as chains of command and copies in triplicate are common to both institutions. Church and state do not always agree, but they do have to take each other into account.

the opposable thumb and the capacity for language) are thought to have developed because they aided the survival of the species, so social characteristics are thought to have developed and endured because they help society survive. They are a positive force. From this viewpoint, institutions are both necessary and desirable. They provide routine ways of successfully solving recurring problems.

Structural-functional theorists point out that stability and predictability are important both for societies and individuals. The classic expression of this point of view comes from Durkheim, who argued that social institutions create a "liberating dependence." By furnishing patterned solutions to our most pressing everyday problems, they free us for more creative efforts. They save us from having to reinvent the social equivalent of the wheel each generation and thus facilitate our daily lives. Moreover, because these patterns have been sanctified by tradition, we tend to experience them as morally right. As a result, we find satisfaction and security in social institutions.

A CONFLICT VIEW OF INSTITUTIONS.   By the very fact that they regulate human behavior and direct choices, institutions also constrain behavior. By producing predictability, they reduce innovation; by giving security, they reduce freedom. Some regard this as a necessary evil, the price we pay for stability.

This benign view of constraint is challenged by conflict theorists. They accept that institutions meet basic human needs, but they wonder, Why *this* social pattern rather than another? Why *this* family system instead of another? To explain why one social arrangement is chosen over another, conflict theorists ask, "Who benefits?"

According to conflict theorists, the development of social institutions is neither natural nor neutral. They argue that social institutions develop to maintain and reproduce a given system of inequality. They see the traditional family institution, for example, as a form of normatively supported inequality. While greater earning power and greater physical strength might enable a man to have power over a reluctant wife and children, how much easier it is for him if his wife and children have been taught that the man is the head of the household and that they *ought* to do what he says. Although the family institution is changing now, for thousands of years this power inequality was a central fact of family life. We call it patriarchy. As in this example, institutions are seen as deliberately fostering and legitimizing unequal benefits for the occupants of some statuses.

From the viewpoint of conflict theory, institutions represent a camouflaged form of inequality. Because institutions have existed for a long time, we tend to think of our familial, religious, and political systems as not merely one way of fulfilling a particular need but as the only acceptable way. Just as a 10th-century Mayan may have thought, "Of course virgins should be sacrificed if the crops are bad," so we tend to think, "Of course women's careers suffer after they have children." In both cases, the cloak of tradition obscures our vision of inequality or oppression, making inequality seem normal and even desirable. As a result, institutions stifle social change and help maintain inequality.

Summary.   Institutions create order and stability; in doing so, they suppress change. In creating order, they preserve the status quo. In regulating, they constrain. In this sense, both conflict and structural-functional theories are right; they simply place a different value judgment on stability and order. The two theoretical prespectives prompt us to ask somewhat different questions about social structures. Structural-functional theory prompts us to ask how an institution contributes to order, to stability, and to meeting the needs of society and the individual. Conflict theory prompts us to ask which groups are benefiting the most from the system and how they are seeking to maintain their advantage. Both are worthwhile questions, and both will be addressed when social structures ranging from deviance to medicine are looked at (in Chapter 8 to 18).

INSTITUTIONS AND TYPES OF SOCIETIES

Institutions give a society a distinctive character. In some societies, the church has been dominant; in others, it has been the family or the economy. Whatever the circumstance, the institutional framework of a society is critical to an understanding of how it works.

The history of human societies is the story of ever-growing institutional complexity. In simple societies, we often find only one major social institution—the family or kin group. Many modern societies, however, have as many as a dozen institutions.

What causes this expansion of institutions? The triggering event appears to be economic. When changes in technology, in physical environment, or in social arrangements increase the level of economic surplus, the possibilities for institutional expansion arise (Lenski 1966). In this section, we sketch a broad outline of the institutional evolution that accompanied three revolutions in production.

HUNTING, FISHING, AND GATHERING SOCIETIES

The chief characteristic of hunting, fishing, and gathering societies is that they have subsistence economies. This means that in a good year they produce barely enough to get by on; that is, they produce no surplus. In some years, of course, game and fruit are plentiful, but there are also many years when starvation is a constant companion.

The basic units of social organization are the household and the local clan, both of which are based primarily on family bonds and kinship ties. Most of the activities of hunting and gathering are organized around these units. A clan rarely exceeds 50 people in size and tends to be nomadic or seminomadic. Because of their frequent wanderings, members of these societies accumulate few personal possessions.

The division of labor is simple, based solely on age and sex. The common pattern is for men to participate in hunting and deep-sea fishing and for women to participate in gathering, shore fishing, and preserving. Aside from inequalities based on age and sex, few structured inequalities exist in subsistence economies. Members possess little wealth; they have few, if any, hereditary privileges; and the societies are almost always too small to develop class distinctions. In fact, a major characteristic of subsistence societies is that individuals are alike. Apart from differences by age and sex, members generally have the same everyday experiences.

HORTICULTURAL SOCIETIES

The first major breakthrough from subsistence economy to economic surplus came with the development of agriculture. When people began to plant and cultivate crops, rather than simply harvest whatever nature provided, stable horticultural societies developed. The technology was often primitive—a digging stick, occasionally a rudimentary hoe—but it produced a surplus.

The regular production of more than the bare necessities revolutionized society. It meant that some people could take time off from basic production and turn to other pursuits: art, religion, writing, and frequently warfare. Of course, the people who participate in these alternate activities are not picked at random; there develops instead a class hierarchy between the peasants, who must devote their full time to food production, and those who live off their surplus.

Because of relative abundance and a settled way of life, horticultural societies tend to develop complex and stable institutions outside the family. Some economic activity is carried on outside the family, a religious structure with full-time priests may develop, and a stable system of government—complete with bureaucrats, tax officers, and a hereditary ruler—often develops. Such societies are sometimes very large. The Inca empire, for example, covered an estimated population of more than 4 million.

AGRICULTURAL SOCIETIES

Approximately 5,000 to 6,000 years ago, there was a second revolution in agriculture, and the efficiency of food production was doubled and redoubled through better technology. The advances included the harnessing of animals, the development of metal tools, the use of the wheel, and improved knowledge of irrigation and fertilization. These changes dramatically altered social institutions.

The major advances in technology meant that even more people could be freed from direct production. The many people not tied directly to the land congregated in large urban centers and developed a complex division of labor. Technology, trade, reading and writing, science, and art grew rapidly as larger and larger numbers of people were able to devote full time to these pursuits. Along with greater specialization and occupational diversity came greater inequality. In the place of the rather simple class structure of horticultural societies grew a complex class system of merchants, soldiers, scholars, officials, and kings—and, of course, the poor peasants on whose labor they all ultimately depended. This last group still contained the vast bulk of the society, probably at least 90 percent of the population (Sjoberg 1960).

One of the common uses to which societies put their new leisure and their new technology was warfare. With the domestication of the horse (cavalry) and the invention of the wheel (chariot warfare), military technology became more advanced and efficient. Military might was used as

CONCEPT SUMMARY
Types of Societies

HUNTING, FISHING, AND GATHERING

Technology:	Very simple—arrows, fire, baskets
Economy:	Bare subsistence, no surplus
Settlements:	None or very small (bands of under 50 people)
Social organization:	All resting within family
Examples:	Plains Indians, Eskimos

HORTICULTURAL SOCIETIES

Technology:	Digging sticks, occasionally blade tools
Economy:	Simple crop cultivation, some surplus and exchange
Settlements:	Semipermanent—some cities; occasionally kingdoms
Social organization:	Military, government, religion becoming distinct institutions
Examples:	Mayans, Incas, Egyptians under the pharaohs

AGRICULTURAL SOCIETIES

Technology:	Irrigation, fertilization, metallurgy, animal power used to increase agricultural productivity
Economy:	Largely agricultural, but much surplus; increased market exchange and substantial trade
Settlements:	Permanent—urbanization becoming important, empires covering continents
Social organization:	Educational, military, religious, and political institutions are well developed
Examples:	Roman empire, feudal Europe, Chinese empire

INDUSTRIAL SOCIETIES

Technology:	New energy sources (coal, gas, electricity) leading to mechanization of production
Economy:	Industrial—few engaged in agriculture or direct production; much surplus; fully developed market economy
Settlements:	Permanent—urban living predominating, nation states
Social organization:	Complex set of interdependent institutions
Examples:	Contemporary United States, Europe, Japan

Even in modern industrial societies, the prosperity of society depends significantly on ability to generate agricultural surplus. In the highly-mechanized agricultural industry in the United States, 2 million farmers can generate enough surplus to feed 250 million people and still leave surplus for export. In few other nations of the world, however, has agriculture taken so much advantage of industrial developments or freed so large a share of the labor force from food production. This 1987 photograph of harvest time in Italy shows the much greater reliance on manual labor that characterizes agriculture in most contemporary societies.

a means to gain even greater surplus through conquering other peoples. The Romans were so successful at this that they managed to turn the peoples of the entire Mediterranean basin into a peasant class that supported a ruling elite in Italy.

INDUSTRIAL SOCIETIES

The third major revolution in production was the advent of industrialization 200 years ago in Western Europe. The substitution of mechanical, electrical, and gasoline energy for human and animal labor caused an explosive growth in productivity, not only of goods but also of knowledge and technology. In the space of a few decades, agricultural societies were transformed. The enormous increases in energy, technology, and knowledge freed the bulk of the work force from agricultural production and, increasingly, also from industrial production. Society's political, social, and economic institutions were transformed. Old institutions such as education expanded dramatically, and new institutions such as science, medicine, and sports emerged.

WHEN INSTITUTIONS DIE: THE TRAGEDY OF THE OJIBWA

The story of modernization is the story of institutional change, of changes in the ways our production, reproduction, education, and social control are socially structured. Sometimes these institutional changes take place in harmony so that institutions continue to support one another and to provide stable patterns that meet ongoing human needs. On other occasions, however, old institutions are destroyed before new ones can evolve. When this happens, societies and the individuals within them are traumatized; societies and people fall apart.

In 1985, Anastasia Shkilnyk chronicled just such a human tragedy when she described the plight of the Ojibwa Indians of western Ontario in the book *A Poison Stronger Than Love*. Although the details are specific to the Ojibwa, her story is helpful in understanding what happened to Native Americans and other traditional societies when rapid social change altered social institutions.

In 1976, Anastasia Shkilnyk was sent by the Canadian Department of Indian Affairs to Grassy Narrows, an Ojibwa community of 520 people, to advise the band on how to alleviate economic disruption caused by mercury poisoning from a paper mill that had polluted nearby lakes and rivers. At the request of the chief and council, she stayed for two and a half years, to assist the band in developing socioeconomic projects and in preparing the band's case for compensation for the damages they suffered from mercury pollution and misguided government policy.

A BROKEN SOCIETY

Grassy Narrows in the 1970s was a community destroyed. Drunken six-year-olds roamed winter streets when the temperatures were minus 40. The death rate for both children and adults was very high compared to the rest of Canada. Nearly three-quarters of all deaths were linked directly to alcohol and drug abuse. A quote from Shkilnyk's journal evokes the tragedy of life in Grassy Narrows.

> Friday. My neighbor comes over to tell me that last night, just before midnight she found four-year-old Dolores wandering alone around the reserve, about two miles from her home. She called the police and they went to the house to investigate. They found Dolores's three-year-old sister, Diane, huddled in a corner crying. The house was empty, bare of food, and all of the windows were broken. The police discovered that the parents had gone to Kenora the day before and were drinking in town. Both of them were sober when they deserted their children.
>
> It's going to be a bad weekend. The police also picked up an eighteen-month-old baby abandoned in an empty house. No one seemed to know how long it had been there. . . . The milk in the house had turned sour. The baby was severely dehydrated and lying in its own vomit and accumulated excrement. Next door, the police found two people lying unconscious on the floor.

The adults in the community were not alcoholics in the sense that they had physiological reactions if they did not drink regularly. Rather, they were binge drinkers. When the wages were paid or the welfare checks came, many drank until they were unconscious and the money was gone. Shkilnyk estimates that on one occasion when $20,000 in wages and $5,000 in social assistance was paid out on one day, within one week $14,000 had been spent on alcohol. The children had as much despair as their parents, and they sought similar forms of escape. Often the children waited until their parents had drunk themselves unconscious and then drank the liquor that was left. If they could not get liquor, they sniffed glue or gasoline—and destroyed their central nervous system so that they could not walk without falling down.

Yet 20 years before, the Ojibwa had been a thriving people. How was a society so thoroughly destroyed?

"Time Zones" by Frank Bigbear, Jr.

OJIBWA SOCIETY BEFORE 1963

The Ojibwa have been in contact with whites for two centuries. In 1873, they signed the treaty that defines their relationship with the government of Canada. In the treaty, the government agreed to set aside reserves for the Indians, to give the Indians the right to pursue their traditional occupations of hunting, fishing, and trapping, and to provide schools.

Generally, this arrangement does not seem to have been disruptive to the Ojibwa way of life. Their reserve was in an area they had traditionally viewed as their own on the banks of the English River in northern Ontario. Despite the development of logging and mining in the areas around them, they had very little contact with the white community except for an annual ceremonial visit on Treaty Day.

The Ojibwa were a hunting and gathering people; the family was the primary social institution. A family group consisted of a husband, a wife, their grown sons and their wives and children, or of several brothers and their wives and children. The houses or tents of this family group would all be clustered together, perhaps as far as half a mile from the next family group.

Economic activities were all carried out by family groups. These activities varied with the season. In the late summer and fall, families picked blueberries and harvested wild rice. In the winter, they hunted and trapped. In all of these endeavors, the entire family participated, everybody packing up and going to where the work was. The men would trap and hunt, the women would skin and prepare the meat, the old people would come along to take care of the children and teach them. They used their reserve only as a summer encampment. From late summer until late spring, the family was on the move.

Besides being the chief economic and educational unit, the family was also the major agent of social control. Family elders enforced the rules and punished those who violated them. In addition, most religious ceremonials were performed by family elders. Although a loose band of families formed the Ojibwa society, each extended family group was largely self-sufficient, interacting to exchange marriage partners and for other ceremonial activities, including, in the old days, warfare with the Sioux.

The earliest influence of European culture did not disrupt this way of life particularly. The major change was the development of the boarding schools, which removed many Indian children from their homes for the winter months. When they returned, however, they would be accepted back into the group and educated into Indian ways by their grandparents. The boarding schools took the children away, but they didn't disrupt the major social institutions of the society they left behind.

THE CHANGE

In 1963, the government decided that the Ojibwa should be brought into modern society and given the benefits thereof: modern plumbing, better health care, roads, and the like. To this end, they moved the entire Ojibwa community from the old reserve to a government-built new community about four miles from their traditional encampment. The new community had houses, roads, schools, and easy access to "civilization." The differences between the new and the old were sufficient to destroy the fragile interdependence of Ojibwa institutions.

First, all the houses were close together in neat rows, assigned randomly without regard for family group. As a result, the kin group ceased to exist as a physical unit. Second, the replacement of boarding schools with a community school meant that a parent (the mother) had to stay home with the child instead of going out on the trap line. As a result, the adult woman overnight became a consumer rather than a producer, shattering her traditional relationship with her husband and community. As a consequence of the women's and children's immobility, men had to go out alone on the trap line. Since they were by themselves rather than with their family, the trapping trips were reduced from six to eight weeks to a few days, and trapping ceased to be a way of life for the whole family. The productivity of the Ojibwa reached bottom with the government order in May 1970 to halt all fishing because of severe mercury contamination of the water. Then the economic contributions of men as well as women were sharply curtailed; the people became heavily dependent on the government rather than on themselves or each other.

What happened was the total destruction of the old patterns of doing things—that is, of social institutions. The relationships between husbands and wives were no longer clear. What were their rights and obligations to each other now that their joint economic productivity was at an end? What were their rights and obligations to their children when no one cared about tomorrow?

The Future

In 1985 the Ojibwa finally reached an out-of-court settlement with the federal and provincial governments and the mercury-polluting paper mill. The $8.7 million settlement was in compensation for damages to their way of life arising from government policies and mercury pollution. The band is using some of this money to develop local industries that will provide an ongoing basis for a productive and thriving society. Today, Ojibwa society has begun the process of healing and recovery.

Summary

Institutions offer stable patterns of responding to stable problems. Some of these stable problems are straightforward and obvious, such as finding enough to eat. Other problems are more subtle but just as important: having something to do each day that is meaningful and having bonds of obligation and exchange with others in the community.

In the case of the Ojibwa Indians and other indigenous peoples of North America, welfare and the supermarket can take care of the first problem, but they cannot take the place of the second. Stable social structures that define our roles relative to others in our environment, that give us assurance of the continuity of the past and the future, are an essential aspect of human society. It is often true, as conflict theorists stress, that any given institutional arrangement benefits one group over another. It is also true, as structural theorists stress, that some institutional arrangement is better than none.

Alcoholism and Native Americans

Unfortunately, the Ojibwa are not exceptional cases. Their tragedy has been played out in tribe after tribe, band after band, all over North America. Compared to the national average, Native Americans are (Podolsky 1986/1987)

- 3.8 times more likely to die from alcoholism
- 4.5 times more likely to have cirrhosis of the liver
- 5.5 times more likely to die in alcohol-related motor vehicle accidents.

To paraphrase C. Wright Mills (Chapter 1), when one or two individuals abuse alcohol, then this is an individual problem, and for its relief we rightfully look to clinicians and counselors. When large

Native Americans are hardly the only subculture in American society to have problems with alcohol abuse. Another is young men. Heavy beer drinking is especially characteristic of the high school and college years, and the expectation of beer drinking is built into many collegiate football games and parties. Although the rise in the drinking age has made this largely illegal, it is still a recurrent pattern supported by subcultural norms and values.

segments of a population have alcohol problems, then this is a public issue and must be addressed at the level of social structure.

THE PROBLEM

There is enormous variety among Native American groups, on this as well as other indicators. Some Native American groups are almost entirely alcohol free; in others, alcoholism touches nearly every family. Nevertheless, the overall level of alcohol abuse is very high (McConnell 1973). As a result, 95 percent of Native Americans report that alcohol abuse is a major problem for their people (Shafer 1989).

High levels of alcohol use are a health problem, an economic problem, and a social problem. Among the related issues are child and spouse abuse, unemployment, teenage pregnancy, birth defects, nonmarital births, and divorce. How can these interrelated problems be addressed?

TWO CONTRASTING APPROACHES: CLINICAL VERSUS STRUCTURAL

The clinical approach to treating alcoholism is based on traditional medical and psychological models: Take one patient at a time and treat his or her symptoms. Many clinical treatment programs use Alcoholics Anonymous as a framework for treatment: Individuals are encouraged to admit that they are alcoholics and to seek the support and help of the AA group and of God in conquering alcoholism. Even when faced with society-wide alcoholism such as exists in some Native American communities, the clinical model still focuses on such solutions as more counselors and better diagnostic care (Weibel-Orlando 1986/87).

A sociological approach to understanding alcoholism on such a scale begins instead with the premise that any widely recurring pattern must be

ISSUES IN SOCIAL POLICY continued

socially structured: According to this perspective, the appropriate strategy for reducing alcoholism among Native Americans is to ask what social structures encourage alcohol use. Conversely, why don't social structures reward sobriety?

The answer depends upon one's theoretical framework. Structural functionalists focus on the destruction of Native American culture and the absence of harmony between their institutions and those of white society. Conflict theorists see the current situation as the result of a violent conflict over scarce resources, a conflict in which victorious Europeans systematically stripped Native Americans of their means of economic production and hence destroyed their society (Fisher 1987).

Regardless of theoretical position, however, the obvious fact is that Native Americans are severely economically disadvantaged. Unemployment is often a way of life, and only 25 percent of the adults are employed on some reservations. Lack of employment is a critical factor in alcoholism in all populations. Having a steady, rewarding job is an incentive to stay sober; it also reduces the time available for drinking, which is essentially a leisure-time activity. Even clinically oriented scholars conclude that "occupational stability is a major factor in maintaining sobriety" (Ronan and Reichman 1986). From this perspective, the solution to high levels of Native American alcoholism must include changing economic institutions to provide full employment, as well as hiring more AA group leaders.

SUMMARY

In many ways, fighting alcoholism is like fighting smallpox. We cannot eradicate the disease by treating people after they have it; we have to prevent its occurrence. When alcoholism is epidemic in a community, it, requires community-wide efforts at prevention. Statuses, roles, and institutions must be reformed so that people have a reason to stay sober.

SUMMARY

1. The analysis of social structures—recurrent patterns of relationships—revolves around three concepts: status, role, and institution.

2. Statuses are of two sorts: achieved or ascribed. The analysis of statuses is concerned with four issues: identification, distribution, consequences, and combinations.

3. Roles define how status occupants *ought* to act and feel. People deviate from these expected role performances because of incompatible roles, inadequate role definitions, unavailability of resources, or inadequate sanctions. In addition, role performances differ because no role is fully scripted and roles must be negotiated.

4. Because societies share common human needs, they also share common institutions. The common institutions are family, economy, government, education, and religion. Each society has some enduring social structure to perform these functions for the group.

5. Institutions are interdependent; none stands alone, and a change in one results in changes in others. A detailed case study of the Ojibwa Indians of Ontario, Canada, shows how changes in economic institutions lead to the disintegration of society and extraordinarily high rates of alcoholism.

6. Institutions regulate behavior and maintain the stability of social life across generations. Conflict theorists point out that these patterns often benefit one group more than others.

7. An important determinant of institutional development is the ability of a society to produce an economic surplus. Each major improvement in production has led to an expansion in social institutions.

8. There are four basic types of societies—hunting, fishing, and gathering; horticultural, agricultural; and industrial—that may be viewed as a rough evolutionary contin-

uum. As societies move up this ladder, they are characterized by larger surpluses, more institutions, and more specialization.

9. When a behavior pattern is widespread, sociologists assume that it must be socially structured rather than the result of personality or individual factors. In the case of high rates of alcoholism among Native Americans, we view it as a public issue rather than a personal problem. Thus, providing jobs and developing new economic institutions would be a more effective solution to the problem than hiring more therapists.

■

SUGGESTED READINGS

Lenski, Gerhard. 1966. Power and Privilege: A Theory of Social Stratification. New York: McGraw-Hill. A major work distinguishing the fundamental characteristics of different types of societies, particularly in terms of socially structured inequality.

Merton, Robert K. 1968. Social Theory and Social Structure. (Enl. ed.) New York: Free Press. Uses structural-functional theory to draw out the basic concepts and relationships and used in the analysis of social structures. Bureaucracies, deviance, religion, and politics are only a few of the illustrations used to show the application of these concepts.

Nye, F. Ivan. 1976. Role Structure and Analysis of the Family. Beverly Hills, CA: Sage. An analysis of the family using the concepts of status and roles. Because it applies the terms to a familiar social structure, it is a particularly accessible piece of sociological analysis.

O'Dea, Thomas F. 1957. The Mormons. Chicago: University of Chicago Press. An interesting and readable soci-ological account of the unique development and growth of Mormonism. The religious organization as a social structure embedded in the society of an isolated people gives uniqueness to the history and development of the Mormon church.

Shkilnyk, Anastasia. 1985. A Poison Stronger Than Love: The Destruction of an Ojibwa Community. New Haven: Yale. An ethnographic community study that focuses on the social structures of a Native American community in Canada. A powerful illustration of the extent to which individual well-being depends on stable institutions.

Spiro, Melford E. 1963. Kibbutz: Venture in Utopia. New York: Schocken Books. An anthropologist analyzes the basic aspects of social structure that were designed early in this century by young Jewish adults in their attempts to create a utopia. Both successes and failures are examined.

5

GROUPS, NETWORKS, AND ORGANIZATIONS

■

Have you ever . . .

Met friends after a long absence and been startled by the changes in them? Perhaps they have been off to college, in the army, or just married and moved away, but you may have found that they had changed so much you hardly knew them. It was not just their appearance but their values and concerns that were altered—and so were yours.

One of the most basic reasons that we change is that we start to associate with new groups of people. When we take a new job, we are often unknowingly making a commitment to a whole lifestyle and outlook. You will become a very different person if your first job after college is with IBM rather than the Sierra Club. Organizations mold us into their sort of people. In this chapter, we look at the different kinds of groups we belong to and how they influence and shape our lives. No one is an island. We are linked to others by complex ties of duty, obligation, and need. These ties have profound impacts on us. If we want to understand why people do what they do, one of our first tasks must be to identify who they do it with—their groups, networks, and organizations.

■

■

113

Sociology is concerned with human behavior and how it is influenced by social structure. Although the concept of social "structure" suggests something firm and unyielding, in fact, a social structure describes ongoing, ever-changing relationships. This means that social structure has an important dynamic element; it is process as well as framework, action as much as pattern (Giddens 1984). In this chapter, we review basic group processes and also three kinds of social structures: the small group, the social network, and the complex organization.

■

GROUP PROCESSES

Some relationships are characterized by harmony and stability; others are made stressful by conflict and competition. We use the term **social processes** to describe the types of interaction that go on in relationships. This section looks closely at four social processes that regularly occur in human relationships: exchange, cooperation, competition, and conflict.

Social processes are the forms of interaction through which people relate to one another; they are the dynamic aspects of society.

EXCHANGE

Exchange is voluntary interaction in which the parties trade tangible or intangible benefits with the expectation that all parties will benefit. A wide variety of social relationships include elements of exchange. In friendships and marriages, exchanges usually include such intangibles as companionship, moral support, and a willingness to listen to the other's problems. In business or politics, an exchange may be more concrete; politicians, for example, openly acknowledge exchanging votes on legislative bills—I'll vote for yours if you'll vote for mine.

Exchange is voluntary interaction in which the parties trade tangible or intangible benefits.

Exchange relationships are based on the expectation that people will return favors and strive to maintain a balance of obligation in social relationships. This expectation is called the **norm of reciprocity** (Gouldner 1960). If you help your sister-in-law move, then she is obligated to you. Somehow she must pay you back. If she fails to do so, then the social relationship is likely to end, probably with bad feelings. A corollary of the norm of reciprocity is that you avoid accepting favors from people with whom you do not wish to enter into a relationship. For example, if someone you do not know very well volunteers to type your term paper, you will probably be suspicious. Your first thought is likely to be, "What is this guy trying to prove? What does he want from me?" If you do not want to owe this person a favor, you will say that you prefer to type your own paper. Nonsociologists might sum up the norm of reciprocity by concluding that there's no free lunch.

The **norm of reciprocity** is the expectation that people will return favors and strive to maintain a balance of obligation in social relationships.

Exchange is one of the most basic processes of social interaction. Almost all voluntary relationships are entered into as situations of exchange. In traditional American families, these exchanges were clearly spelled out. He supported the family, which obligated her to keep house and look after the children; or, conversely, she bore the children and kept house, which obligated him to support her.

Exchange relationships persist only if each party to the interaction is getting something out of it. This does not mean that the rewards must be equal; in fact, rewards are frequently very unequal. You have probably seen play groups, for example, where one child is treated badly by the other children and is permitted to play with them only if he agrees to give them his lunch or allows them to use his bicycle. If this boy has no one else to play with, however, he may find this relationship more rewarding than the alternative of playing alone. The continuation of very unequal exchange relationships usually rests on a lack of desirable alternatives (Emerson 1962).

COOPERATION

Cooperation occurs when people work together to achieve shared goals. Exchange is a trade: I give you something and you give me something else in return. Cooperation is teamwork. It is characteristic of relationships where people work together to achieve goals that they cannot achieve alone. Consider, for example, a four-way stop. Although it may entail some waiting in line, in the long run we will all get through more safely and more quickly if we cooperate and take turns. This does not necessarily mean that all parties will benefit equally from cooperation. When union workers forgo a wage increase to help keep the company from going bankrupt, we say that union and management are cooperating to meet a joint goal: avoiding bankruptcy. It is the workers, however, who have made the sacrifice.

> **Cooperation** is interaction that occurs when people work together to achieve shared goals.

COMPETITION

It is not always possible for people to reach their goals by exchange or cooperation. If your goal and my goal are mutually exclusive (for example, I want to sleep and you want to play your stereo), we cannot both achieve our goals. Similarly, in situations of scarcity, there may not be enough of a desired good to go around. In these situations, social processes are likely to take the form of either competition or conflict.

A struggle over scarce resources that is regulated by shared rules is called **competition** (Friedsam 1965). The rules usually specify the conditions under which winning will be considered fair and losing will be considered tolerable. When the norms are violated, competition may erupt into conflict.

> **Competition** is a struggle over scarce resources that is regulated by shared rules.

Competition is a common form of interaction in American society. Jobs, grades, athletic honors, sexual attention, marriage partners, and parental affection are only a few of the scarce resources for which individuals or groups compete. In fact, it is difficult to identify many social situations that do not entail competition. One positive consequence of competition is that it stimulates achievement and heightens people's aspirations. It also, however, often results in personal stress, reduced cooperation, and social inequalities (elaborated on in Chapters 9–12).

Because competition often results in change, groups that seek to maximize stability often devise elaborate rules to avoid the appearance of competition. Competition is particularly problematic in such informal groups as friendships and marriages. Friends who want to stay friends will not compete for valued objects; they might compete over bowling scores, but they won't compete for the same promotion. Similarly, couples who value their marriage will not compete for their children's affection or loyalty. To do so would be to destroy the marriage.

Many of the good things in life are in short supply: They are scarce resources. Some of the most serious struggles take place over intangible rewards such as respect, prestige, and honor. When the struggle is regulated by norms that specify the rules of fair play, as in a soccer game, we call it competition. When anything goes, we call it conflict.

Conflict is a struggle over scarce resources that is not regulated by shared rules, it may include attempts to destroy or neutralize one's rivals.

A **group** is two or more people who interact on the basis of shared social structure and who recognize mutual dependency.

An **aggregate** is people who are temporarily clustered together in the same location.

A **category** is a collection of people who share a common characteristic.

CONFLICT

When struggle over scarce resources is not regulated by shared rules **conflict** occurs (Coser 1956, 8). Because no tactics are forbidden and anything goes, conflict may include attempts to neutralize, injure, or destroy one's rivals. Conflict creates divisiveness rather than solidarity.

When conflict takes place with outsiders, however, it may enhance the solidarity of the group. Whether we're talking about warring superpowers or warring street gangs, the us-against-them feeling that emerges from conflict with outsiders causes group members to put aside their jealousies and differences to work together. Groups from nations to schools have found that starting conflicts with outsiders is a useful device for redirecting the negative energy of their own group.

Exchange, cooperation, competition, and even conflict are important aspects of our relationships with others. Few of our relationships involve just one type of group process. Even friendships usually involve some competition as well as cooperation and exchange; similarly, relationships among competitors often involve cooperation.

We interact with people in a variety of relationships. Some of these relationships are temporary and others permanent, some are formal and others informal. In the rest of this chapter, we discuss the relationships we have in three kinds of social structures: groups, social networks, and organizations.

GROUPS

What is a group? A **group** is two or more people who interact on the basis of a shared social structure and who recognize mutual dependency. Groups may be large or small, formal or informal; they range from a pair of lovers to IBM. In all of them, members share a social structure specifying statuses, roles, and norms, and they share a feeling of mutual dependency.

The distinctive characteristics of a group stand out when we compare the group to two collections of people that do not have these characteristics. An **aggregate** is people who are temporarily clustered together in the same location (for example, all the people on a city bus, those attending a movie, or shoppers in a mall). Although these people may share some norms (such as moving to the right when passing others), they are not mutually dependent. In fact, most of their shared norms have to do with procedures to maintain their independence despite their close physical proximity. The other nongroup is a **category**—a collection of people who share a common characteristic. Hispanics, welders, and students are categories of people. Most of the people who share category membership will never meet, much less interact.

The distinguishing characteristics of groups hint at the rewards of group life. Group members are the people we take into account and the people who take us into account. They are the people with whom we share norms and values. Thus, groups are a major source of solidarity and cohesion, reinforcing and strengthening our integration into society. The benefits of group life range all the way from sharing basic survival and problem-solving techniques to satisfying personal and emotional needs.

HOW GROUPS AFFECT INDIVIDUALS

When a man opens a door for a woman, do you see traditional courtesy or intolerable condescension? When you listen to heavy metal bands, do you hear good music or mindless noise? Like taste in music, many of the things we deal with and believe in are not true or correct in any absolute sense; they are simply what our groups have agreed to accept as right.

The tremendous impact of group definitions on our own attitudes and perceptions was cleverly documented in a classic experiment by Asch (1955). In this experiment, the group consists of nine college students, all apparently unknown to each other. The experimenter explains that the task at hand is an experiment in visual judgment. The subjects are shown pairs of cards similar to those in Figure 5.1 and are asked to judge which line on Card B is most similar to the line on Card A. This is not a difficult task; unless you need glasses or have forgotten the ones you have, you can tell that line 2 most closely matches the line on the first card.

The experimental part of this research consists of changing the conditions of group consensus under which the subjects make their judgments. Each group must make decisions on 15 pairs of cards, and, in the first few trials, all of the students agree. In subsequent trials, however, the first eight students all give an obviously wrong answer. They are not subjects at all but paid stooges of the experimenter. The real test comes in seeing what the last student—the real subject of the experiment—will do. Will he go along with everybody else, or will he publicly set himself apart? Photographs of the experiment show that the real subjects wrinkled their brows, squirmed in their seats, and gaped at their neighbors; in 37 percent of the trials the naïve subject publicly agreed with the wrong answer, and 75 percent gave the wrong answer on at least one trial.

In the case of this experiment, it is clear what the right answer should be. Many of the students who agreed with the wrong answer probably were not persuaded by group opinion that their own judgment was wrong, but they decided not to make waves. When the object being judged is less objective, however—for example, whether Janet Jackson is better than Guns 'N Roses—then the group is likely to influence not only public responses but also private views. Whether we go along because we are really convinced or because we are avoiding the hassles of being different, we all have a strong tendency to conform to the norms and expectations of our groups. Thus, our group memberships are vital in determining our behavior, perceptions, and values.

INTERACTION IN SMALL GROUPS

We spend much of our lives in groups. We have work groups, family groups, and peer groups. In class we have discussion groups, and everywhere we have committees. This section reviews some of the more important factors that affect the kind of interaction we experience in small groups.

■
FIGURE 5.1
THE CARDS USED IN ASCH'S EXPERIMENT

In Asch's experiment, subjects were instructed to select the line on Card B that was equal in length to the line on Card A. The results showed that many people will give an obviously wrong answer in order to conform to the group.

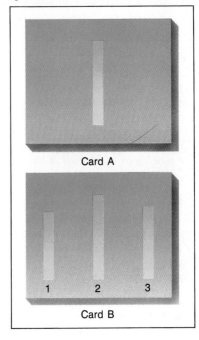
Card A

Card B

■

In these pictures from the Asch experiment, the subject shows the strain and consternation that comes from disagreeing with the judgments of the six other members of the group. This particular subject disagreed with the majority on all 12 trials of the experiment. He is unusual, however, as 75 percent of the experimental subjects agreed with the majority on at least one trial. Subjects who initially yielded to the majority found it increasingly difficult to make independent judgments as the experiment progressed.

Size.   The smallest possible group is two people. As the group grows to three, four, and more, its characteristics change.

Some of the most dramatic consequences of size occur when a group goes from two members (a dyad) to three members (a triad). In a dyad, neither person can leave the group without destroying it. When a third member joins the group, the group becomes much more stable; it can continue to exist if one person dies or just gets mad and quits. This increase in stability is purchased at the cost of decreased importance of each individual group member. Whereas a dyad dies if it allows one person to walk away in anger, a triad can afford to shrug its shoulders. This means triads have less need to compromise or to listen to unhappy members. The move from two to three also makes possible the formation of factions *within* the group (a two-against-one coalition) and the use of majority rule in decision making (Simmel [1908] 1950).

Generally, we find that as groups go from two to three to four and on up, interaction becomes more impersonal, more structured, and less personally satisfying. Consensus tends to be replaced by majority rule and each individual has fewer opportunities to share opinions and contribute to decision making or problem solving.

Proximity.   Dozens of laboratory studies demonstrate that interaction is more likely to occur among group members who are physically close to one another. This effect is not limited to the laboratory.

In a classic demonstration of the role of proximity in group formation and interaction, Festinger and his associates (1950) studied a married-student housing project. All of the residents had been strangers to one another before being arbitrarily assigned to a housing unit. The researchers wanted to know what factors influenced friendship choices within the project. The answer: physical proximity. Festinger found that people were twice as likely to choose their next-door neighbors as friends than they were to choose people who lived only two units away. In general, the greater the physical distance, the less likely friendships were to be formed. An interesting exception to this generalization is that people who lived next to the garbage cans were disproportionately likely to be chosen as friends. Why? Because many of their neighbors passed by their units daily and therefore had many chances to interact and form friendships with them.

Communication Patterns. Interaction of group members can be either facilitated or retarded by patterns of communication. Figure 5.2 shows some common communication patterns for five-person groups. The communication structure allowing the greatest equality of participation is the *all-channel network*. In this pattern, each person can interact with every other person with approximately the same ease. Each participant has equal access to the others and an equal ability to become the focus of attention.

The other two common communication patterns allow for less interaction. In the *circle pattern*, people can speak only to their neighbors on either side. This pattern reduces interaction, but it does not give one person more power than others. In the *wheel pattern*, on the other hand, not only is interaction reduced but also a single, pivotal individual gains greater power in the group. The wheel pattern is characteristic of the traditional classroom. Students do not interact with one another; instead they interact directly only with the teacher, thereby giving that person the power to direct the flow of interaction.

Communication structures are often created, either accidentally or purposefully, by the physical distribution of group members. The seating of committee members at a round table tends to facilitate either an all-channel or a circle pattern, depending on the size of the table. A rectangular table, however, gives people at the ends and in the middle of the long sides an advantage. They find it easier to attract attention and are apt to be more active in interactions and more influential in group discussions. Consider the way communication is structured in the classes and groups you participate in. How do seating structures encourage or discourage communication?

Cohesion. One of the important dimensions along which groups vary is their degree of **cohesion** or solidarity. A cohesive group is characterized by strong feelings of attachment and dependency. Because its members feel that their happiness or welfare depends on the group, the group may make extensive claims on the individual members (Hechter 1987). Cohesive adolescent friendship groups, for example, can enforce dress codes and standards of conduct on their members.

Marriages, churches, and friendship groups differ in their cohesiveness. What makes one marriage or church more cohesive than another? Among the factors that contribute to cohesion are small size, similarity, frequent interaction, long duration, and a clear distinction between insiders and outsiders (Homans 1950; Hechter 1987). Although all marriages in our society have the same size (two members), a marriage where the partners are more similar, spend more time together, and so on will generally be more cohesive than one where the partners are dissimilar and see each other for only a short time each day.

Social Control. Small groups rarely have access to legal or formal sanctions, yet they exercise profound control over individuals. The basis of this

**FIGURE 5.2
PATTERNS OF COMMUNICATION**

Patterns of communication can affect individual participation and influence. In each figure the circles represent individuals and the lines are flows of communication. The all-channel network provides the greatest opportunity for participation and is more often found in groups where status differences are not present or are minimal. The wheel, by contrast, is associated with important status differences within the group.

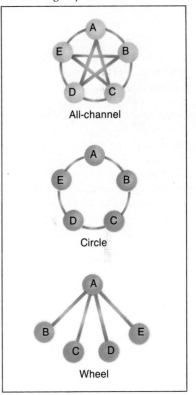

All-channel

Circle

Wheel

Cohesion refers to the degree of attraction members feel to the group.

One of the most powerful mechanisms of social control is the threat of exclusion from valued groups. None of us likes to be rejected, and most of us will go to considerable lengths to avoid the threat of exclusion. This means that we conform: We dress as other group members do, think as they think, and do as they do. This desire to please others in our intimate social circles is the most powerful pressure for conformity. Compared to this, formal sanctions such as fines and jail sentences are relatively ineffective.

control is fear—fear of not being accepted by the group (Douglas 1983). The major weapons that groups use to punish nonconformity are ridicule and contempt, but their ultimate sanction is exclusion from the group. From "you can't sit at our lunch table anymore" to "you're fired," exclusion is one of the most powerful threats we can make against others.

Zurcher (1983) gives an example of how informal social control works in a group of men who meet weekly to play poker. When somebody follows group routines, he is rewarded with a "Good play!" from fellow players. When a player violates the group norm, he is negatively sanctioned. For example, a newcomer to the group violated a group norm that required being a good loser: When he got a bad draw, he swore and threw down his cards. In this case, the dealer picked up the cards without a word and the game went on in total silence. The group figuratively turned its back on the player by pretending he wasn't there. This form of social control is most effective in cohesive groups, but Asch's experiment shows that fear of rejection can induce conformity to group norms even in artificial lab settings.

Decision Making.   One of the primary research interests in the sociology of small groups is how group characteristics (size, cohesion, and so on) affect group decision making. This research has focused on a wide variety of actual groups: flight crews, submarine crews, and juries, to name a few (Davis and Stasson 1988).

Generally, groups strive to reach consensus; they would like all their decisions to be agreeable to every member. As the size of the group grows, consensus requires lengthy and time-consuming interaction so everybody's objections can be clearly understood and incorporated. Thus, as groups grow in size, they often adopt the more expedient policy of majority rule. This policy results in quicker decisions, but often at the expense of individual satisfaction. It therefore reduces the cohesiveness of the group.

Choice Shifts.   One of the most consistent findings of research is that it is seldom necessary to resort to majority rule in small groups. Both in the laboratory and in the real world, there is a strong tendency for opinions to converge. One of the classic experiments on convergence was done over 50 years ago by Sherif (1936). In this experiment, strangers were put into a totally dark room. A dot of light was flashed onto the wall, and each participant was asked to estimate how far the light moved during the experimental period. After the first session, the participants recorded their own answers and then shared them with the other participants. There was quite a bit of variation in the estimates. Then they did the experiment again. This time there was less difference. After four trials, all participants agreed on an estimate that was close to the average of the initial estimates. (The dot of light was, in fact, stationary.)

The convergence effect has been demonstrated in dozens of studies since. Convergence, however, is not always to a middle position. Sometimes, the group reaches consensus on an extreme position. This is called the *risky shift* when the group converges on an adventurous option and the *tame shift* when the choice is extremely conservative. Sometimes these choice shifts depend on persuasive arguments put forward by one or more members, but often they result from general norms in the group that favor conservatism over risk (Davis and Stasson 1988). For example, one might expect the PTA steering committee to choose the safest opinion while members of a terrorist group would choose the riskiest option.

A special case of choice shift is *groupthink*. Groupthink occurs when pressures to agree may be so strong that they stifle critical thinking. In such situations, people do not change; they merely hide their real opinions in order to be supportive. Irving Janis (1982) has documented the role of groupthink in a variety of 20th-century political decisions. For example, in 1962 President Kennedy and his advisers rashly decided to invade Cuba. This so-called Bay of Pigs invasion ended in a disastrous rout for U.S. troops; it was poorly planned and probably foolish in any case. Afterward, nearly every member of the advisory group admitted that they had thought it was a dumb idea, but had hesitated to say so (Schlesinger 1965). As this example illustrates, groupthink often results in bad decisions. Research shows that better decisions usually result when a persistent minority forces the majority to consider the minority's objections (Nemeth 1985).

Summary. Whether the small group arises spontaneously among neighbors or schoolchildren or whether it is a committee appointed to solve a community problem, the operation of the group depends on the quality of interaction among the members. Research suggests that interaction will be facilitated by small size, open communication networks, similarity, and physical proximity. When these circumstances align to produce high levels of interaction, then individual satisfaction, group cohesion, and social control all tend to increase.

TYPES OF GROUPS

Some groups are more important than others in their impact on our lives. All of you, for example, probably belong to a family group as well as to the student body of your college or university. Except for an occasional student activist, membership in the family is far more important than membership in the student body and will have a more lasting effect. Sociologists call small, intimate, and lasting groups *primary groups;* they call large, impersonal groups *secondary groups.*

Primary Groups. **Primary groups** are characterized by intimate, face-to-face interaction (Cooley [1909] 1967). These groups represent our most complete experiences in group life. The closest approximation to an ideal primary group is probably the family, followed by adolescent peer groups and adult friendships. The relationships formed in these groups are relatively permanent and constitute a basic source of identity and attachment.

The ideal primary group tends to have the following characteristics: (1) personal and intimate relationships, (2) face-to-face communication, (3) permanence, (4) a strong sense of loyalty or we-feeling, (5) small size, (6) informality, and (7) traditional or nonrational decision making (Rogers 1960). In addition to the family, friendship networks, coworkers, and gangs may be primary groups. Groups such as these are major sources of companionship, intimacy, and belongingness, conditions that strengthen our sense of social integration into society.

Primary groups are groups characterized by intimate, face-to-face interaction.

Many of the groups that we participate in combine characteristics of primary and secondary groups. The elementary school and its classrooms are secondary groups: they are rationally designed and formally organized to meet specific instrumental goals. On the other hand, they also have some of the characteristics of primary groups, including the development of personal relationships, many of which will last for 6, 12, or even 40 years.

Secondary groups are groups that are formal, large, and impersonal.

Expressive describes activities or roles that provide integration and emotional support.

Secondary Groups.   By contrast, **secondary groups** are formal, large, and impersonal. Whereas the major purpose of many primary groups is simply to provide companionship, secondary groups usually form to accomplish some specific task. The perfect secondary group is entirely rational and contractual in nature; the participants interact solely to accomplish some purpose (earn credit hours, buy a pair of shoes, get a paycheck). Their interest in each other does not extend past this contract. If you have ever been in a lecture class of 300 students, you have firsthand experience of a classic secondary group. The interaction is temporary, anonymous, and formal. Rewards are based on universal criteria, not on such particularistic grounds as your effort or need. The Concept Summary shows the important differences between primary and secondary groups.

Comparing Primary and Secondary Groups.   Primary and secondary groups serve very different functions for individuals and societies. From the individual's point of view, the major purpose of primary groups is **expressive** activity, giving individuals social integration and emotional support. Your family, for example, usually provides an informal support group that is bound to help you, come rain or shine. You should be able to call on your family and friends to bring you some soup when you are down with the flu, to pick you up in the dead of night when your car breaks down, and to listen to your troubles when you are blue.

Because we need primary groups so much, they have tremendous power to bring us into line. From the society's point of view, this is the major function of primary groups: They are the major agents of social control. The reason most of us don't shoplift is because we would be mortified if our parents, friends, or coworkers found out. The reason most soldiers go into combat is because their buddies are going. We tend to dress, act, vote, and believe in ways that will keep the support of our primary groups. In short, we conform. The law would be relatively helpless in keeping all the millions of us in line if we weren't already restrained by the desire to stay

CONCEPT SUMMARY
Differences Between
Primary and Secondary Groups

	PRIMARY GROUPS	SECONDARY GROUPS
Size	Small	Large
Relationships	Personal, intimate	Impersonal, aloof
Communication	Face to face	Indirect—memos, telephone, etc.
Duration	Permanent	Temporary
Cohesion	Strong sense of loyalty, we-feeling	Weak, based on self-interest
Decisions	Based on tradition and personal feelings	Based on rationality and rules
Social structure	Informal	Formal—titles, officers, charters, regular meeting times, etc.

in the good graces of our primary groups. One corollary of this, however, which Chapter 8 addresses, is that if our primary groups accept shoplifting or street fighting as suitable behaviors, then our primary-group associations may lead us into deviance rather than conformity.

The major functions of secondary groups are **instrumental** activities, the accomplishment of specific tasks. If you want to build an airplane, raise money for a community project, or teach introductory sociology to 2,000 students a year, then secondary groups are your best bet. They are responsible for building our houses, growing and shipping our vegetables, educating our children, and curing our ills. In short, we could not do without them.

Instrumental describes activities or roles that are task oriented.

The Shift to Secondary Groups. In preindustrial society, there were few secondary groups. Vegetables and houses were produced by families, not by Georgia Pacific or Del Monte. Parents taught their own children, and neighbors nursed one another's ills. Under these conditions, primary groups served both expressive and instrumental functions. As society has become more industrialized, more and more of our instrumental needs are the obligation of some secondary group rather than of a primary group.

In addition to losing their instrumental functions to secondary groups, primary groups have suffered other threats in industrialized societies. In the United States, for example, approximately 21 percent of all households move each year (nearly 30 percent in the western states). This fact alone means that our ties to friends, neighborhoods, and coworkers are seldom really permanent. People change jobs, spouses, and neighborhoods. One consequence of this breakdown of traditional primary groups is that many people rely on secondary contacts even for expressive needs; they may hire a counselor rather than call their neighbor, for example.

Many scholars have suggested that these inroads on the primary group represent a weakening of social control; that is, the weaker ties to neighbors and kin mean that people feel less pressure to conform. They don't have to worry about what the neighbors will say because they haven't met them; they don't have to worry about what mother will say, because she lives 2,000 miles away and what she doesn't know won't hurt her.

There is apparently some truth in this suggestion, and it may be one of the reasons that small towns with stable populations are more conventional and have lower crime rates than do big cities with more fluid populations—an issue addressed more fully in Chapter 20.

■

SOCIAL NETWORKS

A **social network** is an individual's total set of relationships.

Each of us has memberships in a variety of primary and secondary groups. Through these group ties we develop a **social network**. This social network is the total set of relationships we have. It includes our family, our insurance agent, our neighbors, our classmates and coworkers, and the people who belong to our clubs. Through our social network, we are linked to hundreds of people in our communities and perhaps across the country.

STRONG AND WEAK TIES

Strong ties are relationships characterized by intimacy, emotional intensity, and sharing.

Weak ties are relationships with friends, acquaintances, and kin that are characterized by low intensity and intimacy.

Although our insurance agent and our mother are both part of our social network, there is a qualitative difference between them. We can divide our social networks into two general categories of intimacy: strong ties and weak ties. **Strong ties** are relationships characterized by intimacy, emotional intensity, and sharing. We have strong ties with the people we would confide in, for whom we would make sacrifices, and whom we expect to make sacrifices for us. **Weak ties** are relationships that are characterized by low intensity and intimacy (Granovetter 1973). Coworkers, neighbors, fellow club members, cousins, and in-laws generally fall in this category.

Your social network does not include everybody that you have ever interacted with. Many interactions, such as those with some classmates and neighbors, are so superficial that they cannot truly be said to be part of a relationship at all. Unless contacts develop into personal relationships that extend beyond the simple exchange of services or a passing nod, they would not be included in your social network.

Research suggests that social networks are vital for integration into society, encouraging conformity, and building a firm sense of self-identity. Because of their importance for the individual and society, documenting the trends in social networks has been a major focus of sociological study.

The Relationship Between Ties and Groups. The distinction between strong and weak ties obviously parallels the distinction between primary and secondary groups. The difference between these two sets of concepts is that strong and weak apply to one-to-one relationships while primary and secondary apply to the group as a whole. We can have both strong and weak ties within the primary as well as the secondary group.

A critical part of our social network is our strong ties—the handful of people to whom we feel intense loyalty and intimacy. For many people, family is an important source of strong ties. Although we may not be close to everyone in our family, there are usually a few family members to whom we feel very close. Women are somewhat more apt than men to choose their strong ties from among their family. Many, like these two sisters, will find that these ties provide a lifelong bond that will provide a sense of continuity over the entire life course.

For example, the family is obviously a primary group; it is relatively permanent, with strong feelings of loyalty and attachment. We are not equally intimate with every family member, however. We may be very close to our mother, but estranged from our brother. Similarly, although the school as a whole is classified as a secondary group, we may have developed an intimate relationship, a strong tie, with one of our schoolmates. Strong and weak are terms used to describe the relationship between two individuals; primary and secondary are characteristics of the group as a whole.

Strong Ties.   Although we have a large research literature on strong ties, there is little consensus on how to define them operationally. As a result, different studies yield different pictures of the extent of strong ties. For example, one recent study asked a national sample to name those individuals they could "discuss important matters with." Using this definition, the average individual had only three strong ties (Marsden 1987). Another major study used a definition that included every adult you lived with, engaged in social activities with, or would borrow from or confide in. This study found that the average person had 15–19 ties (Fischer 1982).

Despite these differences, all studies agree on the factors that affect number and composition of strong ties. The most important of these factors is education. People with more education have more strong ties, have a greater diversity of strong ties, and are less reliant on kin. The number of ties also varies by residence and age. Urban residents have more strong ties than rural residents, perhaps in part because they have a greater variety from which to choose. Older respondents consistently report the fewest strong ties. Gender does not appear to make much difference in the number of strong ties that people have, but it does affect the source: Women's ties are more likely than men's to be drawn from the kin group (Marsden 1987; Fischer 1982).

Giving Gifts and Building Ties

Social networks don't come into existence by accident. We build them. Even ties to kin are built; we can choose to strengthen our ties to our brothers and aunts, or we can let those relationships wither. How do we build and sustain these networks? Canadian sociologist David Cheal suggests that one of the vital mechanisms used for sustaining social networks is the giving of gifts. We give gifts on Christmas, Hanukkah, birthdays, Father's Day, anniversaries, Valentine's Day, and on the occasions of births and weddings.

To find out how gift giving affects community ties and intimate networks, Cheal (1988) undertook an intensive study of gift giving in Winnipeg. He did intensive interviewing with a nonrandom sample of 80 people, selected to represent women and men, as well as a variety of ages, social classes, and ethnic backgrounds. He met with each of these people several times over the course of the year (including right after Christmas) to get a full enumeration of every gift they gave or received during the year, to ask about why the gift was given, and to find out about the relationship between giver and receiver.

■

. . . strong ties are marked by many small gifts rather than by extravagant gestures.

Some rather cynical scholars have concluded that people give gifts in order to make the receiver feel obligated. The giver is "buying" a

friend. Cheal argues instead that people use gift giving to reinforce relationships that already exist. Few people in Cheal's sample gave gifts to people they were trying to impress or to people they didn't already know intimately; the vast majority of gifts are given to people who are already part of our social network.

One rather surprising conclusion of his study is that only half of the gifts given in one year were reciprocated in that same year. In many cases, reciprocity exists, but it is diffused throughout the social and kin network: I give a present at your son's wedding, and I expect you to do the same in three years when my daughter gets married. There is more than reciprocity going on, however. Cheal's respondents gauge the size of their gifts by the size of their affection for the recipient, not by the size of the last gift they got. For the most part, however, gifts are small in value, and strong ties are marked by many small gifts rather than by extravagant gestures.

A relatively unsurprising finding is that gift giving occurs largely among women. Women buy 80 percent of the gifts (although sometimes the gifts will be given in their male relatives' name); women also receive many more gifts than men. Bridal and baby showers, of course, are institutionalized settings in which women have traditionally given to other women. Cheal concludes that gift giving is an important way for women to build and maintain networks among themselves as well as with men.

In many social roles, we have normative obligations to one another. Some of the obligations include that we *should* give gifts on occasions such as Father's Day. These gifts serve an important role in symbolizing ties. Gift giving is especially important, however, in reinforcing friendship and kinship ties that are not marked by normative obligation, such as relationships with neighbors or aunts. There are few occasions on which you have a normative obligation to give gifts to these people. If you give them a gift, they can truly say, "Oh, you shouldn't have." The voluntary nature of the gift makes an especially strong statement and is an important way of reinforcing the bonds between giver and receiver.

Consider all the gifts you have given this year—not just obligatory birthday and wedding presents, but the times when, for example, you impulsively picked up flowers at the grocery store and gave them to a friend or to your grandmother. How important are those small gifts in weaving and maintaining your social network?

SOURCE: Cheal 1988.

VOLUNTARY ASSOCIATIONS

In addition to relationships formed through family and work, many of us voluntarily choose to join other groups and associations. We may join the PTA, a bowling team, the Elks, or the Sierra Club. These groups, called **voluntary associations,** are nonprofit organizations designed to allow individuals an opportunity to pursue their shared interests collectively. They vary considerably in size and formality. Some—for example, the Elks and the PTA—are very large and have national headquarters, elected officers, formal titles, charters, membership dues, regular meeting times, and national conventions. Others—for example, bowling teams and quilting groups—are small, informal groups that draw their membership from a local community or neighborhood.

Voluntary associations are an important mechanism for enlarging our social networks. Most of the relationships we form in voluntary associations will be weak ties, but voluntary associations can also be the means of introducing us to people who will become close friends and intimates.

Voluntary associations perform an important function for individuals. Studies document that people who participate in them generally report greater satisfaction and personal happiness, longer life, greater self-esteem, more political effectiveness, and a greater sense of community (Hanks 1981; Knoke 1981; Litwak 1961; Moen, Dempster-McLain, and Williams 1989; Pollock 1982). The correlation between high participation and greater sat-

Voluntary associations are nonprofit organizations designed to allow individuals an opportunity to pursue their shared interests collectively.

The women Shriners in this picture are in many ways typical of the people who belong to voluntary associations: they are middle to upper-middle class, middle-aged, and urban. This picture illustrates another common feature of voluntary associations—sex segregation. As their cheerful expressions indicate, membership in such voluntary associations is generally associated with a greater feeling of integration into one's community and greater personal satisfaction.

isfaction does not necessarily mean that joining a voluntary association is the road to happiness. At least part of the relationship is undoubtedly due to the fact that it is precisely those happy persons who feel politically effective and attached to their communities who seek out voluntary associations. It also appears to be true, however, that greater participation can be an avenue for achievement and lead to feelings of integration and satisfaction.

The Mediation Hypothesis.   An important characteristic of voluntary associations is that they combine some of the features of primary and secondary groups—for example, the companionship of a small group and the rational efficiency of a secondary group. Some scholars have therefore suggested that voluntary associations mediate (provide a bridge) between primary and secondary groups (Pollock 1982). They allow us to pursue instrumental goals without completely sacrificing the satisfactions that come from participation in a primary group. Through participation in voluntary associations, we meet some of our needs for intimacy and association while we achieve greater control over our immediate environment. Take, for example, the sportsman who wishes to protect both wildlife habitat and the right to have guns. This individual can write letters to his member of Congress, but he will believe, rightly, that as an individual he is unlikely to have much clout. If this same individual joins with others in say, the National Wildlife Federation or the National Rifle Association, he will have the enjoyment of associating with other like-minded individuals and the satisfaction of knowing that a paid lobbyist is representing his opinions in Washington. In this way, voluntary associations provide a bridge between the individual and large secondary associations.

Correlates of Membership Participation.   Most Americans belong to at least one voluntary association, and approximately one-fourth participate in three or more. Among those who report membership, a large proportion are passive participants—they belong in name only. They buy a membership in the PTA when pressured to do so, but they don't go to meetings. Similarly, anyone who subscribes to *Audubon* magazine is automatically enrolled in the local Audubon Club, but few subscribers become active members. Because so many of our memberships are superficial, they are also temporary. Most Americans, however, maintain continuous membership in at least one association.

Membership in voluntary associations shows much the same pattern as noted earlier for strong ties. These same factors also tend to affect the kinds of organizations people join (Tomeh 1973):

1. *Urban/rural residence.* Urban residents are more frequently involved in voluntary associations than are rural residents. One reason may be that urban areas offer a greater variety of associations to choose from and less competition from traditional primary groups.
2. *Social class.* Most studies show that people from higher social classes are more involved in voluntary associations than are people from lower classes. Furthermore, the types of organizations joined vary by social class. Upper-class persons join historical societies and country clubs, middle-class persons, civic groups (Chamber of Commerce, hospital auxiliary), and working-class persons, fraternal and veteran's associations.

3. *Age.* Membership in voluntary associations tends to increase continuously through adulthood but begins to decline near retirement age. During early adulthood, the presence of young children has a depressing effect on the involvement of parents, particularly mothers. Age also affects the types of organizations joined. Young people's organizations tend to be almost exclusively expressive in nature; parents are active in youth-oriented groups such as the scouts and the PTA; middle-aged people are more active in civic groups.

4. *Gender.* We find relatively little difference in the number of associations men and women belong to, but major differences in the kinds of organizations they join. In part, this reflects the fact that many voluntary associations are largely or entirely sex-segregated (for example, garden clubs, hospital auxiliaries, the Elks) (McPherson and Smith-Lovin 1986). In general, the associations that women join are smaller, less formal, and more expressive in nature.

5. *Religion.* Church membership and participation is the most widespread and intensive voluntary association in our society. People who are religious belong not only to a church but also to church boards, study groups, sewing circles, and fund-raising committees.

COMMUNITY

In everyday life, we hear a lot of talk about the benefits of having a "sense of community" and mourn the contemporary loss of community. Such commentaries seem to regard community as a good thing, but they usually aren't very specific about what community is.

According to sociologists, a strong community is characterized by dense, cross-cutting social networks (Wellman and Berkowitz 1988). A community is strongest when everybody knows everybody else and when all members of the community are linked to one another through complex and overlapping ties. These ties need not be strong. Research shows that a network of weak ties can have important consequences for a community. As the proportion of people who know each other increases, social control and cohesion increase. Deviance and fear of crime are reduced, better control is exercised over children, and the weak and handicapped are more likely to be cared for (Freudenburg 1986).

A growing body of research shows the importance of voluntary associations and weak ties for community integration. Voluntary associations, especially those that cut across social class and race, create horizontal and vertical links within the community; these links increase the likelihood that community members will feel a sense of cohesion and solidarity, that they will come to one another's aid and conform to community norms (McPherson 1983).

Community cohesion is fostered by many of the same factors that create cohesion in smaller groups: high levels of interaction, stability of membership, similarity, and size. Although it is more difficult to build cohesion in a large, diverse community than in a small, homogeneous one, research shows that a high level of participation in voluntary associations can create a network of weak ties that substantially increases community cohesion (Sampson 1988).

Strong communities are built by dense networks of weak ties. When everybody knows everybody else or at least knows them through a cousin or neighbor, then community norms are reinforced and the community is more likely to be able to work together. This is most easily accomplished in small, stable communities where the residents share much in common.

BUREAUCRACIES AND ORGANIZATIONS

In addition to our involvement in small groups and voluntary associations, most of us are involved with bureaucracies and other large-scale organizations. Our schools, workplaces, hospitals, military, and even churches are large, formal organizations.

These organizations make a major contribution to the overall quality of life within society. Because of their size and complexity, however, they don't supply the cohesion and personal satisfaction that smaller groups do. They may make their members feel as if they are simply cogs in the machine rather than important people in their own right. This is nowhere more true than in a bureaucracy.

BUREAUCRACY

Bureaucracy is a special type of complex organization characterized by explicit rules and a hierarchical authority structure, all designed to maximize efficiency.

Bureaucracy is a special type of complex organization characterized by explicit rules and a hierarchical authority structure, all designed to maximize efficiency. In popular usage, bureaucracy often has a negative connotation: red tape, silly rules, and unyielding rigidity. In social science, however, it is simply an organization in which the social structure has been carefully planned to maximize efficiency.

The Classic View.   Most large, complex organizations are also bureaucratic: IBM, General Motors, U.S. Steel, the Catholic church, colleges, and hospitals. The major characteristics of bureaucracies were outlined 80 years ago by Max Weber ([1910] 1970a):

1. *Division of labor and specialization.* Bureaucratic organizations employ specialists in each position and make them responsible for specific duties. Job titles and job descriptions specify who is responsible for each activity.

2. *Hierarchy of authority.* Positions are arranged in a hierarchy so that each position is under the control and supervision of a higher position. Frequently referred to as chains of command, these lines of authority and responsibility are easily drawn on an organization chart, often in the shape of a pyramid.

3. *Rules and regulations.* All activities and operations of a bureaucracy are governed by abstract rules or procedures. These rules are designed to cover almost every possible situation that might arise: hiring, firing, and the everyday operations of the office. The object is to standardize all activities.

4. *Impersonal relationships.* Interactions in a bureaucracy are supposed to be guided by the rules rather than by personal feelings. Consistent application of impersonal rules is intended to eliminate favoritism and particularism.

5. *Careers, tenure, and technical qualifications.* Candidates for bureaucratic positions are almost always selected on the basis of technical qualifications, such as high scores on civil service examinations, education, or experience. Once selected for a position, persons advance in the hierarchy by means of achievement and seniority.

6. *Efficiency.* Bureaucratic organizations coordinate the activities of a large number of people in the pursuit of organizational goals. All activities have been designed to maximize efficiency. From the practice of hiring on the basis of credentials rather than personal contacts to the rigid specification of duties and authority, the whole system is constructed to keep individuality, whim, and particularism out of the operation of the organization.

Organizational Culture.   Weber's classic theory of bureaucracy almost demands robots rather than individuals. A list of rules that covered every possible situation would be unwieldy and impossibly long. Not surprisingly, therefore, we find that few organizations try to be totally bureaucratic. Instead, organizations strive to create an atmosphere of goodwill and common purpose among their members so that everybody will apply their ingenuity and best efforts to meeting organizational goals (DiTomaso 1987). This goodwill is as essential to efficiency as are the rules. In most organizations, in fact, working exactly according to the rules is considered a form of sabotage. For example, unions of public employees (such as the police) that cannot legally strike, engage in "working to the rule" as a form of protest: They follow every little nitpicky rule and fill out every form carefully. The result is usually a sharp slowdown in work and general chaos.

Sociologists use the term *organizational culture* to refer to the pattern of norms and values that affects how business is actually carried out in an organization. The key to a successful organizational culture is cohesion, and most organizations strive to build cohesion among their members. They do this by encouraging interaction among employees (providing lunchrooms, sponsoring after-hours sports leagues, having company picnics and newsletters, and developing unifying symbols, such as mascots, company colors, or uniforms). This is most clearly apparent when you

■

Many bureaucratic organizations use the company picnic as a strategy to build a positive organizational culture. They hope that the personal ties built during such informal occasions will motivate employees to go beyond the formal rules and to give their best efforts to promoting the company's and their employer's interests. In this picture, Steve Jobs (formerly of Apple Computer and now head of Next Computers) appears at a Next Company picnic barefooted. This just-one-of-the guys informality and family atmosphere may mask the fact that such picnics are good for business.

think about the large bureaucratic organization represented by a university, but it is also characteristic of multinational corporations.

In many organizations, the formal rules have very little to do with the day-to-day activity of the members. In situations as varied as classrooms and shop floors, people evolve their own way of doing business and may have little use for the formal rules (Ouichi and Wilkins 1985); in fact, they may not even know what the rules are. What determines whether an organization works by the rules or not?

A major factor affecting degree of bureaucratization in an organization is the degree of uncertainty in the organization's activities. When activities tend to be routine and predictable, then the organization is likely to emphasize rules, central planning, and hierarchical chains of command. When activities change rapidly in unpredictable ways, there is more emphasis on flexibility and informal decision making (Simpson 1985). This explains why, for example, classrooms tend to be less bureaucratic and ball-bearings factories more bureaucratic.

Criticisms of Bureaucracies.   Bureaucracy is the standard organizational form in the modern world. Organizations from churches to governments are run along bureaucratic lines. Despite the widespread adoption of this organizational form, it has several major drawbacks. Three of the most widely acknowledged are as follows:

1. *Ritualism.* Rigid adherence to rules may mean that a rule is followed regardless of whether it helps accomplish the purpose for which it was designed. The rule becomes an end in itself rather than a means to an end. For example, individuals may interpret a rule stating that the workday ends at 5 P.M. to mean that they cannot work later even if they want to. Overemphasis on rules can stifle initiative and prevent the development of more efficient procedures (Blau and Meyer 1971).
2. *Alienation.* The stress on rules, hierarchies, and impersonal relationships can sharply reduce the cohesion of the organization. This has several drawbacks: It reduces social control, it increases turnover, and it reduces member satisfaction and commitment. All of these factors may interfere with the organization's ability to reach its goals.
3. *Structured inequality.* Critics charge that the modern bureaucracy with its multiple layers of authority is a profoundly antidemocratic organization. In fact, the whole purpose of the bureaucratic form is to concentrate power in one or two decision makers whose decisions are then passed down as orders to subordinates below. Some observers believe that the amassing of concentrated power in the name of efficiency and rationalism is incompatible with a democratic society (Perrow 1986).

Although most organizations use a bureaucratic model, there are two important exceptions: the collectivist organization and the Japanese model of organization. These two alternatives are discussed next.

COLLECTIVIST ORGANIZATIONS

Collective organizations are intentionally designed to avoid the hierarchy and regulation of bureaucracy; instead, they stress high personal involvement, consensus, and democracy. Collectivist organizations offer a variety of services—for example, legal aid, alternative schools, and health care. They also include grass-roots business cooperatives requiring relatively small amounts of capital outlay: bookstores, clothing, newspapers, auto repair, organic food, and alternative energy. They are almost all very small, and they operate in economic arenas where there is little direct competition with corporate actors.

Collectivist organizations have been deliberately designed to be the polar opposite of bureaucratic organizations. They differ in the following ways (Rothschild-Whitt 1979):

1. *Authority*. Collective organizations emphasize democracy and consensus. All members participate in decision making, and the goal is to reach decisions supported by the entire group.

2. *Rules*. There is a marked attempt to minimize the use of rules to run collectives. Instead, decisions are made on an individual basis, taking into account the particular circumstances of each situation.

3. *Social relations*. Alternative organizations strive to maintain primary-group relationships. They often speak of themselves as communities rather than organizations, and they endeavor to create relationships that are holistic, personal, and of value in and of themselves.

4. *Recruitment and advancement*. Hiring and staffing is based largely on such criteria as friendship and shared social and political values. There is no hierarchy of positions and thus no concept of individual advancement.

5. *Status distinctions*. The absence of status distinctions is a central feature of collective organizations. Wage differences occur, but they are largely the result of special circumstances (number of dependents, for example) rather than worth of the individual to the organization: "Through dress, informal relations, task sharing, job rotation, the physical structure of the workplace, equal pay, and the collective decision-making process itself—collectives convey an equality of status" (p. 517).

6. *Specialization*. Little emphasis is placed on specialization and technical expertise. Through job rotation, teamwork, and task sharing, administrative and performance tasks are combined and the division between intellectual and manual work is reduced. Everyone manages and everyone works.

Although laudable in many ways, collectives are not without constraints and social costs. Arriving at consensus and maintaining a high level of communication require the devotion of large amounts of time to staff meetings and discussion. The demand for consensus and full participation means some sacrifice of efficiency. The practice of job rotation and a lack of clear authority further hamper quick and efficient action. Individual costs may be high because of high levels of emotional exchange, the intimacy of face-to-face communication, and the potentials for conflict. It takes a lot of emotional energy to reach and maintain agreement with even half a dozen other individuals.

Generally, the success of collectivist organizations depends on their remaining small (less than 10 people) and unprofitable. When profits and size grow, democracy becomes difficult to sustain. Complete consultation and exchange of information become tedious and inefficient when the group gets larger. As a result, full information is likely to be restricted to a small group of insiders who begin to make decisions without full con-

The **iron law of oligarchy** is the tendency for an elite to dominate an organization.

sultation of all members (Rothschild 1986). The very common tendency for an elite group to come to dominate an organization has been called the **iron law of oligarchy** (Michels 1962).

THE JAPANESE MODEL OF ORGANIZATION

Within the last two decades, Japan has come to dominate dozens of areas of international trade, from automobiles to video recorders. The astounding success of Japanese manufacturers has led to intense scrutiny of Japanese management practices in order to discover their secret (Dore 1973; Marsh and Mannari 1976; Masatsugu 1982).

Because Japanese firms, like their American counterparts, are large and complex, they are run as bureaucracies. They have hierarchies of authority, lots of rules, hiring on the basis of technical qualifications, and many of the other features of classic bureaucratic theory. In addition, however, they have some distinct characteristics that may represent the complex organization of the future. Among these are several practices that move the Japanese bureaucracy in the direction of the collectivist organization. A recent review by Lincoln and McBride (1987) suggests the following unique features of Japanese organizations:

1. *Permanent employment.* Japanese organizations have a strong norm of permanent employment. On leaving school, an employee enters a firm and remains there until retirement. The company makes a lifetime commitment to the employee, and the employee also makes a lifetime commitment to the firm.

2. *Internal labor markets.* Higher-level positions are filled from below from within the same firm. Thus, people can make a lifetime commitment to

Small group responsibility at all levels is a key part of Japanese-style organizations. This is very different from a classic bureaucracy, where the people at the bottom are expected to follow the rules established by their superiors rather than to think for themselves. The bottom-up style of management characteristic of Japanese organizations gives workers a greater investment in their product, and may be a key to higher quality products.

the same firm and still have the opportunity for promotion and upward mobility. This system differs from the common American practice of pursuing careers by changing employers. Because of lifetime commitment and internal labor markets, seniority in the firm and age are highly correlated—and generally highly rewarded.

3. *Relative absence of white-collar/blue-collar distinction.* In Japan, all workers are expected to be committed to the firm, thus all workers work on salary rather than for an hourly wage. There are no separate cafeterias and parking lots for the supervisors and for the line workers. This also means that the internal labor market crosses the white-collar/blue-collar line: Although one might start as a blue-collar worker, seniority is likely to move one into management ranks.

4. *Participatory decision making.* Unlike the classic bureaucratic model where decisions flow in only one direction (down), a more circular pattern of decision making is the norm in Japanese organizations. Suggestions may originate among workers' circles and then rise to the top (called bottom-up management), or they may originate at the top but be implemented only after there is substantial consensus among the workers. This participatory decision-making process is yet another mechanism that reduces the distinction between management and line workers and increases the cohesion and commitment of the employees.

When U.S. scholars first started looking at Japanese organizations, they often attributed the unique features of these organizations to Japan's feudal heritage. Increasingly, however, scholars view Japan's organizational style as the wave of the future rather than a holdover from the past. Unlike the classic bureaucratic model, which pretty much ignores the human component of the workplace, the Japanese organizational form recognizes that complex organizations are *human groups* rather than machines. Thus, it takes into consideration such issues as cohesion and group dynamics. The realization that even corporations such as IBM are groups and are affected by group processes is likely to have a substantial effect on the evolution of bureaucracy in the United States and around the world.

Network Intervention

Group membership furnishes a wide array of benefits for individuals. Research findings in many areas show that individuals who have meaningful ties to multiple groups and organizations are better off in nearly every domain of life. They experience less stress, and they cope with it better when it occurs; as a result, they have longer lives and

People who are all alone are also frequently people with a lot of problems. Belonging to groups, especially primary groups, is associated with better mental and physical health and less deviance. Would this person be any better off if he had a close network of friends? Probably he would. In addition to emotional support, social networks are also an important source of more practical aid. The more people you have in your network, the more likely you are to know someone who knows someone who . . . can get you a job, a place to stay, or a loan.

experience less physical and mental illness (Cobb 1979). Socially integrated individuals are less likely to end their marriages in divorce (Glenn and Supancic 1984) or to engage in abusive family relationships (Gelles and Cornell 1985). In fact, they are in general more likely to be conforming individuals, whose group ties keep them from violating important social norms.

The opposite of the socially integrated individual with a complex social network is the person who is socially isolated, who has few or no ties to others. Such individuals tend to require large amounts of social services and to cause a disproportionate amount of trouble—not just for themselves but also for their communities. When a large proportion of a community lacks social integration, high levels of alcoholism, drug abuse, child neglect, crime, and mental illness are likely to result.

NETWORK INTERVENTION

For these reasons, it has seemed prudent to many at the local and state levels to encourage group participation as a matter of public policy. *Network interventions*, as such policy initiatives are known, take a variety of forms.

1. *Fostering neighborhood networks.* This includes facilitating such neighborhood endeavors as block parties, neighborhood watch, and block parent programs, as well as providing neighborhood centers to encourage interaction of neighbors. It also includes zoning regulations and building codes designed to encourage neighboring in housing projects and apartment buildings (Brownell and Shumacher 1984).

2. *Fostering voluntary association.* As a matter of public policy, many agencies of government supply funding and support facilities for civic and recreational groups, from the scouts to the senior bowlers.

ISSUES IN SOCIAL POLICY continued

3. *Fostering supportive weak ties.* A wide variety of imaginative strategies have been implemented to train people in weak-tie relationships to provide more social support. One program, for example, trained hairdressers (who often receive confidences from their clients while styling hair) to offer more social support (Wiesenfeld and Weis 1979).

4. *Fostering support groups.* A growing method of direct network intervention is providing support groups and hot lines for individuals in special need, such as alcoholics, abused wives, dieters, teen mothers, diabetics, and so on.

CRITICAL ISSUES

Before local governments leap into the social director business, a few critical issues need to be addressed (Rook and Dooley 1985).

1. Artificially fostered support groups may not offer the same kinds of benefits as naturally occurring support groups. Nevertheless, preliminary research on support groups provided for teen mothers shows that it is precisely those young women who had the least natural social support who benefited most from support groups (Unger and Wandersman 1985).

2. Intervention strategies may put the cart before the horse. Perhaps a large part of the relationship between well-being and group membership is due to the fact that healthy, conforming individuals choose to belong to groups. If this is true, encouraging poorly adjusted individuals to join groups will not result in substantial improvements.

3. Group memberships can be a source of stress as well as support. Memberships may demand more time and energy than a person has to give and may end up being a drain rather than a support.

POLICY CONCERNS

Group memberships and strong social networks are beneficial for the individual and for the community (Gottlieb 1981). Should it be public policy to encourage and support such networks? Despite the critical issues just raised, many scholars would answer a cautious yes. There are obvious limitations, however, to the effectiveness of such interventions. Although social networks are helpful, they cannot be used as cheap substitutes for existing social services. Larger and more diverse networks may help people deal with poverty or disability, but they cannot by themselves put food on the table or provide safe neighborhoods (Chapman and Pancoast 1985).

SUMMARY

1. Relationships are characterized by four basic social processes: exchange, cooperation, competition, and conflict.

2. Groups are distinguished from aggregates and categories in that members take one another into account and their interaction is shaped by shared social structure.

3. Group interaction is affected by group size and the proximity and communication patterns of group members. The amount of interaction in turn affects group cohesion, the amount of social control the group can exercise over members, and the quality of group decisions.

4. A fundamental distinction between groups is the extent to which they are primary or secondary. Primary groups are essential to individual satisfaction and integration; they are also the primary agents of social control in society. Secondary groups are generally task oriented and perform instrumental functions for societies and individuals.

5. Each person has a social network that consists of both strong and weak ties. The number of these ties is generally greater for individuals who are urban, middle-aged, and highly educated.

6. Voluntary associations may mediate between the primary and secondary group, providing a bridge that links the individual to larger groups. Voluntary associations combine some of the expressive functions of primary groups with the instrumental functions of secondary groups.

7. A bureaucracy is a rationally designed organization whose goal is to maximize efficiency. The chief characteristics of a bureaucracy are division of labor and specialization, a hierarchy of authority, a system of rules and regulations, impersonality in social relations, and emphasis on careers, tenure, and technical qualifications.

8. Although most contemporary organizations are built on a bureaucratic model, many are far less rational and impersonal than the classic model suggests. All effective bureaucracies rely on an organizational culture to inspire employees to give their best efforts to help meet organizational goals.

9. As a result of the alienation and impersonalization encountered in bureaucratic organizations, antibureaucratic organizations have emerged in recent years. Based on principles of democracy and cooperation, these collectivist organizations minimize the use of rules and authority, status distinctions, and specialization.

10. Japanese organizations fit somewhere between the extreme rationalism of the classic bureaucracy and the people-centered collectivist organizations. Japanese organizations try to maximize employees' commitment to the firm through four mechanisms: lifetime employment, internal labor markets, little distinction between blue- and white-collar workers, and participatory decision making.

11. The positive effects of social networks for individuals and communities are so broad that many government initiatives are designed to support and encourage the development of social networks. These network interventions have positive impacts, but cannot replace direct social services.

SUGGESTED READINGS

Douglas, Tom. 1983. Groups: Understanding People Gathered Together. London: Tavistock. An engaging little book that focuses on the similarity of group processes in teams, families, and other small groups.

Fischer, Claude. 1982. To Dwell Among Friends: Personal Networks in Town and City. Chicago: University of Chicago Press. A report of Fischer's research in northern California, including an excellent overview of sociological concerns about social networks.

Homans, George C. 1950. The Human Group. New York: Harcourt, Brace. A classic that deals with the dynamics of small groups in several different contexts (family, work groups, gangs). The basic processes and structures of groups are drawn out in such a way that application to our own group memberships is made easy and straightforward.

Perrow, Charles. 1986. Complex Organizations: A Critical Essay. (3rd ed.) New York: Random House. A contemporary overview of classic bureaucratic theory and the ways it operates in practice.

Rothschild, J., and Whitt, A. 1986. The Cooperative Workplace: Potentials and Dilemmas of Organizational Democracy and Participation. New York: Cambridge University Press. An overview of a variety of alternative organizations that have sprung up among those dissatisfied with the traditional bureaucratic model.

CONFORMITY AND NONCONFORMITY

CHAPTER 6
THE INDIVIDUAL AND SOCIETY

CHAPTER 7
THE SOCIOLOGY OF
EVERYDAY LIFE

CHAPTER 8
DEVIANCE, CRIME, AND
SOCIAL CONTROL

6

THE INDIVIDUAL AND SOCIETY

PROLOGUE

Have you ever . . .

Wondered how you would have turned out if you had had different parents? You may have considered your friends' families and wondered how you would have turned out if your parents had been richer, you had been an only child, or your parents had been of a different race or ethnicity.

Although you may think that you would have turned out better with different parents, we usually don't have any choice about our parents. As we get older, we have more choices about what relationships we will enter into and what roles we will take on. For example, everyone reading this book has made a choice to go to college and has chosen to enroll in a specific school.

The college choice reflects the complexity of the relationship between individuals and social structures. Your prior circumstances affect your college choice, and your college choice will affect your present and future circumstances. Maybe you would turn out differently if your campus was richer, smaller, and of a different race/ethnicity mix.

As this example illustrates, it is not only in childhood that we are influenced by the social structures and relationships around us. In this chapter we begin to examine the relationship between individuals and social structures. We are concerned with why individuals behave as they do and how this is related to the social structures of which they are a part.

OUTLINE

The previous chapters of this book have focused on macrosociology—analysis of cultures, institutions, social structures, groups, and organizations. This focus on structures should not obscure the fact that the heart of sociology is a concern with *people*. Sociology is interesting and useful to the extent that it helps us explain why people do what they do. It should let us see ourselves, our family, and our acquaintances in a new light.

In this chapter on socialization and the next chapter on the sociology of everyday life, we deal directly with individuals. The two chapters can be viewed as a pair; taken together, they help us to understand the relationship of the individual to society. This chapter looks at how individuals are molded within social structures; the next chapter examines the ways in which individuals interpret and manipulate this molding process.

THE SELF AND SELF-CONCEPT

From the small lump of flesh that is the newborn infant develops a complex and fascinating human being, a human being who is simultaneously much like every other human being and at the same time exactly like no other.

Each individual **self** may be thought of as a combination of unique attributes and normative responses. Within sociology these two parts of the self are called the *I* and the *me* (Mead 1934).

The **I** is the spontaneous, creative part of the self; the **me** is the self as social object, the part of the self that responds to others' expectations. In English grammar, *me* is used when we speak of ourselves as the object of others' actions (She sent me to the office); *I* is used when we speak of ourselves as the actor (I threw spitballs). Sociological use follows this convention.

As this description of the self implies, the two parts may pull us in different directions. For example, many people face a daily conflict between their I and their me when the alarm clock goes off in the morning—the I wants to roll over and go back to sleep, but the me knows it is supposed to get up and go to class. Some of these conflicts are resolved in favor of the me and some in favor of the I. Daily behavior, however, is viewed as the result of an ongoing internal dialogue between the I and the me.

The self is enormously complex, and we are often not fully aware of our own motives, capabilities, and characteristics. The self that we are aware of is our **self-concept.** It consists of our thoughts and feelings about our personality and social roles. For example, a young man's self-concept might include such qualities as: young, male, Methodist, good athlete, poor student, shy, awkward with girls, responsible, American. His self-concept includes all the images he has of himself in the dozens of different settings in which he interacts.

The self and self-concept are social products; they are developed through social relationships. In the following sections, we examine some of these social processes, beginning with a discussion of infancy and the necessity of nurture.

The **self** is a complex whole that includes unique attributes and normative responses. In sociology, these two parts are called the I and the me.

The **I** is the spontaneous, creative part of the self.

The **me** represents the self as social object.

The **self-concept** is the self we are aware of. It is our thoughts and feelings about our personality and social roles.

■

LEARNING TO BE HUMAN

What is human nature? Are we born with a tendency to be cooperative and sharing or with a tendency to be selfish and aggressive? The question of the basic nature of humankind has been a staple of philosophical debate for thousands of years. It continues to be a topic of debate because it is so difficult (some would say impossible) to separate the part of human behavior that arises from our genetic heritage from the part that is developed after birth. The one thing we are sure of is that nature is never enough.

THE NECESSITY OF NURTURE

Each of us begins life with a set of human potentials: the potential to talk, to walk, to love, and to learn. By themselves, however, these natural capacities are not enough to enable us to join the human family. Without nurture—without love and attention and hugging—the human infant is unlikely to survive, much less prosper. The effects of neglect are sometimes fatal, and, depending on its severity and length, neglect almost always results in retarded intellectual and social development.

How can we determine the importance of nurture? There are a few case studies of tragically neglected children, but luckily the instances are rare. Some of the first clinical evidence on the effects of limited social interaction on human development was provided by René Spitz's (1945) study of an orphanage where each nurse was in charge of a dozen or more infants. Although the children's physical needs were met, the nurses had little time to give individual attention to each child.

■

The family is our first experience with group living, and the quality of the experience has lasting influence on our personality and self-concept. If our families shower us with warmth and acceptance, then we will learn to love and to laugh. We will also learn to conform in order to please them. Studies show that love is as important as food and shelter for a child's growth and development.

It would be clearly unethical to examine the consequences of neglect by experimenting on human infants. Harry Harlow, however, has conducted several studies with infant monkeys. One study compared infants who had a wire-covered mother figure with infants who had a terrycloth-covered mother figure such as the one in this picture; both mother figures gave milk. This study found that infant monkeys derived much comfort from cuddling up to the terrycloth mother. Those with the cuddly mother exhibited more normal social behaviors than those with the wire-covered mother figure. Harlow's research shows that simple tactile stimulation is an important element of early experience.

Children who spend the first years of their lives in this type of institutional environment are devastated by the experience. Because of limited personal attention, such children withdraw from the social world; they seldom cry and are indifferent to everything around them. The absence of handling, touching, and movement is the major cause of this retarded development. In time, the children become retarded intellectually and more susceptible to disease and death. Of the 88 children Spitz studied, 23 died before reaching the age of two and a half. Even if they live, Spitz found, socially deprived children are likely to become socially crippled adults.

A number of studies confirm the effects of institutionalized care described by Spitz. Provence and Lipton (1962) compared 75 physically healthy institutionalized infants with a control group of infants raised at home. The institutionalized infants received excellent food and physical care but limited social stimulation. During the first few weeks of life, there was little difference between the two groups. At about three months, however, the institutionalized infants showed increasing signs of retardation. They seldom cried or babbled, lost interest in their surroundings, and by the age of one were noticeably retarded in their language development. Because the infants were healthy to begin with, physical and genetic abnormalities cannot have caused their disabilities. Provence and Lipton concluded that the differences between the control group and the institutionalized infants clearly indicate the devastating effects of deprivation.

Deprivation can also occur in homes where parents fail to provide adequate social and emotional stimulation. Children who have their physical needs met but are otherwise ignored by their parents have been found to exhibit many of the same symptoms as institutionalized infants. Studies of the effects of isolation and deprivation on children suggest that children need intensive interaction with others to survive and develop normally. Much of the evidence for this conclusion, however, is derived from atypical situations in which unfortunate children have been subjected to extreme and unusual circumstances. To assess the limits of these findings and to examine the reversibility of deprivation effects, researchers have turned to experiments with monkeys.

MONKEYING WITH ISOLATION AND DEPRIVATION

For more than 20 years, researchers have been experimenting with deprivation and isolation of infant monkeys. In a classic series of experiments, Harry Harlow and his associates raised infant monkeys in total isolation. The infants lived in individual cages with a mechanical mother figure, which provided milk. Although the infant monkeys' nutritional needs were met, their social needs were not. As a result, both their physical and social growth suffered. They exhibited such bizarre behavior as biting themselves and hiding in corners. As adults, these monkeys refused to mate; if artificially impregnated, the females would not nurse or care for their babies (Harlow and Harlow 1966). These experiments provide dramatic evidence about the importance of being with others; even apparently innate behaviors such as sexuality and maternal behavior must be developed through interaction. On the bright side, the monkey experiments affirm that some of the ill effects of isolation and deprivation are reversible: Young monkeys experienced almost total recovery when placed in a supportive social environment (Suomi, Harlow, and McKinney 1972).

Although it is dangerous to generalize from monkeys to humans, the evidence from the monkey experiments supports the observations about human infants: Physical and social development depends on interaction with others. Even being a monkey does not come naturally. The human ability to walk, to talk, to love, and to laugh all depend on sustained and intimate interaction with others. Clearly, our identities, even our lives, are socially bestowed and socially sustained (Berger 1963, 98). The processes through which interaction with others molds us are discussed in the next section.

SYMBOLIC INTERACTION THEORIES

Sociological theories about the development of the self are dominated by symbolic interaction theory. As noted in Chapter 1, this theory addresses the subjective meanings of human acts and the processes through which people come to develop and communicate shared meanings.

Over the years, two distinct schools have developed within this perspective: the interaction school and the structural school (Biddle 1986; Turner 1985). The **interaction school of symbolic interaction** focuses on the active role of the individual in creating the self and self-concept. The **structural school of symbolic interaction** focuses on the self as a product of social roles. We will review each school separately and then discuss their similarities and differences.

> The **interaction school of symbolic interaction** focuses on the active role of the individual in creating the self and self-concept.

> The **structural school of symbolic interaction** focuses on the self as a product of social roles.

THE INTERACTION SCHOOL

The major premise of the interaction school is that people are actively involved in creating and negotiating their own roles and self-concept. Although each of us is born into an established social structure with established expectations for our behavior, nevertheless we have opportunities to create our own selves. The concepts of the *looking-glass self* and of *role taking* illustrate how this process works.

Looking-Glass Self.   Charles Horton Cooley (1864–1929) provided a classic description of how we develop our self-concept. He proposed that we learn to view ourselves as we *think* others view us. He called this the **looking-glass self** (Cooley 1902). According to Cooley, there are three steps in the formation of the looking-glass self:

> The **looking-glass self** is the process of learning to view ourselves as we think others view us.

1. We imagine how we appear to others.
2. We imagine how others judge our appearance.
3. We develop feelings about and responses to these judgments.

For example, an instructor whose students openly talk to one another or doze during class and who frequently finds herself talking to a half-empty room is likely to gather that her students think she is a bad teacher. She need not, however, accept this view. The third stage in the formation of the looking-glass self suggests that the instructor may either accept the students' judgment and conclude that she is a bad teacher or reject their judgment and conclude that the students are simply not smart enough to appreciate her profound remarks. Our self-concept is not merely a mechanical reflection of those around us; rather it rests on our interpretations of and reactions to those judgments. We are actively engaged in defining our self-concept, using past experiences as one aid in interpreting others' responses. A person who considers herself witty will assume that others are laughing with her, not at her; someone used to making clumsy errors, however, will form the opposite interpretation from the laughter.

We also actively define our self-concept by choosing among potential looking glasses. That is, we try to choose roles and associates supportive of our self-concept (Gecas and Schwalbe 1983). The looking glass is thus a way of both forming and maintaining self-concept.

As Cooley's theory indicates, symbolic interaction considers subjective interpretations to be extremely important determinants of the self-concept. It is not only others' judgments of us that matter; our subjective interpretation of those judgments is equally important. This premise of symbolic interactionism is apparent in a classic statement by W. I. Thomas: If people "define situations as real, they are real in their consequences" (Thomas and Thomas 1928, 572). People interact through the medium of symbols (words, gestures) that must be subjectively interpreted. The interpretations have real consequences—even if they are *mis*interpretations.

Role Taking.   The most influential contributor to symbolic interaction theory during this century is George Herbert Mead (1863–1931). Mead argued that we learn social norms through the process of **role taking.** This means imagining ourselves in the role of the other in order to determine the criteria the other will use to judge our behavior. We use this information as a guide for our own behavior.

Role taking involves imagining ourselves in the role of the other in order to determine the criteria the other will use to judge our behavior.

According to Mead, role taking begins in childhood, when we learn the rights and obligations associated with being a child in our particular family. To understand what is expected of us as children, we must also learn our mother's and father's roles. We must learn to see ourselves form our parents' perspective and to evaluate our behavior from their point of view. Only when we have learned their role perspective as well as our own will we really understand what our own obligations are.

Mead maintained that children develop their role knowledge by playing games. When children play house, they develop their ideas of how husbands, wives, and children relate to one another. As the little boy comes in saying "I've had a hard day; I hope it's not my turn to cook dinner" or as the little girl warns her dolls not to play in the street and to wash their hands before eating, they are testing their knowledge of family role expectations.

Significant others are the role players with whom we have close personal relationships.

In the very early years, role playing and role taking are responsive to the expectations of **significant others**—those people we are very close to and whose good opinion is important to us. Day-care teachers, siblings, and, most of all, parents are important in forming a child's self-concept. As children mature and participate beyond this close and familiar network, the process of role taking is expanded to a larger network that helps them understand what society in general expects of them. They learn what the

Dressing up and playing mommy and daddy are almost universal aspects of childhood. Whether they use their parents' old clothes or enact their fantasies through Barbie and GI Joe, little children act out their own visions of how people ought to behave. Their play is filled with little side dramas where they step out of their temporary roles and discuss what ought to happen next and what the rules of play—and life—are. Mead suggests that this role taking is an essential way that children learn and practice acceptable behavior.

bus driver, their schoolmates, and their employers expect. Eventually, they come to be able to judge their behavior not only from the perspective of significant others but also from what Mead calls the **generalized other**— the composite expectations of all the other role players with whom they interact. Being aware of the expectations of the generalized other is equivalent to having learned the norms and values of the culture. One has learned how to act like an American or a Pole or a Nigerian.

Having learned the norms and values of one's culture does not mean that everyone will behave alike or that everyone will follow the same rules. My significant others are not the same as yours. Not only will our family experiences differ depending on the subculture in which we are reared, but, as we get older, we have some freedom in choosing those whose expectations will guide our behavior. Although we may know perfectly well what society in general expects of us, we may choose to march to the beat of a different drummer.

The **generalized other** is the composite expectations of all the other role players with whom we interact; it is Mead's term for our awareness of social norms.

The Negotiated Self. Role taking and the looking-glass self are ways in which the individual can become an active agent in the construction of his or her own self-concept. The self that emerges is a *negotiated* self, a self that we have fashioned by selectively choosing looking glasses and significant others.

The idea of negotiation suggests that we have an end in view. What is that end? An important one is to protect and enhance our self-esteem. **Self-esteem** is the evaluative part of the self-concept; it is our judgment of our worth compared with that of others. Since we would all like to think well of ourselves, we strive to negotiate a self-concept that reinforces that image. The Focus section in this chapter explores the measurement of self-esteem.

Self-esteem is the evaluative component of the self-concept; it is our judgment about our worth compared with others.

How Is Your Self-Esteem?

	Agree	Disagree
1. I feel that I'm a person of worth, at least on an equal plane with others.	1	2
2. I feel that I have a number of good qualities.	1	2
3. All in all, I am inclined to feel that I am a failure.	1	2
4. I am able to do things as well as most other people.	1	2
5. I feel I do not have much to be proud of.	1	2
6. I take a positive attitude toward myself.	1	2
7. On the whole, I am satisfied with myself.		
8. I wish I could have more respect for myself.	1	2
9. I certainly feel useless at times.	1	2
10. At times I think I am no good at all.	1	2

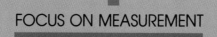

The 10 questions in the box above make up the Rosenberg Self-Esteem Scale (1965), widely used by psychologists and sociologists to measure self-esteem (Bohrnstedt and Fisher 1986; Shamir 1986).

Some have criticized the scale because it has high social-desirability bias; people may distort their answers to provide more positive images. This is not a problem, however, because the question at issue is not whether people really do have anything to be proud of or whether they really are a success or failure. Rather our concern is how they feel about themselves. Since we are asking about subjective interpretations rather than objective facts, this is one scale in which everybody really can be above average.

Some of the more important research findings on self-esteem are the following:

1.   We always think better of ourselves than others do (Wylie 1979). In this sense, the looking-glass self is always a little distorted in our own favor.

2.   Self-esteem turns out to be very stable. Even blows to major role identities, such as the loss of a high-status job, may not result in much loss of self-esteem (Shamir 1986).

When others' responses are ambiguous—and they usually are—we just believe what we want to.

This stability of self-esteem testifies to the skill most of us have in negotiating our self-concepts.

3.   People with high self-esteem are more confident and hence more open to new ideas and new relationships. People with low self-esteem, on the other hand, are defensive and anxious, afraid to challenge themselves or others (Michener, DeLamater, and Schwartz 1986).

We cannot all be above average. Yet studies on topics from intelligence to physical attractiveness show that hardly anybody thinks she or he is below average and large majorities think they are above average. How do people manage to protect their self-esteem? They do so by (1) using the identity salience hierarchy to emphasize roles they do well; (2) being very careful about their choice of looking glasses (Rosenberg 1979); and (3) simply interpreting others' responses in ways that support a positive self-image. When others' responses are ambiguous—and they usually are—we just believe what we want to (Felson 1985).

Summary. According to the interaction school of symbolic interaction, the individual takes an active role in negotiating the self and self-concept. These are not imposed by others or by the social structure; rather they are negotiated by the individual during the process of interacting with others. An important goal in this process is the enhancement of self-esteem.

THE STRUCTURAL SCHOOL

The structural school of symbolic interaction differs from the interaction school by stressing the importance of institutionalized social structures. Unlike the interaction school, which gives the individual a great deal of freedom in negotiating a self-concept, the structural school believes that individuals are constrained and shaped in important ways by society.

Scholars from the structural school focus on institutionalized social roles such as working, parenting, and going to school, and stress the profound ability of these roles to shape both our behavior and our personality. The key concept in structural theory is **role identity,** the image we have of our self in a specific social role (Burke 1980, 18). For example, a woman who is a professor, a mother, and an aerobics student will have a different role identity in each setting. According to structural theorists, her self-concept will be a composite of these multiple identities (Stryker 1981).

> **Role identity** is the image we have of ourself in a specific social role.

The Situated Self. Each of us has multiple role identities, one for each of our major roles. Sometimes this makes it difficult for observers—even ourselves—to decide which is the Real Me. In a sense, there is no Real Me. Instead, we use the concept of **situated identity** to refer to the role identity used in a particular situation. We can use one role identity at home, another at the office, and yet another one when we are out of town.

> **Situated identity** is the role identity used in a particular situation. It implies that our identity will depend on the situation.

The idea of a situated self draws heavily on the analogy of life as a stage. As we move from scene to scene, we change costumes, get a new script, and come out as a different character. A young man may play the role of dutiful son at home, heavy-duty partier at the dorm, and serious scholar in the classroom. None of these images is necessarily false; but because the roles are difficult to carry on simultaneously, the young man does not try to do so. Most of us engage in this practice without even thinking about it. We adjust our vocabularies, topics of conversation, and apparent values and concerns automatically as we talk to elderly relatives, our friends, and our coworkers. In this sense, each of us is like the elephant described by the six blind men; someone trying to find the Real Me might have a hard time reconciling the different views that we present.

Identity Salience Hierarchies. The concept of the situated identity implies that we play one role at a time and ignore the obligations associated with other roles. In practice, however, competing demands often develop that force us to choose between different selves. If your brother's wedding is scheduled for the same weekend that you are offered an interview for a wonderful job, which will you attend? Which self will take priority?

One mechanism for making such choices is the establishment of an **identity salience hierarchy,** a ranking of your various role identities in order of their importance (salience) to you (Callero 1985). Whenever two

> **Identity salience hierarchy** is a ranking of an individual's various role identities in order of their importance to him or her.

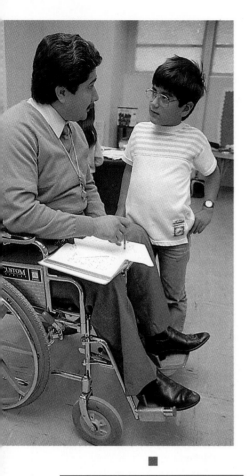

This man occupies many different statuses: he is physically handicapped, he is a teacher, he is a man, he is Hispanic. Each of these statuses provides a role identity, a set of norms that defines how he ought to act. Which takes priority? In some settings, he may react primarily as a man; in others, the teacher role will take the lead. The prominence that our role identities have can change from setting to setting, but we also have an identity salience hierarchy that makes some roles more important than others. Some handicapped people are so overwhelmed by the experience that it becomes their dominant identity; others, such as this teacher, accord it a lower place in their identity hierarchy.

roles come into conflict, you simply follow the role that ranks highest on your list. Research shows that in ranking role identities, we give preference to roles that provide us with the most self-esteem. This reflects two things: the social status associated with a role and our skill in performing it.

Most women, for example, who are both professors and aerobics students will rank being a professor higher in their identity salience hierarchy. A woman who was a very bad professor and very good aerobics student, however, might reverse the order. The relative ranking of mother and professor might be more problematic. Undoubtedly, some women would rank the professor role higher than the mother role; such women would follow the norms of their job in cases of role conflicts. Differences in identity salience hierarchies help explain why two people with the same sets of roles will behave differently (Serpe 1987). Some professor/mothers, for example, will go to the office on Saturday, while some will stay at home.

Social Structure and the Self.   Following their assumption that individual identities are shaped by institutionalized roles, symbolic interactionists from the structural school study the processes through which people who share a social status develop into similar sorts of people. They ask whether being working class as opposed to middle class or being a physician instead of a truck driver produces different patterns of personality and self-concept.

Many studies demonstrate that people who occupy different structural positions tend to have different values and personalities. For example, lower-class individuals are more likely to believe in living for the moment and less likely to think it is worthwhile to save for the future (Lewis 1969). Why is this true? Some insights come from the study, *Tally's Corner*, reviewed in Chapter 2. In this study, Liebow (1967) concluded that "it was unescapable that getting and keeping a job was of low priority" (p. 34) to the street-corner men he studied. Although some scholars have argued that these values are part of a subculture of poverty that is passed down from one generation to the next, structuralists take a different point of view. They would argue that the reason these values reappear in one generation after another is because each generation has faced the same social structure: high unemployment, low education, discrimination. Liebow argues that similarities

> do not result from "cultural transmission" but from the fact that the son goes out and independently experiences the same failures, in the same areas, and for much the same reasons as his father. What appears as a dynamic, self-sustaining cultural process is, in part at least, a relatively simple piece of social machinery which turns out, in rather mechanical fashion, independently produced look-alikes (Liebow 1967, 222–23).

In other words, the structural school argues that people who share social statuses, who experience the same kinds of role constraints and demands in their daily lives, will tend to develop similar personalities and self-concepts. Social class is one of the most important of these structured statuses, and we will return to the topic of class differences in Chapter 9.

CONCEPT SUMMARY
The Two Schools of Symbolic Interaction

	INTERACTION SCHOOL	STRUCTURAL SCHOOL
The self-concept is . . .	Negotiated	Determined by roles
The individual is . . .	Active in creating self-concept; has more freedom to choose self	Less active in creating self-concept; has less freedom to choose self
The self-concept is developed through . . .	Role taking (taking the role of others)	Performing institutionalized roles
Roles are . . .	Negotiated	Allocated
Major concepts	Looking-glass self, role taking, and self-esteem	Role identity, situated identity, and identity salience hierarchy

SYNTHESIS

Despite their differences, the structural and interaction schools have much in common. Scholars from both schools are very much in the symbolic interaction tradition: They agree that meanings are embedded in relationships and that actors have some choices in the process of arriving at meanings. The two schools should not be viewed as opposites but as complements. This relationship is diagrammed in Figure 6.1. As the interaction school suggests, self-concept affects the roles we play; it is also true, as the structural school suggests, that roles affect self-concept. In studying this reciprocal relationship between roles and self-concept, the emphases of the interaction and the structural schools may be regarded as a simple division of labor. Neither school would deny the legitimacy of their other's interests.

FIGURE 6.1

THE RELATIONSHIP BETWEEN THE STRUCTURAL AND THE INTERACTION SCHOOLS OF SYMBOLIC INTERACTION THEORY

The structural school of symbolic interaction theory emphasizes the effect of social structure on self-concept, while the interaction school emphasizes the active part that the individual plays in choosing and defining roles. Symbolic interactionists from both schools believe that the self-concept and social structure are interdependent: The roles we play and their locations in the social structure affect the self-concept we develop; on the other hand, the self is actively involved in role choices.

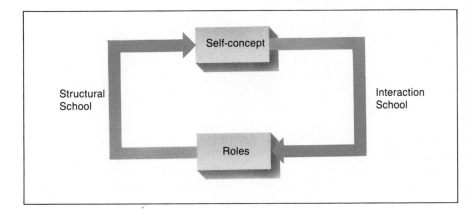

■

ROLE IDENTITY AND SELF-CONCEPT OVER THE LIFE COURSE

Our self-concept and initial social roles are learned in childhood, but we continue to learn new roles and to renegotiate our self-concept throughout our lives. Each time we join a new group or assume a new role, we learn new norms and redefine our identity. Sociologists are interested in two aspects of this process. We are interested in **socialization,** the process of learning the roles necessary for participation in social institutions, and we are interested in how role change affects self-concept and identity. In this section, we begin by reviewing theory and research on early childhood socialization and then move on to discuss role transitions in adulthood. We conclude with a section on resocialization, the process of dramatically altering our self-concept.

Socialization is the process of learning the roles, statuses, and values necessary for participation in social institutions.

EARLY CHILDHOOD

Primary socialization is personality development and role learning that occurs during early childhood.

Early childhood socialization is called **primary socialization.** It is primary in two senses: It occurs first, and it is most critical for later development. During this period, children develop personality and self-concept, acquire motor abilities, reasoning, and language skills, become aware of significant others, and are exposed to a social world consisting of roles, values, and norms.

The Family.   The most important agent of socialization is the family. As the tragic cases of child neglect and the monkey experiments so clearly demonstrate, the initial warmth and nurturance we receive at home are

■

Parents have an enormous capacity to shape their children. Is dad going to put this little girl in a frilly dress that says ''Daddy's princess'' on the front or is he going to put her in overalls that declare ''Big slugger?'' In addition to these ways that parents' expectations shape their children, the form and stability of the family are also important. A two-parent family generally provides more income, more supervision, and more stability than a one-parent family.

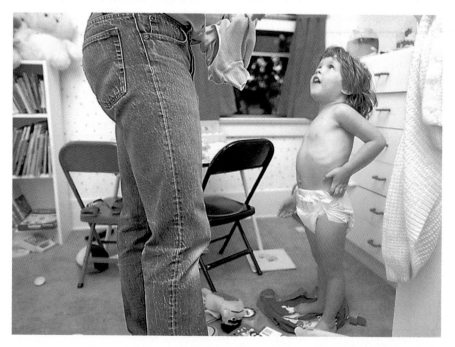

essential to normal cognitive, emotional, and physical development. In addition, our parents are our first teachers. From them we learn to tie our shoes and hold a pencil, and from them we also learn the goals and aspirations that are likely to stay with us for the rest of our lives.

The activities required to meet the physical needs of a newborn provide the initial basis for social interaction. Feeding and diaper changing give opportunities for cuddling, smiling, and talking. These nurturant activities are all vital to the infant's social and physical development; without them, the child's social, emotional, and physical growth will be stunted (Gardner 1972; Lynch 1979; Provence and Lipton 1962; Spitz 1945).

In addition to these basic developmental tasks, the child has a staggering amount of learning to do before becoming a full member of society. Much of this early learning occurs in the family as a result of daily interactions: The child learns to talk and communicate, to play house, and to get along with others. As the child becomes older, teaching is more direct and parents attempt to produce conformity and obedience, impart basic skills, and prepare the child for experiences outside the family.

One reason the family is the most important agent of socialization is that the self-concept formed during childhood has lasting consequences. In later stages of development, we pursue experiences and activities that integrate and build on the foundations established in the primary years. Although the personality and self-concept are not rigidly fixed in childhood, we are strongly conditioned by childhood experiences (Mortimer and Simmons 1978).

The family is also an important agent of socialization in that children inherit many characteristics from their parents. Most important, the parents' religion, social class, and ethnicity influence social roles and self-concept. They influence the expectations that others have for the child, and they determine the groups with which the child will interact outside the family. Thus, the family's ethnicity, class, and religion shape the child's experiences in the neighborhood, at school, and at work.

A critical aspect of family experience that is only now beginning to receive substantial research attention is family stability. A family can be unstable for many reasons: parental or sibling death, parental divorce and remarriage, parents in and out of the labor force, changing neighborhoods. A growing body of research indicates that such change can have a negative effect: The more family instability a child experiences, the more likely he or she is to experience personal and social problems in adolescence (Dornbusch 1989). These negative effects also spill over into adult life. Several recent studies show consistent negative effects on children's well-being when parents divorce: Even when parents' social class and other background variables are controlled, the children of divorced parents tend to achieve less education and to marry earlier, are more likely to have children while unmarried, and are more likely to have their own marriages break up (McLanahan 1985, 1988). The reasons are complex, but one is that a single parent can provide less supervision and one-on-one interaction than can two parents; this means the single parent may have less influence over his or her children. Also, the children of divorce may learn less traditional adult roles; their childhood role taking ("you be the mommy and I'll be the boyfriend") prepares them to replicate their parents' experiences.

As a result of the growing number of families where both parents are in the labor force, children are spending more and more time, starting from a younger age, in schools and other organized care arrangements. Studies show that these school experiences can have positive effects. When there is a low ratio of children to staff and where staff placements are stable, children can build close personal relationships with teachers as well as parents.

Preschools and Day Care.   The increasing participation of women in the labor force has added another social structure to the experience of young children: the day-care center. In 1988, nearly 50 percent of mothers of babies under one year of age were employed. Some of the children with two employed parents are cared for by relatives; in a substantial number of cases, one of their parents works a night or weekend shift so that the parents can take turns caring for their children (Presser 1988). Approximately one-quarter of all preschool children with an employed mother, however, are enrolled in a day-care center.

What are the consequences for children of this experience? Is the day-care center similar to the institutions that Spitz studied in 1945? Will day care stunt the mental, physical, and social growth of the infants and children who spend time there? As the proportion of children who attend day care has grown, so has the empirical research. The answer is that it depends. Generally, research shows that enrollment in high-quality day-care programs has no substantial negative consequences and even some positive effects. For example, a recent study of day-care centers in Sweden showed that children who began their day-care experiences early (before one year of age) scored better on many dimensions than children who didn't attend day care or who started later; children with early day-care experience did better on tests of persistence, independence, school achievement, vocabulary, and low anxiety (Andersson 1989).

There are some important restrictions on these findings, however. For children to prosper in day-care settings, the following conditions probably need to be met: stable placement, stable staff, staff training in child development, and low child-to-staff ratios (for example, one staff member for every four children) (Cole and Cole 1989, 630–32). A large number, perhaps most, day-care centers in the United States do not meet these criteria. Studies show that children placed in low-quality day-care centers (unstable and untrained staff, high child-to-staff ratios) are disadvantaged relative to children who are cared for at home or in high quality day-care centers (Vaughn, Gove, and Egeland 1980). Children placed in low-quality day-care centers have more difficulty attaching themselves to their parents and show fewer competent and more problem behaviors (Berk 1989, 456). Because low-quality day-care centers are also inexpensive, children from low-income families are more likely to experience this inadequate socialization.

SCHOOL-AGE AND ADOLESCENT YOUTH

As children grow older, they participate in more social institutions and develop wider social networks. Between the ages of six and 18, two of these social settings are particularly important: the school and the peer group. Both can play an important part in developing the child's self-concept, social and intellectual skills, and identity. Much of this learning is what sociologists call **anticipatory socialization.** It is learning that prepares us for the roles we are likely to assume in the future. Because of this socialization, most of us are more or less prepared for the responsibilities we will face as employees, college students, parents, spouses or employers. Identities have been established, skills acquired, and attitudes developed that prepare us to accept and even embrace adult roles. This takes place formally in the school system and informally in the peer group.

Anticipatory socialization is role learning that prepares us for roles we are likely to assume in the future.

Schools. In Western societies, schooling has become institutionalized as the natural habitat for children. The central function of schools in industrialized societies is to impart specific skills and abilities necessary for functioning in a highly technological society.

Schools do much more than teach basic skills and technical knowledge, however; they also transmit society's central cultural values and ideologies. Unlike the family, in which children are treated as special persons with unique needs and problems, schools expose children to situations in which the same rules, regulations, and authority patterns apply to everyone. In schools, children first learn that levels of achievement affect status in groups (Parsons 1964, 133). In this sense, schools are training grounds for roles in the workplace, the military, and other bureaucracies in which relationships are based on uniform criteria.

The types of learning that take place in schools and the effects of school structure on individuals are covered in more detail in Chapter 14.

Peer Groups. Both in and out of school, young people spend a lot of time with their peers. This natural tendency to spend time with others like ourselves has been increased in recent years by the growing likelihood of

THE FAR SIDE   By GARY LARSON

Primitive peer pressure

Adolescence is an awkward period in which young people are halfway between childhood and adulthood. As in this picture, they frequently are not very sure what pose to take as they negotiate their way through the dilemmas posed by growing independence. The peer group is an important arena for trying out the various selves that are available and seeing which ones work best.

both parents working outside of the home. This creates a vacuum that is sometimes filled through increased peer interaction.

What are the consequences of peer interaction for socialization and the development of the self-concept? Kids who hang around together tend to look and act a lot alike; they wear the same kind of clothes, have the same kinds of grades and the same levels of deviance, like the same music, and they share many attitudes. This high level of similarity has led many observers to assume that peer pressure has created conformity. The effect of peer pressure, however, has probably been substantially overestimated. Research shows that much of the similarity among group members precedes their joining the group; in other words, they hang around together *because* they share attitudes (Dornbusch 1989).

Peer groups are often thought of as parents' enemies or competitors in terms of influence and as a source of conflict between parents and children. In fact, research shows that most adolescents are more concerned about their parents' opinions than about their friends'. Although, while they are with their friends, they may engage in behavior that their parents would disapprove of, they usually do so only if they think their parents won't find out about it (Dornbusch 1989).

There are, however, three areas of a child's development where peer group socialization has an important influence (Gecas, 1981). First, it has an important effect on the development and validation of the self-concept. Unlike one's family or teachers, one's peers provide a looking glass unclouded by love or duty. Second, the peer group furnishes an important arena for practicing one's skills at role taking. Finally, the peer group is often a mechanism for learning social roles and values that adults don't want to teach. For example, much sexual knowledge and social deviance is learned in the peer group. (Few people learn to roll a joint at their mother's knee.)

Adolescence.   Adolescence is a particularly difficult time for many people. Moving into semiadult roles, changing schools, and physical maturation all require rapid adjustments in self-concept. Whether one is the first or the last to start menstruating, develop breasts, grow tall, or develop body hair, these changes require careful negotiation in order to maintain self-esteem. When these pubertal changes occur simultaneously with changes in social structure (such as the move from elementary school to junior high or the experience of one's parents' divorce), the changes can lead to low self-esteem and a negative self-concept (Simmons et al. 1987). These results may lead to an unfortunate negative spiral: Low self-esteem leads to bad decisions (pregnancy, drug use, theft), which lead to even worse self-esteem. A happy corollary of this scenario, however, is that an adolescent who manages to maintain a positive self-image experiences a positive spiral: High self-esteem leads to good performance, which leads to even higher self-esteem (Gecas 1989).

ADULTHOOD

Adulthood spans as many as 60 years. During this time, individuals go through many role changes. Some of these changes, such as getting a job, getting married, or retiring, are voluntary, and we are more or less prepared for them by anticipatory socialization. Other role changes are more problematic; we lose our jobs, become divorced, or join the army. The roles we occupy in adulthood and the changes that occur in these roles may have substantial effects on our self-concept. In the following section, we review research and theory on how one of our major adult roles—work—affects personality and self-concept. A much more detailed discussion of changes in social roles over the life course appears in Chapter 12.

The Work Role.   The work role is an important one. It determines our income, our prestige in the community, what we do all day, and whom we do it with. Not surprisingly, we find that what people do for a living affects their self-concept and personality.

For example, long-term research by Kohn and his associates indicates that the *nature* of our work affects our self-concept and behavior. The amount of autonomy, the degree of supervision and routinization, and the amount of cognitive complexity demanded by the job have important consequences. If your work demands flexibility and self-discipline, you will probably come to value these traits—at home, in government, and in religion. If your work instead requires subordination, discipline, and routine, you will come to find these traits natural and desirable (Kohn and Schooler 1983). This example of how roles affect personality and self-concept gives empirical support for the structural school of symbolic interaction.

Social standing is another aspect of work that has an important impact on self-concept and behavior. People with little power and few opportunities for upward mobility tend to reject their occupation as a dominant status. Instead they base their self-concept on such nonwork roles as runner or mother, volunteer or motorcyclist. Frequently, however, people are unable to brush aside low achievement in their work roles. As a result, those who have little opportunity or power at work may be bossier, more authoritarian, and more alienated than those whose work provides a validation of their self-worth (Kanter 1977).

Because of the salience of our work role identity, studies demonstrate that losing one's job is sometimes a major blow to the self-concept. Although many people who lose their jobs find ways to protect their self-esteem (for example, by blaming the economy or the government), studies show that unemployment increases depression, anxiety, physical illness, and sleeplessness (Kessler, Turner, and House 1989). It also reduces an individual's sense that she or he is a competent actor who can negotiate what happens (Gecas 1989). Because the threat of unemployment differs substantially by social class, this is another mechanism through which social class affects self-concept.

Role Accumulation in Adulthood.   Generally, adulthood can be viewed as a process of role accumulation: As individuals move from age 20 to 45, many become employed, a spouse, a parent, a church member, a member of a voluntary association, a home owner, and so on. What are the consequences of this accumulation of social roles? Although one might guess that multiple roles increase the opportunity for role conflict, research strongly suggests that role accumulation is a good thing: The more roles people have, the better off they are (Thoits 1986a). For example, women who are married and parents *and* employees show less psychological distress than women who are only married and parents (Thoits 1986a); if they add membership in a voluntary association, they are even better off (Moen, Dempster-Mcclain, and Williams 1989).

Why is role accumulation generally so positive? Each role gives us a role identity and some guidelines about how we ought to behave. The more roles we have, the more areas of our life are governed by such social scripts; this makes us feel certain about what we're doing and why. As a result, people with multiple roles tend to feel less anxiety and a stronger sense of purpose: They know who they are.

RESOCIALIZATION

Resocialization occurs when we abandon our self-concept and way of life for a radically different one.

The development of the self-concept is usually a gradual process over the life course, and who we are at 35 is often only incrementally different from who we were at 25. Sometimes, however, there are abrupt changes in our self-concept, and we must learn new role identities and negotiate a new self-image. **Resocialization** occurs when we abandon our self-concept and way of life for a radically different one. Changing the social behavior, values, and self-concept acquired over a lifetime of experience is difficult, and few people undertake the change voluntarily.

A tragic example of resocialization occurs when people become permanently disabled. Those who become paralyzed experience intense resocialization to adjust to their handicap. All of a sudden, their social roles and capacities are changed. Their old self-concept no longer covers the

The transformation of physical appearance is a powerful symbolic way of leaving one self-concept behind and taking on another. From the traditional buzz cut that recruits receive in the armed forces to the purple mohawk of the punker, physical transformation is an important part of resocialization. It signals to both self and audience that the old self has disappeared and been replaced with a new one.

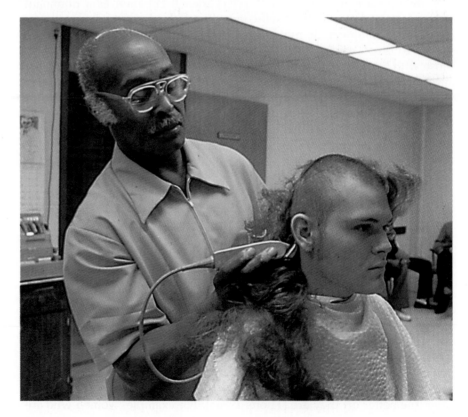

situation. They may have lost bladder and bowel control, be severely limited in their ability to get around, or be incapable of full sexual functioning. If they are young, they must face the fact that they may never marry or become parents; if they are older, they have to reevaluate roles as spouses, workers, or parents. These changes require a radical redefinition of self. If self-esteem is to remain high, priorities will have to be rearranged and new, less active roles given prominence.

Resocialization may also be deliberately imposed by society. When an individual's behavior leads to social problems—as is the case with habitual criminals, substance abusers, and the mentally disturbed—society may decree that the individual must abandon the old identity and accept a more conventional one. Most of those attempting to resocialize people assume that a radical change in self-concept requires a radical change in environment. Drug counseling one night a week is not likely to alter drastically the self-concept of a teenager who spends the rest of the week among kids who are constantly wasted. Thus, the first step in the resocialization process is to isolate the individual from his or her past environment.

This is most efficiently done in **total institutions**—facilities in which all aspects of life are strictly controlled for the purpose of radical resocialization (Goffman 1961). Monasteries, prisons, boot camps, and mental hospitals are good examples. Within them, past statuses are wiped away. Social roles and relationships that formed the basis of the previous self-concept are systematically eliminated. New statuses are symbolized by regulation clothing, rigidly scheduled activity, and new relationships. Inmates are encouraged to engage in self-analysis and self-criticism, a process intended to reveal the inferiority of past perspectives, attachments, and statuses.

Resocialization does not necessarily require a total institution. Alcoholics Anonymous (AA), for example, tries to accomplish resocialization in an out-patient setting: members learn to redefine themselves ("I am an alcoholic. I need help.") and to abandon old friends and form new ones. New members may need to go to a meeting every night or even several times a day, however, in order to sustain this new self-concept. A change in self-concept usually requires a change in social relationships and social activities.

Resocialization is a part of many religious and political conversions. For example, a Hare krishna devotee reports, "When I first joined I was concerned most with my looks and with getting a nice car and a nice apartment. But I eventually came to realize that those material things don't really count that much. . . . Now I realize that this life and body are temporary and miserable" (Snow et al. 1986, 473). This woman has abandoned her old self-concept for an entirely different one. Similarly, people who drop out of school to become full-time environmental activists change their way of life, their social networks, and their self concepts.

Few of us experience resocialization. For most of us, change is gradual and cumulative. We get a new job, fall in with a different circle of friends, and gradually change our lifestyles as we get older. If we change our religion or our politics, it is a modest change that doesn't require much rearrangement of our social relationships or our self-concept. In the "Issues in Social Policy" section of this chapter, we review one of the many sources of incremental change—the mass media.

Total institutions are facilities in which all aspects of life are strictly controlled for the purpose of radical resocialization.

Television—Socialization to Aggression?

The average American child spends five hours a day in front of a television set. During these hours, the child is exposed to a substantial amount of violence and aggression. There are brawls, shootings, shoving matches, hijackings, and verbal threats. It has been estimated that children see as many as 20,000 murders by the time they reach 16.

What do children learn from watching violence on television? In 1969, the National Commission on the Causes and Prevention of Violence concluded that "violence on television encourages violent forms of behavior and fosters moral and social values about violence in daily life which are unacceptable in a civilized society" (Eisenhower

An important element of television drama is violence. Cartoons, soap operas, and sports show people hitting each other, yelling at each other, and wishing each other dead. The most violent form of televised violence, however, is boxing. Mike Tyson and Buster Douglas are real men, drawing real blood, as they deliberately attempt to injure one another in this 1990 fight. Some social science research suggests that watching this kind of violence can desensitize viewers to others' pain, teach techniques of violence, and appear to make violence a socially approved strategy of social interaction.

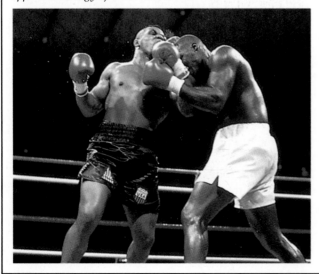

1969, 5). Since 1969, there have been hundreds of additional studies. Some studies find that media violence has strong negative effects, and a few studies find no effect; no studies document a beneficial effect. Although the data are not conclusive, the cumulative research record suggests that watching televised violence significantly increases the probability of aggressive behavior (Levinger 1986).

In one of the most extensive studies of the effect of televised violence on children, Eron interviewed all third-graders in a semirural New York county in 1960. Measures of aggressive behavior came from interviews with parents and teachers as well as fellow students. Each child interviewed was asked to name classmates "who are always starting fights for nothing" or "who were always saying mean things." In 1970, Eron reinterviewed the same children and their classmates, parents, and teachers. He concluded that "the single best predictor of how aggressive a young man would be when he was 19 years old was the violence of the television programs he preferred when he was eight years old" (Eron 1980, 246).

Interestingly, Eron found no association between the watching of televised violence and aggressive behavior among girls. He suggests that this may be because almost all aggressive role models on television are men; few violent women are portrayed. Also, girls are less likely to find the shows believable. Boys, especially the aggressive ones, see the violent shows as realistic, whereas girls are more likely to think that they are just stories.

This study provides an excellent example of why the link between aggression and televised violence is still a matter of debate. Did watching violence on television at age eight cause boys to become aggressive, or did these boys choose to watch violent shows because they were already aggressive at age eight? It may be that watching violence reinforces aggressive behavior among children who already have aggressive tendencies.

ISSUES IN SOCIAL POLICY continued

A review of the many studies of television and aggression suggests that violence is most likely to result in aggressive responses under the following conditions (Comstock 1977): when the violence in the story is (1) rewarded, (2) exciting, (3) real, and (4) justified; and when the perpetrator of the violent act (5) is not criticized for his or her behavior and (6) intends to injure his or her victim.

Much of the violence on television meets these criteria. Often the good guys are as violent as the bad guys, and their behavior is usually portrayed as intentional, justifiable, and rewarded. Most of the violence on television, however, is not real. A major exception to this is contact sports, and the most deliberate example of pure intended violence is professional boxing. Unlike in football or basketball, the object is to hit or injure the other person.

In a clever study, Phillips (1983) examined homicide rates in the United States on the days before and after highly publicized heavyweight fights. He found that homicide rates do indeed increase in the days immediately after a fight. Furthermore, the increase is directly proportional to the amount of publicity a fight receives. After one of the most publicized fights, the so-called Thrilla in Manilla between Ali and Frazier, the homicide rate was 24 percent higher than would have been expected without the fight.

How does television watching encourage violence? There appear to be three mechanisms of encouragement: desensitization, role modeling, and apparent approval. The first path through which television may encourage violence is desensitization. Watching innumerable murders, rapes, and other hostile acts hardens a viewer to others' suffering. People who watch a lot of televised violence are simply not as upset by such events—on the screen or in real life—as people who are less frequent watchers. The second learning mechanism is role modeling. Regardless of whether there is any innate tendency to aggress, the specific techniques of aggression must be learned. People have to learn the swear words, weapons, and styles of violence of their culture. Television offers a comprehensive, free education in the techniques of violence. Finally, televised violence suggests that aggression is a frequent and acceptable means of interaction: "A youngster who is continually bombarded with violence on television may well come to think that aggressive behavior is typical and therefore an appropriate way·to solve life's problems" (Eron 1980, 247).

This evidence concerning the relationship between televised violence and aggressive behavior poses a difficult dilemma for social policy. Would we like to have a society in which people were less aggressive and in which there were fewer acts of violence? Most of us would answer yes. Several organized groups, including the American Medical Association and Americans for Children's Television, would like to eliminate violence from television shows that children are likely to watch. Others oppose any sort of censorship and suggest that it is the parents' responsibility to keep their children from watching violence. To these groups, censorship of television programs is an unwarranted intrusion on individuals' freedom to watch what they choose and perhaps a violation of the networks' right to free speech. Those who oppose censorship note that nearly all of the studies linking television to personal violence are imperfect and that a great deal of controversy exists among social scientists about the magnitude of the impact (for example, Baron and Reiss 1985a, and b; Phillips and Bollen 1985). This disagreement among the experts gives grounds for caution in legislating public policy.

What do you think? Did all those years of watching *Miami Vice, Monday Night Football,* and *Hill Street Blues* increase your own aggressiveness? Would society be better off—would you be better off—if there had been less violence on television when you were growing up?

SUMMARY

1. Sociologists study the ways that social processes and relationships affect the development of the self and the self-concept.

2. Our self is socially bestowed and socially sustained. Through interaction with others we learn to be human— to walk, to love, to talk. Our innate capacities cannot develop without social interaction.

3. Symbolic interaction is the dominant theoretical framework in sociological studies of human development. It emphasizes that learning takes place through subjectively interpreted interaction, and that each of us has a part in constructing and maintaining our own self.

4. The interaction school gives the individual a very active role in constructing the self. The idea of the negotiated self suggests that we use selective interpretations to construct and maintain our self-concept with a special eye to enhancing our self-esteem.

5. The structural school stresses the profound impact of institutionalized roles and statuses on the development of the self-concept. The concepts of role identity and situated identity suggest that our self and self-concept depend in important ways on the situations or roles in which we find ourselves.

6. We learn new roles and renegotiate our self-concept throughout our lives: Primary socialization occurs in early childhood; anticipatory socialization prepares us for future roles; resocialization represents an abrupt change of self-concept.

7. Among the major agents of preadult socialization are the family, the day-care center, school, and the peer group. Of these, the family is the most important. Family background and family stability have strong effects on self-concept.

8. Studies of adult role identities show that work roles affect our self-concept and behavior. Characteristics demanded by one's job (for example, independence and self-discipline) come to be valued outside of work, too. Research generally shows that the more roles you have, the better off you are.

9. Resocialization is so difficult that few people seek it voluntarily. It often requires withdrawal from one's usual social relationships and entrance into a total institution that can control all aspects of one's life.

10. Controversial evidence suggests that a steady diet of televised violence encourages aggressive behavior. It appears to desensitize viewers, teach techniques of aggression, and suggest that aggression is an appropriate solution to life's problems.

SUGGESTED READINGS

Benedict, Ruth. 1961. Patterns of Culture. Boston, Mass.: Houghton Mifflin. Originally published in 1934. A classic that draws on several different cultures to illustrate how behavior and personality are consistent with the culture in which a person is reared. The emphasis is on the continuity of socialization.

Goffman, Erving. 1961. Asylums. Garden City, N.Y.: Anchor/Doubleday. A penetrating account of total institutions and the significance of social structure in producing conforming behavior. Primarily an analysis of mental hospitals and mental patients, although the analysis is applicable to other total institutions.

Heusmann, L. Rowell and Malamuth, Neil (eds.). 1986. Media Violence and Antisocial Behavior. Special issue of Journal of Social Issues, volume 42. A collection of essays that spans the range from pornography to children's cartoons. Included are several articles discussing intervention strategies and regulatory issues.

Kohn, Melvin L., Schooler, Carmi, and Associates. 1983. Work and Personality: An Inquiry into the Impact of Social Stratification. Norwood, N.J: Ablex. A summary of 20 years of research on the impact of work roles on personality and the self-concept. It provides strong evidence in favor of the structural school.

Rosenberg, Morris. 1979. Conceiving the Self. New York: Basic Books. A readable overview of symbolic interaction theory from the point of view of the interaction school.

Zurcher, Louis A. 1983. Social Roles: Conformity, Conflict, and Creativity. Beverly Hills: Sage. A provocative book that applies symbolic interactionism to issues of role choice and role negotiation.

7

THE SOCIOLOGY OF EVERYDAY LIFE

PROLOGUE

Have you ever . . .

Walked into a social situation and asked yourself "What is going on here?" Is this a party or a brawl? Is this a classroom or a group therapy session? Is he or she just being friendly, or is this a sexual overture?

Probably everybody has had the experience of being in a classroom where one student turns a discussion period into a personal confessional. In response to a question about how important is the family, such a student might launch into a long story about how the birth of a first child changed this student's life, perhaps including full details of the delivery, what my mother thought, etc. Most people in the classroom will be embarrassed. They know this is inappropriate.

This embarrassing episode is an example of what happens when someone reaches the wrong answer to the question, "What is going on here?" Unfortunately, a great deal of daily life includes the possibility of such dilemmas. Although culture provides a general pattern for living, much of our day-to-day interaction is problematic. Even after we figure out what is going on, we still find ourselves groping about trying to figure out what is appropriate and what is inappropriate.

The sociology of everyday life is concerned with these processes. It focuses on how individuals analyze their own social settings.

The **sociology of everyday life** focuses on the social processes that structure our experience in ordinary face-to-face situations.

This chapter—a companion to the previous one—examines social structures from the point of view of individual actors. Where chapter 6 covered the development of the self-concept, this chapter looks at the self as it moves through its everyday affairs.

The **sociology of everyday life** focuses on the social processes that structure our experience in ordinary face-to-face situations. This perspective directs our attention away from the larger frameworks that structure our lives toward the processes that structure our behavior in concrete situations. For example, how do we decide what to talk about at the breakfast table? How do we respond when introduced to a stranger? These are the types of concrete situations of interest: They involve specific people in a specific setting.

Concern with everyday life takes us in two rather different directions. One way shows us the ordinary routines of daily life, the patterned social regularities that govern face-to-face encounters. The other directs our attention to the management of problematic situations, where routines and norms provide ambiguous guides to conduct.

THE ROUTINE NATURE OF DAILY LIFE

Everyday life is governed by taken-for-granted routines. The most important routines we use for interaction with others are carried out through talk. We all learn dozens of these verbal routines and can usually pull out an appropriate one to suit each occasion. Small rituals such as

"Hello. How are you?"
"Fine. How are you?"
"Fine."

will carry us through dozens of encounters every day. If we supplement this ritual with half a dozen others, such as "thanks/you're welcome" and "excuse me/okay," we will be equipped to meet most of the repetitive situations of daily life.

To illustrate the degree to which our interaction is governed by taken-for-granted routines, let's look at the routines governing use of physical space.

MANAGING PERSONAL SPACE

Careful observation of routine behavior on sidewalks, in classrooms, and in elevators shows that there are definite norms about the use of space. Like the Supreme Court judge who couldn't define obscenity but knew it when he saw it, we are able to conform to the norms and be offended by their violation even if we are not able to say exactly what these norms are.

Norms about the use of space vary substantially from culture to culture. American norms generally require that people stay farther away from each other than do the norms of other cultures. Each of us has an invisible circle around himself or herself that we regard as our personal space. Only selected others—by invitation only—are welcome within this space. Observation suggests that distances up to 18 inches are reserved for intimates and distances between 18 and 48 inches are reserved for personal but not intimate exchanges (Hall 1969). Most of us are very sensitive to violations of these rules. If we are waiting for an elevator, we typically stand six to eight feet away from strangers; this is not a personal relationship. When we get on a bus with only one other passenger, we generally select a seat several rows away instead of one right next to a stranger.

When people do violate the rules about the use of physical space, when they encroach on our personal space, we experience this as punishing. Take the example of a coworker who comes to within 12 inches of you in a conversation. You back up, he steps forward. You back up again, and he follows again. You are likely to define this as sexual harassment. In any case, you will find such a violation of personal space unpleasant, even threatening.

Riding the Elevator. Goffman (1967) gives a detailed account of the routines we automatically follow in riding elevators. His account conveys the sense of how unknowingly rule bound are so many of our daily encounters.

Goffman likens an elevator ride to a dance, in which the physical positioning of the riders is altered in a patterned way with each addition and subtraction to the number of passengers. The dance is guided by two motifs: Each person faces the front and maintains an equal distance between himself or herself and all other passengers. A woman getting onto an empty elevator may stand wherever she chooses; when the second person gets on, she moves over so that each passenger takes up an opposite side of the elevator; when a third person gets on, all rearrange themselves so that all three are equidistant. The dance continues with every new passenger so that the principle of equal distance is maintained. When passengers start leaving the elevator, the same process is repeated in reverse: People move away from others so that equal distance is maintained as more space becomes available.

The elevator ride also illustrates the routine mechanisms we use to manage physical closeness without intimacy. On crowded elevators or buses or while waiting in ticket lines, we use a device termed *civil inattention* to discourage intimacy. Civil inattention requires a polite acknowledgment of the other's physical presence accompanied by social withdrawal: A nod or other acknowledgment is made, and then the gaze is averted and silence is maintained (Goffman 1963a). If you speak to the person against whom you are squeezed, you are likely to receive a frosty reply or more probably none at all, for you will have violated one of the rules governing social relationships.

Personal Space and Status. Norms about personal space are closely related to social status. The more important you are, the larger is your personal space. This explains several patterned regularities, such as why office size grows with status. It also explains a differential freedom to touch and be touched. Generally, we find that a superior is free to violate an inferior's personal space (Henley 1977). A coach, for example, may pat a player's bottom, but a player is not allowed to pat the coach. Although concerns about inappropriate sexual behavior have reduced the legitimacy of touching, children are touched by adults and women by men more often than the reverse.

Grocery shopping, riding elevators, finding seats in crowded auditoriums—all these and many other mundane activities of everyday life are covered by rituals and spatial norms. This man's enthusiasm for tomatoes led him to violate at least two American norms: he didn't wait his turn and he touched a stranger. As a result, his fellow shopper is rightly surprised and annoyed.

THE IMPORTANCE OF ROUTINE

Routines such as those involving space or greeting acquaintances are so mundane that they may appear to be a foolish topic for scholarly inquiry. Nevertheless, social life depends on routine, on the predictability of others' responses (Goffman 1983). Consider behavior such as driving. Safe passage clearly requires that you and all the other drivers behave in expected ways. In a less life-threatening manner, safe passage through social encounters also depends on routine. If you had no idea what to expect of passersby on the street or sales clerks in the store, each encounter would be potentially disastrous. Because you do know what to expect, you feel relatively confident about your ability to negotiate such encounters smoothly. The routines and rituals of daily life may be very ordinary, but they are not trivial; they are vital for helping us organize and interpret our daily lives. When people do not follow the routines, we usually figure they are trying to cause trouble and we punish them accordingly.

THE SOCIOLOGY OF EVERYDAY LIFE: THE ASSUMPTIONS

The sociology of everyday life is closely identified with the interaction school of symbolic interaction theory. Like that school, it stresses the role of subjective meanings assigned to symbolic communications and the active role of the individual in negotiating roles and identities. Scholars who use the everyday life (EDL) perspective, however, emphasize four additional assumptions: the problematic nature of culture, the dialectic, biography, and thick description.

THE PROBLEMATIC NATURE OF CULTURE

In Chapter 3, we likened culture to a design for living and to a tool kit. If you consider these two images, you will see that they offer subtly different meanings of culture. The "design for living" image suggests a set of blueprints that need only to be correctly followed; the "tool kit" image, on the other hand, suggests a more dynamic approach. You do not follow a tool kit, you *use* it.

The sociology of everyday life is based on the tool kit image. It assumes that day-to-day behavior is not a matter of following clear cultural scripts but of improvising, negotiating, and adjusting to the general outline. From this point of view, culture is problematic.

Culture does furnish a great many rules and rituals, but it is not always clear which rules apply when. Being honest and standing by your friends are both norms; what do we do when telling the truth gets a friend in trouble? This predicament emphasizes that conformity to cultural norms is problematic: It requires a continual stream of choices (Oberschall and Leifer 1986).

THE DIALECTIC

The rules that govern our behavior may contradict each other; they may also contradict our own wishes.

Scholars from the EDL perspective take seriously the I/me split of the self proposed by Mead (Chapter 6). They recognize that, on the sidelines of every social encounter, the I stands ready to assert itself—to barge in and do something impulsive and perhaps selfish. Any concrete situation can be envisioned as a negotiation between these two parts of our self.

This negotiation can be viewed as a dialectic, a process of conflict between individual freedom and social constraint (Bensman and Lilienfeld 1979). Here is a commonplace example: You are hurrying down the sidewalk, late for class, and you pass an acquaintance with a quick "Hi there, Lori, how are you?" Instead of replying as expected, Lori stops and proceeds to tell you that she is real depressed because she has just heard that her mother has cancer. So now what do you do? One aspect of your social self (the me) may tell you that you must pause and show interest and concern. But perhaps your I, the spontaneous, impulsive part of your self, wants to keep hurrying to class. After all, you hardly know Lori, much less her mother. In this case and in many others, your behavior represents a dialectic, a conflict between social convention and individual impulses.

For all of us culture is problematic, offering dozens of potentially conflicting normative prescriptions. Culture is especially problematic for those, such as these two girls, who are caught between two worlds. For all of us, however, life requires a constant stream of choices between alternative cultural imperatives. Everyday life is not just a matter of following the rules; it must be negotiated.

A dialectic is not a simple contradiction but a process in which opposing forces engage, meet, and produce change. Viewing interaction episodes as a dialectic leads to the proposition that social interactions are never completely programmed by social structures. The outcome of a conflict is never fully predictable.

BIOGRAPHY

Each of us possesses a personal history, a biography, that makes us unique. Although we share many things, none of our experiences exactly duplicates the experience of another. Although we may all face similar social constraints, as in the awkward episode of Lori's mother, we will each bring a different self to the dialectic. Because of this, no two encounters are identical.

The uniqueness of each encounter does not mean that there is no patterned regularity in everyday life. Almost all of our daily encounters follow recognizable routines that allow us to interact without awkwardness, even with strangers. These routines explain the similarities in our encounters; biography explains why each one is just a little different from the rest.

THICK DESCRIPTION

The sociology of everyday life uses a methodological technique called thick description. Unlike thin description (who did what when), *thick description* tells us why the actors did what they did and what it meant to them. Thick description requires that we get into the actors' conceptual world, that we understand what is going on in their heads (Geertz 1973).

The switch from thin to thick description brings about an important change in the stance that observers take toward reality. Scholars such as Durkheim and Comte assumed that there exists an objective reality and that the goal of science is to put aside all personal, or subjective, ideas so that this objective reality can be studied. Sociologists of everyday life, on the contrary, assume that there are multiple subjective realities and that the world as I see it is just as real as the world as you see it. Thick description is the attempt to understand the subjective social worlds of individual actors in specific situations (Lincoln and Guba 1985).

The sociology of everyday life is in many ways the application of the interaction school to the mundane encounters of daily life. It stands apart from other branches of sociology, however, because of its emphasis on the problematic nature of culture, the dialectic, biography, and the reality of subjective worlds.

MANAGING EVERYDAY LIFE

Much of our daily life is covered by routines like the "Hi, how are you?" "Fine, you?" "Fine" exchange. Nevertheless, each encounter is potentially problematic, and successful interaction requires selecting the appropriate routine plus the skill and motivation to carry it out.

■

FOCUS ON YESTERDAY

Everday Life for City Kids in 1900

Scholars rely heavily on diaries and other personal histories to penetrate the everyday lives of people in past times (Blee and Billings 1986). These sources are not from a random selection of the past, nor is the information contained in them necessarily objectively true. Even in diaries never intended to be shared, the authors reflect their own points of view, undoubtedly frequently mixed with accounts and disclaimers of various sorts. Nevertheless, scholars of everyday life accept such material as being a true view of life as they experienced it.

In *Children of the City*, David Nasaw (1985) uses this kind of material to unravel the everyday life of children in America's urban centers at the beginning of this century. Although Nasaw cites government reports and sociologists such as Jane Addams, he obviously believes that the truer picture comes from the personal histories. In addition to biographies of the rich and famous, he mines a major new source of data on everyday life: oral history collections of the memories of ordinary women and men. In this way, Nasaw hopes to develop a thick description of what it meant *to the kids* to be a kid in New York or Boston in 1900.

Almost uniformly, reformers and sociologists were alarmed about children's lives in the cities. Their homes were so crowded that they virtually lived in the streets, intimate with prostitutes and bums, at constant risk of death or injury from street traffic. The kids saw it differently.

From the child's point of view, living on the streets meant freedom from adult control. A single block might have hundreds of children living on it. When they all played in the street (and there was no room for them indoors), the streets became theirs. There they organized their own life, freely violating many of their seniors' expectations. They associated with people their parents didn't approve of, played craps and gambled for pennies, and learned things their parents would have preferred they not know. Reformers tried to help children by building playgrounds, but the children were, not surprisingly, unenthusiastic about the adult supervision that went with them.

According to these accounts, one of the best things about city living for children was the opportunity to work and earn money away from their families. These opportunities were especially great for boys: selling newspapers, running messages, selling candy or gum, or shining shoes. Although they were expected to turn all of their income over to their parents—and most boys turned most of it over—the children could easily save out a few pennies or a nickel for themselves. This could be spent in a wide variety of new establishments that courted children's custom—candy stores, hot-dog stands, cheap nickelodeons. One woman reported that when she was a girl she often spent an entire Saturday morning spending a single nickel, walking up and down the aisles of the dime store, picking up and considering one object after another. When clerks questioned her, she just showed them her nickel and they left her alone. Having money of your own made you somebody, gave you rights.

In recollection, the children of the city around 1900 enjoyed great independence. Working was no novelty; children had always had to work. What was new was the variety of jobs to choose from, independence from their parents and often from any adult supervision whatever, personal profit from their work, and exciting places to spend their money.

Which version of children's life in the city is objectively real? The question is of more than historical interest. Children are frequently a population without a voice. People tell us about children instead of children telling us about themselves. Consider how this might affect other contemporary issues about children—for example, the effects of television or day care.

Despite the multitude of norms and rituals that we share, daily life is still problematic and there are countless situations every day that puzzle us. People act in unexpected ways, messages get garbled, and dilemmas confront us. Like the man pictured here, we may have to pause a moment and ask ourselves, "What is going on here?" Negotiating our way through daily living requires real skill in analyzing social settings.

At the beginning of any encounter, individuals must resolve two issues: (1) What is going on here—what is the nature of the action? (2) What identities will be granted—who are the actors? All action depends on our answers to these questions. Even the decision to ignore a stranger in the hallway presupposes that we have asked and answered these questions to our satisfaction. How do we do this?

FRAMES

The first step in any encounter is to develop an answer to the question, "What is going on here?" The answer forms a frame, or framework, for the encounter. A **frame** is a definition of the situation, a set of expectations about the nature of the interaction episode that is taking place.

All face-to-face encounters are preceded by a framework of expectations—how people will act, what they will mean by their actions, and so on. Even the most simple encounter, say, approaching a salesclerk to buy a package of gum, is covered by dozens of expectations: We expect that the salesclerk will speak English, will wait on the person who got to the counter first, will charge exactly the sum on the package and will not try to barter with us, will not comment on the fact that we are overweight or need a haircut. These expectations—the frame—give us guidance on how we should act and allow us to evaluate the encounter as normal or as deviant.

A **frame** is an answer to the question, what is going on here? It is roughly identical to a definition of the situation.

Sometimes our initial framing of events gets us into trouble and, instead of helping us, our definition of the situation only leads to greater perplexity. In such situations, we will have to revise the frame for the encounter and redefine what is going on (Goffman 1974b). Imagine, for example, a police officer coming across a group of rowdy kids. "Now, kids," he says, "you'd better be getting off home." If they respond with obscenities and thrown beer cans, he will reverse his definition of what is going on and prepare for a possibly violent encounter. His initial frame is obviously inappropriate.

   In most of our routine encounters, our frames will be shared with other actors. This is not always the case. We may simply be wrong in our assessment of what is going on, or other actors in the encounter may have an entirely different frame. The final frame that we use to define the situation will be the result of a negotiation among the actors.

IDENTITY NEGOTIATION

After we have put a frame on an encounter, we negotiate an answer to the second question: What identities will be granted? This question is far more complex than attaching names to the actors. Because each of us has a repertoire of roles and identities from which to choose, we are frequently uncertain about which identity an actor is presenting *in this specific situation.*

   To some extent, identities will be determined by the frame being used. If a student visit to a professor's office is framed as an academic tutorial, then the professor's academic identity is the relevant one. If the visit is framed as a social visit, then other aspects of the professor's identity (hobbies, family life, and so on) become relevant.

   In many routine encounters, identities are not problematic. Although confusion about identities is a frequent device in comedy (for example, the films *Being There, Big,* and *Trading Places*), in real life, a few verbal exchanges are usually sufficient to resolve confusion about the actors' identities. In some cases, however, identity definitions are a matter of serious conflict. For example, I want to be considered a status equal, but you wish to treat me as an inferior.

   Resolving the identity issue involves negotiations about both your own and the other's identity. How do we negotiate another's identity? We do so by trying to manipulate others into playing the roles we have assigned them. Mostly we handle this through talk. For example, "Let me introduce Mary, the computer whiz," sets up a different encounter than "Let me introduce Mary, the best party giver I know." Of course, others may reject

Although George Bush undoubtedly spends more time in a suit than in his fishing clothes, this attire symbolizes one of President Bush's salient role identities, "first sportsman." All of us use clothing as a prop to support the roles we play. When we change from pumps to sneakers, from a sportscoat to hip waders, we signal a change in identity. All of us try to affect others' opinions of us by the way we dress and present ouselves.

Dramaturgy is a version of symbolic interaction that views social situations as scenes manipulated by the actors to convey the desired impression to the audience.

■

Even those who have very high self-esteem seek out ways to enhance and maintain their credit with others. Unfortunately, there are very few occasions on which we can wear all of our awards on our shirt. Most of us have to seek somewhat more subtle ways to demonstrate what wonderful people we are.

your casting decisions. Mary may prefer to present a different identity than you have suggested. In which case, she will begin to try to renegotiate her identity.

Identity issues can become a major hidden agenda in interactions. Imagine an incompetent man talking to a competent woman. If the man finds this situation uncomfortable, he may try to define it as a man/woman encounter rather than a competence encounter. He may start with techniques such as "How do you, as a woman, feel about this?" To reinforce this simple device, he will probably follow up with remarks such as "You're so small, it makes me feel like a giant." He may interrupt her by remarking on her perfume. He may also use a variety of nonverbal strategies such as stretching his arm across the back of her chair to assert dominance. Through such strategies, actors try to negotiate both their own and the other's identity.

DRAMATURGY

The management of everyday life is the focus of a sociological perspective called dramaturgy. **Dramaturgy** is a version of symbolic interaction that views social situations as scenes manipulated by the actors to convey the desired impression to the audience.

The chief architect of the dramaturgical perspective is Erving Goffman (1959, 1963a). To Goffman, all the world is a theater. The theater has both a front region, the stage, where the performance is given, and a back region, where rehearsals take place and behavior inappropriate for the stage may appear. For example, waiters at expensive restaurants are acutely aware of being onstage and act in a dignified and formal manner. Once in the kitchen, however, they may be transformed back into rowdy college kids.

The ultimate back region for most of us, the place where we can be our real selves, is at home. Even here, however, front-region behavior is called for when company comes. ("Oh, yes, we always keep our house this clean.") On such occasions, a married couple functions as a team in a performance designed to manage their guests' impressions. People who were screaming at each other before the doorbell rang suddenly start calling each other "dear" and "honey." The guests are the audience, and they too play a role. By seeming to believe the team's act (Goffman calls this "giving deference"), they contribute to a successful visit.

Nonverbal Cues.   A successful act requires careful stage management. Not only must the script be right, but costumes and props and body gestures must support our act.

DRESS.   All of us who have stood in front of our closet wondering what to wear have faced the dilemma of how to present our self. Although most of us have many outfits that meet the necessary criteria of covering our bodies decently and dealing with the climate, we choose among potential outfits based on the impression we would like to create. Concepts such as dressing for success are examples of this. From punk haircuts to cowboy boots, the way we dress furnishes important auxiliary information to our audience; it can either support our act or discredit it.

BODY LANGUAGE. The cues we give through facial expressions, eye contact, and posture can enhance, reinforce, or even contradict the meaning of a verbal communication. For example, when words of affection are accompanied by hugs or caresses, the verbal statements are enhanced and reinforced. When words of encouragement and interest are delivered without looking up from the newspaper, however, the verbal statements are contradicted by actions. Whether intended or unintended, the impression given belies and discredits the verbal communication.

In other cases, gestures and posture may substitute entirely for verbal communication. Anybody who has watched a football game will be familiar with the small drama where a receiver who drops an important pass falls to the ground and drums the turf with his hands. This communicates that he took his failure seriously and he is mad at himself. In effect, it says, "You don't need to bawl me out, Coach, I know I goofed and I feel really bad about it and I'll try my best not to do it again."

CUING STATUS. Nonverbal cues are used extensively to send out messages that would be socially awkward if expressed verbally. Sexual interest is one of these messages. Another is a message about social status. It is difficult to say outright, "You know that I'm more important than you, don't you?" Thus, such messages are sent through nonverbal cues.

Studies of status encounters in laboratories show that the following nonverbal strategies are used to signal dominance: looking directly into the other's eyes while listening and speaking, taking up a lot of physical space (sprawling in one's chair, putting a foot on another chair, leaning an arm across the back of another chair), choosing a seat at the end of the table, interrupting others, and being the first person to speak (Ridgeway, Berger, and Smith 1985). In these last two instances, the timing of the speech acts has an effect independent of their symbolic content. The effectiveness of these strategies is confirmed if we consider the status inferences we would make of a person who did just the opposite: who wouldn't look at us, scrunched up in the corner of the chair, chose an unassuming position at the table, and was hesitant to speak.

Although some nonverbal communication appears to have universal meaning, most nonverbal communication must be framed before it can be accurately understood. A women who takes a long glance up and down a man's body shows that she is interested in his body. Only knowledge of the context will tell you what that means. Is she a doctor looking at him with clinical interest? A tailor? A cannibal? A woman looking for a sexual encounter? An employer sizing up a laborer? As this suggests, a variety of meanings can be associated with the same behavior. The correct interpretation depends on the social context, interactions, and biographies of members.

WHOSE DEFINITION? EX-WIFE AT THE FUNERAL

How we act in any encounter depends in large part on the frame we have developed and the identities we and the other participants have worked out. One of the many processes of negotiation that goes on in social encounters is determining whose definition of the situation will be accepted.

The person who wins this negotiation gains a powerful advantage. A paper by Riedmann (1987) on the role of the ex-wife at the funeral is an insightful illustration of this process.

In this case, a 44-year-old man dies suddenly and accidentally at the home he shares with his new wife of six months. Immediately after the accident, his 20-year-old daughter, who is staying with them, calls her mother to break the news. The ex-wife is terribly upset: She went steady with Bill from age 16 to 22 and was married to him for 20 years; even after the divorce and his remarriage, they remained friends and had lunch frequently. Although they could no longer live together, they shared a concern for their two children and half a lifetime of memories. His parents were almost as close to her as her own; she had spent many summer afternoons with his brothers and their children.

When informed of his death, therefore, she felt bereaved. Her first response was "What? Our dad is dead?" Her definition of the situation was that she had had a death in her family. Acting on this definition, she went over to the home of her parents-in-law. Here she came up against a different definition. From the in-laws' position, it was a death in their family but not in her family. Although they did not say so, they wanted her to leave quickly before the current wife came over.

Over the next few days, the ex-wife again and again ran into the dilemmas posed by contrasting definitions of the situation. The obituary did not mention her as among the relatives left behind. When she went to view the body at the mortuary, she was denied admittance on the grounds that only members of the immediate family were eligible. When the minister asked everybody but the immediate family to leave the graveyard, she was supposed to leave. Although the ex-wife defined Bill's death as a death in her family, it was not a definition commonly shared.

The ex-wife and the new wife formed teams, each trying to pursue its own definition of the situation. The "old family team" (made up of the ex-wife, one of her children, her relatives, and one brother-in-law) and the "new family team" competed to be recognized as the "real family team." At the funeral service itself, each team held down one corner of the lobby. When family and friends entered the lobby, they were faced with the predicament of which team to console first. Since many of Bill's old friends knew the ex-wife well and the new wife not at all, the "old family team" may be considered to have won this round.

Because of legal relationships, in the end the ex-wife was relatively powerless to impose her definition of the situation. The mortician and the priest were paid agents of the "new family team." The ex-wife was ultimately forced to reframe the situation and to recognize her powerlessness to impose her definition of the situation on others.

ETHNOMETHODOLOGY

From the EDL perspective, daily life is a series of problematic encounters. Successful negotiation through this maze of predicaments requires the actor to have some pretty good theories about human nature and how others are likely to act.

How do we arrive at these common-sense theories? The study of the everyday strategies that individuals use to understand their world is called **ethnomethodology.** Generally, *methodology* is the study of scientific and technical procedures such as sampling and statistical analysis; *ethnomethodology* studies folk methods, the procedures you and I use to analyze everyday situations.

Ethnomethodology is the study of the everyday strategies that individuals use to study and organize their world.

The everyday process of understanding our own social world is similar in broad outline to the processes that sociologists use to understand social structure. We begin the interaction episode on the basis of a working hypothesis about what is going on and then watch others' reactions. If the response is consistent with our hypothesis, we feel it is confirmed and keep acting on this basis. If the response suggests that our hypothesis is wrong, however, we reformulate our hypothesis, test it, and watch for new clues. Every social encounter is a little bit like the wheel of science we discussed in Chapter 2, an ongoing process of discovery.

Imagine, for example, meeting your friend John after a period of a couple of months. Your working hypothesis is that nothing has changed since the last time you met. You say, "How's your wife?" John says, "We've separated." Your first hypothesis is obviously wrong, so, to test a new one, you cautiously venture, "That's too bad." "No, it's not," says John. "Our marriage was making us both miserable." Now you are starting to get enough information so that you know how to behave. In the words of Garfinkel (1967), you have "found your feet."

Ethnomethodology is closely linked to the work of Harold Garfinkel, a Harvard-trained sociologist whose central concern is determining the common understandings that individuals use in making sense out of their world. We cover just two of these here: the assumption that appearances are real and that other people know what we know, that they share our symbolic world.

Some of the underlying norms that govern everyday life are not immediately obvious to us, yet we blow up when they are violated. Perhaps one of these people has failed to learn one of the basic norms that governs human relations: Don't ever criticize another person's parents or children or even agree with them when they are critical!

APPEARANCES ARE REALITY

A major hypothesis underlying all our daily interactions is that people are who they appear to be. Our working hypothesis in any interaction episode is that appearances can be trusted: The woman in a police uniform *is* a police officer; the man behind the counter *is* a real salesclerk.

The corollary to this hypothesis is just as important: We assume that others will trust our appearances.

This mutual trust is critical to social interaction. If somebody says they are 22 years old or Catholic, it is considered a hostile act to say, "Prove it." To appreciate the importance of accepting people at their word, you need only recall that one of the surest ways to provoke a fight on the playground is to say, "Oh, yeah?" To challenge another's presentation of self is to undermine the entire basis of social interaction.

SHARED SYMBOLIC WORLDS

Another major working hypothesis that seems to be essential for social relationships is that others share our symbolic worlds. This means that we assume people know what we know and that things have the same meanings for them as they do for us.

One of the ways Garfinkel developed to bring these expectations out in the open was to disrupt normal routines by causing trouble. These deliberate attempts to cause trouble are called *break experiments*. Two examples show how important the assumption of shared meanings is to normal interaction (Garfinkel 1963, 221) In both cases E, the experimenter, is one of Garfinkel's students, acting on orders, and S, the subject, is an unwitting participant.

Case 1: The subject was telling the experimenter, a member of the subject's car pool, about having had a flat tire while going to work the previous day.

    S: I had a flat tire.
    E: What do you mean, you had a flat tire?

The subject appeared momentarily stunned. Then she answered in a hostile way, "What do you mean 'what do you mean?' A flat tire is a flat tire. That is what I meant. Nothing special. What a crazy question!"

Case 2: On Friday night E and her husband were watching television.

    S: I'm tired.
    E: How are you tired? Physically, mentally, or just bored?
    S: I don't know, I guess physically, mainly.
    E: You mean that your muscles ache, or your bones?
    S: I guess so. Don't be so technical.

After some more watching:

    S: All these old movies have the same kind of old iron bedstead in them.
    E: What do you mean?

S: What's the matter with you? You know what I mean.
E: I wish you would be more specific.
S: You know what I mean! Drop dead!

Both of these cases involve violations of our expectation that others know what we know. The key response in both is the subject's angry retort, "What do you mean 'what do you mean?' " In neither case can the subject account for the lack of shared symbolic worlds except that E is crazy, sick, or hostile. The possibility that E really doesn't know what S means doesn't appear to cross S's mind. Notice that in both cases interaction breaks down completely when the assumption of shared meanings is shattered.

■

IDENTITY WORK

Most social scientists wish to go beyond simple descriptions of behavior and ask *why* people do what they do. The answer most often supplied by scholars studying everyday behavior is that people are trying to enhance their self-esteem. One commentator noted wryly that this research assumes an "approval-starved person hot on the trail of a compliment" (Schneider 1981). More generally, we assume that social approval is one of the most important rewards that human interaction has to offer and we try to manage our identities so that this approval is maximized.

Managing identities to support and sustain our self-esteem is called identity work (Snow and Anderson 1987). It consists of two general strategies: avoiding blame and gaining credit (Tedeschi and Riess 1981).

AVOIDING BLAME

There are many potential sources of damage to our self-concept. We may have lost our job or flunked a class; on a more mundane level, we may have said the most embarrassing and stupidest thing imaginable, been unintentionally rude to an older relative, or otherwise made a fool of ourselves. When we behave in ways that make us look bad, that embarrass us and make others think badly of us, then it is important to try to repair the damage.

Most of this repair work is done through talk. We try to explain away our bad behavior by giving *accounts* that will make our mistakes seem excusable or justifiable (Scott and Lyman 1968; Stokes and Hewit 1976).

In an early study of norm violations and how we deal with them, C. Wright Mills (1940, 909) noted that we learn the vocabulary for making excuses at the same time we learn the norms themselves. We learn what the rules are, and we simultaneously learn what kinds of accounts will excuse or justify our violations. If we can successfully explain away our norm violations, then we can reestablish ourselves as the kind of person who normally follows the rules and who deserves to be thought well of by ourselves and others.

The process of excusing our norm violations occurs daily in all types of social settings. One of the most fruitful areas for really innovative accounts occurs in the student role. Students are expected to attend class, study, and turn papers in on time. Many times, however, they don't. How

■

Learning to take criticism and advice without being defensive is one of the hardest tasks that most of us face. How do we take suggestions for improvement while avoiding blame and protecting our self esteem? Generally, effective supervisors and critics will help us in this task. They wil temper their criticism with compliments and note that we are making excellent progress or producing a fine piece of work. This kind of teamwork helps us maintain our self-esteem and contributes to a smooth relationship.

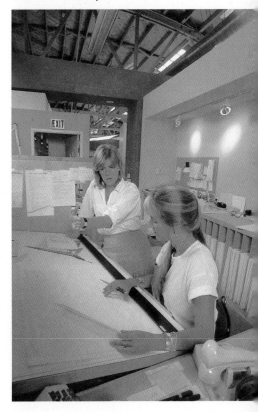

do students try to explain away their norm violations so that they and their teachers maintain a good opinion of them?

Kathleen Kalab, a sociology professor at Western Kentucky University, asked her students to explain in writing why they missed class. Her students' answers show us how identity work takes place. For example, one student said,

> Sorry I wasn't here but Friday my parents called and our entire herd of cattle broke out and were all over the county and then I got to castrate two 500-lb. bull calves. So needless to say I was extremely busy (Kalab 1987, 75).

This student hopes that the teacher will forgive him because he had sacrificed his performance in his student role in order to be a good son.

In a related vein, others argue that they were involved unavoidably in work or athletic events and that doing a good job in these other roles required them to miss class. For example,

> I am really sorry for missing your class Friday. The reason being I was part of my Reserve unit's advance party to Fort Knox. I didn't know this until late Thursday night. So please excuse me for not being here (Kalab 1987, 77).

Or

> I do want to apologize for missing class on Wednesday [date]. I am a nightclerk (it's necessary to help pay out of state) and I worked Sun. and Tues. night as well as staying up all night Mon. for a major test on Tuesday (Kalab 1987, 76).

In all three of these accounts, the students have argued that they missed class *because* they were so hardworking and responsible. They justified their behavior by appealing to another norm. Other students had to rely on illness or oversleeping to account for their behavior. When all else failed, students admitted that they didn't have a very good reason, but apologized and asked for forgiveness.

> I am so sorry I missed your class, among others, Tuesday the [date]. The reason I missed is a simple yet probably unacceptable reason, I slept until 1:45 PM. Not only did I sleep through Sociology, I also slept through these things: Geography, trash pick-up at Poland Hall, maintenance workers sawing down a tree outside my window, my alarm clock (I believe), and many other loud and interesting things. Please see your way clear of forgiving me for this horrible and strange event (Kalab 1987, 79).

Or

> I am sorry to say that I missed your wonderful lecture Friday [date]. I know there is no good reason for this. Especially since I don't have one. I had a terminal case of the LAZIES. Please don't hate me (Kalab 1987, 82).

Accounts such as these are verbal devices we use to try to restore a good image of ourselves, both in our own eyes and in the eyes of others. They help us avoid self-blame for deviant behavior, and they try to reduce the blame that others might attribute to us. If we are successful in this identity work, we can retain fairly good reputations despite a few failures in meeting our social responsibilities.

GAINING CREDIT

Our compliment-starved actor will not be content just to be thought a good sort of person; she wants all the credit she can get. This means that she will employ a variety of verbal devices to associate herself with positive outcomes. Just as there are a variety of ways to avoid blame, there are many ways to claim credit. One way is to link yourself spatially or verbally to situations or individuals that have high status. This ranges from making a $1,000 donation to a political fund-raiser so that you can have a photograph of yourself with the president to aligning yourself verbally with "our" team (when it is winning).

Claiming credit is a strategy that requires considerable tact. Bragging is generally considered inappropriate, and if you pat yourself too hard on the back, you are likely to find that others will refuse to do so. The trick is to find the delicate balance where others are subtly reminded of your admirable qualities without your having actually to ask for or demand praise.

Again, the classroom and the negotiation of the student identity are good sources of examples about how we go about doing positive identity work. In an imaginative study, Daniel and Cheryl Albas (1988) at the University of Manitoba did some systematic analysis of how their students managed their identity when papers were returned. We focus here on how the "aces," the students who have done very well on examinations, manage to claim credit successfully. The aces want to claim all the credit they can, but must somehow avoid the appearance of bragging or being condescending toward the "bombers," their classmates who have done poorly.

The Albases note that the aces differ in the sophistication with which they claim credit. Almost all aces leave their examinations open on their desks with the grade prominently displayed; some go so far as to tap their exams noisily on the desk and otherwise try to draw attention to their scores. In general, however, the aces want more than notice; they want praise. This means that they have to induce others to talk to them about their grades. A crude tactic is simply to walk up to another student and say, "I got 95 percent. What did you get?" Such crude tactics are not very effective. Unless the other student has done as well or better than the ace, he or she will be annoyed, may refuse to answer, and will certainly withhold the desired praise. After an exam or two, aces who use this tactic will find that people are avoiding them. Experienced aces use a variety of more subtle tactics. They start with "Boy, that was a hard exam. I didn't do as well as I thought. How did you do?" This expression of sympathy is likely to elicit both the other student's score and a question about how the ace did. This strategy protects the ace from the criticism of having bragged; the ace gives his or her own score only in response to a question from another.

Being a gracious winner is sometimes harder than being a gracious loser, and it is difficult for aces to interact with bombers in a way that protects the bomber's identity. One strategy that is used is to blame both success and failure on luck. When talking to a bomber, an ace may argue that "it was only luck that I studied the stuff that was on the exam." Through strategies such as this, the ace gets double credit: for being a good student and for being a nice person.

Because the classroom is an explicitly competitive setting, it is an arena that demands a lot of identity work. Every day there are papers, grades, tests, and performances that may reflect either poorly or positively on our self-esteem and our social roles. Whether we squeal with delight when informed of a good grade or just tap our papers meaningfully on our desks, most of us try to get as much credit as we can for our good work.

A CASE STUDY OF IDENTITY WORK: THE HOMELESS

A particularly useful illustration of identity work can be seen in individuals who have what Goffman (1961b) calls *spoiled identities*—identities that are not merely low in status but are actively rejected by society. Examples include the severely handicapped, traitors, and, in some communities, people with AIDS. How do people with spoiled identities sustain their self-esteem?

In 1961, Goffman argued that two general strategies for protecting one's self-esteem in the face of a spoiled identity are (1) physically withdrawing from interaction with higher-status others and (2) trying to pass as a member of some higher-status group. People with AIDS might use these strategies successfully; the homeless cannot. They cannot pass since their clothing and circumstances firmly declare their current status. Physical withdrawal is also difficult: By definition, the homeless have nowhere to go. Lacking these two options, what strategies do these women and men use to negotiate a positive identity?

A recent study among the homeless in Austin, Texas, investigated such identity mechanisms. David Snow and Leon Anderson (1987) ate at the Salvation Army and hung out under bridges and at the plasma center. They listened to homeless people talk about themselves, trying to discover the processes that these people used to negotiate their identities and protect their self-esteem.

PROCEDURES AND CONTEXT

Snow and Anderson used the strategies of participant observation described in Chapter 2 to study homeless people. Just as Eliot Liebow had done for *Tally's Corner*, these two sociologists dressed in their oldest clothes and hung around just to see what was happening. Although their study is of the homeless in one city, they argue that their results are probably applicable to the homeless everywhere. Not only are the homeless a mobile population that drifts from city to city and state to state, but "aside from variations in climate and the availability of free shelter and food, most aspects of life on the street are quite similar from one city to another. We think it is therefore reasonable to expect considerable similarity in basic patterns and process of identity construction and avowal among the homeless" (1987, 1341).

Snow and Anderson did not take notes or use tape recorders while on the street, but they took copious notes after each shift of observation. Although they announced their true identities to some of the street people they talked with, for the most part they passed as fellow homeless. They asked few direct questions, but used an interviewing style that they call "interviewing by comment." For example, instead of asking what a person is doing on the streets, they would say something like "I haven't seen you around." This indirect method of interviewing allowed them to see what the street person would volunteer about himself or herself.

RESULTS

As they analyzed the kinds of stories they heard from the street people in Austin, Snow and Anderson found that they fell into three general categories: role distancing, role embracement, and storytelling. All are verbal strategies that help the homeless maintain their self-esteem and develop a positive identity.

Role Distancing.   Whether we're homeless or not, we occasionally find ourselves playing a role that does us no credit. Students, for example, often have low-status jobs such as working at a fast-food outlet or even sorting laundry at their dormitory. When we have roles that do us no credit, we engage in a process of *role distancing*, explaining to anyone who will listen that this is just temporary and not a reflection of who we really are. We reject this role identity.

Snow and Anderson found that role distancing was one of the most common forms of identity work among the homeless. For example, a 24-year-old man who has been on the street for only a few weeks says, "I'm not like the other guys who hang out down at the 'Sally' [Salvation Army]. If you want to know about street people, I can tell you about them; but you can't really learn about street people from studying me, because I'm different" (1987, 1349).

Role Embracement.   Some of the street people that Snow and Anderson studied had been on the streets for years, and they recognized that this might be a permanent way of life. They coped with this by developing romantic notions of "brethren of the road" and cultivating nicknames such as Boxcar Billy and Panama Red. These people would introduce themselves as bums and tramps; it was one of their salient role identities.

Although it might not appear to be obvious to outsiders, there are degrees of success in performing the role of street person. Those who had embraced the role took pride in their skill at such activities as panhandling and "dumpster diving" (going through trash cans for food, clothing, recyclables, and so on). They also took pride in their independence from conventional constraints and their ability to get food and shelter without toeing the line. These people looked down their nose at those who depended on the Salvation Army to take care of them; a real street person could take care of himself or herself.

Storytelling.   A final form of identity work that the homeless engage in is storytelling. This is most common among those who have been on the street less than four years and who have not yet embraced a street identity. These stories have the purpose of establishing a positive, nonstreet identity by telling others how important one once was or how rich one will be or could easily be. One homeless man who was hanging around a transient

This photograph was taken outside of the Salvation Army in Austin, Texas where David Snow and Leon Anderson did their participant observation study of the homeless. Their research shows that many of the people who hang out at the "Sally" manage to neotiate a positive identity despite being homeless. Getting by without a job, car, money, or house requires a lot of ingenuity, and some longterm homeless take pride in their ability to fend for themselves.

bar bumming cigarettes and beers announced often that he had been offered a job as a mechanic with Harley-Davidson at $18.50 per hour. Others
told stories about the future—how they were going to set up their own
business, inherit a lot of money, or buy extravagant presents for their
families.

Some of these stories were within the realm of reason, but most were
not. Either the story itself was extraordinarily improbable (one man claimed
to have been a guard on the nonexistent Alaska-Siberia border), or the
stories changed so much from day to day that they were no longer believable. Although these unbelievable stories were generally saved for strangers
or chance acquaintances, Snow and Anderson found that tactful audiences
could be relied upon to give deference to the act of storytelling even if they
knew perfectly well that it was all a story. On the street, as well as in more
conventional settings, an unspoken norm is that one doesn't ask too many
questions or challenge a person's stories about himself or herself. In this
way, the street people work together to support one another's identity
claims.

CONCLUSION

The homeless people that Snow and Anderson studied had all the ingredients for the formation of a negative identity: They were hungry, poor,
ragged, homeless, frequently drunk and sick, and unemployed. It is not
too surprising that some of them had negative self-images. More surprisingly, many managed to feel good about themselves. Somehow they had
found it possible to construct a positive identity. Their success in doing so
reaffirms the assumptions made by the interaction school: Even in the face
of a spoiled identity, we can negotiate a positive self-concept.

WHERE THIS LEAVES US

In the 1950s, structural-functional theory dominated sociology, and there
was a great deal of emphasis on the power of institutionalized norms to
determine behavior. Durkheim, with his views on positivism and constraint,
was a favorite classic theorist. Similarly, during this period, the structural
school of symbolic interaction theory clearly dominated the interaction
school, and theorists stressed the power of institutionalized roles to *determine* behavior and personality.

Beginning in the 1960s, sociologists grew increasingly concerned that
this view of human behavior reflected an "oversocialized view of man"
(Wrong 1961). In 1967, Garfinkel signaled rebellion against this perspective
when he argued that the deterministic model presented people as "judgmental dopes" who couldn't do their own thinking.

In the last decade, sociological thinkers have increasingly tended to
view social behavior as more negotiable and less rule bound (Perrow 1986).
This change is most obvious in the sociology of everyday life, but it is also
evident in most other areas of sociology. Studies of mental hospitals, businesses, and complex organizations now suggest that the behavior of actors
may be best understood as a game in which each player chooses a strategy
to maximize her or his self-interest (Crozier and Friedberg 1980). Even

bureaucracies are not seen as wholly deterministic. Employees stress some rules, ignore others, and reinterpret the rest (Fine 1984).

This does not mean that the rules don't make a difference. Indeed, they make a great deal of difference, and there are obvious limits to the extent to which we can negotiate given situations. As W. I. Thomas noted in 1923, "The child is always born into a group of people among whom all the general types of situation which may arise have already been defined and corresponding rules of conduct developed, and where he has not the slightest chance of making his definitions and following his wishes without interference" (cited in Shalin 1986).

The perspective of life as problematic and negotiable is a useful balance to the role of social structure in determining behavior. Our behavior is neither entirely negotiable nor entirely determined.

The Homeless

Over the past five years there has been growing attention to the plight of the homeless in American cities. Estimates of the number of homeless vary from 300,000 to 3 million, depending on the season of the year, the location, and, perhaps more important, on who is doing the counting ("Another Winter" 1989). There is general consensus, however, that the number is embarrassingly large for a rich society such as ours and that the number is growing. As a result, there have been camp-outs on the White House lawn and national marches to encourage federal action. Before we can establish a policy to eliminate homelessness, however, we must have some idea of what causes it. There seem to be two different perspectives: mental illness and structured disadvantage.

THE MENTAL ILLNESS EXPLANATION

In the early 1970s, there was a general move across the country to "deinstitutionalize" the population in state mental hospitals. It was argued that many were being held for little reason and were receiving little treatment. The state would save money and the patients would be happier, it was argued, if they were discharged back into everyday life. As a result, the population of state mental hospitals was dramatically reduced, and tens of thousands of former mental patients were released. In the ensuing years, only the most severely mentally ill have been institutionalized, with the result that many people who are clinically mental ill are out in society; some of them are on the streets (Wright 1988).

Many observers blame the increase in homelessness squarely on the abdication of responsibility by the state hospitals. One observer concluded that "the streets, the train and bus stations, and the shelters have become the state hospitals of yesterday" (cited in Snow et al. 1986). People who hold this position believe that many, if not most, of the homeless are mentally ill. If this position is

The growing problem of homeless families reflects two simultaneous trends, the loss of good working-class jobs and the loss of low-income housing. As a result, a growing number of individuals and families find that they are unable to afford decent housing. Some of the homeless do have personal problems such as mental illess or alcoholism, but many others are simply victims of a changing economy and housing market.

correct, then one solution to homelessness is more mental hospitals.

STRUCTURED HOMELESSNESS

Other scholars argue that, although homelessness isn't likely to improve anybody's mental health,

ISSUES IN SOCIAL POLICY continued

the root cause is lack of opportunity, not mental illness. These scholars point out that (1) a larger proportion of all jobs than ever before pay the minimum wage; (2) the minimum wage remained unchanged from 1972 to 1990 although the cost of living rose 50 percent during that period; and (3) that a substantial portion of the low-cost housing in U.S. cities has been razed to make room for convention centers and domed stadiums (Wright and Lam 1987).

David Snow and Leon Anderson, who have spent more time with the homeless than most policy makers, reject the notion that these people are mentally ill; they are impressed by the resourcefulness the homeless show in obtaining food and shelter and in protecting their self-esteem. They argue that people are homeless because they cannot afford homes (Snow et al. 1986). Even if they were to have jobs, work regularly, and spend responsibly, people who earn the minimum wage find it difficult to find housing. According to federal poverty guidelines, one can afford to spend 25 percent of after-tax income on housing. This means that the average full-time, full-year worker who gets paid $3.80 an hour can afford to pay $125 a month for rent and utilities. Do you know of any places in your community where you can get room, heat, electricity, and water for this price? In most communities, there are fewer and fewer such places as derelict and run-down housing is replaced by urban renewal projects.

According to this perspective, the solution to the problem is building more low-income housing and raising the minimum wage.

DISCUSSION

The social policy dilemma regarding the homeless is an excellent opportunity to apply the sociological imagination. Is homelessness a personal trouble? Can we lay the blame on the illness, disorganization, and character flaws among the homeless themselves? Or, on the other hand, is homelessness the latent dysfunction of social pol-

icy decisions that have systematically reduced the earnings and the housing available to the poor?

The homeless live in a crazy world. When you live in a crazy world, you may need to act crazy in order to get along (Goffman 1971). Although living on the street has been considered an indicator of mental illness, it has been argued that the remarkable resourcefulness of many of the homeless could be taken as an indicator of mental *health* (Wright 1988a).

Snow and Anderson's research shows that many homeless people manage to provide for basic physical needs and maintain a reasonable level of self-esteem. Although many of the homeless can get by in the terrible circumstances in which they find themselves, it is equally obvious that—from anyone's subjective perspective—this is not a good life. Perhaps 40 percent of the homeless are alcoholics, most are malnourished, many are physically ill, and between 10 and 35 percent are mentally ill (Wright 1988a); in many cases, these conditions are the *result* of homelessness, not the cause of it.

It is ironic that homelessness and the Department of Housing and Urban Development (HUD) scandals are simultaneously on the front page of the newspaper. HUD is the federal agency charged with providing low-income housing; instead, it appears to have been more intent on enriching developer's pockets (Moore and Hoban-Moore 1990). As a result, one study showed that in 12 of our largest cities, the percent below the poverty line increased 36 percent while the stock of low-income housing declined by 30 percent (Wright and Lam 1987). Since increasing the availability of low-income housing is the obvious first step toward reducing homelessness, we must hope that the federal government can get its own house in order.

SUMMARY

1. The sociology of everyday life is a perspective that analyzes the patterns of human social behavior in concrete encounters in daily life.

2. Social life depends on routines. Because we share expectations, we can coordinate our behavior with others. Thus, we find that even very mundane aspects of our social relationships, including how we ride on elevators and greet people in the hall, are covered by routine expectations.

3. Four assumptions guide theory and research in this approach to studying human interaction: Culture is problematic; individuals experience a dialectic between freedom and social constraint; each individual is unique, possessing a biography unlike any other individual; and understanding everyday life can be accomplished best through thick descriptions.

4. Deciding how to act in a given encounter requires answering two questions: What is going on here? What identities will be granted? These issues of framing and identity resolution may involve competition and negotiation between actors or teams of actors.

5. Dramaturgy is a perspective pioneered by Erving Goffman. It views the self as a strategist who is choosing roles and setting scenes to maximize self-interest.

6. Ethnomethodology is a perspective linked with Harold Garfinkel. It is concerned with the common-sense assumptions that individuals make about human nature and society in going about their everyday affairs. Two of these assumptions are that appearances are reality and that others share our symbolic worlds.

7. The desire for approval is an important factor guiding human behavior. To maximize this approval, people engage in active identity work to sustain and support their self-esteem. This work takes two forms: avoiding blame and gaining credit.

8. The old image of people as "judgmental dopes" whose actions are determined by culture is being replaced by an image of people as active agents in interpreting culture. This change is reflected in the development of the sociology of everyday life and also in increased emphasis on the negotiated order in bureaucracies and social institutions.

9. The homeless use these three strategies in their identity work: role distancing, role embracement, and storytelling. As a result, many are able to negotiate a positive self-image.

10. Two explanations for increased homelessness are reduced institutionalization for the mentally ill and an increase in low-income jobs accompanied by a decrease in low-income housing. Social policy requires more low-income housing.

SUGGESTED READINGS

Goffman, Erving. 1959. The Presentation of Self in Everyday Life. New York: Doubleday. The book in which Goffman lays out the basic ideas behind dramaturgy. Each of Goffman's books is enjoyable reading and easily accessible to the undergraduate.

Goffman, Erving. 1967. Interaction Ritual: Essays in Face-to-Face Behavior. New York: Doubleday-Anchor. A collection of essays dealing with identity work in a variety of familiar as well as unfamiliar settings.

Momeni, Jamshi (ed.). 1989, 1990. Homelessness in the United States, Volumes I and II. Westport, Conn.: Greenwood. Summarizes local and state-level surveys on homelessness. Essays in these volumes address causes and consequences of homelessness, characteristics of the homeless, and suggested solutions.

Nasaw, David. 1985. Children of the City: At Work and at Play. New York: Oxford. An everyday-life perspective on the lives of urban children at the turn of the last century.

Weigert, Andrew J. 1981. Sociology of Everyday Life. New York: Longman. An introductory sociology book written entirely from the EDL perspective.

DEVIANCE, CRIME, AND SOCIAL CONTROL

Have you ever . . .

Been tempted to do something illegal? Have you, for example, thought how easy it would be to steal something from a department store or from somebody's yard? If you are like a lot of us, you have not only thought about doing something illegal but you *have* done something illegal as well. It may have been as minor as "forgetting" to pay for a pack of gum or as major as "borrowing" a car, but, like most people, you have engaged in some deviance.

A critical question for sociologists is why we don't deviate more often. Why do so many people do what we expect them to so much of the time? A 1987 Pittsburgh scandal exposed four men assigned the job of counting church collections after services who had been systematically stealing from the collection plate. Each week, these men had been walking off with more than $1,000. What is amazing is the thousands of collection-plate counters all over the nation who do *not* make off with the money, despite the very low likelihood that they would be caught.

In this chapter we consider the social forces that compel most of us to conform most of the time. We also consider why some of us go through a period of delinquency and others are habitually deviant.

191

CONFORMITY, NONCONFORMITY, AND DEVIANCE

In providing a blueprint for living, our culture supplies sets of norms and values that structure our behavior. They tell us what we ought to believe in and what we ought to do. Because we are brought up to accept them, for the most part we do what we ought to do and think as we ought to think. Only for the most part, however, since none of us follows all the rules all the time.

Previous chapters concentrated on how norms and values structure our lives and how we learn them through socialization. This chapter considers some of the ways individuals break out of these patterns—from relatively unimportant eccentric behaviors to serious violations of others' rights.

SOCIAL CONTROL

Social control consists of the forces and processes that encourage conformity, including self-control, informal control, and formal control.

An understanding of deviance and nonconformity requires that we first consider what brings about conformity. The forces and processes that encourage conformity are known as **social control**. Social control takes place at three levels:

1. Through self-control, we police ourselves.
2. Through informal controls, our friends and intimates reward us for conformity and punish us for nonconformity.
3. Through formal controls, the state or other authorities discourage nonconformity.

Internalization occurs when individuals accept the norms and values of their group and make conformity to these norms part of their self-concept.

Self-control occurs because individuals **internalize** the norms and values of their group. They make conformity to these norms part of their self-concept. Thus, most of us do not murder, rape, or rob, not simply because we are afraid the police would catch us but because it never occurs to us to do these things; they would violate our sense of self-identity. A powerful support to self-control is **informal social control**, self-restraint exercised because of fear of what others will think. Thus, even if your own values did not prevent you from cheating on a test, you might be deterred by the thought of how embarrassing it would be to get caught. Your friends might sneer at you or drop you altogether; your family would be disappointed in you; your professor might publicly embarrass you by denouncing you to the class. If none of these considerations is a deterrent, you might be scared into conformity by the thought of **formal social controls**, administrative sanctions such as fines, expulsion, or imprisonment. Cheaters, for example, face formal sanctions such as automatic failing grades and dismissal from school.

Informal social control is self-restraint exercised because of fear of what others will think.

Formal social controls are administrative sanctions such as fines, expulsion, and imprisonment.

Whether we are talking about cheating on examinations or murdering people, social control rests largely on self-control and informal social controls. Few formal agencies have the ability to force compliance to rules that are not supported by individual or group values (Scheff 1988). Sex is a good example. In some states, sex between unmarried persons is illegal, and you can be fined or imprisoned for it. Even if the police devoted a substantial part of their energies to stamping out illegal sex, however, they would probably not succeed. In contemporary America, a substantial proportion of unmarried people are not embarrassed about having sexual relations; they do not care if their friends know about it. In such conditions, formal sanctions cannot enforce conformity. Laws that are not supported by broad public consensus—for example, laws governing speeding, distribution of liquor to minors, or seat belt use—are likely to be widely violated.

DEVIANCE VERSUS NONCONFORMITY

People may break out of cultural patterns for a variety of reasons and in a variety of ways. Whether your nonconformity is regarded as deviant or merely eccentric depends on the seriousness of the rule you violate. If you wear bib overalls to church or carry a potted palm with you everywhere, you will be challenging the rules of conventional behavior. Probably nobody will care too much, however; these are minor kinds of nonconformity. We speak of **deviance** when norm violations exceed the tolerance level of the community and result in negative sanctions. Deviance is behavior of which others disapprove to the extent that they believe something ought to be done about it (Archer 1985).

Deviance is Relative.   Defining deviance as behavior of which others disapprove has an interesting implication: It is not the act that is important but the audience. The same act may be deviant in front of one audience but not another, deviant in one place but not another.

Few acts are intrinsically deviant. Even taking another's life may be acceptable in war, police work, or self-defense. Whether an act is regarded as deviant often depends on the time, the place, the individual, and the audience. For this reason, sociologists stress that *deviance is relative.* Some examples: Alcohol use is deviant for adolescents but not for adults; having two wives is deviant for the United States but not for Nigeria; carrying a gun to town is deviant in the late 20th century but was not in the 19th century; wearing a skirt is deviant for an American male but not for an American female.

The sociology of deviance has two concerns: why people break the rules of their time and place and the processes through which the rules get established. In the following sections, we review several major theories of deviance before looking at crime rates in the United States.

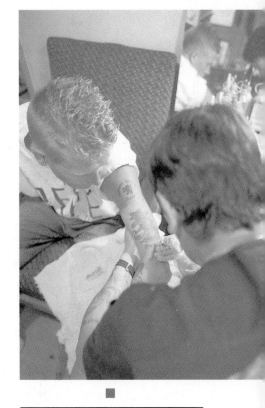

Getting a tattoo isn't against the law and your neighbors probably won't reject you. On the other hand, your mother and father are not likely to be real pleased about it. Tattooing is an example of behavior that steps out of conventional rules without crossing over into deviance. It is an example of nonconformity, but it does not violate any major norms or arouse public disapproval.

■

THEORIES ABOUT DEVIANCE

There are a dozen or more theories about deviant behavior. For the sake of order, we present them in three groups according to our familiar theoretical framework: structural-functional theories, symbolic interaction theories, and conflict theories.

STRUCTURAL-FUNCTIONAL THEORY

In Chapter 1, we said that the basic premise of structural-functional theory is that the parts of society work together like the parts of an organism.

Deviance refers to norm violations that exceed the tolerance level of the community and result in negative sanctions.

From this point of view, deviance is alien to society, an indication that the parts are not working right.

This perspective was first applied to the explanation of deviance by Durkheim in his classic study of suicide ([1897]1951). Durkheim was trying to explain why people in industrialized societies are more likely to commit suicide than are people in other societies. He suggested that in traditional societies the rules tend to be well known and widely supported. As a society grows larger, becomes more heterogeneous, and experiences rapid social change, the norms of society may be unclear or no longer applicable to current conditions. Durkheim called this situation **anomie**; he believed that it was a major cause of suicide in industrializing nations.

Anomie is a situation where the norms of society are unclear or no longer applicable to current conditions.

The anomie idea was broadened to apply to all sorts of deviant behavior in Robert Merton's (1957) **strain theory**. Strain theory suggests that deviance results when culturally approved goals cannot be reached by culturally approved means. This is most likely in the case of our strong cultural emphasis on economic success and achievement. The goals of educational and economic achievement are widely shared. The means to live up to these goals, however, are not. In particular, Merton argued, people from the lower social classes have less opportunity to become successful. They find that the norms about achievement are not applicable to their situation.

Strain theory suggests that deviance occurs when culturally approved goals cannot be reached by culturally approved means.

Of course, not all people who find society's norms inapplicable to their situation will turn to a life of crime. Merton identifies four ways in which people adapt to situations of anomie (see the Concept Summary): innovation, ritualism, retreatism, and rebellion. The mode of adaptation depends on whether an individual accepts or rejects society's cultural goals and accepts or rejects appropriate ways of achieving them.

People who accept both society's goals and society's norms about how to reach them are conformists. Most of us conform most of the time. When people cannot successfully reach society's goals using society's rules, however, deviance is a likely result. One form deviance may take is innovation; people accept society's goals but develop alternative means of reaching them. Innovators, for example, may pursue academic achievement through cheating, athletic achievement through steroids, or economic success through prostitution or selling drugs. In these instances, deviance rests on using illegitimate means to accomplish socially desirable goals.

Other people who are blocked from achieving socially desired goals respond by rejecting the goals themselves. Ritualists slavishly go through the motions prescribed by society, but their goal is security not success. Their major hope is that they will not be noticed. Thus, they do their work carefully, even compulsively. Although ritualists may appear to be over-conformers, Merton says they are deviant because they have rejected our society's values on achievement and upward mobility. They have turned their back on normative goals but are clinging desperately to procedure. Retreatists, by contrast, adapt by rejecting both procedures and goals. They are society's dropouts: the vagabonds, drifters, and street people. The final mode of adaptation—rebellion—involves the rejection of society's goals and means and the adoption of alternatives that challenge society's usual patterns. Rebels are the people who start communes or revolutions to create an alternative society. Unlike retreatists, they are committed to working toward a different society.

CONCEPT SUMMARY
Types of Strain Deviance

Merton's strain theory of deviance suggests that deviance results whenever there is a disparity between institutionalized goals and the means available to reach them. Individuals caught in this dilemma may reject the goals or the means or both. In doing so, they become deviants.

MODES OF ADAPTATION	CULTURAL GOALS	INSTITUTIONAL MEANS
CONFORMITY	Accepted	Accepted
DEVIANCE		
Innovation	Accepted	Rejected
Ritualism	Rejected	Accepted
Retreatism	Rejected	Rejected
Rebellion	Rejected/replaced	Rejected/replaced

SOURCE: Adapted from Merton 1957, 140.

The basic idea of Merton's theory is that, in complex and rapidly changing societies, there are dislocations between ends and means that encourage individuals to commit acts that are defined as deviant (Douglas and Waksler 1982). This theory explicitly defines deviance as a social problem rather than a personal trouble; it is a property of the social structure, not of the individual. As a consequence, the solution to deviance lies not in reforming the individual deviant but in reducing the mismatch between structured goals and structured means.

Two basic criticisms of strain theory have emerged. First, conflict theorists object to its structural-functional roots. Strain theory suggests that deviance results from a lack of integration among the parts of a social structure (norms, goals, and resources); it is viewed as an abnormal state produced by extraordinary circumstances. Conflict theorists, however, see deviance as a natural and inevitable product of competition in a society in which groups have different access to scarce resources. They suggest that the ongoing processes of competition should be the real focus of deviance studies (Lemert 1981).

Second, critics question Merton's assertion that deviance is more characteristic of lower-class people. There is evidence that most lower-class people are able to adjust their goals downward sufficiently so that they can be reached by respectable means (Simons and Gray 1989). In addition, there is overwhelming evidence that many highly successful individuals adjust their goals so far upward that they cannot reach them by legitimate means. The Wall Street scandals of the late 1980s, which revealed that men who earned $500 million a year were cheating to earn still more, are clear evidence that the means-versus-goals discrepancy is not limited to the lower class.

At all ages, whether we conform or get into trouble depends a lot on who we hang around with. Kids who grow up in tough neighborhoods, where good jobs are impossible dreams and getting into trouble is a way of life, are more likely to be delinquent than kids who grow up in better neighborhoods. Although girls generally get in a lot less trouble than boys, growing up in a poor, inner-city neighborhood will make it hard for these pre-teen girls to stay completely out of trouble.

In spite of these criticisms, sociologists continue to find strain theory both interesting and useful as an explanation of deviance. It underscores the sociological view that society, not the individual, is an important cause of deviant behavior.

SYMBOLIC INTERACTION THEORIES

Symbolic interaction theories of deviance suggest that deviance is learned through interaction with others and involves the development of a deviant self-concept. Deviance is not believed to be a direct product of the social structure but of specific face-to-face interactions. There are three forms of this argument: differential association theory, deterrence theories, and labeling theory.

Differential Association Theory.   In the late 1940s, Edwin Sutherland developed a theory to explain the common observation that kids who grow up in neighborhoods where there are many delinquents are more likely to be delinquent themselves. **Differential association theory** argues that people learn to be deviant when more of their associates favor deviance than favor conformity.

How does differential association encourage deviance? There are two primary mechanisms. First, if our interactions are mostly with deviants, we may develop a biased image of the generalized other. We may learn that, of course, everybody steals or, or course, being able to beat other

Differential association theory argues that people learn to be deviant when more of their associates favor deviance than favor conformity.

people up is the most important criterion for judging a person. The norms that we internalize may be very different from those of conventional society. The second mechanism has to do with reinforcements. Even if we learn conventional norms, a deviant subculture will not reward us for following them. In fact, a deviant subculture may reward us for violating the norms. Through these mechanisms, we can learn that deviance is acceptable and rewarded.

Differential association theory stems largely from the structural school of symbolic interaction. People develop a deviant identity because they are thrust into a deviant subculture. The situation determines the identity.

Deterrence Theories.

Many contemporary scholars use some form of deterrence theory to explain deviance. **Deterrence theories** suggest that deviance results when social sanctions, formal and informal, provide insufficient rewards for conformity. Deterrence theories combine elements of structural-functional and symbolic interaction theories. Although they place the primary blame for deviance on an inadequate (dysfunctional) sanctioning system, they also assign the individual an active role in choosing whether to deviate or conform. This theory assumes that the actor assesses the relative balance of positive and negative sanctions and makes a cost/benefit decision about whether to conform or be deviant (Pilavin et al. 1986; Paternoster 1989). When social structures do not provide adequate rewards for conformity, a larger portion of the population will choose deviance.

Empirical studies show that three kinds of rewards are especially important in deterring deviance: instrumental rewards, family ties, and self-esteem.

INSTRUMENTAL REWARDS. Unemployment and low wages are among the very best predictors of crime rates at any age (Devine, Shaley, and Smith 1988; Williams and Flewelling 1988). People with no jobs or with dead-end jobs have little to lose and perhaps much to gain from deviance. People who have or can look forward to good jobs, on the other hand, are likely to conclude that they have too much to lose by being deviant.

FAMILY TIES. Consistent evidence shows that young people with strong bonds to their parents are more likely to conform (Hirschi 1969). Parents are in a very strong position to exert informal sanctions that encourage conformity, and young people who are close to their parents are vulnerable to these informal sanctions. Because divorce frequently results in reduced ties to non-custodial parents, this theory helps explain why youths from broken homes are more likely to be delinquent (Matsueda and Heimer 1987; Sampson and Groves 1989).

SELF-ESTEEM. On a more symbolic level, deterrence theory suggests that people choose deviance or conformity depending on which will do the most to enhance their self-esteem (Kaplan, Martin, and Johnson 1986). For most of us, self-esteem is enhanced by conformity; we are rewarded for following the rules. People whose efforts are not rewarded, however, may find deviance an attractive alternative in their search for positive feedback.

Deterrence theories suggest that deviance results when social sanctions, formal and informal, provide insufficient rewards for conformity.

Although anything is possible, one would be pretty safe in predicting that this boy will manage to stay out of trouble. Why? Because he receives significant rewards for conventional behavior. He has trophies on his mantel, and friends and family who admire him. People who receive many rewards for following the rules are much less tempted by opportunities for deviance.

Especially among lower-class boys, delinquency has been found to be a means of improving self-esteem (Rosenberg, Schooler, and Schoenbach 1989).

According to deterrence theorists, positive sanctions give individuals a "stake in conformity"—something to lose, whether it's a job, parental approval, or self-esteem. When social structures fail to reward conformity, individuals have less to lose by choosing deviance.

Labeling Theory.   A third theory of deviance that combines symbolic interaction and conflict theories is labeling theory. **Labeling theory** is concerned with the processes by which the label *deviant* comes to be attached to specific people and specific behaviors. This theory takes to heart the maxim that deviance is relative. As the chief proponent of labeling theory puts it, "Deviant behavior is behavior that people so label" (Becker 1963, 90).

The process through which a person becomes labeled as deviant depends on the reactions of others toward nonconforming behavior. The first time a child acts up in class, it may be owing to high spirits or a bad mood. This impulsive act is *primary deviance.* What happens in the future depends on how others interpret the act. If teachers, counselors, and other children label the child a troublemaker *and* if she accepts this definition as part of her self-concept, then she may take on the role of a troublemaker. Continued rule violation because of a deviant self-concept is called *secondary deviance.*

This explanation of deviance fits in neatly with the structural school of symbolic interactionism. Deviance becomes yet another role identity that is integrated into the self-concept.

POWER AND LABELING.   A crucial question for labeling theorists is the process by which an individual comes to be labeled deviant. Many labeling theorists take a conflict perspective when answering this question. They assume that one of the strategies groups use in competing with one another is to get the other group's behavior labeled as deviant while protecting its own behavior. Naturally, the more power a group has, the more likely it is to be able to brand its competitors deviant. This, labeling theorists allege, explains why lower-class deviance is more likely to be subject to criminal sanctions than is upper-class deviance.

FROM SIN TO SICKNESS.   In recent years there has been an increasing tendency for behaviors that used to be labeled deviant to be labeled illnesses instead. For example, many now consider alcoholism to be a disease. When a form of deviance becomes accepted as illness, social reaction changes. It is no longer appropriate to put people in jail for being public drunks; instead they are put in hospitals. Physicians and counselors, rather than judges and sheriffs, treat them. The changing relationship between disease and deviance is treated in more detail in Chapter 18.

Individuals who acquire *sick* rather than *bad* labels are entitled to treatment rather than punishment and are allowed to absolve themselves from blame for their behavior (Conrad and Schneider 1980). As you might expect, people in positions of power are more apt to be successful in claiming the sick label. For example, the upper-class woman who shoplifts is likely to

Labeling theory is concerned with the processes by which labels such as *deviant,* come to be attached to specific people and specific behaviors.

be labeled neurotic, whereas the lower-class woman who steals the same items is likely to be labeled a shoplifter. The middle-class boy who acts up in school may be defined as hyperactive, the lower-class boy as a troublemaker.

EVALUATION.   Labeling theory combines elements of symbolic interaction and conflict theory. The deviant label becomes part of the self-concept, affecting further interaction. But this deviant label is imposed by powerful others rather than being self-selected.

The theory has become extremely popular in the last 30 years and has been applied in diverse situations (Chapter 14 discusses labeling in the schools, for example). It does, however, have some important limitations. One critic sums these up by saying that labeling theory gives the impression that this innocent guy was just walking along when, wham, society stuck the label *deviant* on him, and after that he had no choice but to cause trouble (Akers 1968).

More formally, labeling theory is criticized because (1) it doesn't explain primary deviance; (2) its emphasis on the relativity of deviance suggests that the only thing wrong with murder or assault is that someone arbitrarily called it deviant; and (3) it cannot explain repeated deviance by those who haven't been caught, that is, labeled.

CONFLICT THEORY

Conflict theory proposes that competition and class conflict within society create deviance. Class conflict affects deviance in two ways (Archer 1985): (1) Class interests determine which acts are criminalized and how heavily they are punished. (2) Economic pressures lead to offenses, particularly property offenses, among the poor.

Defining Crime.   The conflict perspective on defining crime has already been described in the section on labeling theory. Marxists argue that the law is a weapon used by the ruling class to maintain the status quo (Liska, Chamlin,and Reed 1985). This interpretation fits in with the general Marxist notion that all social institutions, including law, have been created to rationalize and support the current distribution of economic resources.

Supporters of this position note that we spend more money deterring muggers than embezzlers. We give more severe sentences for street crimes than corporate crimes. We are more likely to arrest those who assault members of the ruling class (well-off white males) than we are to arrest those who assault the powerless (nonwhites, women, and the poor) (Smith 1987). Finally, even when people from the upper and lower classes commit similar crimes, those from the lower class are more likely to be arrested, prosecuted, and sentenced (Williams and Drake 1980). The system clearly seems to benefit the upper classes.

Many Marxists deny that crime is more prevalent among the poor. They argue that in fact the well-off are the least conforming group in the population; it is the rich rather than the working class who flout convention (Sorokin and Lundin 1959). Because of their control of the labeling apparatus—the state, the schools, the courts—the upper class has been able to avoid deviant labels.

Posters such as this one were widely distributed in the 1930s in the successful attempt to criminalize marijuana use. Who sponsored this campaign? The answer is on the bottom line of the poster: The Consolidated Brewers Association of America. It doesn't take a financial genius to figure out why the breweries opposed marijuana use. This is one of the more obvious examples of the extent to which what is legal and what is illegal depends more on politics and economics than on unambiguous moral codes.

■

Deterrence theory points out that many young people who grow up in inner-city neighborhoods have little stake in conformity; gang life may offer more rewards than straight life. When this is the case, crime is a rational choice. An implication of this theory is that the solution to high crime rates is to increase the availability of conventional rewards.

Lower-Class Crime.   Although the preceding view of the way crime is defined would be accepted by all Marxists, some believe that the lower class really is more likely to commit criminal acts. One Marxist criminologist has declared that crime is a rational response for the lower class (Quinney 1980). These criminologists generally seem to agree with Merton's strain theory that a means-versus-ends discrepancy is particularly acute among the poor and that it may lead to crime (Greenberg 1985). They believe, however, that this is a natural condition of an unequal society rather than an unnatural condition.

SUMMARY

There are many theories of deviance in the field of sociology. These reflect differences in basic theoretical assumptions as well as differences in the kinds of deviance they try to explain (see the Concept Summary). All, however, are sociological, not psychological or biological, theories: They place the reasons for deviance within the social structure rather than within the individual. In the following sections, we apply these theories as we review major differentials in U.S. crime rates.

CONCEPT SUMMARY
Theories of Deviance

	MAJOR QUESTION	MAJOR ASSUMPTION	CAUSE OF DEVIANCE	MOST USEFUL FOR EXPLAINING DEVIANCE OF
STRUCTURAL-FUNCTIONAL THEORY Strain theory	Why do people break rules?	Deviance is an abnormal characteristic of the social structure.	A dislocation between the goals of society and the means to achieve them	The working and lower classes who cannot achieve desired goals by prescribed means
SYMBOLIC INTERACTION THEORIES Differential association theory	Why is deviance more characteristic of some groups than others?	Deviance is learned like other social behavior.	Subcultural values differ in complex societies; some subcultures hold values that favor deviance. These are learned through socialization.	Delinquent gangs and those integrated into deviant subcultures and neighborhoods
Deterrence theories	When is conformity not the best choice?	Deviance is a choice based on cost/benefit assessments.	Failure of sanctioning system (benefits of deviance exceed the costs)	All groups, but especially those lacking a "stake in conformity"
Labeling theory	How do acts and people become labeled *deviant*?	Deviance is relative and depends on how others label acts and actors.	People whose acts are labeled deviant and who accept that label become career deviants.	The powerless who are labeled deviant by more powerful individuals
CONFLICT THEORY	How does unequal access to scarce resources lead to deviance?	Deviance is a normal response to competition and conflict over scarce resources.	Inequality and competition	All classes: Lower class is driven to deviance to meet basic needs and to act out frustration; upper class uses deviant means to maintain their privilege.

CRIME

Most of the behavior that is regarded as deviant or nonconforming is subject only to informal social controls. **Crimes** are acts that are subject to legal penalties. Most, though not all, crimes violate social norms and are subject

Crimes are acts that are subject to legal or civil penalties.

to informal as well as legal sanctions. In this section, we briefly define the different types of crimes, look at crime rates in the United States, and examine the findings abut who is most likely to commit these crimes.

INDEX CRIMES: MAJOR CRIMES INVOLVING VIOLENCE OR PROPERTY

Each year the federal government publishes the *Uniform Crime Report* (UCR), which summarizes crimes known to the police for eight major index crimes (U.S. Department of Justice 1989a):

- *Murder and nonnegligent manslaughter.* Overall, murder is a rare crime, yet some segments of society are touched by it much more than others; more than 48 percent of all murder victims in 1988 were African American and 75 percent were male.
- *Rape.* Rape accounts for about 7 percent of all violent crimes, and reported rapes have doubled in the last two decades. Nearly 100,000 women were raped in 1988.
- *Robbery.* Robbery is defined as taking or attempting to take anything of value from another person by force, threat of force, violence, or by putting the victim in fear. Unlike simple theft or larceny, robbery involves a personal confrontation between the victim and the robber and is thus a crime of violence.
- *Assault.* Aggravated assault is an unlawful attack for the purpose of inflicting severe bodily injury. Kicking and hitting are included in assault, but increasingly assault involves a weapon. Assault is the fastest-growing category of crime included in the UCR.
- *Burglary, larceny-theft, motor-vehicle theft,* and *arson* are the four property crimes included in the UCR. (Arson has only been added recently and is not covered in the trend data in Figure 8.2.) Property crimes are much more common than crimes of violence and account for 90 percent of the crimes covered in the UCR.

It is a common public perception that crime rates are much higher than they used to be. The accuracy of this perception depends on the time frame one uses and the specific crime. Figures 8.1 and 8.2 depict trends in seven index crimes over the last 20 years. They show that crime rates are indeed higher than they were in 1970—in the case of rape and assault, twice as high. After a general slump in crime rates during the first years of the 1980s, all the UCR index crimes except burglary are again on the rise.

VICTIMLESS CRIMES

Victimless crimes such as drug use, prostitution, gambling, and pornography are voluntary exchanges between persons who desire goods or services from each other.

The so-called **victimless crimes**—such as drug use, prostitution, gambling, and pornography—are voluntary exchanges between persons who desire goods or services from one another (Schur 1979). They are called victimless crimes because participants in the exchange typically do not see themselves as being victimized or as suffering from the transaction: There are no complaining victims.

There is substantial debate about whether these crimes are truly victimless. Many argue that prostitutes, drug abusers, and pornography models

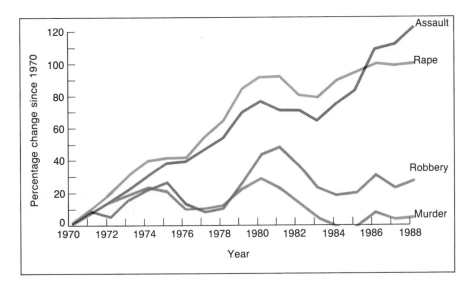

■

FIGURE 8.1
CHANGES IN VIOLENT CRIME RATES, 1970–1988

Violent crime rose during the 1970s. After a dramatic slump in the early 1980s, violent crime rates are again on the upswing. Assault and rape rates are at their highest recorded levels.

SOURCE: U.S. Department of Justice 1989a.

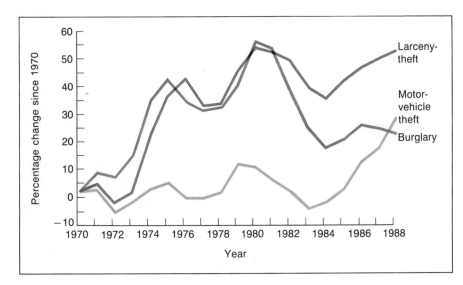

FIGURE 8.2
CHANGES IN PROPERTY CRIMES, 1970–1988

Property crime increased throughout the 1970s. Although all property crime rates dropped in the early 1980s, larceny-theft and motor-vehicle theft rates have returned to or exceeded their previous high levels. Burglary rates remain substantially lower than they were 10 years ago.

SOURCE: U.S. Department of Justice 1989.

are victims (Chapman and Gates 1978; Dworkin 1981): Even though there is an element of choice in the decision to engage in these behaviors, individuals are usually forced or manipulated into it by their disadvantaged class position. Others believe that such activities are legitimate areas of free enterprise and free choice and that the only reason these acts are considered illegal is because of some self-righteous busybodies.

Because there are no complaining victims, these crimes are difficult to control. The drug user is generally not going to complain about the drug pusher, and the illegal gambler is unlikely to bring charges against a bookie. In the absence of a complaining victim, the police must find not only the criminal but also the crime. Efforts to do so are costly and divert attention from other criminal acts. As a result, victimless crimes are irregularly and inconsistently enforced, most often in the form of periodic crackdowns and routine harassment.

■

In 1990, Michael Milken was convicted of securities fraud as part of the on-going Wall Street scandals. Although he may eventually serve time in prison, Milken has already agreed to pay $600 million in fines. Although this sounds like a lot of money, Milken once made $500 million in a single year. Generally this kind of white-collar crime does not generate the same gut reaction as violent crime and there is less public demand to get tough on white-collar criminals.

White-collar crime is crime committed by respectable people of high status in the course of their occupation.

WHITE-COLLAR CRIME

A crime committed by respectable people of high social status in the course of their occupation is called **white-collar crime** (Sutherland 1961).

White-collar crime occurs at several levels. It is committed, for example, by employees against companies, by companies against employees, by companies against customers, and by companies against the public (for example, by dumping toxic wastes into the air, land, or water). In addition to the enormous economic costs of white-collar crime, there are social costs as well. Exposure to repeated tales of corruption tends to breed distrust and cynicism and, ultimately, to undermine the integration of social institutions. If you think that all members of Congress are crooks, then you quit voting. If you think that every police officer can be bought, then you cease to respect the law. Thus, the costs of such crime go beyond the actual dollars involved in the crime itself.

The reasons for white-collar crime tend to be about the same as for street crimes: People want more than they can legitimately get, and the benefits of a crime outrun its potential costs (Coleman, 1988). Differential association also plays a role. In some corporations, organizational culture winks at or actively encourages illegal behavior. Speaking of the insider trading scandals that have rocked Wall Street recently, one observer notes:

> You gotta do it. . . . Everybody else is. [It] is part of the business. . . . You work at a deli, you take home pastrami every night for free. It's the same thing as information on Wall Street. . . . I know you want to help your mother and provide for your family. This is the way to do it. Don't be a schmuck. Nobody gets hurt (cited in Reichman 1989).

The magnitude of white-collar crime in our society makes a mockery of the idea that crime is predominantly a lower-class phenomenon. Instead, it appears that people of different statuses simply have different opportunities to commit crime. Those in the lower statuses are hardly in the position to engage in price fixing, stock manipulation, or tax evasion. They are in the position, however, to engage in high-risk, low-yield crimes such as robbery and larceny. Since most white-collar crime goes undetected or unreported, higher-status individuals are in the position to engage in low-risk, high-yield crimes (Schur 1979).

Marxist critics argue that the absence of white-collar crime statistics from the UCR and the relative absence of white-collar criminals from our prisons reflect the fundamental class bias in our criminal justice system (Braithwaite 1985).

CORRELATES OF CRIME: AGE, SEX, RACE, AND CLASS

Only 20 percent of the crimes reported in the UCR are cleared by an arrest. This means that the people arrested for criminal acts represent only a sample of those who commit reported crimes; they are undoubtedly not a random sample. The low level of arrests coupled with the low levels of crime reporting warn us to be cautious in applying generalizations about arrestees to the larger population of criminals. With this caution in mind, we note that the persons arrested for the criminal acts are disproportionately male, young, and from minority groups. Figure 8.3 shows the pattern

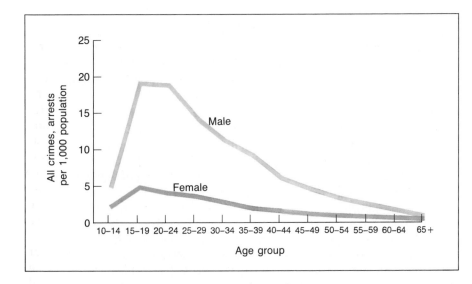

Arrest rates in the United States and most other nations show strong and consistent age and sex patterns. Arrest rates peak sharply for young people ages 15–24; at all ages, men are about five times more likely than women to be arrested.

SOURCE: U.S. Department of Justice 1989; U.S. Bureau of the Census 1989a.

of arrest rates in 1988 by sex and age. As you can see, crime rates, especially for men, peak sharply during ages 15–24; during these peak crime years, young men are about five times more likely to be arrested than women of the same age. Minority data are not available by age and sex, but the overall rates show that African Americans and Hispanics are more than three times more likely than whites to be arrested.

What accounts for these differentials? Can the theories reviewed earlier help explain these patterns?

Age Differences.   The age differences in arrest rates noted in Figure 8.3 are characteristic of nearly every nation in the world that gathers crime statistics (Hirschi and Gottfredson 1983). A great deal of controversy exists over the reasons for the very high arrest rates of young adults, but deterrence theories have the most promise for explaining this age pattern.

In many ways, adolescents and young adults have less to lose than older people. They don't have a "stake in conformity"—a career, a mortgage, a credit rating (Steffensmeier et al. 1989). When young people do have jobs, and especially when they have good jobs, their chances of getting into trouble are much smaller (Allan and Steffensmeier 1989).

Delinquency is basically a leisure-time activity. It is strongly associated with spending large blocks of unsupervised time with peers (Agnew and Petersen 1989; Osgood and Wilson 1989). When there is "nothing better to do," a substantial portion will get in trouble. On the other hand, deviance is deterred by spending a lot of time with one's parents or with conforming peers (Gardner and Shoemaker 1988).

Sex Differences.   The sex differential in arrest rates has both social and biological roots. Women's smaller size and lesser strength make them less likely to use violence or personal confrontation; they have learned that, for them, this is an ineffective strategy. Evidence linking male hormones to aggressiveness indicates that biology also may be a factor in women's lower inclination to engage in violent behavior.

Among social theories of deviance, deterrence theory seems to be the most effective in explaining these differences. Generally, girls are supervised more closely than boys, and they are subject to more social control; this is especially true in the lower class (Hagan, Gillis, and Simpson 1985; Heidensohn 1985; Thompson 1989). Whereas parents may let their boys wander about at night unsupervised, they are much more likely to insist on knowing where their daughters will be and with whom they will be associating. The greater supervision that girls receive increases their bonds to parents and other conventional institutions; it also reduces their opportunity to join gangs or other deviant groups.

These explanations raise questions about whether changing roles for women will affect women's participation in crime. Will increased equality in education, labor-force participation, smoking, and drinking also show up in greater equality of criminal behavior? The evidence shows little tendency for this to happen. It is true that the crime rate for women has increased faster than the crime rate for men in a few areas (vagrancy, disorderly conduct, property crimes), but there has been no increase in women's participation in violent crime.

Differences by Social Class.   The effect of social class on crime rates is complex. Although sociologists have historically held that social class is an important correlate of criminality (Braithwaite 1981; Elliott and Ageton 1980; Thornberry and Farnworth 1982), some studies have found that the relationship is not very strong and in some cases is nonexistent (Hirschi 1969; Johnson 1980; Krohn et al. 1980; Tittle, Villemez, and Smith 1978). Much of the inconsistency appears to center on difficulties in measuring both social class and crime.

Braithwaite's (1981) review of more than 100 studies leads to the conclusion that lower-class people commit more of the direct interpersonal types of crimes normally handled by the police than do people from the middle class. These are the types of crimes reported in the UCR. Middle-class people commit more of the crimes that involve the use of power, particularly in the context of their occupational roles: fraud, embezzlement, price fixing, and other forms of white-collar crime. There is also evidence that the social-class differential may be greater for adult crime than for juvenile deliquency (Thornberry and Farnworth 1982).

Nearly all the deviance theories we reviewed offer some explanation of the social class differential. Strain theorists and some Marxists suggest that the lower class is more likely to engage in crime because of blocked avenues to achievement. Deterrence theorists attribute greater crime among the lower class to the fact that these people may be receiving fewer rewards from conventional institutions such as school and the labor market. All of these theories accept and seek to explain the social class pattern found in the UCR, where, indeed, the lower class is overrepresented. Labeling and Marxist theories, on the other hand, argue that this overrepresentation is not a reflection of underlying social class patterns of deviance but of bias in the law and within social control agencies (Williams and Drake 1980). It also reflects the particular mix of crimes included in the UCR; if embezzlement, price fixing, and stock manipulations were included in the UCR, we might see a very different social class distribution of criminals.

How Deviant Are You?

Because the offenders who find their way into official statistics are such a biased sample of all offenders, many people argue that males, minorities, and lower-class people are getting too much blame for crime. One measurement technique that tries to get at the true differentials in deviance uses self-reports. The following self-report questionnaire was designed by Hindelang, Hirschi, and Weis (1981, 223–26) to measure deviance among high school youths. Try yourself out on it to see how deviant you were at 17.

Place a check next to things you had *ever* done by age 17:

— 1. Been questioned as a suspect by the police about some crime.

— 2. Been held by the police or court until you could be released into the custody of your parents or guardians.

— 3. Been placed on probation by a juvenile court judge.

— 4. Been caught shoplifting by the clerk or owner of a store.

— 5. Been sentenced to a reformatory, training school, or some other institution by a judge.

— 6. Sold something you had stolen yourself.

— 7. Broken into a house, store, school, or other building and taken money, stereo equipment, guns, or something else you wanted.

— 8. Broken into a locked car to get something from it.

— 9. Taken hubcaps, wheels, the battery, or some other expensive part of a car without the owner's permission.

—10. Taken gasoline from a car without the owner's permission.

—11. Taken things worth between $10 and $50 from a store without paying for them.

—12. Threatened to beat someone up if they didn't give you money or something else you wanted.

—13. Carried a razor, switchblade, or gun with the intention of using it in a fight.

—14. Pulled a knife, gun, or some other weapon on someone just to let them know you meant business.

■

If you have never done any of these things, you are exceptional. You are probably also a white female.

—15. Beat someone up so badly they probably needed a doctor.

—16. Taken a car belonging to someone you didn't know for a ride without the owner's permission.

—17. Taken a tape deck or a CB radio from a car.

—18. Broken into a house, store, school, or other building with the intention of breaking things up or causing other damage.

—19. Taken things of large value (worth more than $50) from a store without paying for them.

—20. Tried to get away from a police officer by fighting or struggling.

—21. Used physical force (like twisting an arm or choking) to get money from another person.

—22. Used a club, knife, or gun to get something from someone.

—23. Taken things from a wallet or purse (or the whole wallet or purse) while the owner wasn't around or wasn't looking.

—24. Hit a teacher or some other school official.

—25. Taken a bicycle belonging to someone you didn't know with no intention of returning it.

—26. Tried to pass a check by signing someone else's name.

—27. Intentionally started a building on fire.

—28. Grabbed a purse from someone and run with it.

—29. Forced another person to have sex relations with you when they did not want to.

—30. Taken little things (worth less than $2) from a store without paying for them.

—31. Broken the windows of an empty house or other unoccupied building.

—32. Let the air out of car or truck tires.

—33. Used a slug or fake money in a candy, coke, coin, or stamp machine.

—34. Fired a BB gun at some other person, at passing cars, or at windows of buildings.

—35. Taken things you weren't supposed to take from a desk or locker at school.

—36. Bought something you knew had been stolen.

—37. Broken the windows of a school building.

—38. Taken material or equipment from a construction site.

—39. Refused to tell the police or some other official what you knew about a crime.

—40. Purposely broken a car window.

—41. Picked a fight with someone you didn't know just for the hell of it.

—42. Helped break up chairs, tables, desks, or other furniture in a school, church, or other public building.

—43. Jumped or helped jump somebody and then beat them up.

—44. Slashed the seats in a bus, a movie house, or some other place.

—45. Punctured or slashed the tire of a car.

—46. Destroyed things at a construction site.

—47. Destroyed mailboxes.

—48. Kept money for yourself that you collected for a team, a charity (like the March of Dimes), or someone else's paper route.

—49. Driven away from the scene of an accident that you were involved in without identifying yourself.

—50. Taken mail from someone else's mailbox and opened it.

—51. Broken into a parking meter or the coin box of a pay phone.

—52. Drunk beer or wine.

—53. Drunk whiskey, gin, vodka, or other "hard" liquor.

—54. Smoked marijuana (grass, pot).

—55. Gone to school when you were drunk or high on some drugs.

—56. Pretended to be older than you were to buy beer or cigarettes.

—57. Sold illegal drugs such as heroin, marijuana, LSD, or cocaine.

—58. Driven a car when you were drunk or high on some drugs.

—59. Taken barbiturates (downers) or Methedrine (speed or other uppers) without a prescription.

—60. Used cocaine.

—61. Taken angel dust, LSD, or mescaline.

—62. Used heroin (smack).

—63. Been sent out of a classroom.

—64. Stayed away from school when your parents thought you were there.

—65. Gone out at night when your parents told you that you couldn't go.

—66. Been suspended or expelled from school.

—67. Cursed or threatened an adult in a loud and mean way just to let them know who was boss.

—68. Run away from home and stayed overnight.

—69. Hit one of your parents.

If you have never done any of these things, you are exceptional. You are proabably also a white female. Like the official statistics, self-report measures show differentials by race and sex. Males report nearly twice as much deviance as females; the difference is least on the drug and alcohol items and greatest on the items involving violence. African American youths, especially girls, report somewhat more delinquent acts than white youths of the same sex. This differential is particularly strong for items reflecting violent

personal encounters. Self-report data, however, do eliminate the social class differential. Middle-class youths report as much deviance as lower-class youths (Hirschi 1969; Tittle, Villemez, and Smith 1978). Does this mean that middle-class kids are as deviant as lower-class kids but that they get away with it more? Some scholars believe that this is true; others believe that the lower-class kids really are more deviant than the middle-class kids but that they aren't about to admit it, even on an anonymous questionnaire. These scholars also raise questions about whether the truly deviant (a category that they presume over-represents lower-class kids) are included in these samples (Kleck 1982).

When this self-report was filled out by more than 14,000 youths in Seattle in 1975, it was found that the amount of self-reported deviance was highly related to police contact. Among males with no police record, the average number of items checked was 12; among those with a police (but not a court) record, the average was 22. Among females, the figures were 8 and 12. How did you stack up?

SOURCE: Hindelang, Michael J., Hirsch, Travis, and Weis, Joseph. "Appendix B, The Seattle Self-Report Instrument," pp. 223–26 in Measuring Delinquency.

Differences by Race.   Although African Americans are only 12 percent of the population, they are 57 percent of those arrested for murder, 50 percent of those arrested for rape, and 45 percent of those arrested for assault. Hispanics, who compose about 8 percent of the total population, are between 10 and 15 percent of those arrested for violent crimes. These strong differences in arrest rates are explained in part by social class differences between minority and Anglo populations. Even after this effect is taken into account, however, African and Hispanic Americans are still much more likely to be arrested for committing crimes.

The explanation for this is complex. As we will document in Chapter 10, race continues to represent a fundamental cleavage in American society. The continued and even growing correlation of race with unemployment, inner-city residence, and female-headed households reinforces the barriers between African Americans and whites in American society. An international study confirms that the larger the number of overlapping dimensions of inequality, the higher the "pent-up aggression which manifests itself in diffuse hostility and violence" (Messner 1989). The root cause of higher minority crime rates, from this perspective, is the low quality of minority employment—a factor that leads directly to unstable families and neighborhoods (Sampson 1987; Sampson and Groves 1989).

Poverty and segregation combine to put African American children in the worst neighborhoods in the country, neighborhoods where getting into trouble is a way of life and where conventional achievement is remote (Matsueda and Heimer 1987). Differential association theory thus explains a great deal of the racial difference in arrest rates. Deterrence theory is also important. African American children are much more likely to live in a fatherless home and thus lack an important social bond that might deter deviant behavior. In addition to these factors that may increase the propensity to deviance among minorities, there is also evidence that whether we are talking about troublemaking in school, stealing cars, or petty theft, minority-group members are more likely than Anglos to be labeled deviant and, if apprehended by the police, more apt to be cited, prosecuted and convicted (Unnever, Frazier, and Henretta 1980; Peterson 1988).

THE SOCIOLOGY OF LAW

We have reviewed theories about deviance and examined current findings about crime and criminals. In the last sections of this chapter, we will look at the formal mechanisms of social control. Among the questions of interest are, Why punish? What is a just punishment? How does the criminal justice system work? Can we reduce crime? We begin by taking a broad theoretical overview of the sociology of law.

THEORIES OF LAW

The cornerstone of the formal control system is the law. Generally, law is seen as serving three major functions: It provides formal sanctions to encourage conformity and discourage deviance, it helps settle disputes, and it may be an instrument for social change (Vago 1989). Beyond this simple summary, there is substantial discussion among scholars about how the law operates.

Most citizens, and probably even most sociologists, take a general structural-functional approach to law (Rich 1977). By clearly spelling out expected behaviors and punishing violators, the law helps maintain society. Although some may benefit more than others from particular laws and laws may be unequally enforced, law itself is a good thing, a benefit to society.

Conflict theorists, of course, take a somewhat different position: They suggest that the legal apparatus was designed to maintain and reproduce the system of inequality. Law, in this view, is a tool used by elites to dominate and control the lower orders (Chambliss 1978).

Both perspectives have obvious merit. Although law does serve the general interest by maintaining order, it is not surprising to find that it serves some interests better than others. The relationship between law and inequality is a central concern of sociologists of law. One of the more influential and controversial theories of law is that of Donald Black (1976). Among his propositions are the following:

1. *Quantity of law.* The greater the inequality in society, the more law there will be. A society of equals needs fewer laws than a society with great inequality.

2. *Quality of law.* The law works differently when the victim and offender are status unequals than when they are status equals. When the victim and offender are of equal rank, then the law usually tries to mediate between them rather than punish. For example, in many domestic violence cases, counseling and probation are the preferred strategies. When the victim and the offender are status unequals, then the law takes a more punitive approach. A high-status offender, however, is more likely to be punished with a fine, while a low-status offender will be punished by imprisonment.

WHAT IS JUSTICE?

Justice is an enormously difficult concept to define. Some argue that justice is served when everyone is treated equally; for example, when everyone who commits first-degree murder gets 30 years, no exceptions and no parole. Others believe that justice should be more flexible. They believe that circumstances should make a difference.

In this as in many other fields, Max Weber's contributions are insightful. Weber ([1914] 1954) distinguished between two types of legal procedures: rational and substantive. Rational law is based on strict application of the rules, regardless of fairness in specific cases. Substantive law, on the other hand, takes into account the unique circumstances of the individual case. For example, although the penalty for motor-vehicle homicide might be three years, substantive law might levy a lower penalty on a grief-stricken father who has killed his child than on someone who has killed a stranger.

Studies of actual sentencing outcomes suggest that law tends to be much more substantive than rational. If law were rational, one would expect that sentences would be highly correlated with the nature of the crime; they are not. If law were a tool of the elite, one would expect sentences to be affected by the race and class of the offender and the victim. There is evidence that death penalty decisions *are* affected by the race of the victim; convicted murderers, for example, are less likely to get the death penalty if the victim was black (Kleck 1981). The most general conclusion, however, is that sentencing has only a rough association with the crime or the characteristics of the victim or offender. Decisions seem to depend more on the individual judge than on any characteristic of a particular case.

THE CRIMINAL JUSTICE SYSTEM

The formal mechanisms of social control mentioned at the beginning of the chapter are administered through the criminal justice system. In the United States, this system consists of a vast network of agencies set up to deal with persons who deviate from the law: police departments, probation and parole agencies, rehabilitation agencies, criminal courts, jails, and prisons.

THE POLICE

Police officers occupy a unique and powerful position in the criminal justice system because they are empowered to make arrests in context of low visibility: Often there are no witnesses to police encounters with suspected offenders. Although they are supposed to enforce the law fully and uniformly, everyone realizes that this is neither practical nor possible. In 1988, there were approximately three full-time law-enforcement officers for every 1,000 persons in the nation (U.S. Department of Justice 1989c). This means that the police ordinarily must give greater attention to the more serious crimes. Minor offenses and ambiguous situations are likely to be ignored.

Police officers have a considerable amount of discretionary power in determining the extent to which the policy of full enforcement is carried out. Should a drunk and disorderly person be charged or sent home? Should a juvenile offender be charged or reported to parents? Should a strong odor of marijuana in an otherwise orderly group be overlooked or investigated? The decisions the police make in the initial stages of an investigation are called **street-level justice**. Unlike the justice meted out in courts, street-level justice is relatively invisible and thus hard to evaluate (Smith and Visher 1981).

THE COURTS

Once arrested, an individual starts a complex trip through the criminal justice system. This trip can best be thought of as a series of decision stages. There is considerable attrition as defendants pass from arrest to prosecution to sentencing and punishment. Even in felony cases, as many as 40 to 50 percent of those arrested will not be prosecuted because of problems with evidence or witnesses (Brossi 1979). At the same time, approximately 90 percent of all convictions are the result of pretrial negotiations (Figueira-McDonough 1985). This means that only about 10 percent of criminal convictions are processed through public trials. Thus, the pretrial phases of prosecution are often more crucial to arriving at judicial decisions of guilt or innocence than are court trials themselves. Like the police, prosecutors have considerable discretion in deciding whom to prosecute and on what charges.

Throughout the entire process, the prosecution, the defense, and the judges participate in negotiated plea bargaining. The accused is encouraged to plead guilty in the interest of getting a lighter sentence, a reduced charge, or, in the case of multiple offenses, the dropping of some charges. In return, the prosecution is saved the trouble of assembling evidence sufficient for a jury trial.

There is a great deal of discretion in police work. In most situations, the police officer is out on her or his own, away from supervision and direction, and must make snap decisions about whether to pursue violations or let them go. Because we recognize that there are not enough police officers to pursue every violation, we hope officers will use good judgment about what kinds of violations and violators are worth pursuing and will not let prejudice or bias affect their decisions.

Street-level justice consists of the decisions the police make in the initial stages of an investigation.

Getting Tough on Crime: How and Why?

Crime rates have gone up in the last 20 years, especially those crimes of violence that people fear most. Recent surveys demonstrate that nearly half of all Americans are afraid to walk at night in their own neighborhoods (Gallup Report 1989a). As a result of this fear, the topic of crime evokes a gut-level response in most Americans, and there is strong public demand to "get tough on crime." In this section, we start by examining theories of punishment and then review current penal practices in the United States.

Punishment Rationales.   Any assessment of prisons and punishment must come to grips with the issue: Why are we doing this? Before we can assess the adequacy of punishment, we need to be clear about its purpose. There seem to be five major rationalizations for punishment (Conrad 1983):

1. *Retribution.* Society punishes offenders to revenge the victim and society as a whole; this is a form of revenge and retaliation.
2. *Reformation.* Offenders are not punished, but rather are corrected and reformed so that they will become conforming members of the community.
3. *Specific deterrence.* Punishment is intended to scare offenders so they will think twice about violating the law again.
4. *General deterrence.* By making an example of offenders, society scares the rest of us into following the rules.
5. *Prevention.* By incapacitating offenders, society keeps them from committing further crimes.

Today, social control agencies in the United States represent a mixture of these different philosophies and practices.

Prisons.   For most people, getting tough on crime means locking criminals up and throwing away the key. Over 80 percent of the American public wants to make it harder for people convicted of violent crimes to get parole (Gallup Report 1989b). In response to this public demand, the rate of imprisonment has risen in the last 10 years (see Figure 8.4). In 1987,

FIGURE 8.4

RATES OF IMPRISONMENT PER 1,000 INDEX CRIMES AND PER 100,000 POPULATION

Since 1970, there has been a sharp upturn in our use of prison sentences to control crime. Both the number of prisoners per crime and the number of prisoners per 100,000 population have doubled since 1970. The consequence is a "crisis in penalty." The economic and social costs of imprisonment may be so high that we must consider alternative strategies.

SOURCE: U.S. Department of Justice 1989b, 6; U.S. Bureau of the Census 1989a, 183.

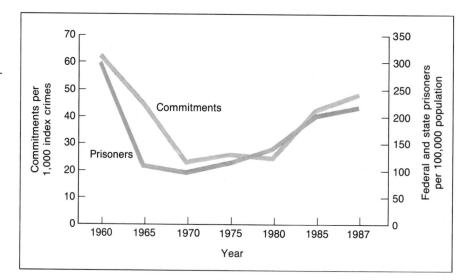

Prisons are total institutions where inmates are assigned numbers, wear identical uniforms, live in identical cells, and follow the same routines. They are also environments full of anger, hatred, violence, boredom, and insecurity. In this totally negative environment, prisons become warehouses for the deviant and the violent. They are unlikely environments for rehabilitation.

there were twice as many prison commitments per 1,000 index crimes as there were in 1970 (U.S. Department of Justice 1988, 6).

As a result, prison populations are soaring. In 1988, there were 627,402 people in state and federal prisons—nearly double the number in 1980. Disproportionately these prisoners are young men who are uneducated, unskilled, poor, and black. The latest figures shows that 27 percent are under age 25, 47 percent are black, and only one-third have graduated from high school. More than four in five have been in prison before (U.S. Bureau of the Census 1989a, 184).

The sharp increase in the use of prison to control crime has resulted in a crisis in prison conditions. Many facilities are housing twice as many inmates as they were designed to hold. These overcrowded conditions have been shown to be the chief determinant of violence in prisons (Gaes and McGuire 1985). As a result, court orders in more than 30 states have required prisons to reduce crowding and improve prison conditions. This is an enormously expensive undertaking. The costs are so huge that one observer has called this a "crisis of penalty" (Young, cited in Currie 1989). Most observers agree that "a total commitment to the incarceration of all adult felons . . . cannot be sustained in practice" (Mushane et al. 1989, 137). Do we really want to spend billions and billions of dollars to build more prisons to warehouse a growing proportion of those convicted of crime? Do we need to?

A growing number of empirical studies demonstrate that the certainty of getting caught has more deterrent effect on crime than the length of the sentence (Klepper and Nagin 1989). These findings suggest that we are pursuing the wrong strategy. Rather than building more prisons to warehouse criminals for longer periods of time, we need to put more money into law enforcement. Today, most experts agree that increasing the certainty that criminals will be caught will reduce crime more than will clobbering the few that we do catch.

Community-Based Corrections.   Another approach to solving the prison crisis is to change the way we punish convicted criminals. Only one quarter of the convicted offenders under the jurisdiction of social control agencies are actually in jail or prison. The other three quarters are on probation or parole. The public has been generally negative about probation and parole, believing—often rightly—that probation has meant giving criminals a "slap on the wrist" and parole has meant letting criminals out without effective supervision.

As the cost of imprisoning larger numbers of people balloons to crisis proportions, there has been increased interest in effective community-based corrections. New intensive supervision probation (ISP) programs are being used across the country. They include curfews, mandatory drug testing, supervised halfway houses, mandatory community service, frequent reporting and unannounced home visits, restitution, electronic surveillance, and split sentences (incarceration followed by supervised probation) (Lurigio 1990). These programs are alleged to cost only half as much as imprisonment and to be more likely to result in rehabilitation (Mushane et al. 1989). Such claims are still being evaluated.

Social Change.   The conservative approach to confronting crime has generally been to increase penalties for convicted criminals. This approach

Not everyone who commits a crime comes from a bad neighborhood or suffers economic disadvantage. Delinquency, in fact, seems to show relatively little correlation with social class. Nevertheless, economic disadvantage can mean that adolescent delinquency turns from an occasional leisure-time activity into a permanent way of life. One strategy for reducing crime is to provide opportunities for better school performance, better jobs, and economic advancement.

dominated the 1970s and 1980s, which is why prison populations have soared. An alternative approach, which may be gaining renewed momentum, is to address the social problems that give rise to crime. A leading criminologist advocates four major strategies for reducing crime (Currie 1989):

1. Reduce inequality and social impoverishment.
2. Replace unstable, low-wage, dead-end jobs with decent jobs.
3. Enact a supportive national family policy.
4. Increase the economic and social stability of communities.

These strategies would require a massive commitment of energy and money. They are not only expensive but also politically risky. While law-and-order advocates want to get tough on crime by sending more criminals to jail, a policy incorporating Currie's four strategies would channel dollars and beneficial programs into high-crime neighborhoods. Such a policy calls for teachers, not police officers, and good jobs rather than more prisons.

Observers from all sociological perspectives and all political parties recognize that social control is necessary. They recognize that soaring rape and assault rates and the explosion of drug-related crimes are serious problems that must be addressed. The issue is how. The sociological perspective suggests that crime can be addressed most effectively by examining social institutions rather than individual criminals. We consider the implications of this perspective for drug policy in the Issues in Social Policy section.

Fighting the War on Drugs

By almost anybody's standards, drug use is a problem in the United States. Drugs are the number one national problem, according to public opinion polls, and objective evidence suggests that the public might be right. Drugs are very much a part of rising crime rates: Half of those in prison have been convicted of a drug-related crime or were daily users of drugs before their offense. Drugs are also a critical part of the growing inner-city health crisis: Over 10 percent of newborns have been affected by their mother's prenatal drug use; intravenous drug use is a major avenue for the spread of AIDS.

As a result of concern about drugs, the federal government has launched a "war on drugs." Public policy issues in this war are twofold: Should we combat demand or supply? Should we legalize drugs or increase the penalties?

Greater education about potential harm from drug use and the advent of cheap crack cocaine have changed the social class composition of drug users. There are fewer recreational, middle-class users and a growing number of drug abusers among the urban lower class. Strategies necessary to reduce drug abuse among the despairing inner-city poor may be a great deal more expensive than those aimed at the middle-class.

SUPPLY VERSUS DEMAND

Currently, about 70 percent of U.S. government effort in the drug war goes into law enforcement. Such enforcement is aimed at reducing the *supply* of drugs by reducing drug imports into the United States and by jailing drug dealers. The attempt to destroy Colombian cocaine cartels is one part of this battle. The other part is fought on the streets, where police combat the gangs who distribute drugs. The number of drug busts has been increasing 25 percent per year, but it has not made a serious dent in the distribution of drugs in the United States.

An alternative approach is to reduce the *demand* for drugs. This could occur in three ways: education programs to reduce the number of people who try drugs or use drugs recreationally; social reforms to reduce the conditions (school failure, joblessness, despair, gangs) that encourage drug use; and treatment programs for those who

are already drug abusers. Only the first of these alternatives is getting much financial support.

Education programs that publicize the health dangers of drug use have curbed illicit drug use among the middle class. Studies of college students show steadily declining proportions who use drugs. The result of declining middle-class use and the simultaneous emergence of cheap crack cocaine is a growing social class differential in drug use: the war on drugs is increasingly a lower-class issue. This means that further progress toward reducing the demand for drugs will have to target relief of social and economic conditions that make drug use and drug dealing so attractive.

ISSUES IN SOCIAL POLICY continued

PUNISHMENT VERSUS LEGALIZATION

Some observers think that the war on drugs is so impossible to win that we should just legalize the stuff and quit worrying about it. Others believe that we need stiffer penalties.

Within the past year, several prominent observers, both Republican and Democrat, have come out in favor of legalization—usually only of marijuana. Among the arguments in favor: Marijuana is a relatively harmless drug, perhaps no more harmful than alcohol; legalization would reduce the likelihood that users would get involved with traffickers in other illegal drugs; legalization would enable us to tax use and control quality and quantity. Opponents argue that marijuana is far from harmless, and they cite evidence that long-term marijuana use is implicated in mental illness. Since drug use is increasingly concentrated in the lower class, critics charge that legalization is another way of turning our backs on the poor. Finally, they argue that criminalization deters the timid and the conventional from using drugs and that this is a good thing (Goode 1989).

In fact, the legalization or criminalization of marijuana is irrelevant to the larger issue. Legalizing marijuana would enable middle-class youths (who are disproportionately the users of marijuana) to escape penalties. It would not affect the epidemic of crack cocaine that is affecting America's inner cities.

SUMMARY

The sharp increase in drug use and drug-related crimes in America's inner cities is the symptom of larger, underlying problems. Although some people cry out for harsher penalties for users and dealers alike, how many years in jail are appropriate for a 10-year old user? Do we really want to give the death sentence to a 12-year-old dealer? The seriousness of the issues probably does merit a "war"—but a war on poverty and disadvantage as well as a war on drugs.

SUMMARY

1. Most of us conform most of the time. We are constrained to conform through three types of social control: (1) self-restraint through the internalization of norms and values, (2) informal social controls, and (3) formal social controls.

2. Nonconformity occurs when people violate expected norms of behavior. Acts that go beyond eccentricity and that challenge important norms are called deviance. Crimes are a specific kind of deviance for which there are formal sanctions.

3. Deviance is relative. It depends on society's definitions, the circumstances surrounding an act, and the particular groups or subcultures one belongs to.

4. All three major theoretical perspectives in sociology have implications for the explanation of deviance. Structural functionalists use strain theory to blame deviance on social disorganization; symbolic interactionists propose differential association, deterrence, and labeling theories, which lay the blame on interaction patterns that encourage a deviant self-concept; Marxists and other conflict theorists find the cause of deviance in inequality and class conflict.

5. Most crimes are property crimes rather than crimes of violence. Although crime rates dropped in the early 1980s, all index crimes have been rising in the last few years.

6. Many arrests are for victimless crimes—acts for which there is no complainant. Such crimes are the most difficult and costly to enforce.

7. The high incidence of white-collar crimes, those committed in the course of one's occupation, indicates that crime is not merely a lower-class behavior.

8. Males, minority group members, lower-class people, and young people are disproportionately likely to be arrested for crimes. Some of this differential is due to their greater likelihood of committing a crime, but it is also explained partly by their differential treatment within the criminal justice system.

9. The sociology of law is concerned with how law is established and how it works in practice. Law reflects economic and political institutions and operates differently depending on social class. In practice, legal decisions are highly variable rather than determined by formal rules.

10. The criminal justice system includes the police, the courts, and the correctional system. Considerable discretion in the execution of justice is available to authorities at each of these levels.

11. The U.S. faces a "crisis of penalty," as our "get-tough" approach to crime is populating prisons far beyond capacity. Evidence suggests that longer sentences may not be necessary. Alternatives to imprisonment include community-based corrections and social change to reduce the causes of crime.

12. Most of the effort in the war on drugs is targeted against supply rather than demand. The social class differential in drug abuse is increasing, and reducing demand for drugs will require social reform that reduces joblessness, school failure, and despair.

SUGGESTED READINGS

Ben-Yehuda, Nachman. 1985. Deviance and Moral Boundaries. Chicago: University of Chicago Press. A wide-ranging coverage of deviance from witchcraft and the occult to cheating in science. A nice balance to the usual emphasis on criminal deviance.

Chamblis, William J., and Seidman, Robert B. 1982. Law, Order, and Power. Reading, Mass.: Addison-Wesley. A major text from the conflict perspective.

Cohen, Stanley. 1985. Visions of Social Control: Crime, Punishment, and Classification. Cambridge, England: Polity Press. A thoughtful book that considers the rationales that we use to justify punishment and the evidence supporting them. Cohen draws a provocative distinction between doing justice and doing good.

Elliott, Delbert, Huizinga, David, and Ageton, Suzanne. 1985. Explaining Delinquency and Drug Use. Beverly Hills: Sage. A research report on this most familiar form of deviance. It includes a good introductory coverage of symbolic interactionist theories of deviance.

Goode, Erich. 1989. Drugs in American Society. (3rd ed.) New York: Knopf. A textbook on drugs and drug use in the United States, covering everything from alcohol to heroin. A balanced and informed approach.

Vago, Steven. 1989. Law and Society. (2nd ed.) Englewood Cliffs, N.J.: Prentice-Hall. Covers the sociology of law, including a historical treatment of theories of the law as well as contemporary issues.

UNIT THREE

DIFFERENTIATION AND INEQUALITY

CHAPTER 9
STRATIFICATION

CHAPTER 10
RACIAL AND
ETHNIC
INEQUALITIES

CHAPTER 11
SEX AND
GENDER

CHAPTER 12
DIFFERENTIATION
AND INEQUALITIES

9

STRATIFICATION

Have you ever . . .

Considered where the kids you went to high school with are now? Some may have gone to Harvard, some to major state universities, some to community colleges, and some to vocational-technical schools. Some may be working on assembly lines, and some may be selling shoes; some may already have two children; some may be on welfare.

What determines which path people will take? Are the people who go to Harvard really that much smarter than those who are selling shoes? Or are they harder working or maybe luckier? Or did their parents have more money? Consider what the future holds for those who go to major universities compared with those who are selling shoes or working on assembly lines. Their lives are bound to be very different; they already are very different.

This chapter considers how occupations are assigned and what the consequences are for individuals and societies. It also considers the issue of fairness and how Americans deal with the significant inequalities that exist all around them. How did the kids who drove their parents' old Ford station wagons cope with the knowledge that some kids got new Camaros for their 16th birthday? As you read this chapter, you might consider how well it explains the origins and destinations of your high school senior class and how its explanations compare with those that you yourself have offered.

STRUCTURES OF INEQUALITY

Inequality exists all around us. Maybe your mother loves your sister more than you or your brother received a larger allowance than you did. This kind of inequality is personal. Sociologists study a particular kind of inequality called stratification. **Stratification** is an institutionalized pattern of inequality in which social statuses are ranked on the basis of their access to scarce resources.

If your parents gave your brother more money because they decided he was nicer than you, this inequality is not stratification. Inequality becomes stratification when two conditions exist:

1. The inequality is *institutionalized*, backed up by long-standing social norms about what ought to be.
2. The inequality is based on membership in a status (such as oldest son or blue-collar worker) rather than on personal attributes.

The scarce resources that we focus on are generally of three types: material wealth, prestige, and power. When inequality in one of these dimensions is supported by widely accepted and long-standing social norms and when it is based on status membership, then we speak of stratification.

TYPES OF STRATIFICATION STRUCTURES

Stratification is present in every society that we know. All societies have norms specifying that some categories of people ought to get more wealth, power, or prestige than others. There is, however, wide variety in the ways in which inequality is structured.

A key difference among structures of inequality is whether the categories used to distribute unequal rewards are based on ascribed or achieved statuses. As noted in Chapter 4, *ascribed statuses* are those that are fixed by birth and inheritance and are unalterable during a person's lifetime. *Achieved statuses* are optional ones that a person can obtain in a lifetime. Being African American or female, for example, is an ascribed status; being an ex-convict or a physician is an achieved status.

Every society uses some ascribed and some achieved statuses in distributing scarce resources, but the balance between them varies greatly. Stratification structures that rely largely on ascribed statuses as the basis for distributing scarce resources are called **caste systems;** structures that rely largely on achieved statuses are called **class systems.**

Caste Systems.   In a caste system, whether you are rich or poor, powerful or powerless, depends entirely on who your parents are. Whether you are lazy and stupid or hardworking and clever makes little difference. Your parents' position determines your own.

This system of structured inequality reached its extreme form in 19th-century India. The level of inequality in India was not very different from that in many European nations at the time, but the system for distributing rewards was markedly different. The Indian population was divided into

---

Stratification is an institutionalized pattern of inequality in which social statuses are ranked on the basis of their access to scarce resources.

Caste systems rely largely on ascribed statuses as the basis for distributing scarce resources.

Class systems rely largely on achieved statuses as the basis for distributing scarce resources.

castes, roughly comparable to occupation groups, that differed substantially in the amount of prestige, power, and wealth they received. The distinctive feature of the caste system is that caste membership is unalterable; it marks one's children and one's children's children. The inheritance of position was ensured by rules specifying that all persons should (1) follow the same occupation as their parents, (2) marry within their own caste, and (3) have no social relationships with members of other castes (Weber [1910] 1970b).

Class Systems.   In a class system, achieved statuses are the major basis of unequal resource distribution. Occupation remains the major determinant of rewards, but it is not fixed at birth. Instead, you can achieve an occupation far better or far worse than that of your parents. The amount of rewards you receive is influenced by your own talent and ambition or their lack.

The primary difference between caste and class systems is not the level of inequality but the opportunity for achievement. The distinctive characteristic of a class system is that it permits **social mobility**—a change in social class. Technically, mobility that occurs from one generation to the next is **intergenerational mobility.** Change in occupation and social class during an individual's own career is **intragenerational mobility.** Both kinds of mobility may be downward as well as upward.

Social mobility is the process of changing one's social class.

Intergenerational mobility is the change in social class from one generation to the next.

Intragenerational mobility is the change in social class within an individual's own career.

■

How much should these men be paid for removing garbage? Removing garbage is both unpleasant and vital, but since almost anybody can do it, the pay can be quite low. Critics of this structural-functional theory suggest that the generally low wages of garbage collectors has more to do with their lack of power than their lack of skill.

Even in a class system, ascribed characteristics have an influence. Whether you are male or female, Hispanic or non-Hispanic, Jewish or Protestant is likely to influence which doors are thrown open and which barriers have to be surmounted. Nevertheless, these factors are much less important in a class than in a caste society. Because class systems predominate in the modern world, the rest of this chapter is devoted to them. The following three chapters then address structured inequality based on race and ethnicity, sex, and age and show how these ascribed characteristics interact with class to determine life chances.

CLASSES—HOW MANY?

A class system is an ordered set of statuses. Which statuses are included, and how are they divided? Two theoretical answers to these questions are presented here.

Marx.   Karl Marx (1818–1883), who was writing during the early phase of industrialization, concluded that industrialized society would become polarized into just two classes. We could call them the haves and the have-nots; Marx called them the bourgeoisie (boor-zhwah-zee) and the proletariat. The **bourgeoisie** are those who own the tools and materials necessary for their work—the means of production; members of the **proletariat** do not. They must therefore support themselves by selling their labor to those who own the means of production. In Marx's view, **class** is determined entirely by one's relationship to the means of production.

> The **bourgeoisie** is the class that owns the tools and materials for their work—the means of production.

> The **proletariat** is the class that does not own the means of production. Members of this class must support themselves by selling their labor to those who own the means of production.

> **Class** refers to a person's relationship to the means of production.

Relationship to the means of production obviously has something to do with occupation, but it is not the same thing. According to Marx, your college instructor, the manager of the Sears store, and the janitor are all proletarians, because they work for someone else. Your garbage collector is probably also a proletarian who sells his labor to an employer; if the collector owns his own truck, however, then he is a member of the bourgeoisie. The key factor is not income or occupation but whether individuals control their own tools and their own work.

Marx, of course, was not blind to the fact that in the eyes of the world managers of Sears stores are regarded as more successful than truck-owning garbage collectors. Probably managers think of themselves as being superior to garbage collectors. In Marx's eyes, this is **false consciousness**— a lack of awareness of one's real position in the class structure. Marx, a social activist as well as a social theorist, hoped that managers and janitors could learn to see themselves as part of the same oppressed class. If they developed **class consciousness**—an awareness of their true class identity— he believed a revolutionary movement to eliminate class differences would be likely to occur.

> **False consciousness** is a lack of awareness of one's real position in the class structure.

> **Class consciousness** occurs when people are aware of their relationship to the means of production and recognize their true class identity.

Weber: Class, Status, and Power.   In fact, of course, Marx was wrong about the polarization of society. Instead of a polarization between rich and poor, a whole new middle class of managers and university-trained professionals developed. Max Weber, who wrote 50 years later than Marx, thus believed that we needed a more complex system for analyzing classes. Instead of Marx's one-dimensional ranking system, which provided only two classes, Weber proposed three independent dimensions on which

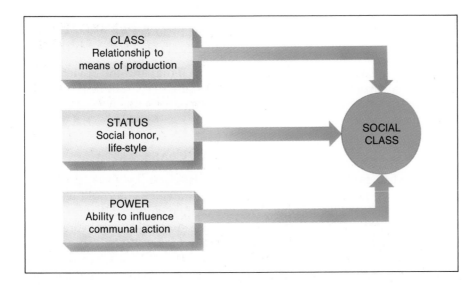

FIGURE 9.1
WEBER'S MODEL OF SOCIAL CLASS

Weber identified three independent dimensions of stratification. This multidimensional concept is called social class.

people are ranked in a stratification system (see Fig 9.1). One of them, as Marx suggested, is class. The second is **status,** or social honor, expressed in life-style. Unlike people united by a common class, people united by a common life-style form a community. They invite one another to dinner, marry one another, engage in the same kinds of recreation, and generally do the same things in the same places. The third dimension is **power,** the ability to get others to act against their wishes, the ability to overcome resistance.

A **status** is a specialized position within a group.

Weber argued that although status and power often follow economic position, they may also stand on their own and have an independent effect on social inequality. In particular, Weber noted that status often stands in opposition to economic power, depressing the pretensions of those who "just" have money. Thus, for example, a member of the Mafia may have a lot of money, may in fact own the means of production (a brothel, a cocaine manufacturing plant, a casino)—but this person will not have social honor.

Power is the ability to direct others' behavior, even against their wishes.

Most sociologists use some version of Weber's framework to guide their examination of stratification systems. Rather than speaking of class (the Marxian dichotomy), we speak of *social* class. **Social class** is a category of people who share roughly the same class, status, and power and who have a sense of identification with one another. When we speak of the upper class or of the working class, we are speaking of social class in this sense.

Social class is a category of people who share roughly the same class, status, and power and who have a sense of identification with each other.

Social class differs from *class* in two ways. First, it recognizes the importance of status and power as well as class. Second, it includes the element of self-awareness. Although people may be ignorant of their class situation, they are usually well aware of their social class position, often using it as an important means to map the social world and their own place in it. People recognize that they are similar to others of their own social class, but different in important ways from those in other social classes. The manager of the Sears store and the garbage collector, for example, are likely to be aware that they are members of the middle and working class, respectively.

FIGURE 9.2
SOCIAL CLASS IDENTIFICATION IN THE UNITED STATES

Social class is a very real concept to most Americans. They are aware of their own social class membership: They feel that, in a variety of important respects, they are similar to others in their own social class and different from those in other social classes. The great majority of Americans place themselves in either the working or the middle class.

SOURCE: Davis, James Allan, and Smith, Tom W. 1986.

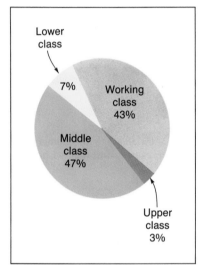

Socioeconomic status (SES) is a measure of social class that ranks individuals on income, education, occupation, or some combination.

INEQUALITY IN THE UNITED STATES

Stratification exists in all societies. In Britain, India, and the Soviet Union alike, social structures ensure that some social classes routinely get more rewards than do others. This section considers how the system works in the United States.

MEASURING SOCIAL CLASS

If you had to rank all the people in your classroom by social class, how would you do it? There are many different strategies you could use: their incomes, their parents' incomes, the size of their savings accounts, or the way they dress and the cars they drive. Some students would score highly no matter how you ranked them, but others' scores might be very sensitive to your measurement procedure. The same thing is true when we try to rank people in the United States; the picture of inequality we get depends on our measurement procedure.

Self-Identification.   A direct way of measuring social class is simply to ask people what social class they belong to. Given our definition of social class as a self-aware group, people should be able to tell you which social class they are in. Sure enough, when we ask Americans, "Which of the following social classes would you say you belong to?" fewer than 1 percent say they don't know. Hardly anybody says, "What do you mean, 'social class'?" and even fewer tell you that we don't have social classes in the United States. The concept of social class is meaningful to most Americans, and they have an opinion about where they fit in the hierarchy.

The results of a 1986 survey are presented in Figure 9.2. As you can see, only tiny minorities see themselves as belonging to the upper and lower classes, and the bulk of the population is split nearly evenly between working- and middle-class identification. Studies show that the difference between working- and middle-class identification has important consequences, affecting what church you go to, how you vote, and how you raise your children. Some of these differences are discussed in later parts of this book.

Socioeconomic Status (SES).   An alternative way to measure social class is by **socioeconomic status (SES),** which ranks individuals on income, education, occupation, or some combination of these. SES measures do not produce self-aware social class groupings, but result in a ranking of the population from high to low on criteria such as years of school completed, family income, or occupation.

Many scholars use occupation alone as their indicator of social class position. The device most often used to rank occupations is the Occupational Prestige Scale. The scale is based on survey research in which large random samples are given lists of occupations and asked "to pick out the statement that best gives your own personal opinion of the general standing that such a job has. Excellent, good, average, somewhat below average, or poor." The prestige of an occupation rests on the overall evaluation that

■

TABLE 9.1
PRESTIGE OF SELECTED OCCUPATIONS

Prestige scores are based on survey research asking about the general standing of occupations. The same rankings have been found in the United States since 1927.

OCCUPATION	1963
Physician	93
College professor	90
Lawyer	89
Dentist	88
Public school teacher	82
Accountant for large business	81
Artist	78
Electrician	76
Trained machinist	74
Welfare worker	74
Police officer	72
Bookkeeper	70
Carpenter	68
Mail carrier	66
Plumber	63
Barber	63
Truck driver	59
Store clerk	56
Restaurant cook	55
Coal miner	50
Janitor	48
Garbage collector	39
Shoe shiner	34

SOURCE: Hodge, Siegel, and Rossi. 1964. "Occupational Prestige in the United States, 1925–63." American Journal of Sociology 70 (3), table 1. © 1964 by the University of Chicago.

sample respondents give to each occupation. Repeated tests have shown that this procedure yields consistent results; the same ordering of occupations has been demonstrated on American samples since 1927 as well as in other Westernized societies, from urban Nigeria to Great Britain (Hodge, Siegel, and Rossi 1964; Hodge, Treiman, and Rossi 1966). And in spite of the fact that the question is specifically about *men* who hold these occupations, occupations are ranked the same way for women, too (Bose and Rossi 1983). Thus, we can be confident that the scale produces a reliable ordering of occupations (see Table 9.1 for a partial list of ranked occupations).

ECONOMIC INEQUALITY

All contemporary class systems have very high levels of inequality. In the United States, income inequality has been substantial since the beginning of the republic. Despite wars on poverty, large-scale increases in educational attainment, and a fourfold increase in the number of two-earner households, inequality in the distribution of household income has changed little. The poorest 20 percent continues to receive only 4 percent of all

FIGURE 9.3
INCOME INEQUALITY IN THE UNITED STATES, 1988

Distributions of income in the United States show little change in income inequality since World War II. Forty-six percent of the total income in the United States goes to the richest 20 percent of the population whereas the poorest 20 percent of the population consistently receives only 4 percent.

SOURCE: U.S. Bureau of the Census 1989g.

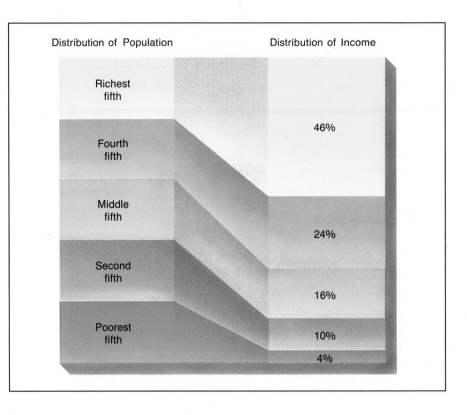

personal income, whereas the richest 20 percent receives 46 percent—or 11 times more (see Figure 9.3).

The inequality documented by income distribution is actually an underestimate of inequality. If we measure material inequality by the distribution of *wealth*—all that the person and the person's family have accumulated over the years (savings, investments, homes, land, cars, and other possessions)—we find that the richest 20 percent of households held 75 percent of all wealth in 1984, the last year for which the government published data. A significant portion of Americans never accumulate any assets, and the richest 2 percent owned fully 26 percent of all assets in 1984 (U.S. Bureau of the Census 1986). Historical research suggests that this unequal distribution of wealth is a long-standing pattern in the United States, dating back at least to 1810.

THE CONSEQUENCES OF SOCIAL CLASS

The following chapters point out the influence of social class in a number of areas—among them religious affiliation and participation, divorce, prejudice and discrimination, and work satisfaction. Here it suffices to say that almost every behavior and attitude we have is related to our social class. Do you prefer bowling to tennis? What kind of movies do you like (they call them films in the upper class)? Would you rather drink beer or sherry? These choices and nearly all the others you make are influenced by your social class. Knowledge of a person's social class will often tell us more about an individual than any other single piece of information. This is why "What do you do for a living?" almost always follows "Glad to meet you."

Can Money Buy Happiness?   Some social class differences are merely subcultural differences in tastes and life-styles. If you prefer football or even all-star wrestling to the symphony, there is no objective way to say that your tastes are worse than those who subscribe to elite culture; they are just different. On many dimensions, however, social class differences are more meaningful. Consider the following:

■ People with incomes below $7,500 a year are nearly twice as likely to be overweight as those with incomes of $40,000 or more (U.S. Bureau of the Census 1989a).

■ People with incomes of less than $10,000 a year are more than twice as likely to have been the victim of a violent crime as those with incomes over $30,000 (U.S. Department of Justice 1989c).

■ Infants whose mothers fail to graduate from high school are twice as likely to die before their first birthday as infants born to mothers with college degrees (Bertoli et al. 1984).

■ People who fail to graduate from high school are twice as likely to get divorced within the first five years of marriage as those who complete at least one year of college (Martin and Bumpass 1989).

On these and many other indicators, the better off are not just different, they are also healthier and happier. The differences between social classes go far beyond tastes in recreation to fundamental differences in the quality of life.

Change and Continuity in the Consequences of Social Class.   Levels of income inequality have changed little since World War II, and differences in wealth have been remarkably constant over 180 years. Nevertheless, there have been some striking changes in the consequences of social class. We can see the clearest evidence in two studies of Middletown (Muncie, Indiana), the first done in 1924–25. After the original investigation, the researchers concluded that social class

> is the most significant single cultural factor tending to influence what one does all day long throughout one's life: whom one marries; when one gets up in the morning; whether one belongs to the Holy Roller or Presbyterian church; or drives a Ford or a Buick; whether or not one's daughter makes the desirable high school Violet Club; or one's wife meets with the Sew We Do Club or with the Art Students' League; whether one belongs to the Odd Fellows or to the Masonic Shrine; whether one sits about evenings with one's necktie off; and so on indefinitely throughout the daily comings and goings of a Middletown man, woman, or child (cited in Caplow and Chadwick 1979).

In 1972, another team of investigators went back to see how Middletown had changed in the ensuing 50 years. The second study found a dramatic decline in social class differences (see Table 9.2). The working class still got up a little earlier and still placed less stress on independence, but there was a marked convergence on all measures except the directly economic one—percentage unemployed.

 As the differentials reported on obesity, infant mortality, victimization, and divorce demonstrate, social class still does make a big difference.

TABLE 9.2

CHANGES IN LIFE-STYLES BY SOCIAL CLASS IN MIDDLETOWN BETWEEN 1924 AND 1972

Differences in social class declined sharply in Middletown between 1924 and 1972. With the exception of unemployment, the life-styles of working-class families and business-class families were much more similar in 1972 than they were in 1924.

	1924	1972
Percentage of families rising before 6 A.M. on workdays		
Business class	15%	31%
Working class	93	38
Percentage of families where husband unemployed in last year		
Business class	1	4
Working class	28	25
Percentage of families with a working wife		
Business class	3	42
Working class	44	48
Percentage of mothers wanting their children to go to college		
Business class	93	90
Working class	23	83
Percentage of parents stressing independence in children		
Business class	46	82
Working class	17	68

SOURCE: Caplow and Chadwick. 1979. "Inequality and Life-Styles in Middletown, 1920–1978." Social Science Quarterly 60 (3). Reprinted with permission of The University of Texas Press and authors.

Nevertheless, the difference is less than it was 65 years ago. To some extent, this is a result of the major increases in real income that have been experienced in this country since 1924. The increases have been particularly important for those who were barely keeping their heads above water. Although the cars, televisions, and homes of the working class are not of the same quality as those of the middle class, the working class does have them. An additional factor in reducing some of the major differences in life chances is the extension of public services. Public schools, the GI Bill, and veterans' benefits have helped reduce some of the severer consequences of lower social class. As we will document later in this chapter, however, some pockets of truly disadvantaged people still exist.

Conclusion.   Social class is important in American society. It affects our attitudes, behaviors, values, health, and opportunities. Although some social class differences have been reduced through federal programs and through mass culture, many important differences—including very substantial income inequality—remain. Next we look at the factors that explain this continuing inequality.

EXPLANATIONS OF INEQUALITY

Michael Jackson earned $32 million in 1989, Joe Montana earned $2 million, George Bush earned $200,000, and the average police officer and teacher earned about $30,000; some 30 percent of Americans live in families where the annual income is less than $10,000. How can we account for such vast differences in income? Why isn't somebody doing anything about it?

We begin our answers to these questions by examining the social structure of stratification—that is, instead of asking about Michael and Joe and George, we ask why some *statuses* routinely get more scarce resources than others. After we review these general theories of stratification, we will turn to explanations about how individuals are sorted into these various statuses.

STRUCTURAL-FUNCTIONAL THEORY

The structural-functional theory of stratification begins (as do all structural-functional theories) with the question: Does this social structure contribute to the maintenance of society? This theoretical position is represented by the work of Davis and Moore (1945), who conclude that stratification is necessary and justifiable because it contributes to the maintenance of society. Their argument begins with the premise that each society has essential tasks (functional prerequisites) that must be performed if it is to survive. The tasks associated with shelter, food, and reproduction are some of the most obvious examples. They argue that we may need to offer high rewards as an incentive to make sure that people are willing to do these tasks. The size of the rewards must be proportional to three factors:

1. *The importance of the task.* When a task is very important, very high rewards may be necessary to guarantee that it is done.
2. *The pleasantness of the task.* When the task is relatively enjoyable, there will be no shortage of volunteers and high rewards need not be offered.
3. *The scarcity of the talent and ability necessary to perform the task.* When relatively few have the ability to perform an important task, high rewards are necessary to motivate this small minority to perform the necessary task.

Let us apply this reasoning to two tasks, health care and reproduction. The tasks of the physician require quite a bit of skill, intelligence beyond the average, long years of training, and long hours of work in sometimes unpleasant and stressful circumstances. To motivate people who have this relatively scarce talent to undertake such a demanding and important task, Davis and Moore would argue that we must hold out the incentive of very high rewards in prestige and income. Society is likely to determine, however, that little reward is necessary to motivate women to fill the even more vital task of reproducing and raising a new generation. Although the function is essential, the potential to fill the position is widespread (most women between 15 and 40 can do it), and the job has sufficient noncash attractions that no shortage of volunteers has arisen.

In many ways, this is a supply-and-demand argument that views inequality as a rational response to a social problem. This theoretical position is sometimes called consensus theory because it suggests that inequality is the result of societal agreement about the importance of social positions and the need to pay to have them filled.

Criticisms. This theory has generated a great deal of controversy. Among the major criticisms are these: (1) High demand (scarcity) can be artificially created by limiting access to good jobs. For example, keeping medical schools small and making admissions criteria unnecessarily stiff reduce

A Community Without Inequality?

In 1920 a group of 90 young Jewish pioneers from Poland set up a commune in Palestine that attempted to eliminate inequality. Their successes and failures, described in a 1956 book by Melford Spiro, *Kibbutz: Venture in Utopia*, illuminate how difficult it is to eliminate inequality.

The Goals

The settlers of Kiryat Yeddidum were Marxists. They hoped that by abolishing private property and investing ownership and control of the means of production in the entire community that they could eliminate all inequality—inequality of status and power as well as inequality in wealth, inequality between women and men as well as inequality between classes. They took the following steps.

1. *All property belonged to the community.* Even the clothes they wore were not their own. Each week they checked out a different suit of clothing from the community laundry. In the beginning, they went so far toward equality that everybody got the same size!

2. *The emphasis was on community rather than on individuals.* Each couple or single person had a sparsely and identically furnished room for sleeping, but all activity beyond sleeping was expected to be communal: communal toilets, showers, dining rooms. It was regarded as selfish to want to be by yourself.

3. *Jobs were rotated.* Not all jobs are equally prestigious. People who manage have more power than those who milk cows; people whose work produces substantial profit have more prestige than those who do the laundry. In order to equalize these elements of inequality, job assignments were temporary and were rotated annually. Thus, one might manage one year, scrub toilets the next, and drive a tractor the third.

The Outcome

Did it work? Partially. The settlers established equality in material wealth, but not in prestige. The major difficulty was job rotation. Not everyone had the skills to do accounting. More important, in an agricultural community with a low level of mechanization, much of the work was so physically demanding that sex and age made a difference in how effective a worker was. Because the commune was living on the edge of subsistence, it could not afford to be less than totally efficient in allocating labor. Thus, strong men worked in the fields where they made an immediate contribution to the community's livelihood, and women and old men worked in the laundry or the kitchen or scrubbed toilets. Out of economic necessity, these assignments, with their obvious inequalities in prestige, existed year after year rather than being rotated. These inequalities were bitterly resented.

Assessment

What lessons about the possibility of establishing equality can we draw from this attempt? First, the experience of Kiryat Yeddidum tells us that equality in material rewards is easier to establish than equality in prestige. Second, inequality in prestige *is* important; those with low status will find it galling. Third, equality in status and prestige probably does rest on effective job rotation.

Effective job rotation is very difficult to implement, however. Recognizing this difficulty, most groups and societies striving for equality have concentrated on equalizing differences in material wealth. Most have also been content to try to eliminate class inequality without tackling the more difficult issues of gender and age inequalities. These issues are addressed in more detail in Chapters 11 and 12.

supply and increase demand for physicians. (2) Social class background, sex, and race or ethnicity probably have more to do with who gets highly rewarded statuses than do scarce talents and ability. (3) Many highly rewarded statuses (rock stars and professional athletes, but also plastic surgeons and speech writers) are hardly necessary to the maintenance of society.

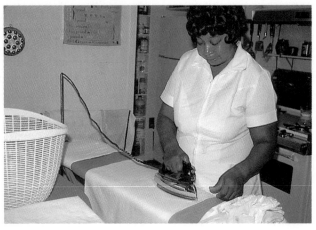

THE CONFLICT PERSPECTIVE

A clear alternative to the Davis and Moore theory is given by scholars who adhere to conflict theory. They explain inequality as the result of class conflict rather than as a result of consensus about how to meet social needs. We review traditional Marxist thought first and then describe more recent applications of conflict theory to the study of inequality.

Marxist Theory. Marx argued that inequality was rooted in private ownership of the means of production. Those who own the means of production seek to maximize their own profit by minimizing the amount of return they must give to the proletarians, who have no choice but to sell their labor to the highest bidder. In this view, inequality is an outcome of private property, where the goods of society are owned by some and not by others. In Marxist theory, stratification is neither necessary nor justifiable. Inequality does not benefit society; it benefits only the rich.

Although Marx did not see inequality as either necessary or justifiable, he did see that it might be nearly inevitable. The reason lies in the division of labor. Almost any complex task, from teaching school to building automobiles, requires some task specialization: Some people build fuel pumps and others install them, some teach algebra and others teach poetry. To make such a division of labor work effectively, somebody has to coordinate the efforts of all the specialists. Individuals who do this coordination are in a unique position to pursue their own self-interest—to hire their own children in preference to others', to give themselves more rewards than they give others, and generally to increase the gap between themselves and those they coordinate. Marx's patron and coauthor, Friedrich Engels, explained it this way:

> It is therefore the law of the division of labor that lies at the basis of the division into classes. But this does not prevent the division into classes from being carried out by means of violence, and robbery, trickery and fraud. It does not prevent the ruling class, once having the upper hand, from consolidating its power at the expense of the working class, from turning its social leadership into an intensified exploitation of the masses (Engels [1880] 1965, 79).

Which job is the hardest? Which one pays the most? Ironically, people who work the hardest often earn the least; they earn the least income and the least honor. A more critical problem for structural functional theory is the issue of how these two jobs are assigned. Would you feel safe in concluding that the woman who has to iron for a living has less talent and ability than the white-collar worker? Critics point out that social class background and race are often more important than ability in determining who gets the good jobs and who gets the bad jobs.

Modern Conflict Theory.   During the early days of industrialization when Marx was writing, ownership and control were inseparable: Those who owned the factories also managed them. In modern capitalism, however, ownership may be divided among dozens or even thousands of stockholders, while management control is concentrated among a handful of expert managers. Thus, in the modern economy, control may exist independent of ownership (Wright 1985).

Modern conflict theory goes beyond Marx's emphasis on ownership to consider how control may affect the struggle over scarce resources (Grimes 1989). It shares with earlier Marxist theory the idea that those in control are able to oppress those who work for them by claiming the profits from their labor (Wright 1985). Conflicts of interest and manipulation of the less powerful by the more powerful are still the bases of inequality.

Criticisms.   There seems to be little doubt that people who have control (through ownership or management) systematically use their power to extend and enhance their own advantage. Critics, however, question the conclusion that this means that inequality is necessarily undesirable and unfair. This is certainly a debatable assumption. First, people *are* unequal. Some people are harder working, smarter, and more talented than others. Unless forcibly held back, these people will pull ahead of the others—even without force, fraud, and trickery. Second, coordination and authority *are* functional.

A CONTEMPORARY SYNTHESIS

Structural-functional theory and conflict theory address important issues in the explanation of inequality; each also has a blind side. Structural-functional theory disregards how power may be used to create and enhance inequality; conflict theory generally ignores the functions of inequality.

In 1989, Beegley provided a general theory of contemporary stratification that pulls together some ideas from structural-functional and conflict theory. His synthesis rests on three major points:

1. *Power is the major determinant of the distribution of scarce resources.* People who have power, whether because of ownership or because of control, will use that power to enhance, protect, and extend their resources. For example, they will try to shape the labor market in ways that benefit themselves.

2. *The distribution of power (and hence of scarce resources) is socially structured.* The level of poverty in a society, the salaries of rock stars, and the opportunities to get ahead depend on public and private policies. For example, if professional schools require annual tuitions of $15,000 and more a year, then it is almost automatic that most of the professionals of the next generation will come from today's advantaged families. One implication of this idea is that, if we wanted to, we could change this policy and increase access to professional statuses.

3. *Individuals can make a difference.* As we saw when we looked at the development of the self-concept, individual behavior is not wholly determined by social structures. Individual characteristics such as talent and ambition play a role. Thus, scarce talents and abilities may allow some to rise to the top despite a disadvantaged position in the social structure.

CONCEPT SUMMARY
A Comparison of Three Models of Stratification

BASIS OF COMPARISON	STRUCTURAL-FUNCTIONAL THEORY	CONFLICT THEORY	BEEGLEY'S SYNTHESIS
1. Society can best be understood as . . .	Groups *cooperating* to meet common needs	Groups *competing* for scarce resources	Groups competing for scarce resources
2. Social structures . . .	Solve problems and help society adapt	Maintain current patterns of inequality	Determine opportunities and their allocation
3. Causes of stratification are . . .	Importance of vital tasks, unequal ability, pleasantness of tasks	Unequal control of means of production maintained by force, fraud, and trickery	Inequalities in power
4. Conclusion about stratification . . .	Necessary and desirable	Difficult to eliminate, but unnecessary and undesirable	Inevitably built into social structure; no value judgment
5. Strengths . . .	Consideration of unequal skills and talents and necessity of motivating people to work	Consideration of conflict of interests and how those with control use the system to their advantage	Value free; recognizes that structure is more important than individual talents
6. Weaknesses . . .	Ignores importance of power and inheritance in allocated rewards; functional importance overstated	Ignores the fuctions of inequality and importance of individual differences	Applies to modern capitalist societies

The first two of Beegley's points are drawn from modern conflict theory, the third from structural functionalism. Although his theory does allow a role for scarce talents and abilities, it focuses on the social structure of power as the major determinant of inequality.

Conclusion.   So, why *do* Michael Jackson and Joe Montana make so much money? Neither Jackson nor Montana appears to be engaged in force, fraud, or trickery or to be using his authority to exploit others. Beegley's theory suggests an explanation for their earnings. First, of course, Jackson and Montana are very good at what they do (see Beegley's third point). At least as important, however, is the fact that entertainment is a huge industry in the United States, which supports Beegley's second point. Finally, and this is Beegley's first point, the people who *control* the entertainment industry (as opposed to those who merely work in it) have incomes that dwarf Jackson's and Montana's. One of the reasons, in fact, that Jackson makes more than Montana is that, over the years, he has acquired control of his own production; Joe Montana still works for the owner of the 49ers. Although it takes a stretch of the imagination to see Montana as exploited, the professional football strike of the 1988 season illustrates the conflict of interest between management and labor even at this level. The fact that the players lost and the owners won also illustrates Beegley's first point: Those in control have the resources to protect and maintain their advantage.

THE DETERMINANTS OF SOCIAL CLASS POSITION

With each generation, the social statuses in a given society must be allocated anew. Some people will get the good positions and some will get the bad ones; some will receive many scarce resources and some will not. In a class system, this allocation process depends on two things: the characteristics of the individuals (their education, aspirations, skills, and so on) and the characteristics of the labor market. We refer to these, respectively, as micro- and macro-level factors that affect achievement.

MICROSTRUCTURE: STATUS ATTAINMENT

If *Sports Illustrated* gave you the job of predicting the top 20 college football teams in the country next year, you could go to the trouble of finding out the average height, weight, and experience level of each team's members, the dollars allocated to the athletic department, the years of coaching experience, and the attendance at games. From this information you could devise some complex system of predicting the winners. You would probably do a better job for a lot less trouble, however, if you predicted that last year's winners will be this year's winners. The same thing is true in predicting winners and losers in the race for class, status, and power. The simplest and most accurate guess is based on social continuity.

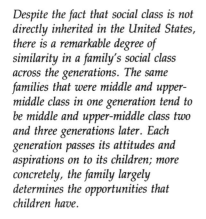

Despite the fact that social class is not directly inherited in the United States, there is a remarkable degree of similarity in a family's social class across the generations. The same families that were middle and upper-middle class in one generation tend to be middle and upper-middle class two and three generations later. Each generation passes its attitudes and aspirations on to its children; more concretely, the family largely determines the opportunities that children have.

American culture values achievement rather than ascription, and occupations are not directly inherited. Yet people tend to have occupations of a status similar to that of their parents. How does this come about? The best way to describe the system is as an **indirect inheritance model.** Parents' occupations do not directly cause children's occupations, but the family's status and income determine children's aspirations and opportunities.

The **indirect inheritance model** argues that children have occupations of a status similar to that of their parents because the family status and income determine children's aspirations and opportunities.

Inherited Characteristics: Help and Aspirations.   The best predictor of your eventual social class is your education—and the best predictor of your education is your parents' education. A small part of this is directly financial. Better educated parents are more often able to afford their children's college expenses. Most of the impact of parents' education, however, is less direct. If your parents graduated from college or have middle-class jobs, then you have probably always assumed that you, too, would go to college. You automatically signed up for algebra and chemistry in high school. If your parents didn't graduate from high school and tend to think that education is a necessary evil, then you probably bypassed algebra for a shop or sewing class.

The atmosphere of the home and the parents' support and encouragement may have important effects on the child's success. Bright and ambitious lower-class children may find it hard to do well in school if they have to study at a noisy kitchen table amidst a group of people who think that their studies are a waste of time; middle-class children with even modest ambitions and intelligence may find it hard to fail within their very supportive environment.

The Wild Cards: Achievement Motivation and Intelligence.   The social class environment in which a child grows up is the major determinant of educational attainment. There are, however, two wild cards that keep education from being directly inherited: achievement motivation and intelligence. Neither of these factors is strongly related to parents' social class, and both act as filters that allow people to rise above or fall below their parents' social class (Duncan, Featherman, and Duncan 1972).

Achievement motivation is the continual drive to match oneself against standards of excellence. Students who have this motivation are always striving for A's, are never satisfied with taking easy courses, and have a real need to compete. Not surprisingly, students with high achievement motivation do better than others in school.

Achievement motivation is the continual drive to match oneself against standards of excellence.

High achievement motivation appears to be the major reason for the remarkable social mobility of many recent Asian American immigrant groups in the United States. For example, Vietnamese-Americans are twice as likely to be enrolled in college as the average American (Gardner, Robey, and Smith 1985). Simply put, they try harder; they want to succeed more. With this kind of drive, some individuals from disadvantaged backgrounds can make it.

Intelligence is another important factor in determining educational and occupational success (Duncan, Featherman, and Duncan 1972). Because intelligent people are born into all social classes, intelligence is a factor that allows for both upward and downward intergenerational mobility. (Chapter 14 looks at the issue of social class and intelligence in greater detail.)

Summary.   The indirect inheritance model summarizes the processes of individual status attainment. It shows how some people come to be well prepared to step into good jobs, while others lack the necessary skills or credentials. By themselves, however, skills and credentials do not necessarily lead to class, status, or power. The other variable in the equation is the labor market.

MACROSTRUCTURE: THE LABOR MARKET

If there is a major economic depression, you will not be able to get a good job no matter what your education, achievement motivation, or aspirations. The character of the labor market and the structure of occupations it provides have a significant effect on individual achievements.

Within the last 80 years, the occupational structure of the United States has changed rapidly. As Figure 9.4 shows, the proportion of positions at the top has expanded dramatically during this century, providing opportunities for upward mobility. Despite this general improvement, the labor market is not equally open to all workers. Women and minorities especially have been virtually shut out of some high-earning occupations. No matter what their talents and credentials, they have found the labor market inhospitable. Between 1960 and 1980, the racial compositions of the National Basketball Association shifted from 80 percent white Americans to 80 percent African Americans. This shift was not because African American basketball players all of a sudden got a lot better; it was a function of the changed structure of the labor market. Employers were finally willing to hire African American players.

Labor market theorists suggest that the U.S. has a **segmented labor market:** one labor market for good jobs (usually in the big companies) and one labor market for bad jobs (usually in small companies). Women and minorities are disproportionately directed into companies with low wages, low benefits, low security, and short career ladders. (The contemporary economic structure is discussed in more detail in Chapter 16.)

Summary.   The stratification structure of any society depends upon both macro- and micro-level processes. Some aspects of inequality are best ex-

The **segmented labor market** parallels the dual economy. Hiring, advancement, and benefits vary systematically between the industrial core and the periphery.

■

FIGURE 9.4
THE CHANGING OCCUPATION STRUCTURE, 1900–1990

Since the turn of the century the occupational structure of the United States has shifted away from farm labor. Today there are many more white-collar, professional, and managerial jobs.

SOURCES: U.S. Bureau of the Census 1975, 139; U.S. Department of Labor 1990, 30.

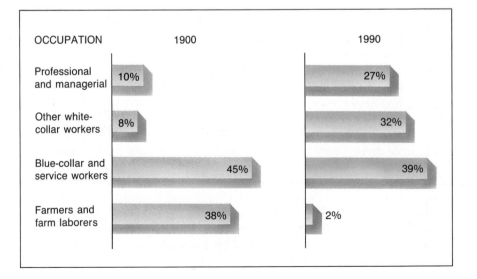

OCCUPATION	1900	1990
Professional and managerial	10%	27%
Other white-collar workers	8%	32%
Blue-collar and service workers	45%	39%
Farmers and farm laborers	38%	2%

plained on the macro level. For example, if we want to know what percent has good jobs or why some groups have bad jobs despite their credentials, then we look at the structure of the labor market and how it is changing. If we want to know which individuals are prepared to take the good jobs, then we need to look at micro-level processes that determine individual characteristics.

THE AMERICAN DREAM: IDEOLOGY AND REALITY

A system of stratification is an organized way of ensuring that some categories of individuals get more social rewards than others. As we have seen, sometimes this means a great disparity not only in income but also in health, honor, and happiness. Yet, in most highly stratified systems, there are no revolutionary movements, the rich aren't always fearing attack, and the poor don't sit around stoking the fires of resentment. For the most part, inequality is accepted as fair and natural, even as God-given.

This consensus about inequality indicates the role of the normative structure in reinforcing and justifying a system of stratification. Each system furnishes an **ideology**—a set of norms and values that rationalizes the existing social structure (Mannheim 1929). The ideology is built into the dominant cultural values of the society—often into its religious values. For example, the Hindu religion maintains that a low caste in this life is a punishment for poor performance in a previous life. If you live well in this life, however, you can expect to be promoted to a higher caste in the next life. Thus, the Hindu religion offers mobility (extragenerational mobility, we might call it) and also an incentive to accept one's lot in life. To attack the caste system would be equivalent to saying that the gods are unfair or this religion is stupid.

In the United States, the major ideology that justifies inequality is the *American Dream*, which suggests that equality of opportunity exists in the United States and that your position in the class structure is a fair reflection of what you deserve. That is, if you are worthy and if you work hard, you can succeed; since your position comes entirely from your own efforts, no one but you can be blamed for your failures. The upper class is the most likely to believe that America is a land of opportunity and that everybody gets a fair shake, but most others believe this, too. There are, to be sure, some grumblers, especially among minority groups, such as the disenchanted person who stated, "The rich stole, beat, and took. The poor didn't start stealing in time, and what they stole, it didn't value nothing, and they were caught with that!" (Huber and Form 1973).

The grumblers, however, are few, and most of them are less interested in changing the rules of the game than in being dealt into it. A survey of American adults found that equality was a dirty word: Fewer than 20 percent agreed that "it would be a good thing if the president decided to distribute all the money in the United States equally among all the population" (Bell and Robinson 1978).

Americans believe in "fair shares" rather than in "equal shares" (Ryan 1981). They believe that people who work harder and people who are smarter deserve to get ahead. A typical attitude toward the wealthy is represented by the comments of one unemployed laborer: "If a person keeps his mind to it, and works and works, and he's banking it, hey, good luck to him!" (cited in Hochschild 1981, 116).

The preparation that you receive for the labor market—your education, training, and aspirations—have an enormous impact on whether you get a good or bad job. Nevertheless, your fate ultimately depends on the job market. If the aerospace industry is in a slump, even aeronautical engineers may be unemployable. Even in a booming economy, many labor markets implicitly discriminate against people on the basis of their age, sex, race, or ethnicity. These market factors are critical for understanding why some groups consistently have worse jobs and lower earnings than others.

An **ideology** is a set of norms and values that rationalizes the existing social structure.

VARIATIONS ON A THEME: THE RICH, THE WORKING CLASS, AND THE POOR

The United States is a middle-class nation. If given only three categories for self-identification, more than two-thirds of the population considers itself middle class. American norms and values are the norms and values of the middle class. Everybody else becomes a subculture. This section briefly reviews the special conditions of the nonmiddle class in America.

THE UPPER CLASS

In 1988, it required a family income of "only" $85,640 a year to put one in the richest 5 percent. Thus, a variety of more-or-less ordinary salespersons, doctors, lawyers, and managers in towns across the nation qualify as being very rich compared with the majority. Although their incomes are nothing to sneeze at, most of this upper 5 percent is still in the middle class, albeit the upper-middle class. Like members of the working class, they would have a hard time making their mortgage payments if they lost their jobs.

The true upper class is the top 5 percent of the top 5 percent. There are nearly half a million millionaires in the United States—people whose assets total over $1 million. At the very top of the heap are the nearly 5,000 whose *earnings* in a single year top $1 million.

Every year *Forbes* magazine provides a glimpse at the very rich by providing profiles of the richest 400 people in the United States. (A review of the top 10 for 1989 appears in Table 9.3.) The average person who made it into the Forbes 400 was a 63-year-old white male with a degree from an Ivy League school. He made his fortune in manufacturing, the stock market, or media. Forty percent inherited their way to the top. Of the 217 who were self-made, few went from rags to riches; most got an excellent start:

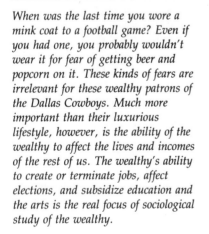

When was the last time you wore a mink coat to a football game? Even if you had one, you probably wouldn't wear it for fear of getting beer and popcorn on it. These kinds of fears are irrelevant for these wealthy patrons of the Dallas Cowboys. Much more important than their luxurious lifestyle, however, is the ability of the wealthy to affect the lives and incomes of the rest of us. The wealthy's ability to create or terminate jobs, affect elections, and subsidize education and the arts is the real focus of sociological study of the wealthy.

■

TABLE 9.3
THE 10 RICHEST PEOPLE IN THE UNITED STATES, 1989

Each year Forbes *magazine publishes a list of the 400 richest people in the United States. About 40 percent of these fabulously wealthy individuals inherited their fortunes; the other two-thirds are largely individually responsible for generating their vast wealth. Their major avenues to riches were the stock market, manufacturing, and the media.*

NAME, AGE	COLLEGE	ESTIMATED NET WORTH	MAJOR WEALTH SOURCE
John Kluge, 75	Columbia	$5.2 billion	Metromedia; self-made; began a radio station in Washington, D.C.
Warren Buffett, 59	Columbia	4.2	Stock market; self-made, with help from a $100,000 family investment fund
Sumner Redstone, 66	Harvard	2.9	National Amusements, Inc. (MTV, The Movie Channel); took over father's small chain of drive-in theaters
Ted Arison, 65	None	2.9	Carnival Cruise Lines; started own business when immigrated to U.S., but father is largest shipowner in Israel
Ronald Perelman, 46	Wharton	2.8	Finance (leveraged buyouts); self-made, but as a child sat in on father's business deals
Samuel Newhouse, 61 Donald Newhouse, 60	None given None given	5.2	Advance Publication, inherited from their father but greatly expanded by sons
Barbara Cox Anthony, 64 Anne Cox Chambers, 61	None given None given	5.0	Inherited Cox Communications from their father
H. Ross Perot, 57	Annapolis	2.4	Electronic Data Systems; self-made, started as a salesperson at IBM

SOURCE: "The Forbes Four Hundred" 1989, 152–56.

They had at least middle-class parents with business experience who sent their children to excellent schools. For example, William Henry Gates III dropped out of school at 19 to found Microsoft, a company that produces an extremely popular software package. At 33, he has a net worth of $1.25 billion. Gates, who got a perfect 800 on the math portion of the SAT, is obviously very smart in addition to being extraordinarily hardworking. He did not make it on grit and talent alone, however. He had all the right background: His father is a prominent attorney in Seattle; his mother is on the University of Washington Board of Regents; the college he dropped out of was Harvard ("The Forbes" 1989, 182–84).

The very rich not only have many more choices in their lives than do those whose next mortgage payment depends on their keeping their job but they also have the capacity to affect large numbers of others through their choices. By controlling media resources, contributing money to political campaigns, building museums, or deciding to open or close manufacturing plants, they have the power to affect the lives of millions of ordinary citizens. The power that they wield over others gives us an intense interest in their politics and attitudes, yet we know relatively little about the lives of the very rich. Although occasionally their stories and pictures appear in the news, they are not available to social researchers. They do not participate in Gallup polls, nor do they hang out in public places where their behavior can be observed. If you watch "Life-Styles of the Rich and Famous," you will know about as much about the lives of the rich as a social scientist does.

The one aspect of the rich that has been extensively studied is their attitudes toward inequality. A social scientist who has made a career out of studying elites concludes that the people at the top "share a consensus about the fundamental values of private enterprise, limited government, and due process of law. . . . [They] believe in equality of opportunity rather than absolute equality" (Dye 1983, 273). As conflict theory would suggest, they are interested in maintaining a system that has been good to them.

The Working Class

Who are the members of the working class? The answer is determined partly by occupation, partly by education, and partly by self-definition. Generally, the working class includes those who work in blue-collar industries and their families. They are the men and women who work in chemical, automobile, and other manufacturing plants; they load warehouses, drive trucks, and build houses. Although they sometimes receive excellent wages and benefits, it is the working class that suffers 10–15 percent unemployment during economic recessions and slumps.

To find out what life was like for the working class, sociologist David Halle (1984) spent seven years studying the blue-collar employees of a New Jersey chemical plant. His participant observation study involved hanging around in the plant itself and going to taverns, football games, and Christmas parties. Because of his own sex, Halle found it easier to observe working-class men than women, so his conclusions focus primarily on men. His work suggests that the following dimensions make working-class life distinct from that of the middle class: education, job and economic prospects, leisure, and gender differences.

Education.   The working class is more highly educated than it used to be. A majority are probably high school graduates. Still, an eleventh-grade education is more common than a year of college. More importantly, many of these people did not do well in school, and they did not absorb the school's middle-class values.

> What was school like? It was horrible, horrible! . . . They [the teachers] were cuckoos. They gave you *Romeo and Juliet* to read, and I looked at it and I said, "What is this! What has this got to do with me?" I looked at the flyleaf. . . . And I saw Joe Smith's name from three years ago. I knew he was digging ditches now, so I said to myself, "This book didn't do anything for him. What's it going to do for me?" (Halle 1984, 49).

Although there are working-class women and men who read Shakespeare and discuss existentialism, much more common are the people who aren't interested in elite culture. Halle found that these men were painfully aware of the low prestige associated with their taste, but they were really much more interested in football than opera. Although sensitive about his lack of cultured interests, the typical worker excused himself as "just a working slob."

Economic Prospects.   Quite a few members of the working class have incomes as good or better than the lower-middle class. Some make as much or more than public school teachers and people in retail sales. As a result, they live in the same neighborhoods as these members of the lower-middle class. Their economic prospects differ from their white-collar neighbors, however, in two ways. First, they have little or no chance of promotion. The barrier between manual labor and management is virtually impassable. The height of one's earning power may be reached at age 25. Second, layoffs and plant closings expose them to more economic uncertainty. As a result of low prospects and economic uncertainty, members of the working class tend to place a higher value on security than others. One aspect of this is home ownership. Nearly three quarters of the working class own their own homes. For most, it is their major financial asset and their only effective savings plan. Their resulting interest in property taxes, property values, and neighborhood maintenance drives much of their political activity.

Leisure. Most working-class jobs are not enjoyable. Although middle-class workers may have a hard time separating their leisure time from their work time (going to the office on Saturdays, taking their work home with them, or having business dinners), members of the working class have no difficulty separating work from leisure—and they much prefer leisure. According to Halle, the working-class man does his work without joy and lives for his leisure. The high point of his life is going hunting and fishing with his friends, having a few drinks in the tavern after work, watching football on Sunday afternoons, and fooling around in his yard. When he dreams of the future, he dreams of his new boat or maybe a cabin in the mountains; he doesn't dream of a better job.

Gender Differences. Scholars of working-class life emphasize the sharp differences between the worlds of men and women. As the description of leisure activities suggests, men's leisure interests lie largely in sex-segregated activities: watching football, going hunting, drinking in taverns. Even when social activity is based on couples, the women will talk in the kitchen and the men in the den. Although lack of common interests may damage some marriages, social class is not strongly related to marital happiness. One worker explains his recipe for a happy marriage:

> We [his wife and he] do a lot together. We both bowl, and we go out to eat together, and go to parties. I'm happy.
>
> My wife is very liberal. She doesn't bother if I'm out, and I don't bother if she's out. I know she's with her girlfriends or something. She doesn't mind if I come home late unless it's very late, maybe 2:00 or 3:00 in the morning. . . .
>
> There are some things you can't do. Like my wife doesn't mind if my friends come over to play cards so long as it's not every night. Once or twice a week is OK, but not every night. Then she'll say, "No way!" because she has to clean up afterward, sweep and clean away cigarette butts and all that. That's a lot of work (Halle 1984, 57).

Gender segregation of leisure activities is not confined to the working class, but working-class women and men appear to have less in common than their middle-class counterparts. Perhaps more important, the working class is more likely to hold norms suggesting that men and women ought to be different and that they "naturally" will have different interests and roles.

Summary.   Income is an inadequate criterion to distinguish the working from the middle class. The working class is often less well off than the middle class, but the primary distinctions are in occupation, education, and lifestyle rather than in income. This may change in the future. As Chapter 16 will document, the jobs that have provided relative affluence for the unionized working class are declining. In their place are minimum-wage service jobs that will push a growing sector of the working class to the poverty level.

THE POOR IN AMERICA

Each year, the U.S. government fixes a poverty level that is calculated to be the amount of money a family would need to meet the minimum requirements of a decent standard of living. The poverty level adjusts for family size, and in 1988, the poverty level for a family of four was $12,091 (U.S. Bureau of the Census 1989g). Under this definition, 31.9 million people, 13 percent of the population, were classified as poor in 1988.

Who Are the Poor?   Poverty cuts across several dimensions of society. It is found among white Americans as well as nonwhites, in rural areas as much as in urban centers, in families as well as in single households. As Table 9.4 indicates, nearly half (46 percent) of the poor in 1988 were too old or young to work. Of those in the working ages, a substantial proportion could not earn a wage that would lift them out of poverty.

A significant portion of the women and children who live in poverty do so simply because they have no husband or father in their house. Granted that having a man in the house is no guarantee of being out of poverty (12.1 million male-headed families are below the poverty level), it does significantly decrease the likelihood of being in poverty: Seven percent of all male-headed families are below the poverty level, whereas 37 percent of all female-headed families are below that level.

Although some categories of people, such as minorities or those in female-headed households, top the poverty charts year after year, a recent study shows that there is less continuity than one might suppose in the individual experience of poverty. A study of a large sample of Americans between 1969 and 1978 found that one quarter of all Americans were poor at least one year between 1969 and 1978, but only one-third of those who were poor in 1978 had been poor for eight or more of those 10 years. The persistently poor fell into one of two categories: They were elderly or they lived in households headed by a black woman (Duncan 1984).

How Poor Are the Poor?   An important issue that arises in discussing American poverty is how poor the poor actually are. Two concepts are important here: absolute poverty and relative poverty. **Absolute poverty** means the inability to provide the minimum requirements of life. **Relative poverty** means the inability to maintain what your society regards as a decent standard of living.

The poor in America come in both forms. Those who live at or close to the poverty level have a roof over their head and food to eat. On the other hand, their car is broken down and so is the television, the landlord is threatening to evict them, they are eating too much macaroni, and they cannot afford to take their children to the doctor or the dentist. Although

Absolute poverty is the inability to provide the minimum requirements of life.

Relative poverty is the inability to maintain what your society regards as a decent standard of living.

■

TABLE 9.4
THE POPULATION BELOW THE POVERTY LEVEL IN 1988

Many of the people below the poverty level in 1988 were unable to work. Many of those who were able to work could not have earned a wage that would put them above the poverty level.

	MILLIONS OF PEOPLE	PERCENTAGE OF POVERTY POPULATION	PERCENTAGE OF GROUP IN POVERTY
Total	31.9	100%	13%
Race and Hispanic origin			
White	20.8	65	10
Black	9.4	29	32
Hispanic origin[a]	5.4	17	27
Residence			
Central cities	13.7	43	18
Other urban	9.5	30	8
Nonmetropolitan	8.7	27	16
Living in families			
Male headed	12.1	38	7
Female headed	12.1	38	37
Living alone			
Male	2.8	9	18
Female	4.2	13	23
Children under 15	11.0	35	20
People over 65	3.5	11	12

SOURCE: U.S. Bureau of the Census 1989g, table 17.
[a]Hispanics may be of any race. Because almost all Hispanics are also included in counts of the white or black population, total numbers add to more than 100 percent.

they may not be absolutely poor, they are deprived in terms of what Americans regard as a decent standard of living. There are also Americans who are absolutely poor: the homeless and the truly disadvantaged.

THE HOMELESS.   There are at least 300,000 homeless people in the United States. Many of them are single adults, but 23 percent are families with children. Not only do they lack a roof over their heads but 37 percent also eat one meal a day or less ("Another Winter" 1989). They are homeless, hungry, and often ill. By any standards, they are absolutely poor. As discussed earlier (Chapter 7), some of these people are mentally ill or have alcohol problems; many are simply unable to match their low earning ability with high rents.

THE TRULY DISADVANTAGED.   At the very bottom of the social class hier archy is a group that has been called the **underclass,** a group that is un-employed and unemployable, a miserable substratum that is alienated from American institutions (Myrdal 1962). This underclass in America is dis-proportionately black. It is a group characterized by high nonmarital bir-thrates, high drug use, high murder rates, and high unemployment rates (Wilson 1987). Children born in this environment start at the bottom and

The **underclass** is the group that is un-employed and unemployable, a miser-able substratum that is alienated from American institutions.

Most college students feel poor. Their money runs out before the end of the month, they buy gas $5 at a time, and they are always in debt and overcharged on their Visa. This poverty is generally only temporary and very relative, however. There are many Americans who are truly poor. They are not only without income, but they are alienated from American society. They may be illiterate or nearly so, cut off completely from the major currents of American life, and living one day at a time. The indirect inheritance process makes it extremely unlikely that these children will break out of their parents' social class.

they will undoubtedly stay there. When a researcher asked some young Italian boys from the underclass what they expected to be doing in 20 years, he got the following replies (MacLeod 1987, 61):

STONEY: Hard to say. I could be dead tomorrow. Around here, you gotta take life day by day.

FRANKIE: I don't f------ know. Twenty years. I may be f------ dead. I live a day at a time. I'll probably be in the f------ pen.

SHORTY: Twenty years? I'm going to be in jail.

None of these young men mentioned work as part of their future. All of them use a lot of drugs; all are just barely literate; few will graduate from high school. Their futures seem very likely to be as bleak as they predict.

Causes of Poverty.   Earlier in this chapter, we said that both micro- and macro-level processes are at work in determining social class position. The causes of poverty are simply a special case of these larger processes. At the micro level, poverty is explained by the hypothesis that there is a "culture of poverty"; at the macro level, poverty is explained by the lack of an adequate structure of opportunity.

THE CULTURE OF POVERTY: BLAMING THE VICTIM?   The indirect inheritance model suggests that people born into poverty are likely to stay there: They have poorer preparation for school, lower aspirations, and less help at every step of the way.

An additional mechanism that has been proposed to explain the inheritance of poverty is what anthropologist Oscar Lewis (1969) called the **culture of poverty.** Lewis argued that in rich societies, people who are poor develop a set of values that protects their self-esteem and maximizes their ability to extract enjoyment from dismal circumstances. This set of values—the "culture of poverty"—emphasizes living for the moment rather than thrift, investment in the future, or hard work. Recognizing that success is not within their reach, that no matter how hard they work or how thrifty they are, they will not make it, the poor come to value living for the moment. Like Stoney and Frankie, they live one day at a time.

The culture-of-poverty hypothesis fits neatly into American ideology, and a substantial majority of Americans agree that the poor are poor because of their values. In a recent survey, the two reasons most often endorsed as causes of poverty were that the poor "are not motivated because of welfare" and "lack of drive and perseverance" (Smith and Stone 1989). Blaming failure—or success—on personal characteristics, however, overlooks the role of social structure in shaping both values and opportunities.

THE STRUCTURE OF OPPORTUNITY.   The culture-of-poverty hypothesis implicitly blames the poor for perpetuating their condition. Critics of this hypothesis suggest that we cannot explain poverty by looking at micro-level processes. To understand poverty, they argue, we need to look at the structures of opportunity. If there are no jobs available, then we don't need to psychoanalyze people in order to figure out why they are poor.

Two structural issues are particularly critical for understanding contemporary poverty: the changing labor market and the growing link between education and wages. As we documented in Figure 9.4, the shift from an agricultural to an industrial society produced major structural pressure for upward mobility earlier in this century. Now, at the end of the century, the de-industrialization of America is squeezing the lower middle of the American occupational structure and creating structural pressure for downward mobility among the traditional working class: Good jobs have virtually disappeared for the high school graduate who has no advanced training. Instead of the good union jobs that their parents held, today's high school graduates often find themselves working at dead-end jobs for the minimum wage. A little arithmetic shows that the minimum wage means poverty.

This macrostructural approach to poverty suggests that a major cause of poverty is the absence of good jobs. The issue is a critical one, and we will look at the changing occupational structure in more detail in Chapter 16.

The **culture of poverty** is a set of values that emphasizes living for the moment rather than thrift, investment in the future, or hard work.

Reducing Inherited Equality in the United States

If the competition is fair, inequality is acceptable to most Americans. The question is how to ensure that no one has an unfair advantage. Social policy has taken three different approaches to this: taxing inheritances, outlawing discrimination, and creating special education programs.

ESTATE TAXES

The policy regarding estate taxes is designed to reduce the direct inheritance of social position, to create greater equality at the start of the race. There is substantial consensus that although it is acceptable for ambitious, lucky, or clever persons to amass large fortunes, it is not fair that their children should start their race with such a large advantage. Thus, since 1931, the United States has had a progressive estate tax. The maximum tax has varied over the years from 50 to 90 percent of the estate.

In fact, however, inheritance taxes have not significantly reduced unequal advantage. If wealthy individuals die at 70, their children are already middle aged. The $80,000 the parents spent to give them the best private education money could buy, the new homes they bought for the children when they married, the businesses they set them up in, the trusts they set up for their grandchildren—none of these are part of the estate. By the time the parents die, the children have already been established as rich themselves (Lebergott 1975). Unless we ban private schools, transfers of money to one's children, and giving one's children good jobs, this inheritance is outside the scope of public policy.

OUTLAWING DISCRIMINATION

Antidiscrimination and affirmative-action laws are not aimed at reducing the inequalities that one starts the race with; rather they attempt to ensure

Headstart programs and special education programs cannot reasonably be expected to yield equality of opportunity. If the children in these two pictures all went to the same school, their achievements would probably be very different. Equality of opportunity can only be achieved where there is already substantial equality in background. When children come to school from very unequal backgrounds, their achievements in school are likely to repeat the patterns of their parents.

ISSUES IN SOCIAL POLICY continued

that no unfair obstacles are thrown in the way during the race. Antidiscrimination laws have some effect. Able people have been and still are held back unfairly. If the race itself is not rigged, however, those who work very hard and are very able may overcome the handicaps they begin with. Because people start out with unequal backgrounds, however, they do not have an equal chance of success just by running the same course.

EDUCATION

Education is widely believed to be the key to reducing unfair disadvantages associated with poverty. Pre-kindergarten classes designed to provide intellectual stimulation for children from deprived backgrounds, special education courses for those who don't speak standard English, and loan and grant programs to enable the poor to go to school as long as their ability permits them to do so—all these are designed to increase the chances of students from lower-class backgrounds getting an education.

The programs have had some success. During the last 20 years, colleges and universities saw more students from disadvantaged backgrounds than they used to. Because students spend only 35 hours a week at school, however, and another 130 hours a week with their families and neighbors, the school cannot reasonably overcome the entire disability that exists for disadvantaged children. A study entitled *Summer Learning* documents the fact that disadvantaged children learn less quickly than advantaged children during the school year. Per-

haps more important, they forget more during the summer. Their home environments do not include trips to the library and other activities that encourage them to use and remember their school work. Consequently, for every step forward they take at school, they slide back half a step at home during the summer (Heyns 1978).

CONCLUSION

This review of programs designed to reduce unfair advantages or disadvantages leads to the conclusion that the family is at the root of the inheritance of both advantage and disadvantage. As long as some people are born in tenements or shacks, as long as their parents are uneducated and have bad grammar and small vocabularies, and as long as they have no encyclopedias or intellectual stimulation—while others are born to educated parents with standard speech patterns who flood them with intellectual stimulation and opportunity—there can never be true equality of opportunity. To some extent, the pursuit of equal opportunity will come at the expense of the family: Any attempt to reduce inheritance of status requires weakening the influence of parents on their children.

In any culture, individuals espouse values that conflict with one another and values that are so idealistic that few attempt to live by them. America's ambivalent feelings about inequality are no exception. Do we want equal opportunity badly enough to pay the costs, or will it remain, like marital stability, an ideal but not a reality?

SUMMARY

1. Stratification is distinguished from simple inequality in that (1) it is based on social roles or membership in social statuses rather than on personal characteristics, and (2) it is supported by norms and values that justify unequal rewards.

2. Marx believed that there was only one important dimension of stratification: class. Weber added two further dimensions. Most sociologists now rely on Weber's three-dimensional view of stratification, which embraces class, status, and power.

3. Inequality in income and wealth is substantial in the United States and has changed little over the generations. This inequality has widespread consequences and affects every aspect of our lives. Although the negative consequences of being working class or lower class are less than they were 50 years ago, the lower class and working class continue to be disadvantaged in terms of health, happiness, and life-style.

4. Structural-functional theorists use a supply-and-demand argument to suggest that inequality is a functional way of sorting people into positions; inequality is necessary and justifiable. Conflict theorists believe that inequality arises from conflict over scarce resources, in which those with the most power manipulate the system to enhance and maintain their advantage.

5. Beegley provides a contemporary synthesis of conflict and structural-functional theories. His theory argues that power and social structure are critical factors, but it allows some role for individual characteristics.

6. Allocation of people into statuses includes macro and micro processes. At the macro level, the labor market sets the stage by creating demands for certain statuses. At the micro level, the status attainment process is largely governed by indirect inheritance.

7. There is a great deal of continuity in social class over the generations. In the United States, this inheritance of social class is indirect and works largely through education. Achievement motivation and intelligence, however, are factors that allow for upward and downward mobility.

8. In spite of high levels of inequality, most people in any society accept the structure of inequality as natural or just. This shared ideology is essential for stability. In the United States, this ideology is the American Dream, which suggests that success or failure is the individual's choice.

9. Approximately 13 percent of the American population is below the poverty level. Many of the poor are children or elderly. Although some part of poverty may be due to micro-level processes (the culture of poverty and indirect inheritance), the structure of opportunity determines how extensive poverty is in a society.

10. Because families pass their social class on to their children, any attempt to reduce inequality must take aim at the intergenerational bond between parents and children and must reduce the ability of parents to pass on their wealth and values.

SUGGESTED READINGS

Beegley, Leonard. 1989. The Structure of Stratification in the United States. Boston: Allyn & Bacon. A stratification textbook that reviews other theories about inequality in addition to Beegley's own. This very up-to-date text covers racial and gender inequality as well as social classes.

Halle, David. 1984. America's Working Man. Chicago: University of Chicago Press. An ethnographic study of men who work at a New Jersey chemical plant. Halle's book covers family, leisure, and life-style, as well as issues related directly to blue-collar labor.

Hochschild, Jennifer. 1981. What's Fair? American Beliefs About Distributive Justice. Cambridge, Mass.: Harvard University Press. Addresses the issue of why there is so little support for redistribution among America's poor. The answer is found in loosely structured interviews with several dozen Americans, including both the poor and the rich. Their own words provide the body of this readable and provocative book.

Lenski, Gerhard. 1966. Power and Privilege: A Theory of Social Stratification. New York: McGraw-Hill. A major work distinguishing the fundamental characteristics found in different types of societies, particularly in terms of socially structured inequality.

Patterson, James T. 1986. America's Struggle Against Poverty, 1900–1985. Cambridge, Mass.: Harvard University Press. A history of poverty, poor people, and poverty legislation in the United States during this century.

Ryan, William. 1981. Equality. New York: Pantheon Books. An impassioned argument for "equal shares" instead of "fair shares." Ryan argues that too much inequality exists in the United States and that we should plan policy to increase equality in material wealth.

Wilson, W. Julius. 1987. The Truly Disadvantaged: The Inner City, the Underclass, and Public Policy. Chicago: University of Chicago Press. A strong statement about the growing American underclass by one of the nation's most prominent experts. Wilson argues convincingly for new government programs to put a floor under all citizens.

10

RACIAL AND ETHNIC INEQUALITIES

PROLOGUE

HAVE YOU EVER . . .

Read the graffiti on the walls of a public rest room? If you have, you know that racism is alive and well in the United States. Racial and ethnic slurs are common in America's public places.

Although there are obvious signs of progress, most minority Americans must cope daily with the disadvantage of minority status. Many people remain prejudiced; in overt as well as covert ways, they discriminate. These people are not all rednecks, not all Archie-Bunker-type bigots. Instead, racism is alive and well on college campuses. Some incidents make the national news. In 1987, for example, a racial name-calling incident provoked a small-scale race riot on the campus of Columbia University. In 1989, a fraternity at Tulane paraded in blackface, causing a furor on campus. Since 1986, there have been racial incidents at 250 colleges ranging from "hate-filled graffiti to the repeated destruction of anti-apartheid shanties" ("Lessons from Bigotry 101" 1989, 48).

College-educated people tell surveyors that they are not prejudiced and do not discriminate. Nevertheless, race remains a very important source of intergroup tension and hostility in the United States and none of us is immune to this tension. In this chapter, we consider how class and race have interacted to produce this tension, and we examine prospects for the future.

OUTLINE

RACE, ETHNICITY, AND INEQUALITY

In Chapter 9, we reviewed the general picture of inequality in the United States and examined theories of inequality based on achieved characteristics. We also, however, need to consider differences in rewards and life chances that are associated with ascribed characteristics. In Chapters 10, 11, and 12, we examine three such ascribed characteristics: race and ethnicity, sex, and age. In each case, we deal with the differences in life chances that exist by virtue of ascribed characteristics and consider whether these differences can be explained by the usual processes of social class or whether some other processes are at work. In short, we ask whether the greater poverty of blacks, Hispanics, and Native Americans can be explained by color-blind forces of educational and occupational attainment or whether it is in some way a direct product of being black, Hispanic or Native American. To the extent that the latter is true, we need to introduce some new ideas to explain how ascribed statuses work in a class system.

RACE AND ETHNICITY

A **race** is a category of people whom we treat as distinct on account of physical characteristics to which we have assigned *social* importance.

An **ethnic group** is a category whose members are thought to share a common origin and to share important elements of a common culture.

A **race** is a category of people whom we treat as distinct on account of physical characteristics to which we have assigned *social* importance. An **ethnic group** is a category whose members are thought to share a common origin and to share important elements of a common culture—for example, a common language or religion (Yinger 1985). Both race and ethnicity are handed down to us from our parents, but the first refers to the genetic transmission of physical characteristics whereas the second refers to socialization into cultural characteristics.

Although race is based loosely on physiological characteristics such as skin color, both race and ethnicity are socially constructed categories. Both individual self-identity and institutional forces play a role in the creation and maintenance of racial and ethnic statuses. For example, in 1930, the U.S. Bureau of the Census declared that those with Mexican background should be classified as nonwhite. The Mexican government complained, and the bureau reversed itself. Now the census bureau defines Hispanic Americans as an ethnic group, declaring that Hispanics can be of any race (Petersen 1988). The 1980 census revealed that there were 6.7 million people who claimed Native American (American Indian) as their ethnic group, but only 1.4 million who claimed it as their race (Lieberson and Waters 1988). More recently, the shift from "black" to "African American" is an example of changing from a racial to an ethnic group identification. As these examples illustrate, racial and ethnic statuses are not fixed. Over time individuals may change their racial and ethnic identification, and society, too, may change the statuses it recognizes and uses.

Race and ethnicity *could* be of primary importance to sociologists as the basis of subcultures. Sociologists could (and some do) focus on differences in musical preferences, language use, and values. Overshadowing these subcultural differences among racial and ethnic groups, however, is the issue of inequality. In the United States today, African Americans, Hispanics, and Native Americans do not simply comprise subcultures, they comprise *disadvantaged* subcultures. In the rest of this chapter, we analyze the types and degree of disadvantage involved.

CASTE AND CLASS: RACISM AS A SPECIAL CASE OF STRATIFICATION

How do we explain the development and persistence of racial and ethnic inequalities? Most contemporary scholars use some form of conflict theory. In the conflict over scarce resources, this theory suggests, historical circumstances (such as slavery, technological advantage, and so on) gave some groups an edge over others. In order to maintain and enhance this advantage, the advantaged groups created social institutions that perpetuated and rationalized the status quo.

As we have seen, the indirect inheritance model built into our family and educational institutions is one way to maintain advantage. In addition, however, racial advantages have been maintained through *racism*, an ideology that justifies and rationalizes racial differences. **Racism** is a belief that inherited physical characteristics determine the presence or absence of socially relevant abilities and characteristics and that such differences provide a legitimate basis for unequal treatment.

A major question for scholars of racial and ethnic inequality today is how important a part racism plays in the maintenance of contemporary racial disadvantages.

The Semicaste Model. Early theorists of stratification confidently expected that industrialization would be followed by the virtual elimination of castelike ascribed statuses in favor of achieved status. Clearly, however, ascribed characteristics such as race and sex continue to be important in allocating scarce resources in our society. Many scholars of race relationships in the United States believe that we have a combination of two stratification systems, class and caste. This **semicaste structure** is a hierarchical ordering of social classes within racial categories that are also hierarchically ordered (see Figure 10.1).

As in a full caste system, race represents an unchangeable status associated with unequal evaluation of worth. The analogy extends to the mechanisms for maintaining separation between the categories. The barriers between races are maintained in the same ways as in the Indian caste system described in Chapter 9: All children are assigned the racial category of their parents (or, in the case of mixed parentage, of their nonwhite

Racism is a belief that inherited physical characteristics determine the presence or absence of socially relevant abilities and characteristics and that such differences provide a legitimate basis for unequal treatment.

A semicaste structure is a hierarchical ordering of social classes within racial categories that are also hierarchically ordered.

■

**FIGURE 10.1
THE SEMICASTE MODEL**

Race and ethnicity are factors in the stratification system of the United States. There is a social class hierarchy within each race, but there is also a castelike barrier between them. Upper-class nonwhites are not as upper class as upper-class whites and the lowest positions in the social class hierarchy are reserved for nonwhites.

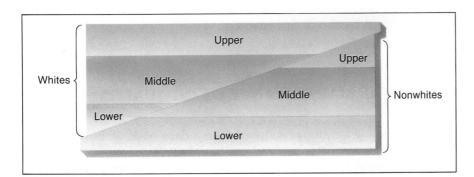

■

TABLE 10.1

INCOME DISTRIBUTIONS AMONG FAMILIES BY RACE, 1988

United States income data support the semicaste model. The wealthiest 20 percent of black families receive 50 percent of all black family income, a figure very comparable to the 46 percent received by the wealthiest 20 percent of white families. Nevertheless, wealthy white families have larger incomes than wealthy black families and poor black families have much lower incomes than poor white families.

	PERCENTAGE OF INCOME RECEIVED		UPPER LIMIT OF INCOME FIFTH	
	Black	White	Black	White
Poorest fifth	3%	4%	$ 5,900	$12,600
Second fifth	8	10	12,000	23,000
Third fifth	15	16	21,200	35,000
Fourth fifth	25	24	36,100	52,100
Richest fifth	50	46	61,600[a]	87,700[a]
Median Income			19,800	34,200

SOURCE: U.S. Bureau of the Census 1989g. Tables 1 and 5.

[a]For this highest income category, the cutoff establishing the top 5 percent is reported rather than the top income.

parent), intermarriage between races is frowned on (was in fact illegal in many states in the United States until 1967), and residential segregation has discouraged contact between the races. These mechanisms ensure the maintenance of inherited castelike status from one generation to the next.

Unlike the Indian system, however, there are social class groupings within each race. Data from 1988 (Table 10.1) show that, although the median income of white families is nearly double that of black families ($34,200 versus $19,800), each race displays a very similar pattern of inequality. In both the white and black populations, the wealthiest 20 percent of families get nearly half of all income. We can also see another implication of the semicaste model in this table; wealthy blacks have less money than wealthy whites, poor blacks are much poorer than poor whites.

American scholars have hotly debated whether race (caste) or class is most important for understanding the structure of inequality in the United States. The operation of general processes of stratification noted in Chapter 9 is surely important, but the condition of minorities cannot be understood in social class terms alone. Rather, as the semicaste model suggests, both race and class are important (Allen and Farley 1986). We will return to this issue in the final section of this chapter.

■

SEPARATE AND UNEQUAL: THE MAINTENANCE OF INEQUALITY

How is it possible for groups to interact on a daily basis within the same society and yet remain separate and unequal? In this section, we introduce sociological concepts that help us understand how societies maintain and reinforce group differences.

MAJORITY AND MINORITY GROUPS

Rather than speaking of white and black or Jew and Arab, sociological theories of intergroup relations usually refer to majority and minority groups. A **majority group** is a group that is culturally, economically, and politically dominant. A **minority group** is a group that is culturally, economically, and politically subordinate. Although minority groups are often smaller than majority groups, this is not always the case. In the Union of South Africa, for example, whites are the majority group, although they make up only 15 percent of the population, because they control all major political, economic and social institutions. Relations between majority and minority groups may take one of four general forms: conflict, accommodation, acculturation, or assimilation.

Conflict.   Following the definition in Chapter 5, **conflict** is a struggle over scarce resources that is not regulated by shared rules; it may include attempts to neutralize, injure, or destroy one's rivals. In European contact with the native populations of North America, the scarce resource was land, and open conflict was the means used to achieve it. In other instances, racial conflict is less violently expressed through laws requiring segregation or forbidding social, political, or economic participation by the minority group.

Accommodation.   When the two groups coexist as separate cultures in the same society, we speak of **accommodation**. They are essentially parallel cultures, each with its own institutions. Canada's French and English provinces and Switzerland's German, Italian, and French cantons are examples of this type of relationship. Although the two cultures are seldom equal, the relationship between them is not based on direct subordination. The idea of parallel cultures is sometimes referred to as *pluralism*.

Acculturation.   Another possible outcome of intergroup contact is for the minority group to adopt the culture of the majority group. This process is called **acculturation**. It includes learning the language, history, and manners of the majority group; it may even include accepting its loyalties and

A **majority group** is a group that is culturally, economically, and politically dominant.

A **minority group** is a group that is culturally, economically, and politically subordinate.

Conflict is a struggle over scarce resources that is not regulated by shared rules; it may include attempts to destroy or neutralize one's rivals.

Accommodation occurs when two groups coexist as separate cultures in the same society.

Acculturation occurs when the minority group adopts the culture of the majority group.

■

Despite major changes in race relations over the past 25 years, racism still flourishes in America. In January, 1987 a group of white youths attacked a group of black youths who had ventured into Howard Beach, a white neighborhood. In an effort to escape a brutal beating, one black youth ran into the path of an oncoming car and was killed. The white youths' chants of "nigger, go home" and the subsequent anger in both the white and black community show substantial racial tension still exists in the United States.

values as one's own. As middle-class blacks in the United States have learned, however, acculturation does not necessarily mean acceptance.

Assimilation. When the minority group is fully integrated into the institutions of society and ceases to be a subordinate group, we speak of **assimilation**. This usually includes going to the same schools, living in the same neighborhoods, belonging to the same social groups, and being willing to marry one another. Under conditions of full assimilation, members of a minority group cease to be defined as a distinct group.

Assimilation is the full integration of the minority group into the institutions of society and the end of its identity as a subordinate group.

Full assimilation is a relatively rare form of intergroup contact. Whether we look at Nigeria, the Soviet Union, Belgium, or the United States, we see that groups remain separate and often unequal after generations of living in the same society. This separatism is achieved through processes that promote what sociologists call **social distance**. Social distance is operationally defined by questions such as "Would you be willing to have members of this group as good friends?" It is a measure of the degree of intimacy and equality in the relationship between two groups.

Social distance is the degree of intimacy in relationships between two groups.

Two processes that encourage social distance even when physical distance is absent are prejudice and discrimination. Most societies also use segregation, or physical distance, as an aid to maintaining social distance.

PREJUDICE

The foundation of prejudice is stereotyping, a belief that people who belong to the same category share common characteristics—for example, that athletes are dumb or that blacks are naturally good dancers. **Prejudice** moves beyond stereotyping in that it is always a negative image and it is irrational. It exists in spite of the facts rather than because of them (Pettigrew 1982). A person who believes that all Italian Americans are associated with the Mafia will ignore all instances of the law-abiding behavior of Italian Americans. If confronted with an exceptionally honest man of Italian descent, the bigot will rationalize him as the exception that proves the rule.

Prejudice is irrationally based negative attitudes toward categories of people.

A startling example is the decision by the United States to intern its West Coast Japanese American citizens during World War II. The decision to go ahead with the internment in spite of the lack of evidence is a fascinating study in the irrationality of prejudice. Said General John Dewitt (1943): "The very fact that no sabotage has taken place to date is a disturbing and confirming indication that such action will be taken."

Prejudice is a powerful obstacle to the kinds of interaction that might reduce intergroup barriers. It ensures that when people from different groups interact, they see not each other but only their conception of what the other is like. What causes prejudice? We review three factors: cultural norms, institutional patterns, and personal factors.

Cultural Norms. We learn to hate and fear through the same processes that we learn to love and admire. Prejudice is a shared meaning that we develop through our interactions with others. Most prejudiced people learn prejudice when very young at the same time they are internalizing other social norms. This prejudice may then grow or diminish depending on whether groups and institutions encountered during adulthood reinforce these early learnings (Wilson 1986).

Institutional Patterns. Prejudice arises from and is reinforced by institutionalized patterns of inequality. In a stratified society, we tend to rate ourselves and others in terms of economic worth. If we observe that no one pays highly for a group's labor, we are likely to conclude that the members of the group are not worth much. Through this learning process, members of the minority as well as the majority group learn to devalue the minority group (Stolte 1983).

Prejudice is also powerfully reinforced by patterns of segregation and discrimination. A child growing up in a society where racial separation is well established in housing, schooling, and work is very likely to learn to devalue members of the minority group—especially if this separatism is accompanied by differential social class rankings.

Personal Factors. Personality factors cannot explain widespread prejudice (Stone 1985). Nevertheless, some people are more prone to prejudice than others. Three factors that dispose such people to prejudice are authoritarianism, frustration, and beliefs about stratification.

Authoritarianism is a tendency to be submissive to those in authority and aggressive and negative toward those lower in status (Pettigrew 1982). Regardless of their own race or ethnic group, authoritarians in the United States tend to be strongly anti-black and anti-Semitic.

Frustration is another characteristic associated with prejudice. People or groups who are blocked in their own goal attainment are likely to blame others for their problems. This practice, called **scapegoating**, has appeared time and again. From the anti-Chinese riots in 19th-century California to anti-Jewish atrocities in Nazi Germany, setbacks for majority group members often result in attacks against the minority group.

Finally, prejudice is more likely among individuals who believe strongly in the American Dream. People who subscribe to the view that we can all get ahead if we work hard and that poor people have only themselves to blame are substantially more likely to attribute poverty or disadvantage to personal deficiencies. In the case of disadvantaged minorities, these people believe that the disadvantage is the fault of undesirable traits within the minority group (Kluegel and Smith 1983; Pettigrew 1985).

THE SELF-FULFILLING PROPHECY

An important mechanism for maintaining prejudice is the **self-fulfilling prophecy**—where acting on the belief that a situation exists causes it to become real. A classic example is the situation of women in feudal Japan (or in more recent Western cultures). Because women were considered to be inferior and capable of only a narrow range of social roles, they were given limited education and barred from participation in the institutions of the larger society. The fact that they subsequently knew nothing of science, government, or economics was then taken as proof that they were indeed inferior and suited only for a role at home. And, in fact, most women were unsuited for any other role. Having been treated as inferiors had made most of them ignorant and unworldly. The same process reinforces boundaries between racial and ethnic groups.

Prejudice is a negative and irrational attitude toward others. Because it is based on feelings and values rather than facts or experiences, prejudice is often difficult to eliminate. This man almost certainly learned racial hatred before he learned his ABCs. Instead of trying to change people's beliefs, most public policy is designed to prevent acts of discrimination and to eliminate public demonstrations of racism such as cross burnings or swastikas on synagogues.

Authoritarianism is the tendency to be submissive to those in authority coupled with an aggressive and negative attitude toward those lower in status.

Scapegoating occurs when people or groups who are blocked in their own goal attainment blame others for their failures.

The **self-fulfilling prophecy** occurs when acting on the belief that a situation exists causes it to become real.

America's Concentration Camps

One of the darkest blots on the U.S. conscience is the relocation of 123,000 Japanese Americans during World War II. Although not as extreme as the enslavement of African Americans or the extermination of Native Americans, the relocation startles and shames because it occurred only 50 years ago. It brings home the reality that racism in a virulent form was alive and well very recently; it is not something our nation left behind with the last century.

Anti-Japanese racism was strong on the West Coast almost from the beginning of Japanese settlement. The relative economic success of the Japanese immigrants only strengthened the resentment. Thus, when Japan bombed Pearl Harbor in December 1941, there were immediate demands to do something about the Japanese in the United States—two-thirds of whom were U.S. citizens. During this period, Japanese Americans huddled in front of their radios, eager to hear the news but afraid to go out into the streets, to school, or to work. In fear, they burned or destroyed all their ties to Japan—books, letters, Bibles, and clothing (Sone 1953).

There were relatively few hostile incidents, but the fears turned out to be justified. In February 1942, President Roosevelt signed Proclamation 9066, the document that gave the army the right to do what it thought necessary to protect national security. The army's solution was the relocation of the West Coast Japanese Americans.

The people were given less than two months to sell all their belongings or to find a trusted white American to care for their property. Dealers in second-hand goods roamed like vultures through Japanese neighborhoods, trying to buy cheaply from people who had no time to look for a decent price. One woman remembers her mother breaking every piece of a treasured set of china rather than sell it for $15 (Houston and Houston 1973). Long-term land leases were voided, and many lost their homes and businesses. Things left behind were vandalized or stolen.

The army had as little time to prepare as did the Japanese Americans, and initially the internees were confined on fairgrounds, housed in exhibition halls and barns. Within six months, however, large relocation camps had been thrown up in isolated regions of the Western United States—Tule Lake, Manzanar, Minedoka. The inmates themselves provided all the labor in the camps; they were cooks, nurses, and even internal security forces. The weather was awful, and the conditions were Spartan at best.

Almost immediately, decent women and men began to try to undo the damage. Through the American Friend's Service Committee (a Quaker organization), Japanese college students were sent to the East Coast to resume their studies. Efforts were made to find jobs and relocate families in the Midwest and the East. As a result, the camps were entirely empty before the war itself ended. And although it did not come close to covering actual losses, the U.S. government paid out $37 million in property damages to the internees.

In fear, they burned or destroyed all their ties to Japan—books, letters, Bibles, and clothing.

One of the tactics the government used to defuse anti-Japanese sentiment and to integrate the Japanese Americans into American society was to encourage their enlistment in the armed forces. It is hard to imagine the gall it took for a recruiter to enter an internment camp and urge young men to serve their country. Nevertheless, young men did volunteer and did serve with distinction in Europe and the Pacific, even in the army of occupation. For its size, the all-Nisei (American-born Japanese) 100th Battalion and 442nd

Regimental Combat Team was the most decorated combat team in the war. Memorial services for dead soldiers were held in internment camps as well as at Arlington National Cemetery.

The deed of relocating Japanese Americans was shameful. Not a single act of sabotage or espionage was ever uncovered to justify the incarceration of a single individual, much less the entire West Coast Japanese American population (Girdner and Loftis 1969). Although wartime fear was a factor, so was racism; there was no move to imprison German Americans or Italian Americans. Racism plus fear resulted in the violation of the constitutional rights of more than 100,000 U.S. citizens. In

evaluating our acts and our principles, it is useful to remember that we were not the only ones evacuating people of Japanese ancestry. Canada and Mexico also evacuated West Coast Japanese. In the case of Canada, it was done far less humanely than in the United States. For example, the Canadian government confiscated all the goods of Japanese Canadian citizens, sold them at sacrifice prices, and gave the people back the money minus a sales commission. It broke up families by putting the men into work crews and sending the women, children, and the elderly to fend for themselves in abandoned ghost towns (Kogamawa 1981). Having company in a disgraceful act does

not reduce the burden, but it does make it clear that racism is not a particularly American character fault.

After decades of wrangling about whether or not the U.S. government was at fault in interning Japanese Americans, in September of 1987 the U.S. Congress finally approved the extension of formal apologies to Japanese Americans interned during World War II. The bill also authorizes $20,000 in reparation to each person of Japanese ancestry who was "relocated, confined, held in custody, or otherwise deprived of liberty or property." So far, however, no funds have been earmarked to pay these reparations.

DISCRIMINATION

Treating people unequally because of the categories they belong to is **discrimination**. Prejudice is an attitude; discrimination is behavior. Often discrimination follows from prejudice, but it need not. Figure 10.2 shows the possible combinations of prejudice and discrimination. Most individuals fit into the two consistent cells: They are prejudiced, so they discriminate (bigots); or they aren't prejudiced, so they don't discriminate (friends). Some people, however, are inconsistent, usually because their own values are different from those of the dominant culture. Fair-weather friends do not personally believe in racial or ethnic stereotypes; nevertheless, they discriminate because of what their customers, neighbors, or parents would say. They do not wish to rock the boat by acting out values not shared by others. The fourth category, the timid bigots, have the opposite characteristics: Although they themselves are prejudiced, they hesitate to act on their feelings for fear of what others would think (Merton 1949).

Public policy directed at racism is aimed almost entirely at reducing discrimination—allowing fair-weather friends to act on their fraternal impulses and putting some timidity into the bigot. As Martin Luther King, Jr., remarked, "The law may not make a man love me, but it can restrain him from lynching me, and I think that's pretty important" (cited in Rose 1981, 90).

SEGREGATION

The mechanisms of prejudice and discrimination may be carried out between groups in close, even intimate, contact; they create social distance between groups. Differences between groups are easier to maintain, how-

Discrimination is the unequal treatment of individuals on the basis of their membership in categories.

■

FIGURE 10.2
THE RELATIONSHIPS BETWEEN PREJUDICE AND DISCRIMINATION

Prejudice is an attitude; discrimination is behavior. They do not always go hand in hand. Some people act on their attitudes, whereas others curb their behavior to conform to community standards. Fair-weather friends are unprejudiced people who will discriminate anyway; timid bigots are prejudiced people who are deterred from discrimination by community standards.

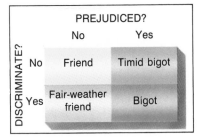

Segregation refers to the physical separation of minority and majority group members.

Institutionalized racism occurs when the normal operation of apparently neutral processes systematically produces unequal results for majority and minority groups.

ever, if social distance is accompanied by **segregation**—the physical separation of minority and majority group members. Thus, most societies with strong divisions between majority and minority groups have ghettos, barrios, Chinatowns, or Little Italies, where, by law or custom, members of the minority group live apart.

INSTITUTIONALIZED RACISM

Once well established, disadvantage can be perpetuated without explicit reference to race or ethnicity. The persistence of racial disadvantage through apparently neutral social processes is called **institutionalized racism**. It means that apparently color-blind forces such as educational attainment and majority rule produce systematically unequal results for members of majority and minority groups. Institutionalized racism works in two primary ways:

1. *The indirect inheritance model.* The normal operation of the status attainment process described in the last chapter ensures that patterns of inequality established in past generations persist: Poorly educated parents tend to have poorly educated children. When a group starts out far behind the majority in terms of social class, the indirect inheritance process makes it enormously difficult to catch up.

2. *Majority rule.* In the United States, racial and ethnic minority groups are, in fact, numerical minorities. This means that their voting power is often insufficient to allow them to be heard. Political structures further weaken their vote. For example, when city council or school board members are elected on a citywide basis, it is difficult for numerically small groups to elect representatives. When elections are held by district, however, residentially concentrated minorities are more likely to be represented (Vedlitz and Johnson 1982).

For much of American history, *institutionalized racism* was overshadowed by simple *racism*. Today, however, this more subtle form of racism is an important cause of continuing race and ethnic inequalities.

EXTRAORDINARY SOLUTIONS

Prejudice, discrimination, and segregation are what might be called ordinary solutions that societies use to maintain boundaries between majority and minority groups (Daniels and Kitano 1970). If they fail, however, or if the minority group is seen as particularly threatening, extraordinary solutions may be invoked: apartheid, concentration camps, expulsion, or extermination. All too often, the history of intergroup relations is the study of extraordinary solutions.

RACIAL AND ETHNIC GROUPS IN THE UNITED STATES

The United States and, indeed, the entire Western Hemisphere comprise an ideal location for the study of racial and ethnic relations. For 400 years, floods of immigrants from diverse backgrounds have jostled against one another—assimilating, accommodating, and conflicting. Some have come to escape persecution, some have come to strike it rich, some were dragged here, and some were here in the first place. In this section, we give a snapshot of each of the major racial and ethnic groups in the United States.

WHITE IMMIGRANTS

The earliest immigrants to North America were English, Dutch, French, and Spanish. By 1700, however, English culture was dominant on the entire Eastern seaboard. The English became the majority group, and everybody else, regardless of degree or number, became a minority group in North America.

The Melting Pot. The extent of interaction and assimilation among white ethnic groups led some idealistic observers to hope that a new race would emerge in North America, where "individuals of all nations are melted into a great race of men" (Crèvecouer [1782] 1974). The final form of the melting-pot image was provided by an English Jew, Israel Zangwill, in his 1909 play *The Melting Pot:*

> There she lies, the great melting pot—listen! Can't you hear the roaring and bubbling? There gapes her mouth—the harbor where a thousand mammouth feeders come from the ends of the world to pour in their human freight. Ah, what a stirring and seething—Celt, Slav, and Teuton, Greek and Syrian, black and yellow— . . . Jew and Gentile (cited in Rose 1981, 64).

Anglo Conformity. In fact, careful observers suggest that the melting pot never existed. Instead of a blending of all cultures, what has occurred is a specific form of acculturation—**Anglo conformity**, the adoption of English customs and English language. To gain admission into U.S. society, to be eligible for social mobility, one has to learn to speak correct English, become restrained in public behavior, work on Saturday and worship on Sunday, and, in general, act like the American version of English people.

The Future of White Ethnicity. For more than 100 years white ethnics emphasized their integration into American society and many children were proud to have given up their parents' old-country ways. When African Americans, Hispanics, and Native Americans began to assert pride in their distinct cultures, however, white ethnics demonstrated a resurgence of ethnic awareness. Between 1960 and 1980 there was an explosion in the number of Americans of Italian, Greek, Norwegian, and Polish descent who claimed that they were not fully assimilated after all and that their ethnic culture was still distinct and vibrant (Fishman 1985b).

Generally, scholars have been skeptical of these claims on the part of white ethnics. Rates of intermarriage are so high among white ethnics that the intergenerational transmission of distinct ethnic cultures is nearly broken. For example, although 94 percent of Italians age 65 and over are Italian on both sides of their families, only 18 percent of those younger than five have two parents of Italian decent (Alba 1985). Correspondingly, a growing segment of the white population identifies with no single ethnic group: They are simply Americans (Lieberson 1985). Consequently, observers attribute the recent surge in ethnicity claims to increased competition from

Many white Americans still claim some ethnic identity; they say they are Polish, or Norwegian, or German. Although a small proportion will dance with the Norwegian Club or go to the Greek parade, most white ethnics know little of their ethnic heritage beyond the name. Even this form of ethnic identification is waning. High rates of intermarriage mean that an increasing proportion of the white population have such complex ethnic heritages that they give up trying to figure it out and just call themselves, "Americans."

Anglo conformity is the process of acculturation in which new immigrant groups adopt the English language and English customs.

groups of color rather than to a real revival in white ethnic subcultures (Nielsen 1985).

Summary.   To a significant extent, ethnicity has ceased to be a basis for stratification among white, Gentile, non-Hispanic Americans. Although ethnic differences do exist and assimilation is not complete for white ethnics, these differences are not related to structured inequality. Rather, feelings of group identity among Poles, Czechs, Germans, and Swedes often provide a basis for cohesion and solidarity, processes that produce a stronger, not a weaker, community.

The integration of 80 percent of the population from diverse sets of backgrounds and conditions is a remarkable achievement. Yet it leaves out a significant portion of Americans. Here we consider the other 20 percent: the nonwhites, the Hispanics, and the Jews.

AFRICAN AMERICANS

African Americans are the largest racial minority in the United States, representing one-ninth (or 12 percent) of the entire population. Their importance goes beyond their numbers. Next to Native Americans, African Americans have been the greatest challenge to the United States' view of itself as a moral and principled nation.

The history of black Americans has two essential elements that distinguish it from the history of other ethnic groups. First, black immigration was involuntary; blacks came as slaves, not as settlers. Second, black Americans are almost uniformly descendants of people who have been here since the founding of the nation, having roots in this country deeper than those of the Swedish, Norwegian, Italian, Irish, and German settlers who followed them.

At the beginning of the 19th century, more than 90 percent of the blacks in the United States were slaves, mostly in the rural South. Occasionally, they knew a skilled trade; more often, they were laborers. The limited evidence available suggests that slave families were usually stable two-parent families and had health and life expectancies similar to those of lower-class white Americans (Sowell 1981).

As the Civil War approached, southern society became more defensive about its "peculiar institution" and increasingly afraid of slave uprisings. For the first time, education of blacks was banned, and it appears that conditions affecting health and life expectancy deteriorated in this period (Eblen 1974). The Civil War and emancipation did little to change these conditions. Rather, 4 million illiterate slaves were freed to go out and support themselves in a land ravaged by war. They began their career in freedom as a poor, rural, and southern people; they remained poor, rural, and southern until World War II.

In many ways, World War II was a benchmark for blacks in the United States. The move from the rural South to the industrial North and Midwest that had begun during World War I was greatly accelerated. The defense effort sharply increased the demand for labor and made possible some real gains in income for blacks relative to whites. In addition, the Nazi slaughter of 6 million Jews in the name of racial purity deeply shocked the Western world, causing a renewed soul searching about racism in the United States.

Compared with the century before, the years following World War II have seen rapid social change: segregation banned in the armed forces (1948), school segregation outlawed (1954), the Civil Rights Act passed (1964), affirmative-action laws passed (1968). For the first time, blacks appeared on television, on baseball diamonds, in ballet companies, and on the Supreme Court. In the following sections, we review some evidence about the differences in life chances for black and white Americans. In many cases, comparisons over time show that these differences have been significantly reduced.

Political Change.   For nearly 100 years after the Civil War, black political rights existed on paper only. It took the Civil Rights Act of 1964, subsequent voter registration laws, and the civil rights activism of the late 1960s to make these political rights effective. The results have been dramatic, and black voters are now an active and influential political force, especially in the Democratic party. Black political leadership is growing along with this group's voters. Several major cities that do not have a black majority (for example, Seattle, New York, and Los Angeles) have elected black mayors; 1989 saw the election of the first black governor (L. Douglas Wilder in Virginia).

Education.   The racial gap is also being reduced in education. In 1940, young white adults were nearly four times more likely to have graduated from high school as blacks of the same age (39 versus 11 percent). By 1988, only 7 percentage points separated white and black rates of high school graduation (87 and 80 percent, respectively). Unfortunately, the racial gap

Black Americans have had the right to vote since 1864 (a right, incidently, not granted to Native Americans until 1924). Until the civil rights movement of the 1960s, however, many blacks were too intimidated to use their voting rights. Martin Luther King played an important role in the effort to secure black voting rights by giving black and white Americans a vision of racial equality and a sense that justice could be achieved.

in high school graduation has closed at about the same time as this level of education has been bypassed as the route to success. The educational gap remains wide at higher levels: Among young adults, blacks are only half as likely as whites to have graduated from college. Thus, despite improvement, significant educational differences remain between white and black Americans.

Economic Disadvantage.   Black income continues to lag behind white income. In 1964, the median income for black families was only 54 percent of the income for white families. By 1987 this figure had only increased to 56 percent. This striking economic disadvantage is due to two factors: black workers earn less than white workers, and black families are less likely to have two earners.

FEMALE-HEADED FAMILIES.   About half of the gap between black and white family incomes is due to the fact that black families are less likely to include an adult male. Nearly half (43 percent) of black families have a female head, compared to 13 percent of white families. This fact has led some commentators to engage in "blaming the victim," arguing that poverty is the result of bad decisions by black women and men. In fact, the primary reason for high rates of female headship is high male unemployment and low male income. Female headship is a *response* to low earnings rather than a cause of it.

LOW EARNINGS.   One of the reasons why blacks earn less than whites is that they are more than twice as likely to be unemployed. In 1990, black unemployment was 12 percent compared to 5 percent for whites; among those under 25, the figures were 23 and 10 (U.S. Department of Labor 1990). Even when employed, however, blacks earn less than white workers.

On the average, black workers have less education and experience than comparable white American workers. A recent analysis, however, concludes that these differences in background and experience account for no more than half of the earnings gap between black and white Americans (Farley 1985). The other half is the result of a pervasive pattern of discrimination that produces a very different occupational distribution and a very different earnings picture for black and white Americans. Thanks largely to government employment opportunities, there is a growing black middle class (Hout 1986). Nevertheless, blacks are 33 percent of the nation's garbage collectors and 44 percent of all maids (Pettigrew 1985).

Continued Concerns.   Between 1940 and 1970, there were major improvements in nearly every arena for black Americans: Civil rights, income, and education all improved. During the last decade, however, little progress has been made and a large black-white gap persists virtually unchanged ("Black-White Gap" 1989). In fact, being black is a better predictor of poverty and unemployment today than it was 25 years ago (Lichter 1988). Among the symptoms of concern ("American Black" 1989):

■ *Health.* Black infants are twice as likely as white infants to die before their first birthday, and between 1987 and 1989 black life expectancy actually decreased.

- *Crime.* One in four black men aged 15 to 24 is in jail or under correctional supervision. Homicide has become a leading cause of death for young men, and black men stand a 1-in-10 chance of dying from homicide.
- *Family Structure.* Neary half of all black families are headed by women and over half of all black children are born to unmarried women.
- *Unemployment.* Black unemployment rates are twice as high as white unemployment rates.
- *Education.* Rates of college enrollment have declined for black males.

These multiple responses to poverty and lack of opportunity create a vicious circle that may perpetuate or even increase the disadvantage of blacks. Louis Sullivan, Secretary of the U.S. Department of Health and Human Services has declared that, "Not since slavery has so much calamity and ongoing catastrophe been visited" on the black population ("American Black" 1989).

How do we reconcile this troubling picture with the general improvements noted earlier? Many perceive a fissure in the black population: on the one hand, a working- and middle-class population that is increasingly integrated into American society; on the other, an black underclass that has not been included in the overall improvement. In fact, for them the situation has deteriorated. This black underclass has been left behind by the more prosperous of all races (W. J. Wilson 1978).

There have been real improvements for black Americans in the last 20 years; income, education, and political power have increased. Nevertheless, there is a substratum of black society that has not participated in these improvements, a group that experiences extraordinarily high rates of illegitimacy, female headship, and poverty. Thus, although some black Americans are able to use the educational system to pursue the American dream, an important segment continues to be alienated from the economic benefits of American society.

HISPANICS

Hispanics or Latinos are an ethnic group rather than a racial category, and a Hispanic may be white, black, or some other race. This ethnic group includes immigrants and their descendants from Puerto Rico, Mexico, Cuba,

■

On nearly every dimension that we use to measure disadvantage, one of the Hispanic groups comes out at the bottom. Mexican-Americans have the lowest education of any racial or ethnic group and Puerto Ricans have the highest rate of female-headed households. A significant part of the Hispanic disadvantage is due to recent immigration and lack of facility with the English language. Success in school will enable this young girl to move rather quickly into the mainstream of American life.

and other Central American or South American countries. Hispanics constitute 8 percent of the U.S. population. The largest group of Hispanics is of Mexican origin (62 percent), with 13 percent from Puerto Rico and the remaining 25 percent from Cuba and elsewhere. The various Hispanic groups live in different parts of the country and have different cultural backgrounds and levels of social and economic integration.

Cubans.   The first wave of Cuban immigrants came to Florida after the Cuban Revolution of 1960; they were largely middle class or professionals. Cuban immigrants who arrived in subsequent waves represent much lower average economic and educational levels. As a result, the economic status of the Cuban population of the United States is worse now than it was a decade ago. Despite having educations almost equal to those of the average American and despite a high proportion of male-headed families, Cubans lag substantially behind other Americans in average income.

Puerto Ricans.   Since the Spanish-American War in 1898, Puerto Rico has been a commonwealth of the United States. Its people are citizens of the United States, free to move back and forth between Puerto Rico and the mainland. Some Puerto Ricans, like many of the recent Cuban immigrants, face the double jeopardy of being Hispanic and black. They are perhaps the poorest racial or ethnic group in the United States, and a full 38 percent of Puerto Rican families live below the poverty level (Valdivieso and Davis 1988).

Mexican Americans.   The Mexican American population of the United States is very diverse. Many Mexican Americans are not immigrants; their ancestors were here when the United States annexed the Southwest in 1848. Following annexation, there have been three waves of immigrants. The first wave, between 1900 and 1930, was caused by civil unrest in Mexico and labor demand in the United States. The second wave, between 1942 and 1950, brought thousands to the United States under the bracero (contract labor) program to fill jobs opened by absent servicemen and the relocation of Japanese Americans. The third wave, from 1960 to the present, is due to the substantial wage differences between Mexico and the United States. Following the first two waves of immigration, massive deportations took place—1 million in 1951 alone. Despite the fact that the third, and current, wave of immigration is largely illegal, there has been little effective control of it. Deportation is relatively rare, and the U.S. border patrol has been helpless to stem the rising tide of job-seeking immigrants. (Recent legal responses to illegal immigration and its impact on the U.S. population are discussed in the Issues in Social Policy section of Chapter 19.)

Socioeconomic status.   It is misleading to describe the socioeconomic status of Hispanics as if they were a single group. Their experiences in the United States have been and continue to be very different. Recent evidence suggests that their economic and political experiences may be growing more divergent rather than becoming more similar (Portes and Truelove 1987). Although Cubans are becoming increasingly assimilated, as signaled by a very high rate of American citizenship, the Mexican American population is not.

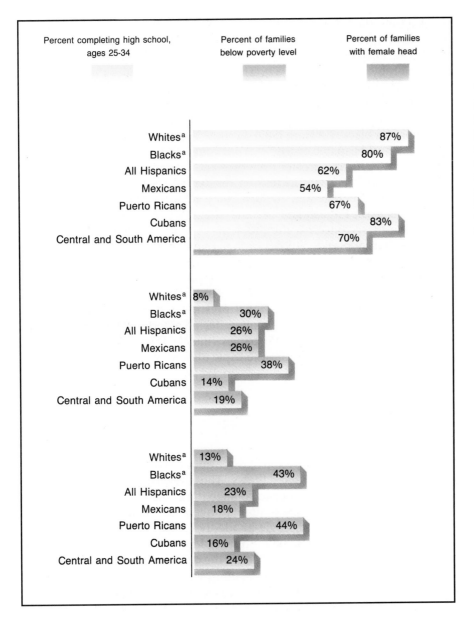

Percent completing high school, ages 25-34

Whites[a]	87%
Blacks[a]	80%
All Hispanics	62%
Mexicans	54%
Puerto Ricans	67%
Cubans	83%
Central and South America	70%

Percent of families below poverty level

Whites[a]	8%
Blacks[a]	30%
All Hispanics	26%
Mexicans	26%
Puerto Ricans	38%
Cubans	14%
Central and South America	19%

Percent of families with female head

Whites[a]	13%
Blacks[a]	43%
All Hispanics	23%
Mexicans	18%
Puerto Ricans	44%
Cubans	16%
Central and South America	24%

FIGURE 10.3

EDUCATION, POVERTY, AND FAMILY STRUCTURE BY RACE AND HISPANIC ORIGIN, 1988

On all of these measures of disadvantage, a Hispanic ethnic group comes out at the bottom. A significant portion of this disadvantage, however, can be traced to recent immigration and poor English skills.

SOURCE: Valdivieso and Cary 1988; United States Bureau of the Census 1989 b and c.

[a]Each racial category includes people of all ethnic backgrounds, including Hispanics.

Figure 10.3 compares the various Hispanic groups to one another and to the overall white and black populations on three measures: education, poverty, and family structure. (Because race and Hispanic origin are overlapping categories, Hispanics are included twice in this and other tables—once under their ethnic group and again under their racial identification.) On each of these measures, a Hispanic group comes out at the very bottom. On this table, Mexican Americans are the poorest educated racial or ethnic group; Puerto Ricans are the most likely to live in poverty and in female-headed households.

Special Concerns for Hispanics.   As a result of continuous streams of poorly educated, non-English-speaking immigrants, mostly from Mexico but also from the Caribbean and Central America, the Hispanic population is the fastest-growing ethnic group in the United States. If current growth continues, Hispanics are expected to constitute 18 percent of the U.S. population by 2030 (Davis 1982). This rapid growth raises three concerns for the status of Hispanics: First, because the new immigrants are young and poorly educated, the socioeconomic position of the Hispanic population is falling. Between 1980 and 1988, Hispanic poverty rates grew faster than those for blacks (O'Hare 1989). Second, a growing Hispanic population has raised non-Hispanic concerns about competition over jobs and cultural change, thus spurring greater prejudice and discrimination. Finally, rapid growth is associated with increasing residential segregation (Massey and Denton 1988). Segregation, in turn, may retard the rate at which new immigrants learn English and become integrated into American society.

Despite these concerns, the problems of white Hispanics are substantially less than of blacks. Studies of the assimilation process show that the castelike barrier separating races operates much less dramatically in the case of ethnicity. For white Hispanics, the problem is largely one of class. As a result, by the second and third generation, Hispanics are able to translate education into occupational prestige and they are able to leave segregated barrios (Massey and Mullen 1984; Neidert and Farley 1985). The exception is the 7 percent of Hispanics (mostly Puerto Ricans and other Caribbean islanders) who suffer the triple disadvantage of being Hispanic, poor, and black (Massey and Bitterman 1985).

JEWS

Between 1880 and 1920, outbreaks of violent anti-Semitism in Russia and Poland resulted in the emigration of three quarters of the Jewish population of Eastern Europe to the United States. These Jewish immigrants were the poorest of all immigrant groups to come to the United States in this period. In the crowded slums of Manhattan's lower East Side, they established their own institutions and single-handedly created the U.S. garment industry. One of these men, Levi Strauss, lent his name to what is now classic American clothing. By the turn of the century, 234 of the 241 garment factories in New York were owned and operated by Jews (Sowell 1981).

First through hard work and then by zealous application to education, these Jewish immigrants pulled themselves out of the lower class. Despite the very real prejudice and discrimination they faced, their rate of upward mobility was twice as high as that of other immigrant groups (Peterson 1978). By 1950, Jews far exceeded other Americans in education and income; in that year, 25 percent of all Jewish men had a college degree, compared with 10 percent of all men in the United States.

Despite what seems the perfect example of the American success story, Jews have remained a minority group. Until the last decade, Jews were commonly excluded from clubs and colleges across the country. This overt discrimination is now much reduced (though not completely eliminated), and assimilation appears to be nearing completion for Jews. An increased level of intermarriage (nearly one-third of all Jews now marry Gentiles) suggests that Jews may soon cease to be regarded as a minority group (Reiss 1980, 333).

ASIANS

The Asian population of the United States (Japanese, Chinese, Filipinos, Koreans, Laotians, and Vietnamese) more than tripled between 1970 and 1985, yet it still constitutes only 1.5 percent of the total population. The Asian population can be broken into three segments, the 19-century immigrants (Chinese and Japanese), the post-WWII immigrants (Filipinos, Asian Indians, and Koreans), and the recent refugees from Southeast Asia (Kampucheans, Laotians, and Vietnamese).

Americans of Japanese and Chinese descent have surpassed the educational achievements of white Americans, and it appears that many of the more recent streams of Asian immigrants will follow the same path. For example, although many of the Southeast Asian refugees who came to the United States between 1975 and 1984 began their American lives on welfare, 42 percent of Vietnamese youth aged 20–24 are enrolled in school compared with 24 percent of the white population the same age (Gardner, Robey, and Smith 1985).

Because of their educational success, Asians are often held up as an example of what hard work can accomplish. It is important to remember just how hard work it was and continues to be. In the early years of this century, Japanese and Chinese immigrants were faced with virulent racism. White Americans were so threatened that many states passed laws forbidding Japanese immigrants from owning land; from 1906 to 1947, federal laws singled out Japanese immigrants and said that they could *never* become United States citizens (Jiobu 1988). The Focus in this chapter recounts a particularly striking example of discrimination against Japanese Americans.

Discrimination is not all in the past. Asian American applicants are less likely to be accepted to elite colleges and universities than white Americans with the same credentials; many observers attribute this to a quota system,

■
_____

Asian Americans experience a great deal of frustration about being held up as a "model minority," whose successes are used to illustrate and justify American structures of opportunity. Many Asians point out that they succeeded despite terrible obstacles and that they still suffer dscrimination in employment opportunities as well as outright violence and abuse. As this student's shirt suggests, Asians feel that the "model minority" image is patronizing and manipulative, and they resent bitterly that the racism they felt and still feel is so glibly overlooked.

similar to that used 50 years ago to keep Jewish students from dominating elite schools (Nakanishi 1989). Discrimination can also be more direct. In 1982 two unemployed autoworkers beat to death a Vietnamese man because they thought he was Japanese and they blamed the Japanese for the loss of their jobs. The startling thing in this case was that the judge found their stress understandable and sentenced them only to three years of probation (Saigo 1989).

Although Asian Americans appear to demonstrate that racial barriers can be surmounted, their hard work, strong families, and high educational achievements hide the economic discrimination they experience. A recent study by the U.S. Civil Rights Commission concluded that "native-born Asian men were less likely to be in management positions than their white counterparts and that highly educated native-born Asian men in all five groups [Chinese, Filipinos, Japanese, Asian Indians, and Koreans] were earning less—in most cases, substantially less—than similarly qualified white men" (Suzuki 1989, 16). In short, Asian Americans have been denied the opportunities that their educational achievements should have opened for them.

NATIVE AMERICANS

Native Americans (American Indians) are one of the smallest minority groups in the United States (about 0.5 percent of the entire population), and nearly half of their members live in just four states: Oklahoma, Arizona, California, and New Mexico. Native Americans are widely regarded as our most disadvantaged minority group. Incomes of husband-wife families are

Like the white ethnics pictured earlier, Native Americans put on traditional dress and dance at festivals; unlike white ethnics, they do not easily slip into the mainstream of American life when they exchange their ceremonial attire for jeans. Although we have relatively little statistical data on Native Americans, they are clearly one of the most disadvantaged minority groups in the United States.

10 to 20 percent lower for Native Americans than for black Americans (Sandefur and Sakamoto 1988). Likewise, Native Americans suffer the highest rates of alcoholism and premature death of any racial or ethnic group in the United States.

Within this general picture of low social and economic status, there is enormous variability. Native Americans represent more than 200 tribal groupings, with different cultures and languages. Some have been successful: fish farmers in the Northwest, ranchers in Wyoming, bridge builders in Maine. In urban areas, Native Americans experience less racial segregation than do other nonwhite groups (Bohland 1982), and have entered the professions and other occupations of modern industrial society.

More than any other minority, however, Native Americans have remained both unacculturated and unassimilated. It is clear that Native American culture is not simply different from the dominant culture; in many ways it is a shattered culture. Those who cling to earlier values face a severe case of anomie, since the means to achieve the old goals are gone forever. In addition, prejudice and discrimination may stand in the way of achieving the new goals. The story of Ojibwa described in Chapter 4 represents an extreme case of what has happened to Native American culture.

EQUALITY: PROSPECTS AND CHALLENGES

The United States is a land of immigrants. At a rough guess, at least 97 percent of our population is descended from people who moved to this land within the last few hundred years. We have discussed the current situations of many of these groups individually. At this point we want to consider the broader picture. In this final section, we examine the ethnic and racial fabric of the United States. As a society, how much progress are we making toward assimilation? What are the prospects for the future?

RESIDENTIAL SEGREGATION

Residential segregation is an important indicator of assimilation. High levels of segregation suggest that racial and ethnic groups do not feel comfortable with one another and wish to reduce interaction. Moreover, segregation is an important mechanism for maintaining inequality. Since good jobs, good schools, and good housing are all spatially specific, restricting a group's residential patterns is an important way to restrict their access to these benefits.

Sociologists measure segregation by the extent to which groups are represented equally in the census tracts within a city. In a city with a population that is 80 percent Anglo and 20 percent Hispanic, perfect integration exists when each census tract is 80 percent Anglo and 20 percent Hispanic. The segregation index varies from 0 to 100 and can be interpreted as the proportion of the smaller group that would have to move to create total integration.

A recent study by Massey and Denton (1988) calculated segregation indexes based on data from the 1980 census. They separated the population into four groups—Anglos, Hispanics (excluding the 7 percent who claimed

■

TABLE 10.2

RESIDENTIAL SEGREGATION OF BLACKS, HISPANICS, AND ASIANS AND OTHER RACES

Residential segregation remains high in both the suburbs and the central cities of the United States. Segregation is moderate for both Hispanics and Asians and other races but much higher for blacks.

	Percent of Minority Group Members Who Would Have to Move to Achieve Full Integration with Anglos	
	CENTRAL CITIES	SUBURBS
Blacks	69%	57%
Hispanics	45	38
Asians and other races	41	38

SOURCE: Massey and Denton 1988, 604.

black as their race), Blacks, and Asians and other races—and calculated a segregation score for each minority group relative to the Anglo majority. Table 10.2 shows their results for both central cities and suburbs.

Residential segregation from Anglos is substantial for all three groups, but blacks are far more segregated than either Hispanics or Asians. A full 69 percent of central-city blacks would have to move to create racial integration, compared to 45 percent of the Hispanics and 41 percent of Asians and other races. For all three minority groups, suburbanization reduces but does not eliminate racial segregation. When these groups move to the suburbs, they are likely to move to segregated suburbs.

Historical studies suggest that these high levels of residential segregation are not new; they have existed since at least 1940 and have changed relatively little (Farley 1985). Such segregation is not established by law, but neither is it a historical accident. It occurs partially as a result of social class segregation of neighborhoods, but it also occurs because whites have exerted economic and political pressure, including violence and intimidation, to keep minorities "in their place" (Hirsch 1983).

Massey and Denton found that the reasons for segregation differ by group. Among white Hispanics and Asian Americans, income and occupation are important predictors of segregation. Once new immigrants improve their socioeconomic status, they are able to move into integrated neighborhoods. The same is less true for black Americans. Even if they have the same status characteristics as their white Hispanic or Anglo neighbors, black Americans are much more likely to remain segregated. Massey and Denton concluded that "blacks experience a consistent, powerful, and highly significant penalty in the process of spatial assimilation" (1988, 621).

INTERMARRIAGE

We defined assimilation as the full integration of a minority group into majority culture and institutions and the end of group membership as a basis for social relationships. The ultimate indicator of assimilation is intermarriage, and intermarriage rates tell us much about the degree of separatism that exists among racial and ethnic groups.

■

TABLE 10.3
INTERMARRIAGE RATES OF AMERICAN-BORN WOMEN

Intermarriage rates suggest that there remains a strong sense of ethnic identity, even among white ethnic groups. The odds of a Dutch woman marrying a Dutch man, for example, are 10 times greater than for a non-Dutch woman. Within-group marriage is especially strong for Hispanics and blacks. The odds that a black woman will marry a black man are 33,000 times greater than for a non-black woman!

Group	Relative Odds of In-Group Versus Out-Group Marriage
Irish	4
German	5
French	6
Scottish	6
English	8
Welsh	8
Swedish	8
Dutch	10
Danish	14
Polish	16
Native American (American Indian)	16
Hungarian	19
Italian	19
Norwegian	21
Czech	27
Russian	61
Spanish—Other	175
Portuguese	180
Mexican	742
Puerto Rican	3,468
Black	32,998

SOURCE: Lieberson and Waters 1988, 1730.

In 1988, Lieberson and Waters published calculations of intermarriage rates for white and nonwhite ethnic groups based on the 1980 census. Lieberson and Waters measured assimilation by asking about the relative odds that a man will be married by a woman from his own group as opposed to a woman from other groups. For example, "How much larger are the odds that a Welsh woman will choose a Welsh man than will a non-Welsh woman?" Some of their findings are presented in Table 10.3.

For every ethnic group, Lieberson and Water's data show that marriage within ethnic groups remains substantial. Poles, Swedes, and Norwegians still show pronounced tendencies to marry within their own ethnic group. A German woman, for example, is five times more likely to marry a German man than is a non-German woman. The startling numbers at the bottom of the table, however, show that these tendencies toward within-group marriage among European ethnics are swamped by separatism displayed by racial minorities. A black woman is 33,000 times more likely to marry a black man than is a non-black woman! Mexican American women are "only" 742 times more likely to marry a man from their own ethnic group.

These differences provide a clear demonstration of the continued role of race and, to a much smaller extent, ethnicity in American society. These intermarriage data suggest that, racially at least, our society is more characterized by separatism than by assimilation.

THE UNIQUE DISADVANTAGE OF BLACKS

Nearly every group that came to the United States started at the bottom. Yet some, such as the Jews, the Japanese and Chinese, the Irish, and the Italians have made it. Their levels of education and income are comparable to and in some cases higher than average. Although these groups continue to show a pronounced tendency to marry within their group, they have nevertheless been substantially assimilated into American society.

This leads to the obvious question about why black Americans are still so substantially disadvantaged. The answers are complex and not at all clear. One important reason is that the historical circumstances of black Americans were very different from those of white immigrants. One scholar of racial and ethnic assimilation in the United States concludes that:

> It is a serious mistake to underestimate how far the new Europeans have come in the nation and how hard it all was, but it is equally erroneous to assume that the obstacles were as great as those faced by blacks or that the starting point was the same" (Lieberson 1980, 383).

Of perhaps more interest to us now is why blacks remain so seriously disadvantaged in American society. What can society do to end this disadvantage? To simplify a complex debate, we offer three sociological perspectives, each of which points to a different solution.

1. *Eliminate racism.* Some scholars believe that racism is the root of black disadvantage. If this is true, then the solution lies in affirmative-action programs, laws against discrimination, and education to reduce prejudice. Once racism is ended, equality of opportunity will exist, and African Americans will have the same chance as other ethnic groups. This perspective is attractive to conservatives because it requires the least social change.

2. *Reduce social class inequality.* Some observers believe that although racism was the historical cause of black disadvantage, it is now maintained through the color-blind forces of the indirect inheritance model. According to this perspective, the solution lies in Head Start programs, better education, and more job programs—strategies that will reduce the inequality between classes and reduce the inheritance of social class. This liberal perspective requires basic changes in our social class, educational, and economic systems.

3. *Dismantle capitalism.* Conflict theorists see the maintenance of racial disadvantages as part of a deliberate strategy carried out by the capitalist (bourgeois) class. In a divide-and-conquer strategy, capitalists encourage racial divisions among the working class. This is the *segmented labor market* that we referred to in the last chapter. By restricting all the good working-class jobs to white Americans, the capitalists have bribed the white working class to support the system. Capitalists are thus able to exploit the minority working class without having to fear working-class solidarity. According to this radical perspective, the solution is the dismantling of capitalist

How should government policy address the problem of racial disadvantage? Some observers think we need to attack racism and race-specific problems, others believe that we need to attack the general problems of unemployment, deteriorating housing, and poor education. The latter strategy is more attractive politically because it would benefit all Americans. If not accompanied by decreases in racism, however, it could increase rather than decrease racial disadvantage.

institutions and an increase in the control that African Americans have over the means of production. As African American activist Stokely Carmichael said in 1965, what we need is not rights, but *power*.

Conclusion

Only 25 years ago, blacks were subject to violence for registering to vote, using "white" drinking fountains, or attending "white" colleges. Only 50 years ago, all the West Coast Japanese Americans were rounded up and put in camps. The last major massacre of Native Americans occurred only 100 years ago.

Viewed from this perspective, the changes in the last 25 years have been enormous. Racial and ethnic discrimination is illegal, prejudicial attitudes are less common and less tolerated, and there are signs of progress in most social and economic areas. Nevertheless, prejudice, discrimination, and disadvantage still exist for most American minority groups. Although the most vicious expressions of prejudice have declined, minority group members still face significant disadvantages in day-to-day living in the United States. We conclude this chapter with an Issues in Social Policy section that considers the liberal agenda for reducing these disadvantages.

ISSUES IN SOCIAL POLICY

An Agenda for the Black Underclass

There have been real gains for many black Americans in the last 40 years. There is an increasingly strong black middle class that wields more economic and political power than ever before. Nevertheless, there is growing consensus that the condition of the black *poor* has been substantially deteriorating. Whether this poorest third of the black population is called the ghetto underclass or the inner-city poor, the point is the same: Joblessness is up, female-headed households are up, crime and homicide rates are up, drug use is up, and so on. The physical concentration of so many social problems has created explosive levels of social disorganization in poor, black neighborhoods. Twenty years ago they were poor; now they are poor and hopeless (Billingsley 1989).

Why the change? It is not because white America has grown more racist. Although racism remains a factor that limits black progress in the United States, all of the evidence suggests that racism is falling, not rising (Firebaugh and Davis 1988). Instead, the reasons lie in America's changing economy and its differential effect on the black middle and lower class. A key factor is the de-industrialization of America, which has hurt all classes and races that depended on jobs in the manufacturing sector. Many of the good factory jobs that drew blacks to Detroit, Chicago, and Buffalo after World War II have disappeared forever. A second factor is the shift of economic activity from the central city to the suburbs. Ironically, a third factor contributing to the disintegration of inner-city black communities is the existence of more opportunities for middle-class blacks (Billingsley 1989; Wilson 1988). As better-off blacks have moved to the suburbs, they have taken with them much of the stability and civic energy that previously held black communities together despite relatively high levels of poverty. With their depar-

ture, the inner city has become virtually isolated from major social institutions. Children may grow up without having known *anybody* who holds a regular job; consequently, they don't know how to get a job or how to keep one (Wilson 1988, 60–61).

For a variety of reasons, both practical and moral, the problem posed by the ghetto underclass must be addressed by public policy. It is, however, a problem so complicated that it seems to defy solution. To put it in its bleakest form: How much good can a Head Start program do for a youngster whose father is in jail, whose mother is a drug addict?

William Julius Wilson (1987), one of the most prominent African American scholars in America, takes the second of the three approaches outlined on p. 276. He argues that the solution is a national job policy directed toward creating full employment and better jobs for *all* Americans. His vision includes a substantially higher minimum wage, universal health care, retraining programs, relocation assistance, and public child care.

Wilson's agenda is obviously controversial. It is far more liberal than even most Democrats are likely to endorse. Nor is there universal scholarly agreement that jobs are the solution. Conservatives believe the jobs are there but that the blocked opportunities created by racism have established a "culture of poverty" that makes the underclass unemployable. Radicals believe that the only way to achieve the goal of good jobs for all is to dismantle capitalist institutions. Tragically, *none* of these agendas is being pursued with any vigor. Like the Reagan administration before it, the Bush administration has recommended cutting social programs for the poor.

◼

SUMMARY

1. Race and ethnicity are both passed on from parent to child, but race refers to the genetic transmission of physical characteristics and ethnicity refers to socialization into distinct cultural patterns.

2. Race and ethnicity interact with social class to determine an individual's position in the hierarchy of life chances. Prejudice, discrimination, and segregation tend to decrease as groups improve their educational and economic position.

3. Four basic patterns of contact between majority and minority groups are conflict, assimilation, accommodation, and acculturation.

4. Prejudice is an attitude; discrimination is behavior. Prejudice is difficult to change because it is irrational; thus, most social policy is aimed at reducing discrimination.

5. Although prejudice and discrimination are more typical of some kinds of individuals than others, these pervasive social patterns cannot be explained by individual characteristics. Instead, institutionalized patterns of segregation, racism, and inequality help perpetuate disadvantage from one generation to the next.

6. Despite significant progress, black Americans continue to experience serious disadvantage on indicators such as health, crime, unemployment, and family structure. The black underclass has been left behind by the more prosperous of all races.

7. On indicators of poverty, educational attainment, and female-headed families, some Hispanic groups are at great disadvantage. Hispanic disadvantage appears to stem largely from recent immigration and poor facility with the English language.

8. Asian-Americans have shown remarkable social mobility through education, but still earn less than white Americans with the same credentials. Although we have little solid information, Native Americans are one of our most disadvantaged minority groups.

9. Overall assimilation of U.S. racial and ethnic groups is assessed on two indicators: segregation and intermarriage. Both segregation and within-group marriage are relatively high in American society, suggesting that race and ethnicity continue to be important. On both indicators African Americans are at a unique disadvantage.

10. Three perspectives offer insights on disadvantages experienced by racial and ethnic minorities: the racism perspective (eliminate racism); the social class perspective (reduce social class inequality; and the conflict perspective (eliminate capitalism).

11. William J. Wilson argues that the situation for the black underclass has deteriorated substantially. His agenda for the future, from the social class perspective, consists of a national job policy.

◼

SUGGESTED READINGS

Feagin, Joe R. 1989. Racial and Ethnic Relations, (3rd ed.) Englewood Cliffs, N.J.: Prentice-Hall. A current textbook that covers theoretical issues and includes a separate chapter on each of the major race and ethnic groups in the United States.

Horowitz, Ruth. 1983. Honor and the American Dream: Culture and Identity in a Chicano Community. New Brunswick, N.J.: Rutgers University Press. An absorbing account of a Mexican American community in Chicago.

Lieberson, Stanley, and Waters, Mary. 1988. From Many Strands: Ethnic and Racial Groups in Contemporary America. New York: Russell Sage. Covers intermarriage rates, economic attainment, and cultural differences among white ethnics as well as minority groups. A good book if you want to see how the Poles or Czechs or Danes have done in America.

Liebow, Elliot. 1967. Tally's Corner. Boston: Little, Brown. This classic study provides an insightful look at how poverty and lack of opportunity affect family and personal life in urban slums.

Shkilnyk, Anastasia. 1985. A Poison Stronger Than Love: The Destruction of an Ojibwa Community. New Haven: Yale. An ethnographic community study that focuses on the social structures of a Native American community in Canada.

Wilson, William J. 1987. The Truly Disadvantaged: The Inner City, the Underclass, and Public Policy. Chicago: University of Chicago Press. A controversial book by one of America's leading African American scholars.

11

SEX AND GENDER

Have you ever . . .

Heard the story about the boy and his father who were out in the country for a drive? The father lost control of the car, and it crashed into a tree. The father was killed outright, and the son was seriously injured. An ambulance brought the boy to the hospital, and a surgeon was called to do emergency surgery to save the boy's life. After seeing the boy, however, the shaken surgeon refused to operate, saying, "I cannot operate on him—he's my son." Question: How can that be when the boy's father is dead?

Perhaps the answer is obvious to most of you now: The surgeon was the boy's mother. But when this riddle first appeared 15 years ago, it stumped a lot of people.

The roles of women and men have changed in the last decades. Nevertheless, enough truth is left in our old stereotypes about men and women to give most people pause for at least a few seconds when presented with this riddle. (A few dyed-in-the-wool traditionalists may even be permanently stumped!) In this chapter, we examine some of the roles played by women and men and try to put them in sociological perspective.

SEXUAL DIFFERENTIATION

Men and women are different. Biology differentiates their physical structures, and cultural norms in every society differentiate their roles. In this chapter, we describe some of the major differences in men's and women's lives as they are socially structured in the United States. We will be particularly interested in the extent to which the ascribed characteristic of sex has been the basis for structured inequality.

SEX VERSUS GENDER

Sex is a biological characteristic, male or female.

Gender refers to the expected dispositions and behaviors that cultures assign to each sex.

Gender roles refer to the rights and obligations that are normative for men and women in a particular culture.

In understanding the social roles of men and women, it is helpful to make a distinction between gender and sex. **Sex** refers to the two biologically differentiated categories, male and female. It also refers to the sexual act that is closely related to this biological differentiation. **Gender,** on the other hand, refers to the expected dispositions and behaviors that cultures assign to each sex. Although biology provides two distinct and universal sexes, cultures provide almost infinitely varied gender roles. Each man is pretty much like every other man in terms of sex—whether he is upper class or lower class, black or white, Chinese or Apache. **Gender roles,** however, are a different matter. The rights and obligations, the dispositions and activities, of the male gender role are very different for a Chinese man than for an Apache man. Even within a given culture, gender roles vary by class, race, and subculture. In addition, of course, individuals differ in the way they act out their expected roles. Some males play an exaggerated version of the "manly man," whereas others display few of the expected characteristics.

Social scientists are more interested in gender roles than in sex. They want to know about the variety of roles that have been assigned to women and men and, more particularly, about what accounts for the variation. Under what circumstances do women have more or less power, prestige, and income? What accounts for the recent changes that have occurred in gender roles in our society?

CROSS-CULTURAL EVIDENCE

A glance through *National Geographic* confirms that there is wide variability in gender roles across cultures. The behaviors we normally associate with being female and male are by no means universal. Despite the wide variety across human cultures, there are two important universals: In all cultures, child care is a female responsibility, and in all cultures women have less power than men.

In spite of the fact that women do substantial amounts of work in all societies, often supplying much of the food as well as taking care of stock, children, and households, women universally have less power and less value. A simple piece of evidence is parents' almost universal preference for male children. Table 11.1 includes data on sex preference for six nations. In these nations, parents who have a preference prefer a boy to a girl by

■

TABLE 11.1

CROSS-CULTURAL DIFFERENCES IN SEX PREFERENCE

Most cultures have a strong preference that a new baby be a boy. This preference is even stronger for firstborn children.

"When a family has several children, both sons and daughters equally, and a new child is coming, is it preferable that the new child be a boy, either one, or a girl?"

	BOYS	GIRLS	EITHER	BOY/GIRL RATIO
Argentina	33%	3	63	11/1
Chile	56	5	39	11/1
India	78	5	17	16/1
Bangladesh	91	2	8	46/1
Israel (non-Europeans)	44	4	52	11/1
Nigeria	67	2	31	34/1

SOURCE: Inkeles and Smith 1974.

a margin never lower than 10 to 1 and as high as 46 to 1. This preference is less strong in modern industrial nations, but parents in the United States prefer their first child to be a boy by a 2 to 1 margin (Pebley and Westoff 1982).

Determinants of Women's Status.   There are no known societies where women have more power than men, but important variations exist from society to society in the amount of women's power and status. In some societies, their status is very low, whereas in others it approaches equality. Three key factors determine women's status in any society: (1) the degree to which women are tied to the home by bearing, nursing, and rearing children; (2) the degree to which economic activities in a society are compatible with staying close to home and caring for children; and (3) the degree of physical strength necessary to carry on the subsistence activities of the society.

Until the sharp fertility declines of the last 200 years, the first factor showed relatively little variability: Most women in most societies were more or less continually tied close to home by pregnancy and subsequent responsibility for nursing and rearing children. The degree to which women could participate in the economic life of their society and contribute to subsistence depended substantially on the second and third conditions. When economic activities required little physical strength and could be carried on while caring for children, women made major contributions to providing subsistence for their families and communities (Chafetz 1984).

As a result of these factors, women have the highest status in gathering and simple horticultural societies (Quinn 1977). In these societies, the major subsistence activities (gathering and simple hoe agriculture) are compatible with women's child-related roles, and women may be responsible for as much as 60–80 percent of a society's subsistence (Blumberg 1978). Moreover, their economic activities make them an active part of their community and increase their likelihood of being involved in community and group decisions.

These three factors help explain most of the important differences in women's status across societies, and they allow us to understand why women's status was low during industrialization but now shows signs of rising. Industrialization moved work away from home and made it difficult for women to be economically productive while bearing and rearing children. Reduced fertility, however, has allowed women to leave the household and increase their participation in society's economic and public life. As a result, the status of women is improving. Nevertheless, men remain substantially advantaged in status and power. In the rest of this chapter, we discuss the reasons this is so and the prospects for change.

GENDER ROLES OVER THE LIFE COURSE

In some things, such as table manners, we expect men and women to be alike. A great many characteristics, however, are *gendered*—considered more appropriate for one sex than another. We expect women and men to like different activities, to have different personalities and skills, and to perform different tasks. Many of these differences are normative—that is, we think men and women *ought* to think and act in specific, different ways. People who violate these norms may receive sanctions from friends and family. More important, if they have internalized society's norms, individuals who violate gender norms will feel guilty and uncomfortable.

Gender differences begin with pink and blue blankets in the hospital nursery and extend throughout life. In this section, we provide an overview of some of the basic differences in American gender roles over the life course. Later, we will address the issue of male/female inequalities in scarce resources and some explanations for them.

DEVELOPING A GENDERED IDENTITY

Early Childhood Socialization.   Chapter 6 pointed out that we begin to develop a sense of our self-identity by seeing ourselves through others' eyes—the looking-glass self. One of the first elements youngsters distinguish as part of their looking-glass self is their gender identity. By the age of 24 to 30 months, they can correctly identify themselves and those with whom they come into contact by sex, and they have some ideas about what this means for appropriate behavior (Cahill 1983).

Because young children are not capable of complex thinking, they tend to develop very rigid ideas of what it means to be a boy or a girl. These ideas are often highly stereotyped: "Boys don't play with dolls!" or "Ladies don't drive trucks!"

Young children develop strong stereotypes for two reasons. One is that the world that they see is highly divided by sex: In their experience, women usually don't drive trucks, and boys usually don't play with dolls. The other important determinant of stereotyping is how they themselves have been treated. Substantial research shows that parents treat boys and girls differently. They give their children gender-appropriate toys, they respond negatively when their children play with cross-gender toys, they allow their boys to be active and aggressive, and they encourage their daughters

Despite many changes in American gender roles, boys and girls still tend to experience large doses of traditional gender role socialization. Boys are more likely to want to race motocross and girls are more likely to want to play with dolls. Although some of these differences may be due to our genetic heritage, studies show that parents' and teachers' expectations have a tremendous influence on the degree to which children ascribe to and act out traditional roles. Dad and mom, after all, provided this motorcycle, not nature.

to play quietly and visit with adults. If parents do not exhibit gender-stereotypic behavior and if they do not punish their children for cross-gender behavior, however, the children will be less rigid in their gender stereotypes (Berk 1989).

As a result of this learning process, boys and girls develop pretty strong ideas about what is appropriate for girls and what is appropriate for boys. Because males and male behaviors have higher status than female behaviors, boys are punished more than girls for exhibiting cross-gender behavior. Thus, little boys are especially rigid about their ideas of what girls and boys ought to do. Girls are freer to engage in cross-gender behavior, and by the time they enter school, many girls are experimenting with boyish behaviors.

Differences in Aptitudes and Personality.   If you ask young children what they are like, boys will tell you that they are independent and aggressive and adventurous; girls will often tell you that they are gentle, cooperative, and quiet. They are responding to gender stereotypes. Considering how strongly children hold these stereotypes and how much pressure there is from others to encourage gendered behavior, it is surprising that the actual differences in boys and girls are quite small.

A review of thousands of studies over the last several decades points to the following differences between boys and girls (Berk 1989):

- Boys are better in spatial ability, are more active and aggressive, and are better at mathematics (after junior high).
- Girls have better verbal skills, are more fearful and anxious, more compliant and dependent, and less likely to have developmental or behavior problems.

The most impressive thing about these sex differences in personality and cognitive ability is that they are so small. Most of these differences have declined over time, and today sex is a very poor predictor of either math scores or personality among children (Deaux 1985).

There are few differences in level of education between women and men. Women are as likely as men to graduate from high school and college, and just as likely to get postgraduate degrees. The primary sex difference is in type of education. If you had to guess which of these students was in electrical engineering and which in English, you would do well to take sex into consideration. Although women students are going into engineering and computer sciences in greater proportions than before, the traditional sex differences in college majors persist.

EDUCATION

Of particular concern to sociologists are those aspects of gender identity that are critical for achievement. Generally, research shows that girls and boys (and their parents and teachers) expect better performances on gender-appropriate tasks. Girls expect to be better at English and art; boys expect to be better at mechanical things, math, and athletics. Not surprisingly, therefore, SAT scores and other measures of performance show that boys excel in math and that girls outscore boys in verbal proficiency. The boys' advantage in math is far stronger than the girls' advantage in verbal skills, especially at the upper end. Thirteen times as many boys as girls score over 700 on the quantitative portion of the SAT. (Benbow and Stanley 1983).

Over the last generation, girls and boys have become much more similar in their scholastic aptitudes and in their curriculum choices (Jacobs 1989). Nevertheless, significant differences remain. Figure 11.1 shows the in-

FIGURE 11.1
SELECTED COLLEGE MAJORS BY SEX, COLLEGE FRESHMEN, 1989

In the last 20 years, there has been a substantial narrowing of the sex gap in educational focus. Nevertheless, engineering continues to be largely a male preserve while education attracts a disproportionate number of women undergraduates. Since engineers earn roughly three times what teachers make, this difference in educational direction is one reason why women earn so much less than men.

SOURCE: Astin and Associates 1989.

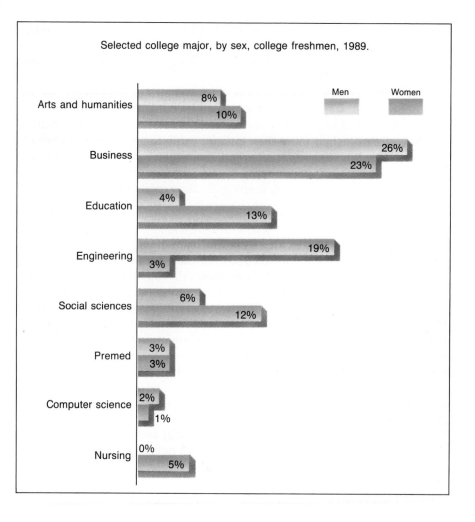

Selected college major, by sex, college freshmen, 1989.

tended major of a large national sample of 1989 college freshmen. Women and men are nearly equally likely to choose business, premedicine, or arts and humanities majors. The most striking differences are in education and engineering: Males are six times more likely than females to choose engineering, while women are over three times more likely than men to choose education. Since engineers make a great deal more money than teachers, these differences in educational aspirations have implications for future economic well-being.

LABOR-FORCE PARTICIPATION

In 1990, 93 percent of men compared with 74 percent of women aged 25–54 were in the labor force (U.S. Department of Labor 1990). This gap is far smaller than it used to be, but probably larger than it will be in the future (Figure 11.2). Recent studies show no sex differences at all in the proportion

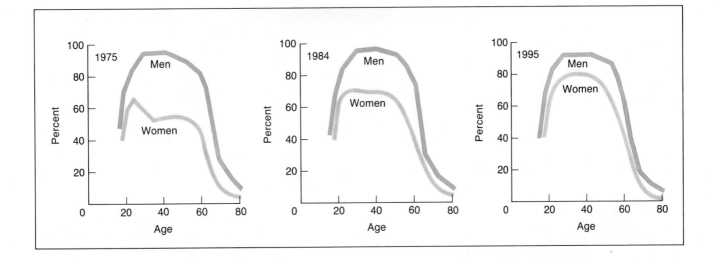

of male and female college students who expect to be employed at age 25 or age 50 (Affleck, Morgan, and Hayes 1989). Although most young women expect to be mothers, they also expect to be full-time, permanent members of the labor force.

Although women and men are nearing equality in the proportion employed, our norms still send out very different messages about the importance of employment. There is no ambiguity about a man's role: His major adult role continues to be provider. Although his wife may work, the moral responsibility for supporting the family falls on his shoulders. Women, however, receive mixed messages about the importance of work and family. Just 25 years ago, the majority of the American public considered it wrong for women with children to work; now only a minority feels this way. Labor-force participation is still more of an option than an obligation for women, however, and women are far less likely than men to be sanctioned by their friends and neighbors for their inability to support their families. They will, however, be sanctioned if their employment results in neglect of their children's or husband's needs. American norms make it clear that, although employment is an acceptable option, their families should be women's primary obligation.

Differences in norms about the importance of work and about the types of work appropriate for women and men have dramatic consequences for the types of work men and women actually do and for their earnings (Bielby and Bielby 1989). These differences will be the topic of later sections in this chapter.

■

FIGURE 11.2

LABOR-FORCE PARTICIPATION RATES OF MEN AND WOMEN AGED 16 AND OVER, 1975 TO 1995

In the 20 years between 1975 and 1995, two major changes will occur in labor-force participation: Men's and women's rates will become very similar, and fewer of either sex will work past age 60.

SOURCE: U.S. Department of Labor 1986a.

FAMILY ROLES

Although society has changed dramatically in the last half century, the vast majority continue to marry, become parents, and take on family roles. These family roles are sharply gendered: husband and wife, mother and father have different obligations and different rights.

Parenting.   Because of modern contraceptives, childbearing is a choice for most women rather than a biological imperative. This "choice" is not made in a vacuum, however. In fact, enjoyment of small children and the wish to be a mother are both normative expectations for women. Until very recently, women who did not want families were regarded as unnatural, unwomanly. There is now greater tolerance for deliberate childlessness, but 90 percent of American women nevertheless expect to have children (U.S. Bureau of the Census 1989j). The decision to have children has enormous economic, social, and emotional consequences.

If children are to be born, then women, of course, must be the ones to bear them. Culture cannot redistribute this role. Subsequent care of the child, however, is not so clearly a biological imperative. Nevertheless, all societies, including our own, have viewed this as a female responsibility. The last few years have seen increased emphasis on fathers' involvement with their children, and some modest shifts in child-care responsibility have occurred. The increase in the proportion of fathers changing diapers, however, has been overshadowed by the increase in the number of children being raised by single mothers. The major responsibility for child-care in most American households rests on the mother.

Household Production.   In addition to child-care, home and family are the site of a substantial amount of domestic work. Clothes must be purchased and washed; meals must be purchased, prepared, and cleaned up after; houses must be taken care of and lawns mowed. In addition, family relationships require work: Somebody has to make sure Grandmother is okay, plan holiday dinners, buy wedding presents for nieces and cousins, and generally keep the family together. Almost all of this work is women's work in our society (Thompson and Walker 1989). There have been some changes in attitude, but relatively few changes in behavior (LaRossa 1988).

Summary.   Marriage and parenthood do not dominate women's lives the way that they did a generation ago (McLaughlin and Associates 1988). Women are marrying later and having children later; growing (though still small) proportions will never marry or have children. More important, marriage and parenthood no longer signal withdrawal from other spheres of activity. Nevertheless, family roles remain sharply gendered, and getting married and especially becoming a parent continue to be powerful forces for differentiating male and female experience.

CONCLUSION

One hundred years ago, to be a male rather than a female meant a tremendous difference in one's day-to-day life. Today, this is less true. For the most part, both girls and boys expect to spend a large portion of their adult life in the labor force, and they expect significant equality in social relationships. Nevertheless, very substantial differences still remain in their access to such scarce resources as income and power. We address these inequalities in the next section.

Contemporary gender roles ask fathers to do much more for their children than just support them economically and play catch on Saturday afternoons. Today we expect dads to change diapers, cook dinners, and listen to their children's troubles—many of the tasks that were left primarily to mothers only a generation ago. Unfortunately, nearly forty percent of America's children live apart from their fathers. As a result, the overall picture may be one of less rather than more fathering.

WHO BENEFITS?
SOCIAL INEQUALITIES BETWEEN WOMEN AND MEN

In terms of race and social class, women and men start out equal. The nurseries of the rich as well as the poor contain about 50 percent girls. Nevertheless, the proportion of women who live in poverty is nearly twice that of men. This section examines some of the structured social inequalities that exist between women and men.

ECONOMIC INEQUALITIES

In 1989, women who were full-time, full-year workers earned 65 percent as much as men. Why do women earn less than men? The answers fall into two categories: workplace segregation and different earnings.

Workplace Segregation.   Women are employed in different jobs than men (see Figure 11.3), and the jobs women hold pay less than the jobs men hold. The major sex differences in Figure 11.3 show that women dominate clerical jobs, whereas men dominate blue-collar jobs. The clerical and sales jobs occupied by nearly one-half of the female labor force are generally nonunion and poorly paid, with low benefits and few promotional opportunities. Although the blue-collar jobs dominated by male workers also have few promotional opportunities, many are unionized and have high hourly wages and good benefit packages. The proportion of men and women in professional and managerial jobs is nearly equal. Generally, though, men are doctors and women nurses; men manage steel plants and women manage dry-cleaning outlets.

Studies of sex segregation in the workplace show that there has been marginal improvement in the last 70 years. Using an index of segregation that varies from 0 to 100 (the same index of segregation that was used to measure housing segregation in Chapter 10), Jacobs (1989) reports that sex segregation in the labor force fell by 23 percent between 1910 and 1986. In 1910, 74 percent of the women would have had to be reassigned to achieve occupational integration; in 1986, 57 percent of women would have had to change jobs.

There are three primary reasons why women and men have different jobs: gendered jobs, different qualifications, and discrimination.

GENDERED JOBS.   Because of historical circumstances, many jobs in today's labor market are regarded as either "women's work" or "men's work." Construction work, warehousing, and much manual labor is almost exclusively men's work; nursing, library work, medical technology, and typing are largely women's work. These occupations are so strictly sex segregated that many men or women would feel uncomfortable working in a job where they were so clearly the "wrong" sex. It is not so much that employers discriminate but that they receive so few cross-sex applications.

A growing number of jobs that used to be reserved for men—such as insurance adjusters, police officers, and bus drivers—have been opened

FIGURE 11.3
**DIFFERENCES IN OCCUPATION BY
SEX, 1990**

Men and women continue to be employed in very different occupations in the United States. The most striking differences are in technical, sales, and clerical work where women predominate and in various blue-collar jobs held primarily by men. Within categories, men typically hold higher-status positions than women.

SOURCE: U.S. Department of Labor 1990.

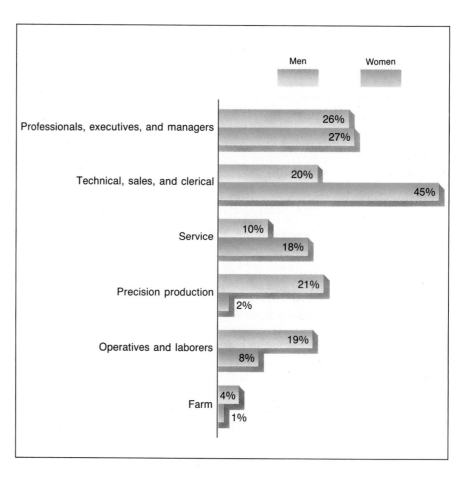

up to women in the last decade. Research shows, however, that this is not because women have increased their access to good jobs. Rather, women have moved into jobs that men are abandoning because of deteriorating wages and working conditions (Reskin 1989).

DIFFERENT QUALIFICATIONS.   There are relatively few sex differences in the *quantity* of education attained in the United States. Men and women are about equally likely to graduate from college and even to get master's degrees. By the year 2000, women are expected to outnumber men among people getting the doctorate (U.S. Department of Education 1989).

The primary educational difference has been in field of study. Although these differences are smaller than they used to be, women continue to prepare themselves to work in relatively low-paying fields, such as education, while men are more likely to choose more lucrative fields.

Probably more important than differences in educational qualifications are differences in experience and on-the-job training. Because many women have taken time out of the labor force for childbearing and childrearing, they have less labor force experience and lower seniority than men their own age (Marini 1989). Perceiving that women will be less likely to be long-term employees than men, employers have invested less in training women.

As a result, women employees have lower qualifications than men. Both of these factors mean that women are less likely to be promoted into management positions.

DISCRIMINATION. Although men and women have somewhat different occupational preparations, a large share of occupational differences is due to discrimination by employers (Bielby and Baron 1986). Employers reserve some jobs for men and some for women on the basis of their own stereotypes. This covers not only major occupational differences (men drive forklifts and women type) but also very minor distinctions in job titles. Within the same objective task, men and women will be given different titles—women will be executive assistants and men doing the same tasks will be assistant executives, often at a much higher pay scale.

Why do employers discriminate? An important reason is that they believe in gender stereotypes. They believe that men are competent and analytical and that women are emotional and timid. It is not surprising, then, that they prefer to hire men for managerial or other responsible positions. There is also some evidence that employers (largely male) are responding in part to the wishes of their male employees who want to avoid competition with women (Bielby and Baron 1986).

Several studies document that an important reason that men and women have different jobs is that women are less likely to be promoted. For example, a recent study of women engineers found that, within five to 10 years of getting out of school, they were already significantly behind their male peers. In terms of education and experience, these women were identical to their male counterparts. What they did "wrong" was that they were women—by gender as well as sex. Although as well qualified as the men in their firms, they were less aggressive and self-confident. As a result, they were passed over for promotion (Robinson and McIlwee 1989).

Same Job: Different Earnings: Not all jobs are substantially sex segregated. Some, such as flight attendant, teacher, research analyst, contain considerable proportions of both men and women. Generally, however, men earn substantially more than women even within the same occupation (see Table 11.2), and these same-occupation wage differences are a major source of sex inequities (Brown, Moon, and Zoloth 1980; Stevenson 1975).

Within integrated occupations, such as hotel managers or law, men tend to be in high-paying firms and women tend to be in low-paying firms (Blau 1977). Men tend to be in large firms and women in small. These differences in type of firm reflect the segmented labor market. The gist of this concept is that *where* you work may be as important as what you do in determining your income and opportunity.

Why are women more likely than men to end up working in small, low-profit firms? An important reason is that their family responsibilities interfere with their ability to maximize their careers. More often than men, women have to choose a job close to home so that they can drop children off at the baby-sitter or take them to the doctor during lunch hour. They are more likely to quit their jobs because of childbearing or because their husband's job requires a move, and they are very unlikely to be able to move to a different city in order to take advantage of a career opportunity.

TABLE 11.2
SEX DIFFERENCES IN EARNINGS FROM THE SAME OCCUPATION

Even when women have the same occupation as men, they tend to earn substantially less money. In part because of their family responsibilities, women tend to be employed in smaller and lower-paying firms. They also experience substantial discrimination in both employment and promotion opportunities

| | MEDIAN EARNINGS | | MALE/FEMALE |
OCCUPATION	MALES	FEMALES	RATIO
Accountants	$34,867	$22,960	1.52
Engineers	40,309	32,506	1.24
Natural scientists and mathematicians	39,420	30,970	1.27
Computer equipment operators	23,066	16,849	1.37
Lawyers and judges	54,190	38,650	1.40

SOURCE: U.S. Bureau of the Census 1989f, pp. 161, 165.

In the contemporary labor force, few jobs require sex-specific abilities, such as being able to lift 100 pounds. As a result, there are a growing number of jobs that include women and men. Just having the same job, however, does not produce equal earnings. Even among full time, full-year employees with the same occupational title, women earn substantially less than men. As women's employment becomes a life-long role and fewer women take sustained periods off for childrearing, some of this earnings gap may be reduced.

Recognizing these family claims on women employees, employers are less likely to hire them for jobs requiring long career tracks or geographical moves, less likely to invest in training for them, and less likely to promote them. As a result of these processes, women accountants are more likely than men to be keeping the books for Joe's Garage and men accountants are more likely than women to be keeping the books for IBM.

Studies show that discrimination against women employees is strongest when the women are married and mothers. Never-married or long-divorced women and nonmothers are more likely to get hired for jobs with longer career ladders and more promotion opportunities. Partly as a result of the greater opportunities that are open to them, women with fewer family ties earn more than women with husbands and children (Peterson 1989).

Because *some* women drop out of the labor force for family reasons, employers are reluctant to hire women employees, promote them, or invest in them. This pattern of behavior affects all women, even those who intend to work for 40 years or who are the sole support for themselves or their families (Marini 1988).

POWER INEQUALITIES

As Max Weber pointed out, differences in status and power are as important as differences in economic reward. When we turn to these rewards, we again find that women are systematically disadvantaged. Whether we are talking about business or church or the family, we find that women are less likely to be given positions of authority.

Unequal Power in Social Institutions.   Women's subordinate position is built into most social institutions. From the church to the family, we find that norms specify that women's roles are subordinate to men's. The Bible's New Testament, for example, urges, "Wives, submit yourselves unto your own husbands" (Ephesians 5:22); the traditional marriage vows require women to promise to obey their husbands; until 1919, women were not allowed to vote in the United States. In almost every institution, traditional norms have specified that men should be the leaders and women the followers.

In politics, prejudice against women leaders is declining—although it is still quite strong. Whereas women represent 53 percent of the voters, they comprise only 12 percent of all state legislators and only 5 percent of the U.S. Congress. Only a minority of people (17 percent) now say that they would not consider voting for a woman for president, but by a very large margin the public believes that a man would do a better job as president than a woman (Gallup Report 1984).

Within the family, ideas about leadership roles have also been changing (see Table 11.3). In 1962, a survey of Detroit mothers found that only 32 percent disagreed with the statement that "Most of the important decisions in the family should be made by the man of the house." When these same women were reinterviewed in 1980, 71 percent disagreed (Thornton, Alwin, and Camburn 1983). American norms now call for relative equality in the status of husbands and wives, but the reality is that men continue to have substantially more power in families than women.

Unequal Power in Interaction.   As we noted in Chapter 7, even the informal exchanges of everyday life are governed by norms. That is, they are patterned regularities, occurring in similar ways again and again. Careful attention to the roles men and women play in these informal interactions shows some rather clear differences—all of them associated with women's lower status in our society.

◾

TABLE 11.3
GENDER ROLES: CHANGE AND CONTINUITY

There have been substantial changes in men's and women's attitudes. Nevertheless, about half of Americans still prefer a traditional division of labor, and nearly a quarter believe that women should stay out of the labor force and let men make the decisions at home.

		MALE	FEMALE
Do you approve or disapprove of a married woman earning money in business or industry if she has a husband capable of supporting her?			
Percent approve	1938	19%	25%
	1972	62	66
	1986	78	76
If you were taking a new job and had your choice of a boss, would you prefer to work for a man or woman?			
Percent preferring a woman	1953	2	8
	1987	9	19
Most of the important decisions in the life of the family should be made by the man of the house.			
Percent disagree	1962	NA	32
	1980	NA	71
It is better for everyone if the man is the achiever outside the home and the woman takes care of the home and family.			
Percent agree or strongly agree	1977	68	62
	1986	47	47

SOURCE: Simon and Landis 1989; Thornton, Alwin, and Camburn 1983.

NA Not Asked

An easy example is that women smile more (Goffman 1974a). They smile to offer social support to others, and they smile to express humility. Watch carefully the next time you observe class presentations. If you are the speaker, you will notice that the women in the class smile at you more than the men. If you are part of the audience, note that nervous women speakers will smile at their audience more than equally nervous men.

Evidence of the different roles men and women play in interaction comes from analysis of informal conversations. Although we don't generally think of them this way, conversations involve a division of labor between a listener and a speaker. To qualify as a conversation, the two roles must alternate. Often, this is accomplished effortlessly. We wait until the speaker has finished a sentence or idea, and then we start speaking. If the listener enters too soon, he or she interrupts the speaker. When this occurs, the speaker may graciously cede the floor, or the speaker may keep on talking so that the interrupter must quit and subside back into the listener role.

As the scenario implies, the speaker role is the most powerful. The speaker dominates the listener. By holding the floor, the speaker controls the flow of information and prevents the listener from expressing an opinion. Length of speaking time and the ability to reject others' attempted interruptions are both important clues to relative status.

Studies of informal conversation show that men regularly dominate women in verbal interaction (Fishman 1978). This is empirically demonstrated in a variety of ways. Men take up more of the speaking time. Men interrupt women more often than women interrupt men—and, most important, they are more often successful interrupters. Finally, we find women providing more support roles in conversation. One important mechanism for this support is called "back channels," remarks such as "I see" or "mm-hmm" that are inserted into the speaker's turn without attempting to interrupt. They signify assent and interest. Women are also more concerned than men about being nonthreatening in conversation; they are more placating and less assertive. They are more likely to state their opinions as questions ("Don't you think the red one is nicer than the blue one?") and to follow their opinions by tag questions ("I like the red one better. Don't you?").

Laboratory studies pairing men and women with different status characteristics (for example, male teacher/woman student; woman teacher/male student) show that this conversational division of labor is largely a function of differential status (Kollock, Blumstein, and Schwartz 1985; Wagner, Ford, and Ford 1986). When clear-cut situational factors, such as a student/teacher situation, give women more status in a conversation, they cease to exhibit low-status interaction styles. Nevertheless, a recent study of conversations between physicians and their patients shows that patients are much more likely to interrupt women physicians than men physicians (West 1984). It would appear that the lower status accorded to women in our society cannot be overturned merely by changing their occupations.

THE OTHER SIDE: MALE DISADVANTAGE

Women are at a substantial disadvantage in most areas of conventional achievement, and, in informal as well as formal interactions, they have

Girls' play is generally less competitive than boys' play, and it is less likely to be governed by formal rules, such as those that govern sport. The skills that girls develop in cooperation and negotiation follow them into adult life. Studies of informal interaction between women and men show that women are more apt than men to smile and to give signals of verbal support.

less status than men. They pay for their disadvantage in higher levels of mental illness and poverty (see Chapter 9). Men, too, face some disadvantages from their traditional gender role.

Mortality.   Perhaps the most important difference in life chances is life itself. In 1987, men in the United States could expect to live 71.5 years and women 78.3 years. On the average, then, women live seven years longer than men. Although a small part of this difference may be biological (Waldron 1983), the social contribution to differential life expectancy begins at a very early age and continues through the life course. At high school and college ages, males are nearly three times more likely than females to die. Some of this difference is due to the greater likelihood, even at this age, of males dying of cancer and heart disease; to a significant extent, however, it has to do with the more dangerous life-style (particularly drinking and driving) associated with masculinity in our culture.

The sex differential in life expectancy is more complex than the greater risk taking of young men. One prominent mortality specialist attributes 80 percent of the sex differential to cardiovascular (heart) disease—a disease of the middle-aged and elderly (Preston 1976). Evidence suggests that men's disadvantage in heart disease is not because men experience more stress than women but because, under the same levels of stress, men are more vulnerable to heart disease than women. Current thinking attributes men's greater risk of heart disease to the male gender role's low emphasis on nurturance and emotional relationships. Where women's personalities and relationship characteristics seem to protect them from this consequence of stress, lack of social support appears to leave men especially vulnerable to stress-related diseases (Nathanson 1984). This suggests that, despite increasing female participation in politics and the labor force, women's life expectancy will continue to remain substantially higher than men's. The sex differential in mortality is likely to decline only when differences in personality and dispositions are reduced.

Social Integration. The low emphasis on nurturance and expressiveness in the male role appears to reduce men's interest in and ability to form close relationships with their children, other kin, and friends. Maintaining family relationships is usually viewed as women's work, and when men end up without women to do this work for them (never married, divorced, or widowed), they also frequently end up alone. Surveys demonstrate that children express more affection toward their mothers than their fathers—a differential that extends to old age, when fathers see less of their children than do mothers (Hoyt and Babchuk 1983; Norman and Harris 1981). It is not all a case of "poor Dad," however, since men are socialized to depend less on interpersonal contacts (Chappell and Havens 1980) and are not as dissatisfied as women by the lack of close friends or kin. Nevertheless, men's disadvantaged position in terms of intimacy and affiliation leaves them less supported in a variety of crises: widowhood, financial troubles, divorce, and separation (Kessler and McLeod 1984; Stroebe and Stroebe 1983; Wallerstein and Kelly 1980). Ultimately, this leaves them substantially disadvantaged in health.

In addition, the focus of the male gender role on achievement and success can prove stressful. Even men who are successful by any reasonable standard may feel pressured by the constant striving, and those who fail often compensate by excessive aggressiveness in other spheres. This constant emphasis on achievement, coupled with a normative demand to be confident and self-assured, may lead men to assume the exaggerated version of masculinity we call macho. Anybody who has watched a 15-year-old boy take on the swagger of confidence when it is obvious that he is very unsure of himself will recognize the strains posed by the masculine role. Assuming that the boy manages to perfect his acting of the role, the world of conventional achievement may be his oyster, but he will have sacrificed something on the way. This sacrifice will be reflected in higher rates of heart disease, a suicide rate that is three times higher than women's, and an alcoholism rate that is five times higher (U.S. Bureau of the Census 1989a).

SUMMARY

An observer reviewing the evidence on differential life chances by sex comes to the inevitable conclusion that men have the advantage in class, status, and power. Although there are individual exceptions, men as a category have more prestige, more income, and more power than women. One consequence of this is that five times more female-headed than male-headed households are living in poverty. Men pay a price, however, in terms of foregone intimacy and higher mortality. Many changes have occurred in the last decades, and most of them have reduced the differences between women and men. However, in two areas—life expectancy and earnings—the gap between men and women is as large as or larger than it was 30 years ago.

The fact that women bear all the children is due to physical differences between men and women. Most of the differences in life chances, however, are socially structured. How do these differences arise?

■

PERSPECTIVES ON SEX STRATIFICATION

In all societies, including our own, women have less status than men do. Nevertheless, the gap between women and men now receives less normative support than it used to, and there are many signs of change. What explains women's lower status, and what factors explain recent changes?

FUNCTIONAL THEORY: DIVISION OF LABOR

The structural-functional theory of sex stratification is based on the premise that a division of labor is often the most efficient way to get the job done. In the traditional sex-based division of labor, the man does the work outside the family and the woman does the work inside the family. Functionalists have argued that this division of labor is functional because specialization will (a) increase the expertise of each sex in its own tasks; (b) prevent competition between men and women, which might damage the family; and (c) strengthen family bonds by making men dependent on women and vice versa.

As Marx and Engels noted, any division of labor includes the seeds of control and domination. In this case, the division of labor has a built-in disadvantage for women: Because women's speciality is the family, they have fewer contacts, less information, and fewer independent resources. Because this division of labor contributes to family continuity, however, structural functionalists have seen it as necessary and desirable.

Structural-functional theories of sex stratification are still popular among conservative factions of the population, especially the religious fundamentalists. Those groups that opposed the Equal Rights Amendment (ERA), for example, argued that it was best if women and men had different roles. For example, Phyllis Schlafly argued that

> Every successful country and company has one "chief executive officer." None successfully functions with responsibility equally divided between cochairmen or copresidents. The United States has a president and a vice-president. They are not equal. The vice-president supports and carries out the policies enunciated by the president. . . . The experience of the ages has taught us that this system is sound, practical, and essential for success. . . . If marriage is to be a successful institution, it must likewise have an ultimate decision maker, and this is the husband (Schlafly 1977).

As Table 11.3 shows, nearly half of the American population continues to believe that a sex-based division of labor is best.

CONFLICT THEORY: SEGMENTED LABOR MARKETS

According to conflict theorists, women's disadvantage is not a historical accident, nor is it designed to benefit society. Rather, it is designed to benefit men as a group. In addition, contemporary sex differences are designed to benefit the capitalist class.

It is relatively easy to see how women's lower status can benefit men, but how can it benefit capitalists? The answer lies in the segmented labor market. The segmented labor market is two tiered and sharply gendered. It creates one set of jobs for women and another, better set of jobs for men. In doing so, capitalists divide the working class and bribe working-class men into a coalition against working-class women. Further, the female labor force can be used to provide a cushion against economic cycles: Women can be laid off during slack times and hired back when employment demands are up (Bonacich 1972; England and Dunn 1988).

MAINTAINING INEQUALITY

Functionalist and conflict theories provide overarching ideas about why sex stratification arose and whom it benefits. On a more mundane level, however, we need to understand the basic processes that maintain inequality in everyday life. We cover three basic processes through which inequality is maintained: socialization, learned expectations, and prejudice and discrimination.

Socialization.   With a few rare exceptions, today's Americans were raised under more or less traditional gender norms. As a result, we share norms

Gender roles have changed substantially in the last generation, but continuity with the past remains strong. The odds of finding a female doctor giving instructions to a male nurse are much, much lower than the odds of observing this traditional cast of characters. In many ways, public opinion also supports a traditional division of labor. The occasional female governor or mayor or the growing handful of female business executives belies the fact that many women continue to be mired in traditional female occupations.

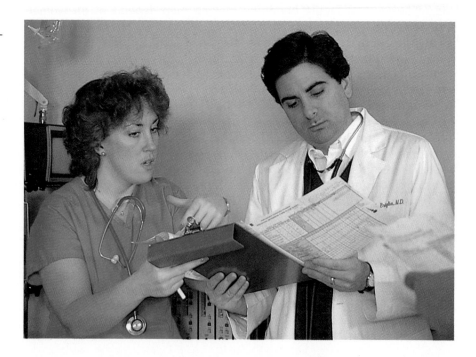

about the appropriateness of men's provider role and women's domestic role. Most of us have integrated some of these ideas about gender-appropriate behavior into our self-concept. As employees and employers, as mothers and fathers, as husbands and wives, as church members, and as students, these gendered roles affect our aspirations and our behaviors. Although some women buck the system by applying for jobs in the priesthood or driving heavy equipment (and are often rebuffed for doing so), the majority of women and men follow the prepared script. Differential socialization effectively perpetuates the system of inequality that currently exists. On the other hand, changes in socialization are also producing new generations with less traditional expectations.

Learned Expectations.   If two strangers are thrown together in an airplane or a waiting room, they will not start their relationship with a blank slate. Rather, they will find cues in each other's dress, manner, age, race, and sex to frame their interaction. Although subsequent conversations may cause them to change this framework, it is likely that their presuppositions will color the course of the relationship.

Expectation states theory argues that status characteristics (race, sex, class) create expectations in others about probable abilities and social status. When people act on the basis of these expectations, the expectations are confirmed (Berger, Rosenholtz, and Zelditch 1980). For example, if there are no other cues about status, a man and a woman set in an interactive situation are likely to assume that the other possesses characteristics stereotypically associated with their sex. This means she will assume that he is competent and aggressive, and he that she is nurturant and sensitive. It also means he will assume that he has higher status than she, and the whole style of their interaction will follow from these assumptions. As a result, he will dominate her and she will defer, and any observer would conclude that he does in fact have higher status.

Expectation states theory is an extension of earlier ideas about the self-fulfilling prophecy. It has been developed to explain the findings, noted previously, that men usually dominate women in daily interaction. Although laboratory studies demonstrate that this dominance pattern can be reversed when women's higher status is clearly established (Wagner, Ford, and Ford 1986), such clear status cues are usually missing in real-life encounters. Where cues about actual competence are absent or ambiguous, expectation states give men the edge.

These expectation states have a powerful influence in day-to-day interaction, affecting exchanges with salesclerks, friends, colleagues, and supervisors. They affect the likelihood that women will be hired as managers as well as the likelihood that they will be touched, called by their first name, or interrupted. An implication of this research is that when women move away from the kitchen and the typing pool, they will have to demonstrate superiority clearly in order to be treated as equals.

Prejudice and Discrimination.   An understanding of women's status can gain much from an analogy to race relations. Women can be viewed as a minority group and men as the majority (dominant) group. The same mechanisms that help maintain boundaries between racial groups also

Expectation states theory argues that status characteristics create expectation states in others about probable abilities and social status. When people act on the basis of these expectations, the expectations are confirmed.

maintain boundaries between the sexes: prejudice, discrimination, self-fulfilling prophecies, and segregation. The analogy extends to the use of labels to keep minority groups in their place. Just as black men were called boys to remind them of their inferior status, middle-aged women continue to be called girls. Is this just a friendly term that doesn't have any political meaning, or is it a subtle suggestion that women are not full grown-ups with responsibilities equal to men's? Although people who use the term *girls* usually deny any negative intent, the fact that this usage is most common toward women in lower-status occupations (for example, typists and housewives) suggests that it is a mechanism for reinforcing status.

Sexism is a belief that men and women have biologically different capacities and that these form a legitimate basis for unequal treatment.

SEXISM.   One of the most important mechanisms for keeping women in their place is **sexism**—the belief that women and men have biologically different capacities and that these differences form a legitimate basis for unequal treatment.

Conflict theorists explain sexism as part of the general strategy of stratification. Whenever any group has access to class, status, or power, its first step is to try to exclude others from it. If it can exclude others categorically (that is, on the basis of category membership such as sex or race), the need to compete individually is reduced. Sexism, then, is a means of restricting access to scarce resources.

Sexual harassment consists of unwelcome sexual advances, requests for sexual favors, or other verbal or physical conduct of a sexual nature.

SEXUAL HARASSMENT.   A special form of discrimination that is especially problematic for female workers and students is **sexual harassment**—unwelcome sexual advances, requests for sexual favors, and other unwanted verbal or physical conduct of a sexual nature. Harassment may be just an annoyance. It may, however, turn into real discrimination. The courts use the following guidelines to determine when unwelcome sexual advances constitute unlawful discrimination (Switzer 1989):

- *Quid pro quo harassment.* This occurs "when an employee's [or student's] submission to unwelcome sexual conduct becomes an explicit or implicit condition of employment, or when personnel actions such as promotion, transfer, compensation, or discipline are determined on the basis of an employee's response to such conduct."
- *Hostile environment.* A hostile environment develops when there is "unwelcome sexual conduct which unreasonably interferes with an individual's job performance or creates an intimidating, hostile, or offensive work environment."

Sexual harassment ranges from subtle hints about the rewards of being more friendly with the boss or teacher to rape. In the less severe instances (and sometimes even in the severe instances), the subordinate may be reluctant to make, literally, a federal case of it. New federal laws protecting male as well as female workers, however, have removed the legitimacy of this form of discrimination and may well help reduce it.

FEMINIST THEORIES

Generally, all feminist theories share the view that gender inequalities are socially rather than biologically constructed and that they should be eliminated (Sapiro 1986). Within this general framework, however, there are

Women of Color: "And Ain't I a Woman?"

During the first half of the 19th century, many civic-minded northern women were active in the movement to abolish slavery. The discrimination they experienced in trying to speak out against slavery radicalized many of these women, who soon realized that they couldn't free anyone else while they were not free themselves. As a result, in the 1840s, some women split away from the abolitionist movement to promote women's rights. Many who stayed within the ranks of the abolitionist movement thought that once rights were extended to black men, they would surely be extended to white and other women.

Of course, many activists continued to work hard for both the end of slavery and for women's rights. One of the most eloquent speakers on the women's rights circuit was a former slave who took the name Sojourner Truth. In response to male hecklers who claimed that women were weak and needed the protection of a dependent position, she responded:

> The man over there says women need to be helped into carriages and lifted over ditches, and to have the best place everywhere. Nobody ever helps me into carriages or over puddles, or gives me the best place—and ain't I a woman?

> Look at my arm. I have ploughed and planted and gathered into barns, and no man could head me—and ain't I a woman? I could work as much and eat as much as a man—when I could get it—and bear the lash as well!

And ain't I a woman? I have born thirteen children, and seen most of 'em sold into slavery, and when I cried out with my mother's grief, none but Jesus heard me—and ain't I a woman? (cited in Flexner 1972, 90–91).

Despite Sojourner Truth's effective advocacy of women's rights, many women of color have found the struggle for women's rights and that for minority rights to be an uneasy combination.

Women of color face a two-pronged dilemma. First, they have not benefited from the sheltered position of traditional women's roles. As Truth so eloquently illustrated, nobody held doors for them or protected them from heavy work. Women of color have always worked hard outside the home: At the turn of the century, married African American women were 6 times more likely than married white women to be employed (Golden 1977). Nevertheless, they faced the economic and civic penalties of being women. Thus, they have had

less to lose and more to gain from abandoning traditional gender roles. On the other hand, women of color face a potential conflict of interest: Is racism or sexism their chief oppressor? Should they work for an end to racism or an end to sexism? If they choose to work for women's rights, they may be seen as working against men of their own racial and ethnic group.

Current income figures indicate that sex is more important than race is determining women's *earnings:* The difference between Hispanic, black, and Anglo women is relatively small compared to the difference between women and men. This suggests that fighting sex discrimination should be more important than fighting racial discrimination. But this conclusion overlooks the fact that the total *income* of women and their children depends to a significant extent on the earnings of their husbands and fathers. Black women and children are three times more likely than white women and children to live below the poverty level. The reason, of course, is the low earnings and employment of black and Hispanic men. From this perspective women of color could advance their cause most effectively by fighting racial and ethnic discrimination.

The dilemma remains a real one. The women's rights movement is seen as a middle-class white social movement; racial and ethnic movements have been seen as men's movements. No matter which side the woman of color chooses, she is likely to be seen as a traitor to one side or the other.

many varieties of feminism. Some feminists fit comfortably into conventional political positions, but others take extremely radical positions. Here we outline three general classes of feminist theory.

Liberal Feminism.   Liberal feminists rest their case for equality on the same grounds that men have been using for centuries—that all people are created equal, endowed with inalienable rights to pursue life, liberty, and happiness, and so on.

These feminists want to apply standard moral and political values to women. They do not want to change society drastically or turn society's values upside down; they just want to extend basic rights one further step. Although their modest proposals occasionally give rise to real conflict with those who oppose the extension of these rights, liberal feminism is not a radical program.

Socialist Feminism.   Socialist feminists use a Marxist framework to explain differences between the status of men and of women. Women are the proletarians in the sexual division of labor, men the bourgeois (Engels [1884] 1972). This perspective suggests that men control the means of production and keep women in a dependent position by force, fraud, and trickery. Men had the initial advantage because of their greater physical strength and women's frequent pregnancies, but the advantage has been maintained by institutionalized norms and values that keep women in an inferior position.

This doesn't mean that individual men are scheming to subordinate women through force, fraud, and trickery (though some are), but that social institutions are set up to preserve power differentials between men and women. Thus, decent and compassionate men may want to preserve tra-

The feminist movement is very diverse. On the one hand are the business and professional women who fight for equal rights in the legislature and courtroom. On the other hand, radical feminists want to dismantle the entire set of social institutions, which they see as embodying principles of male domination. One issue that unites nearly all feminists is defense of legal abortion, a woman's right to choose.

ditional family roles because they have been taught to value them rather than because they help restrict women's opportunities.

These theorists believe that women's inequality is rooted in the institutions of private property and the means of production. As a result, private property, including the exclusive ownership of children, must be eliminated to create equality for women. They argue, for example, that women will never achieve equal status as long as the children they bear are regarded as their individual property and responsibility.

Socialist feminism is obviously a more radical approach than liberal feminism. It suggests that the problem is not the access of women to conventional institutions, but the institutions themselves.

Radical Feminism.   The most extreme of all feminist theories is radical feminism. Those who adopt this perspective argue that men, not institutions, are the problem. They see all of history as a more or less successful domination of men and men's ideas over women and women's ideas. Since they define men as the problem, they do not believe that changing social institutions will help. The solution they advocate is separation of women from men—severing all heterosexual relationships and creating a separate women's culture. They believe such a culture will be characterized by specifically female virtues—nurturance, sharing, and intuition (Sapiro 1986).

Summary.   Most American feminists fall within the liberal camp. They want greater equality for women within conventional social institutions, and they are not interested in revolutionizing society or setting up a sex-segregated culture. Although socialist and radical theorists are a distinct minority, their views are influential and have a tendency to expand continually the areas of concern for liberal feminists.

■

CONCLUSION

A recent study asked a crosssection of 1,400 Americans what were the most memorable events and changes that had occurred in their lifetimes. Very few women respondents and only five men mentioned changes in gender roles as one of these major changes (Schuman and Scott 1989). Yet, with few exceptions, changes in gender roles have affected more of us more deeply and personally than the Kennedy and King assassinations or the Vietnam War.

Changing gender roles have brought stress to many people—to men who have had to give up rights and power and also to women. Women who grew up in an era when being a good mother and housekeeper was a sufficient goal are troubled to find that society no longer regards this as enough. Generally, the changes in gender roles mean that both women and men must add new roles, while retaining many of their traditional obligations. For women, the remodeled gender role may appear in the superwoman complex. Each woman is expected to maintain a well-kept house, prepare elegant meals, and have cheerful and clean children; she must belong to the PTA, be a room mother, and have a successful career. There is a parallel in the postfeminist superman role: Each man is supposed to have a successful career as well as be a gourmet cook, a sensitive lover, and a dad who begins a life of total involvement with his children by going to Lamaze classes and staying in the delivery room (Gerzon 1982).

In the short run, the increasing role demands on both men and women may create role strain, a feeling that too much is being demanded. In the long run, many expect that changed gender roles will produce more well-rounded human beings. The greater flexibility of gender roles may increase our freedom to choose the roles that we play well and that suit our interests.

It would be a mistake, however, to think that the past has been swept away. In many respects, continuity with the past is much more important than change. This is especially true at home. The kids and the house are still largely her responsibility; breadwinning and the lawn are his responsibility.

The lack of responsiveness of family roles to the other changes is a source of frequent conflict in American marriages, and the family is increasingly being identified as the most critical frontier for women's equality (Curtis 1986; Hartmann, 1981). In fact, it may be in the family that gender-role stereotypes are the most resistant to change, where women physicians and typists are equally unable to override expectations that the children and household are their responsibility and that their husband should assume the dominant role in interaction.

ISSUES IN SOCIAL POLICY

Pornography and Violence Toward Women

In any metropolitan newspaper, headlines announce such news as "Woman Stabbed and Sexually Assaulted," or "South Side Rapist Adds 19th Victim." Fear of attack is an everyday experience for most women. They are fearful if they have to walk to their cars after dark, fearful of entering dark apartments or offices, and often fearful when they are alone in a strange neighborhood or even in their own home (Warr 1985).

These fears are not unfounded. There were nearly 100,000 rapes reported to the police in 1988. It is estimated that one-fourth of all women are raped or sexually assaulted sometime during their lifetime (Malamuth and Donnerstein 1984).

Violence toward women adds another dimension to the discussion of sex differences and gender roles: Women are, and have cause to be, afraid of men; the opposite is seldom true. This

Does pornography exploit women? Does it encourage people to view women as sexual objects and implicitly sanction rape and sexual violence? These questions are at the heart of the current debate over pornography legislation. Many women feel that the struggle for equal rights must go beyond the battle for equal wages; they also want freedom from fear of victimization.

inequality in fear has profound consequences for the quality of life. Equality in incomes and opportunity without equal freedom from fear is only half a loaf.

Violence toward women has many causes. One of the causes that is currently being much discussed as a matter of public policy is pornography.

PORNOGRAPHY AND VIOLENCE TOWARD WOMEN: THE EVIDENCE

The link between pornography and violence toward women is a case study of how difficult it is to examine complex human behavior with social science methods. We cannot stage rapes in the laboratory. Nor is a survey including questions such as "How much pornography are you exposed to?" and "Did you rape or consider raping anybody in the last year?" likely to turn up good evidence. Thus, the evidence linking sexually explicit material to violence toward women is generally weak.

The results of major studies support, though they do not prove, a link between some kinds of pornography and some aspects of violence toward women. Specifically, laboratory studies of male college students demonstrate that young men who are exposed to sexually explicit materials for one hour per week for six weeks become more callous toward women (Check 1985; Zillman and Bryant 1982). They are more likely to accept the rape myth (that women who say no really mean yes and that women enjoy rape), less likely to sympathize with victims, and less likely to believe the rapist should be punished. When the material included sexual violence or degradation, these effects were more marked (Check 1985). Although there is no proof that these attitudes lead to acts of aggression, it seems likely that such attitudes can foster or legitimize rape.

ISSUES IN SOCIAL POLICY continued

THE ISSUES

Some levels of pornography offend almost everyone, and one could get general agreement that such material constitutes a menace to society—for example, pictures of sexual torture and dismemberment or sexual acts involving very young children. The difficult issue is where, along a continuum running from naked statues in the park to the extremes of sexual sadism, to draw the line.

In the United States, two constitutional freedoms are crucial in defining obscenity: freedom of speech and freedom of the press. Neither right is absolute, but our constitution requires that we err on the side of underregulation rather than overregulation. Nevertheless, when speech or publications constitute a clear and present danger, they may be regulated.

The question, then, is whether some pornographic materials constitute a serious harm to some segments of society, women and children in particular, such that they should be declared obscene and regulated by the state.

The 1986 Attorney General's Commission on Pornography reviewed hundreds of studies and interviewed dozens of expert witnesses on both sides. At the end, it acknowledged that it did not have enough information to prove a linkage between violent and degrading pornography and violence toward women. It did, however, conclude that there was enough evidence of a link between pornography and violence toward women that a prudent government should act to reduce the danger to its citizens. As a result, the commission made 92 recommendations to federal, state, and local governments to restrict publication and dissemination of degrading and violent pornography (U.S. Department of Justice 1986).

These recommendations are very controversial and are opposed by many. Opposition comes from two sources. First, many people argue that any restriction of freedom of the press will put a chill on freedom of speech (Linz, Penrod, and Donnerstein 1986). They argue that once a precedent for censorship has been established, the authority of the Constitution's protection is fatally undermined. From this point of view, only the most compelling evidence of terrible social damage would be sufficient to justify censorship of any kind. This brings up the second point: the quality of the evidence. Data gathered in dozens of studies using a variety of study designs suggest that pornography can change men's *attitudes* toward rape. It is an inference rather than a fact that these attitudes create a climate that encourages and supports acts of rape. For many people, this evidence is not strong enough to justify censorship.

Perhaps not surprisingly, pornography is the public issue with the biggest gender gap. Public opinion data show that 51 percent of women are "very concerned about the amount of pornography in this country," but only 27 percent of men share their concern (Public Opinion 1986b). Because of their personal involvement in this issue, women are much more likely than men to accept the pornographic/rape linkage as strong enough to justify public action.

As with most issues of social policy, empirical evidence is insufficient to decide the case. Policy, in fact, is always in part a matter of values. Policy is also a matter of politics. Which side has the most evidence may be less important than which side has the most power.

■

SUMMARY

1. Although there is a universal biological base for gender roles, a great deal of variability exists in the roles and personalities assigned to men and women across societies. Universally, however, women have had less power than men.

2. From earliest childhood, females and males integrate ideas about sex-appropriate behavior into their self-identity. Nevertheless, differences in aptitudes and personality are surprisingly small and are declining.

3. Women and men are growing more similar in their educational aspirations and attainments and in the percentage of their lives that they will spend in the work force. Family roles remain sharply gendered. Parenting and household production remain largely female responsibilities.

4. Women earn 65 percent as much as men because of workplace segregation and because they are paid less for doing the same work. Workplace segregation is achieved through gendered jobs, different qualifications, and simple discrimination. Women get paid less than men for the same work because they work for smaller, less profitable firms and because their family responsibilities interfere with career development.

5. Women's subordinate position is built into family, religious, and political institutions. Although some of this

has changed, men disproportionately occupy leadership positions in social institutions. They even dominate women in conversation.

6. Men also face disadvantages due to their gender role. These include higher mortality and fewer intimate relationships.

7. Functional theorists argue that a division of labor between the sexes builds a stronger family and reduces competition. Conflict theorists stress that men and capitalists benefit from a segmented labor market that relegates women to lower-status positions.

8. Sex stratification is maintained through socialization and learned expectations and by the same types of mechanisms used to maintain boundaries between racial groups: prejudice, discrimination, and sexism.

9. Feminist theories come in several forms: liberal, socialist, and radical. All types of feminists share a belief that gender inequalities are socially constructed and should be eliminated.

10. Violence against women is an important element of the disadvantage that women face. Although there is some evidence that certain kinds of pornography may encourage attitudes toward women that invite or condone rape, control of pornography conflicts with constitutional rights.

■

SUGGESTED READINGS

Chafetz, Janet S. 1984. Sex and Advantage. Totawa, N.J.: Rowman and Allanheld. A review of historical and cross-cultural evidence regarding women's status. Well written and accessible to the nonspecialist.

Epstein, Cynthia. 1988. Deceptive Distinctions: Sex, Gender, and the Social Order. New Haven: Yale University Press. An analysis of the relative importance of biology and culture in producing current sex differences. Epstein shows how a continued emphasis on biological differences helps perpetuate traditional disadvantages for women.

Gerzon, Mark. 1982. A Choice of Heroes: The Changing Faces of American Manhood. Boston: Houghton Mifflin. Looks at changing gender roles from the male perspective and provides a nice balance to the usual emphasis on women's roles.

Goffman, Erving. 1976. Gender Advertisements. New York: Harper & Row. An entertaining yet powerful

look at the ways advertising distorts women. The photographs in this book are dated now, but you won't have difficulty thinking of contemporary equivalents.

McLaughlin, Steven and Associates. 1988. The Changing Lives of American Women. Chapel Hill: University of North Carolina Press. A review of the major changes in women's lives in the last decade—in employment, marriage and divorce, childbearing, sexual behavior, and attitudes.

Reskin, Barbara and Hartmann, Heidi. 1986. Women's Work, Men's Work: Sex Segregation on the Job. Washington, D.C.: National Academy. A collection of articles about one of the most critical areas for discrimination against women—occupations and earnings.

Sapiro, Virginia. 1986. Women in American Society. Palo Alto, Ca.: Mayfield Publishing Company. A text book in women's studies designed for undergraduates. A thorough review of American gender inequalities.

12

AGE DIFFERENTIATION AND INEQUALITIES

Have you ever . . .

Experienced age discrimination? Of course you have. When you were in high school, you were turned away from R-rated movies because you weren't old enough and didn't bring your mother; you were told that you weren't old enough to buy liquor, cigarettes, or rent a car; you weren't old enough to work in some establishments or on some shifts. Many of those reading this book still aren't legally entitled to drink, smoke, or rent a car. You can go to jail and join the army and pay taxes, but you do not have a full set of rights.

Age discrimination is pervasive in our society, but it has seldom created much public outcry. Most young people have enough on their plates already without starting a social movement to improve their legal rights. All they have to do, after all, is just wait a few years.

In this chapter, we consider how age is socially structured in our society. In addition to considering norms for age-appropriate behavior, we will also consider structured inequalities between age groups. How are they created and maintained?

All of the other bases of differentiation that we have looked at (class, race, ethnicity, sex) tend to be mutually exclusive. To be white means you will never be black; to be female means you will never be male; to be born middle class probably means that you will always be middle class. Age, however, presents a very different picture. We move through age categories sequentially, casting off one and going on to the next. We move from childhood through adolescence into adulthood and finally into old age. Because some behaviors and attitudes are considered appropriate for one age category and not for another, we change our roles as we age. This chapter is about the social transitions that accompany physical aging and the differences in roles and life chances that are associated with membership in an age category.

AGE DIFFERENTIATION

THE SOCIOLOGICAL STUDY OF AGE

In all cultures, people have been assigned different roles according to age. At a minimum, all societies distinguish between the young, the adult, and the elderly. Some role differentiation by age is inevitable, especially at the two extremes. Children cannot perform as well as adults; the elderly experience declining strength and endurance as they age.

But what is young? What is elderly? We can measure age in many ways. We can measure simple chronological age—whether a person has reached the 20th or 50th birthday. There is a certain merit to this measurement, since people of the same chronological age share many experiences. For example, everybody who is now 65 shares a rememberance of World War II and of a childhood without television. Nevertheless, it is important to recognize that just because people are the same age does not mean they have reached the same place, have traveled a similar way to get there, or are going in the same direction (Pearlin 1982). In addition, chronological age may be a poor indicator of physical condition or emotional and intellectual maturity. Some 70-year-olds are in wheelchairs, but some are on the tennis courts. And some 25-year-olds are independent, whereas others are still bringing their laundry home to mother (Neugarten and Neugarten 1986, 37).

The systematic physical and psychological changes associated with aging are not of primary interest to sociologists. Rather, we are concerned with social norms and roles that structure the behavior of people in different age categories. In short, we want to know what is implied when we tell someone to "act your age." What norms govern age-related behavior, and what roles are considered appropriate for particular age groups? Finally, we want to consider whether the rights and privileges associated with age roles represent a pattern of structured inequality. Is there a consistent pattern of unequal reward by age that is justified by age norms?

AGE AND SOCIAL STRUCTURE

Aging and age expectations are, in large part, products of social structure. In our own society, critical points in the age distribution are 6, 16, 18, 21, and 65. These ages represent points at which social structures treat you differently or declare that you have different rights or responsibilities. You must go to school, you may drive, you must register for the draft, you may vote, you may drink, or you may draw retirement benefits. These significant ages are products of culture not biology. Because these culturally designated points vary from one society to the next, so does the experience of growing up and aging.

Modern bureaucracies are giving the aging experience more and more formal structure. Especially during the first 21 years, there are a great many explicit formal expectations of what we should be doing and not doing at each age (Saraceno 1984). At 10, for example, one should be in the fifth grade—not the fourth or the sixth, but exactly in the fifth grade. Although they do not disappear, these age-graded expectations become far less rigid after high school graduation. Nevertheless, at the other end of the life course, institutionalized social structures affecting pension benefits create age norms about retirement.

Because age requirements have been built into modern bureaucracies, age norms have become institutionalized. The experience of being 16 or 35 or 65 depends not only on your own physical and mental vigor but also on the social structures in which you participate. As a result, the aging process and all of the transitions involved in growing up and growing old differ across societies, and within societies, by class, race, and sex.

The Life-Course Perspective.   A key concept in the sociological approach to age is the **life course**, "the age-related transitions that are socially created, socially recognized, and shared" (Hagestad and Neugarten 1985, 35). The life-course perspective implies no necessary or universal experience with aging; rather, it is concerned with how aging is socially structured.

This approach to aging takes explicit account of the fact that the experience of aging is somewhat different for each generation. The life choices available to your grandparents are no longer available to you, and those of your children will be different again. For this reason, sociological studies of aging focus on unique experiences of a **cohort**, a category of individuals who share a particular experience at the same point in time. For example, we might study the birth cohort of 1930 or the marriage cohort of 1990. Application of the cohort perspective to experience with the Great Depression has shown that the experience was very different for those who were young children in 1930 than for those who were teenagers (Elder 1974). For the youngest children, poverty and uncertainty were the conditions they were born into, and the post–World War II prosperity seemed to them to represent progress and security. Those who were older at the time of the depression, however, saw a cyclical pattern in which prosperity was erased and then returned. Even 40 and 50 years later, these people are still saving their old socks in case hard times return. Thus, these cohorts will experience old age differently because of the different paths they took to get there.

> **Life course** refers to the age-related transitions that are socially created, socially recognized, and shared.

> A **cohort** is a category of individuals who share a particular experience at the same point in time—for example, all of those who were born in 1930 or who married in 1990.

AGE NORMS IN THE UNITED STATES

Age norms center on the behaviors and attitudes expected of us when we "act our age." These age norms are much less specific than those associated

Normative standards for childhood are very different in our own affluent society than they are in most of the rest of the world. We believe it is appropriate for children to do such small tasks as setting the table and putting away their toys, but we are appalled at the amount of heavy labor required of these children in Colombia. Freeing children from labor is a luxury that many developing societies cannot afford.

with sex, and generally few sanctions are associated with violating them (Marini 1984). Nevertheless, these norms guide the behaviors of the majority of individuals so that those who are out of step will feel set apart from their age-mates. In this section, we describe the general norms about age roles in the United States. These norms are the roadmap that social structures use to guide our journey from childhood to old age.

THE ROLE OF CHILDREN

The norms of childhood establish a rather clear set of rights and responsibilities for children. Legal rights include health care, freedom from physical abuse, freedom from labor, and access to state-provided education. Children's rights also include being shielded from bad language, sexuality, worry, and danger. The obligations of the contemporary child are to play and to accomplish certain developmental tasks, such as learning independence and self-control, as well as mastery of the school curriculum. These obligations are not wholly the child's, however, for if the child fails to meet them, the fault will be attributed to the parents or the school rather than to the child.

The norms governing expectations for childhood have changed. Gone are the days when we expected children to turn over their paychecks to Mom and Dad. Children are no longer expected to do much work and, in fact, are legally barred from employment. Contemporary norms specify that parents give to children, not vice versa. Nevertheless, childhood is seldom the oasis that our ideal norms specify. A sizable fraction of children are physically or emotionally abused by their parents; current estimates suggest that one out of four girls experiences sexual abuse during childhood (Finkelhor 1986). Nearly one-fifth of children will grow up in poverty.

An important change in the social structure of the child's world is the sharp increase in the proportion of children who grow up in single-parent households: Twenty percent are born to single mothers, and it is estimated that fully 59 percent of all children born in the 1980s will spend some time in a single-parent household before they are 18 (Glick 1984). This rapid and extensive change in the primary social structure of childhood is likely to change the experience of childhood in ways only partially understood. It is likely, however, to reduce the protection from harsh reality that our ideal norms specify.

ADOLESCENCE/YOUNG ADULTHOOD

Adolescence is often a period of irresponsibility. Because society has little need for the contributions of youth, it encourages a concern among young people for trivialities—such as concern over personal appearance and the latest music. Yet, because adolescence is a temporary state, the adolescent is under persistent pressure. Questions such as "What are you going to do when you finish school?" "What are you going to major in?," and "How serious are you about that girl [or boy]?" have an urgent reality that creates strain.

What are the rights and obligations of adolescence? Basically, there appear to be four (Campbell 1969):

1. Adolescents are supposed to become independent of their parents. The change from family to peer groups as a source of esteem is the first step in this process.

2. They are supposed to experiment with new roles and behaviors, to test their values and the worth of social roles. Throughout childhood they have taken their parents' word for what is valuable and normative. During adolescence they either make these values their own or discard them.

3. They are supposed to acquire adult skills. These include social skills (how to work in committees and how to meet and impress new people, for example) and technical skills (how to make change, type, and differentiate equations, for example).

4. Last, but not least, they are supposed to have fun. If they do not (if they stay home on Friday nights, if they are always serious and never silly), they will be violating a norm and will surely be sanctioned by their peers. Their parents will begin to worry about them, and they may find themselves seeing a psychologist.

Thus, in spite of the fact that society does not appear to expect much of adolescents, they are under a great deal of role strain. Indeed, adolescence is one of the most stressful stages in the life course. Survey data show that adults are twice as likely to pick adolescence as the worst rather than the best time of their lives (Harris and Associates 1975),

ADULTHOOD

The role of adult in our society carries with it more rights and responsibilities than any other age role. Within each institution—family, education, religion, politics, economy—adults are expected to carry the load. They also reap many of the benefits. Not only are their rights and responsibilities greater within each institution but also adults are involved in more institutions than other age categories. It is a stage of maximum engagement in social structures.

Adult roles differ substantially by sex. Although this is less true today than it was 50 years ago or even 20 years ago, the experience of moving across the age span differs for women and men. Women marry earlier and have children earlier than men; they also retire earlier. The meaning of various adult roles also differs for women and men. The decision to become a parent, for example, is much more significant for women's roles than for men's; entering and leaving the labor force, too, generally means different things for men and women.

The Transition to Adulthood.   Some societies have **rites of passage**, formal rituals that mark the end of one age status and the beginning of another. In our own society, there is no clear point at which we can say that a person has become an adult.

In psychology, adulthood may be defined by responsibility and maturity. The sociological concept of adulthood, however, focuses on social roles. Although expectations vary by sex, adulthood means that a person adopts at least some of the following roles: being employed and supporting oneself and one's dependents, being out of school, marrying, having children, voting, being a church member. Some of these social roles are voluntary and people may be considered adults if they never marry, never vote, never join a church, or, in the case of women, never hold a paid job (Hogan and Astone 1986). Nevertheless, the majority of people follow the conventional route of adulthood: They make the transition to adulthood by finishing school, getting a job, marrying, and raising a family.

Much of the research on the transition to adulthood focuses on the sequencing of these four transitions. The normative and most common transition sequence is to finish school, then to get a job, a spouse, and

Rites of passage are formal rituals that mark the end of one status and the beginning of another.

Rites of passage mark the end of one status and the beginning of another. In our society, rituals such as graduations and weddings continue to have symbolic significance, but the transitions they mark are less clear than they used to be. When as many as half of all couples cohabit before their weddings, when many people receive advanced degrees years after they have married and borne children, the transition to adulthood becomes somewhat fuzzy.

■

TABLE 12.1

THE CHANGING TRANSITION TO ADULTHOOD

In the last generation, the transition to adulthood has been postponed by two to three years. As a result of growing educational demands and a changing economy, young people are less quick to start their own families and are spending more years in school and with their parents.

	1970	1985–88
Median age at first marriage (women)	20.6	23.0
Median age at childbearing (women)	24.3	26.3
Percent aged 18–21 in school	39.8	43.8
Percent aged 18–24 still living with parents	47.3	54.4

SOURCE: U.S. Bureau of the Census 1989a, 49, 62, 86, 128; U.S. Bureau of the Census 1989e, 63.

children—in that order. Three major changes have occurred in this sequence in the last two decades. First, all four transitions occur much closer together than they used to. Men born in 1907 had an average of 18 years between the first and last of these transitions; the span was only eight years for men born in 1947 (Hogan 1981). Second, the order of these transitions is much more variable than it used to be. Increasing numbers of men and women marry and even have children before they finish school; some have children before they marry. Third, on the average, these transitions are occurring at later ages. Age at marriage is up, age at finishing education is up, and age at leaving home is up (see Table 12.1).

Middle Age. The busiest part of most adult lives is between the ages of 20 and 45. There are often children in the home and marriages and careers to be established. This period of life is frequently marked by role strain and role conflict, simply because so much is going on at one time. Middle age, that period roughly between 45 and 65, is by contrast a quieter and often more prosperous period. Studies show that both men and women tend to greet the empty nest and then retirement with relief rather than regret (White and Edwards 1990; Goudy et al. 1980).

The norms of our society suggest that people should have achieved most of their life goals by the time they reach middle age. Thus, middle age is a period of assessment (Neugarten 1968). It is a time for evaluating one's own situation—family, career, standard of living, physical appearance—relative to the norms of society. For some people this evaluation results in what is called the midlife crisis—an awareness that goals not yet reached are probably forever beyond reach. More positively, people recognize that youthful norms are no longer as applicable as they used to be, and they reorganize life's priorities (Tamir 1982). Good looks and a slim body may no longer be so important, and health and satisfaction may become more so.

ADULTS 65 AND OVER

Older adults, those 65 and over, are extremely diverse, defying easy categorization. For the most part, they are retired, although 16 percent of the men and 7 percent of the women are in the labor force. Social norms

FOCUS ON RESEARCH

Do You Get Better with Age?

As we move from age 20 to 40 to 60, our lives change in more or less predictable ways. We leave home, form families, work, and retire. In early adulthood, the process is largely one of role acquisition; in middle and old age, it is a process of role loss. According to some symbolic interactionists, the addition of roles in adulthood should improve our self-concept, whereas the loss of roles in later life should decrease it. Others suggest that adulthood is a period of growth and maturation so that older individuals become more, not less, satisfied with themselves and their roles.

A recent study by Walter Gove, Suzanne Ortega, and Carolyn Style (1989) addresses this issue. They asked a national random sample to read a list of adjectives and check the ones that described them. The adjectives measured four dimensions of self-concept:

- *Competent:* hardworking, well organized, self-confident, strong, logical, and intelligent
- *Supportive:* helpful, flexible, considerate, content
- *Calm:* not emotional, not nervous, not frustrated
- *Cooperative:* not lazy, not disorganized, not stubborn.

Because they reasoned that these characteristics might be affected by social class, race, and sex, they adjusted for these factors. The adjusted results are presented in Figure 12.1. They show clearly that older people feel better about themselves than younger people: Young people rate themselves as relatively

uncooperative, incompetent, uncalm, and unsupportive. In contrast, the older respondents feel very positive about their identities.

These results suggest that, despite the high esteem in which youth is held in our society, youth is not all wonderful, and growing old is not altogether a bad thing. In fact, getting older seems to be associated with getting better—with being a nicer and more capable person. These results led Gove, Ortega, and Style to conclude that maturation is more important than role loss in affecting self-concept.

In interpreting these data, however, the authors run into a serious problem. These are *cross-sectional*

■

FIGURE 12.1
**DIFFERENCES IN SELF-CONCEPT
BY AGE**

A large national study shows that older people report substantially better self-concepts than younger people. Older people report that they are more competent, supportive, calm, and co-operative. It is possible that today's older generation always had these positive traits, but the study's authors conclude that people tend to develop these characteristics as they grow older.

SOURCE: Adapted from Gove, Ortega, and Style 1989.

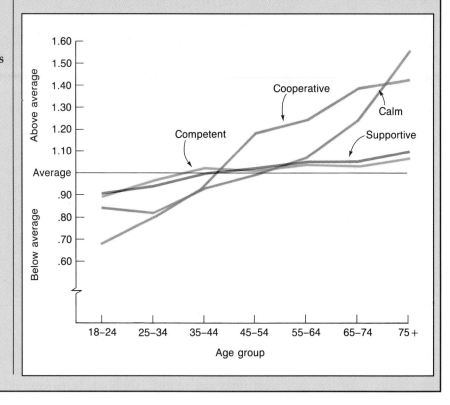

data. That means that the respondents who are 65 to 74 are of an entirely different generation than those who are 18 to 24. This raises the very realistic possibility that these people did not become more cooperative, competent, and so forth with age—but that their generation was always more competent and cooperative.

Whenever we look at age differences from a cross-sectional sample, we face two possibilities: that the differences are the result of *age ef-* *fects* or *cohort effects.* The age effect takes the data at face value and hypothesizes that, as today's young people age, they will become more competent, cooperative, supportive, and calm. The cohort effect suggests that these are permanent generational differences and will not change with age—that even at 65, today's young people will feel uncooperative, unsupportive, uncalm, and incompetent.

Gove, Ortega, and Style choose to believe that their results show an age effect. They conclude that maturation does bring about positive changes. They support their conclusion by citing survey research from as far back as 1957 showing the same pattern. In the final analysis, however, the choice of a cohort or an age interpretation rests on theory. Which interpretation makes the most sense to you? Do you expect to get better with age?

are more explicit about what they are not supposed to do than about what they are supposed to do. This has led some commentators to suggest that being elderly is a roleless role—an absence of both rights and duties. The socially appropriate role for the elderly is to be nonproductive, nonaggressive, and noncompetitive, but also independent and out of their children's hair—and homes, except when invited.

Some observers suggest that the comparative rolelessness of the elderly reduces life satisfaction. Nevertheless, one of the most consistent findings in research on the elderly is that retirement is generally a positive stage in the life course (Medley 1976). Although some women and men may require a little adjustment (as one woman said, "I'm getting twice as much husband for half as much money!"), almost all believe that their new leisure is legitimate (that is, normatively approved) and do not feel badly about not having more demanding social roles. As long as they stay healthy, older adults report high levels of life satisfaction. The best predictors of satisfaction among the elderly are the same factors that predict satisfaction at every other stage of the life course: good health, adequate income, and a satisfying family life (Larson 1978; Medley 1976).

LIFE CHANCES AND INEQUALITIES

Society is run mainly by adults between the ages of 30 and 65. These adults control jobs, industry, education, and wealth. In the following sections, we examine the extent to which youth and the elderly can be considered structurally disadvantaged relative to this middle-aged group.

THE STATUS OF YOUTH

Legal Restrictions. In law, people under 18 are called infants (Sloan 1981). They are not responsible for their contracts (thus, they usually are not allowed to make any), and they are considered less responsible than adults for their bad deeds. Just as legal statutes once declared women and minority members incapable of self-government, the law still declares the

Young people are frequently disadvantaged in the labor market. Although an occasional young man gets a good job working construction, a large proportion of young people have to settle for the minimum wage in supermarkets and fast food franchises. Although these wages might be acceptable to those who are still living at home and just working for pocket money, low wages and high unemployment pose a hardship for young people who must support themselves or their families.

young to be incapable. As you may be painfully aware from personal experience, young people have few legal rights. Their rights to drink, drive, work, own property, and marry are abridged. They have to pay adult prices, but cannot see adult movies. In church, school, and industry, they find there are age barriers they must pass before they are allowed full participation. Unlike the case of women and minorities, there is no movement to reduce inequality for teenagers. The voting age was reduced from 21 to 18 in 1970, but the drinking age has been raised to 21. Once again, we face the irony of staffing our armed forces with young people we will not trust with a beer. Although raising the drinking age springs from the praiseworthy objective of reducing deaths from drinking and driving, it is nevertheless a reminder that many people believe the young cannot make responsible decisions and need to be protected.

For the most part, these age-related rules reflect society's belief that age is a reasonable indicator of competency; moreover, it is one that is easy and efficient to administer. Thus, instead of devising some test of maturity before voting privileges are granted, society uses the simple rule of thumb: Under 18 is not mature, but 18 and over is mature enough for this purpose.

Although there is growing sentiment that neither ethnicity nor sex are good guides to competency, no such change of sentiment has occurred about the utility of age for making relevant judgments about youth. In fact, discrimination against youth may be the last bastion of approved inequality before the law. The Supreme Court, in siding with parents who wished to prohibit a teenage daughter's abortion, concluded that "the rights of children cannot be equated with those of adults" (Justice Powell in *Bellotti* v. *Baird* [1979], cited in Eglit 1985, 532). These age rules receive very high consensus from society, and little, if any, pressure exists to repeal them.

Economic Status.   Owing to underdeveloped work skills, limited experience, desire for part-time or flexible schedules, and also owing to simple discrimination, a very large share of American youth earn the minimum wage. Even this wage is under a two-pronged assault. First, the law that raised the minimum wage in 1990 provides for a subminimum training wage; this training wage is targeted largely at young people. The second assault on youthful earnings is a very high rate of unemployment: In 1990 when 5 percent of the civilian labor force was unemployed, the unemployment figure was 16 percent for those aged 16–19 and 10 percent for those 20–24 (U.S. Department of Labor 1990). For African American youth, these figures are 27 and 19 percent, respectively. As a consequence, families headed by people under 25 (3 million in 1988) are three times more likely to be in poverty than the average family.

Crime.   Failure to integrate youth fully into major social structures is reflected in several indices of social disorganization. Although youth are underrepresented among voters and workers, they are overrepresented in accident and crime statistics. In 1988, people under age 24 represented only 20 percent of the population, but they accounted for 43 percent of the rape arrests, 41 percent of the arrests for aggravated assault, 45 percent of murder arrests, and 72 percent of arrests for motor-vehicle thefts (U.S. Department of Justice 1989a).

A recent study shows that these youthful crime rates are strongly related to the availability of employment for juveniles and the quality of work (wages) for young adults (Allan and Steffensmeier 1989). Although some observers downplay the importance of youthful unemployment or low wages, assuming that the problem will solve itself as individuals age, the clear message is that failure to include young people in the labor market has severe consequences for society as well as for the young people themselves.

School. Prior to age 16, nearly all American youth are enrolled in school full time; at ages 20–21, one-third are still enrolled in school. Thus, educational roles play an enormous part in structuring the experience of young people. Not only does education provide the basic structure of life (when to get up, where to go, when to come home, and what to do with most of one's waking hours) but school roles are also critical for identity. The best predictor of adolescent self-esteem is performance at school: Students who do well in school feel competent and confident, whereas poor students feel less competent. Because of its dominant role in young people's lives, what happens at school tends to affect other dimensions of life. For example, young men who get low rewards at school have been found to be more likely to pursue delinquent careers; those who get rewarded at school, on the other hand, are more likely to stay out of trouble (Rosenberg, Schooler, and Schoenbach 1989).

Youth Subculture. In Chapter 3, we said that culture was a set of patterned responses for dealing with the common problems that a society faces. In a parallel vein, a subculture may be distinguished as a set of patterned responses to problems that are unique to a particular group within society. Youth is such a group.

The primary characteristics of youth subculture are an emphasis on passive escape types of entertainment (music, home videos, television, movies) and on style. Style, as embodied in the youth subculture, has been described as having three major elements: (1) image—appearance created by costume, accessories such as hairstyle, and jewelry; (2) demeanor—made up of expression, gait, and posture (how the image is delivered); and (3) argot—special vocabulary and how it is delivered (Brake 1985, 12). Although youth itself is an ascribed status, the style of youth must be achieved. Mastery of this style can be an important basis of self-esteem that partially compensates for youths' disadvantaged position in society's economic and political institutions.

Youth subculture is basically a leisure-time activity. As such, its most extreme manifestations occur among those with the most leisure time— the unemployed, the unmarried, the nonparents, those not going to school. Young people who play one or more of these other roles may participate in the youth subculture during their leisure hours, but the youth subculture will have a marginal influence on their lives.

There is some debate about the origins and merits of youth subculture. Some Marxist analysts see youth subculture as a synthetic creation, a mass-marketing strategy beamed out to millions of bored youth on the airwaves of MTV, created to exploit youth for the profit of a few. In this view youth subculture is indeed false consciousness, a sense of belongingness and

Adolescence is a period in which children grow more independent of their parents. Although parental support and approval remain very important, the peer group also becomes an important source of self-esteem. In the peer group, young people experiment with behavior and language that their parents would probably disapprove of. Although some children model smoking, drinking, and swearing directly on their parents' behavior, many learn these behaviors independently in the peer group.

control that is entirely false to the economic and social reality. Others see elements of authenticity in youth subculture, noting that rock and roll and music videos and other elements of style give youth a chance to express themselves and their interests.

Summary.   Young people are systematically excluded from participation in many of our society's institutions. In some cases, they are excluded by formal rules, such as restrictions on drinking, driving, or renting a car. In other cases, they are excluded because there is no room for them, as in the labor force. In terms of class, status, and power, youth rank significantly behind older adults. To a larger extent, this inequality represents stratification: The lower status of youth is justified by institutionalized norms applicable to an entire category of individuals. For most of us, this lower status is temporary: We get jobs, get married, finish school, have children, and generally become plugged into society. For the minority who never become integrated into society's economic and social structures—and these are disproportionately racial and ethnic minorities—the lower status of youth becomes permanent.

THE STATUS OF THE OVER 65

Although they may have less power than they used to, the elderly in our own society do not seem to be particularly disadvantaged—as long as they keep their health. The following sections review some of the basic findings about the elderly in the United States.

Health, Life Expectancy, and Changing Definitions of "Old."
Perhaps the most important change in the social structure of the population over 65 is that it is now a common stage in life—and often a long one. The average person reaching 65 can now expect to live 17 more years—19 if a woman and 15 if a man. Most of these years will be healthy years. Certainly most people at 65 and 70 experience some loss of energy and physical stamina, but a remarkably large proportion experience no major health limitations. In fact, only one-third of those over *85* report that their health places major limitations on their activities (Neugarten and Neugarten 1986, 35).

For this reason, it is convenient to divide the over 65 population into two rough categories, often called the "young old" and the "old old." The "old old" refers to those whose loss of physical stamina seriously limits their ability to take care of their homes and themselves. In the following pages, we generally refer to the condition of the "young old," those whose status can be regarded as more socially than physically determined.

Income.   The economic condition of the elderly has improved sharply over just the last 30 years. In 1959, 35 percent of the population over 65 had incomes below the poverty level; in 1988, this figure was only 12 percent. This improvement is directly related to increases in Social Security, expanded coverage of private pension plans, and a more comprehensive system of benefits for the elderly. As a result of this system, the proportion of the aged below the poverty level is no greater than the proportion of the entire population that is poor. (See Chapter 9 for a review of poverty data.)

Retirement.   The growing adequacy of Social Security and pension coverage has meant substantial reductions in labor-force activity of older workers. Between 1970 and 1990, the percent of men over 65 who were still in the labor force dropped from 27 to 12 percent; at ages 55–64, labor force participation dropped from 83 to 67 percent. Older women's labor force participation rates however, have remained relatively constant over this period at about 45 percent (U.S. Department of Labor 1990).

Studies show that the primary predictors of early retirement are poor health, a physically demanding job, and a mentally unrewarding job. Not surprisingly, people whose jobs require hard physical labor and provide little mental stimulation quit as soon as they can afford to; those who have mentally challenging jobs are more likely to stay at work (Hayward et. al 1989).

The jobs that encourage early retirement are disproportionately working-class jobs. Since the working class is less likely to have the savings necessary to cushion retirement, many find that they cannot really afford to be out of the labor force. As a result, an increasing number of retired workers reenter the labor market. The average person now retires 1.3 times rather than simply once. Reentry jobs are usually much less demanding, and they pay a substantially lower salary than preretirement jobs (Hayward, Grody, and McLaughlin 1988).

Postretirement Incomes.   Although only 12 percent of the population over 65 is below poverty, the other 88 percent is not all that wealthy. The average person experiences only a minor income loss in the years immediately following retirement, but there are two dark spots in this picture. First, over one quarter of the population experiences an income drop of over 50 percent following retirement. Those people who were living close to the economic margin during middle age—who accumulated no assets,

Most older people "age in place"— that is, they remain in the same neighborhood and the same house that they have lived in for 40 years. Nevertheless, a growing number of elderly have taken advantage of their new prosperity, earlier retirement, and longer life expectancy to move to Arizona and other retirement meccas of the sunbelt. "Snowbirds," such as these women, have resulted in rapid growth for communities such as Sun City, Arizona—a community where three quarters of the population is over 65 and where some neighborhoods have zoning ordinances specifying that no one under 50 can buy a house!

who didn't pay off a home mortgage, and who contributed relatively little to either Social Security or a pension fund—find that retirement brings poverty or near poverty. These people are disproportionately women and minorities, people whose work-life earnings are low. Second, widowhood produces a severe economic blow for most older women, many of whom find that a substantial portion of their retirement income dies along with their husband (Holden, Burkhauser, and Feaster 1988).

Discrimination.   In the past, mandatory retirement regulations forced some people out of the labor force regardless of their physical ability, economic need, or desire to work. In 1986, however, federal legislation outlawed mandatory retirement except for a few cases (such as police officers) where age-related abilities are considered legitimate bases for discrimination.

A far more important problem than mandatory retirement is age discrimination that begins during middle age, when women and men over 40 are considered too old to learn new skills or take new jobs. Age-based discrimination is particularly hard on people who need a new job after 40. This is why affirmative-action legislation uses age 40 to define when age discrimination begins. One recent study examined what happened to men who were laid off after plant closings. The results showed that workers over 55 had to wait twice as long to find a new job as workers under 45 and that the new jobs of older workers were substantially worse than the new jobs of younger workers (Love and Torrence 1989).

Political Power.   Age and even infirmity in no way abridge one's legal rights. The elderly are more likely to vote than other age groups (see Chapter 16), and this makes them a potentially powerful group. There is no evidence, however, that the older population acts together as a cohesive voting bloc. Cleavages of race, class, and sex work against such unity. Major political victories for the aged, most recently the defeat of threatened decreases in Social Security, owe more to broadly based interest groups such as organized labor than they do to senior-based political groups (Hudson and Strate 1986).

Honor and Esteem.   Societal rewards distributed by stratification systems go beyond income and power. They also include esteem or social honor. It is in this regard that the status of the elderly has been most seriously at issue. Our idealized version of the past holds that the elderly used to be highly regarded and respected. Careful examinations of cross-cultural and historical data, however, suggest that the elderly seldom have as much prestige as younger adults (Stearn 1976) and that, historically, our attitude toward the elderly has been ambivalent at best (Achenbaum 1985). Hags, crones, dirty old men, and other negative stereotypes of older people crowd our literature. Whether scheming hags or dear old things, the elderly are seldom regarded with respect and admiration (Cool and McCabe 1983).

Many studies document negative stereotypes about the elderly. Survey research among college students, for example, shows that older people are considered to be less competent, less flexible, and slower to learn than middle-aged or younger people (Levin 1988). These stereotypes about older

people form the basis of **ageism**—the belief that chronological age determines the presence or absence of socially relevant characteristics and that age therefore legitimizes unequal treatment. Although the bulk of the American public strongly favors public programs for the elderly, they also hold opinions that systematically devalue the older person.

In our society, many circumstances work to reduce the esteem in which we hold the elderly. Age is associated with reductions in vigor and physical beauty, both of which are highly prized in our society (Streib 1985). Moreover, because of rapid expansion of the educational system within the last decades, older people are substantially less well educated than younger adults: In 1988, only 54 percent of those over 65 had completed high school. In a society where knowledge and education are taken as indications of intelligence and worth, the elderly are considered less worthy than others. Finally, because the over 65 are generally outside of the mainstream of economic competition, they seldom receive the prestige of active earners (Rosow 1974). Together these three factors mean that, although individual older people may have good incomes, good health, and be politically active, they will often find themselves being patronized and condescended to by younger individuals.

Social Integration.   We have defined adulthood as a period of maximum integration into social institutions. This involvement in social institutions is gradually reduced during old age. Active parenting is the first role to drop off, followed by the work role. Many, especially women, also experience the loss of the marital role through the death of their spouses. The world of church, of family and friends and community, however, often

In the contemporary United States, retirement is a generally satisfactory stage in the life course. Blessed with good health, adequate incomes, and leisure time, many people between 65 and 75 find that life is very enjoyable. Although few have the physical stamina they had 20 or 30 years ago, increases in health and income have dramatically improved the quality of life for the population over 65. Inevitably, old age will take some of the fun out of life, but recent data show that two-thirds of those over 85 say that physical disability is not a problem.

Ageism is the belief that chronological age determines the presence or absence of socially relevant characteristics and that age therefore legitimates unequal treatment.

remains vitally active, at least until the advent of old, old age when health limitations restrict activities.

Studies of older people demonstrate that one of the most important predictors of life satisfaction is their relationships with close friends. These are usually age peers and often, at the end of the life course, brothers and sisters. Interestingly, close ties with their children are not a uniform blessing (Lee 1985). Especially when age starts to become a serious handicap, ties with children become tinged with dependency and ambivalence (Sokolovsky and Cohen 1981). Because ties with age peers usually lack this element, they tend to be more gratifying.

Summary.   An assessment of the status of the elderly over the last 30 years would show very substantial economic improvements. With this improvement in economic circumstances has come much greater independence from their families, better health, and greater community involvement. Nevertheless, among the "old old" a substantial group are "ill fed, ill housed, ill clothed, and just plain ill" (Hess 1985, 329). This group is disproportionately female and minority.

INTERGENERATIONAL BONDS

Relations between age groups, as with relationships between the sexes, are qualitatively different from relationships between races or classes. Generations are intimately tied to one another through family. Some people have worried that geographical mobility and the increased role of the state in providing support for dependents might weaken these intergenerational ties. In this respect, as in many others, the rumor of the death of the family has been much exaggerated.

Youth and Parents: The Generation Gap.   The relationship between teens and their parents is not as bad as is often suggested. Although many families go through a prolonged period of conflict, both parents and children being relieved when they are able to live apart, they maintain a strong bond and many common values (Dornbush 1989). Dozens of studies of college students demonstrate that apparent differences are more often in style than in substance and that young people and parents agree about basic values. As Mark Twain is alleged to have said, "When I was a boy of 14, my father was so ignorant I could hardly stand to have the old man around. But when I got to be 21, I was astonished at how much the old man had learned in seven years."

Adults and Their Parents.   At the other end of the age scale, sociological concern has focused on the nature of the relationship between older people and their children and grandchildren. Empirical studies document a reassuring level of family commitment and involvement across the generations. One study confirmed that 60 percent of those over 65 had seen at least one of their children the previous week, and fully 53 percent of those over 85 had seen a child the previous day (U.S. Bureau of the Census 1989a, 37).

The nature of intergenerational relationships between adult children and their older parents depends very substantially on the ages of the generations. When the older generation falls into the "young old" category, the older generation is, on the average, still providing more help for their children than children are for their parents (Neugarten and Neugarten 1986). They are helping with down payments and grandchildren's college educations or providing temporary living space for children who have divorced or lost their jobs.

As the senior generation moves into the "old old" category, however, relationships must be renegotiated (Mutran and Reitzes 1984). Even in the "old old" category, most people continue to be largely self-sufficient, but eventually most need help of some kind—shopping, home repairs, and social support. A critical difficulty is that many of the children to whom they would turn for this kind of help are themselves no longer young. This gives rise to what has been called the generation squeeze, where the middle generation is caught between demands for support, social or financial, from both their children and their parents. This so-called sandwich generation may suffer substantial role strain.

Summary. Family ties across the generations make inequality between age strata qualitatively different than class inequality. Because of intimate ties across the age span, age stratification has not and is not likely to result in polarized political groups that seek their own goals at the expense of other age groups. Nevertheless, there is competition among age groups. The competition between youth and age for shares of the public purse is described in the next section.

Family ties are important at all stages of the life course. In addition to ties of obligation and affection, we often find our parents and children to be good companions because they are a lot like us. They often share our values and our life-styles. As we get older, we find that they also share our memories. Together, this older man and his middle-aged son can laugh over shared adventures and shake their heads over family disasters of 50 years ago.

THE CHANGING BALANCE OF YOUTH AND AGE

CHANGES IN THE AGE DISTRIBUTION

The United States has historically been a society with a youthful population. As indicated in Figure 12.2, in 1820 fully 58 percent of America's population was under 20. Now, this proportion is down to 29 percent. At the other end of the age spectrum, the proportion of the population over 65 has increased more than sixfold in the last 170 years, from 2 to 13 percent.

Ironically, the increased proportion of the population that is over 65 is due not to decreased mortality but to decreased fertility. In a high-fertility population, the proportion of the elderly is always small. If each couple has six children and their children have six children and so on, then there are many more young than old people. This is roughly the situation that prevailed in 1820, when the average American woman bore 6.7 children. When fertility is relatively low, however, and each woman has only one or two children, then the elderly generation is about the same size as the children's generation—or even larger. The result is that an increasing proportion of the population is elderly and a decreasing proportion of the population consists of children.

Although fertility change is the major determinant of our changing age structure, increased life expectancy does play a part. The last decade has witnessed an unprecedented and largely unanticipated increase in life expectancy among the elderly. Thus, a part of the growth in the elderly population has to do with their lower mortality.

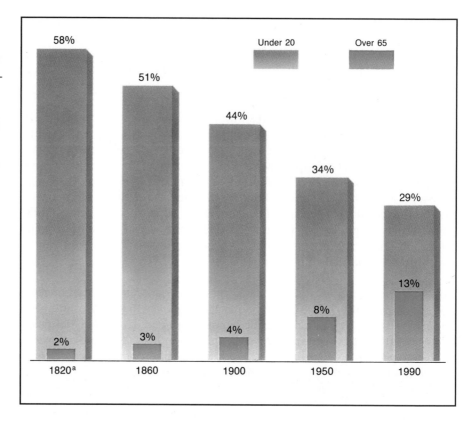

■
FIGURE 12.2
CHANGING U.S. AGE DISTRIBUTION,
1820–1990

In 1820, there were 29 children for every person over age 65. In 1990, there were approximately two children for every older person. Partly as a result of this shift, investment in children consumes a much smaller part of society's resources today.

[a]Data for 1820 are based on the white population only.

SOURCE: U.S. Bureau of the Census 1988, 1975.

Relative Shares of the Public Pot

The ratio of children to old people was 29 to 1 in 1820; in 1990, it was only 2.2 to 1. In numerical terms, then, the relative power of young people has declined substantially. If numbers were the only criterion, we would still expect youth to retain advantages over age. In point of fact, however, older people vote and children do not. Children have various representatives to act in their interests (parents, social workers, and so on), but they are basically disenfranchised. One result is that, increasingly, children lose out in the battle for scarce public resources (Preston 1984).

This is clearly illustrated by the types of budget cuts made at the federal level in the last few years. Federal expenditure on child-related programs (Aid to Families with Dependent Children, Head Start, food stamps, child nutrition, child health, and aid to education) is only one quarter the size of federal expenditures on programs for the elderly. When figured on a per-capita basis, the federal government spends 9 percent as much on the average child as it does on the average person over 65 (Preston 1984). This situation has been gradually worsening. The major programs hit by recent federal cutbacks on social expenditures have been child-related programs. Programs for the elderly, especially Social Security, have become too politically risky to cut, and they have remained largely immune to major decreases in social spending.

A consequence of these changes is that the condition of children in the United States has deteriorated, whereas the condition of the elderly has

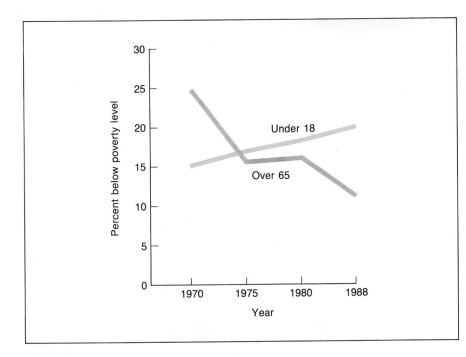

FIGURE 12.3

CHANGING LEVELS OF POVERTY AMONG YOUTH AND THE ELDERLY, 1970–1988

In the last 18 years, the poverty rate for the elderly had declined sharply but the poverty rate for children has increased. As a result, children are now substantially more likely than the elderly to live in poverty.

SOURCES: Data from 1970, 1975, and 1980 are from U.S. Bureau of the Census 1982, 11. Data for 1988 are from U.S. Bureau of the Census 1989g.

improved. Figure 12.3 compares changes in poverty rates between 1970 and 1988. These data show that poverty has increased among children and decreased among the elderly. Within 18 years, we went from a society in which the elderly were 64 percent *more likely* than children to be poor to a society in which the elderly are 45 percent *less likely* to be poor.

Why have children become less advantaged than the elderly? Several explanations have been suggested. An obvious one is that, although everybody has parents, not everybody has children. Some childless people have little sympathy with the problems of providing for children. A related explanation is that of family norms: In the United States we generally believe that parents are obligated to support their children but that children are not obligated to support their parents. We have given the government the responsibility for allocating resources to the elderly, and it does so relatively even handedly. Distribution of resources to children, however, still rests largely with their parents and varies widely, depending on the earnings of their parents and whether children live with one or two parents. Some observers have also wondered if the decreasing benefits to children might not reflect the fact that 24 percent of the population under 15 is Hispanic or African American, double the percentage in the entire population (Torres-Gil 1986).

Probably the most important factor behind the increased proportion of children in poverty, however, is the growing proportion who, through nonmarital birth or parental divorce, do not have a father to help in their support (Pifer 1986). That such children remain in poverty reflects society's norms about family responsibility. As long as we agree that children's poverty is largely their parents' responsibility the status of children and the elderly is likely to remain unequal.

EXPLANATIONS FOR AGE STRATIFICATION

In everyday usage, most people rely on a physiological explanation of age stratification. The young and the old have less status because they are less competent and less productive. To some extent this explanation is correct. It does not, however, explain the cross-cultural or historical variations in the status of age groups. Conflict and structural-functional perspectives, as well as modernization theory, furnish insightful explanations about why age stratification exists and varies across societies.

STRUCTURAL-FUNCTIONAL PERSPECTIVE

The structural-functional perspective focuses on the ways in which age stratification helps fulfill societal functions. From this perspective, the restricted status of youth is beneficial because it frees them from responsibility for their own support and gives them time to learn the complex skills necessary for operating in society.

At the other end of the age scale, the functionalist perspective is the basis for **disengagement theory.** The central argument of this theory is that the aged voluntarily disengage themselves from active social participation, gradually dropping roles in production, family, church, and community even before actual disability connected with age requires it. This disengagement is functional for society because it makes possible an orderly transition from one generation to the next, avoiding the dislocation caused by people dropping dead in their tracks or dragging down the entire organization by decreased performance. It is functional for the individual because it reduces the shame of declining ability and provides a rest for the weary. Disengagement theory is a perfect example of why functional theory is sometimes called consensus theory: The lack of participation of

Disengagement theory, a functionalist theory of aging, argues that the aged voluntarily disengage themselves from active social participation.

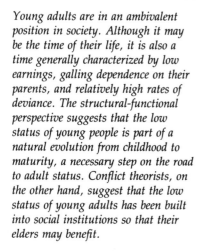

Young adults are in an ambivalent position in society. Although it may be the time of their life, it is also a time generally characterized by low earnings, galling dependence on their parents, and relatively high rates of deviance. The structural-functional perspective suggests that the low status of young people is part of a natural evolution from childhood to maturity, a necessary step on the road to adult status. Conflict theorists, on the other hand, suggest that the low status of young adults has been built into social institutions so that their elders may benefit.

CONCEPT SUMMARY
A Comparison of Three Explanations of Age Stratification

	MAJOR ASSUMPTIONS	CONCLUSIONS ABOUT YOUTH	CONCLUSIONS ABOUT ELDERLY	OVERALL EVALUATION
Structural-Functional Theory	Age groups cooperate for common good	Youth's exclusion from full social participation is for good of self and society	Elderly disengage voluntarily; good for self and society	Currently adequate to explain status of elderly, but not compelling for status of youth
Conflict Theory	Age groups compete over scarce resources	Youth excluded so that others may benefit	Elderly excluded so that senior positions open up for younger adults	Useful to explain status of youth; not useful to today's elderly
Modernization Theory	Changes in institutions alter the value of special resources that age groups hold (land, labor, and knowledge)	Unspecified; by implication, status goes down because labor not necessary	Status of elderly has decreased because traditional bases of power have eroded	Useful to explain low social honor of elderly and youth

the aged is agreed on by both the aged and others and is to the benefit of all (Hendricks and Hendricks 1981).

CONFLICT PERSPECTIVE

The conflict view of age stratification produces a picture of disengagement that is far less benign—a picture of simple rejection and discrimination springing from competition over scarce resources. These resources are primarily jobs but also include power within the family. Conflict theorists suggest that barring youth and older people from the labor market is a means of categorically eliminating some groups from competition and improving the prospects of workers between 25 and 65.

There is empirical evidence to support this view. Early in American history, few people retired. Not only could they not afford to, but their labor was still needed. As immigration provided cheap and plentiful labor, the need for the elderly worker decreased. In addition, as unions established seniority as a criterion for higher wages, older workers became more expensive than younger ones. In response to these trends, management instituted compulsory retirement to get rid of older workers. The mandatory retirement rules occurred long before Social Security, in an era when few employees had regular pension plans. Thus, compulsory retirement usually meant poverty for the older worker (Atchley 1982).

It was not until 1965 that social structures such as Social Security and private pensions began to make retirement a desirable personal alternative. Between 1959 and 1985, the proportion of the elderly who were poor declined dramatically, from 35 percent to 12 percent. At the present time, retirement suits both the aging worker and the economic system. As the growing elderly population becomes an increasing burden on a shrinking working-age population, however, conflict may once again emerge between the generations over economic interests (an idea discussed more fully in the Issues in Social Policy section at the end of this chapter). The good health and relative prosperity of some of the "young old" population may cause the entire older population to be viewed as a new leisure class, whose motor homes and trips to Arizona are being paid for by an overburdened working generation (Bengston et al. 1985).

MODERNIZATION THEORY

Modernization theory of aging argues that the elderly have low status in modern societies because the value of their traditional resources has eroded.

According to the **modernization theory of aging,** the elderly have low status in modern societies because the value of their traditional resources has eroded. This is due to three simultaneous events: the decline in importance of land (disproportionately owned by the elderly) as a means of production, the increasing productivity of society, and a more rapid rate of social change (Cowgill 1974).

Decline in Importance of Land.   When land is the most vital means of production, those who own it have high status and power. In many traditional societies, land ownership is passed from father to son. This gives fathers a great deal of power even if they live to an age when they are physically much less able than their sons. This explanation, of course, applies only in a society where wealth resides in transferable property, either land or animals. In a hunting-and-gathering society—for example, the Plains Indians of the 19th century—where there is little accumulated wealth, status comes from physical prowess, and consequently the elderly have much lower status.

Level of Productivity.   In societies with low levels of productivity, it is not feasible to exclude either the young or the elderly from productive activity. Everyone's labor is needed. In industrial societies, however, productivity is so high that many people can be freed from direct production. They can study, they can do research, they can write great novels, or they can do nothing at all. In such a society, the labor of youth and the elderly becomes expendable: Society doesn't need it anymore.

Speed of Change.   Technological knowledge has grown at an ever-accelerating pace. Since most of us learn the bulk of our technological skills when we are young, this rapid change produces an increasing disadvantage for older workers (Cohn 1982). Their technical skills become outdated. In times of less rapid change, their greater reliability was a virtue; now their mental skills are growing old faster than their physical skills. Thus, rapid social change works to the disadvantage of the elderly.

EVALUATION

Although both youth and the aged have lower status than adults in midlife, their experiences are rather different. Thus, theories that explain the status of youth may not be as effective in explaining the status of the elderly (see The Concept Summary).

Overall, it would appear that all three theories can contribute to understanding the status of youth. Certainly, as functional theorists suggest, it is beneficial for youth and society if they are protected from full responsibilities while very young. Nevertheless, the continued disadvantage of young adults and their subsequent poverty, lack of social integration, and deviance are hardly functional for themselves or society. In this case, it seems appropriate to attribute their low status to the systematic disadvantages they face in competing for scarce resources controlled by an older generation. Part of this disadvantage stems, as modernization theory suggests, from devaluation of their traditional resource: the capacity for low-skill, physically demanding work.

The status of the elderly is harder to account for. Modernization theory is not really applicable to the rising economic status of the elderly, though it may explain their low social honor. Nor does conflict theory seem adequate to explain the economic status of the elderly: Their rising status has not been wrested from any other age group through a competition over scarce resources. Rather, at this point in history, the disengagement of the older worker seems mutually attractive to younger and older people. The improved economic status of the elderly and the expansion of government programs to provide health care and other services to this group appear to rest on a consensus across the entire age span that this is appropriate. Obviously, such a consensus is based on the ability of a productive society to be generous without it hurting too much. The grounds for such a consensus may not always exist.

CROSS-CUTTING STATUSES: AGE, GENDER, AND RACE

We began the section on stratification by examining inequalities in life chances. So far we have dealt with unequal life chances by social class, race and ethnicity, sex, and age. On each of these dimensions, we have been able to demonstrate that there is a hierarchy of access to the good things in life and that some groups are substantially disadvantaged.

When a person has a lower status on more than one of these dimensions, we speak of **double or triple jeopardy.** This means that disadvantage snowballs. Black teenagers are twice as likely as white teenagers to be unemployed; old women are more likely than old men to be poor. In this section, we review briefly the special problems of old age by gender and race and ethnicity.

Double or triple jeopardy means having low status on two or three different dimensions of stratification.

AGING AND GENDER

Aging poses special problems for women. First is the problem of the double standard of aging: The signs of age—wrinkles, loose skin, gray hair—are considered more damaging for women than for men. The classic stereotype of the middle-aged man who leaves his middle-aged wife for a younger woman is not without foundation. When men of middle age remarry, they generally marry women who are 10–15 years younger than they are. Middle-aged women are seldom able to remarry at all; in fact, fewer than 25 percent of women who are divorced after 35 will find another husband. For this

The quality of life one experiences in old age probably has less to do with age than it does with social class, sex, and race and ethnicity. Those who are most disadvantaged in old age are those who were close to the poverty line during their earning years. Even among relatively affluent retirees, widowhood often means sharp reductions in an older woman's income.

reason, aging presents some special problems for women; age is associated with greater decreases in prestige and esteem for women than for men.

The life expectancy gap between men and women also makes the experience of old age very different for women than men. On the average, women live about seven years longer than men. Taken together with the fact that women are usually two years or so younger than their husbands, this works out to a 9-year gap between when her husband dies and when she dies. This mortality difference has enormous consequences for the quality of life. First, it means that most men will spend their old age married, have the care of a spouse during illness, and be able to spend their last years at home being cared for by their spouse. The average woman, on the other hand, will spend the last 10 years of her life unmarried, will spend most of these years living alone with no one to care for her, and is more likely to be cared for in a nursing home during her last illness.

Sex differences in mortality mean that old age is disproportionately a society of women. Above age 75, there are nearly twice as many women as men. The decreasing availability of men in older age groups has consequences for social roles. It means that, as people get older, heterosexual contacts, whether through marriage or in bridge groups, are less important for structuring social life. It also means that fewer of the elderly are married and more of them live alone (Soldo 1981). The feminization of old age is an increasing component of the poverty of old age. Female-headed households are poorer than male-headed households at all ages, and the elderly are no exception. When the elderly population rose out of poverty in the last three decades, female-headed households were disproportionately left behind.

MINORITY AGING

Minorities earn substantially less during their peak years than do Anglos, and this means they are less likely to have accumulated assets such as home ownership to cushion income loss during retirement. There is no evidence, however, that the economic or health status of minorities gets worse in old age (Ferraro 1989). Instead, health and income differentials by race remain pretty constant between middle and old age.

The most significant link between minority status and aging is that minorities are less likely to live to experience old age! Whereas 75 percent of white males can expect to survive until they are 65, only 58 percent of black males will live until retirement age. For women, the figures are 86 and 75 percent, respectively (U.S. Bureau of the Census. 1989a, 72).

ISSUES IN SOCIAL POLICY

Social Security—In Need of an Overhaul?

The Social Security system is our nation's most comprehensive program for dealing with the elderly. The system is much misunderstood. It is only in part the insurance program it is advertised to be. A person pays into it all his or her working days and draws out from it after retirement on the basis of years of work and level of contribution. From the beginning, however, the system has been paying beneficiaries out of current earnings. In practice, it is a systematic program of intergenerational transfers in which the currently productive generation decides on the level at which it is willing to be taxed to provide a particular standard of living for the elderly.

In all cultures, adults of working age produce goods that are used for the benefit of themselves and their dependents. In traditional societies, the family is the distribution network, the adults being responsible for their own children and their own parents. In modern industrial societies, this burden has been shifted in part to the state. The state collects taxes from the working population and redistributes them to dependents, depersonalizing the exchange process. Social Security does what the family was expected to do in previous times. In some ways, it does it better. It regularly gives a guaranteed sum of money: It entails no feeling of obligation on the part of the aged and no feeling of direct resentment on the part of the working generation. Workers may grumble about taxation and government inefficiency, but they don't resent their own parents. The changing age composition of the population, however, raises serious questions about whether the program can continue.

THE AGE STRUCTURE

As demonstrated in Figure 12.2, the elderly have become a growing portion of the U.S. population.

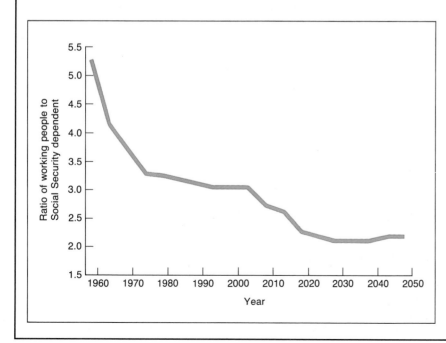

FIGURE 12.4

RATIO OF EMPLOYEES PER SOCIAL SECURITY DEPENDENT, 1960–2050

In 1960, there were five people working for every person over 65 who was drawing a Social Security check. By the year 2030, there will be only two earners for every person over 65. The result is sharply higher payroll taxes and a burgeoning pension industry.

SOURCE: Bouvier 1980.

ISSUES IN SOCIAL POLICY continued

Owing to continued low fertility and improvements in life expectancy among the elderly, this proportion is expected to grow even larger.

In the United States, the problem will be most severe around 2030. At this time, the huge baby-boom generation will be over 65, and the proportion 65 and older will climax at 18 percent of the total population. The biggest baby-boom crop will be wanting to retire and live off the taxes of the younger workers. Because of the low birth rates in the 1970s and 1980s, however, there won't be very many of these younger workers. As Figure 12.4 demonstrates, in 1960 there were over five workers per social security recipient; by 2030, the ratio of workers to recipients will be down to two. This changing age structure will impose a heavy burden on the working-age population, and it raises questions about the viability of the current Social Security system.

THE CURRENT DILEMMA

Recognizing the fiscal dilemma posed by the changing age structure, Congress tried, in 1983, to head off the coming crisis by passing new laws. It sharply raised payroll taxes—so that the baby boomers could pay ahead of time for their own retirement—and it raised the age at which workers could draw full retirement benefits to age 67 beginning in 2017. This adjustment has been almost too successful: In the 1989 fiscal year, Social Security taxes generated a surplus of $55 billion. Projections suggest that the Social Security fund will "grow monstrously. By the year 2030, it will own nearly one-sixth of everything in America" ("Fixing Social Security" 1990, 54). At $12 trillion, the Social Security pool will be perilously large, and politicians are gearing up for a battle over who will control these enormous assets between now and when you are eligible to claim them.

The burden posed by the changing age structure goes beyond the fiscal issue. Even if the baby boomers save for their retirement, who will produce the goods and services that they will be able to afford to buy? A change from five workers per retiree to two workers per retiree implies the need for immense increases in productivity if this diminishing pool of workers is to keep up with demand.

As a result of these dilemmas posed by a changing age structure, many observers are concluding that the current Social Security system is unworkable. One likely solution is to encourage longer work lives by raising further the age at which full benefits can be drawn. This will keep more people in the productive workforce and reduce the number drawing benefits. We may also see the diversion of some workers from Social Security into private pension plans so that the federal government can reduce its involvement in managing the nation's retirement savings.

SUMMARY

1. Age roles are less highly structured than many others. Although there are accepted criteria for "acting your age," there are few sanctions for violating these norms.

2. The meaning of age depends on social structure and thus varies across time and societies. The institutionalization of age-linked criteria in bureaucracies such as school or Social Security systems has increased the uniformity of experience by age.

3. Two perspectives are important to the sociological study of age: the life-course perspective and the cohort perspective. They alert us to focus on the changing relationships of individuals to social structures as they age and the ways this process can differ from one cohort to the next.

4. Childhood, adolescence, and old age are almost role-less roles. We expect very little from people in these age

groups and specify few obligations for them. The ages from 20 to 65, however, are crowded with obligations, and role strain may result.

5. Young people suffer many structured inequalities and are not well integrated into society's institutions. Among the consequences of this are a high crime rate and the development of a youth subculture that emphasizes style and passive escape.

6. The population over 65 is better off now than perhaps it has ever been. Although the older population still suffers from low honor, improvements in health and in economic circumstances have sharply decreased the disadvantages associated with age. The disadvantages of aging are more pronounced for women and those who were living on the economic margin during their working years.

7. There have been major changes in the U.S. age distribution. Owing to reduced fertility and, to a lesser extent, increased life expectancy, the proportion of the population over 65 is growing rapidly and the proportion under 20 is declining.

8. As indexed by the poverty rate, children are more disadvantaged than the elderly. This is due to two factors: the greater willingness to support the elderly out of the public purse and the increasing proportion of children whose fathers do not help support them.

9. Modernization theory, structural functionalism (disengagement theory), and conflict theory provide competing explanations of why the young and the elderly tend to have lower status in our society. Right now conflict theory seems more appropriate to explaining the disadvantage of youth and structural-functional theory more appropriate to explaining the improved status of the elderly.

10. Because of changes in fertility, the burden of supporting a growing retired population will fall on a declining working-age population. Thus, the Social Security system stands in need of an overhaul.

SUGGESTED READINGS

Binstock, Robert, and Shanas, Ethel. (eds.). 1983. Handbook of Aging and the Social Sciences. (2nd ed.) New York: Van Nostrand Reinhold. A collection of theoretical and empirical articles. Although some are technical, it offers an excellent overview of social science approaches to aging.

Kertzer, David, and Schaie, K. Warner. (eds.). 1989. Age Structuring in Comparative Perspective. Hillside, N.J.: Erlbaum. A collection of articles showing how the experience of age from childhood to old age is socially structured around the world.

Modell, John. 1989. Into One's Own: From Youth to Adulthood in the United States, 1920–1975. Berkeley: University of California Press. A social history of the transition to adulthood. Modell draws from a variety of sources—from True Confessions to census data—to describe and explain how growing up has changed.

Pifer, Alan, and Bronte, Lydia. (eds.). 1986. Our Aging Society: Paradox and Promise. New York: Norton. A wide-ranging collection that covers special problems of aging among women and among minorities. It includes several good pieces on public policy and aging.

Sokolovsky, Jay. (ed.). 1983. Growing Old in Different Cultures. Belmont, Ca.: Wadsworth. An introduction to the anthropology of aging; a good overview of the historical and cross-cultural background.

UNIT FOUR

SOCIAL INSTITUTIONS

CHAPTER 13
THE FAMILY

CHAPTER 14
EDUCATION

CHAPTER 15
POLITICAL
INSTITUTIONS

CHAPTER 16
ECONOMIC
INSTITUTIONS

CHAPTER 17
RELIGION

CHAPTER 18
HEALTH AND
MEDICINE

13

THE FAMILY

Have you ever . . .

Stopped to consider how many of the people in your family you would choose as friends? If you are like the average person, there are some people in your family whom you really like, people you would seek out whether you were obliged to or not. You might, however, be able to identify one or two family members whom you really don't like very well, people you would not choose as your friends. Probably ties of family loyalty bind you to these people so that you would come to their aid if they needed you, you would feel badly if they had troubles, or you would expect them to help you if you had problems. But you wouldn't shed any tears if you did not see them for the next 10 years.

The family is a remarkable arrangement for binding people together with ties of obligation. Your obligations to your parents, brothers, sisters, and children will bind you to them long after you have ceased to live together in the same household—and, to a significant extent, regardless of the affection between you. You may be able to divorce a spouse or end a friendship, but there is no such thing as an ex-child or an ex-brother. These relatives are with you forever.

The poet, Robert Frost, once said that "home is the place where, if you have to go there, they have to take you." As we grow up and achieve economic independence, most of us choose not to live with our parents, brothers, and sisters. In times of unemployment, bereavement, divorce, and trouble, however, family members can usually be counted on to provide a sanctuary. Although we hope we will not need them, it is nice to know they are out there.

This chapter begins a six-chapter section on social institutions. We cover the five basic institutions—family, education, government, economy, and religion—and one relatively new institution, medicine. *Institutions* are enduring and complex social structures that provide ready-made arrangements to meet human problems (see Chapter 4). The chief characteristic of institutions is their stability. Their major function is to produce continuity in social organization from one generation to the next. Yet institutions are also responsive. Old ones adapt, evolve, and change; new ones emerge to meet new needs.

The paradox of change and continuity is perhaps nowhere as clear as in our first institution—the family. In many ways, the American family of 1990 is similar to the family of 1890, yet there have been dramatic changes. In order to place these changes in perspective, we find it useful to look at the variety of family forms across the world. What is it that is really essential about the family, and what kinds of structures are possible to meet these needs? How is the structure of the family affected by surrounding institutions?

■

MARRIAGE, FAMILY, AND KINSHIP: BASIC INSTITUTIONS OF SOCIETY

UNIVERSAL FAMILY FUNCTIONS

In every culture, the family has been assigned major responsibilities, typically including (Murdock 1949; Pitts 1964):

1. Replacement through reproduction
2. Regulation of sexual behavior
3. Economic responsibilities for dependents—children, the elderly, the ill, and the handicapped
4. Socialization of the young
5. Ascription of status
6. Provision of intimacy, belongingness, and emotional support

Because these activities are important for individual development and the continuity of society, every society provides some institutional pattern for meeting them. No society leaves them to individual initiative. Although it is possible to imagine a society in which these responsibilities are handled by religious or educational institutions, most societies have found it convenient to assign them to the family.

The importance of these tasks varies across societies. Status ascription is a greater responsibility in societies where social position is largely inherited; regulation of sexual behavior is more important in cultures without contraception. In our own society, we have seen the priorities assigned to these family responsibilities change substantially over time. In colonial America, the family's primary responsibilities were care of dependent children and replacement through reproduction; the provision of emotional support was a secondary consideration. More recently, however, some of the responsibility for socializing the young has been transferred to schools and day-care centers; financial responsibility for the dependent elderly has been shifted to the government. At the same time, intimacy has taken on increased importance as a dimension of marital relationships.

Unlike most social structures, the **family** is a biological as well as a social group—a relatively permanent group of persons linked by ties of blood, marriage, or adoption, who live together and cooperate economically and in the rearing of children. This definition includes both the single- and the two-parent family. The important criteria for families are that their members are bound together—if not by blood, then by some cultural ceremony such as marriage or adoption that ties them to each other relatively permanently—and that they assume responsibility for each other.

The family is a subset of a larger set of relatives—the kin group. A **kin group** is the set of relatives who interact on the basis of a shared social structure. The kin group need not include all of a person's blood relatives. In the Trobriand Islands, social relationships are organized around mother's kin rather than father's so that only the relatives on her side of the family would fall into a person's socially defined kin group; among the Zulu, kinship is organized around male siblings. In our society, the group we call kin covers both our mother's and father's side of the family, but seldom extends beyond first cousins. In addition to blood relatives, most Americans include their in-laws as part of their kin group.

Marriage is an institutionalized social structure that provides an enduring framework for regulating sexual behavior and childbearing. Many cultures tolerate other kinds of sexual encounters—premarital, extramarital, or homosexual—but all cultures discourage childbearing outside marriage. In some cultures, the sanctions are severe and almost all sexual relationships are confined to marriage; in others, marriage is an ideal that can be bypassed with relatively little punishment.

Marriage is important for childrearing because it imposes socially sanctioned roles on parents and the kin group. When a child is born, parents, grandparents, and aunts and uncles are automatically assigned certain normative obligations to the child.

The **family** is a relatively permanent group of persons linked by ties of blood, marriage, or adoption, who live together and cooperate economically and in the rearing of the children.

A **kin group** is the set of relatives who interact on the basis of shared social structure.

Marriage is an institutionalized social structure that provides an enduring framework for regulating sexual behavior and childbearing.

Around the world, the family is a central social institution. Although families have different tasks in some cultures than in others, in all cultures family members are charged with the responsibility for taking care of one another. Parents must take care of children and wives and husbands of each other. As this photograph of a family in Ecuador shows, the family is also often a primary source of personal warmth and satisfaction.

This network represents a ready-made social structure designed to organize and stabilize the responsibility for children. Children born outside marriage, by contrast, are more vulnerable. The number of people normatively responsible for their care is smaller, and, even in the case of the mother, the norms are less well enforced. One consequence is higher infant mortality for illegitimate children in almost all societies, including our own.

Marriage, family, and kinship are among the most basic and enduring patterns of social relationships. Although blood ties are important, the family is best understood as a social structure defined and enforced by cultural norms.

CROSS-CULTURAL VARIATIONS

Families universally regulate sexual behavior, care for dependents, and offer emotional and financial security. That is where the universals end, however. Hundreds of different family forms can be used to fill these roles. Children can be raised by their grandmothers or their aunts; wives can have one husband or three; children can be cared for at home or sent to boarding school; the aged can be put out in the cold to die or put on Social Security. This section reviews some of the most important variations in the ways cultures have fulfilled family functions (The Focus at the end of this section describes in some detail the unique family system of a 19th-century utopian community.)

A **nuclear family** consists of a husband, a wife, and their dependent children.

Family Patterns.   The basic unit of the family is the wife-husband pair and their children. When the married pair and their children form an independent household living apart from other kin, we call them a **nuclear family.** When they live with other kin, such as the wife's or husband's parents or siblings, we refer to them as an **extended family.**

An **extended family** exists when the wife-husband pair and their children live with other kin and share economic and childrearing responsibilities with them.

Extended families are found in all types of societies, although they are defined as the ideal family form only in premodern, nonindustrialized societies. Where extended families occur in the United States, they are often the result of financial hardship.

Neolocal residence occurs when norms of residence require that a newly married couple take up residence away from their relatives.

Residence Patterns.   Whether a society favors nuclear or extended families has a great deal of influence on where a newly married couple will live. By definition, the nuclear family lives by itself; this is called **neolocal residence.** Extended families, however, may exhibit a wide variety of residence patterns. They may live with the wife's relatives (**matrilocal residence**), with the husband's relatives (**patrilocal residence**), or in some unique combination. Like the extended family itself, complex residence patterns are gradually being displaced by the neolocal pattern of the nuclear family. There are still hundreds of small societies that prescribe complex residence patterns, but the great majority of the world's population now lives in societies practicing neolocal residence.

Matrilocal residence occurs when norms of residence require newly married couples to take up residence with the wife's kin.

Patrilocal residence occurs when norms of residence require a newly married couple to take up residence with the husband's kin.

Courtship Patterns.   As it does for all recurring behaviors, culture furnishes a set of standards for how and when to select a mate. It also specifies the extent to which parents and kin are involved (Goode 1959; see Figure 13.1).

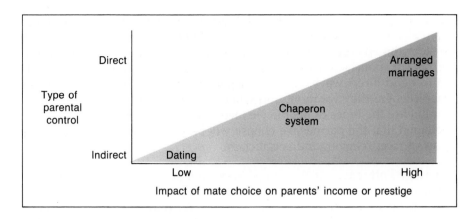

FIGURE 13.1
**TYPES OF COURTSHIP SYSTEMS
AND THEIR DETERMINANTS**

*Parental control over courtship is
more direct when the child's mate selection directly affects the parents.*

Whenever marriage has a strong impact on families or communities, it is unlikely that mate selection will be left up to individuals. When dowries or bride prices are exchanged, when the new spouse will move in with relatives, or when prestige is strongly related to family ties, then the activities leading to marriage are likely to be controlled by parents and kin. Under these circumstances, mate selection is based on the interests of the kin group rather than on any emotional bond between the young people. Love between a couple is regarded as a lucky accident and more likely follows than precedes marriage.

In the extreme case, this may mean that the family arranges a marriage between young people who have never met each other. In less extreme cases, chaperoning and careful supervision, especially of girls, gives some scope for individual choice while ensuring that young people will meet only those who are socially and economically acceptable to their parents. In extended family systems, family control of mate selection is important because marriage affects the economic interests of kin groups. Where the young people will live by themselves, however, and where the kin group's economic interests are not affected by the young people's choices, there is a corresponding decrease in the family's involvement in choosing children's mates (Lee and Stone 1980).

■

*Where the choice of marriage partners
affects the economic welfare of the
parents or the community, courtship
practices are likely to be closely
supervised. Among the Old Order
Amish, one form of supervision is the
requirement that the buggies used by
courting couples must be open so that
others can supervise their behavior.
Only after a couple is married are
they entitled to the privacy afforded by
a covered buggy.*

In our own society, dating and courtship are relatively free of direct parental control. We have considerable freedom of choice and need not consider the wishes of others, including our parents, in choosing dating partners or spouses. Parental influence is still important, however, in both indirect and direct ways. Where our parents live, where they send us to school, where they vacation, and what activities they engage in all serve to influence the types of people we meet. Such arrangements increase the likelihood that the partner we choose will be acceptable to our parents in terms of race, religion, and social class.

Marriage Patterns.   In the United States and much of the Western world, a marriage form called **monogamy** is practiced; each man may have only one wife (at a time), and each woman may have only one husband. Many cultures, however, practice some form of **polygamy**—marriage in which a person may have more than one spouse at a time. The most frequent pattern, that practiced by the 19th-century Mormons, is to allow a man to have more than one wife at a time (**polygyny**). Less frequently, the form is **polyandry,** where a woman may have more than one husband at a time.

Viewed cross-culturally, polygyny has been the most popular marriage pattern. In a study of 250 cultures, Murdock (1949, 1957) found that 75 percent prefer polygyny as a marriage pattern, 24 percent prefer monogamy, and only 1 percent prefer polyandry. In the contemporary world, polygyny is most common in African societies. In the period 1960–1977, approximately 24 percent of married African men had more than one wife (Welch and Glick 1981). The practice of polygyny is, of course, restricted by the nearly equal number of men and women in a society; if some men have more than one wife, other men will have to go without. Thus, even in societies where polygyny is the preferred marriage pattern, the majority of men have only one wife—and even though a clear majority of cultures favor polygyny, the great majority of the population of the world lives in cultures that practice monogamy.

Polygyny is by definition an extended family system. It tends to be best adapted to preindustrial societies in which both geographic and social mobility are limited. It is also characteristic of societies in which wealth depends on kinship ties. Polygyny enhances a man's wealth by bringing in more dowries, providing more women and children for labor, and producing more heirs (Reiss 1980). Everywhere polygyny is practiced, it tends to become an important symbol of the prestige and status of the wealthy. Monogamy, on the other hand, tends to flourish when there are other means to demonstrate wealth and status and when the costs of children exceed their economic benefits.

Authority Patterns.   Both in and out of the family, human societies have been characterized by **patriarchal authority;** the oldest male of the family typically controls economic resources, makes decisions, and has the final say in all matters related to the family. Although the influence or authority of wives varies from one society to another, there are no societies in which the cultural norms specify **matriarchal authority** and few in which the norms specify equality of authority. Increasingly, however, contemporary Western societies are coming to accept a new norm of **egalitarianism,** in which spouses jointly share in decision making, control of family resources,

---

Monogamy is marriage in which there is only one wife and one husband.

Polygamy is any form of marriage in which a person may have more than one spouse at a time.

Polygyny is a form of marriage in which one man may have more than one wife at a time.

Polyandry is a form of marriage in which one woman may have more than one husband at a time.

Patriarchal authority is normatively approved male dominance.

Matriarchal authority is normatively approved female dominance.

Egalitarianism emphasizes equality in decision making, control of family resources, and childrearing.

Group Marriage in the 19th Century

The United States in the late 19th century was remarkably tolerant. The moral code of the dominant culture stressed premarital chastity and monogamy. Nevertheless, dozens of sectarian groups with very different ideas of sexual and familial morality emerged and briefly prospered. The Mormons are the only one of them to have survived to the present day; and, as pointed out in Chapter 4, one of the conditions of their survival was the adoption of the family structure of the dominant culture.

The Oneida community was one of the most successful and most daringly different of these 19th-century groups. Oneida was founded in 1847 by a Yale-trained theologian named John Humprey Noyes. It began as a group of 20 to 30 in Oneida, New York, and grew to 300 children and adults before it disbanded in 1879.

Noyes's community was based on the principles of Christian communism. (Acts 2:32–35 offers biblical support for Christian communism.) In the Oneida community, there was no private property, and monogamy, the exclusive ownership of a spouse, was not allowed. Although Noyes recognized that the early Christians applied the communistic principle only to material goods:

Yet we affirm that there is no intrinsic difference between property in persons and property in things. . . . The new command is, that we love one another, and that, not by pairs, as in the world, but *en masse*. We are required to love one another fervently. The fashion of the world forbids a man and woman who are otherwise appropriated to

love one another fervently. But if they obey Christ they must do this (Noyes [1869] 1961, 625–27).

In the Oneida community, the practice of group marriage meant that all men were considered married to all women. Oneida, however, was hardly the place to go if one was looking for sex without commitment. Entrance into the community required signing over all of one's worldly goods to the community as well as embracing a life of considerable physical toil, and group marriage was not simply a matter of sleeping around. Rather, the selection of sexual partners was done through a committee. At Oneida, all members lived together in a big mansionlike house. The women each had a private bedroom, whereas the men all slept together in a dormitory. When a man wished to sleep with a particular woman, he submitted a written request, to the committee, which then referred it to the woman. The request could be denied by the woman on personal

This photograph of the Oneida community depicts the women and men of the community on a free afternoon in front of the Mansion House. Note that the women wore pantaloons under their short skirts and bobbed their hair, styles which were unconventional for the time. Oneida was obviously economically successful as a community, a major factor that contributed to group marriage lasting as long as it did.

grounds or by the committee on the ground that too much particularism was developing in this relationship and that the brother did not show himself willing to love all his sisters. During the first two decades of the community's existence, the Oneidans avoided having children. They wished to establish both their economy and their family structure before adding the burden of children. During these 20 years they practiced a form of contraception called *coitus reservatas,* in which the man does not ejaculate. Since this technique takes a great deal of willpower and some practice, it is reported that young men were required to sleep only with women past childbearing age until they had perfected the technique. (In a parallel practice, younger women were encouraged to sleep with older men. In this case, greater spiritual growth was given as the reason.) The teaching method must have worked reasonably well, as only two children were born during this period.

Between 1869 and 1879, the Oneidans produced 59 children. The women and men who became parents were "scientifically" matched by a committee. The selection process was designed to produce children with superior mental and physical abilities. The children were nurtured by their mothers for the first 12 months and then were raised in a communal nursery. As with spouses, there was to be no exclusive attachment; adults were supposed to love all children equally. The children of Oneida apparently got exceptional care; their infant mortality rate was very low, and their educational training was excellent.

In 1879, the Oneida community disbanded. A major cause for the breakup was the erratic leadership provided by Noyes. Additional problems included the management of an increasingly large household and diversified economic enterprises. The problems were internal rather than external; the community

never received a great deal of harassment from outsiders. It even advertised for visitors and sold Sunday lunches to day-trippers from New York who came up to satisfy their curiosity about these strange people. The community's hard work and economic success, as well as a strategic willingness to buy locally and help neighbors, meant that its members were generally well regarded in upstate New York in spite of their odd family system.

When the community disbanded, many members stayed on in Oneida, most of them legally marrying one of the other members. The financial enterprises of Oneida were incorporated and divided among the members. One of these enterprises, the Oneida Silver Manufacturing Company, is still a successful corporation supplying tableware for millions. If you look, you'll probably find Oneida silverware in your own kitchen.

SOURCE: Whitworth 1975.

and childrearing. Even in the societies where equality is most highly developed, however, husbands continue to have more power than wives and are less involved in childrearing.

The American Family in Perspective.   The American or, more generally, the Western European family is nuclear and neolocal; it is characterized by independence in mate selection; marriages are monogamous. These basic outlines of the American family have remained relatively constant. In 1790 as well as in 1990, these characteristics distinguished our family form from that of Hindus or Kenyans or Chinese. In the remainder of this chapter, we will talk about some of the rather dramatic changes in the American family that have occurred within this basic framework.

THE AMERICAN FAMILY OVER THE LIFE COURSE

On nearly every dimension of American family life, there have been remarkable changes in attitude and behavior in recent decades. A few statistics set the stage:

- *Divorce.* The most recent estimates suggest that a whopping 64 percent of all first marriages will end in divorce (Martin and Bumpass 1989).
- *Non-marital Births.* Nearly one quarter of U.S. babies are born to unmarried mothers; the figure is 61 percent for black infants (U.S. Bureau of the Census 1989a).
- *Parenting.* Approximately 60 percent of American children will spend at least some part of their childhood in a single-parent home (Bumpass 1984).
- *Working mothers.* Over 50 percent of mothers are back in the labor force before their child's first birthday (U.S. Bureau of the Census 1989a).

These changes in family life have been felt, either directly or indirectly, by all of us. Is the family a dying institution, or is it simply a changing one? In the following sections, we use a life-course framework to examine some of the major family roles, how they are changing, and what these changes mean for societal and individual well-being.

DATING AND MATE SELECTION

We do not have matchmakers or formally arranged marriages in our society, and at first glance it appears as if everybody is on their own in their search for a suitable spouse. On further reflection, however, we see that parents, schools, and churches are all engaged in the process of helping young people pair up with suitable partners. Schools and churches hold dances and other social events designed to encourage heterosexual relationships; parents and friends introduce somebody "we'd like you to meet." The average person begins to date at about age 14, and if you are too far behind that, your parents and friends will start to worry about you. Although dating may be fun, it is also an obligatory form of social behavior—it is normative.

Recent Trends. In the 1950s, teenagers dated in order to find a spouse. Many did so very quickly, and over 50 percent of American women were

Romantic love is the ideal that Americans use to judge their dating relationships against. Although love and physical attraction can cross many barriers, most people fall in love with people who are similar to themselves in terms of education and social class background. As this picture of college students suggests, we also tend to fall in love with people we see regularly—people we work with and people we go to school with.

married before their 21st birthday. In the ensuing 30 to 40 years, all of this has changed. Teenagers no longer date with the expectation of settling down early, and dating is no longer an activity restricted to the teenage years. Nearly one-third of women and one-half of men are unmarried at ages 25–29. Although not all of these people are looking for a spouse, most are looking for at least a temporary partner.

Two trends have been responsible for the changes in dating patterns. First, people are making first marriages later in life. In the short span between 1970 and 1985, the average age at first marriage rose from 20.6 to 23.0 for women, from 22.5 to 24.8 for men. Second, high divorce rates mean that more people are marrying a second and even a third time. Today only about 50 percent of all weddings are first marriages for both the bride and groom. As a result of these two trends, courtship and dating are often activities of 28- or 35-year-olds as well as 16-year-olds.

Narrowing Down the Field.   Over the course of one's single life, one probably meets thousands of potential marriage partners. How do we narrow down the field?

Factors important in determining original attraction include propinquity, homogamy, and physical attractiveness. Obviously, you are unlikely to meet, much less marry, someone who lives in another community or another state. **Propinquity,** or spatial nearness, operates in more subtle ways, however, by increasing the opportunity for continual interaction. It is no accident that so many people end up marrying coworkers or fellow students. The more you interact with others, the more likely you are to develop positive attitudes toward them—attitudes that may ripen into love (Homans 1950).

Propinquity is spatial nearness.

Spatial closeness is also often a sign of similarity. Research demonstrates that people tend to be drawn to others like themselves—people of the same class, race, religion, age, and interests. Of course, there are exceptions, but faced with a wide range of choices, most people choose a mate similar to themselves (Rawlings 1978). This tendency is called **homogamy.**

Homogamy is the tendency to choose a mate similar to oneself.

Advertisers have sought to convince people that physical attraction is the major determinant of whether one gains attention or love from the opposite sex. Although it isn't as important as the media suggest, research has found that physical attractiveness is important in gaining initial attention (Elder 1969; Walster et al. 1966). When you first meet somebody, all you have to go on is the outside packaging; if that is attractive, it may prompt a closer look. Its importance in the courtship process, however, normally recedes after the first meeting.

Dating is likely to progress toward a serious consideration of marriage if the couple discover similar interests, aspirations, anxieties, and values (Reiss 1980). When dating starts to get serious, couples begin sharing information about marriage expectations. Do they both want children? How do they feel about traditional marriage roles for men and women? If he expects her to do all the housework and she thinks that idea went out with the hula hoop, then they will probably back away from marriage.

This description of the courtship process is diagrammed in Figure 13.2 as a set of filters that gradually narrows down the field of eligibles (Kerckhoff and Davis 1962). At each stage in the courtship process, the screens in the funnel become a little finer, and the pool of eligibles is finally reduced to the one best person. Is mate selection really all that sensible? Probably not. Some people do follow this sensible set of steps from top to bottom, but others jump to the final choice without passing through all the filters. Some get married in the fever of love at first sight, and some are caught by unexpected pregnancies.

Dating can be viewed as a shopping trip in which each person is evaluating the available goods and searching for the best bargain. Each is trying to get the most in return for personal assets (looks, talents, money). If this sounds too crass, consider the times you have heard someone say, "I know he can do better than that" or "She's throwing herself away on him." These statements basically imply that the shopper has bought overpriced merchandise and should have done a little more shopping around. A commitment to marriage is likely to occur when the individual decides that a particular person is the best buy in the market (Adams 1979).

The Sexual Side of Courtship. Some of the more important norms surrounding dating behavior are concerned with the amount of acceptable sexual contact. In the United States, we have seen two revolutions in premarital sexual norms and behavior. The first occurred in the 1920s, when there was a major increase in the proportion of both women and men who engaged in premarital sexual intercourse (Kinsey 1948, 1953). The second began in the late 1960s. Studies of adolescents and college students indicate that this second revolution has two components: an increase in permissiveness and a decline of the double standard.

All major surveys have found increases in permissiveness in recent years; more people engage in sex before marriage, and fewer see anything wrong with it. Increasingly, both men and women believe that a strong commitment is unnecessary for a sexual relationship to be acceptable. Moreover, these changes in the last decade have been more pronounced for women than for men, with the result that men and women are now much more alike in both attitudes and levels of experience.

A major national survey shows that nearly three quarters of all unmarried women have had sexual intercourse by the time they reach their early 20s (Pratt 1984). Although no national surveys have asked young men the same question, it seems likely that the rate is at least as high or probably higher. These figures suggest that for the majority—though not all—of Americans, dating involves sex. Although American norms have changed to the point where few see anything wrong about this, it nevertheless raises two potential problems: pregnancy and sexually transmitted diseases.

PREGNANCY.   Study after study demonstrates that unmarried people and especially young unmarried people take great risks with sex. Less than half of all unmarried couples use contraception at first intercourse, regardless of how old they are (Pratt 1984), and many wait a year or more to begin using effective birth control. One expert has estimated that only 44 percent of all sexual acts committed by unmarried 15 to 19-year-olds and just 77 percent of those committed by unmarried 20- to 24-year-olds are covered by contraception (Westoff 1988). The result is very high rates of unwanted

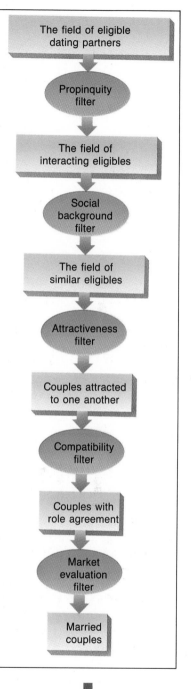

FIGURE 13.2
PROCESS OF SELECTING A MATE

Mate selection can be viewed as a series of filters that help us narrow the field of eligibles to one or two people who share our interests and expectations—and who seem to be a good bargain.

SOURCE: Kerckoff and Davis 1962.

pregnancy. Somewhere between one-third and one-half of American women become pregnant at least once between the ages of 15 and 19. Almost all of these pregnancies are unwanted and more than half (58 percent) end in abortion. Even at ages 20 to 24, one-third of all pregnancies end in abortion (U.S. Bureau of the Census 1989a, 70).

SEXUALLY TRANSMITTED DISEASES.   In the past 20 years we have witnessed a reduced age for beginning sexual activity and more years of single life before and between marriages. The result is more years of nonmarital sexual activity. Usually this means more partners, and this in turn makes sexually transmitted diseases more likely. Of most concern, of course, is exposure to AIDS (Acquired Immunodeficiency Syndrome). It is estimated that 400,000 American heterosexuals now carry the HIV virus that may grow into AIDS, and public health officials note that AIDS is now growing faster among the heterosexual than the homosexual population. Nevertheless, studies show that few heterosexuals are very worried about it, and campaigns urging safe sex and condom use have largely fallen on deaf ears.

Cohabitation.   Another major change in the mate selection process is the significant rise in **cohabitation**—living together without legal marriage.

■

TABLE 13.1
WHO ARE THE COHABITORS?

Rates of cohabitation have increased dramatically in the last generation. Cohabitation is more common among people with low educational attainment; it is also more common among those people whose parents' marriage is not intact.

	PERCENT UNDER 45 WHO EVER COHABITED
TOTAL	25%
Sex	
Male	27
Female	24
Age	
19–24	25
25–29	34
30–34	34
35–39	18
40–44	11
Race/Ethnicity	
White	25
Black	29
Hispanic	21
Education	
Less than 12 years	31
12 years	24
More than 12 years	26
Parents' Marriage Intact?	
Yes	22
No	32

SOURCE: Bumpass and Sweet 1989.

In 1988, approximately 2.3 million couples in the United States were co-habiting. One study found that the chances that an individual would *ever* live in a cohabiting relationship had increased 400 percent for men and 1200 percent for women within the last 25 years (Bumpass and Sweet 1989). Differentials in the likelihood of cohabiting are displayed in Table 13.1.

Cohabitation is an increasingly common stage of the courtship process, and approximately half of all recently married couples cohabited before they were married (Bumpass and Sweet 1989). Interestingly, the evidence suggests that the trial-marriage aspect of cohabitation is not very effective: Divorce rates are significantly *higher* for couples who cohabited before marriage (Booth and Johnson 1988). Generally, observers attribute this to the fact that the kind of people who flout convention by cohabiting are the same kind of people who are likely to get a divorce.

MARRIAGE AND MARITAL RELATIONS

Despite the seeming disorganization of the dating process, nearly 95 percent of Americans end up married at least once by the time they reach 45. A sizable proportion also get divorced at least once, but most of the people who divorce eventually remarry. As a result, the majority of Americans spend the bulk of their adult years in the married state. What is it like?

Gender Roles in Marriage. Marriage is a sharply gendered relationship. Both normatively and in actual practice, husbands and wives, mothers and fathers have different responsibilities. Although many things have changed, American norms specify that the husband *ought* to work; it is still considered his responsibility to provide for his family. Although two-thirds of all wives between ages 25 and 65 are employed, this change has not yet been incorporated into our norms about women's roles. Few people believe wives have a moral obligation to be employed. One survey found that only one-third of adults believed that women without children have an obligation to be employed (Huber and Spitze 1983).

Similarly, norms specify that the responsibility for housework falls on the wife, not the husband. Although attitude surveys indicate this norm is changing, the actual division of labor remains virtually unchanged whether the wife works or not (Spitze 1986). As a result, wives who work, and especially mothers who work, often end up with a severe case of role overload. One adaptation families make to this overload is to lower their standards for cleanliness, meals, and other domestic services. They eat at McDonald's, let the iron gather dust, and vacuum once a week instead of every day.

In addition to these important continuities in marital gender roles, there have also been some important changes. American norms now specify an egalitarian authority pattern. Only a minority of husbands still expect to "wear the pants" in the family, and most wives expect to be considered equals in the marital relationship. This equality is probably seldom achieved in practice. In many marriages, husbands still have more power than wives to decide where the family will live, how much housework, meal preparation, and child care they do, and how much they can spend on themselves. Nevertheless, egalitarianism is the standard against which a growing number of wives and husbands compare their marriages.

Many commentators feel that childless couples are America's new elite. Dubbed DINKS (Double Income, No Kids), these couples have levels of affluence and leisure unattainable by those who sacrifice income and leisure to raise children. Although children continue to provide rewards, there is decreasing normative pressure to become parents. It is estimated that one quarter of today's young women will remain childless.

■
TABLE 13.2
FREQUENCY OF SEXUAL INTERCOURSE PER MONTH IN THE EARLY YEARS OF MARRIAGE

The frequency with which married couples engage in sexual intercourse steadily declines after the first year of marriage for most couples. Couples attribute this decline to such things as work, childrearing, fatigue, and familiarity.

YEAR OF MARRIAGE	AVERAGE	RANGE
First	14.8	4–45
Second	12.2	3–20
Third	11.9	2–18
Fourth	9.0	4–23
Fifth	9.7	5–18
Sixth	6.3	2–15

SOURCE: Greenblat 1983, 292.

Sexual Roles in Marriage: A Changing Script.   In few areas of our lives are we free to improvise. Instead, we learn social scripts that direct us toward appropriate behaviors and away from inappropriate ones. Sex is no exception. Unfortunately, we know relatively little about the sexual script for marriage partners and about how it has changed. All the attention in the sexual revolution has gone to young people. Did the revolution pass married folks by, or have sexual roles changed within marriage as well as outside it?

The few serious studies that have been done find that frequency of sexual activity seems to have changed very little among married people in the last 30 years (Gagnon 1977; Gagnon, Roberts, and Greenblat 1978). There have, however, been two notable trends. One is an increase in oral sex, a practice that was limited largely to unmarried sexual partners and the highly educated in earlier decades. The second is that women have reached parity with men in their probability of having an affair. The double standard has disappeared in adultery, and recent studies suggest that 50 percent of both men and women have had an extramarital sexual relationship (Thompson 1983).

One of the most consistent findings about sexuality in marriage is that the frequency of intercourse declines steadily with the length of the marriage (see Table 13.2). The decline appears to be nearly universal and to occur regardless of the couple's age, education, or situation. After the first year, almost everything that happens—children, jobs, commuting, housework, finances—reduces the rate of marital intercourse (Greenblat 1983).

Oh, it's getting worse all the time. Maybe it's three or four times a month now instead of three or four times a week. But I guess it's natural—it's like "I'm tired, you're tired, let's forget it" (cited in Greenblat 1983, 296).

Sex has become less important now—in the beginning there was a feeling that newlyweds screw a lot; therefore, we ought to. It was great and I loved it, but now I think that other things have become more important as we found other things that are satisfying to do besides sex (cited in Greenblat 1983, 297)

The overall conclusion drawn from Greenblat's research is that, after the first year of marriage, sex is of decreasing importance to most people. Nevertheless, satisfaction with both the quantity and quality of one's sex life is essential to a good marriage (Blumstein and Schwartz 1983).

What Makes It Good?   A lasting marriage and a good marriage are not necessarily identical. At the end of this chapter, we'll talk about the frequency of divorce and what leads to the failure of a marriage. At this point we want to take a more positive approach. How satisfactory are marriages and why?

If we ask the public a simple question, "Overall, how satisfied are you with your marriage: very satisfied, pretty satisfied, or not too satisfied?," about two-thirds will tell us that they are very satisfied with their marriages. This suggests that marriage is a pretty satisfactory arrangement for most people. Paradoxically, one reason for these high levels of reported marital happiness is our high divorce rate. In the contemporary United States, people who are unhappy in their marriages get a divorce. The people who stay married are thus a select group who have good marriages.

Although most studies show that marital happiness peaks during the honeymoon and takes a moderately downhill course after that, the majority of middle-aged people report that their marriages are very satisfactory. Agreement on gender roles is more important than high income in creating a happy marriage, and couples who share the same values and life-style have an easier task in creating a happy as well as lasting marriage. Many people, both youthful and middle-aged, list their spouse as their best friend—the person they are most comfortable confiding in and who gives them the most emotional support.

Studies of marital happiness reveal two consistent determinants of marital satisfaction: years married and gender-role agreement (Glenn 1990). During the 1980s, a half dozen studies demonstrated that marital happiness is pretty much a downhill slope. Whether they have children or stay childless, most couples experience a decline in satisfaction within the first years of marriage. Another important determinant of marital happiness is agreement on gender roles. Disagreement over gender roles can take place in several arenas: Do both partners agree on the importance of the wife's career? Do they agree on who should do the housework and take care of the children? Failure to agree on these fundamental aspects of marriage gives rise to dissatisfaction.

PARENTING

In the past, the majority of couples entered marriage with the expectation of becoming parents—often immediately. This link between marriage and parenthood is being broken in two ways: non-marital births and delayed childbearing. Nearly one quarter (22 percent) of all births in the United States are to unmarried women. In addition, many married women are choosing to postpone childbearing until 5 or even 10 years after their first marriages. Today, 25 percent of American women ages 30 to 34 are still childless (U.S. Bureau of the Census 1989j). Although most still intend to have children eventually, childbearing is no longer seen as an inevitable consequence of marriage.

Currently, the average number of children born to American women is approximately two. This small family size is due largely to changes in the role of women and changes in the security of family roles. Although the average woman does not yet place career roles over family roles, women today desire economic security and more personal freedom, both of which are adversely affected by taking time out for childbearing (McLaughlin and Associates 1988). If the divorce rate remains high and if women's labor-force participation rises—both of which appear likely—then having children will grow even less attractive.

The Decision to Have a Child: A Leap of Faith.   The decision to become a parent is a momentous one. Children are extremely costly, both financially and in terms of emotional wear and tear. Recent estimates suggest that it may cost as much as $150,000 to raise a middle-class child to adulthood. Parenthood, however, is one of life's biggest adventures. Few other undertakings require such a large commitment of time and money on so uncertain a return. The list of disadvantages is long and certain: It costs a lot of money, takes an enormous amount of time, probably disrupts all your usual activities, and causes at least occasional stress and worry. And once you've started, there is no backing out; it is a lifetime commitment. What are the returns? You hope for love and a sense of family, but you know all around you are parents whose kids cause them heartaches and headaches. Parenthood is really the biggest gamble most people will ever take. In spite of this, or maybe because of it, the majority of people want and have children.

Who's Watching the Baby?   Probably the central question for the American family today is child care. Relatively high rates of divorce, non-marital births, and mothers' labor-force participation have threatened our previous childrearing structures. Obviously we need to reconsider the question, "Who's watching the baby?"

In the traditional American family, there was little question about who was watching the baby: Mom. To a significant extent this is still true today. Nevertheless, over two-thirds of married mothers are now in the labor force and a full 50 percent of mothers return to the labor force before their child reaches its first birthday. This means that families must come up with alternative child-care arrangements. For most families, this does *not* mean day care. Approximately half of all preschoolers are cared for by relatives while their mother is at work; about one out of five children of employed, married mothers is cared for by his or her father (Presser 1989). Frequently, this arrangement involves not day care but *night* care. Nearly one quarter

Traditionally, parenting has been a sharply gendered behavior and the roles of mothers and fathers were very different. Mothers spent much more time with children than did fathers. Today, approximately 50 percent of American mothers are back in the labor force before their child's first birthday and children of married parents are likely to spend nearly equal time with dad and mom. Nevertheless, many childcare activities remain disproportionately mothers' responsibility.

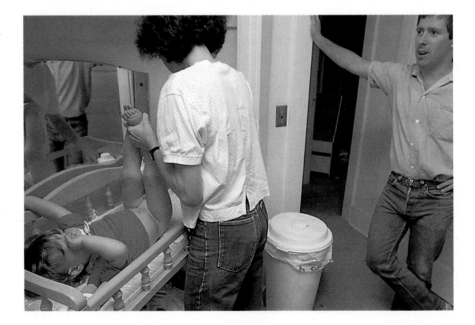

of all two-earner couples with children work alternate shifts so that one of them can be home with the children.

There is growing emphasis on the father's role in child care. Both women and men expect that fathers will do more than play catch with their children on Saturday afternoons and provide economic support for them. They expect fathers to change diapers and take part in the day-to-day responsibility for child care. Studies show that attitudes have changed faster than actual behavior, but there is little doubt that the parenting responsibilities of married parents are less sharply divided by sex than before (LaRossa 1988).

The dilemma, of course, is that fewer than 60 percent of American children live with both of their parents. Figure 13.3 shows living arrangements of U.S. children. Nearly 24 percent live with a single parent, most often their mother, and another 14 percent are being raised in a stepfamily situation. How does parenting work in these families?

Single Parents.   Before they reach the age of 18, an estimated 59 percent of all U.S. children born in the 1980s will spend some time living with a single parent. Of those whose parents divorce and remarry, nearly half will experience the breakup of the second marriage, too (Bumpass 1984; Glick 1984).

Most single parenting is done by mothers: Nearly seven out of eight single-parent families in the United States are headed by women. There has been a slight increase in father custody after divorce, especially when the children are older or are boys. This has been more than offset, however, by the formation of single-mother families through non-marital births.

These changes in family experience have had a negative impact on children. In more than 25 percent of all cases, the noncustodial parent disappears entirely from the child's life: no child support and no visits. In many other cases, both contact and child support are sporadic. As a result, the child's economic and social welfare often depends on a single adult.

■
FIGURE 13.3
LIVING ARRANGEMENTS OF CHILDREN UNDER 18 IN THE UNITED STATES, 1988

Current rates of illegitimacy and divorce have substantially reduced the likelihood that a child will grow up with both parents. These estimates from 1988 show that only a little over half of all American children under the age of 18 live with both of their parents.

SOURCE: Adapted from U.S. Bureau of the Census 1989d. 59; Moorman and Hernandez 1989.

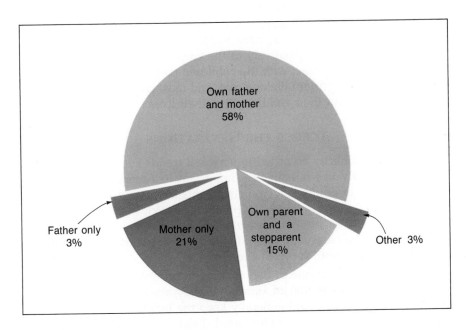

Own father and mother 58%

Father only 3%

Mother only 21%

Own parent and a stepparent 15%

Other 3%

A single parent can provide less time and less money than two parents, and children reared in single-parent families are more likely to be raised in poverty and less likely to get effective supervision. As a result, studies show that, on the average, they do less well in school, marry earlier, are more likely to have nonmarital births, and report more social and psychological problems (Amato and Keith 1990; McLanahan and Booth 1989).

Stepparenting.   An estimated 14 percent of all children in the United States are being raised in a stepfamily situation, most frequently by their mother and a stepfather (Moorman and Hernandez 1989). If parenting is difficult, stepparenting is more so. In addition to the problems all parents face, stepparents often have to contend with an ex-husband or an ex-wife, plus the trials of giving equal love and attention to his children, her children, and their children. As a result, both stepparents and stepchildren indicate more conflict and stress in stepfamilies than in original families. One way stepfamilies relieve this stress is by encouraging teenage stepchildren to leave home as soon as possible; the other "solution" is a divorce rate that is nearly double the divorce rate for families without stepchildren (White and Booth 1985).

The Empty Nest: Crisis or Release?   For the first 18 years or so of their lives, children usually live under the same roof as at least one of their parents. More years of schooling and the postponement of marriage have extended the period that young adults stay with their parents: In 1988, 54 percent of all men ages 18 to 24 were still living at home, up from 43 percent in 1970.

The reason adult children are staying at home longer has more to do with economics than it does with lack of independence. Studies show that children are more eager to leave home than parents are to have them go. Traditional parents are especially likely to expect that their children will stay at home until they get married (Goldscheider and Goldscheider 1989).

Nevertheless, the majority of parents look forward to their children's eventual departure. This doesn't mean that they want their children to disappear from their lives—far from it. One recent study shows that although parents respond positively to the empty nest, this is true only if they retain frequent contact with their children (White and Edwards 1990). Parenthood is an important lifelong role, and most parents want and have frequent contact with their children all of their lives.

ACROSS THE GENERATIONS

Despite all the publicity accorded to very real trends such as divorce and illegitimacy, family ties remain very important to Americans. Over two-thirds of American adults talk to their parents at least once a week; one-fifth talk to a parent every day (Gallup Reports 1989c). In addition, siblings keep in touch with each other, and grandchildren keep in touch with their grandparents. The parent-child bond is the strongest family relationship, and it stays strong until very old age.

It has been said that one of the most important roles that women play in American families is that of *kinkeepers*. They send the birthday cards, organize family parties, and generally keep the family in touch with one another. One result of this gender-based division of labor is that women are usually closer to their relatives than men are and that female relatives are closer to each other than are male relatives. The mother-daughter and sister-sister bonds are substantially closer than the father-son and brother-brother bonds (Gallup Reports 1989c).

MINORITY FAMILIES

Most of what we have said about the American family is true of all types of families, regardless of race or ethnicity. There are, however, two ways in which African American and Hispanic families are distinct: higher rates of female headship and higher reliance on an extended kin network.

Historically, disadvantaged minority groups (blacks, Hispanics, Asians) have compensated for economic marginality through an extensive kin-based support network. They have been more likely to live in extended families, to live close to their relatives, and to exchange significant economic and social support with kin. The strong extended family reflects subcultural norms about family roles and responsibilities as well as a "resilient response to socioeconomic conditions of poverty and unemployment" (Taylor 1986, 67).

In the relatively recent past, the stronger extended family system among minority Americans more or less made up for higher rates of female headship. Today, however, the rates of female headship are much higher, and there is consensus that the old safety net of extended family doesn't work as well (Billingsley 1989). This is a special problem for black families. Black women have higher rates of non-marital births (61 percent of black infants are born to unmarried women), lower marriage rates, and higher divorce rates. The result is that 43 percent of all black and 23 percent of all Hispanic families are female headed compared to only 13 percent of all white families (see Figure 13.4).

The chief cause of high rates of female headship is the weak position of minority males in the labor force (Schoen and Kluegel 1988; Tucker and Taylor 1989). The breadwinner role continues to be the central male role in the family: If he isn't working regularly, isn't bringing in a steady pay-check, then he has only a marginal place in the family. When male un-

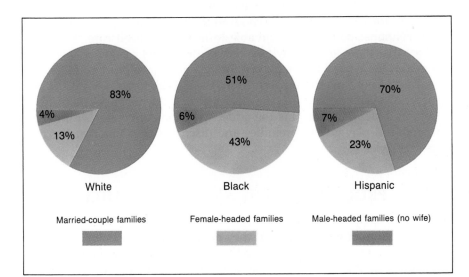

FIGURE 13.4
FAMILY TYPES BY RACE AND HISPANIC ORIGIN, 1988

Minority families, but especially black families, have high rates of female headship. The primary underlying cause of these high rates is the disadvantaged position of the minority male in the labor market.

SOURCE: U.S. Bureau of the Census 1989.

employment rates are high, marriage rates go down and divorce rates go up. Thus, the key to strengthening minority families lies in changing the structure of economic opportunity.

ALTERNATIVE FAMILY FORMS

The family institution provides a blueprint for much of our adult lives. Although there is more flexibility than ever before, most of us expect to follow the normative path: to get married and have children. Not everybody fits this mold, however, and it is appropriate to consider what the family institution means to two categories that may have been left out of some of the previous discussion but who are nevertheless affected by the family institution: the never married and the homosexual.

Staying Single.   In 1988, approximately 5 percent of the population aged 40–45 had never married; most of these people will never marry. Some of them would have married if their health or choices had been better, but perhaps half *chose* the independence of remaining single (Austrom and Hanel 1985). Some of these never-married persons have children; most of them do not. Yet nearly all of them have parents, brothers and sisters, nieces and nephews. Although we know relatively little about unmarried men, a recent study of never-married women showed that they are very close to their families. They baby-sit, act as godmothers, and carry a vastly disproportionate share of the load in taking care of aging parents. In fact, for many of these never-married women, their obligations to their parents were what kept them single (Allen 1989).

Homosexual Families.   Analysis of the family institution often focuses exclusively on heterosexuals. A little reflection, however, will show that most of the issues discussed in this chapter—mate selection, intergenerational ties, and even childrearing—are relevant to the millions of Americans who are largely or entirely homosexual in their sexual preference. Almost all have traditional family ties: They are close to their parents and perhaps brothers and sisters; many have long-term partners despite the lack of normative support for their unions. A substantial minority have children, many from previous marriages. Several states have recently opened the doors for legal adoption of children by homosexuals, reasoning that unconventional homes are preferable to institutionalized care. Estimates suggest that there are somewhere between 6 and 14 million homosexual parents in the United States (Bozett 1987). There have been no large, national studies of how these parents and their children fare. Available evidence, however, suggests that they face the same dilemmas of other single-parent and step families plus the added problems of coping with neighborhood and playground prejudice and discrimination aimed at the parents' life-styles.

PROBLEMS IN THE AMERICAN FAMILY

There are couples who swear that they never have an argument and never disagree. These people must certainly be in the minority, however, and most intimate relations involve some stress and strain. We become con-

A small but growing proportion of all families are headed by homosexuals. John Rios and Don Harrelson were united by a minister two years ago, and together they are raising Jacob and Jennifer, John's children from a previous marriage. Don has already raised two children whom he adopted thirteen years ago in one of the first recognized homosexual adoptions. Jacob introduces Don Harrelson as his father's husband.

cerned when these stresses and strains affect the mental and physical health of the individuals and when they affect the stability of society. In this section, we cover two problems in the American family: violence and divorce.

VIOLENCE IN FAMILIES

Child abuse is nothing new, nor is wife battering. These forms of family violence, however, didn't receive much attention until recent years. In a celebrated court case in 1871, a social worker had to invoke laws against cruelty to animals in order to remove a child from a violent home. There were laws specifying how to treat your animals, but no restrictions on how wives and children were to be treated. In recent years, however, we have become much more aware of and less tolerant of abuse and violence.

The incidence of abuse is hard to measure. The social desirability bias on this question is enormously high. Nevertheless, a series of studies by scholars at Rhode Island University provides a relatively reliable set of figures on abuse. Table 13.3 shows the percent of the population reporting severe violence in the year prior to being interviewed. The operational definition of "severe violence" is if one or more of the following was reported: kicked, bit or hit with fist; hit or tried to hit with some object; beat up; threatened with a gun or a knife; used a gun or a knife. Using this definition, 10.7 percent reported severe violence from a parent to a child, 4.4 percent reported severe violence from a wife to a husband, and 3 percent reported severe violence from a husband to a wife (Straus and Gelles 1986).

These data show somewhat surprising evidence about sex and abuse: Spouse abuse is more likely to be husband abuse than wife abuse. Generally, however, observers believe that wife abuse is more serious. A blow from a woman is much less likely to cause physical damage than is a blow from a man. A previous study by this team suggests that child-to-parent abuse is approximately on the same level as these others: about 3 percent per year. Girls and boys are equally likely to direct violence toward their parents, but mothers are more apt than fathers to be the victims (Cornell and Gelles 1982).

Family violence is not restricted to any class or race. It occurs in the homes of lawyers as well as the homes of welfare mothers. Studies suggest that violence is most typical in families with multiple problems: unemployment, alcohol and drug abuse, money worries, stepchildren, physically or mentally handicapped members, or members who were abused themselves as children (Gelles and Straus 1988). Although these problems can occur in any social class, it is also true that lower-class families are more likely to experience unemployment and money worries that add to the difficulty of coping with normal family stresses. For example, this couple sounds as if they might have had trouble even if there had been no money troubles; with money troubles, they had a violent home:

> My husband wanted to think of himself as the head of the household. He thought that the man should wear the pants in the family. Trouble was, he couldn't seem to get his pants on. He had trouble getting a job and almost never could keep one. If I didn't have my job as a waitress, we would have starved. Even though he didn't make no money, he still wanted to control the house and the kids. But it was my money, and I wasn't about to let him spend it on booze or gambling (Gelles and Straus 1988, 82).

■
TABLE 13.3
VIOLENCE IN THE AMERICAN FAMILY

Nobody likes to admit that they have behaved violently and tried to hurt members of their families. As a result of strong social desirability bias, these figures probably seriously underestimate the amount of violence that actually occurs in American families.

PERCENT REPORTING SEVERE VIOLENCE	
Parent to child	10.7%
Wife to husband	4.4
Husband to wife	3.0

SOURCE: Adapted from Strauss and Gelles 1986 and Cornell and Gelles 1982.

Solutions to family violence are complex. The first step, however, is to make it clear that violence is inappropriate and illegal. New laws against spousal rape and other forms of family violence may clarify what used to be rather fuzzy norms about whether family violence was appropriate (Straus and Gelles 1986).

DIVORCE

In the United States, more than 2 million adults and approximately 1 million children are affected annually by divorce. The **divorce rate,** calculated as the number of divorces each year per 1,000 married women, has risen steadily in the post–World War II period, and it stood at 22 in 1985—that is, 22 out of 1,000, or 2.2 percent of all married women in the United States, divorce annually. Another way of looking at divorce is to calculate the probability that a marriage will *ever* end in divorce—the **lifetime divorce probability.** Of marriages begun in 1890, for example, the proportion ever ending in divorce was approximately 10 percent (Cherlin 1981). Experts estimate an astounding 64 percent of first marriages contracted in the last decade will end in divorce (Martin and Bumpass 1989). Figure 13.5 shows the trend in lifetime divorce probability over the last century.

Which Marriages End in Divorce?   Nearly two-thirds of recent first marriages are expected to eventually end in divorce, but one-third will last. For second marriages the odds of failure are a little bit higher. What are the factors that make a marriage more likely to fail? Table 13.4 displays some of the predictors of marital failure within the first five years of marriage. A review of empirical results over the last decades suggests that six factors are especially important (White 1990):

The **divorce rate** is calculated as the number of divorces each year per 1,000 married women.

Lifetime divorce probability is the estimated probability that a marriage will ever end in divorce.

FIGURE 13.5
CHANGING PROBABILITY OF DIVORCE, 1870–1985

There has been a dramatic increase in the likelihood that marriages will end in divorce. For those who first married after 1980, it is now expected that two-thirds will divorce.

SOURCE: Adapted from Cherlin 1981. (Reprinted by permission, Harvard University Press) and Martin and Bumpass 1989.

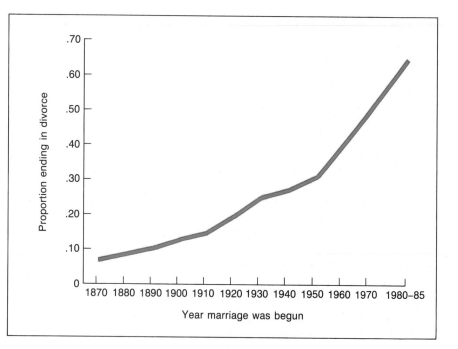

■

TABLE 13.4
PROBABILITY OF MARRIAGE BREAKING UP WITHIN THE FIRST FIVE YEARS

The probability that a first marriage will ever end in divorce is about 64 percent. If we limit our focus to the first five years of marriage, about 23 percent of all first marriages and 27 percent of second marriages end in this period. Divorce is more likely for those who marry young, those with low levels of educational attainment, blacks, and those who had a child before the marriage.

	FIRST MARRIAGES	SECOND MARRIAGES
Total	23%	27%
Age at marriage		
14–19	31	40
20–22	26	26
23–29	15	27
30+	14	14
Education		
Less than 12 years	33	36
12 years	26	26
13 years or more	16	22
Children before marriage		
No	21	24
Yes	36	28
Race		
White	22	26
Black	36	43
Hispanic	24	28

SOURCE: Martin and Bumpass 1989.

■ *Age at marriage.* Probably the best predictor of divorce is a youthful age at marriage. Marrying as a teenager or even in one's early 20s *doubles* one's divorce probability relative to those who marry later. Not surprisingly, if you are already on a second marriage before your twentieth birthday, your chances of failure are very high. (see Table 13.4).

■ *Parental divorce.* People who were raised in single-parent families because their parents divorced are more likely to divorce themselves.

■ *Premarital childbearing.* Having a child before marriage reduces the stability of subsequent marriages. Premarital conception followed by a postmarital birth, however, does not seem to increase the likelihood of divorce.

■ *Education.* The higher one's education, the less likely one's marriage is to end in divorce. Part of this is because people with higher educations are likely to come from two-parent families, avoid premarital childbearing, and marry later. Independent of these other factors, however, higher education does reduce the chances of divorce.

■ *Race.* Black Americans are substantially more likely than white Americans (Hispanic or non-Hispanic) to end their marriages in divorce. Even if we restrict the comparison to women who marry late, go to college, and have no premarital births, black women are twice as likely as white women to divorce (Martin and Bumpass 1989).

- *Bad behavior*. As you might expect, alcohol and drug abuse, adultery, and abusive behavior are all predictors of divorce. Surveys that ask newly divorced people what happened in their marriages find that these bad behaviors crop up frequently. One woman said, "He was running around and the first time we had sex after the baby's birth, he gave me VD." Another said, "He's a liar and a cheater and a gambler " (Booth and Associates 1984). Although many people just drift apart and cite irreconcilable differences, nearly one-third of the people who seek divorce have a specific and important grievance (Kitson and Sussman 1986).

Societal-Level Factors.   Age at marriage, premarital childbearing, education, and bad behavior affect whether a particular marriage succeeds or fails. These personal characteristics, however, cannot account for why close to 64 percent of all marriages fail. The shift from a lifetime divorce probability of 10 to 64 percent within the last century is a social problem, not a personal trouble, and to explain it we need to look at social structure.

The change in marital relationships is probably most clearly associated with changes in economic institutions. The shift from an industrial and agricultural to a service economy, a change detailed in Chapter 15, has revolutionized the technologies and relationships essential to production. One result of this revolution is that an earner's chief economic asset is education and experience. You can walk away from a marriage and taken these assets along; the same is not true with land, which is often tied up in family relationships. Another result is the increased opportunity for women to support themselves outside of marriage.

Women and men are less and less impelled to marry or to stay married by economic necessity. Since no incentive for marriage more effective than economic need has arisen to replace this factor, marriages have less institutional support than before.

HOW SERIOUS ARE PROBLEMS IN THE AMERICAN FAMILY? A THEORETICAL APPROACH

In Chapter 4 we noted that some people view institutions as constraints that force people into uncomfortable and perhaps oppressive relationships; others see institutions as providing the stability and comfort frequently associated with old shoes. This conflict of views is nowhere more present than in the case of the family.

Theoretical viewpoints sharply influence perceptions of the health of the modern family (Adams 1985). If the family is an oppressive institution, then divorce is a form of liberation; if the family is the source of individual and community strength, then divorce undermines society. In this section we briefly review some of the major criticisms of the contemporary family and conclude with a perspective on the future.

Loss of Commitment.   Critics argue that a major problem with the American family, and some would argue with American culture, is an accent on individual growth at the expense of commitment. This criticism is most likely to come from structural functionalists, who traditionally stress the subordination of individual to community needs, but it also comes from symbolic interactionists concerned with stable personal identity.

CHAPTER 13 THE FAMILY

The most prominent symptom of the alleged emphasis on individual happiness and growth at the expense of long-term commitment is the rapid rise in the number of women who are raising children on their own. Because men don't want to be tied down by wives and children and because wives don't want to be tied down by husbands, fathers have walked away and mothers have let them, even encouraged them, according to this perspective. The result is that the basic family unit, in the sense of long-term commitment to sharing and support, is the mother-child pair. Husband-wife and father-child relationships are increasingly seen to be temporary and even optional. For many critics this increasingly voluntary nature of family ties is dysfunctional, reducing the stability of the family and reducing its ability to perform one of its major tasks: caring for children. Among the ill consequences these critics note are the increasing proportion of women and children in poverty.

Oppression.   Critics from a conflict perspective are more apt to criticize the family for its oppression of women and children. They point to the lower power of women and children relative to men, working women's inability to get help with the housework, and to the number of women and children who suffer abuse in the family. For example, Denzin (1984, 487–88) declares, "A patriarchical, capitalist society which promotes the ownership of firearms, women, and children; which makes homes men's castles; and which sanctions societal and interpersonal violence in the forms of wars, athletic contests, and mass media fiction (and news) should not be surprised to find violence in its homes. . . . Violence directed toward children and women is a pervasive feature of sexual divisions of labor which place females and children in subordinate positions to adult males."

From this perspective, the family is not particularly changed for the worse: It has traditionally been an oppressive institution maintained by force and fraud. These critics do note the development of greater egalitarianism in the contemporary family, but generally find these changes too slow.

The major developing problem from this perspective is that women's and children's independence from husbands-fathers in the family is coming before their independence in the marketplace. The solution they recommend is equal opportunity and equal pay for women and state support for children in the form of family allowances.

Perspectives on the Future.   Some of the functions performed by the traditional family, such as care of the dependent, are not as important today as they used to be. Nevertheless, the family continues to perform vital functions for society and individuals.

The family is the central socializing agent, the arena in which we develop our self-concept, learn to interact with others, and internalize society's norms. Without the strong bonds of love and affection that characterize family ties, these developmental tasks are difficult if not impossible. Thus, the family is essential for the production of socialized members, people who can fit in and play a productive part in society.

The nuclear family and the larger kin group are also important for individuals, not just in childhood, but throughout the life course. To cite just a few examples, people with close ties to their kin report greater satisfaction with their life, their marriages, and their health; they are less likely to abuse their children or get divorced; and they are more likely to be able to ride out personal and family crises (LaVee, McCubbin, and Patterson 1985; McGhee 1985; Rosenthal 1985).

Given these benefits that the family gives to both the individual and society, it would seem to be a reasonable goal to keep and support the family, while simultaneously reducing some of its more oppressive features. This goal is not impossible. Despite current rates of divorce, illegitimacy, childlessness, and domestic abuse, there are signs of health in the family: the durability of the mother-child bond, the frequency of remarriage, the frequency with which stepfathers are willing to step in and support other men's children, the frequency with which elderly persons rely on *and get* help from their children.

There is no doubt that the family is changing. When you ask a young man what his father did when he was growing up, you are increasingly likely to hear, "What father?" or "Which father?" These recent changes must be viewed as at least potentially troublesome. At present we have no institutionalized mechanisms comparable to the family for giving individuals social support or for caring for children. The importance of these tasks suggests that the family and especially children need to be moved closer to the top of the national agenda. The policy issue in this chapter addresses one aspect of this agenda: the relationship between divorce and child poverty.

Divorce, Poverty, and Family Policy

Divorce is not a universally negative experience. It frees many adults and children from violent and conflictual homes; it gives many adults a chance to start again. On the other hand, rising divorce rates bear a significant portion of the blame for rising rates of poverty among women and children. In this section, we review the connection between divorce and poverty and then discuss available policy options.

DIVORCE AND POVERTY

Empirical data in the United States reveal a substantial link between divorce and poverty. There are three reasons. First, poor families are more likely to divorce than well-off families.

Second, divorce reduces family income—especially for women and children. A simple example shows how this can happen. Say that a couple has one child and a total family income of $42,000 (the husband earns $25,000, and the wife earns $17,000). Each family member has a per-capita income of $14,000. After the divorce, the mother will usually get custody of the child, and the father will be ordered to pay 17 percent ($4,250) of his gross income in child support (Beller and Graham 1986). After the breakup, the husband will have a per-capita income of $20,750, and the wife and child will have a per-capita income of $10,625. In short, his per-capita income will go up substantially, while his ex-wife and child will experience a drop of nearly one-third in their per-capita income (Hoffman and Duncan 1988).

A third factor linking divorce to poverty is that fewer than 50 percent of noncustodial parents regularly pay child support (Weitzman 1985). When this occurs, the economic damage of divorce is often even greater.

Rising divorce rates are the primary cause of rising rates of female headship (Wojtkiewicz, McLanahan, and Garfinkel 1990), and rising rates of female headship are the primary cause of rising rates of poverty among women and children. In 1989, nearly one out of four children was living below the poverty line, compared to one in eight only 20 years ago. Because childhood poverty has been shown to have significant negative effects on nearly every dimension of life, from educational attainment to mental health (Acock and Kiecolt 1989), increasing childhood poverty is perceived to be a serious problem.

POLICY INITIATIVES: MAKING DADS PAY

Public policy has been directed primarily at the third link in the chain between divorce and poverty: making dads pay. In 1988, federal legislation was passed to increase noncustodial parents' support of their children. This legislation sets higher minimum child support awards and, more important, sets new enforcement procedures. Beginning in 1994, every parent who is required to pay child support will have the amount automatically deducted from his or her paycheck. The easy passage of this legislation reflects the strong consensus about "a father's first responsibility: He must support his children, even if he no longer lives with them and even if he marries again" (Cherlin 1990, 2).

This new legislation represents a moral victory rather than a solution, however. Because many of the fathers whose children are in poverty have low earnings, their contributions will not help much. One study estimated that full enforcement would reduce the number of children receiving welfare by only 25 percent (McLanahan, Garfinkel, and Watson 1986).

THE DEEPER ISSUE: GENDER AND THE FAMILY

A primary reason that divorce increases childhood poverty is that children normally live with their

---

ISSUES IN SOCIAL POLICY continued

lower-earning parent (their mother) after divorce. In the example given here, for instance, per-capita income would have been unchanged—with everybody still getting approximately $14,000—if the child had lived with the father after divorce and the mother had paid 17 percent of her income in support.

This raises several deeper issues about gender and the family. Although we could "solve" the poverty problem by giving custody of children to their higher-paid parent, this overlooks a critical linkage between family and the labor market:

Women are paid less *because* they have parented more. Getting custody and earning less both reflect the fact that, on the average, women devote more time to their families and less time to their careers than do men. The root cause of women's and children's poverty is the gender-based division of labor in the family (Scanzoni 1989). An intact marriage disguises women's and children's dependence on their husbands and fathers under the cloak of a division of labor. Divorce brings this dependence out in the open.

SUMMARY

1. Marriage, family, and kinship are the most basic institutions found in society. In all societies, these institutions meet such universal needs as regulation of sexual behavior, replacement through reproduction, child care, and socialization.

2. Cross-cultural comparisons demonstrate that the structure and function of the family vary considerably. Preindustrial economies tend to place greater emphasis on extended families, on family participation in mate selection, and on male dominance. In industrial societies, norms prescribe a nuclear family, individual choice in mate selection, and more egalitarian authority patterns.

3. Major changes in the U.S. family include the increased probability of divorce, increased illegitimacy, increased single parenting, and increased labor-force participation by wives and mothers.

4. Because of postponement of marriage and high divorce rates, dating is no longer just a teenage activity. Sexual relations are a common aspect of contemporary courtship, producing high rates of unwanted pregnancy and an increased risk of sexually transmitted diseases. Cohabitation is a common courtship stage.

5. Marriage and family roles continue to be sharply gendered, and agreement on gender roles is crucial for marital satisfaction. Men's breadwinning role and women's child-care and housekeeping roles are changing slowly, and there has been an increase in wives' and mothers'

labor-force participation and increased normative support for egalitarian authority patterns.

6. Parenting has changed substantially. Divorce and non-marital births mean many children do not live with both of their parents. It is also likely that their mother is employed. As a result of dilemmas about child care, American women are choosing to have relatively few children.

7. Family roles are important to most Americans. Although few parents and children want to live together after the children grow up, the ties remain important. Family members tend to keep in close contact and provide substantial support to one another.

8. Minority families are distinct from majority families on two dimensions: higher rates of female headship (this is especially true for African American families) and stronger extended kin networks. Poor economic prospects for minority males are the major cause of higher rates of female headship.

9. Family violence is relatively commonplace in American homes. It is more characteristic of parent-child relationships than of husband-wife relationships. It is strongly related to multiple family problems.

10. It is estimated that 64 percent of first marriages will end in divorce. Factors associated with divorce include age at marriage, parental divorce, premarital childbearing, education, race, and bad behavior. Reduced eco-

nomic dependence on marriage underlies many of these trends.

11. Perceptions of the health of the family depend on the theoretical orientation of the viewer. Two problems are loss of commitment and inequality within the family.

12. Divorce is the primary cause of rising rates of poverty for women and children. Recent public policy tackles this issue by raising child support awards and enforcing them more strictly. At a deeper level, the poverty of women and children is an outgrowth of the gender-based division of labor in the family.

SUGGESTED READINGS

Cherlin, Andrew. (ed.). 1988. The Changing American Family and Public Policy. Washington, D.C.: Urban Institute Press. This collection of six essays is a rich mixture of factual information and recipes for public policy. Topics such as divorce, fatherhood, day care, and gender-role change are addressed.

Gelles, Richard, and Straus, Murray. 1988. Intimate Violence. New York: Simon & Schuster. A report on the decade-long Rhode Island University study of family violence. Written for a lay audience, the book covers incidence of violence and also prescriptions for public policy.

Kephart, William M. 1987. Extraordinary Groups: The Sociology of Unconventional Life-Styles. (3d ed.) New York: St. Martin's Press. A fascinating tour of some of the most interesting variations in U.S. family practices within subcultures and countercultures, both past and present: the Oneidans, Mormons, Amish, gypsies, Shakers, and Hutterites. Painless and interesting sociology.

McLaughlin, Steven D., and Associates. 1988. The Changing Lives of American Women. Chapel Hill: University of North Carolina Press. Based on a large national survey commissioned by the editors of *Cosmopolitan*, this book attempts to analyze the causes and consequences of changing gender roles, particularly as they relate to the family.

14

EDUCATION

PROLOGUE

Have you ever . . .

had doubts about whether college was worth it? Going to school is hard work, it is expensive, and it is stressful. For most of us, going to school means nearly constant pressure. Even on Saturdays and Sundays, we really ought to be starting that term paper or studying. There are no legitimate days off when you're a college student. If you go ahead and take two or three days off, you'll probably have to pay for it with an all nighter at exam time.

For the majority of college students, going to school also means sacrifice of income. Although there are a growing number of students who work parttime and even fulltime, the majority of college students earn much less than they would if they were able to devote full effort to earning.

Given the work, the stress, and the poverty, why are you and 13 million others going to school? Most of us go to school because we expect to receive an economic payoff. We expect to earn more money and have more satisfying and respected jobs if we graduate from college. These are realistic expectations. If you get a college degree, you will have substantially increased your earning power.

Despite these inducements, only about one-third of young high school graduates are enrolled in college. Those who are not enrolled are most likely to be from the lower or working class. Thus the pattern of college enrollments virtually guarantees that the social class structure of the next generation will be like this generation. The role of education in reproducing inequality is at the heart of the sociological study of education.

The **educational institution** is the social structure concerned with the formal transmission of knowledge. In this chapter, we describe the educational institutions of the United States, how they relate to other institutions, and how they affect our personal lives and life chances.

Education is one of our most enduring and familiar institutions. Most of us spend at least 12 years going to school, and some spend 16 or even 20 years as students. When we include the teachers, secretaries, janitors, and administrators who work in the schools, 65 million Americans are directly involved in education every day; three out of every 10 Americans are either enrolled in school or employed within the educational system. Even those not actually in the system are involved as taxpayers, parents, or former students.

There are many critics of our educational institutions. These critics are chiefly concerned with two issues: equity and quality. Those concerned about equity argue that the schools do too little to create equality of opportunity and are actually a chief agent in reproducing social and economic inequality (Bowles and Gintis 1976). Those concerned about quality, on the other hand, tend to focus on average outcomes such as SAT scores.

These are both legitimate concerns and raise important questions about the characteristics of the schools and the purposes they serve. Why is such a large part of our lives and our dollars devoted to education? What purposes are being achieved? Who benefits?

DEVELOPMENT OF U.S. EDUCATION

During the earliest years of this nation, there was little consensus on the form that education should take. Charity schools for paupers and immigrants, private schools, military academies, and church schools existed alongside free public schools. Although most people managed to pick up enough education to achieve basic literacy, there was no coherent, formal system. During the 19th century, however, education changed dramatically. Consensus developed on the desirability of free public schools, and schooling expanded rapidly.

THE ESTABLISHMENT OF THE PUBLIC SCHOOLS

At the beginning of the American republic, most jobs did not require literacy. Education was an unnecessary luxury and hence was enjoyed more often by the children of the elite than by the average child. During the 19th century, however, education came to be viewed by all classes as such a critical necessity that attendance became compulsory. There were three major forces impelling the growth of the public schools during the 19th century: parental demand, labor demand, and social control demands.

Parental Demand.   From very early in American history, the ability to read and write was seen as essential for reading the Scriptures and being an informed citizen. As a result, rural parents established schools almost as soon as they established churches. The curriculum in these schools focused on basic intellectual skills such as reading, writing, and arithmetic rather than on vocational training. They were public institutions that reflected the dominant cultural and social values of the communities that established and supported them.

Labor Demand.   As industrialization developed during the 19th century, so did organized labor. As the working class became more self-conscious about its disadvantaged position, organized labor became a strong advocate for the public schools as a way to provide upward mobility for its children. The labor-versus-capitalist battle also affected the curriculum. Where the capitalists wanted vocational training to prepare working-class children for working-class jobs, organized labor wanted an academic curriculum that would enable its children to leave the working class.

Social Control Demands.   Rapid urbanization and very high rates of immigration in the late 19th century raised many concerns about social control. Compulsory schooling was seen as a way to get kids off the streets and out of trouble. New York, for example, established reform schools for delinquent children in 1823, several years before they considered establishing public schools for nondeliquent children (Katz 1987). The schools were also considered a way to ensure the rapid Americanization of immigrants. The demand for schools as a form of social control came from elites rather than from the average citizen.

Almost from the beginning, people from different social classes and different political perspectives have wanted different things from education. The content of education has been and continues to be "contested terrain" (Edwards 1979). Whether we want excellence for a few, opportunity for all, or social control are still issues being debated.

THE EXPANSION OF SCHOOLING

By the turn of the century, compulsory school attendance was established by law everywhere but the South (Richardson 1980). These laws were not always well enforced, but schooling through the eighth grade was well

The expansion of education has been accompanied by increasing standardization. From our first achievement test in elementary school through the SAT and then graduate school entrance exams, the mark-sense form and the no. 2 pencil are a familiar part of life in the schools. Because standardized test scores determine college entrance, there is increasing pressure on school districts to teach the standard curriculum that will prepare their students for these examinations.

entrenched across most of America by 1900. High schools, however, were substantially behind. By 1910, fewer than 10 percent of America's 18-year-olds had a high school diploma, and it was not until the 1930s that high school education became common (Parelius and Parelius 1987). Even in 1950, only half of America's young adults had graduated from high school. If your grandparents graduated from high school, they were part of a minority. Today, however, nearly 90 percent of young adults have a high school diploma.

The expansion of secondary and college education is largely a phenomenon of the post-World War II years (see Figure 14.1). Numerous social conditions contributed to this expansion. The GI Bill sent millions of veterans of World War II, the Korean War, and the Vietnam War to college. In the 1960s, expanded federal loan programs and the development of the

FIGURE 14.1

EDUCATIONAL ACHIEVEMENT OF PERSONS 25 AND OLDER BY RACE AND ETHNICITY, 1940–1988

Among whites, the proportion of adults graduating from high school has tripled in the last 50 years; among blacks, the increase in education is even more dramatic. Nevertheless, blacks and Hispanics continue to be disadvantaged in terms of quantity of education.

SOURCE: U.S. Bureau of the Census 1975, 380; U.S. Bureau of the Census 1989a, b, and c.

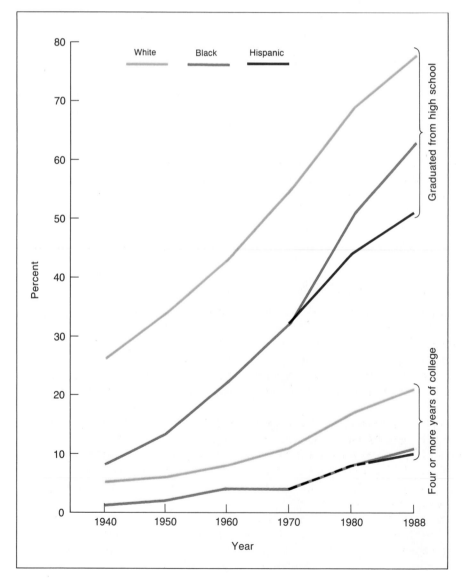

community college system also helped bring a college education within reach of more Americans.

This expansion of education has occurred unevenly. Blacks, Native Americans, and Hispanics have all experienced a great deal of difficulty participating in this expansion. These groups have generally been offered less education, worse education, segregated education, and more oppressive education. Until 1954, when the Supreme Court's decision against the Topeka, Kansas, Board of Education outlawed racially segregated schools, many minority Americans attended poorly funded, segregated schools. Hispanics and Native Americans faced added hurdles of mandatory deculturation. Native American children were educated at boarding schools that sought to Americanize them. In the Southwest, laws that made it illegal to teach in any language but English effectively disenfranchised Mexican American children (San Miguel 1987). All minority children studied from textbooks that either omitted or maligned their people, their culture, and their history. As a result, only 50 to 60 percent of today's black, Hispanic, and Native American adults over age 25 have completed high school. Including these disadvantaged segments of society in the expansion of the public school system is an unfinished project.

■

INEQUALITY AND THE SCHOOLS

The central concern of the sociology of education in the last 40 years has been the link between education and stratification (Hallinan 1988). This concern exists on both micro and macro levels. On the micro level, we want to know what happens to individual children—how the school experiences of working-class and middle-class children differ. On a macro level, we want to understand whether the structure of the schools to which we send our children affects their learning.

SOCIAL CLASS AND SCHOOLING

Children from disadvantaged backgrounds are likely to experience economic hardships that work against them in all their daily experiences in school. They are likely to lack a set of encyclopedias and a home computer. Futhermore, it is likely that their parents will be too caught up in the struggles of day-to-day living to have the time or energy to help them with their studies. Paying the bills may be more important than trying to improve their children's SAT scores.

The differences are far more subtle than simple economics. Poorly educated parents, for example, are less likely to attend parent/teacher conferences, are less comfortable talking to their children's teachers, and are less able and often less willing to help their children with their schoolwork. The way this adds to the disadvantage of their children is illustrated in the comments of one working-class mother:

My job is here at home. My job is to raise him, to teach him manners, get him dressed and get him to school, to make sure that he is happy. Now her [the

Children enter school with very unequal backgrounds. Some have been taken to the library and read to, while others have been abandoned to the company of the television; some have been playing learning-readiness games on their computer while others have been playing in dirty stairwells. These inequalities pose an insuperable obstacle to equal educational opportunity. As a result, studies show that the benefits of education go disproportionately to those who had the advantages to start with.

teacher's] part, the school's part, is to teach him to learn. Hopefully, someday he'll be able to use all of that. That is what I think is their part, to teach him to read, the writing, any kind of schooling (Lareau, 1987, 79).

This mother's remarks reveal several attitudes that are more common among lower- and working-class parents than among middle-class parents. First, the mother sees a division of labor between home and school; she does not think it is her responsibility to review homework or reinforce school-taught skills. Reading and writing are things you do at school, not at home. Second, she *hopes* the boy can use the skills. Obviously she isn't very sure that school will do him any good, and this uncertainty is likely to affect the boy's enthusiasm for learning. Third, this mother's emphasis on manners illustrates the repeated social science finding that working-class parents give more attention to being quiet and polite and less attention to independent thinking than do middle-class parents (Alexander et al. 1987).

   In addition, children of the middle and upper-middle classes have more of what has been called **cultural capital**—social assets, such as familiarity and identification with elite culture (Bourdieu 1973). They are more likely to have been introduced to art, music, and books at home and to define themselves as cultured people. This doesn't mean that they all prefer Beethoven to the Grateful Dead, but it does mean that they accept books and reading as a natural and important part of life. This cultural capital will help them to do well in school (DiMaggio and Mohr 1985; Teachman 1987), and it may influence how effectively they are able to translate their education into occupational success.

Cultural capital refers to social assets such as familiarity and identification with elite culture.

SOCIAL CLASS AND LIFE IN THE SCHOOLS

To understand how social class background translates into educational experiences, we need to look at two processes in the schools: cognitive development and tracking. Each is critical to eventual educational attainment, and each has been shown to be affected by social class background.

Cognitive Development.   One of the major processes that takes place in schools, of course, is that students learn. When they graduate from high school, many can use a computer, write essays with three-part theses, and even differentiate equations. In addition to learning specific skills, they also undergo a process of cognitive development wherein their mental skills grow and expand. They learn to think critically, to weigh evidence, to develop independent judgment. The extent to which this development takes place is related to both school and home environments.

An impressive set of studies demonstrates that cognitive development during the school years is enhanced by complex and demanding work without close supervision and by high teacher expectations. Teachers and curricula that furnish this setting produce students who have greater intellectual flexibility and higher achievement test scores. They are also more open to new ideas, less authoritarian, and less prone to blind conformity (Miller, Kohn, and Schooler 1985, 1986).

Unfortunately, the availability of these ideal learning conditions varies by students' social class. Studies show that teachers are most demanding when they are of the same social class as their students: The greater the difference between their own social class and that of their pupils, the more rigidly they structure their classrooms and the fewer the demands they place on their students (Alexander, Entwisle, and Thompson 1987). As a result, students learn less when they are from a lower social class than their teacher. Because the social class gap tends to be largest when youngsters are the most disadvantaged, this process helps to keep them disadvantaged.

Tracking.   When students enter first grade, they are sorted into reading groups on the basis of ability. This is just the beginning of a pervasive pattern of stratification in the schools. By the time they are out of elementary school, some students will be directed into college preparatory tracks, others into general education (sometimes called vocational education), and still others into remedial classes.

Tracking is the use of early evaluations to determine the educational programs a child will follow. Ideally, tracking is supposed to benefit both the gifted and the slow learners. By having classes that are geared to their levels, both should learn faster and both should benefit from increased teacher attention. Instead, one of the most consistent findings from education research is that assignment to a high-ability group has positive effects whereas assignment to a low-ability group has negative effects (Hallinan and Sorenson 1986; Shavit 1984).

Tracking occurs when evaluations relatively early in a child's career determine the educational programs the child will be encouraged to follow.

There are several reasons for this. One important reason that students assigned to low-ability groups learn less is because they are taught less. They are exposed to less material, asked to do less homework, and, in general, not given the same opportunities to learn. One study found that the average student in high-track English classes was asked to do an average of 42 minutes of homework a night; in low-track English classes, the average was 13 minutes (Oakes 1985).

In addition, there are less formal processes. Students who are assigned to high-ability groups receive a strong affirmation of their academic iden-

■

FOCUS ON MEASUREMENT

Measuring Mental Ability

■ How many legs does a Kaffir have?

■ Who wrote *Great Expectations?*

■ Which word is out of place? sanctuary—nave—altar—attic—apse

■ If you throw the dice and 7 is showing on top, what is facing down? 7—snake eyes—boxcars—little joes—11

If you have answered 2, Dickens, attic, and 7, then you get the highest possible score on this test. What does that mean? Does it mean that you have genetically superior mental ability, that you read a lot, that you shoot craps? What could you safely conclude about a person who got only two questions right?

The standardized test is one of the most familiar aspects of life in the schools. Whether it is the California or the Iowa Achievement Test, the SAT or the ACT, students are constantly being evaluated. Most of these tests are truly achievement tests; they measure what has been learned and make no pretense of measuring the capacity to learn. IQ tests, however, are supposed to measure the innate capacity to learn—mental ability. People who rank highly on one kind of test tend to rank highly on the other, though, and both are effective predictors of grades and educational attainment (Jencks et al. 1972). They are used for guiding students into various tracks and for college placement. In short, they are important; people use them to make real decisions about real people. On these tests, African American, Hispanic, and Native American students consistently score below Anglo students

and working-class students score substantially below middle-class students. Because the test scores are used to determine track placement and college admissions, these differences in test scores help ensure that the statification patterns of the next generation will look very much like those of this generation.

■

Just as the body does not develop fully without exercise, neither does the mind.

The obvious question is whether these tests are fair measures. Are African American, Hispanic, Native American, and working-class youths lower in mental ability than middle-class or Anglo youths?

Before we can answer this question, we must first ask another: What is mental ability? Most scholars recognize that it is a combination of genetic potential and prior social experiences. It is an aspect of personality, "the capacity of the individual to act purposefully, to think rationally and to deal effectively with his environment" (Wechsler 1958, 7).

Do questions such as those that opened this section measure any of these things? No. We can all imagine people who act purposefully, think rationally, and deal effectively with the environment but do not know who wrote *Great Expectations* and are ignorant about dice or church architecture. These people may be foreigners, they may have lacked the opportunity to go to

school, or they may have come from a subculture where dice, churches, or 19th-century English literature is not important.

For this reason, good IQ tests try to measure reasoning ability as well as knowledge. These nonverbal tests are supposed to measure the ability to think and reason without the assumption of formal educational opportunity. Examples of items from such a nonverbal test are reproduced on the facing page. Do these nonverbal tests achieve their intention? Do they measure the ability to reason independent of years in school, subcultural background, or language difficulties? Again, the answer seems to be no.

There are two ways in which these tests are not culture free. The first is that they reflect not only reasoning and knowledge but also competitiveness, familiarity with and acceptance of timed tests, rapport with the examiner, and achievement aspiration. Students who lack these characteristics may do poorly even though their ability to reason is well developed.

The more serious fault with such nonverbal tests is their underlying assumption. Reasoning ability is not independent of learning opportunities. How we reason, as well as what we know, depends on our prior experiences. The deprivation studies of infant monkeys and hospitalized orphans (see Chapter 6) demonstrate that mental and social retardation occurs as a result of sensory deprivation. Just as the body does not develop fully without exercise, neither does the mind. Thus, reasoning capacity is not culture

Culture-Free Intelligence Tests?

What can we conclude about your intelligence from your score on this simple test? Does a high score mean that you are naturally intelligent, or have some of your experiences in life and in school prepared you for these kinds of problems? Increasingly scholars believe that it is impossible to make an intelligence test that is free of cultural influences.

SOURCE: From Frames of Mind: *The Theory of Multiple Intelligences* by Howard Gardner © 1983 by Howard Gardner. Reprinted by permission of Basic Books, Inc., Publishers.

free; it is determined by the opportunities to develop it. For this reason, there will probably never be an IQ test that will not reflect the prior cultural experiences of the test taker.

An IQ test score is a mixture of natural ability, exposure to appropriate stimuli, and drive to excel. A high score means that a person is likely to be a success in school, and a low score means that a person is likely to do poorly in school. Does the low score also mean that the person is stupid or lacks mental ability? No. It may mean that, but it may also mean that the student has lacked the opportunity or encouragement to learn. Since these elements cannot be untangled, many educators now recommend that IQ tests be used not as measures of natural ability but as measures of cultural deprivation. If this interpretation is generally accepted, then the test will begin doing what its originator intended nearly 100 years ago—identifying those who need help to live up to their potential.

What do you think? What are the benefits of knowing a child's mental ability—and do they exceed the harm that might be done if an IQ score wrongly identifies a child's mental ability?

1. From the array of four, choose that form that is identical to the target form.

Target form

(a) (b) (c) (d)

2. From the array of four, choose that form which is a rotation of the target form.

Target form

(a) (b) (c) (d)

3. (For a, b, c) Indicate whether the second form in each pair is a rotation of the first or is a different form.

(a)

(b)

(c)

Answers: 1. d   2. d   3(a). same   3(b). same   3(c). different

Community and junior colleges serve a wide variety of purposes. Some schools focus on a traditional college curriculum for transfer to 4-year schools, some emphasize vocational training—such as the training these young men are receiving to operate computer-controlled industrial robots, while other community colleges focus on adult service courses such as basic word processing, home decorating, and budget management. These multiple purposes and multiple audiences make the community college curriculum "contested terrain."

tity; they find school rewarding, have better attendance records, cooperate better with teachers, and develop higher aspirations. These characteristics increase their performance still more, producing an upward spiral of advantage (Gamoran and Mare 1989). The opposite occurs with students placed in low-ability tracks. They get fewer rewards from their efforts, their parents and teachers have low expectations for them, and there is little incentive to work hard. Many will cut their losses and look for self-esteem through other avenues such as athletics or delinquency (Rosenberg, Schooler, and Schoenbach 1989). As Figure 14.2 shows, the result is a downward spiral of academic performance (Vanfossen, Jones, and Spade 1987).

Research is very clear on the outcomes of tracking: It benefits those in the advanced groups and decreases the performance of those in the lowest groups. The question of how tracks are assigned is thus a critical one. Which students get to be in the highest tracks? Students are likely to be assigned to a higher track when they meet one or more of these criteria: (a) They have high academic performance, especially on standardized tests; (b) they aspire to go to college; (c) they behave well in school.

None of these criteria is obviously discriminatory by social class. Yet this set of neutral and reasonable criteria produces systematic disadvantage for kids from lower socioeconomic backgrounds. Because they received less preschool stimulation, children from disadvantaged backgrounds start the first grade already behind, and they never catch up: Their scores on standardized tests start low and stay low. Because their parents did not attend college, the children are less likely to aspire to go to college themselves. Finally, the combination of low achievement and low aspiration tends to alienate children from the school, and they generally have more behavior problems. As a result, social class is a powerful predictor of track assignment.

There are, however, two important factors that work to dilute the effect of social class (Gamoran and Mare 1989). First, African Americans are more likely than white Americans from the same social class background to aspire

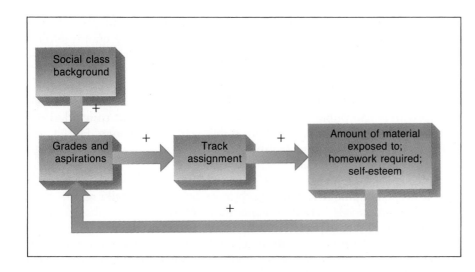

■
**FIGURE 14.2
THE TRACKING PROCESS**

The tracking system has a feedback loop that produces an upward spiral of advantage for middle-class children and a downward spiral of disadvantage for lower-class children.

to go to college. This means that schools are more likely to place African American children in college tracks than their test scores alone would warrant. As a result, the tracking process has been found to *reduce* the inheritance of disadvantage by race (Gamoran and Mare 1989). Second, being in the top third of one's class is probably more important than one's absolute score on standardized tests. For administrative convenience, nearly every school divides its students into ability groupings. If your scores are only average but your classmates' scores are even worse, you are likely to get into the high-ability track of your school (Gamoran and Mare 1989). Because schools tend to be segregated by social class, this structural factor ensures that some working-class children get college preparatory training.

SUMMARY.   There is no doubt that tracking benefits those in the high-ability groups and systematically lowers the achievements of those in low-ability groups, nor is there any doubt that track assignment is related to social class. The result is that tracking plays a critical role in reproducing social class. If this is true, why do we keep doing it? The answer from a conflict perspective is obvious: It perpetuates the current system of inequality. From a structural-functional viewpoint, the answer is that it facilitates administration. A first-grade teacher cannot teach reading to 35 students simultaneously, so she must divide them into groups; homogeneous ability groups are easier to work with. Tracking (stratification) is thus necessary and justifiable, according to this view.

DOES THE SCHOOL MAKE A DIFFERENCE?

In 1988, the state of Arkansas, one of the poorest states in the nation, spent only $2,400 per pupil on public education; New Jersey spent $6,900 per pupil. The same variation appears on a smaller scale within states, as taxpayers in well-off areas produce higher tax revenues. Better-financed districts can afford better facilities and better teachers. The question is, How much difference does expenditure make? The answer appears to be "not much." The social class characteristics of students pretty much determine the average achievement at a school; knowing about libraries and

Most schools offer a variety of athletic, vocational, and hobby activities for their students. The idea is that strengthened friendship networks and extracurricular activities will provide incentives for better attendance and more attention to school. In fact, studies show that students who are involved in extracurricular activities are less likely to drop out. One of the reasons smaller schools are more effective is that there are more opportunities for participation in such activities. When there are only 150 kids in the senior class, nearly everybody can find a spot somewhere on a team or club.

laboratories does not add very much (Heyns 1986; Hallinan 1988). Nevertheless, three types of schools may have an effect on the quality of education: Catholic schools, integrated schools, and effective schools. Each has been the topic of substantial debate and research.

Are Catholic Schools Better? In the 1980s, a major controversy developed over the publication of a two-volume study that concluded that Catholic schools do a better job than public schools (Coleman, Hoffer, and Kilgore 1982; Coleman and Hoffer 1987). The reason Catholic school students do better is threefold:

- *Curriculum.* Catholic schools teach more basics, especially math.
- *Higher expectations.* They demand more homework, emphasize study habits, have higher expectations, and have better discipline.
- *Parental involvement.* Parents of Catholic school students attend more PTA meetings, are more active in school governance, and work more closely with their children's teachers.

There appears to be little doubt that Catholic schoolchildren do perform better. The question is whether this result can be reproduced in the public schools. Changing the curriculum is relatively easy, though by itself it may have little or even a detrimental effect (see the Issues in Social Policy section at the end of this chapter). The critical difference is probably parental involvement. Because sending one's children to Catholic school takes extra thought and extra money, only parents who care about their children's education send their children to Catholic schools. It is probably parental caring rather than Catholic education that produces the big difference.

Are Racially Integrated Schools Better? In 1966, a controversial but influential report concluded that black students learned substantially better in integrated schools and white students learned no worse (Coleman 1966). That study was part of the social science arsenal that was used to promote busing. During the ensuing decade, however, there has been little real progress in school desegregation. While some schools have become less racially segregated because of busing, other schools have become *more* segregated as a result of changing patterns of residential segregation.

Recent evidence continues to support the conclusion that students who attend schools with a large black majority learn less and drop out more. The problem is social class more than race: Mostly black schools include a disproportionate share of youngsters from disadvantaged family backgrounds. Although a good school might be able to absorb and help a small proportion of disadvantaged students, an entire student body of disadvantaged children (regardless of race) tends to overwhelm the school. Discipline and control become more important than teaching, and the good students suffer along with the bad.

The "Effective School." Despite the almost overwhelming odds that many inner-city schools face, some of them have excellent records. A recent body of research asks about the characteristics of these "effective schools." The answers appear to be that these schools have (Bryk 1988):

- A strong, required basic core
- Discipline and order
- Smaller size
- Committed teachers
- Positive climate.

The last two points are critical. Teaching math for 90 minutes a day and putting a police officer in the corridor will not achieve an effective school. A positive climate, where both teachers and students feel that discipline is fair and in their best interests, is essential. Punitive law-and-order reforms are not likely by themselves to create effective schools.

In the United States, we like to believe that our public elementary and secondary schools offer equal opportunity and give children from every social class a good start in life. In fact, as we have seen, the schools have swallowed a rat named "disadvantage" that they cannot digest, and it moves through the system relatively unchanged. The evidence on tracking suggests that the schools may even increase the degree of inequality that exists among students. What happens when we move to the college level, a level where school is voluntary and explicitly depends on aspirations and ability to pay tuition?

COLLEGE

WHO GOES AND WHERE?

Approximately one-third of all high school graduates between the ages of 18 and 24 are enrolled in colleges or universities. This means that two-thirds are not enrolled. Twenty percent of high school graduates ages 25–29 have graduated from college; this means that 80 percent have not. Thus, although you and many of the people you know have gone to college, you should recognize that you are in the minority. Who is this minority that goes to college?

The easiest answer is that these students are the ones who applied (Manski and Wise 1983). In the United States, there is a college placement available for everybody who graduated from high school. The chief requirement is not grades but aspirations and financial backing. Both, of course, are strongly related to social class. Empirical studies show that parents' socioeconomic status is the best predictor of whether a student will go to college (U.S. Department of Education 1985).

Community Colleges Versus Four-Year Schools. There were 11 million undergraduates in the United States in 1989. Over one-third of these students (36 percent) were enrolled in community colleges rather than in four-year colleges or universities (Astin 1989). These two-year schools have mixed purposes, and it is here that the old conflict between vocational and academic training is most visible today. Some two-year schools focus on postsecondary vocational training in business, medical technology, or skilled trades; others emphasize academic courses for transfer to a four-year school.

We tend to speak of "going to college" as if it were a homogenous experience. In fact, there is wide diversity in the extent to which colleges offer access to traditional collegiate life. This community college in Austin, Texas is obviously designed for the highly motivated. There is no beautiful campus, no football team, and no frills. It is not surprising that studies show that intelligence and achievement motivation are more important determinants of success at community colleges than four-year schools.

The vast majority of students who attend community colleges intend to transfer to a four-year school in order to complete their degrees. Studies show, however, that students who start their college careers at a two-year school are less likely to graduate than *comparable* students who start at a four-year school (Dougherty 1987). Freshman and sophomore dropout rates are higher in community colleges; at junior and senior levels, transfer students from community colleges are more likely to drop out than students who have begun their careers at four-year schools.

There are many reasons why this is true. Most important, as Table 14.1 shows, freshmen who start at community colleges are, on the average, less well prepared than those who go to four-year schools: They earned lower grades in high school, they have less academic self-confidence and lower aspirations, they get less financial help, and they are more often first-generation college students. There are also school factors to contend with. Community colleges rarely have dormitories, athletic events, or other means to integrate students into an academic community. Thus, student attachment to the college is lower.

Students who stick to it and finish two years at a community college face additional barriers when trying to transfer to a four-year school. The level of competition jumps rather suddenly, and most transfer students experience a significant drop in their grades. They also frequently face loss of some credit hours because of transfer problems. When these discouraging experiences are added to their continuing financial problems, it is not surprising that community college transfer students have higher dropout rates (Dougherty 1987).

The higher dropout rates from community colleges have made community colleges the center of a bitter debate. Conflict theorists argue that the community college is simply another level of the tracking process—a way of *seeming* to open up the opportunity for higher education to nonelites

■

TABLE 14.1

A COMPARISON OF FRESHMEN ATTENDING TWO-YEAR AND FOUR-YEAR COLLEGES, 1989

On the average, students who attend two-year colleges have weaker academic preparation and fewer family resources than students who go to four-year schools. Two-year schools give students who otherwise might be excluded a chance to go to college, but it is still an uphill battle.

	TWO-YEAR SCHOOLS	FOUR-YEAR SCHOOLS
ACADEMIC ASPIRATIONS		
Planning to get a bachelor's degree	82%	96%
Planning to get a graduate degree	41	66
ACADEMIC BACKGROUND		
An A average in high school	10	25
Believe themselves in the top 10 percent in academic ability	35	60
Father graduated from college	28	44
FINANCIAL BACKGROUND		
Receive financial help from parents	72	83
Work more than 15 hours a week	45	39
Median family income	$35,500	$42,800

SOURCE: Astin and Associates 1989.

without really having to share anything with them. The structural-functionalist view is that the two-year school "is perhaps the most effective democratizing agent in higher education" (cited in Dougherty 1987). There is some evidence for both points of view. On the functionalist side: (a) Intelligence has been shown to be a better predictor of success in two-year than in four-year schools: (b) two-year schools make college attendance possible for many people whose family responsibilities, geographic location, or economic circumstances preclude their going to a major uni-

■

One of the important changes taking place in American education today is that it is breaking out of the 5 to 21 age range. A growing proportion of all college students are "non-traditional"—over 25, parents, in the full-time labor force, and sometimes all of these simultaneously. Night classes at this community college in Charlotte, North Carolina attract a wide audience of adults who are seeking to increase their skills and supplement their credentials.

versity. Evidence about lower graduation rates suggests, however, that the state must put extra resources into two-year colleges so that they make it possible for students to *graduate* from college, not just attend. Such a change would include establishing better transfer programs, improving student integration into campus life, and raising student and teacher expectations.

Minority Enrollment.   The period of the 1970s saw higher minority enrollment in colleges and universities. Not only did civil rights activism encourage minority aspirations but expanded federal loan programs also made it more feasible to fulfill those aspirations. In the intervening years, high school graduates who were Hispanics or black females continued to increase their college participation (see Figure 14.3). This apparent increase in the equity of college enrollments masks two concerns. First since only 60 percent of Hispanic young people have graduated from high school, their overall rate of college participation is much lower than that for black or white Americans. A second cause for concern is the *falling* enrollment rate for black men. Their enrollment rates dropped from 30 to 25 percent in the last 18 years. This drop appears to be greatest for black men from low-income backgrounds: ("Black and Hispanic" 1990). Although some of the blame for the drop can be placed on reductions in federal college support programs for low-income students, the singling out of black men also reinforces the conclusion that they represent a particularly disadvantaged segment of the population.

EDUCATION, EARNINGS, AND OCCUPATION

For many people, the chief objective of a college education is the attainment of a good job and higher earnings. This objective has been and continues to be realistic. In 1987, the average college graduate, male or female, earned nearly 40 percent more *annually* than the average high school graduate.

FIGURE 14.3

PERCENTAGE OF HIGH SCHOOL GRADUATES AGES 18 TO 24 ENROLLED IN COLLEGE, BY RACE, ETHNICITY, AND SEX, 1970 AND 1988

Comparisons by sex, race, and ethnicity show increasing similarity in the likelihood that high school graduates from each category will attend college. A cause for concern is the declining enrollment rates for black males.

SOURCE: American Council on Education 1990. NA Data for Hispanics not available in 1970.

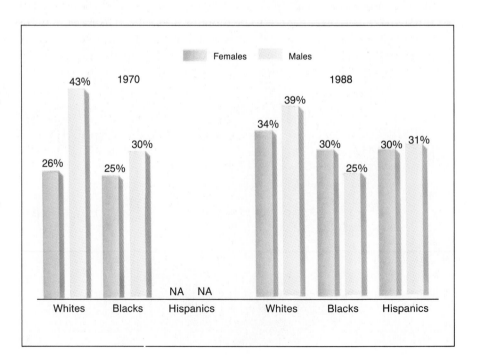

Some of this additional income is related to background characteristics rather than years in school—that is, people who complete college generally have higher high school test scores and higher-status parents. These factors would have raised their income even if they had not completed college. Nevertheless, college continues to pay a handsome profit.

Differences by Sex and Race.   At every educational level, white males' earnings far exceed those of other race/sex categories. Among full-time, full-year workers, black men have to have a college degree to earn as much as white men with a high school diploma. Women, black and white, have to achieve postgraduate college educations to earn as much as white male high school graduates (see Table 14.2). Although a college education does not erase these inequalities, generally blacks and women experience equal or better *proportional* return on educational investment compared to white males.

At the baccalaureate level, the proportional return on a college degree is about the same regardless of sex or race: College graduates earn between 36 and 42 percent more annually than do their counterparts who have only a high school diploma. At the postgraduate level, the highest proportional returns go to black men, who increase their annual earnings by an additional 35 percent if they complete at least one year of graduate education.

Outlook for the Future.   During the 1970s and early 1980s, new college graduates faced a tough labor market. The combination of the baby boom and increased college attendance meant that there were large numbers of college graduates looking for a relatively small number of entry-level positions. As a result, many graduates had to begin their careers in entry-level positions for which they were overqualified or that were outside their field of study.

In the early 1990s, the picture looks much brighter. Two factors are improving job prospects for today's college graduates: the growth in labor market demand for college graduates and the relatively small number in

■

TABLE 14.2
ECONOMIC RETRUNS OF ADDITIONAL EDUCATION, 1987

For all groups there is a substantial economic payoff for educational attainment after high school. Full-time full-year workers who completed college annually earned between 36 and 42 percent more than high school graduates. The impact of post graduate education on earnings is especially strong for black male workers.

	FEMALE		MALE	
	White	*Black*	*White*	*Black*
Median Total Money Income for Full-Time, Full-Year Workers 25 and over with:				
4 years of high school	$16,674	$15,582	$26,046	$18,920
4 years of college	23,749	21,140	35,701	26,550
5 + years of college	29,793	26,415	42,063	35,815
Percent Increase in Income for Going from:				
4 years of high school to 4 years of college	42%	36%	37%	40%
4 years of college to 5 + years of college	25	25	18%	35%

SOURCE: U.S. Bureau of the Census 1989f.

their birth cohorts. As a result, the financial benefits of a college degree have improved markedly (Griffith, Frase, and Ralph 1989). Some analysts estimate that new cohorts of college graduates (that's you!) can expect to raise the earnings differential between themselves and high school graduates to 70 percent (Lee and Bryk 1989).

WHAT'S THE BOTTOM LINE?
WHAT WILL COLLEGE DO FOR ME?

A major incentive for college attendance is the belief that it will pay off economically. The evidence clearly supports this belief. As Table 14.3 shows, people who graduate from college have better jobs, experience lower unemployment, and have higher incomes than those with less education. In this sense, your investment in a college education will pay off.

It can pay off in other ways too. It is a value judgment to say that a college education will make you a better person, but it is a value judgment that the majority of college graduates is willing to make. Survey after survey demonstrates that people feel very positively about their college education, believing that it has made them better and more tolerant people (Bowen 1977).

Whether it makes you a better person or not, a college education is likely to have a lasting effect on your knowledge and values. If you finish college, you will sit through 30 to 45 different courses. Even the least dedicated student is bound to learn something from these courses. In addition, students learn informally. Whether you go to college in your hometown or across the country, college will introduce you to a greater diversity of people than you're likely to have experienced before. This diversity will challenge your mind and broaden your horizons. As a result

■

TABLE 14.3

SOCIOECONOMIC CONSEQUENCES OF EDUCATION, 1988

Education pays off in terms of good jobs and good income. The differences shown in this table, however, are not all directly related to additional years of schooling; that is, people who graduated from college have, on the average, higher high school grades and more background advantages than those who graduated from high school only. These circumstances may have as much to do with their achievements as do their additional years of schooling.

EDUCATION	PERCENT WITH MANAGERIAL OR PROFESSIONAL OCCUPATION	PERCENT UNEMPLOYED	MEDIAN INCOME OF FULL-TIME FULL-YEAR WORKERS (MALE)
Less than 4 years of high school	6%	10%	$19,288
Exactly 4 years of high school	13	5	26,045
1–3 years of college	27	4	30,129
4 or more years of college	67	2	39,967

SOURCE: U.S. Bureau of the Census 1989a, 391, 394; U.S. Bureau of the Census 1989g, Table 11.

of formal and informal learning, college graduates are more knowledgeable about the world around them, more tolerant and less prejudiced, more active in public and community affairs, less traditional in their religious and gender-role beliefs, and more open to new ideas than those who don't have a college degree (Weil 1985; Funk and Willits 1987).

Higher education is an excellent investment, one that would be justified on the basis of the monetary returns alone. When one also considers the nonmonetary rewards—the contributions to intellectual and social growth—there is "no doubt that American higher education is well worth what it costs" (Bowen 1977, 448).

■

A CASE STUDY: THE JAPANESE MODEL

In the last decade, America's public school system has received a lot of bad press. Standardized scores for America's children are down compared to their own earlier scores, and they compare very unfavorably with those of children in the rest of the world. American employers and college professors complain that high school graduates lack basic skills. In addition to being accused of being too soft, the schools are also accused of being unfair. Before assessing the American educational system, let us put it in perspective by taking a look at an educational system that is sometimes held up as a model.

The Japanese educational system looks a lot like ours on the surface. Over 90 percent of children ages 15–17 are enrolled in high school, and substantial proportions go on to college. Nevertheless, the system differs from ours in three fundamental ways: more schooling, more explicit tracking, and a stronger link between school performance and jobs.

Although the U.S. and Japanese educational systems are superficially similar, from the first grade on, Japanese children have a very different experience in the schools. In the early grades, Japanese schools place less emphasis on academic basics and more emphasis on learning cooperation and positive attitudes. The uniforms that Japanese schoolchildren wear symbolize commitment to group identification and loyalty, values that apply in kindergarten and industry.

from ours in three fundamental ways: more schooling, more explicit tracking, and a stronger link between school performance and jobs.

More Schooling.   In Japan, the school year is 240 days long compared to 180 days in the United States. Since students spend so much more time in school, it is not surprising that they learn more. In the first and second grades Japanese students probably receive less academic instruction than our students; their primary task in these early grades is to learn appropriate attitudes about learning and cooperation. Once they start their academic curriculum in the third grade, however, they get a very heavy dose of the basics. Their homework demands are much heavier than those of American students.

More Explicit Tracking.   In Japan, public high schools are formally differentiated by purpose and status: There are top-notch college prepatory high schools, average college prepatory high schools, vocational schools, and general education schools. You cannot get into a top-notch university unless you go to a top-notch high school (Rosenbaum and Kariya 1989).

High school assignment is based on an examination taken at age 15. Your score on this examination affects which high school you go to, which will in turn determine which—if any—college you can go to, and ultimately what job you get. As a result of the overwhelming importance of this single test, Japanese students study very hard for it. Most parents who aspire to a college education for their children make major financial sacrifices to send their children to special "cramming" schools called jukos. These cramming schools may run until 10 at night several days a week. If you want to go to college, you have to decide early enough to study hard for your examination. You cannot decide at 18 that you really want to go to college after all.

Link Between Education and Jobs.   Unlike the American student, the Japanese student doesn't need to write up a résumé and start knocking on doors when he or she is ready to start working. At both the college and the vocational high school level, schools have contracts with employers (Rosenbaum and Kariya 1989). These agreements specify, for example, that Ido Vocational High School will send 45 students to Sony for work on its video recorder assembly line or that Ido Community College will send the company 10 computer technicians. This link between school and labor market covers the best jobs available: the jobs with big companies, better wages, more security, and higher benefits. School performance and teacher recommendations cast a long shadow over one's life. Again, there is relatively little forgiveness in the system. Unless you were well behaved and hardworking in school, you are likely to find yourself at a substantial disadvantage in the labor market.

■

THE U.S. SYSTEM: THEORETICAL VIEWS

Compared to Japan's, our educational system is less demanding, more flexible, and more forgiving. We try to keep students' options open as long as we can. Community colleges and other institutions welcome nontraditional students who decide at age 25 or 35 or 45 that they would like to go to college. The link between school and labor market is also much looser; students who cut up in school can become serious and get a good job. To many Americans, these traits appear to be an advantage of our system. They appeal to our desire to give everybody an equal chance and a second and even a third chance.

Does our system actually accomplish these goals? In the following section, we review structural-functional and conflict perspectives on American education. This format offers an opportunity to review both the accomplishments and the weaknesses of our educational system and to put them into a larger theoretical perspective.

THE STRUCTURAL-FUNCTIONAL PERSPECTIVE OF AMERICAN EDUCATION

A structural-functional analysis of education is concerned with the consequences of educational institutions for the maintenance of society. It points out both how education contributes to the maintenance of society and how educational systems can be forces for change and conflict.

The Functions of Education.   The educational system has been designed to meet multiple needs. Major manifest (intended) functions of education include cultural reproduction, social control, assimilation, training and development, selection and allocation, and promotion of change.

■ *Cultural Reproduction.* Schools transmit society's culture from one generation to the next by teaching the ideas, customs, and standards of the culture. We learn to read and write our language, we learn the pledge of allegiance, and we learn history. In this sense, education builds on the past and conserves traditions.

■ *Social Control.* Second only to the family, schools are responsible for socializing the young into patterns of conformity. By emphasizing a common culture and instilling habits of discipline and obedience, the schools are an important agent for encouraging conformity.

■ *Assimilation.* Schools function to assimilate persons from diverse backgrounds. By exposing students from all ethnic backgrounds, all regions of the country, and all social backgrounds to a common curriculum, they help create and maintain a common cultural base.

■ *Training and Development.* Schools teach specific skills—not only technical skills such as reading, writing, and arithmetic but also habits of cooperation, punctuality, and obedience.

■ *Selection and Allocation.* Schools are like gardeners; they sift, weed, sort, and cultivate their products, determining which students will be allowed to go on and which will not. Standards of achievement are used as criteria to channel students into different programs on the basis of their measured abilities. Ideally, an important function of the school system is to ensure the best use of the best minds. The public school system is a vital element of our commitment to equal opportunity.

■ *Promotion of Change.* Schools also act as change agents. Although we do not stop learning after we leave school, the transmission of new knowledge and technology is usually aimed at school children rather than at the adult population. In addition, the schools promote change by encouraging the development of critical and analytic skills and skepticism. Schools, particularly colleges and universities, are also expected to produce new knowledge.

Latent Functions and Dysfunctions.   In spite of its many positive outcomes, a system as large and all-encompassing as education is bound to have consequences that are either unintended or actually negative. They include generation gaps, custodial care, youth cultures, rationalization of inequality, and perpetuation of inequality.

- *Generation Gap.* As schools impart new knowledge, they may drive a wedge between generations. Courses in sociology, English, history, and even biology expose students to ideas different from those of their parents. What students learn in school about evolution, cultural relativity, or the merit of socialism may contradict values held by their parents or their religion.
- *Custodial Care.* Compulsory education has transformed schools into settings where children are cooped up seven to eight hours a day, five days a week, for nine months of the year (Bowles 1972). Young people are kept off the streets, out of the labor force, and, presumably, out of trouble in small groups dispersed throughout communities in special buildings designed for close supervision. This enables their elders to command higher wages in the labor market and relieves their parents of the responsibility of supervising them.
- *Youth Culture.* By isolating young people from the larger society and confining them to the company of others their own age, educational institutions have contributed to the development of a unique youth culture. This youth culture is fractured into half a dozen subcultures, some of which stress athletics, some popularity, some grades, and some partying. Youth culture does not arise spontaneously; to a very significant extent it is fostered and created by the school structure: Grades, tracking, formal athletic programs, sponsored social activities—all help to divide the student body into the same types of cliques from one generation to the next.
- *Rationalization of Inequality.* One of the chief consequences of life in the schools is that young people learn to expect unequal rewards on the basis of differential achievement. Schools prepare young people for inequality. Some consider this preparation undesirable in that it leads young people to believe that all inequality is earned, that it is a fair response to unequal abilities.
- *Perpetuation of Inequality.* As noted in earlier sections of this chapter, abundant evidence exists that ascriptive characteristics of students (race, sex, and social class) have an impact on how students are treated in school. The evidence supports the conclusion that schools perpetuate inequality and function to maintain and reinforce the existing social class hierarchy. From the functionalist point of view, this is a latent dysfunction of the schools—an unfortunate and unintended consequence that should be rectified.

A structural-functional analysis begins with the premise that any ongoing institution of society must be contributing to the maintenance of society. The enumeration of the functions of education clarifies what some of these contributions are. Although there are unanticipated side effects, both positive and negative, functionalists tend to concentrate on how education benefits society and individuals.

THE CONFLICT PERSPECTIVE ON AMERICAN EDUCATION

Conflict theories of education look much like structural-functional theories, except in their value judgments on the final product. Conflict theorists agree that education reproduces culture, socializes young people into patterns of conformity, sifts and sorts, and rationalizes inequality. Since conflict theorists see the social structure as a system of inequality designed to benefit the rich at the expense of the rest of us, however, naturally they see any institution that reproduces this culture in a negative light. Three of the major conflict arguments are summarized here.

The **hidden curriculum** of schools socializes young people into obedience and conformity.

Education as a Capitalist Tool. Some conflict theorists argue that mass education developed because it benefited the interests of the capitalist class. Capitalists demanded educated workers not only because literacy made workers more effective but also because they had been taught obedience, punctuality, and loyalty to the economic and political system (Bowles and Gintis 1976). The schools, they argue, developed to meet this demand.

To support this argument, theorists point to the schools' **hidden curriculum,** which socializes young people into obedience and conformity. This curriculum—learning to wait your turn, follow the rules, be punctual, and show respect—prepares young people for life in the industrial working class (Dale 1977).

There is a great deal of controversy over this argument. Certainly capitalists and industry have tried to affect the content of schooling in ways

In all societies, education is an important means to reproduce culture. Children not only learn neutral skills such as reading and writing, they also learn about their heritage. In America, this means that we learn about George Washington and the American Revolution; in China, it means learning about Mao Zedong and the Communist Revolution. In all societies, education tends to be a conservative force that teaches repect for the past.

supportive of their interests. Most recently this has taken the form of demanding more basic skills—better reading, writing, and arithmetic skills—rather than more obedience. Nevertheless, the school system does prepare young people to accept inequality and hierarchy, and this does make it easier for their employers to control them.

Credentialism.   One supposed outcome of free public education is that merit will triumph over origins, that hard work and ability will be allowed to rise to the top. Conflict theorists, however, argue that the shift to educational credentials as the mechanism for allocating high-status positions has had little impact on equalizing economic opportunity. Instead, a subtle shift has taken place. Instead of inquiring who your parents are, the prospective employer asks what kind of education you have and where you got it. Because these educational credentials are highly correlated with social class background, they serve to keep undesirables out. Conflict theorists argue that educational credentials are mere window dressing; apparently based on merit and achievement, credentials are often a surrogate for social class background. The use of educational credentials to measure social origins and social status is called **credentialism.**

> **Credentialism** is the use of educational credentials to measure social origins and social status.

As the level of education in society increases, educational requirements also must rise to maintain the status quo. This credential inflation can be seen in nursing, in public school teaching, and in government. Jobs that used to require a high school diploma now require a bachelor's degree; jobs that used to require a bachelor's degree now require a master's degree. Because the elite increases its pursuit of higher degrees as quickly as the lower class increases its pursuit of a high school diploma, no real change

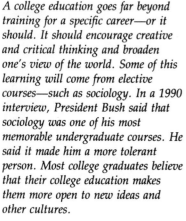

A college education goes far beyond training for a specific career—or it should. It should encourage creative and critical thinking and broaden one's view of the world. Some of this learning will come from elective courses—such as sociology. In a 1990 interview, President Bush said that sociology was one of his most memorable undergraduate courses. He said it made him a more tolerant person. Most college graduates believe that their college education makes them more open to new ideas and other cultures.

occurs. Credentialism, it is argued, is a way of manipulating the educational system for the benefit of the well-off (Collins 1979).

Reproduction of Inequality. Both the "capitalist tool" and "credentialist" arguments imply that the elite is scheming to keep down the masses. Conflict theory, however, has a much broader application that does not require the assumption of a manipulative elite. The heart of the conflict perspective of education—as of the conflict perspective on any institution—is that those who benefit from the system seek to perpetuate it.

The people who benefit from today's educational system are the middle- and upper-middle-class parents whose children get good public educations that allow them access to colleges and universities and ultimately to good jobs. These parents are not scheming to put down the masses, but they are trying to protect their children and their schools. As a result, middle-class parents oppose any redistricting plans that would enlarge the proportion of disadvantaged children in their schools. They oppose untracking plans that would remove their high-track children's current advantage. More than three quarters of Americans say they are willing to raise their taxes in order to provide better schools, more Head Start programs, and reduce disadvantage (Gallup Report 1989d). None of them, however, wants to reduce their own advantage.

CONCLUSION

Most contemporary sociological analyses of schooling focus on the role of the school in reproducing social class advantage and disadvantage. These analyses illuminate the ways that a lower social class background puts children at a disadvantage that is magnified rather than eliminated by school processes.

Schools are a vitally important institution. In 1988, the U.S. spent $308 *billion* on education; over 60 million children and young adults were enrolled; over 3 million people are employed by the schools. Perhaps more important, the schools play a vital role in determining the character of future generations. They provide new citizens, new workers, new parents.

For all of these reasons, we must care about how well the schools are doing their job. From many points of view, the answer appears to be "poorly." In the concluding section of this chapter, we address a critical issue in social policy: how to improve quality without sacrificing our commitment to equity.

Balancing Equity and Excellence

In 1983, the 18-member National Commission on Excellence in Education issued a report that was extremely critical of U.S. education. The report indicated that 13 percent of all 17-year-olds and as much as 40 percent of minority youths are functionally illiterate. In a comparison of U.S. students with students from 21 other nations, Americans scored the worst on seven out of 19 achievement tests and never came in either first or second. The commission argued that the problem was caused not by factors beyond our control but simply by lack of insight and will. The solutions recommended included (1) a more demanding sequence of basic courses, (2) longer school days and school years, and (3) higher standards for school achievement.

Generally, the call for excellence in education has been well received. By 1984, 17 states had instituted competency testing for high school graduation and seven more were in the process of implementing it. Increasingly, however, policymakers are facing the dilemma posed by the potentially conflicting demands of equity and excellence (Alexander, Natriello, and Pallas 1985).

WHEN EXCELLENCE BACKFIRES

Will more basics, more time, and higher standards improve the quality of education? The answer is, "on the average, yes."

There are, however, two latent dysfunctions of the excellent campaigns: increased labeling and increased high school dropouts. As with almost everything else in the school system, the greatest benefits of the excellence campaigns are likely to go to those who already are achieving. Why is this so? An important reason is that a standard core curriculum increases labeling. Increased standardization of courses makes it easier to compare individuals and hence makes it easier for the student and others to come up with an overall ranking of the individual's ability. This labeling has particu-

larly negative consequences for the low-achieving student. In a sense, the back-to-basics movement denies that there are a variety of kinds of useful abilities for adults to have in our society and singles out conventional academic ability as the only relevant one.

The second problem with the excellence campaign is their potential for increasing the dropout problems. Despite the sharp expansion in education in the last decades, a substantial minority of the population has not graduated from high school. In 1988, fully 14 percent of all young adults aged 25–29 had not graduated from high school; this figure was 21 percent among blacks and 41 percent among Hispanic young adults (U.S. Bureau of the Census 1989c).

These dropouts pose a potentially major social and economic problem. One study summarized the issues:

> Dropping out of high school is associated with an array of individual and social costs. For the individual, failure to complete high school is associated with limited occupational and economic prospects, disenfranchisement from society and its institutions, and substantial loss of personal income over his or her lifetime. For society, premature school-leaving is associated with increased expenditures for government assistance to individuals and families, higher rates of crime, and maintenance of costly programs for purposes such as employment and training. (Steinberg, Blinde, and Chan 1984, 113)

For all of these reasons, the dropout problem is a social policy issue. It is an issue that the reports on excellence ignore altogether. An important question for policymakers is whether steps made to increase excellence—higher standards, more basics, longer school years or school days—will increase the dropout problem. If imposition of higher standards increases the SAT scores of those students who remain but doubles the dropout rate, especially among minority or disadvantaged

ISSUES IN SOCIAL POLICY continued

students, will we have gained? Or, as one recent report claims, will this be a "blueprint for failure" (McDill, Natriello, and Pallas 1986, 139)?

THE ISSUE

The implementation of higher standards, especially the implementation of standard competency tests for graduation or promotion, is bound to have disproportionate effects on disadvantaged students. If these recommendations are directly implemented, they will tighten rather than loosen the strong chain of interconnected problems that reproduces poverty and disadvantage (McDill, Nutriello, and Pallas 1986).

The issue then becomes how to increase excellence without sacrificing equity—how to increase the scores and achievement of all of our students without losing half along the way.

Recent research suggests several strategies. First, raise teacher expectations. This inexpensive mechanism has been found to raise attendance and performance levels of both good and poor students. This change should especially benefit poor students, many of whose teachers have such low expectations for them that they give them a passing grade only for attendance or for not causing trouble. Second, reduce the size of schools. In smaller schools, teachers have greater ability to influence students and, perhaps as important, students have greater ability to influence their schools. They have more opportunities for extracurricular activities that will enhance their attachment to school. Third, build some flexibility into the system so that youth who work, marry, or bear children can participate.

The educational institution is a complex one with many goals and widely varying constituencies. Without some attention to this variability, even the most laudable plans are likely to go awry. Careful forethought is necessary if the latent dysfunctions are not to overwhelm the possible good.

"If an unfriendly foreign power had attempted to impose on America the mediocre educational performance that exists today, we might well have viewed it as an act of war."

In 1983, an American commission on education concluded that American education was in terrible shape. We are, they argued, being swept over by a "tide of mediocrity." As a result, many educators are pressing for tougher educational standards and a return to basics. The consequences of this trend for an already high dropout rate are a cause of concern.

SUMMARY

1. During the 19th century, a consensus developed that public education was so desirable that it should be compulsory. Contributing factors were parental demand, labor demand, and demands for social control.

2. Elementary education was universal by 1900, but high school education didn't become commonplace until the 1930s. College education expanded dramatically after World War II. African Americans, Hispanics, and Native Americans have not been full participants in the expansion of education.

3. The sociology of education is largely concerned with the link between education and stratification.

4. Social class affects preparation for school, attitudes toward school, and thus school performance and deportment. Students from lower-class backgrounds are more likely to end up tracked into low-ability groups; this process builds on previous disadvantage so that disadvantage snowballs.

5. Compared to social class effects, school effects are relatively weak. Greater Catholic school success is probably due to more caring parents rather than to any characteristics of the schools. Schools with a majority of students from disadvantaged backgrounds (regardless of racial composition) retard student achievement. Effective schools are characterized by a positive attitude, not by get-tough policies.

6. About one-third of U.S. high school graduates between 18 and 24 are enrolled in college. Nearly half of these are enrolled in two-year schools. Two-year schools give students a chance to attend college, but still leave many obstacles in the students' way. Minority enrollments are rising, with the notable exception of African American men.

7. College pays off handsomely in terms of more income, more job security, and better jobs. New cohorts of college graduates should do even better than previous cohorts.

8. Japanese education differs from American in three ways: more schooling, more explicit tracking, and a stronger link between school performance and jobs.

9. Structural-functional theories of education argue that education performs many functions (cultural reproduction, social control, teaching of specific skills, selection of students for future adult roles, and promotion of change); failure to equalize opportunity for the disadvantaged is a latent dysfunction.

10. Conflict theory suggests that education helps maintain inequality in three ways: the hidden curriculum, credentialism, and the reproduction of inequality. Most contemporary analyses of education focus on the role of education in reproducing advantage and disadvantage.

11. Attempts to improve the quality of America's schools by stiffening requirements may backfire if they simultaneously increase the already high (14 percent) dropout rate. Three strategies that might raise achievement levels without encouraging dropping out among disadvantaged students are to raise teacher expectations, to reduce school size, and to maintain flexible curriculums and schedules for youths who marry, work, or bear children.

SUGGESTED READINGS

Coleman, James, and Hoffer, Thomas. 1987. Public and Private High Schools: The Impact of Communities. New York: Basic Books. The latest "Coleman report," again igniting a major public policy debate. Coleman and Hoffer argue that Catholic schools do it better.

Eysenck, H. J., and Kamin, Leon. 1981. The Intelligence Controversy. New York: Wiley. A short but readable book in which two leading experts in the field of intelligence testing vigorously debate the issue of heredity versus environment in intelligence through attack and counterattack, addressing such topics as the validity of IQ tests, the relationship between race and intelligence, and how intelligence is formed throughout childhood.

Oakes, Jeannie. 1985. Keeping Track: How Schools Structure Inequality. New Haven: Yale University Press.

This critical study of the tracking process in the schools concludes that tracking seriously reduces the schools' ability to provide equal education and social opportunities to disadvantaged youngsters.

Parelius, Robert, and Parelius, Ann. 1987. The Sociology of Education. (2nd ed.) Englewood Cliffs, N.J.: Prentice-Hall. A comprehensive text that covers some of the same issues included in this chapter, plus more on professionalization and life in the schools.

San Miguel, Guadalupe. 1987. Let Them All Take Heed. Austin: University of Texas Press. An impassioned study of the processes by which Hispanic students were kept out of education for a century after the U.S. annexed Texas.

15

"Staten Island Ferry Summer of 1986" by James Pile

PROLOGUE

Have you ever . . .

wondered what would happen if they held an election and nobody came? Voters in the United States are notoriously apathetic. Compared to other democracies, our citizens don't appear to care very much. Our apathy makes a startling contrast against the two thirds turnout in Peru's recent election—in the face of threats by the Shining Path guerrillas that they would cut off the right hand of anybody seen voting!

It is possible that you do vote. You may even have donated to a political cause, appeared in a demonstration, or written to your Congressional representative. The odds aren't good though. Only about one third of people under 25 voted in the last presidential election.

Why are Americans so apathetic? There are two reasons. They don't think that their vote counts—that anybody cares what they think. Second, they don't see much difference between the candidates or the parties. Who cares who wins?

In this chapter we will examine the basis for these opinions. We will identify major political actors and ask who makes the decisions. We will also look at rates of individual participation and see whether participation makes a difference. In the course of the chapter we may confirm some of your reasons for not voting, but we also provide some ideas that may increase your ability to affect political decisions.

OUTLINE

POWER AND POLITICAL INSTITUTIONS

POWER

Jeff wants to watch "The Cosby Show" while John wants to watch "Return of the Vampire Bats"; fundamentalists want prayer in the schools and the American Civil Liberties Union wants it out; state employees want higher salaries and the citizens want lower taxes. Who decides?

Whether the decision maker is Mom or the Supreme Court, decision makers who are able to make and enforce decisions have power. Formally, **power** is the ability to direct others' behavior, even against their wishes. To the extent that Mom's decision determines what Jeff and John do, she has power; if the Supreme Court's decision affects prayer in the school, then it has power. As these examples illustrate, power occurs in all kinds of social groups, from families to societies.

Although both mothers and courts have power, there are obvious differences in the basis of their power, the breadth of their jurisdiction, and the means they have to compel obedience. The social structure most centrally involved with the exercise of power is the state, and that is the focus of this chapter. Before we begin, however, we give a broad overview of two kinds of power, coercion and authority, as well as a closely related phenomenon—influence.

Coercion.   The exercise of power through force or the threat of force is **coercion.** The threat may be of physical, financial, or social injury. The key is that we do as we have been told only because we are afraid not to. We may be afraid that we will be injured, but we may also be afraid of a fine or of rejection.

Power through coercion may or may not be legitimated by social norms and values. If the IRS sends you a letter saying that they will throw you in jail if you don't pay up, you generally accept this as legitimate; the activities of the mugger who takes the same amount of money are not legitimate. Similarly, although it has been generally acceptable to threaten your children ("Clean your room or you cannot go out") and even to spank them, it is considered unacceptable to threaten your spouse.

Authority.   Threats are sometimes quite effective means of making people follow your orders. They tend to create conflict and animosity, however, and it would be much easier if people would just agree that they were supposed to do whatever it was you told them. This is not as rare as you might suppose. This very commonplace kind of power is called **authority** and refers to power that is supported by norms and values that legitimate its use. When you have authority, your subordinates agree that, in this matter at least, you have the right to make decisions and they have a duty to obey.

In a classic analysis of power, Weber distinguished three bases on which this agreement is likely to rest: tradition, extraordinary personal qualities (charisma), and legal rules.

Power is the ability to direct others' behavior, even against their wishes.

Coercion is the exercise of power through force or the threat of force.

Authority is power supported by norms and values that legitimate its use.

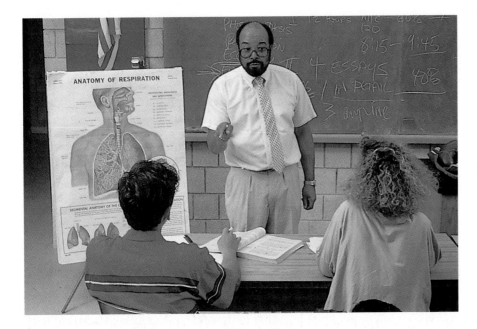

Power is an important part of all institutions and most social relationships. Teachers have power over their students, parents have power over their children, and coaches have power over their players. Teacher/student power inequalities are built into institutionalized statuses and supported by widely shared norms. In most cases, students agree that teachers have the right to set the syllabus and the course requirements. In addition to this institutionalized authority, many good teachers also influence their students outside of the classroom.

TRADITIONAL AUTHORITY. A right to make decisions that is based on the sanctity of time-honored routines is **traditional authority** (Weber [1910]/ 1970e, 296). Monarchies and patriarchies are classic examples of this type of authority. For example, only 30 years ago, the majority of women and men in our society believed that husbands ought to make all the major decisions in the family; husbands had authority. Today, most of that authority has disappeared. Traditional authority, according to Weber, is not based on reason; it is based on a reverence for the past.

CHARISMATIC AUTHORITY. When individuals are given the right to make decisions because of perceived extraordinary personal characteristics, this is **charismatic authority** (Weber [1910]/1970e, 295). These characteristics (often an assumed direct link to God) put the bearer of charisma on a different level from subordinates. Gandhi's authority was of this form. He held neither political office nor hereditary position, yet he was able to mold national policy in India. On a much smaller scale, one of John Humphrey Noyes's strongest assets in leading the Oneida community (see Chapter 13) was his personal attractiveness to both women and men.

Charismatic authority may be very powerful, gaining followers' loyalty as well as obedience. By nature, however, it is an unstable form of power; it resides in an individual and is therefore mortal. If efforts are made to pass on charisma—if, for example, it is argued that charisma is a property of the son as well as the father—then charismatic authority evolves into traditional authority.

RATIONAL-LEGAL AUTHORITY. When decision-making rights are allocated on the basis of rationally established rules, we speak of **rational-legal authority.** This ranges all the way from a decision to take turns to a decision to adopt a constitution. An essential element of rational-legal authority is

Traditional authority is the right to make decisions for others that is based on the sanctity of time-honored routines.

Charismatic authority is the right to make decisions that is based on perceived extraordinary personal characteristics.

Rational-legal authority is the right to make decisions that is based on rationally established rules.

that it is impersonal. You do not need to like or admire or even agree with the person in authority; you simply follow the rules.

Rational-legal authority is the kind on which our government is based. When we want to know whether the president or the Congress has a right to make certain decisions, we simply check our rule book: the Constitution. As long as they follow the rules, most of us agree that they have the right to make decisions and we have a duty to obey.

SUMMARY.   Analytically, we can make clear distinctions among these three types of authority. In practice, the successful exercise of authority usually combines two or more (Wrong 1979). An elected official who adds charisma to the rational-legal authority stipulated by the law will have more power; the successful charismatic leader will soon establish a bureaucratic system of rational-legal authority to help manage and direct followers.

All types of authority, however, rest on the agreement of subordinates that someone has the right to make a decision about them and that they have a duty to obey it. This does not mean that the decision will always be obeyed or even that each and every subordinate will agree that the distribution of power is legitimate. Rather, it means that society's norms and values legitimate the inequality in power. For example, if a parent tells her teenagers to be in at midnight, they may come in later. They may even argue that she has no right to run their lives. Nevertheless, most people, including children, would agree that the parent does have the right—even the obligation—to supervise her children.

Because authority is supported by shared norms and values, it can usually be exercised without conflict. Ultimately, however, authority rests on the ability to back up commands with coercion. Parents may back up their authority over teenagers with threats to kick them out of the house or take the car away. Churches back up their authority by threats to excommunicate. Teachers back up their authority with threats to flunk, suspend, or expel students. Employers can fire or demote workers. Thus, authority rests on a legitimation of coercion (Wrong 1979).

Influence.   A concept closely related to power but separate from it is **influence.** The wielder of influence has no right to make the decision and no ways to compel obedience; instead the person must rely on persuasion and personal appeals. Influence occurs when you try to persuade people to change their opinion, party, or creed (or when you try to sell them a vacuum cleaner).

Influence is the ability to affect others' decisions through persuasion and personal appeals.

Influence is not institutionalized; it rests on an individual appeal based on personal or ideological grounds rather than on social structure. It is typically the strategy of groups that are structurally powerless. People without the right to order an action may be reduced to: "Won't you do it for little old me?" Even people who have a great deal of power must often use influence if they want to affect actions outside the scope of their authority. The president of the United States, for example, has no authority to compel Congress to support his legislative proposals. To get congressional approval, he must try to exercise influence. He calls individual senators on the telephone, invites them to dinner, and generally courts their favor, using personal appeals and persuasive arguments to move them to his position.

CONCEPT SUMMARY
Power

CONCEPT	DEFINITION	EXAMPLE FROM FAMILY
Power	Ability to get others to act as one wishes in spite of their resistance; includes coercion and authority	"I know you don't want to mow the lawn, but you have to do it anyway."
Coercion	Exercise of power through force or threat of force	"Do it or else . . ."
Authority	Power supported by norms and values	"It is your duty to mow the lawn."
Traditional authority	Authority based on sanctity of time-honored routines	"I'm your father, and I told you to mow the lawn."
Charismatic authority	Authority based on extraordinary personal characteristics of leader	"I know you've been wondering how you might serve me, . . ." (unlikely)
Rational-legal authority	Authority based on submission to a set of rationally established rules	"It is your turn to mow the lawn; I did it last week."
Influence	Not power but ability to persuade others to change their decisions	"I don't feel very well today; would you help me mow the lawn?"

As this example suggests, influence and power often exist side by side. For example, many parents first try to influence their children to do what they want and use authority and then coercion as last resorts. In bureaucracies, there are patterns of influence as well as authority. Thus, who eats lunch with whom may be more important in determining decision making than are the formal rules of authority.

POLITICAL INSTITUTIONS

Power inequalities are built into almost all social institutions. In institutions as varied as the school and the family, roles associated with status pairs such as student/teacher and parent/child specify unequal power relationships as the normal and desirable standard.

Political institutions are institutions concerned with the social structure of power; the most prominent political institution is the state.

In a very general sense, **political institutions** are all those institutions concerned with the social structure of power. This general definition includes many of the institutions of society. The family, the workplace, the school, and even the church or synagogue have structured social inequality in decision making. The most prominent political institution, however, is the state.

THE STATE

THE STATE AS THE DOMINANT POLITICAL INSTITUTION

The **state** is the social structure that successfully claims a monopoly on the legitimate use of coercion and physical force within a territory.

The **state** is the social structure that successfully claims a monopoly on the legitimate use of coercion and physical force within a territory. It is usually distinguished from other political institutions by two characteristics: (1) Its jurisdiction for legitimate decision making is broader than that of other institutions, and (2) it controls the use of coercion in society.

Jurisdiction.   Whereas the other political institutions of society have rather narrow jurisdictions (over church members or over family members, for example), the state exercises power over the society as a whole.

Generally states have been considered to be responsible for gathering resources (taxes, draftees, and so on) to meet collective goals, arbitrating relationships among the parts of society, and maintaining relationships with other societies (Williams 1970). As societies have become larger and more complex, the state's responsibilities have grown. A recent poll (see Figure 15.1) indicates that the majority of Americans think the government is also responsible for such things as taking care of the elderly and keeping prices under control.

The dominant political institution is the state. Although fathers have power and biology teachers have power, only the state can legitimately arm its authority figures with M-16s. Coercion and threats of coercion are important weapons used by the state in backing up its authority. Although most of us pay our taxes and obey the laws without any direct threat, we are all aware of the state's ability to fine or imprison should we stray from the rules.

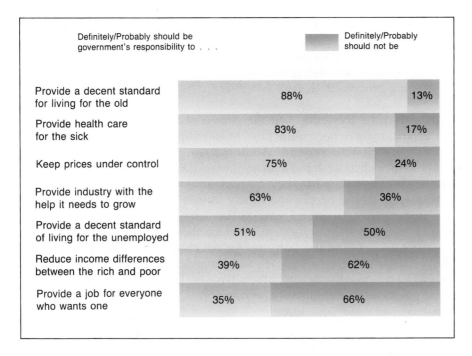

Definitely/Probably should be
government's responsibility to . . .

Definitely/Probably
should not be

Provide a decent standard for living for the old	88%	13%
Provide health care for the sick	83%	17%
Keep prices under control	75%	24%
Provide industry with the help it needs to grow	63%	36%
Provide a decent standard of living for the unemployed	51%	50%
Reduce income differences between the rich and poor	39%	62%
Provide a job for everyone who wants one	35%	66%

FIGURE 15.1

Question: On the whole, do you think it should or should not be the government's responsibility to . . .

SOURCE: Survey by National Opinion Research Center, General Social Survey, February–April, 1985.

Coercion.   The state claims a monopoly on the legitimate use of coercion. To the extent that other institutions use coercion (for example, the family or the school), they do so with the approval of the state. In recent years, the state has withdrawn approval of physical coercion between husband and wife, has sharply restricted the amount of physical punishment that is legitimate for parents to administer to children, and has generally declared physical punishment illegitimate within the school system. As a result, the state is increasingly unique as a legitimate user of coercion.

The state uses three primary types of coercion. First, the state uses its political power to claim a monopoly on the legitimate use of physical force. It is empowered to imprison people and even impose the death penalty. This claim to a monopoly on legitimate physical coercion has been strengthened in recent years by the declining legitimacy of coercion in other institutions, such as the home and the school. Second, the state uses taxation, a form of legitimated confiscation. Finally, the state is the only unit in society that can legally maintain an armed force and that is empowered to deal with foreign powers.

DEMOCRATIC VERSUS AUTHORITARIAN SYSTEMS

A variety of social structures can be devised to fulfill the functions of the state. Here we review the two basic political forms: democracy and authoritarian systems.

Democracy.   There are several forms of **democracy,** many of them rather different from that of the United States. All democracies, however, share two characteristics: There are regular, constitutional procedures for changing leaders, and these leadership changes reflect the will of the majority.

In a democracy, there exist two basic groups: the group in power and one or more legal opposition groups that are trying to get into power. The

Democracy is a political system that provides regular, constitutional opportunities for a change in leadership according to the will of the majority.

rules of the game call for sportsmanship on both sides. The losers have to accept their loss and wait until the next constitutional opportunity to try again, and the winners have to refrain from eliminating or punishing the losers. Finally, there has to be public participation in choosing among the competing groups.

Authoritarian Systems. In the course of human history, democratic governments have been quite rare. Most people in most times have lived under **authoritarian systems.** Authoritarian governments go by a lot of other names: dictatorships, military juntas, despotisms, monarchies, theocracies, and so on. What they have in common is that the leadership is not selected by the people and legally cannot be changed by them.

Authoritarian structures vary in the extent to which they attempt to control people's lives, the extent to which they use terror and coercion to maintain power, and the purposes for which they exercise control. Some authoritarian governments, such as monarchies and theocracies, govern through traditional authority; others have no legitimate authority and rest their power almost exclusively on coercion.

> **Authoritarian systems** are political systems in which the leadership is not selected by the people and legally cannot be changed by them.

In the Spring of 1990, Violetta Chamorro succeeded Daniel Ortega as a democratically elected president of Nicaragua. The triumph of democracy may be more apparent than real, however. Within ten weeks of her inauguration, virtual civil war was once again raging in the streets of Managua. Many nations inaugurate democratic governments; many fewer are able to sustain them. The impoverished and war-torn Central American nation is not a likely candidate for successful democracy.

CONDITIONS FOR DEMOCRACY

Whether a nation has a democratic or an authoritarian government is not simply a matter of cultural values. Instead, research suggests that three conditions are necessary for democracy to flourish: low inequality in income, competing interest groups, and an absence of fundamental cleavages. (The Focus section in this chapter asks whether these conditions can be met in the Soviet Union.)

Low Inequality in Income. No observer could fail to notice that contemporary democracy is found almost exclusively in the wealthier nations of the world. Careful study, however, suggests that it is not wealth by itself that predicts successful democracy but income equality. Muller (1988) looked at 55 nations' political history during the 20th century. He concluded that all kinds of countries *started* a democratic system in the 20th century but that the only ones that survived as democracies were those that had relatively low levels of income inequality. This explains why democracies in Latin America and Africa tend to be so fragile and so soon superseded by military governments and dictatorships.

The reasons that relative income equality is necessary to sustain democracy are complex. Where inequality is low and differences between social classes are relatively small, citizens are likely to feel that they can improve their lot by working within the system. Where there is a gulf between rich and poor, however, the poor are more likely to believe that drastic measures are necessary: They are likely to reject the small incremental changes characteristic of democracy in favor of revolution.

Competing Interest Groups. Democracy is a mechanism for arbitrating among competing groups. It can flourish only in a society in which there are many competing groups, each comprising less than a majority (Williams 1970, 271). The fracturing of the population into competing groups has two

FOCUS ON ANOTHER CULTURE

Can the Soviet Union Be Democratic?

Russia has had an authoritarian political system for 1,000 years. Before the Communist party took power early in this century, Russia was a monarchy headed by a Czar. By 1990, however, the Soviet Union was flirting with the idea of democracy. Across Eastern Europe, dictators were being deposed and democracy was declared. In the Soviet Union itself, Mikhail Gorbachev was steering the Communist party toward a less authoritarian position, and the people were demanding democracy.

Does the USSR Meet Democratic Prerequisites?

The question is whether the Soviet Union meets the prerequisites for democracy: relatively low income inequality, competing interest groups, and an absence of fundamental cleavages. The latter prerequisite may be an insuperable barrier.

The Soviet Union is composed of 15 republics, many of which were annexed by force rather than choice. Not only do many of these republics resent the Russians but some are strongly opposed to other republics and ethnic groups within the Soviet Union. The violent ethnic strife between the Azerbaijanis and the Armenians is but one example. The total lack of trust between some pairs of republics and between many republics and the Soviet government means that democracy may be impossible. If given a vote, many Republics would withdraw from the Soviet Union altogether. In fact, the Baltic Republics—Latvia, Lithuania, and Estonia—are trying to do so

even before they have been granted a vote. It does not seem likely that the Soviet Union can meet the criterion of an absence of fundamental cleavages. In fact, it seems very unlikely that the Soviet Union can sustain itself as a nation if it moves to a democratic government.

The stirrings of democracy signalled the crumbling of the Soviet empire. In 1990 the Soviet republic of Lithuania unilaterally declared itself an independent nation; more republics are likely to follow.

An Additional Barrier . . . Patience

There is an additional barrier to democratic government: a total absence of democratic heritage. From

the czars to the party chiefs, Russians have been ruled by authoritarian leaders. They have never known the discipline of self-governance (Kennan 1989). Like many oppressed peoples, they are likely to expect that democracy would mean that the people have "won" over the elite. In fact, of course, a democracy contains winning and losing coalitions, winning and losing interest groups.

Unless people have the patience and commitment to tolerate losing, democracy cannot be sustained. This tolerance is sometimes hard to come by even in a stable and wealthy society such as our own. In a society that has been "economically, socially, and spiritually damaged by 50 years of terror, corruption, and stagnation" (Kennan 1989), tolerance is very likely to be in such short supply that democracy is impossible. People are likely to want results *now;* they are very likely to put results ahead of democracy. If a military leader or party chief offers faster results than the ballot box, an impatient public may prefer results. This attitude is already apparent. In approving extraordinary powers for President Gorbachev, one delegate said, "We are tired of social tension. . . . We need a person who can have real power . . . the quicker the better" ("Soviets" 1990).

These problems of course, are not unique to the Soviet Union. The Philippines, Nicaragua, and many other nations experimenting with democracy today face very similar dilemmas. In all these cases, democracy may be a very fragile institution.

vital consequences for democracy. First, it means that no single group can win a majority of the votes without negotiating and compromising with other groups to build a coalition. Second, it means that since each group is a minority group, effective safeguards for minority political groups are in the interest of everybody. Both of these characteristics help support the rules of good sportsmanship that are essential to a democracy.

Studies of democratic stability suggest that the behavior of the "out" groups is critical to sustaining democracy (Weil 1989). If the out groups are divided or ineffective, they will not be perceived as offering a realistic opportunity for winning elections, and the public will become impatient and disillusioned with the democratic process.

Absence of Fundamental Cleavages.   Although competing interest groups are vital for sustaining democracy, it is equally vital that these interest groups have basically compatible values. When groups emerge that are not merely competitive but bitterly opposed to the existence of one another, they are not likely to be able to abide by the rules of the game. For example, a party dedicated to the overthrow of the government or the elimination of some minority group would be neither a gracious winner nor a gracious loser. Class conflict, racial or ethnic conflict, and religion are but a few of the dimensions that have historically been sources of major cleavages. In U.S. history, the Civil War was the result of such a cleavage, and the secession of the South demonstrated that the issues were too vital for it to maintain the pretense of being a gracious loser. The existence of major cleavages between blacks and whites in South Africa or between Catholics and Protestants in Northern Ireland are additional examples of cleavages that make democracy difficult.

■

POLITICAL PARTIES IN THE UNITED STATES

Sustained democracy requires an effective opposition but the absence of fundamental cleavages. Generally, this means that democracy rests on an effective system of political parties. A **political party** is an association specifically organized to win elections and to secure power over the personnel and policies of the state.

A **political party** is an association specifically organized to win elections and secure power over the personnel and policies of the state.

THE TWO-PARTY SYSTEM

In democratic systems, political parties are voluntary associations with open recruitment—membership is by self-designation. In many democratic societies, there are four or five or even a dozen political parties competing for votes and legislative seats. Such a proliferation of splinter groups often makes it hard for any one group to win firm control of the government, and thus they must govern through coalitions. The United States is virtually unique in having a relatively stable two-party system, each representing a loose coalition of competing interest groups.

The two-party system is not mandated by the Constitution, which indeed does not mention parties at all. Rather, the character of American political parties can be seen as an outgrowth of our formal system of government and the heterogeneity of our population.

In order to win a presidential election in the United States, a candidate must appeal to the majority of the population. In a nation as diverse as the United States, this means that he (or, less often, she) must appeal to a broad spectrum of potential voters. In 1988, Jesse Jackson could not win his party's nomination only by appealing to African American voters. As this picture of candidate Jackson milking a cow demonstrates, he also needed the support of Iowa farmers.

Formal Structure and the Winner-Take-All Rule.   An important characteristic virtually unique to the American brand of democracy is the winner-take-all rule. In most European democracies, legislative seats are apportioned according to the popular vote. A party getting 10 percent of the vote gets 10 percent of the legislative seats. In the United States, a group that got only 10 percent of the vote would come out with nothing. Thus, to gain any representation at all in our system, the small group must ally itself with others in a coalition that may ultimately appeal to a majority of the voters. The winner-take-all rule has prevented radical or special-interest groups from gaining political power or even having an effective voice. As one observer remarked, these groups have run up against the "50 percent wall" (Przeworski 1985).

Heterogeneity.   In a homogeneous nation, broad national appeal might be attained with a very specific, even extreme, program of action. In a heterogeneous society, however, majority backing can be gained only by a program that combines and balances the interests of many smaller groups— farmers, labor, Hispanics, big cities, conservationists, heavy industry, and so on. The strength and stability of American political parties is thus partly attributable to the diversity of the American population and its many cross-cutting interest groups.

PARTY AFFILIATION

In spite of the fact that both of the major political parties in the United States are necessarily centrist, there are philosophical distinctions between them. Traditionally, the Democratic party has been more likely to support the interests of the poor and the working class, and the Republican party has been more likely to support policies favoring economic growth. Because of these characteristics, the Republicans tend to attract people with higher incomes and the Democrats tend to attract minority and lower-income voters as well as some highly educated liberals (see Table 15.1).

■

TABLE 15.1
PARTY IDENTIFICATION

Although American parties are not closely tied to social class, the better-off tend to be Republicans, and the poor and nonwhite tend to be Democrats. The growing proportion who identify themselves as independent tend to be young, well educated, and Anglo.

"In general, would you call yourself a Democrat, a Republican, or what?"

	DEMOCRAT	REPUBLICAN	INDEPENDENT
Race/ethnicity:			
Anglo	38%	32%	30%
Black	75	8	17
Hispanic	51	23	26
Education:			
Less than 12 years	52	22	26
High school graduate	44	28	28
Some college	39	33	28
College graduate	34	36	30
Income:			
Under $15,000	51	22	27
$15,000–24,999	43	28	29
$25,000–39,999	41	30	29
$40,000 and over	34	37	29

SOURCE: The Gallup Poll 1989.

A growing proportion of voters aligns itself with neither party. These independents are not themselves a political party, but have declared an intent to vote on the basis of the issues rather than party loyalty. When the 29 percent of the voters who call themselves independents go to the polls, however, they usually have to choose between a Democratic and a Republican candidate.

WHY DOESN'T THE UNITED STATES HAVE A WORKERS' PARTY?

The United States is almost alone among Western democracies in not having a party that explicitly supports the interests of the working class. As a direct result, it is almost alone among Western democracies in not having national health insurance, not having family allowances, and not having a comprehensive system of unemployment benefits (Quadagno 1990). Working-class interests have been diluted and compromised in Democratic party platforms, and there has been no clear political voice for the working and lower classes. There have been few congressional representatives whose reelection depended on whether they supported a working-class agenda; certainly there have been no presidents who felt that the workers were their unique political constituency. As a result, no one has spoken very loudly or very often for labor.

In nearly every other democratic society, there is a Labor or Socialist party that stands for the redistribution of society's wealth, greater equality, and social welfare programs for the working and lower classes. Why is the United States an exception?

Three answers are usually given. First, U.S. labor unions tend to be organized around a specific craft and sometimes even limited to a specific region, and there has been little success in creating superunions that would represent the interests of labor as a whole (Quadagno 1990). One of the reasons is that the heterogeneity of American society results in many cross-cutting loyalties for American workers. Race and ethnicity, religion, and regional subcultures interfere with labor solidarity. Perhaps more important are the great inequalities that exist within the working class. Unionized workers in manufacturing, the so-called aristocracy of labor, earn four times more than the working poor who labor at the minimum wage. These wage differences reduce the likelihood that workers will share an economic and political agenda (Form 1985).

Second, worker complacency has been traced to the astounding abundance of the American economy. Although our abundance is accompanied by significant disparities in income, our standard of living is luxurious by almost any comparison. As a 19th-century socialist noted with chagrin in describing the failure of the United States to sustain a socialist movement: "On the reefs of roast beef and apple pie, socialist utopias of every sort are sent to their doom" (Sombart [1906] 1974, 87).

Finally, of course, there is the ideology of the American Dream (Chapter 9). The American working class has not been interested in absolute equality but in equality of opportunity. Because they believe that they can make it within the current system, they have not wanted to reduce the privileges associated with success.

Very early in this century, labor unions often aligned themselves with radical platforms favoring redistribution of wealth; at midcentury, they were less radical but solidly Democratic. In 1990, only about half of union members are members of the Democratic party. This collapse of working-class liberalism has led some observers to speculate that any future pressure for redistribution will come from the minimum-wage service sector and from the unemployed, groups that so far have shown little political muscle (Form 1985).

Every four years, each of the major political parties holds a convention to write a platform and select a presidential and vice-presidential nominee. There are many, many more women and minority delegates at these conventions than there were 20 or 30 years ago, but the delegates continue to represent organized interest groups rather than the party rank and file. There aren't very many working-class faces at either the Republican or Democratic conventions.

WHO GOVERNS?
MODELS OF AMERICAN DEMOCRACY

POLITICAL ACTORS: PUBLICS AND PACS

The political process involves many actors. These can be viewed roughly as a pyramid (see Figure 15.2). As we move from the top to the bottom of the pyramid, actors increase in number, but decrease in political effectiveness (Lehman 1988). The state occupies the top of the pyramid, and the political parties we have just discussed occupy the next level. Below these two major actors are two additional levels: interest groups and publics.

Publics. A **public** is a category of citizens who are thought to share a common political agenda. For example, Hispanics, women, farmers, and small business owners are each a distinct public.

The distinctive feature of a public is that it is not organized. It is a *category* not a *group*. This means that it is a relatively ineffective political

A **public** is a category of citizens who are thought to share a common political agenda.

FIGURE 15.2
THE U.S. POLITICAL PROCESS

The political process occurs at several levels. As we move from unorganized publics to organized interest groups to political parties to the state, the number of actors becomes smaller and their capacity to act effectively in pursuing their self-interest grows.

SOURCE: Adapted from Lehman 1988.

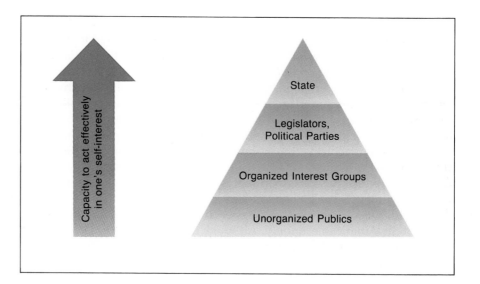

actor. Although individual members of a public may affect political decisions through their votes, their donations to political causes, and even their answers to public opinion polls, lack of organization reduces their impact. Power requires organization; it requires that a public become a self-conscious interest group that can speak for all members.

Interest Groups.   A group or organization that seeks to influence political decisions is called an **interest group** (Welch et al. 1990). There are thousands of interest groups in the United States, from the PTA to the Tobacco Growers of America. Some of these interest groups, such as the PTA, are multi-purpose organizations: Affecting government policy is only one part of their purpose. Other interest groups, such as the National Rifle Association, exist largely in order to affect political decisions.

An **interest group** is a group or organization that seeks to influence political decisions.

Interest groups use two strategies to affect political decisions: lobbying and financial contributions. Lobbyists try to "educate" legislators or officials about the need to protect their group's interests. Some interest groups can afford to hire permanent lobbyists who work year-round in their behalf; other interest groups rely on volunteer letter writers to bring their position to legislators' attention. In each case, lobbyists are able to say that they are not speaking just for themselves, but also for the thousands or millions of people who belong to their organization.

Another way for interest groups to affect political decisions is to provide financial help for political candidates who agree with their point of view. Because of widespread concern that candidates were being "bought" by big donors, however, federal election reforms have limited the amount of money that individual donors could give to campaigns. For example, an individual cannot donate more than $1,000 to any single U.S. Senate election and no more than $17,500 to all Senate races in a single year (Welch et al. 1990).

To circumvent this law, interest groups have formed Political Action Committees (PACs). If each member of an interest group funnels his or her donation into a PAC, a huge war chest can be accumulated. Although PACs, like individuals, are limited in the amount they can give to specific candidates, the U.S. Supreme Court has ruled that they can spend *unlimited* amounts working on behalf of candidates of issues. That is, they can give the candidate only $5,000, but they can spend millions on the candidate's behalf.

The PAC is a powerful vehicle for giving an interest group political clout. The richer the PAC, the more likely it is to get its candidates elected. Also, of course, the richer the PAC, the more likely it is that some needy candidate will be pursuaded to favor the PAC's position in exchange for financial support. The PAC has proven to be such an effective instrument, that no interest group can afford to be without one. There is a FishPAC, a BeefPAC, a cigarPAC, a PAC for the National Organization for Women, and even a PAC for the alcohol industry, called—you guessed it—the Six-PAC (Welch et al. 1990).

FOUR MODELS

Students of the U.S. political process agree that the process involves a variety of political actors, each pursuing different agendas. Some of these actors are bigger, better funded, and better organized than others. Which ones are spinning their wheels, and which ones are effective in getting their way? Put another way: "Who governs?" To answer this question, we turn to four models of the democratic process.

The Pluralist Model. The pluralist model of American government focuses on the processes of coalition and competition that take place in state and federal governments. A vital part of this model is the hypothesis of shifting allegiances. According to pluralist theorists, different coalitions of interest groups arise for each decision. For example, labor unions will ally themselves with automakers in favoring tariffs against Japanese imports; when it comes to domestic issues such as wages, however, these two groups will oppose each other. This pattern of shifting allegiances keeps any interest groups from consistently being on the winning side and keeps political alliances fluid and temporary rather than allowing them to harden into permanent and unified cliques (Dahl 1961, 1971). As a result of these processes, pluralists see the decision-making process as relatively inefficient but also relatively free of conflict, a process in which competition among interest groups keeps any single group from gaining significant advantage.

Critics believe that the pluralist model is naïve at best. They argue that, although all of these interest groups may be skirmishing in Congress, the real decisions are being made in higher circles. At worst, critics argue, the pluralist model "obscures and shelters the citadels of domination" by refusing to recognize the controlling hand of the ruling class (Bowles and Gintis 1986).

The **power elite** consists of the people who occupy the top positions in three bureaucracies—the military, industry, and the executive branch of government—and who are thought to act together to run the United States in their own interests.

The Power-Elite Model.   Theorists associated with the power-elite model wave aside the competition among organized interest groups as the middle levels of power. Power-elite theorists contend that there is a higher level of decision making where an elite makes all the major decisions—in its own interests. In his classic work, *The Power Elite*, C. Wright Mills (1956) defined the **power elite** as the people who occupy the top positions in three bureaucracies: the military, industry, and the executive branch of government. From these "command posts of power" and through a complex set of overlapping cliques, these people share decisions having at least national consequences (Mills 1956, 18).

The power-elite theory is a positional theory of power. It argues that individuals have power by virtue of the positions they hold in key institutions. If the interests of these individuals and institutions were in competition with one another, this model would not be significantly different from the pluralist model. The key factor in the elite theory is that these elites share a common worldview and act together to promote their own interests (Orum 1987).

The suggestion that individuals occupying the top positions represent a unified elite is supported by evidence of a strong similarity in background among the top members of the three bureaucracies. They have gone to the same colleges and prep schools, summered at the same resorts, skied at the same lodges, and joined the same clubs. One recent study used a generous definition of "top position" to identify 5,800 individuals as the power elite. The majority of the elite are white men who had graduated from 12 prestigious private universities; fewer than 5 percent of the elite were women, only 20 individuals on the list were black, and only 25 percent had graduated from a public university (Dye 1986).

That an upper class exists in America and that this upper class is highly overrepresented in the power elite seems unarguable (Domhoff 1983). The critical question is whether there is any evidence that this collection of top position holders acts together to promote the interests of the upper class.

The Conflict/Dialectic Model.   A Marxist version of class conflict is at the root of the conflict/dialectic model. Like the power-elite model, the conflict/dialectic model features an elite that runs the show. The Marxist elite differs from the power elite in two ways. First, the Marxist elite is made up of a much smaller group of people: the people who actually own the means of production. Managers, bureaucrats, and generals are not considered to be members of the Marxist elite; they are rather tools of the elite. Second, Marxists do not require a unified elite tied together by social custom and tradition. Instead, they recognize that there will be factions within the elite with competing economic interests. For example, financiers like high interest rates; automobile manufacturers do not (Roy 1984). The Marxist elites include more of what political scientist Dye (1986) calls cowboys: They are aggressive about making and keeping their money, and they don't care much for fancy manners and old school ties. As a result, the Marxist elite includes built-in competition that may ultimately weaken it and lead to change.

Another difference between the conflict/dialectic and power-elite models is the tension they see between the elite and nonelites. Marxists argue that

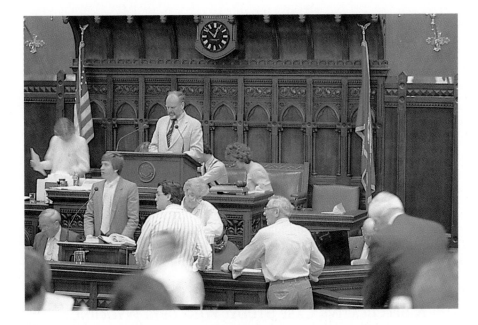

The pluralist model of American politics stresses the importance of Congress and the state legislatures as arenas for making decisions. Floor debates, such as this one in the Connecticut House, are seen as occasions where competing interest groups vie for votes and power. According to this model of the American political process, no side consistently wins and there is a shifting balance of power.

the working class has its own resources for power: class consciousness and the possibility of class action. The power of the subordinate class can be likened to that of a sleeping rattlesnake; the snake is not hurting you now, but you want to be certain not to awaken it. Thus, the conflict/dialectic model sees underlying tensions between the elite (dominant class) and the nonelite that are largely missing from the power-elite model.

A further element of this model is its emphasis on the dialectic as the process of social change. As noted in earlier chapters, the dialectic suggests that social change will emerge as a result of contradictions and conflicts within and between social institutions. Marxists believe that

> social institutions, economic systems, and political institutions contain inherent contradictions. These produce conflicts and strains that eventually lead to the transformation of those institutions and systems. *Contradictions* are thus engines of social change and their analysis is central also to understanding the dynamics of political power (Whitt 1979, 84).

In terms of the American political structure, the dialectic suggests that the elite has to be constantly on its toes to ward off the potential consciousness and power of the subordinate class in a climate of shifting economic and political conditions. Change rather than stability is the key to the conflict model. Whereas the power-elite model sees the elite striving to maintain privilege, the conflict model envisions a more rough-and-tumble battle in which both sides strive to structure change for their benefit. This conflict occurs within as well as between classes.

The State Autonomy Model.   A growing number of scholars argue that the government bureaucracy is a powerful, independent actor in political decisions. The federal government employs 3 million people directly.

In addition, its policies determine the employment of tens of millions of additional people who work for national defense contractors, state and local governments, schools, and social welfare agencies. In 1986, the federal government collected over $848 billion in revenue and spent over $1 trillion! It seems only common sense to suppose that the state is in a powerful position to get what it wants. The state autonomy model suggests that the state (meaning the federal bureaucracy) is a powerful, independent actor that pursues its own agenda. This agenda is not class linked (as in the power-elite model) but is linked to the maintenance and extension of bureaucratic power.

In this model, the state maintains its power by playing elites off against publics and interest groups (Clegg, Boreham, and Dow 1986). In order to avoid being captured by the elite, government bureaucrats need to promote the power of nonelites. Only when the nonelites are relatively strong can the bureaucrats occupy a central role as mediator. According to this theory, then, the state's search for a powerful mediating role is a mechanism for increasing the voice of nonelites.

A Speculative Case Study: Who gets Wyoming?

The different implications of the models can be illustrated by speculation on how each would envision the political decision to strip-mine in Wyoming. If the large and virtually untouched deposits of coal in Wyoming can be mined, the United States won't face an energy shortage for a long time. However, the process will be dirty, destructive of the environment, and disruptive of the current use of the land as well as of the economic and social life of the small communities currently in the area. The land containing the coal deposits is controlled largely by the U.S. Bureau of Land Management (BLM). How will the decision be reached about what to do?

The pluralist model would envision competition among various interest groups: cattle ranchers, the environmentalists, and coal companies. Each group will seek allies among other groups, such as federal agencies, the Wyoming government, Indian reservations, and the railroads, and will put together a broad coalition to block the competing groups or, less probably, to get its own way. Ultimately, no side will win a clear victory, and some compromise will be reached.

The power-elite model would suggest that while all this is going on, the heads of the energy company and the Interior Department will be sharing lunch at their club and deciding how to run their program. The elites will act together. Often they work together even without planning to do so; they simply have similar interests and values.

The conflict/dialectic model would assume that the elite is divided, not unitary. The firms representing the various oil, natural gas, and coal interests will be in competition with one another. Those who don't have mineral rights in Wyoming are likely to favor restrictive policies on strip mining there. Regardless of who wins this round, however, the debate over strip mining will probably mobilize previously unorganized publics—environmentalists, ranchers, recreational developers—who may become powerful interest groups in future debates. They will have awakened the rattlesnake.

Finally, the state autonomy model would assume that the BLM, the Department of Energy, the National Parks Service, and other federal agencies are operating in a way designed to maintain and enhance the power of their own agencies. These federal agencies would oppose any energy developments that would take land out of federal control and pass it into private control. On the other hand, if becoming an active public watchdog over energy development created an expanded role for their agencies, they would probably favor it.

SUMMARY AND EVALUATION: WHO *DOES* GOVERN?

These four models are divided on several points. Are the elites divided? Are there shifting coalitions? Does an elite make all the decisions? Research in the United States supports two conclusions. First, there is little evidence for the pluralist expectation of shifting allegiances. Instead, research shows that business elites are relatively unified. Studies of PAC contributions show that business interests are unified by shared conservatism: They act together as a class to support probusiness candidates (Neustadtl and Clawson 1988; Clawson and Neustadtl 1989). Second, there are only a few issues in which other interest groups in the United States have the unity or resources to challenge the power of business effectively (Korpi 1989). In the United States, redistributive programs—such as civil rights or social security—have been passed under two conditions: A sense of crisis caused the elite to favor the change, or the elite disagreed among themselves (Jenkins and Brent 1989). There is little evidence that any other interest group—either the state or the working class—has the resources or the unity to challenge a unified business class.

A final point is important. Although there are some important differences among the four major models of decision making in the United States (see the Concept Summary), a notable feature of all four is that organized entities—businesses, unions, PACs, government agencies—rather than individuals are the key actors. Individuals play a very small role unless they represent or are represented by one of these organizations (Laumann, Knoke, and Kim 1985).

INDIVIDUAL PARTICIPATION
IN AMERICAN GOVERNMENT

Democracy is a political system that explicitly includes a large proportion of adults as political actors. Yet it is easy to overlook the role of individual citizens while concentrating on leaders and organized interests. This section describes the American political structure and process from the viewpoint of the individual citizen.

WHO PARTICIPATES?

The average citizen is not politically oriented. A significant proportion of the voting-age population (approximately one-third in 1988) does not even

■

CONCEPT SUMMARY

Comparison of Four Models of American Political Decision Making

	PLURALIST	POWER-ELITE	CONFLICT/ DIALECTIC	STATE AUTONOMY
Basic units of analysis	Interest groups	Institutional elites	Classes	Government bureaucracy
Source of power	Situational; depends on issue	Positional; top positions in bureaucracies	Class based; ownership of means of production	Control of personnel and budget of government
Distribution of power	Dispersed among competing diverse groups	Concentrated in relatively homogeneous elite	Held by dominant class, potentially available to lower class	Held by bureaucrats
Limits of power	Limited by shifting and cross-cutting loyalties	No identifiable limits to elite domination	Limited by class conflict and contradiction among social institutions	Limited if elite is unified and nonelites are unorganized.
Role of the state	Arena where interest groups compete	One of several sources of power	Captured by the ruling class	A major source of power

register to vote; of those people who do register, many do not vote. In recent presidential elections, 40 to 50 percent of the voting-age population has not bothered to go to the polls. Electoral participation declines markedly as one gets closer to the local level, and often only 20 to 25 percent vote in local elections.

Voting is in many ways the easiest and most superficial means of participating in politics. If we include letter writing, returning congressional questionnaires, and making campaign contributions as elements of political activity, we will have to conclude that less than 20 percent of U.S. citizens take an active part in politics. And, of course, only a very small proportion take part to the extent of running for or occupying elective office.

The studies demonstrating low levels of political participation and involvement pose a crucial question about the structure of power in American democracy. Who participates? If they are not a random sample of citizens, then some groups probably have more influence than others. Studies show that voters differ from nonvoters on social class and age.

Social Class.   One of the firmest findings in social science is that political participation (indeed, participation of any sort) is strongly related to social class. Whether we define participation as voting or letter writing, people with more education, more income, and more prestigious jobs are more likely to be politically active. They know more about the issues, have stronger opinions on a wider variety of issues, and are much more likely to try to influence the nature of political decisions. This conclusion is supported by data on voting patterns from the 1988 election (see Table 15.2). The higher the level of education, the greater the likelihood of voting; those who have graduated from college are twice as likely to vote as those who have not completed high school.

It should be stressed that lower voting participation by underprivileged groups is not a characteristic of all democratic systems. Rather, the low participation of the poor and the working class in the United States can be attributed to the absence of a political party that directly represents their interests (Zipp, Landerman, and Luebke 1982). In European political systems with pro-worker parties, this class differential in political participation is largely absent. In the United States, however, there is no exclusive political vehicle for the working class or the poor. If our political parties were not so centrist, it is possible that voter interest would be higher.

Age. Another significant determinant of political participation is age. There is a steady increase in political interest, knowledge, opinion, and participation with age. One-third of all voters in the 1988 election were 55 or older. Even in the turbulent years of the Vietnam War, when young antiwar demonstrators were so visible, young adults were significantly less likely to vote than were the middle-aged. In that period, young adults engaged in other forms of political participation that did, in fact, influence

■

TABLE 15.2
PARTICIPATION IN THE 1988 ELECTION

Political participation is greater among people who are older, better educated, and non-Hispanic

	PERCENTAGE REGISTERED	PERCENTAGE ACTUALLY VOTING
Total	67%	57%
Education		
8 years or less	48	37
9–11 years	53	41
12 years	65	55
13–15 years (college)	74	64
16 or more years (college graduate)	83	78
Race/Ethnicity		
White	68	59
Black	64	52
Hispanic[a]	36	29
Age		
18–24	48	36
25–34	58	48
35–44	69	61
45–64	76	68
65 +	78	69

SOURCE: U.S. Bureau of the Census 1989k.
[a]Underestimates participation among eligible voters; 32 percent of Hispanics ineligible to register because they are not citizens.

political decisions. In most time periods, however, the low participation of younger people at the polls is a fair measure of their overall participation.

Race and Ethnicity.   Political participation is no longer strongly related to race. In fact, after social class has been taken into consideration, it seems likely that being African American increases political participation. African Americans are more apt than whites to want changes made in the system, and they turn to political participation as a means to effect these changes (Guterbock and London 1983, 440).

Hispanics, however, are less likely to vote than other Americans (see Table 15.2). Their low participation is traceable partly to low socioeconomic status, but much of the apparent low participation of Hispanics is an artifact of the measurement procedure: One-third of the voting-age population of Hispanics consists of aliens (legal as well as illegal), and these people are not eligible to register or to vote.

The data on voting patterns demonstrate that establishment people are more likely than others to try to influence political decisions. These people are middle aged, middle to upper class, well educated, and with vested economic interests. They are the people who have the highest stake in preserving the status quo. Thus, differential patterns of participation give added weight to conservative positions and reduce the voice of the dissatisfied.

Differentials in Office Holding.   By law, almost all native-born Americans over the age of 35 are eligible to hold any office. In practice, elected officials tend to be white men from the professional classes. Thus, for the most part, the political activities of other groups (women, minorities, non-elites) have been directed at choosing the white elite males to represent them. This practice has been changing, however; African Americans, Hispanics, and women (though not nonelites) are increasingly holding elected office, especially at local levels. In 1989, for example, Virginia elected America's first African American governor, and there were more than 300 African American mayors in the United States, 10 of whom were from some of the largest cities in the nation, such as New York, Los Angeles, and Philadelphia ("The Rise" 1989). Still, only about 5 percent of all state legislators are African American, and only 15 percent are female. The proportions in Congress are much smaller (U.S. Bureau of the Census 1989a).

WHY PARTICIPATE?

Scholars of voting behavior suggest that calculations of personal costs and benefits are an important factor in determining whether we vote and whom we vote for. This is part of a general perspective called **social choice** (or sometimes exchange) **theory,** which argues that individual decisions from voting to marriage are based on cost/benefit calculations.

Social choice theory (or exchange theory) argues that individual decisions are based on cost/benefit calculations.

Voting.   The costs of voting in the contemporary United States are not high: Polling places are usually conveniently located and they are open at

hours during which most people can find time to go. Many states, however, require a preliminary procedure of registering to vote that may demand a visit to a government office between 8 A.M. and 5 P.M. Plus, of course, there is the bother of reading the paper and watching the news and figuring out what the issues are. Any trouble is too much trouble when you cannot see that it matters much one way or the other who wins.

An important factor reducing incentive to vote is the centrist nature of American political parties. Their platforms are so similar that it is unlikely that one party's victory will mean personal prosperity and the other disaster. This lack of effective choice helps to explain why political participation is so much lower in the United States than it is in many European democracies and why, in contrast to these other nations, the American working class is less likely to vote than the middle class (Bollen and Jackman 1985; Davis 1986).

Political Alienation.   As social choice theory suggests, an important determinant of whether citizens participate in political decision making is their judgment of the usefulness of the exercise. Citizens who believe they can influence outcomes through their participation are apt to be active. Those who suffer from **political alienation**, who believe that voting is a useless exercise and that individual citizens have no influence on decision

In the United States, all citizens over the age of 18 have the right to vote. A surprisingly large proportion of the population chooses not to exercise this right. The pattern of political decisions reflects the fact that the people who are most apt to vote are establishment-types of people: middle-aged, better off, and well-educated. If less advantaged segments of the population would increase their political participation, the nature of U.S. political decisions might change.

Political alienation is a belief that voting is a useless exercise and that individual citizens have no influence on decision making.

making, are not going to be active. Alienated voters are likely to think that their vote doesn't count, that no one cares what they think, and that the system is run for the benefit of the few. Opinion poll results show that alienation has increased substantially among voters since the mid 1960s (see Figure 15.3), and it has contributed to the overall decline in voter participation.

CONSEQUENCES OF LOW PARTICIPATION

Elite theorists see popular elections as little more than games designed to delude the masses. Since real decisions aren't made in Congress, much less by the governor or the mayor, the level of participation is irrelevant. These theorists point out that opinion polls show a drop in political alienation immediately after elections (Ginsberg and Weissberg 1978), and they interpret elections as a ritualized form of participation that serves to confirm the legitimacy of the system.

This is probably unduly cynical. Democracy *does* matter. Studies of Western Europe demonstrate that the existence of a unified workers' party is one of the most powerful predictors of the generosity of a nation's social welfare programs (Korpi 1989). Similarly, the size of old-age pensions has been shown to be directly related to the size of the elderly voting bloc (Pampel and Williamson 1985).

People who want to have an effective voice in shaping government policy need to do more than vote: They need to *organize*. Nevertheless, simply going to the polls makes you hard to ignore. The strong correlation between participation and social class means that the government is unrepresentative of the whole and, in particular, that it underrepresents the poor and the poorly educated.

15.3

POLITICAL ALIENATION IN THE UNITED STATES, 1966–1989

Political events of the last 25 years have left an increasing number of Americans feeling alienated. A majority now feel helpless to affect the course of government.

SOURCE: Harris Survey 1989b.

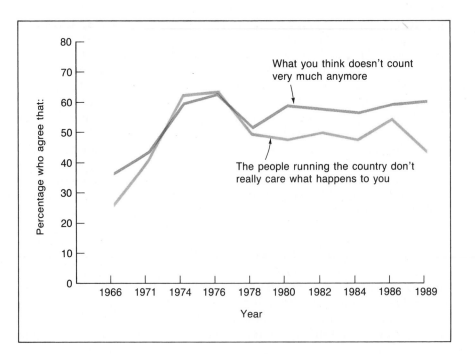

Why Can't We Control Guns?

On January 17, 1989, Patrick Edward Purdy used an automatic assault rifle to open fire on an elementary school playground in Stockton, California. Five children were killed and 30 others were wounded. This incident galvanized public demand for gun control.

For at least 50 years, public opinion polls have indicated that the public favors stronger gun control. Gun control proposals range from a seven-day waiting period to outright bans on certain kinds of weapons. Following the Stockton inci-

dent, national polls showed that three quarters of the public favored an outright ban on the manufacture, sale, or possession of cheap handguns (so-called Saturday night specials), plastic guns, and automatic assault guns (Gallup Report 1989a). Yet any legislation against guns remains highly unlikely. Why?

The answer has to do with the relative power of organized interest groups versus unorganized publics. The issue pits the gun lobby, specifically the National Rifle Association (NRA), against a silent majority. The National Rifle Association provides a variety of services to its members and the public; it is a leading provider of classes on safe use of firearms. Its major purpose, however, is to provide what the association's own brochures describe as "the strongest, most formidable grassroots lobby in the nation" (cited in Welch et al. 1990, 137).

The NRA has opposed any restrictions on the right to bear arms. Recently the NRA did concede that citizens had no right to own surface-to-air missiles (McGuigan 1989), but they passionately defend the public's right to own machine guns and assault rifles. The NRA argues that banning assault rifles would only take them away from law-abiding citizens. President George Bush, a lifelong member of the NRA, has sided with the organization in opposing a ban on assault rifles.

The issue of gun control is a textbook example of how a small but very well-organized minority can determine policy when a much larger public remains unorganized. In fact, it is an example of a lobby that outruns even its members' wishes: A recent poll of the members of the NRA showed that 60 percent of them favor outlawing assault rifles (Harris Survey 1989a). Proponents of gun control are largely unorganized. Although the majority favor gun control, they are not passionate about it—certainly not anywhere near as passionate as are the members of the NRA.

What is a political candidate to do? A vocal minority makes it perfectly clear that it will do all in its power to defeat any legislator favoring gun control. On the other hand, gun-control proponents are not so passionate. Although they may take a candidate's position on gun control into account, they will balance it against the candidate's position on defense, abortion, drug control, and taxes. A candidate seeking votes is likely to conclude that he or she will lose more votes by favoring than opposing gun control. One U.S. congressman, for example, defined gun control as a "political loser" (Jeffe and Jeffe 1989).

It is not at all clear that stricter gun control would reduce violence in the United States (Wright 1988). We are a violent society, divided by deep racial and class barriers. A ban on Rambo-style guns would do little to reduce the 30,000 deaths that occur each year because of firearms. The issue, nevertheless, provides a dramatic illustration of how a well-organized and vocal minority can hold government policy hostage. This example is but one of a hundred cases where government policy goes against public wishes, even against the public interest, because legislators respond to organized interest groups rather than to the public.

SUMMARY

1. Power may be exercised through coercion or through authority. Authority may be traditional, charismatic, or rational-legal. Influence is less effective than power since it does not allow one person to compel another's obedience.

2. Any ongoing social structure with institutionalized power relationships can be referred to as a political institution. This definition includes the family, the school, and the church, but the most prominent political institution is the state.

3. The state is distinguished from other political institutions because it claims a monopoly on the legitimate use of coercion and it has power over a broader array of issues.

4. Democracy is not just a matter of having the right values; it also requires a supportive institutional environment. Such an environment is characterized by competing interest groups, the absence of fundamental cleavages, and low income inequality.

5. The stable two-party system is a product of our heterogeneous population and of the formal structure of government. It results in the creation of two centrist parties, each representing a coalition of interest groups.

6. Although the Democrats tend to attract working-class and minority voters and Republicans tend to attract better-off voters, both U.S. political parties are necessarily centrist. Unlike many other democracies, the United States has no working-class party.

7. Political effectiveness depends on organization. Interest groups, especially those with political action committees (PACs) have far more influence on policy than do members of unorganized publics.

8. There are four major models describing the American political process: the pluralist model, the power-elite model, the conflict/dialectic model, and the state autonomy model. None of them suggests that the average voter has much power to influence events.

9. Political participation is rather low in America; fewer than half of the people of voting age vote in most national elections, and fewer yet take an active role in politics. Political participation is greater among those with high social status and among middle-aged and older people—categories that are more likely to support the status quo.

10. Poltical participation is based on individual calculation of costs and benefits. When costs of participating are low and the benefits relatively high, people will vote.

11. U.S. failure to enact stricter gun control laws despite strong public support illustrates how a highly organized minority (the NRA) can have more power to affect political decisions than a much larger, but unorganized, public.

Suggested Reading

Domhoff, G. Williams. 1983. Who Rules America Now? Englewood Cliffs, N.J.: Prentice-Hall. A classic updated, by a scholar who has spent 20 years chronicling the antics of the power elite.

Dye, Thomas R. 1990. Who's Running America? The Bush Era (5th ed.) Englewood Cliffs, Prentice-Hall. A name-naming review of the elite. Applicable to nearly any theoretical framework.

Mills, C. Wright. 1956. The Power Elite, New York: Oxford University Press. One of the most important discussions of the relationships among three areas of power in America: government, business, and the military. Mills, a conflict theorist, argues that a small elite of individuals makes the decisions that control American society.

Orum, Anthony. 1989. Introduction to Political Sociology: The Social Anatomy of the Body Politic. (3rd ed.) Englewood Cliffs, N.J.: Prentice-Hall. A contemporary textbook in political sociology. Orum covers the political process in communities as well as nations and shows how the ideas discussed in this chapter apply to the local level.

Welch, Susan, Gruhl, John, Steinman, Michael, and Comer, John. 1990. Introduction to American Government. (3rd ed.) St. Paul: West. A popular political science text that provides over 20 chapters of details on how interest groups, PAC, and parties work.

16

ECONOMIC INSTITUTIONS

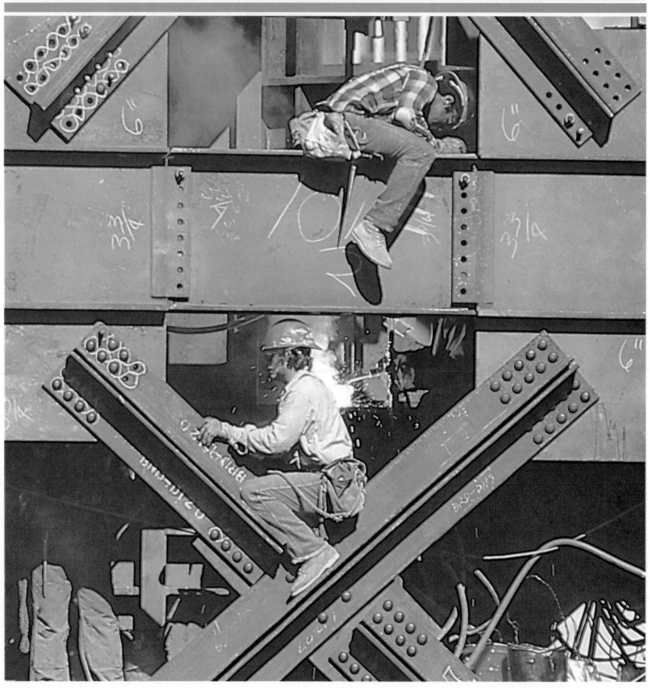

Have you ever . . .

Seriously tried to imagine what it might have been like to live in the United States 200 years ago? You would probably have lived on an isolated farm. You would have had, on the average, eight children, two to three sets of clothes, a one-room house, and 35 years of life expectancy. Life would probably have been hard and short.

In the 1990s the situation is very different. You are much more likely to work in a crowded office than on an isolated farm. You have far more clothes than you have children (a situation for which you are probably thankful). This transition from rural to urban, from poor to relatively well off can be traced directly to the transformation of our economy.

What does the future hold? Will you be better off than your parents' generation? Will you be able to buy a house before you are 35? Retire before you are 65? Pay back your student loans? Some students borrow up to $75,000 to finance their education; they are betting that the future economy will be at least as good as today's. Whether this is a good bet depends to a large extent on the productivity of our economy and how successfully the U.S. can compete with Asia and a newly mobilized Eastern Europe. More than any other institution, the economy will determine our future prosperity and life-styles.

Economic institutions are social structures concerned with the production and distribution of goods and services.

Economic institutions are social structures concerned with the production and distribution of goods and services. Such issues as scarcity or abundance, guns or butter, craftwork or assembly lines are all part of the production side of economic institutions. Issues of distribution include what proportion goes to the worker versus the manager, who is responsible for supporting nonworkers, and how much of society's production is distributed on the basis of need rather than effort or ability. The distribution aspect of economic institutions intimately touches the family, stratification systems, education, and government.

Sociology is not concerned with the intricate workings of economic systems. Such issues as monetary policy, inflation, and the national debt are all left to the discipline of economics. Some understanding of such issues is required, of course. For example, do high interest rates lead to an increase or decrease in income inequality? Sociologists, however, focus on the enduring pattern of norms, roles, and statuses that make up the economic system (Turner 1972).

In this chapter, we look at the economic system from two points of view. At the macroeconomic level, we examine the social structures of economic institutions and their relationships to other social institutions. Then we turn to an examination of the microeconomic level, looking at the economic system from the point of view of the individual. In the case of economic institutions, this means jobs and the organization of work. We close the chapter with a detailed examination of the often uneasy relationship between labor and technology.

TYPES OF ECONOMIC INSTITUTIONS

All societies must deal with the problems of producing and distributing goods. At a minimum, each must produce food, clothing, and shelter and must institutionalize some set of rules for distributing them. From a historical and cross-cultural point of view, we distinguish three major types of economic institutions: preindustrial, industrial, and postindustrial. They differ from one another in the typical organization of work as well as in the kind and amount of goods produced.

Preindustrial Economic Structures. In a simple society, most goods are produced by the clan or family unit. There may be limited barter or trade, but most of the goods consumed by a family are also produced by it. The family also serves as the distribution system. Family ties obligate the more productive to share with the less productive; thus, children, the elderly, and the sick are provided for by ties of family responsibility.

Preindustrial economic structures were characteristic of Europe until 500 years ago and are still typical of many societies. Although the economies vary in complexity, their dominant characteristics are:

1. Production units are small, and settlements are small and widely dispersed.
2. The major sources of energy are human and animal power, occasionally supplemented by primitive waterwheels.

Primary production involves direct contact with natural resources—fishing, hunting, farming, and forestry. Until a few hundred years ago, the vast majority of human beings were involved in extracting these raw materials. Because primary production is almost necessarily rural production, it usually entails small, kin-based communities and a close association between work and other aspects of life.

3. The vast majority of the labor force is engaged in **primary production,** extracting raw materials from the environment. Prominent among primary production activities are farming, herding, fishing, foresting, hunting, and mining. As late as 1900, 36 percent of the U.S. labor force was engaged in primary production.

Primary production consists of extracting raw materials from the environment.

In large part because of limited energy resources, preindustrial economies do not produce much more than they need. Some have produced enough surplus to support giant cities such as Rome, Cairo, and Tenochtitlán, as well as artistic and scholarly elites, but this standard of living for the few required great inequality. It also required that the great majority of the population continue to give constant attention to primary production.

For the average person, a preindustrial economy means a close integration of work with all other aspects of life. Work takes place at or near home in family or neighborhood units. Some observers who deplore modern industrial work organization (assembly lines, time clocks, and so on) have romanticized preindustrial work organization as a situation in which people set their own pace, organize their own work, and have the satisfaction of seeing the results of their own labor. In fact, the average person in preindustrial societies probably works very hard; and if the impetus to go to work is the needs of the stock or the amount of work to be done, there is little individual choice about working. Getting to organize one's work is probably limited to deciding which end of the field to weed first, and the products of one's labor are undoubtedly too few to give rise to a great deal of satisfaction. Nevertheless, a preindustrial style of work organization does offer flexibility and variety. Its content and tempo change with the seasons; the hectic pace of the harvest is followed by the relative relaxation of harness mending and stock tending in the winter. All too often, it is also followed by malnutrition in the early spring, as last season's small surplus dwindles (Wrigley 1969).

INDUSTRIAL ECONOMIC STRUCTURES

Industrialization means a change in both the organization and the content of production. Its major characteristics are:

1. Large and bureaucratically organized work units
2. Reliance on new sources of energy (gasoline, electricity, coal, steam) rather than on muscle power
3. A shift to **secondary production,** the processing of raw materials.

Secondary production consists of the processing of raw materials.

For example, ore, cotton, and wood are processed by the steel, textile, and lumber industries; other secondary industries will turn these materials into automobiles, clothing, and furniture. Obviously, some part of the labor force must still produce ore, cotton, and timber, but the proportion in primary production drops steadily as greater use of nonmuscle energy decreases the labor requirements for primary production.

The shift from primary to secondary production is characterized by growing surpluses. Even with substantial inequalities in distribution, this abundance generally leads to better education, better health, and a higher standard of living for the entire population. Other changes, however, are not so desirable: population growth, the assault on the environment, and the growth of cities. (Many of these problematic aspects of industrialization are covered in Unit 5, which deals with change.) In spite of its drawbacks, industrialization has been eagerly sought by most societies. As a means of increasing productivity and the standard of living, its advantages have been unquestioned.

POSTINDUSTRIAL ECONOMIC STRUCTURES

Tertiary production consists of the production of services.

Postindustrial development rests on a third stage of productivity, **tertiary production.** This stage consists of the production of services.

The tertiary sector includes a wide variety of occupations: physicians, schoolteachers, hotel maids, short-order cooks, and police officers. It includes everyone who works for hospitals, governments, airlines, banks, hotels, schools, or grocery stores. None of these organizations produces tangible goods; they all provide services to others. They count their production not in barrels or tons but in numbers of satisfied customers.

The tertiary sector has grown very rapidly in the last half-century and is projected to grow still more. As Figure 16.1 illustrates, only 19 percent of the labor force was involved in tertiary production in 1920; by 1956, the figure had grown to 49 percent and by 2000 is expected to include a full 76 percent of the labor force. Simultaneously, the portion of the labor force employed in primary production has been reduced to almost nil, and the proportion employed in secondary production has halved. These shifts do not mean that primary and secondary production are no longer important. A large service sector depends on primary and secondary sectors that are so efficiently productive that large numbers of people are freed from the necessity of direct production.

The expansion of the tertiary sector is largely a post–World War II phenomenon, and the consequences of this change for societies and in-

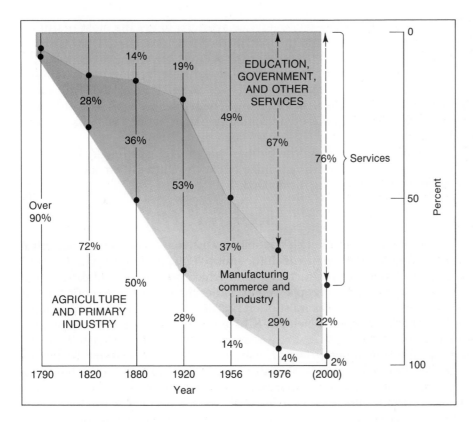

■
FIGURE 16.1
**CHANGING LABOR FORCE
IN THE UNITED STATES**

Since 1900, the labor force in the United States has changed drastically. The proportion of workers engaged in primary production has declined sharply while the proportion engaged in service work has expanded greatly.

dividuals are not yet fully understood. Some of these changes are addressed later in this chapter when we discuss the changing nature of work in the United States.

■

CAPITALISM AND SOCIALISM

In the modern world, there are basically two types of economic systems: capitalism and socialism. Because economic systems must adapt to different political and natural environments, however, we find few instances of pure capitalism or pure socialism. Most modern economic systems represent some variation on the two and often combine elements of both.

CAPITALISM

Capitalism is an economic system in which most wealth (land, labor, equipment, money) is private property; both the production and the distribution of goods are carried out on a for-profit basis. Ideally, such an economic system harnesses individual self-interest to the broader goal of increasing overall productivity and efficiency. For example, Josiah Wedgwood devised a better way to make pottery. He invested his own capital into a factory, where his new system (a precursor to today's assembly line) produced pottery faster and better than his competitors. In order to avoid bankruptcy, his competitors also began to use the more efficient technique.

Capitalism is the economic system in which most wealth (land, capital, and labor) is private property, to be used by its owners to maximize their own gain; this economic system is based on competition.

In a capitalist economy, everyone attempts to get the most return on what they have to offer in the marketplace. For most of us, what we have to offer is our labor. We try to maximize our rewards (wages, benefits, satisfaction) by making our labor more valuable (getting more training, working harder). The money we get in exchange for our labor will enable us to buy food, shelter, and clothing. The harder we work and the more we have invested in our own training, the more money we'll have, or so the story goes.

Capitalism is based on competition and individual struggle. It assumes that if each of us tries to maximize our own returns, then society's total productivity will also be maximized.

SOCIALISM

Socialism is an economic structure in which the group (or its representative, the state) owns the means of production and in which production and distribution are managed for the group's welfare rather than private profit; this economic system is based on cooperation.

Cooperation, rather than competition, is the basis of socialism. **Socialism** is an economic system in which the group (or its representative, the state) owns the means of production and in which production and distribution are managed for the group's welfare rather than for private profit. In past centuries, socialism was most often practiced by small communal groups. As you have read, the Oneidans (Chapter 13) practiced a form of Christian socialism.

In the contemporary world, socialism most often appears as *state socialism*. Private property is abolished or restricted and decisions about production and distribution are made by government bureaucracies. Ideally, these bureaucracies will use labor and capital efficiently to produce goods that society needs and the people demand. The major purpose of a socialist economy, however, is not high productivity but equitable distribution.

The creed of pure socialism is "from each according to ability, to each according to need." An explicit goal of socialism is to eliminate unequal rewards as the major incentive for economic activity. In a pure capitalist economy, people who cannot compete in the marketplace—the handicapped, the elderly, children—must depend on charity or their families; they are left out of the economic system. Socialism explicitly includes all citizens, regardless of whether they have labor that they can trade for goods and services.

MIXED ECONOMIES

Many societies in the late 20th century represent a mixture of both capitalist and socialist economic structures. In many nations, services such as the mail and the railroads and key industries such as steel and energy have been socialized. These moves to socialism are rarely the result of pure idealism. Rather, public ownership is often seen as the only way to ensure continuation of vital services that are not profitable enough to attract private enterprise. Other services—for example, health care—have been partially socialized because societies have judged it unethical for these services to be available only to those who can afford to pay for them. Education is a socialized service, but it went public so long ago that few recognize the public schools as one of the first socialized industries.

In the case of many socialized services, general availability and progressive tax rates have gone far toward meeting the maxim "from each according to ability, to each according to need." There are still inequalities

The primary goal of socialist economies is equitable distribution, not high productivity. Many state socialist nations have achieved this equality at rather low levels of productivity. In order to improve productivity, the Chinese government has experimented with free markets where farmers can sell surplus goods for profit. Such free markets have been enormously successful, boosting farm productivity and income and improving food availability.

in education and health care, but many fewer than there would be if these services were available on a strictly cash basis. The United States has done the least among major Western powers toward creating a mixed economy. Although the long-term shift in the United States has been toward greater socialization of services, some of this commitment has been reduced during the Reagan/Bush years. The future mix of socialist and capitalist principles in the U.S. will reflect political rather than strictly economic conditions.

THE POLITICAL ECONOMY

Although all institutions are interdependent, the link between economic and political institutions is particularly strong. In fact, earlier generations often referred to the two as a single institution—the political economy. Marxist scholars, of course, focus on the extent to which governments serve economic elites. Of equal interest is the question we address in this chapter: To what extent can contemporary socialist and capitalist economies be regarded as *political* economies—economies in service of political goals and political elites.

The Political Economy of State Socialism.   By definition, state socialism is a political economy. The state rather than private enterprise owns and controls production and distribution. It makes an enormous difference, however, whether the state is democratic or authoritarian. Democratic socialism, such as that practiced in Sweden, has been achieved with the support of the people. The economy is in many ways controlled by the voters.

Communism is socialism grafted onto an authoritarian political system. It is a socialist economy guided by a political elite and enforced by a military elite (Ebenstein 1980). The goals of socialism (equality, efficiency) are still there, but the political form is authoritarian rather than democratic. Many contemporary Marxists bitterly reject the traditional Soviet and Chinese brand of communism as an "antidemocratic perversion of socialism" (Stephens 1980), run at the expense of the workers instead of for the benefit of the workers (Oppenheimer 1985). These critics allege that the inefficiencies and inequalities rampant in communism have everything to do with authoritarianism and excessive bureaucratization and nothing to do with socialism as an economic system.

In Poland, Romania, the Soviet Union, and throughout the former communist bloc, the last few years have revealed widespread agreement that these critics have a point. Authoritarianism is being replaced by democracy, and some economic decision making is being transferred from the state to the market. In the Soviet Union, this restructuring of the socialist economy is called *perestroika*. The goal of such restructuring is not to abandon socialism but to shift production decisions from the political to the economic units—to reduce the political domination of the economy. Factory managers are expected to respond to the market instead of to directives from central planners. The goal, or manifest function, of these reforms is to make production more efficient. The latent function, however, will be to shift power from government bureaucrats to those people who run factories or agricultural collectives (Nee 1989).

The U.S. Political Economy.   It is not only under state socialism that the government interferes with the economy. Probusiness critics argue that the U.S. economy has been captured by government and that excessive regulation and interference reduce the ability of capitalism to respond to market forces. On the other hand, critics from the left argue that government has been captured by economic elites and that it pursues pro-business interests to the detriment of other citizens.

This debate has already been addressed to some extent in the previous chapter, and we will not expand on it here except to note that the relative merits of the arguments depend largely on two factors. The first factor is the segment of the economy we examine. In the industrial core, there are often cozy relationships between business and government that work for the benefit of business. The so-called military/industrial complex is one such relationship. On the periphery, on the other hand, small businesses are much more likely to be hemmed in by unwanted government interference than they are to have any influence over government. The second factor is the level of government we examine. At the federal level, government has considerable power over business, large and small. The situation is very different at the local level. Major corporations dwarf many cities in their assets and power, and local governments are often in a subservient position with regard to these businesses, having to bargain tax packages, zoning exceptions, and environmental quality to gain or retain jobs that improve the health of the local economy.

The Multinationals.   The link between political and economic actors is of particular concern when the economic actors become international actors. The large international companies (mostly American in origin)—the **multinationals** such as International Telephone and Telegraph, IBM, and General Motors—are so large that they dwarf many national governments in size. Their ability to move capital, jobs, and prosperity from one nation

Multinationals are large corporations that operate internationally.

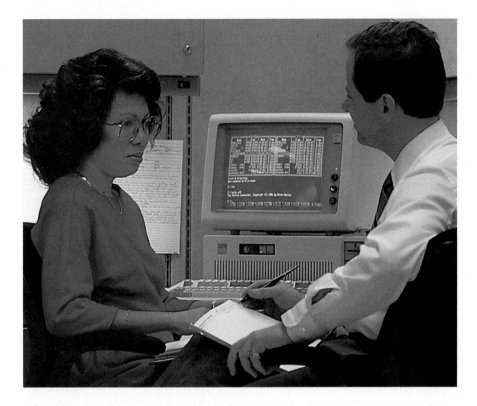

The majority of American workers are employed in the service sector (tertiary industry). We don't grow anything, harvest anything, or make anything. Like these bank auditors, growing numbers of us work in financial, health, education, or government institutions. We move money, ideas, paper, and people around, but we do not produce tangible products. This vast superstructure of tertiary workers, however, rests on a highly productive agricultural and industrial labor force that can supply us with all the food, computers, and other tangible goods that we need.

to another makes them political actors. Unlike the government, however, they are motivated by a search for profit rather than by the national interest.

There is a great deal of debate about the possible effects, good and ill, of such international economic enterprises. A few observers hope that ties of international finance will help create a more interdependent (and peaceful) world (Tannenbaum [1968] 1979). Less sanguine observers make two criticisms of the link between multinationals and U.S. foreign policy; they argue that economic interests direct foreign policy in order to pursue their own economic gains and that the government manipulates the multinationals in order to pursue its political agenda. Both concerns have a foundation in fact. Most recently, trade embargoes and economic sanctions against the Union of South Africa, Sandinista Nicaragua, Manuel Noriega's Panama, and Iraq are examples of a *political* economy.

The political and economic acts of the U.S. have enormous ramifications on the governments and economies of other nations of the world. Chapter 22 focuses on these interconnections and covers such issues as Third World debt, international development, and the role of multinationals.

THE DUAL ECONOMY IN THE U.S.

The U.S. economic system can be viewed as a **dual economy.** Its two parts are the complex giants of the industrial core and the small, competitive organizations that form the periphery. These two parts are distinguished

A **dual economy** consists of the complex giants of the industrial core and the small, competitive organizations that form the periphery.

from each other on two dimensions: the complexity of their organizational forms and the degree to which they dominate their economic environment (Baron and Bielby 1984).

THE INDUSTRIAL CORE: CORPORATE CAPITALISM

In classic capitalism, the market is peopled with a large number of small producers who are competing among themselves for labor, customers, and capital. This competition is what makes the market efficient. To a very significant extent, however, this competition is absent in today's industrial core. In place of the small, independent producers of the last century, we have a tightly knit group of industrial giants. The increase in size and interdependence has significantly changed the way capitalism operates.

Size of Units.   There are more than 250,000 businesses in the United States, but most of the nation's capital and labor are tied up in a few giants that form the industrial core. The largest U.S. companies—General Motors, Exxon, Ford, and IBM—control billions of dollars of assets and employ hundreds of thousands of individuals. These giants loom large on both the national and international scene: They exceed many nations of the world in wealth and population.

Interdependence.   Both the ownership *and* control of these large corporations have been divided up into small pieces; ownership has been split into stocks and control into boards of directors. Although some ordinary citizens own stocks, the majority of stockholders and the majority of directors come from the very wealthiest part of society (Roy and Bonacich 1988). Wealthy capitalists no longer face each other as competitors but as co-owners and codirectors. They all tend to own some AT&T stock, some IBM stock, and some R. J. Reynolds stock; they sit on the same boards of directors.

The result of shared ownership and control is that the capitalist class is increasingly cooperative rather than competitive (Roy and Bonacich 1988). This cooperation has economic and political consequences: It reduces competition and hence productivity and efficiency, and it makes the capitalist class a more potent political force (Mizruchi 1989).

THE COMPETITIVE SECTOR: SMALL BUSINESS

The competitive sector of the U.S. economy is made up largely of small businesses that are family owned or operated by a small group of partners. They are usually characterized by few employees, economic uncertainty, relatively little bureaucratization of management and authority, and particularism in hiring, firing, and promotion. The chief examples of these kinds of businesses are farming, small banks and retail stores, and restaurant and repair services. Some small manufacturing companies continue to meet these criteria. This segment of the competitive sector is what Marx called the petit (pronounced petty) bourgeois. The **petit bourgeois** are those who use their own modest capital to establish small enterprises in which they and their family provide the primary labor (Bechhofer and Elliott 1985).

One hundred fifty years ago, Marx predicted that the economy would become polarized into wealthy capitalists and impoverished workers. The

The **petit bourgeois** are those who use their own modest capital to establish small enterprises in which they and their family provide the primary labor.

Ohlson's gas station and general store is in many ways a classic example of the American small business: It is a family activity, it is located in a small town, and it requires largely blue-collar job skills. Such enterprises are seldom very prosperous. They do, however, offer independence, variety, and challenge—all the ingredients that go into producing satisfied workers.

disappearance of the small business class would be "the last act of the tragedy" (cited in Steinmetz and Wright 1989, 982). Yet this class has not disappeared. After steadily declining for over 100 years, it has recently reestablished itself at a solid 15 percent of the labor force.

This type of business has offered an especially important avenue of opportunity for minority Americans. Koreans, Hispanics, and African Americans who doubt their ability to get hired and make a successful career with a major corporation may nevertheless achieve moderate prosperity by operating neighborhood grocery stores, laundries, and fast-food franchises.

Who are the petit bourgeois? Some are professionals (doctors, lawyers, consultants), but many are blue-collar workers who own their own trucks, do independent contracting, own hamburger franchises, or have their own beauty salons. The people who work for themselves tend to be older and better educated and tend to live in smaller communities than do people who engage in the same occupations for a wage (Form 1982). Many of those who own their own businesses live on the edge of economic disaster; failure is just around the corner, and they may soon be working for someone else again. Nevertheless, owning one's own business is enormously attractive to many Americans. There is a real possibility of economic success; but more important, there is the opportunity for independence. Furthermore, the economic pitfalls that face the self-employed are not significantly greater than those facing the average blue-collar worker, for whom layoffs and unemployment are common experiences. Although many of the smallest businesses fail, the competitive sector contains many secure and profitable small businesses.

Informal Economy. An important sector of the periphery is the underground or **informal economy.** This is that part of the economy that escapes the record keeping and regulation of the state. It includes illegal activities such as prostitution, selling drugs, and running numbers, but it

The **informal economy** is that part of the economy that escapes the record keeping and regulation of the state.

also includes a large variety of legal but unofficial enterprises such as home repairs, housecleaning, and garment subcontracting. Often referred to disparagingly as "fly-by-night" businesses, enterprises in the informal sector are nevertheless an important source of employment. This is especially true for those segments of the population who would like to avoid federal record keeping: illegal aliens, those aliens whose visas do not permit working, senior citizens and welfare recipients who don't want their earnings to reduce their benefit levels, adolescents too young to meet work requirements, and many others (Portes and Sassen-Koob 1987).

THE SEGMENTED LABOR MARKET

Parallel to the dual economy is a dual labor market, generally referred to as a **segmented labor market,** in which hiring, advancement, and benefits vary systematically between the industrial core (the corporate sector) and the periphery (the competitive sector).

In the industrial core, firms generally rely on what are called internal labor markets. Almost all hiring is done at the entry level, and upper-level positions are filled from below. At all levels, credentials are critical for hiring and promotion. Within core firms, there are predictable career paths for both blue- and white-collar workers. Employment is generally secure, and benefits are relatively good. Wages and benefits are best in the very largest firms (Villemez and Bridges 1988).

In the competitive sector, on the other hand, credentials are less important, career paths are short and unpredictable, security is minimal, and benefits are relatively low. However, bureaucratization and red tape are less pervasive in the competitive sector, and both workers and managers have more freedom in their work.

The competitive sector offers a haven of employment for those who do not meet the demands of the corporate sector: those who do not have the required credentials, who have spotty works records, or who want to work part time. As a result, a disproportionate number of minorities and women work in the competitive sector. Because keeping a job and getting a promotion are governed almost exclusively by personal factors rather than by seniority or even ability, however, this sector is less likely to promote minorities or women; there is no affirmative-action officer in Joe's Café. The predominance of women and minorities in the competitive sector is an important reason for the relatively small gains shown by affirmative-action programs. The programs have been effective within the corporate sector, but many of the people to whom the programs are directed are not in that sector.

The **segmented labor market** parallels the dual economy. Hiring, advancement, and benefits vary systematically between the industrial core and the periphery.

The garment industry is part of the competitive sector of the economy, and it offers a classic example of the segmented labor market. The garment industry historically has relied on poorly paid immigrant and female labor. Employees are usually paid on a piece rate, and they receive no job security, no health insurance, no retirement, no career ladder.

WORK IN THE UNITED STATES

From the individual's point of view, economic institutions mean jobs. For some, jobs are just jobs; for others, they are careers. Either way, spending 40 years in the world of work makes this world central to most people's lives.

Employment and Unemployment

In the contemporary United States, approximately two-thirds of all adults are in the labor force at any given time. Labor force participation is higher for men than women, but the gap is closing rapidly.

The labor force includes the unemployed as well as those actually working. Over the last 40 years, unemployment has averaged about 5 percent of the labor force. Unemployment hit a postwar peak in 1983 with 10 percent unemployed; in 1990, unemployment had dropped to 5 percent. As noted in Table 16.1, minorities are much more likely than whites to experience unemployment: Black Americans experience more than twice as much unemployment as whites and Hispanics fall about halfway between black and white Americans.

Employment is a critical necessity for most people. It determines their status in their families and communities, it provides their income, and it structures their lives. Unemployment, then, is a critical problem, and dozens of studies show that involuntary unemployment has negative effects on mental and physical health. It is associated with alcoholism, family violence, and depression (Horwitz 1984).

Unemployment depends on two sets of factors: individual factors (education, race, skill) and structural factors (such as whether one works in the construction or the health care industry, the competitive sector or the corporate core) (Baron 1984). Those most vulnerable to unemployment are minorities and blue-collar workers (Schervish 1983). The degree of their vulnerability, however, varies by economic sector.

Unemployment due to involuntary layoffs is much higher in the industrial core than it is in the periphery. The degree of bureaucratization in the core, however, seems to ensure that a last-hired, first-fired principle operates, and there is little evidence of racial discrimination in this sector's unemployment (Cummings 1987). In the peripheral sector, we find more evidence of racial discrimination.

The Structure of Work: Occupations

Aside from the simplest consequences of working (income and filling up 40 hours of your time each week), what you do at work is probably as important as whether you work. Your income, status, security, and work satisfaction will be very different if you are a retail sales clerk working at the minimum wage rather than a teacher, for example.

Professions.   Occupations that demand specialized skills and creative freedom are **professions.** Their distinctive characteristics include (1) the production of an unstandardized product, (2) a high degree of personality involvement, (3) a wide knowledge of a specialized technique, (4) a sense of obligation to one's art, (5) a sense of group identity, and (6) a significant service to society (Gross 1958).

The definition of professions was originally developed for the so-called learned professions (law, medicine, college teaching). It applies equally well, however, to artists, dancers, and potters.

■
TABLE 16.1
UNEMPLOYMENT RATES, 1990

Overall unemployment rates fell from close to 11 percent in 1983 to 5.2 percent in 1990. Nevertheless, some pockets of the population, especially racial and ethnic minorities, continue to face very high unemployment. Not counted in these figures are all of the people who are working part time because they cannot find a full-time job.

Percentage of the Civilian Labor Force Over 16 Unemployed, by Race/Ethnicity

White	4.6%
Black	10.5
Hispanic[a]	7.8
TOTAL	5.3

[a]Hispanics may be of any race.
SOURCE: U.S. Department of Labor 1990, 38–39.

Professions are occupations that demand specialized skills and creative freedom.

■

White-collar workers appear across nearly the entire spectrum of occupational prestige. They range from the top executives of major firms down to minimum-wage clerks in government offices. This commodities broker with Charles Schwabb is typical of the upper end of the white-collar spectrum. His job demands a college education, ability to do independent thinking, and excellent communication skills. Although it is a high stress job, it also is a very well paid job that provides intrinsic as well as extrinsic rewards.

There is a great deal of variability in the rewards that professionals achieve. Some, such as physicians and lawyers, receive very high income; dancers and potters may earn very little. The major reward that all professionals have shared, however, is substantial freedom from supervision. Because their work is nonroutine and requires personal judgments, professionals have been able to demand—and get—the right to work their own hours, do things their own way, and arrange their own work lives.

Freedom from supervision remains the most outstanding reward of professional work, but it is a reward that is being eroded. Increasingly, people in the professions work for others within bureaucratic structures that constrain many of the characteristic aspects of professionalism.

What Color Is Your Collar?   Fifty years ago, the color of your collar was a pretty good indication of the status of your job. People who worked with their hands wore blue (or brown or flannel) collars; managers and others who worked in clean offices wore white collars. Those days are past. The labor force is far more diversified, and some of the old guidelines no longer work. The bagger at Safeway wears a white shirt and tie; the librarian wears blue jeans and sandals. Yet the librarian is a white-collar worker and the bagger is not.

Traditional white-collar workers are managers, professionals, typists, salespeople—those who work in clean offices and are expected to be able to think independently. Blue-collar workers are people in primary and secondary industry who work with their hands; they farm, assemble telephones, build houses, and weld joints. Although some blue-collar workers earn more than some white-collar workers, their jobs are characterized by lower incomes, lower status, lower security, closer supervision, and more routine.

Fifty years ago, this simple, two-part division of the labor force included most workers. These days it leaves out a growing category of low-skilled, low-status workers. Some have called these people the pink-collar workers, but they as often appear in company-supplied brown polyester suits or turquoise jackets. They fry hamburgers, stock K-Mart shelves, and collect money at the ''U-Serv'' gas station. An important characteristic of the jobs these workers hold is that they have a short or nonexistent career ladder and they pay the minimum wage or close to it.

OCCUPATIONAL OUTLOOK

As the graph in Figure 16.1 indicated, the outlook for the future is for greater expansion of the tertiary sector and even more reductions in employment in secondary and primary production. What will this mean for the kinds of jobs that are available in the future? Some of the changes projected between 1988 and 2000 are illustrated in Table 16.2

Some traditional occupational categories are expected to suffer major declines. The occupations with the largest projected decreases include both blue- and white-collar jobs: Stenographers and teachers will have a harder time finding jobs, as will sewing machine operators and farmers. The declining opportunities in these occupations reflect a variety of factors: changing age structure, loss of American jobs due to migration of industry overseas, and new technology.

■
TABLE 16.2
THE SHIFTING JOB MARKET: PROJECTED CHANGES BETWEEN 1988 AND 2000ᵃ

The demand for labor is expected to grow between 1988 and 2000, but opinion differs over the kinds of jobs that will be available for future workers. Although some observers note with satisfaction the growth of high-skill positions, others point with concern to the fact that many of the fastest growing jobs are low-skill and low-wage jobs.

| | CHANGES 1988–2000 | |
	PERCENT	NUMBER OF NEW JOBS
The five fastest-growing jobs relative to their size in 1988		
Paralegals	75%	62,000
Medical assistants	70	104,000
Home health aides	68	160,000
Radiologic technicians	66	87,000
Data processing equipment repairers	61	44,000
The five fastest-growing jobs in absolute number		
Salespersons, retail	19	730,000
Registered nurses	39	613,000
Janitors and cleaners	19	556,000
Waiters and waitresses	31	551,000
General managers and top executives	16	479,000

ᵃThese projections are from the moderate series, which assumes no major changes in general economic trends.
SOURCE: Silvestri and Lukasiewicz 1989, 60.

The issue of most controversy is what kind of new jobs the economy will offer. Optimistic observers point to the fact that executive and professional jobs are growing faster than average and point to the high quality and good pay of these new jobs as indicators of what awaits today's college graduates. Others focus on the rapid increase in what one critic has called "McJobs." Although not all entail selling hamburgers, many are low-status jobs with low wages and no benefits: health aides, waiters and waitresses, custodians and maids. The facts about the occupational outlook are presented in Table 16.2, which shows the five jobs that are expected to grow the most in absolute number and the five jobs that will grow the most in percentage terms (that is, in relation to their size in 1988). This list suggests that there will be growth at all educational and status levels. Big growth is expected for managers and top executives and for many highly-trained support personnel (paralegals, nurses, radiological technicians, data processing equipment repairers). Unfortunately, the list also suggests that some of the fastest growing occupations are in the low-paying end of the service sector: home health aides, janitors and cleaners, waiters and waitresses. Between 1988 and 2000, nearly three-quarters of the new jobs in the rapidly growing service sector will be in food service, health service, and cleaning and building service (Silvestri and Lukasiewicz 1989).

Both the optimists and the critics are correct in their expectations for the future: There is rapid growth in good jobs for college graduates and those with technical training, but there is also rapid growth in bad jobs.

The fastest-growing jobs today in the United States are in the service sector. Many of these are what have been called "McJobs." They are minimum-wage jobs offering few benefits and very limited career ladders. Our future job market appears to be splitting in two very different directions: high-technology jobs that require advanced education and low-skill service jobs. The decline of good-paying working-class jobs is a major concern.

Where there is no growth and even decline is in good jobs for those who lack technical training or a college degree. The losers in the transformation of the labor market are likely to be the traditional working class men and women who did skilled manual labor.

THE MEANING OF WORK

For most people, work is essential as the means to earn a livelihood. As noted in Chapter 9, one's work is often the most important determinant of one's position in the stratification structure and, consequently, of one's health, happiness, and life-style.

Work is more than this, however. It is also the major means that most of us use to structure our lives. It determines what time we get up, what we do all day, whom we do it with, and how much time and energy we have left for leisure. Thus, the nature of our work and our attitude toward it can have a tremendous impact on whether we view our lives as fulfilling or painful. If we are good at it, if it gives us a chance to demonstrate competence, and if it is meaningful and socially valued, then it can be a major contributor to life satisfaction.

Work Satisfaction.   American surveys consistently find that the large majority (over 80 percent) of workers report satisfaction with their work (Gallup Report 1989d). Although such a report may represent an acceptance of one's lot rather than real enthusiasm, it is remarkable that so few report dissatisfaction.

Studies of job satisfaction concentrate on two kinds of rewards that are available from work. **Intrinsic rewards** arise from the process of work; you experience them when you enjoy the people you work with and feel pride in your creativity and accomplishments. **Extrinsic rewards** are more tangible benefits, such as income and security; if you hate your job but love your paycheck, you are experiencing extrinsic rewards.

Intrinsic rewards are rewards that arise from the process of work; they include enjoying the people you work with and taking pride in your creativity and accomplishments.

Extrinsic rewards are tangible benefits such as income and security.

Ideally, work would be most satisfying if it provided high levels of both intrinsic and extrinsic rewards. A review of dozens of studies shows that the most satisfying jobs are those that offer (1) autonomy and freedom from close supervision, (2) good pay and benefits, (3) job security, (4) opportunity for promotions, (5) use of valued skills and abilities, (6) variety, (7) interesting work, and (8) occupational prestige (Mortimer 1979). There is, however, a great deal of variability in the extent to which these attributes are attached to jobs. Some jobs score high on all of them and some score low on nearly all of them.

Generally, the most satisfied workers are those in the learned professions, people such as lawyers, doctors, and professors. These people have considerable freedom to plan their own work, to express their talents and creativity, and to work with others; furthermore, their extrinsic rewards are substantial. The least satisfied workers are those who work on automobile assembly lines. Although their extrinsic rewards are moderately high, their work is almost completely without intrinsic reward; they have no control over the pace or content of the work and are generally unable to interact with coworkers. A survey of automotive assembly-line workers showed that only 8 percent would choose the same occupation again, whereas 93 percent of urban university professors would choose the same occupation (Kohn 1972). In between these extremes, professionals and skilled workers generally demonstrate the greatest satisfaction; semiskilled, unskilled, and clerical workers indicate lower levels of satisfaction.

Alienation.   Another dimension of the quality of work life is explicitly Marxist: **Alienation** occurs when workers have no control over their labor. Workers are alienated when they do work that they think is meaningless (push papers or brooms) or immoral (build bombs) or when their work takes their physical and emotional energies without giving any intrinsic rewards in return. Alienated workers feel *used*.

The factory system of the mid 19th century was the ultimate in alienation. In 1863, a mother gave the following testimony to a committee investigating child labor:

> When he was seven years old I used to carry him [to work] on my back to and fro through the snow, and he used to work 16 hours a day. . . . I have often knelt down to feed him, as he stood by the machine, for he could not leave it or stop (cited in Hochschild 1985, 3).

This child was truly an instrument of labor. He was being used, just as a hammer or a shovel is, to create a product that would belong to someone else.

Although few of us work on assembly lines any more, modern work can also be alienating. Service work, in fact, has its own forms of alienation. In occupations from nursing to teaching to working as flight attendants, not merely our bodies but also our emotions become instruments of labor. To turn out satisfied customers, we must smile and be cheerful in the face of ill humor, rudeness, or actual abuse. Studies of individuals in these occupations show that many have trouble with this emotional work. After smiling for eight hours a day for pay, they feel that their smiles have no meaning at home. They lose touch with their emotions and feel alienated from themselves (Hochschild 1985).

The kind of work that we do determines what we do all day, who we do it with, and, not least, how much income and prestige we have. For these reasons, our jobs are one of our most critical roles, and our jobs spill over to affect what we do at home and in our communities. Studies show that people who have flexibility and independence at work are also flexible and independent at home. On the other hand, people whose work requires rigid authority may be more authoritarian at home.

Alienation occurs when workers have no control over the work process or the product of their labor; they are estranged from their work.

Alienation is not the same as job dissatisfaction (Erikson 1986). Alienation occurs when workers lack control. It is perfectly possible that workers with no control, but with high wages and a pleasant work environment, will express high job satisfaction. Marxist scholars believe that job satisfaction in such circumstances is a sign of false consciousness (Halaby 1986).

Self-Direction at Work.   A key aspect of work that relates to both job satisfaction and alienation is self-direction. A 20-year program of studies by Kohn and his associates shows that the degree of self-direction in our work affects satisfaction, alienation, and our personalities.

Self-direction has three components: job complexity, degree of supervision, and degree of routinization. Low-routine, low-supervision, and high-complexity jobs provide the greatest satisfaction and give the greatest opportunity for self-expression. Such work includes not only that of college professors but also that of blue-collar workers with flexible jobs requiring active decision making. On the other hand, high-routine, high-supervision, and low-complexity jobs such as working on an assembly line or running groceries over a scanning machine give the least satisfaction and the most alienation.

These job characteristics also affect personality. In studies in the United States and Japan, Kohn and his associates have consistently demonstrated that people who have more self-direction at work have greater mental flexibility, more trust, and greater receptivity to change; they also have lower levels of authoritarianism, conservatism, fatalism, self-depreciation, and conformity (Kohn and Schooler 1983; Naoi and Schooler 1986).

TECHNOLOGY AND THE FUTURE OF WORK

The productivity of workers and the quality of their work experience are often tied directly to the tools they work with. Some work technologies, such as the assembly line, increase alienation while they increase productivity. Others, such as the photocopier, appear to be unmixed blessings. The rapid introduction of computerization and automation has had far-reaching effects on the nature of work.

Many people argue that the new technology is inescapably antilabor. These critics point out three negative effects of technology on labor: de-skilling, displacing workers, and greater supervision.

1. *De-skilling.* Many observers believe that increased mechanization has reduced the skill level needed for many jobs to the point where it is difficult to take pride in craft or a job well done. The process of automating a job so that it takes much less skill than it used to is called *de-skilling*. De-skilling occurs at all levels of labor, not just on the assembly line. For example, in the days before word processors, photocopiers, and self-correcting typewriters, good typists could take pride in their work. With the new technologies, almost anyone can turn out decent-looking copy.

An important element of the de-skilling process is that it reduces the scope for individual judgment. In hundreds of jobs across the occupational spectrum, computers make decisions for us. In the sawmill industry, for example, a computer now assesses the shape of a log and decides how it

The Luddites: Down with Machines!

Since the dawn of the industrial era, there has been tension between labor and technology. In 1675, weavers rioted against the introduction of looms that could allegedly do the work of 20 people, and in 1768 sawyers in London destroyed a mechanized sawmill. The most widely known revolt of labor against machinery, however, was the Luddite uprising in England between 1811 and 1816.

Wool was a major part of the English economy in the early 19th century. It was largely a home industry, and in Lancashire nearly every home was engaged in wool production. The work was tedious and difficult. Particularly difficult was the last stage in which a worker wielding 50-pound shears finished the fabric by cutting off all the nubs. Being able to handle these shears for 88 hours a week (the standard work week) required great strength and skill. It was an esteemed occupation.

In 1811, finishing machines were introduced to do this work. Each machine replaced six men. Not only were the men out of a job but also the skills developed over a lifetime were made worthless. As use of the machines spread through the valley, large numbers of men were thrown out of work, and their families starved. On the horizon were more machines to take over other phases of wool production. Added to this, England was engaged in the Napoleonic Wars with their trade embargoes and the subsequent high price of food. The classic ingredients for insurrection were in place. The focus of the workers' anger was the machines, and their response was to destroy them.

In 1811, a young man named Ned Ludd, or Lud or maybe Ludlam, is alleged to have broken up his father's hosiery loom because he resented a rebuke. The incident, which may have been imaginary, coincided with the eruption of machine-breaking demonstrations, and the labor movement came to be called the Luddites.

◼

Now, almost every year a new technology is developed that can reduce even further the dependence of industry on human labor.

In the early 19th century, any organization of labor was illegal. Nevertheless, laborers met secretly at taverns and later in the woods to plan well-organized attacks. A body of men with blackened faces would break into a shop and destroy all of the machinery. As the movement progressed, it became less disciplined and owners too were assaulted and their homes looted. It was, said one observer, collective bargaining by riot.

The government was uncertain how to respond. There were a few liberals who were sympathetic with labor. Lord Byron, for example, wrote that "however much we may rejoice in any improvement in ye arts which may be beneficial to mankind; we must not allow mankind to be sacrificed to improvements in Mechanism" (cited in Reid 1986). The hard-liners won, however, and troops were sent in to restore order. Leaders and alleged leaders of the Luddites were hanged or deported to the far corners of the empire.

The Luddite movement caused hardly a pause in the increasing use of machines to replace workers. Now, almost every year a new technology is developed that can reduce even further the dependence of industry on human labor. Although we have unemployment insurance, early retirement schemes, and welfare to cushion the blows, the process still causes human misery as valuable skills are debased and employment is lost. If we use the term *Luddite* to include all of those who "resist mechanization, automation, and the like, and who are the supposed enemies of 'progress' where the adoption of labour-saving devices is concerned" (Thomis 1970, 12), there are probably plenty of people who remain Luddites in spirit.

should be cut to get the most board feet of lumber from it. An important element of skill and judgment honed from years of experience is now made worthless. According to the chief proponent of this argument, the central process in de-skilling is the separation of mind and hand (Braverman 1974).

This photograph shows robotic welding in a Renault-Alliance factory in Kenosha, Wisconsin. Studies show that, on the average, a robotic welder can do the work of 1.5 men per shift—and the robot can work 3 shifts per day. The replacement of human labor with robots and other computerized tools saves money, reduces human error, and frees people from dangerous and unpleasant work. All too often, however, it frees them from any work at all. Displacement of human labor with machines raises serious questions about the future of the industrial working class.

2. *Displacement of the labor force.* One of the most critical complaints about automation is that it replaces people with machines. A few examples suffice. Computerization in grocery stores has resulted in sharp reductions in employment by eliminating inventory clerks and pricing/repricing personnel, as well as reducing the skill level in cashiering to the point that an average 15-year-old could do it. In the automobile industry, it is estimated that one of the new robots can replace 1.5 men per shift—and the robot can work three shifts a day (U.S. Department of Labor 1985, 1986b).

In industry after industry, more sophisticated technology has made sharp inroads into the number of hours of labor necessary to produce goods and services. Many have concluded that fear of job loss is one of the reasons why employees seldom complain about the de-skilling aspects of their jobs. If they still have a job, they are happy about it (Vallas and Yarrow 1987).

3. *Greater supervision.* Computerization and automation give management more control over the production process. More aspects of the production process are determined by management through its computerized instructions and less is determined by the employees. Computers also keep more complex and thorough records on employees (Rule and Attewell 1989). For example, the scanner machines used in grocery stores do more than keep inventory records and add up your grocery bill. They also keep tabs on the checker by producing statistics such as number of corrections made per hour, number of items run through per hour, and average length of time per customer.

Whether new technologies are an enemy of labor may depend on which laborer we ask. From the standpoint of professionals in the knowledge industries (education, communications), new technology is undoubtedly a boon. Computers have expanded their job opportunities and enhanced their lives. Those whose work is being replaced rather than aided by computers, however, are less likely to see anything wonderful about it. Those most adversely affected by these developments are women and less-skilled workers (Gill 1985). The policy implications of these changes on the labor force are discussed in the Issues in Social Policy.

ISSUES IN SOCIAL POLICY

Postindustrialization or De-laborization?

Twenty years ago, postindustrialization was talked of as if it meant the coming of the golden age. Dirty smokestack industries with dangerous jobs were expected to be replaced by clean, high-technology jobs so that the environment would be better, workers would be happier, and life would be rosy.

Experience has been far less positive (Summers 1984). The smokestack industries have indeed faded away. In community after community across the U.S., industries that manufactured steel, automobiles, tires, or electrical appliances have closed

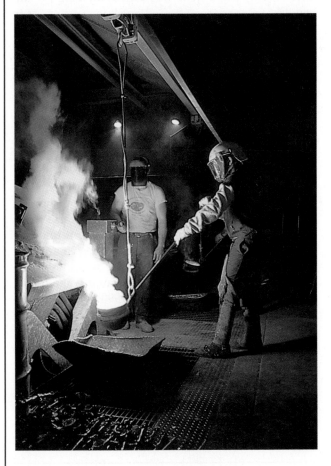

down, and millions of working-class men and women have been thrown out of work. The clean, new jobs have not materialized. As a result, whole communities are unemployed. In these communities, financial institutions are choked by repossessed cars and houses and motor homes; there is nobody to pay taxes or foot the bill for education or social welfare services.

The U.S. economy is in the process of being restructured. Some call it postindustrialization and emphasize the boom in the high-technology and knowledge industries. Others call it "de-laborization" (McQueen 1982). They stress that industry (just as agriculture before it) has learned how to produce more and more goods with fewer and fewer people. Just as one farmer with a combine can cover 400 acres, one computer operator can run an entire assembly line. Industry has learned to get along without people. Can people learn to get along without industry?

There are, of course, new jobs and new industries. Analysts call this new labor market the "hour-glass" market. It is wide on the top and on the bottom but very slim in the middle. An unemployed steelworker is obviously not in a good position to compete for an opening for an electrical engineer, a lawyer, or a computer programmer. He or she *can* get a job behind the automotive counter at K-Mart or as a custodian at the office park. This means trading a secure job with a decent salary, health insurance, and a pension for a minimum-wage job with no benefits and little security. It means losing the house, skimping on the children's health care, and going on food stamps.

The consequences of "de-laborization" are substantial. Not only individual workers but entire communities are impoverished. Further, the national economy is undergoing a parallel process of reverse development: Like a Third World country, we export raw materials such as logs and wheat and import manufactured products such as VCRs and automobiles. People in Mexico or Japan or

ISSUES IN SOCIAL POLICY continued

Korea have jobs manufacturing products for the U.S. market while American workers are making hamburgers.

PUBLIC POLICY OPTIONS

What can public policy do to protect America's jobs? There are three general policy options: the conservative free-market option, new industrial policies, and the social welfare option (Hooks 1984).

The Conservative Free-Market Approach

Generally, business leaders and conservatives argue that the solution is to reduce wages and benefits. If labor is cheap, they argue, business will have less incentive to automate or to move assembly plants to Mexico.

By default, this policy has been implemented. In communities across the nation, managements have used threats of plant closings to force wage concessions and reduce benefits. Labor unions are reduced to negotiating benefit protection in the face of wage reductions; in many cases, they have even failed to do this. Because so many workers have been afraid of losing their jobs, organized labor's power has been sharply reduced. Thus, one result of "de-laborization" is the reduced economic circumstances of workers who still have jobs.

New Industrial Policies

Liberals argue that private profit should not be the only goal of economic activity and that the state should see to it that economic decisions protect communities' and workers' interests (Genovese 1989). Among the specific policies recommended are: (a) federal trade policies that make American-made goods more competitive in international markets and that reduce the advantage that foreign-made products have in the U.S.; (b) vigorous state investment in industries that will provide the largest number of decent jobs; (c) government over-sight of mergers and plant closings to make sure plants behave responsibly; and (d) state support for worker efforts to buy and manage their own industries.

Social Welfare Policies

New industrial policies are designed to keep people working; social welfare policies are aimed at protecting those who are thrown out of work. Among the policies recommended are (Blakely and Shapira 1984): (a) six-month notification of plant closings; (b) paid leave for soon-to-be-displaced employees who look for alternative jobs; (c) retraining programs for displaced workers; (d) relocation assistance for displaced workers; and (e) substantially more generous unemployment benefits.

CONCLUSION

De-industrialization is not unique to the U.S. It has been experienced by all the Western industrialized nations. An analysis of their experiences suggests that the most effective policy would combine social welfare programs with a new industrial policy (Hooks 1984). In 1990, however, the U.S. is still firmly in the conservative camp. A 1988 bill to require a two-month notification of plant closings was vetoed by President Reagan, though Congress later overrode the veto. In 1989, a bill to raise the minimum wage was opposed by President Bush because it would make labor too expensive and send jobs to Mexico. A compromise was finally worked out that allowed the minimum wage to be raised to $3.80 an hour in April 1990 and $4.25 in April 1991 with the condition that employers could use the old minimum wage ($3.35) as a "training wage" for new employees for the first six months of their employment (Haugen and Mellor 1990). Because of the enormous barriers to getting any part of the social welfare or new industrial policies passed at the federal level, many analysts believe that the real action is likely to occur at the state level.

■ SUMMARY

1. The economic institution has a profound effect on other institutional structures, particularly government, stratification systems, education, and the family. Changes from preindustrial to industrial to postindustrial economies have thus had profound effects on social organization.

2. The tertiary sector of the economy has expanded rapidly and is expected to employ three quarters of the labor force by 2000. The tertiary sector includes highly paid professional occupations as well as custodians and retail sales clerks.

3. Capitalist economies are based on competition, socialist economies on cooperation. Capitalist economies are designed to maximize productivity, and socialist economies emphasize equality of distribution. Many modern societies are mixed; they try to balance productivity and equality.

4. The operation of an economic system depends on the political structure in which it operates. Socialism in combination with an authoritarian government is called communism. The former communist bloc is now trying to unlink socialism from authoritarianism.

5. In the U.S., critics allege that the political/economic link is problematic for two reasons: the politically powerful use the economic system to maintain their advantage and the economic system has too much power over government, nationally and internationally.

6. The United States has a dual economy containing two distinct parts: the industrial core and the competitive sector at the periphery. These are paralleled by a segmented labor market.

7. Economic projections show substantial changes in occupations in just the next 10 years. The largest number of new jobs will be in highly trained professions or in low-status, low-wage service positions. The major losers will be those who have occupied traditional blue-collar jobs.

8. Scholars look at the individual meaning of work from two perspectives: work satisfaction and alienation. Although most U.S. workers report satisfaction with their work, Marxists often argue that they are nevertheless alienated because they are estranged from the products of their labor.

9. Critics argue that automation and computerization have had three ill effects on labor: de-skilling jobs, reducing the number of jobs, and increasing control of workers. Nevertheless, some occupations have grown or been made easier through new technology.

10. The U.S. is becoming de-industrialized, losing many of the good jobs that kept the working class afloat. Three major approaches to relieving this problem are: the conservative free-market option, new industrial policies and the social welfare option. Although it has negative effects for the working class, the U.S. seems to be pursuing the free-market option.

■ SUGGESTED READINGS

Dix, Keith. 1988. What's a Coal Miner to Do? The Mechanization of Coal Mining. Pittsburgh: Pittsburgh University Press. An analysis of one of the industries hardest hit by de-industrialization. Keith takes a historical look at the development of new equipment throughout this century and how it has affected the miners and communities that have depended on work in the mines.

Dolbeare, Kenneth M. 1984. Democracy at Risk: The Politics of Economic Renewal. Chatham, N.J.: Chatham House. An integrated approach to the political as well as economic problems lying behind America's current economic problems and low industrial productivity.

Halle, David. 1984. America's Working Man: Work, Home, and Politics Among Blue-Collar Property Owners. Chicago: University of Chicago Press. An ethnography of the blue-collar workers in a single plant in New Jersey, using the workers' own words to illuminate issues such as alienation, de-skilling, and class consciousness.

Hochschild, Arlie R. 1985. The Managed Heart: The Commercialization of Human Feelings. Berkeley: University of California Press. A study of alienation in service occupations, with detailed examination of how flight attendants handle emotion work.

Kalleberg, Arne, and Berg, Ivar. 1987. Work and Industry: Structures, Markets, Processes. New York: Plenum. A book written for scholars but that is accessible to an educated public. Kalleberg and Berg discuss how the structure of work affects income inequality, worker satisfaction, and labor markets.

■ PHOTO ESSAY: **Sports: An Emerging Institution?**

Most of us are introduced to sports as very young children: we throw balls, jump ropes, and run sack races. During our school years, all of us participate in team sports as part of physical education classes and many choose to participate in intramural school sports. After the school years, many of us become less active in sports. Nevertheless, golf, swimming, tennis, and bowling are often important leisure activities well into the last stage of the life course.

If you are like most people, you enjoy sports. You play tennis, softball, or swim, and spend some Sunday afternoons happily vegging out while catching a game in front of your television. Even if you do not know that Louis Sullivan is the Secretary of the U.S. Department of Health and Human Services, you probably know who Jackie Joyner-Kersey, Joe Montana, Michael Jordan, and Steffi Graf are.

For most of us, sports are something we do in our leisure time. We watch sports on TV, go to games and meets, and play tennis or golf in the time left after school or work. For most of us, sports are a reason to spend money—not make money; they are a form of play. Does this mean sports are trivial? Short reflection will tell you that the answer is no.

Some have suggested that sports, far from being trivial, are in the process of becoming an institution in contemporary society. Let's review the definition of an institution and see if sports qualify. Chapter four defined an institution as a social structure that has three general characteristics: It endures for generations, includes a complex set of statuses, roles, norms and values, and it meets a basic human need.

The first two of these criteria are relatively easy for sports to meet. The history of the Olympic Games tells us that sports have been an enduring part of human society. In fact, sports are probably a universal aspect of human societies. Most societies play some kind of ball games, and it is difficult to imagine a society in which children do not compete in some version of the 50-yard dash.

Sports also meet the criterion of having a complex set of values and norms. In addition to specific rules that govern each sport, the entire field of sports is governed by a common set of norms and values that can be summarized by the injunction, "be a good sport." This maxim means that you should be a cheerful loser and a gracious winner, play fair, and give your best effort. According to the norms of sports, not doing your best to win is almost as damning as cheating. If you are behind 44 to 12 and it is impossible for you to win, you still have to try. If you give up, this is taken as a demonstration of lack of character.

The critical question, then, is whether sports meet a basic human need. Is it essential to the fabric of society?

In American society, sports are an important part of life at both the micro and the macro level. Although many of us are spectators rather than players and few earn a living at it, sports play an important part in all of our socialization experiences. Cast your mind back to your elementary and high school experiences. Were you the last one chosen for softball teams or were you a standout athlete? Did

■ PHOTO ESSAY: **Sports: An Emerging Institution?**

■

Sports reinforce the values of teamwork and cooperation and encourage fitness. As a result, nearly every government in the world has concluded that sports are functional. Both communist and capitalist nations, dictatorships and democracies have encouraged sports among their people. Although these Vermont parents may think that baseball is training their son for a uniquely American way of life, the functions of team sports are valued in every country of the world.

you dread or look forward to dodge ball? Whichever category you were in, these experiences undoubtedly had a lasting effect on your self-concept and self-esteem. Sports also may have helped you stay out of trouble, and taught you important lessons about the importance of practice and teamwork, and of winning and losing graciously.

At the macro level, many observers believe that sports serve vital functions for society. Among the functions attributed to sports are reinforcing norms and values important to society, helping to integrate society, and

channeling hostility and aggression. For example, sports are an important mechanism for teaching and reinforcing central societal norms of competition and teamwork. Sports metaphors, such as "There is no 'I' in TEAM," teach us that success is achieved by putting the group above individual glory. Slogans like "Winners never quit and quitters never win" reinforce values of competition and working hard to get ahead. These lessons are also taught in church, school, and family, but they are reinforced effectively on the playing field. The importance of

these lessons and the role of sports in symbolizing and integrating communities are important reasons why nearly every twentieth-century nation has encouraged athletics.

The role of sports in reproducing social structures, including inequality, provides additional evidence that sports is an emerging institution. Conflict theorists have argued that sports play a role in reproducing class relations and supporting racism and sexism. For example, it has been suggested that school athletics is a form of tracking that schools use for lower-class and minority students. These young people are directed toward athletics—instead of academics—as a road to success. However, only a very small minority of high school athletes are able to support themselves through athletics. In fact, one recent source suggests that only one of 12,000 high school athletes will earn money as a professional athlete; among those who make it, the average professional career lasts only three years ("Career Statistics" 1990).

The importance of sports in contemporary society can be illustrated by a comparison between sports and religion. In the Middle Ages, communities built huge, expensive cathedrals. Although only used extensively on Sunday mornings, they were a potent symbol of their communi-

One of the major criticisms of sports is that they encourage sexism. First, sports offer a highly visible arena for demonstrating that males can, on the average, lift more, hit harder, and run faster than women. Second, women and girls have often been excluded from sports participation, restricted to the role of cheerleading on the side lines. The sex barriers have not disappeared in sports, but they have been falling. Many high schools have had to close down their cheerleading corps because the girls are too busy playing on their own teams.

■ PHOTO ESSAY: **Sports: An Emerging Institution?**

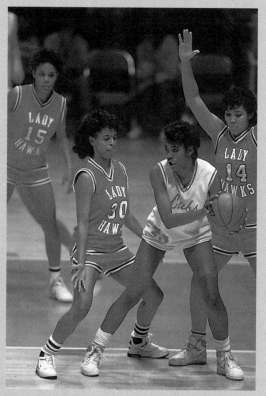

If asked to say whether sports are a good thing or a bad thing most Americans would give you an answer that would be compatible with structural-functional theory. Their answers would point to the role of sports in building character and reinforcing important values. As these photographs suggest, participation in sports can help develop character traits such as competitiveness, learning how to push yourself, learning how to work with a team, and learning how to put a good face on taking second place instead of first.

ties. In contemporary society, communities are more apt to build domed stadiums. These facilities also are huge and expensive, often used only one day a week. Like the cathedrals of the Middle Ages, the stadiums symbolize what our society holds dear. The parallels can be extended almost indefinitely. Consider, for example, whether criticism of ignorance of your community's athletic team might be viewed as a contemporary version of religious heresy.

Sports are very big business. They are also universal, lasting and complex. Realistically, however, sports are not as essential to our well being as the family or the economy. For the most part, sports duplicate functions that are served by other institutions: They reinforce lessons, patterns, and symbols that are also found in the family, economy, school, and government. We conclude that sports are an important but secondary institution.

Sports has critics as well as admirers. One of the criticisms of organized sports is that they may damage instead of improve athletes' health. Life-threatening injuries are most common in gymnastics and football, but participants in many sports may damage their longterm health by using steroids or tearing muscles and ruining joints. A conflict perspective is most often used to explain what happens when players are encouraged to push themselves too far for the glory (profit) of the coach, team, school, or franchise.

17

RELIGION

HAVE YOU EVER . . .

Seriously considered what the concept *God-given rights* means? Most people who use this phrase appear to imply that God was the real author of the U.S. Bill of Rights. They seem to believe that the right to bear arms, the right to freedom of speech, and the right to assemble were handed down to our founding fathers much as God handed Moses the Ten Commandments on Mount Sinai. (Is it just a coincidence that there are 10 of each?)

The Declaration of Independence claims that "all men are created equal, that they are endowed by their Creator with certain unalienable Rights, that among these are Life, Liberty, and the pursuit of Happiness." The rights spoken of are not religious rights, such as forgiveness or salvation; they are political, economic, and civil rights (Garrett 1987).

The issue of God's role in economic and political affairs has been controversial for 4,000 years, and it continues to be a vital contemporary issue. All around the globe, revolutions and civil wars are fought in the name of "God-given" rights and religion: Sikhs fight Hindus in India, Moslems fight Jews in Palestine, Christians fight Moslems in Lebanon, Protestants fight Catholics in Northern Ireland, and liberation theologists struggle against oppression in Latin America. Many of these struggles are about economic and political rights as much as about religion, but each side uses religion as a means of building internal unity and of rationalizing domination or rebellion.

We need not go halfway around the world to find evidence that religion is involved in the turmoil of public life. Current U.S. battles about abortion, prayer in the schools, state funding for parochial schools, and public support for Christmas displays are examples of the many areas in which religion and politics overlap. In this chapter, we introduce the basic concepts of the sociology of religion and consider their implications for American society.

Religion is an important part of social life. It is intertwined with politics and culture, and it is intimately concerned with integration and conflict. At the microsociological level, sociologists examine the consequences of religious belief and involvement for the lives of ordinary people. On a macrosociological level, sociologists examine how society affects religion and how religion affects society. Of particular concern is the contribution of religion to social order and social change.

THE SCIENTIFIC STUDY OF RELIGION

Religion is a system of beliefs and practices related to sacred things that unites believers into a moral community.

The first step in studying religion is to agree on what it is. How can we define religion so that our definition includes the contemplative meditation of a Buddhist monk, the speaking in tongues of a modern Holy Roller, the worship of nature in Native American cultures, and the formal ceremonies of the Catholic church? Sociologists define **religion** as a system of beliefs and practices related to sacred thing that unites believers into a moral community (Durkheim [1915] 1961, 62). This emphasis on the sacred allows us to include belief systems that invoke supernatural forces as explanations of earthly struggles (Stark and Bainbridge 1979, 121), as well as those that give personal qualities to the forces of nature. It does not include, however, belief systems such as Marxism or science that do not emphasize the sacred.

Sociologists who study religion treat it as set of beliefs. As with beliefs about the desirability of monogamy or democracy, our concern is not whether the beliefs are true or false. The scientific study of religion does not ask whether God exists, whether salvation is really possible, or which is the true religion. Rather, it examines the ways in which culture, society, and class relationships affect religion and the ways in which religion affects individuals and social structure.

WHY RELIGION? SOME THEORETICAL ANSWERS

Religion is a fundamental feature of all societies. Whether primitive or advanced, each society has forms of religious activity and expressions of religious behavior. Why? The answer appears to lie in the fact that every individual and every society must struggle to find explanations of events and experiences that go beyond personal experience. The poor man looks around him and wonders, "Why me?" The woman whose child dies in its sleep wonders, "Why mine?" The community struck by flood or tornado wonders, "Why us?" Beyond these personal dilemmas, people may wonder why the sun comes up every morning, why there is a rainbow in the sky, and what happens after death. Individuals and societies struggle with questions like these, searching for meanings and explanations. The answers vary widely from culture to culture, but each culture furnishes answers that help individuals understand their place in the universe. Many of these answers are given by religion.

Religion helps us interpret and cope with events that are beyond our control and understanding; tornadoes, droughts, and plagues become meaningful when they are attributed to the workings of some greater force

Although religion is common to all cultures, the forms that religious activity can take vary widely. This Trappist Monk, a member of a Roman Catholic religious order in France, spends much of his day in meditation, silence, and fasting. His austere monastic life is a very different application of religious belief than that required of The Holy Ghost People, who include the unusual practice of handling live poisonous snakes as part of their religious rituals. This particular practice is a demonstration of their faith that God will protect them and they will not be harmed.

(Spilka, Shaver, and Kirkpatrick 1985). Beliefs and rituals develop as a way to control or appease this greater force, and eventually they become patterned responses to the unknown. Rain dances may not bring rain, and prayers may not lead to good harvests; but both provide a familiar and comforting context in which people can confront otherwise mysterious and inexplicable events. Regardless of whether they are right or wrong, religious beliefs and rituals help people cope with the extraordinary events they experience.

Within this general sociological approach to religion, there are two distinct theoretical perspectives. One school, associated with Durkheim, sees religion as a thinly disguised worship of society, serving to create and maintain social solidarity. The second school, associated with Weber, views religion as an intellectual force that may challenge society as well as support it. Let us briefly examine both of these schools.

DURKHEIM: RELIGION AS THE WORSHIP OF SOCIETY

Durkheim's approach to the study of religion is based on the structural-functional perspective. He assumed that if religion is universal, then it must meet basic needs of society; it must serve important functions. Durkheim began his analysis of religion by trying to identify what was common to all religions.

The Elementary Forms of Religion.   Durkheim ([1915] 1961) compared religions from all over the world and concluded that all share three elements, which he called the elementary forms of religion: (1) a distinction between the sacred and the profane, (2) a set of beliefs, and (3) a set of rituals.

THE SACRED AND THE PROFANE.   A central component of all religions is the division of human experience into the sacred and the profane. The **profane** represents all that is routine and taken for granted in the everyday world, things that are known and familiar and that we can control, understand, and manipulate. The **sacred,** by contrast, consists of the events and things that we hold in awe and reverence—what we can neither understand nor control.

In premodern societies, a large proportion of the world is viewed as sacred. Many events are beyond control and manipulation. As advances in human knowledge increase a society's ability to explain and even control what was previously mysterious, fewer and fewer events require supernatural explanations; less is held sacred. When an event can be explained without reference to supernatural forces, then it is no longer sacred. This process of transferring things, ideas, or events from the sacred to the profane is called **secularization.** Science and technology have been major contributors to secularization. They have given us explanations for lightning, rainbows, and death that rely on physical rather than supernatural forces.

BELIEFS, MYTHS, AND CREEDS.   A second common dimension to all religions is a set of beliefs about the supernatural. Religious beliefs center around uncertainties associated with birth, death, creation, success, failure, and crisis. They become part of the worldview constructed by culture as a rationale for the human condition and the recurrent problems experienced. As beliefs become organized into an interrelated set of assumptions about the supernatural, they form the basis for official religious doctrines, which find expression in the rituals of the church.

RITUALS.   Religion is a practice as well as a belief system. It brings people together to express through ritual the things they hold sacred. In contemporary Christianity, rituals are used to mark such events as births, deaths, weddings, and Christ's birth and resurrection. In an earlier era, when most people lived off the land and life was more uncertain, planting and harvest were occasions for important rituals in the Christian church; they are still important ritual occasions in many religions.

The **profane** represents all that is routine and taken for granted in the everyday world, things that are known and familiar and that we can control, understand, and manipulate.

The **sacred** consists of events and things that we hold in awe and reverence—what we can neither understand nor control.

Secularization is the process of transferring things, ideas, or events from the sacred realm to the profane.

The Functions of Religion.   Durkheim argued that these elementary forms of religion serve functions for individuals and for society as a whole. For individuals, the beliefs and rituals of religion offer support, consolation, and reconciliation in times of need. On ordinary occasions, many people find satisfaction and a feeling of belongingness in religious participation. This feeling of belongingness is the moral community, or community of believers, that is part of the definition of religion.

On a societal level, Durkheim argued, the major function of religion is that it gives tradition a moral imperative. This means that most of the central values and norms of any culture are taught and reinforced through its religion. These values and norms cease to be merely the usual way of doing things and become the only moral way of doing them. They become sacred. When a tradition is sacred, it is continually affirmed through ritual and practice and is largely immune to change.

Within this functionalist perspective, the worship of God is seen as a barely disguised worship of society (Durkheim, in O'Dea 1966, 12). Religion is seen as a means of lending supernatural authority to traditional practices, a way of giving usual practice the unchallengeable standing of supernaturally established law.

Weber: Religion as an Independent Force

Durkheim looked at the forms of religion and asked about the kinds of functions they perform: the consequences of religion for individuals and society. Weber shared this interest, but he was also concerned with the processes through which religious answers are developed and how their content affects society.

For most people, religion is a matter of following tradition; people worship as their parents did before them. To Weber, however, the essence of religion is the search for knowledge about the unknown. In this sense, religion is similar to science; it is a way of coming to understand the world

Ritual is an important part of all religions. Ritual occasions such as Passover Seders and Easter masses bring people together as a community of believers and reaffirm their shared values. Even those people who are not particularly devout in their beliefs find the traditional ritual comforting. For many of us, as for these Jews, our religion is also part of our ethnic heritage; participating in religious rituals is an important means of tying us to our cultural heritage.

Charisma refers to extraordinary personal qualities that set the individual apart from ordinary mortals.

around us. And as with science, the answers provided may be uncomfortable; they may challenge the status quo as well as support it.

Where do the answers to questions of ultimate meaning come from? Often they come from a charismatic religious leader. **Charisma,** you will recall from Chapter 15, refers to extraordinary personality qualities that set the individual apart from ordinary mortals. Because these extraordinary characteristics are often thought to be supernatural in origin, charismatic leaders are often able to be the agents of dramatic change in individuals and society. Charismatic leaders include Christ, Muhammad, and, more recently, John Humphrey Noyes (Oneida community), Joseph Smith (Mormonism), and Jim Jones (People's Temple). Such individuals give answers that often disagree with traditional answers. Thus, Weber saw religious inquiry as a potential source of instability and change in society.

In viewing religion as a process, Weber gave it a much more active role than did Durkheim. This is most apparent in Weber's analysis of the Protestant Reformation.

The Protestant Ethic and the Spirit of Capitalism.   In a classic analysis of the influence of religious ideals on other social institutions, Weber ([1904–05] 1958) argued that the Protestant Reformation paved the way for bourgeois capitalism.

Three ideas found in early Protestantism were critical: an emphasis on hard work and doing one's earthly duty, a stress on individualism, and a belief in rationalism. These elements were most developed among the Puritans. They rejected hymn singing and religious ritual as an emotional rather than a rational approach to understanding God. For them religion was not a matter of making a joyful noise but a serious business that emphasized hard work and rational rather than emotional assessment of the Scriptures. Their serious approach to life and religion led to an emphasis on plain living and a rejection of earthly pleasures and vanities.

The result was what Weber called the Protestant ethic, a belief that work, rationalism, and plain living are moral vitures, while idleness and luxury are sinful. Although this ethic was developed for religious reasons, one of its latent functions is the tendency for those who live by it to get rich. The close relationship between religion and wealth was acknowledged by the founder of the Methodist church, John Wesley:

> Religion must necessarily produce both industry and frugality, and these cannot but produce riches. But as riches increase, so will pride, anger, and the love of the world in all its branches. . . . Is there no way to prevent this—this continual decay of pure religion? We ought not to prevent people from being diligent and frugal; we must exhort all Christians to gain all they can and to save all they can; that is, in effect to grow rich (cited in Niebuhr [1929] 1957, 70).

In the Protestant ethic, wealth was an unintended consequence of behavior directed by religious motives. According to Weber, however, it was not long before wealth became an end in itself. At this point, the moral values underlying early Protestantism become the moral values underlying early capitalism: (1) Work is moral and everybody should work hard; (2) rational cost/benefit calculations should be the basis of business decisions; (3) profits should be reinvested rather than spent on luxuries; and

(4) wealth rather than aristocratic lineage is the best indicator of people's importance in society.

In the more than 80 years since Weber's analysis, other scholars have explored the same issues, and many have come to somewhat different conclusions. Some argue that the spirit of capitalism arose from class antagonisms set into motion by the decline of feudalism and that the Protestant Reformation was a part, not a cause, of the rise of capitalism. Nevertheless, 80 years of scholarship have not changed Weber's major contribution to the sociology of religion: the idea that religion is not merely a passive supporter of the status quo but can be an important element in social change.

MODERN CONFLICT THEORY: BEYOND MARX

Like Durkheim, Marx saw religion as a supporter of tradition. This support ranges from relatively mild injunctions that the poor and oppressed should endure rather than revolt (blessed be the poor, blessed by the meek, and so on) and that everyone should pay taxes (give unto Caesar) all the way to the extreme endorsement of inequality implied by a belief in the divine right of kings.

Marx differed from Durkheim by interpreting the support for tradition in a negative light. Marx, an atheist, saw religion as a delusion deliberately fostered by the elite—a sort of shell game designed to keep the eyes of the downtrodden on the hereafter so they would not notice their earthly oppression. This position is hardly value free, and much more obviously than either Weber's or Durkheim's, it does make a statement about the truth or falsity of religious doctrine.

Modern conflict theory goes beyond Marx's interpretation of religion as the opiate of the masses. The major contribution of Marxism to the analysis of religion is the idea of the dialectic—that contradictions build up between existing institutions and that these contradictions lead to change. Sometimes contradictions between other institutions erupt into religious expression. On other occasions, the basic tension is between society and religion. This tension is addressed in the next section of the chapter.

■

TENSION BETWEEN RELIGION AND SOCIETY

A society's religion is a part of its culture, its traditional ways of doing things. The Muslim religion is an integral part of Middle Eastern culture, just as Judeo-Christianity is an important part of Western culture. Despite this overlap between culture and religion, there is a universal tension between them.

Each religion is confronted with two contradictory yet complementary tendencies: the tendency to reject the world and the tendency to compromise with the world (Troeltsch 1931). When a religion denounces adultery and fornication, does the church categorically exclude adulterers and fornicators, or does it adjust its expectations to take common human frailties into account? If "it is easier for a camel to go through the eye of a needle than for a rich man to enter the kingdom of God," must the church require that *all* members forsake their worldly belongings?

How religions resolve these dilemmas is central to their eventual form and character. Scholars distinguish two general types of religious organizations: church and sect. The *church* represents the successful compromisers, and the *sect* represents the virtuous outsiders.

Churches are religious organizations that have become institutionalized. They have endured for generations, are supported by society's norms and values, and have become an active part of society. Their involvement in society does not necessarily mean that they have compromised essential values. They still retain the ability to protest injustice and immorality. From the abolition movement of the 1850s to the sanctuary movement for Central American refugees or the antinuclear movements of the 1980s, church members have been in the forefront of social protest. Nevertheless, churches are generally committed to working with society. They may wish to improve it, but they have no wish to abandon it.

Sects are religious organizations that reject the social environment in which they exist (Johnson 1957). Religions that reject sexual relations (Shakerism), automobiles (Amish), or monogamy (19th-century Mormonism) are examples of sects that differ so much from society's norms that their relationships with the larger society are often strained. They reject major elements of the larger culture and are in turn rejected by it.

The categories of church and sect are what Weber referred to as *ideal types*. The distinguishing characteristics of each type are summarized in the Concept Summary. Although no church or sect may have all of these characteristics, the ideal types serve as useful benchmarks against which to examine actual religious organizations.

CHURCHLIKE RELIGIONS

Within the general category of churches are two major types: the ecclesia and the denomination.

Ecclesia. The most institutionalized of all religious structures is an **ecclesia**—a religious organization that automatically includes every member of a society. People do not join ecclesiae; membership comes with citizenship (Becker, in Yinger 1957, 149). The Roman Catholic church in Europe was an ecclesia during the Middle Ages; Iran and Israel have many of the characteristics of a modern ecclesia. Ecclesiae represent the highest degree of religious institutionalization. Little tension exists between the religion and society—the religion is fully assimilated into society. The fate of the church and the fate of the nation are wrapped up in each other, and the church is vitally involved in supporting the dominant institutions of society.

Denominations. Religious organizations that have accommodated to society and to other religions are **denominations** (Robertson 1970). Most of the largest religious organizations in the United States fit this definition: Catholic, Jewish, Lutheran, Methodist, and Episcopalian. Their clergy meet together in ecumenical councils, their members pray together at commencements, and they generally adopt a live-and-let-live policy toward one another. Denominations have adjusted to the existing social structure of society. They support and are supported by the other institutional structures. This endorsement of the broad and basic fabric of the social order

---

Churches are religious organizations that have become institutionalized. They have endured for generations, are supported by society's norms and values, and have become an active part of society.

Sects are religious organizations that reject the social environment in which they exist.

An ecclesia is a churchlike religious organization that automatically includes every member of a society.

Denominations are churchlike religious organizations that have accommodated to society and to other religions.

■

CONCEPT SUMMARY

Distinctions Between Churches and Sects

Church and sect are ideal types against which we can assess actual religious organizations. Many religious organizations combine some characteristics of both. Nevertheless, Catholicism and Lutheranism are obviously churches, whereas the Old Order Amish have many of the characteristics of a sect.

	CHURCHES	SECTS
Degree of tension with society	Low	High
Attitude toward other institutions and religions	Tolerant	Intolerant; rejecting
Type of authority	Traditional	Charismatic
Organization	Bureaucratic	Informal
Membership	Establishment	Alienated
Examples	Catholics, Lutherans	Jehovah's Witnesses, Amish

assures members that the ways of both their religion and their society are moral and just.

Structure and Function of Churchlike Religions. Ecclesiae and denominations tend to be formal bureaucratic structures with hierarchical positions, specialization, and official creeds specifying their religious beliefs. Leadership is provided by a professional staff of ministers, rabbis, or priests, who have received formal training at specialized schools. These leaders are usually arranged in a hierarchy from the local to the district to the state and even the international level. Religious services almost always prescribe formal and detailed ritual, repeated in much the same way from generation to generation. Congregations often function more as audiences than as active participants. They are expected to stand up, sit down, and sing on cue, but the service is guided more by ceremony than by the emotional interaction of participants.

Generally, people are born into churchlike religions rather than being converted to them. People who change churches, who become Methodists instead of Lutherans, Catholics instead of Presbyterians, usually do so for practical reasons. They marry somebody of the other faith, the other church is nearer, or their friends go to the other church (Roof 1989). Although churches usually do not actively recruit new members, they have confirmation classes for adults and children to educate newcomers to the doctrines of their adopted faith. Individual commitment is based more on tradition or intellectual commitment than on the emotional experience of conversion.

Denominations tend to be large in size and to have well-established facilities, financial security, and a predominantly middle-class membership.

As part of their accommodation to the larger society, they generally allow the Scriptures to be interpreted in ways that are relevant to modern culture. Because of these characteristics, denominations are frequently referred to as *mainline churches*, a term denoting their centrality in society.

SECTLIKE RELIGIONS

Within the category of religious organizations that have greater tension with society, there is a great deal of variability. We can distinguish three levels of tension. First are cults, with the greatest tension, then sects, and finally established sects. The latter begin to approach institutionalization.

Cults.   A religious organization that is independent of the religious traditions of society is a **cult** (Stark and Bainbridge 1979). Examples of cults in the United States are Scientology, the Moonies, and the Hare Krishna. Each of these religions is rather foreign to the Judeo-Christian tradition of the United States: They have a different God or Gods or no God at all; they don't use the Old Testament as a text.

Because they do not support the religious heritage of society, cult movements challenge the moral community of established religions. They are in a high degree of tension with society and often the object of strong social disapproval.

A **cult** is a sectlike religious organization that is independent of the religious traditions of society.

Stoned rastafarians . . . very stoned. The Ras Tafari, a Jamaican cult movement, originated in 1930 among lower-class men as a semi-religious, semi-political movement. The Rastas are violently anti-white; they regard former Emperor Haile Selassie of Ethiopia as God and advocate the return of blacks to Africa. Today, the Rastas are largely unemployed Jamaicans residing in crowded, blighted areas. Street meetings twice a week and Sunday services typically include speech making, singing, and, for some, getting stoned.

Cults tend to arise in times of societal stress and change, where established religions do not seem adequate to explaining the upheavals that individuals experience. Because they are so alien to society's institutions, however, cults are of little assistance in helping people cope with their everyday lives. Instead, they often urge their members to alter their lives radically and to withdraw from society altogether. Because of the radical changes they demand, cults generally remain small, and many fail to survive more than a few years.

Sects.   Within the general category of sectlike religions, those called sects occupy a medium position. They reject the social world in which they live, but they embrace the religious heritage of society. The Amish are an excellent example: They base their lives on a strict reading of the Bible and remain aloof from the contemporary world.

Sects often view themselves as restoring true faith, which has been mislaid by religious institutions too eager to compromise with society. They see themselves as preservers of religious tradition rather than innovators. Like the Reformation churches of Calvin and Luther, they believe they are cleansing the church of its secular associations. However offbeat in comparison to mainline churches, if a religious group in the United States uses the Bible as its source of inspiration and guidance, then it is probably a sect rather than a cult.

Established Sects.   A sect that has adapted to its institutional environment has become an **established sect.** An established sect often retains the belief that it is the one true church, but it is less antagonistic to other faiths than are sects.

An **established sect** is a sect that has adapted to its institutional environment.

Whereas sects often withdraw from the world in order to perserve their spiritual purity, established sects are active participants. Frequently, the motivation for this participation in the world is to spread their message, to make converts, and to change social institutions. To the extent they are successful at these goals, they reduce the tension between themselves and society. To effect social change, they must have lobbying groups and participate in political, economic, and educational institutions. To spread their message and make converts, they must associate with many outsiders.

The Mormons are a classic example of an established sect. In the last 160 years, they have increased their accommodation to the larger society: They have abandoned plural marriage, left the seclusion of a virtual ecclesia in Utah, and spread throughout the world seeking converts. Mormons nevertheless retain many characteristics of sectlike religions, including lack of a paid clergy and an emphasis on conversion. These characteristic organizational features are covered in the next section.

Structure and Function of Sectlike Religions.   The hundreds of cults and sects in the United States exhibit varying degrees of tension with society, but all are opposed to some basic societal institutions. Not surprisingly, these organizations tend to be particularly attractive to people who are left out of or estranged from society's basic institutions—the poor, the underprivileged, the handicapped, and the alienated. For this reason, sects have been called "the church of the disinherited" (Niebuhr [1929]

1957). Not all of the people converted to sectlike religions are poor or oppressed. Many are middle-class people who are spiritually rather than materially deprived. They are individuals who find established churches too bureaucratic; they seek a moral community that will offer them a feeling of belongingness and emotional commitment (Barker 1986).

Sect membership is often the result of conversion or emotional experience. Members do not merely follow their parents into the church; they are reborn or born again. Religious services are more informal than for churches, and even in such established sects as the Mormon or Christian Scientist, congregation members may be called on to give testimony of religious experience.

Leadership remains largely unspecialized, and there is little, if any, professional training for the calling. Lay ministers assume part-time responsibility for administering religious rituals, conducting services, and teaching the gospel. The religious doctrines emphasize otherworldly rewards, and the Scriptures are viewed as of divine origin subject to literal interpretation.

Sects and cults share many of the characteristics of primary groups: small size, informality, and loyalty. They are relatively closely knit groups that emphasize conformity and maintain significant control over their members. Members may be required to observe specific norms related to patterns of dress (Amish, Oneida), speech (Quaker), use of modern technology (Amish), and so on. These requirements are symbolic reminders to community members of their religious identity. They function to foster cohesion and reinforce group identity.

Many, if not all, of the churches in the world today started out as sects. Over the centuries, they grew and became part of the institutional structures of society. Not all sects, of course, adjust and become assimilated in this way. Some remain established sects, antagonistic to many institutions in the general society; others suffer eventual extinction.

CASE STUDIES OF SECTLIKE RELIGIONS

Concepts such as church and sect are useful for highlighting the essential sociological characteristics of religions. They help us to see that religions as different in content as the Amish and the People's Temple share sociologically relevant characteristics, such as smallness and rejection of society.

Old Order Amish.   A sect that developed from the Protestant reform movement in Switzerland in 1520 and that migrated to Lancaster County, Pennsylvania, in 1727 is the Old Order Amish. This sect believes in the Scriptures as the literal word of God, in adult rather than infant baptism, and in strict separation from the ways of the world (Hostetler 1963).

The Amish pride themselves on being a "peculiar" people who follow the Bible rather than the ways of the world. As a result, they differ sharply from the other residents of Pennsylvania in dress and behavior. The Amish use Bible verses to support a clothing style that is modest, shows a distinction between the sexes, and does not appeal to vanity. All women dress alike in dark-colored skirts, blouses, matching aprons, and homemade bonnets (following a biblical injunction that women who pray with their heads uncovered are dishonored), and none wears jewelry. Men too must

The Old Order Amish pride themselves on being a "peculiar" people. They have managed to successfully withdraw from the ways of the modern world that surrounds them by adopting a life-style based on self-sufficiency. They reject modern conveniences, make almost all of their goods by hand, and are excellent farmers. This photograph of a large family saying grace before their meal shows the typical dress worn by members of the Amish community.

all dress alike, in jackets that have no lapels, no outside pockets, and no buttons. Zippers are forbidden except in utilitarian work clothes. These distinctive dress patterns serve a vital function; they constantly remind members of the group that they are outside the ways of the world. Neither the Amish nor their neighbors are likely to forget that they are a peculiar people.

The Amish reject almost all modern conveniences. They are not allowed to have rugs, electricity, telephones, or any modern appliances except sewing machines. Most important, they are not allowed to use automobiles. Instead, both farm equipment and pleasure vehicles are horse drawn. The Amish are forbidden to dance, to go to movies, to live in cities or towns, to serve in the military, to go to court, to join any association other than the church or to go to public school.

Both boys and girls attend Amish schools for eight years. They learn reading, writing, and arithmetic from teachers who have had the same eighth-grade education. The purpose of education is to allow the Amish to read the Bible and to manage farm accounts. Any further learning is considered not only unnecessary (for the Bible is the source of all knowledge) but actually wrong, as it will expose youth to the ways of the world and make them unhappy with Amish society. All adults, however, are expected to be able to read and study the Bible. The Amish have no established clergy; the leadership positions in the church are established by lot. Thus, every man in the community is expected to be familiar with the Bible and with church doctrine.

The Amish have managed to escape from secularization almost completely for more than 400 years. They have withdrawn physically—in the 18th century moving all the way from Germany to Pennsylvania—to escape the influence of the world. They seek neither converts nor worldly influence; they wish only to be left alone.

Whether the Amish can continue to ward off the world is questionable. Busy highways and the increasing price of land are challenging the Amish way of life. More direct challenges are offered by the draft, taxes, and education. For example, the Amish refuse to pay Social Security taxes, believing that such a plan indicates distrust of God's care. After much legal skirmishing, Congress exempted the Amish from the taxes and benefits of Social Security. More troubling is education. In Pennsylvania, officials have long since worked out an accommodation to allow the Amish to have their own schools without state-certified teachers and to have their children stop at the eighth grade. Population pressure (the Amish often have eight children), however, is pushing the Amish and their way of life into other states, which are unwilling to make this accommodation. The governments of Iowa and Nebraska have levied heavy fines on Amish families who refuse to send their children to public schools.

As a result of these changes, the Amish are finding it increasingly difficult to remain aloof from the world. Amish young people inevitably see some of the pleasures available in American society, and many are reluctant to turn their back completely on dancing, driving, and other amusements. As a result, many Amish communities now allow their young people a year in the larger world, hoping that they will get their curiosity out of their system and be willing to return to the Amish way of life.

People's Temple.   In 1978, the world was fascinated and appalled when 912 people died in Jonestown, Guyana, after drinking cyanide-laced Kool-Aid on the direction of their "bishop" and "father," Jim Jones.

The early career and beliefs of Jones (1931–78) are unclear. He himself said in later years that he used a religion in which he did not believe to spread the gospel of communism and social justice. At the time he began preaching, however, he appeared to be a Christian crusader. After traveling the circuit of poor black and white neighborhoods in Indianapolis, Jones—who had no formal theological training—raised $55,000 to start the People's Temple. Jones's temple, affiliated with the Disciples of Christ, appealed particularly to the poor and black. Jones preached racial integration, opened soup kitchens, distributed clothes to the needy, found jobs for ex-addicts and ex-convicts, and started nursing homes. In recognition of his social services to the community, he was named director of the Indianapolis Human Rights Commission.

Jones justified his activism by reference to the New Testament. Christ, he said, would not recognize his church if he found it to consist only of praying and singing on Sunday mornings. Christ, he said, demanded action. A favorite text was Matthew 25:35–40: "For I was hungered and ye gave me meat, I was thirsty and ye gave me drink; I was a stranger and ye took me in; Naked and ye clothed me; I was sick and ye visited me; I was in prison and ye came to me. . . . Verily I say unto you, Inasmuch as ye have done it unto one of the least of these, my brethen, ye have done it unto me." Thus, the so-called Jonestown cult began as a sect, nourished and supported by Christian tradition.

Many sects begin as antithetical to society's institutions but gradually reduce this tension. The People's Temple followed the opposite course. An antagonistic relationship developed between Jones and a group called

Concerned Relatives, which used every legal (and some illegal) means to discredit Jones and pull their relatives away from his influence (Hall 1987). As a result of this tension, Jones became ever more paranoid and secretive, finally retreating with 912 members of his flock to Jonestown in the jungles of Guyana on the northern coast of South America.

Like many sect and cult founders, Jones was a charismatic leader. His followers believed that he spoke directly with God; indeed, they came to believe he was the Messiah. The faith of his followers rested partly on standard brainwashing procedures; Jones kept temple members tired and busy, cut off from their nontemple friends, and frightened. As a result, they suspended their critical faculties. In addition, however, his followers had a Christian heritage, and they believed that Christ would come again. Why not this man? Why not this place and time? Jones used the Christian heritage of his followers to manipulate them, but in fact, early in his career, he abandoned Christianity and the Bible's God, whom he disparagingly called the sky God. "What's your sky God ever done? . . . He never gave you a bed and He never provided a *home*. But I, *Your socialist worker God*, have given you *all* these things" (cited in Reiterman 1982, 148–49).

The members of his congregation hungered for salvation and a heavenly reward. They also sought respite from the hardship of Jonestown. Thus,

---

The People's Temple was a Christian-based sect founded by Jim Jones. It advocated social activism among the poor and the curing of earthly problems through socialism. For this reason, sect membership appealed disproportionately to the poor, the black, and the alienated in society. Jones became so alienated from American society and so paranoid about spies that he moved his entire congregation to the jungles of Guyana. There, his beliefs and practices became more bizarre and paranoid. In 1978, he decreed mass suicide for his entire congregation.

when they were ordered to drink the poison in November 1978, more than 900 (including 200 children) did so. The temple's property was willed to the Communist party of the Soviet Union.

The Jonestown "cult" was, up until its last year, similar to many other sects. It was a religion of the disinherited, and it was led by a charismatic leader. Its congregation formed a strong moral community that bound its members so tightly that they could not conceive of any disloyalty; their whole existence became one with temple membership. Although initially based on Christian tradition, the doctrine and rituals of the group became increasingly cultlike during the last year.

The amount of coercion and intimidation at Jonestown clearly distinguishes it from other sectlike religions in the United States. Yet violence does not in itself make a religion a cult. The witch hunts and inquisitions of the Middle Ages, the Holy Wars of Islam, self-immolation by Buddhist monks in Saigon, and numerous other kinds of martyrdoms remind us that violence is often part of ecclesiae and denominations as well as of cults and sects.

LIBERATION THEOLOGY AND SOCIAL JUSTICE

Churches tend to be part of the world, while sects tend to withdraw from the world. Ironically, this gives churches much more incentive for radical political activism. A recent survey of U.S. Christian leaders asked them to indicate whether the primary goal of the church should be to "bring people to Jesus" or to "help the poor." The results showed that 95 percent of those leaders who called themselves fundamentalists said that their primary mission was bringing people to Jesus; only half of the Catholic and mainline Protestant leaders chose this option (Lerner, Rothman, and Lichter 1989). For the other half, social justice was more important or as important as bringing people to Jesus.

The link between religious activism and political and economic activism is most marked in *liberation theology*, a religious movement associated with Latin American Catholicism. Liberation theology aims at the creation of democratic, Christian socialism that eliminates poverty, inequality, and political oppression.

The harnessing of a moral community to politics establishes a powerful team. One South American organizer notes that:

> People do not come to [meetings] when there is no praying and singing. They come four or five times to organize practical things, but nothing further will come of it. When, however, people pray and sing, when they feel themselves together, when the gospel is read and, *on this basis*, concrete actions are organized and the national situation is analyzed, then the group remains united (emphasis added; cited in Neuhauser 1989, 239).

The priests who are active in liberation theology may spend more time picketing than praying, more time organizing than saving souls. This radical activity has caused controversy in the church and, in 1987, the Pope ordered Catholic priests and nuns to stay out of politics. Many have disregarded the order, facing the perils of excommunication as well as the

In 1980, Archbishop Oscar Romero, an outspoken critic of army repression and death squads, was assassinated in El Salvador while saying mass. His assassination is widely attributed to top officials of the rightwing government. Romero, one of the most potent symbols of liberation theology, is widely regarded as a hero and saint by the people of Central America. Each year, the anniversary of his assassination is marked by demonstrations and processions.

perils of political activism under violent circumstances. Every year in Central America there are new incidents of religious workers (Episcopalians and Mennonites as well as Catholics) killed by right-wing guerrillas. In November 1989, six Catholic priests and their household staff were killed in El Salvador by government agents trying to stop their organizing among the poor. Two of these priests were also sociologists. One of them, Dr. Segundo Montes, wrote shortly before his death that "I consider it a duty to work for human rights; it is the duty of every human being who has the sensibility and sensitivity to the suffering of people. As a Christian who follows the God of Life and who is against the idols of death, . . . I want to live with the people who suffer and deserve more." Of the conflict in Central America, he wrote that "the establishment of a real democracy, together with economic development for the majority, are both indispensable for the achievement of an authentic and durable peace" (cited in "Observing" 1990).

The dilemmas of social justice are not so acute in the United States, and today the church in the U.S. has more visibility as a conservative than as a radical political actor. It is worth remembering, however, that the civil rights movement of the 1960s was based largely in the African American church and that the Southern Christian Leadership Conference took the lead in securing African American political and economic rights. Some of the contemporary issues that generate church/state tensions in the United States are addressed in the Issues in Social Policy section at the end of this chapter.

An analysis of the role of religion in the world suggests that both Marx and Durkheim overestimated the conservative force of religion. Religion does much more than simply support the status quo; it can be an active agent for change. Time and again, its moral community has been the foundation for political organization; its ideals can be the basis of political and economic ideals.

■

RELIGION IN THE UNITED STATES

When asked what religion they belong to, only 8 percent of the people in the United States say they belong to no church. Most people are able to identify themselves not only as religious but also as affiliated with some particular religious organization. Most (59 percent) call themselves Protestants, but 27 percent are Catholics and 2 percent are Jews (see Figure 17.1). Within the category of Protestants and among the 4 percent of the population who belong to other religious faiths, there is a great deal of variability. The *Yearbook of American and Canadian Churches* lists more than 200 religious organizations, and researchers have identified more than 500 cult movements and more than 400 sects in the United States (Stark and Bainbridge 1981).

Despite their differences, the three major religions in the United States embrace a common Judeo-Christian heritage. They accept the Old Testament, and they worship the same God. They rely on a similar moral tradition (the Ten Commandments, for example), which reinforces common

■
FIGURE 17.1
RELIGIOUS AFFILIATION
IN THE UNITED STATES

Although nearly 90 percent of Americans call themselves Protestant, Catholic, or Jewish, there are more than 200 religious organizations in the United States and as many as 1,000 cults and sects.

SOURCE: The Gallup Report 1987.

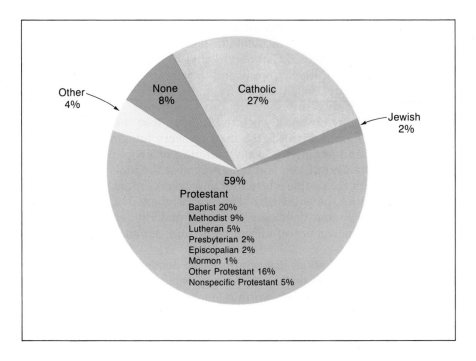

values. This common religious heritage supplies an overarching sense of unity and character to U.S. society—providing a framework for the expression of our most crucial values concerning family, politics, economics, and education.

WHO IS RELIGIOUS?

Although almost everybody expresses a belief in God, some people are consistently more likely than others to emphasize the role of religion in their lives. These patterns of religious commitment are summarized in Table 17.1. The data come from a national probability sample of adults interviewed in 1989.

Two-thirds of the adults in this country are members of churches or synagogues, and 42 percent are found in church on a weekly basis. A clear majority (55 percent) define religion as very important to their lives. On both measures of religiosity (church attendance and importance of religion), people who live in the Midwest and the South report greater religiosity than people who live in the West or the East.

The most striking differences in religiosity, however, are found by age and sex. Older people and women report greater attachment to religion than do younger people and men. These differences are highly reliable and have been reported in national studies over several decades (Greeley 1979, 120). Young adults, particularly those under the age of 30, are approximately three times more likely to indicate no religious preference than are those over 50; they are less likely to be members of a congregation, they have lower weekly attendance than adults in other age groups, and they are less likely to view religion as very important to their lives.

A question that has consistently interested students of religious affiliation is the relationship between socioeconomic status and religiosity. To

TABLE 17.1
RELIGIOUS PARTICIPATION AND ATTITUDES, 1987–89

There are some pronounced patterns in U.S. religiosity. Men are less religious than women, young people are less religious than their elders, westerners are less religious than people in other regions, Jews are less religious than people of other religions. The well educated go to church, but they are not otherwise as religious as the less well educated.

	PERCENTAGE OF ADULTS WHO	
	Attended Church or Synagogue Last Week	*Say Religion Is Very Important*
National	42%	55%
Region:		
Midwest	46	56
South	49	64
East	38	47
West	31	49
Age:		
Below 30	31	44
30–49	41	52
50 and older	49	65
Sex:		
Male	36	45
Female	47	64
Education:		
Grade school	41	66
High school	41	55
College	43	49
Religion:		
Protestant	43	61
Catholic	52	52
Jewish	NA	30

SOURCE: The Gallup Report 1987, 1989.

many people, it has seemed logical that religion should appeal disproportionately to the poor, who may stand in greater need of hope and help in dealing with this world. Empirical research, however, demonstrates that the relationship between religion and social class is more complex. As the data in Table 17.1 indicate, people with a college education are as likely to attend church as are people with a grade school education. They are, however, significantly less likely to say that religion is important to them. Higher-status people also belong to somewhat different religious organizations. They are more often members of churchlike religions, whereas lower-class individuals are more often members of sects and cults.

Why does religion appeal to some groups more than others? After examining several competing explanations, Roof and Hoge (1980) concluded that religious involvement for adults is strongly associated with community attachment and conventional values. People who are involved

The Cult of George Washington

In 1776, when the American colonies declared independence, many considered democracy a radical and frightening experiment. It was feared that without the tradition of aristocracy and monarchy, government might deteriorate into mob rule and domination by popular tyrants. The Founding Fathers were deeply afraid of investing power in any man, for they believed that power was incompatible with liberty. Yet, if they wanted to fight a war, they needed a general.

Into this situation came George Washington. Washington was *not* a charismatic leader. In fact, he was something of a cold fish. He was stern and distant, not warm in his affections. Nor was he particularly bright. Thomas Jefferson said of him that his mind was not "of the very first order. . . . It was slow in operation, being little aided by invention or imagination, but sure in conclusion." Today, we might call him a plodder. Nor did he have any previous military experience. His major qualification for office was that he didn't want the job. When it was forced on him, he said, "Lest some unlucky event should happen, I beg it may be remembered by every gentleman in this room, that I, this day, declare with utmost sincerity, I do not think myself equal to the command I am honored with." His humility turned out to be appropriate, for his generalship was not brilliant and his armies met with many defeats.

Still, within weeks of his appointment as commander of the Continental Army, Washington began to be an object of near worship.

"Memorial to George Washington" painting on glass

George III's pictures were taken down and George Washington's put in their place. The music to "God Save the King" was retained, but the words were changed to "God Save Great Washington." In the end, many would have been glad to give him voluntarily the kingship they had feared he would demand.

◼

If God was on their side, then Washington must be God's agent on earth; he was widely proclaimed to be the American Moses.

Why did the cult of Washington develop? There appear to be three reasons. One is the colonists' belief that God was on their side. If God was on their side, then Washington must be God's agent on earth; he was widely proclaimed to be the American Moses. Ministers told their congregants that it would be a sin not to support the war. Second, Washington was a symbol for a union that did not yet exist. The Articles of Confederation had little authority. No structure or institution represented the United States—only Washington symbolized the fledgling nation's unity. Finally, in an atmosphere of near paranoia about the abuse of power, Washington's indifference to power, the relief with which he relinquished his command and his presidency, made him a hero.

By the time of his death, Washington was virtually deified. One of his eulogists said:

Did he, like Caesar, after vanquishing his countrymen's foes, turn his conquering armies against that country? Far, far otherwise. Before the great Council of our Nation, the PATRIOT-HERO appeared, and in the presence of numerous, admiring spectators, resigned his victorious sword into the hands of those who gave it.

AUGUST Spectacle! Glorious Example! For my own part, I never contemplate it but each fiber vibrates with rapture, and the vital current trembles through every artery of my frame.

The cult of Washington is a homegrown example of Durkheim's theory about the functions of religion. By worshiping Washington, the colonists were worshiping themselves—their nation and the virtues they believed it embodied.

SOURCE: Schwartz 1983.

in their communities—who belong to voluntary associations and civic groups and are integrated into their neighborhoods—tend to extend that involvement to religious participation. Liberal attitudes toward sexual morality, gender roles, civil liberties, and drug use, however, tend to be inconsistent with church involvement. These factors help explain why well-educated people participate in church despite their lack of enthusiasm for it and why young people are less likely to participate or believe.

U.S. CIVIL RELIGION

In addition to their common religious heritage, Americans also share what has been called a civil religion (Bellah 1974, 29). **Civil religion** is a set of institutional rituals, beliefs, and symbols sacred to the nation. In the United States, these include giving the pledge of allegiance and singing the national anthem, as well as folding and displaying the flag in ways that protect it from desecration. In many American homes, the flag or a picture of the president is displayed along with a crucifix or a picture of the Last Supper.

Civil religion has the same functions as religion in general: It is a source of unity and integration, providing a sacred context for understanding the nation's history and current responsibilities (Wald 1987). To a significant extent, we have made liberty, justice, and freedom sacred principles; as a result, the American way of life—our economic and political system—has

Civil religion is the set of institutionalized rituals, beliefs, and symbols sacred to the nation.

Many observers, including Marx, have thought that religion ought to appeal disproportionately to the poor and the disadvantaged. Although the poor and disadvantaged are more likely than others to be fervent in their beliefs, studies show that churchgoing is correlated more strongly with being conventional than with being disadvantaged. It is characteristic of people who are involved in their communities, belong to other voluntary associations as well, and hold traditional values.

become not merely the usual way of doing things but also the only moral way of doing them, a way of life that is blessed by God.

Not surprisingly, African Americans and other disadvantaged minorities have been less likely to endorse civil religion (Woodrum and Bell 1989). The recent elevation of Martin Luther King, Jr. to secular sainthood, as evidenced by state and federal holidays honoring his birth, is a step toward making civil religion more inclusive of all Americans.

SECULARIZATION: RELIGIOUS DECLINE?

Many scholars have argued that the long-term trend in the Western world is toward *secularization*, the decline of religious influence in social life. Secularization has three dimensions (Dobbelaere 1981):

1. The growing isolation of the church from other institutions, particularly government and the schools
2. The increasing accommodation of churches to changing social values—for example, by tolerating homosexuality, women ministers, birth control, abortion, and divorce
3. The reduced importance of religion for individuals.

The evidence on secularization is mixed, and the picture one gets depends on the historical era one chooses for comparison. Descriptions of colonial times suggest that U.S. religious history is far from one ongoing fall from grace. In 1776, it is estimated that only 10–12 percent of the population belonged to a church (Stark and Finke 1988). In 1779, a traveling preacher told of meeting a man in the backwoods of Delaware and asking him, "Do you know Jesus Christ?" "Can't say as I do," replied the man. "He must not live in these parts." Even as late as the mid 19th century, it was generally held that Sunday stopped at the Missouri River (Phares 1964).

■

TABLE 17.2
CHANGING RELIGIOUS COMMITMENT, 1947 TO 1989

Over the last 40 years there has been little decline in outward religious observance. There has, however, been a substantial drop in the proportion who say that religion is very important to their lives, and there has been a sharp decrease in the proportion who think that the Bible is the actual word of God.

	1947–1952	1986–1989
Belong to a church or synagogue	76%	67%
Attended church last week	46	42
Have no religion	6	8
Believe in God	94	94
Religion is very important to their own lives	75	57
Believe Bible is actual word of God, to be taken literally word for word[a]	65	37

SOURCE: Gallup Report 1987, 1989d.
[a]The first measure on this variable was taken in 1963.

Compared to 1776, the U.S. is a very religious nation. Compared to 1950, however, we find signs of decline in individual religiosity (see Table 17.2). Although there has been little change in church participation or belief in God, the proportion who say religion is very important to their own lives has dropped substantially, and there has been a sharp decrease in the proportion who believe that the Bible is the actual word of God.

Overall, it appears that science, industrialization, and the development of the modern state *have* eroded the centrality of the church. Science has attacked the validity of religious explanations, industrialization has made life on earth much more pleasant and the hereafter subsequently less attractive, and the state has replaced the church as the chief charitable institution (Wuthrow 1988). Of course, not all groups have benefited equally from industrialization and the solicitude of the state. The church has stayed strong for the poor and for those for whom religion symbolizes ethnic identity (Stark and Bainbridge 1985).

FUNDAMENTALISM AND THE NEW CHRISTIAN RIGHT

One of the most striking changes in religion today is the vitality and growth of the fundamentalist churches compared with mainline denominations.

Fundamentalists can be found in all religions; there are fundamentalist Catholics, Baptists, Jews, Muslims, and Lutherans. Their common aim is to reverse the accommodation of the church to the secular world and to bring the church back to its tension with society. The split between the fundamentalists and the modernists is one of the most significant religious cleavages in the United States. On many social and political issues, it is much more important than whether one is Catholic or Protestant. For example, consider the issue of creationism in the schools. Fundamentalists generally favor a requirement that the Genesis story be taught in the schools along with, or even instead of, evolutionary theory. They believe that the two theories are incompatible, and they wish to make certain that students are exposed to Judeo-Christian theory. Leaders of established churches are generally not in favor of creationism in the schools. They have interpreted the Genesis story as a parable rather than as literal truth, and they see no contradiction between scientific evolution and religion. One Catholic authority, for example, notes: "We're more concerned with God as the creator of the world than with how he created. . . . So long as whatever is taught in the schools allows room for that interpretation, there's no problem" (Rev. Thomas Gallagher, Secretary for Education, U.S. Catholic Conference, cited in Bollier 1982, 196).

The New Christian Right.   The New Christian Right is a loose coalition of fundamentalists who believe that American government and social institutions must be made to operate according to Christian principles. They believe the United States is God's chosen instrument to fight communism and that it is a Christian obligation to be politically active in making the United States a Christian nation. Two quotes give a flavor of this mixture of Christianity and political activism:

> The idea that religion and politics don't mix was invented by the Devil to keep Christians from running their own country (Jerry Falwell, cited in Bollier 1982, 54).

> Not voting is a sin against God. . . . Perverts, radicals, leftists, Communists, liberals, and humanists have taken over the country because Christians didn't want to dirty their hands in politics (Pat Robertson, cited in Bollier 1982, 70).

The New Christian Right is best understood as a political rather than a religious movement. It uses normal political processes—lobbying, campaign contributions, and getting out the vote—as means of influencing public policy. In doing so, of course, it is building onto the existing foundations of civil religion.

Despite this link to established values and despite the growth in fundamentalist religions, the movement has had more publicity than power. Fundamentalists differ among themselves on matters of religious conviction; they are also divided on political issues such as abortion, gun control, military defense, and pornography (Moore and Whitt 1986; Shupe and Stacy 1982). This divisiveness, plus the centrist nature of American political parties, has reduced the actual political power of the New Christian Right.

TELEVANGELISM

Increasingly, people find it possible to enjoy religious participation at the touch of a dial. Televised ministries are aired on 221 stations (a growth of 71 percent) and reach a regular audience of 13 million people weekly (Martz 1987). There are perhaps another 1,500 religious radio broadcasters in the United States.

People who tune in to religious broadcasts are similar to those who attend churches: They are older, mostly female, Protestant, and disproportionately from the southern and midwestern regions of the country.

They also tend to have less education and a lower socioeconomic status (see Table 17.3).

Evangelist means literally to spread the gospel. Televangelists spread the gospel on television. There is little controversy about this goal, and everyone agrees that these ministries help to make religion available to those who otherwise would be shut off from participation: the elderly, the physically handicapped, and other isolated individuals.

Televangelism has been the target of two major criticisms, which come almost entirely from nonviewers. First, some have criticized it for failing to fulfill one of the major functions of traditional religion: bringing people together into a moral community. Since most people who listen to televangelists also attend church, however, this criticism has relatively little merit. More important is the argument that televangelists have used their

■

TABLE 17.3
WHO WATCHES TELEVISED RELIGION?

People who watch religious broadcasts on television are disproportionately older, nonwhite, poorly educated, and low income. These are also the same people who are most likely to attend church.

	PERCENTAGE FREQUENT VIEWERS	PERCENTAGE NON VIEWERS
Total	18%	39%
Age		
18–29	5	60
30–49	12	44
50–65	28	29
Over 65	33	21
Sex		
Male	16	43
Female	19	37
Race		
White	16	43
Nonwhite	26	20
Education		
Less than high school	29	25
High school graduate	17	39
Some college or none	12	49
Household Income		
Under $15,000	26	29
$15,000–$24,999	17	36
$25,000–$35,000	13	48
Over $35,000	9	54
Church Attendance		
Once a week	23	30
Less than once a week	12	51

SOURCE: U.S. Bureau of Census 1989a, 56.

One of the biggest changes in religious activity in America in the 1980s is the use of electronic media to broadcast religious messages into people's homes. Jerry Falwell, shown here in his television studio preparing his weekly broadcast of The Old Time Gospel Hour, reaches an estimated audience of 547,000 households weekly. Televangelists such as Falwell are charismatic leaders who combine sophisticated technology with organizational resources to spread the word. Their success has been monumental, and some believe televangelism may bring far-reaching changes to American culture.

powers of persuasion to bilk a naïve audience. One calculation showed that the average televangelist spends 21 percent of his or her airtime soliciting funds (Frankl 1984). As a result, it is estimated that the major televangelists pull in more than $100 million every year (Martz 1987).

In the late 1980s, the televangelist industry was rocked by scandals involving sex and financial fraud: Jimmy Swaggart and Jim and Tammi Bakker fell from grace. Far from alienating their chief audiences, however, the scandals had strong negative effects only on those who already had negative opinions (Gallup Reports 1989d). It appears that these scandals are only a temporary embarrassment to televangelism and that the media will continue to be an important means by which to reach a religious audience.

Which Religions Are Protected by Government?

In a 1944 case, the Supreme Court concluded that it was illegal to ban the Jehovah's Witnesses from going from door to door to distribute religious material and raise money. In reaching this decision, Justice Jackson argued that citizens have the right "to believe anything they want, however bizarre those beliefs may appear to others" (Richardson 1988). Justice Jackson went further and argued that the "mental and spiritual poison" that "false prophets" disseminate is beyond the reach of the law (Robbins 1986). Not everyone agrees that religion is beyond the law, however, and it is not surprising to find that the more bizarre your beliefs, the less likely you are to have your religious rights supported by courts of law. We briefly cover three court cases.

PARENT'S RIGHTS

The right to free religious expression means that one has the right to speak on street corners or dis-

tribute booklets about one's faith; certainly it has meant the right to raise one's children in one's own faith. Is there a limit to this right? Say you believe in human sacrifice. Do you have a right to raise your children in this religion? To demand their sacrifice? Most people would probably say that you do not have this right. But how do we draw the line between the rights of this religion and those of Presbyterianism?

A recent court case involved a divorced mother who was raising her children in an extreme fundamentalist commune that emphasized corporal punishment as a means of exorcising the devil. The children's father and maternal grandparents sued for custody of the children—and received it. The judge allowed the mother visitation rights, but ordered her not to make "any comments to the minor children with regard to her religious beliefs, whatsoever, under the penalties of contempt." He argued that the Good Life Pentecostal Church had "adopted systems of corporal punish-

"Man's Law & God's Law" by Claudia DeMonte

ISSUES IN SOCIAL POLICY continued

ment and fear to force obedience and submission of her children to the doctrine of her church. . . . When [religious] beliefs threaten the health and well-being of children, then the courts have a duty to act to remove children from such abuse" ("York Woman" 1990). This decision has been appealed.

RACISM AND RELIGION

In 1982, the U.S. Supreme Court ruled that Bob Jones University did not qualify as a religious organization for tax purposes because it publicly espoused racism. The IRS reasoning, which the Supreme Court accepted, was that a religious organization must be a charitable organization and a charitable organization must support public policy. Since racism is a contradiction of U.S. public policy, it followed that Bob Jones University was not a religious organization! Although many people probably were pleased to see Bob Jones University get into trouble for its racist practices, this decision raises a troubling issue: Will only those religious organizations that do not create tension between religion and society be regarded as "real" religions (Richardson 1988)?

FORCIBLE DEPROGRAMMING

If your child falls under the "undue influence" of a charismatic leader and becomes a member of the Moonies or a cult such as the People's Temple,

what can you as a parent do about it? Some parents have hired deprogrammers to kidnap their children and focibly deprogram them. Should this be legal? Proponents argue that the right to "free religious expression" doesn't apply to new religious movements that use brainwashing techniques; they believe that their children did not make an informed, free choice. Legal scholars who support deprogramming argue that the first amendment does not cover "coerced" cultist beliefs (Delgado 1984). Opponents, however, wonder how the courts can decide whether someone's religious beliefs are based on informed choice (Shepard 1985): Does a child raised as a Jew make an informed choice not to believe in Christ, does a Catholic child make an informed decision to do so?

CONCLUSION

Issues such as prayer in the schools and creationism pit two establishment groups against one another. The broader issues of state support for religion arise when we look at *which* religions the state supports. Which religions' prayers are we considering for the schools? Which religions are granted legitimacy by the Internal Revenue Service? The answers suggest that underlying current controversies about school prayer and abortion is a high level of consensus in the U.S. about which religions are appropriate and which are not.

SUMMARY

1. The scientific study of religion concerns itself with the consequences of religious affiliation for individuals and with the interrelationships of religion and other social institutions. It is not concerned with evaluating the truth of particular religious beliefs.

2. There are two distinct viewpoints about the role of religion in society. One, associated with Durkheim, sug-

gests that religion provides support for the traditional practices of a society and is a force for continuity and stability. The other, associated with Weber, suggests that religion generates new ideas and challenges the institutions of society.

3. All religions are confronted with a dilemma: Should the religion reject the secular world, or should it compromise with the world? The way a religion resolves this question determines its form and character. Those who make adaptations to the world are called churches, whereas those who reject the world are called sects.

4. The primary distinction between a cult and a sect is that a cult is outside a society's traditional religious heritage whereas a sect often sees itself as restoring the true faith of a society. Both tend to be primary groups characterized by small size, intense we-feeling, and informal leadership.

5. Because churches are more in the world, they are more likely to be involved in political affairs. Liberation theology aims to create democratic, Christian socialism that eliminates poverty, inequality, and oppression. The church's moral community has often been the foundation for political organization.

6. The great majority of Americans consider themselves religious. Age and sex are the best predictors of religiosity; college-educated people attend church or synagogue as often as others but are less likely to say religion is very important in their lives.

7. Civil religion is an important source of unity for the American people. This "religion" holds our nation sa-

cred: It is composed of a set of beliefs (that God guides the country), symbols (the flag), and rituals (the pledge of allegiance) that many Americans of all faiths hold sacred.

8. There is mixed evidence on the progress of secularization. Compared to 1950, religion today does appear to have less influence on social life.

9. Fundamentalist churches that stress a return to basic religious principles have grown in influence. The political arm of the fundamentalist churches, the New Christian Right, seeks to bring religion into government, education, and all social institutions.

10. Despite recent scandals, televangelism remains a strong form of religious ministry. For the most part, televangelism reaches an audience already heavily involved in the church. Viewers are older, mostly female, Protestant, lower in socioeconomic status, and from the South or Midwest.

11. Most church/state issues pit two establishment groups against one another. The deeper issues of religious freedom arise when we consider unpopular or bizarre religions that do not enjoy public support.

■

SUGGESTED READINGS

Beckford, James A. 1985. Cult Controversies: The Societal Response to New Religious Movements. London: Tavistock Publications. An excellent overview and description of the most recent and controversial cults in America and Europe. Includes the Children of God, International Society for Krishna Consciousness, Scientology, and the Unification church. Readable and informative.

Kephart, William M. 1987. Extraordinary Groups: An Examination of Unconventional Life-Styles. (3rd ed.) New York: St. Martin's Press. Provides a very good overview of specific utopian groups and religious sects in America. Includes coverage of modern communes and gypsies as well as religious sects: the Amish, Oneidans, Shakers, Mormons, and Father Divine movement.

Pope, Liston. 1942. Millhands and Preachers. New Haven, Conn.: Yale University Press. A classic study of the confrontation between economic and religious forces in a textile mill strike in the South in 1929. An

illuminating narrative of the very real tension between religion and society.

Wald, Kenneth D. 1987. Religion and Politics in the United States. New York: St. Martin's Press. A readable and informative treatment of church/state tensions. Examines the historical and contemporary influence of religion on American politics.

Weber, Max. [1904–05] 1958. The Protestant Ethic and the Spirit of Capitalism. New York: Scribner's. An influential essay on the relationship between religion and economics. Argues that early Protestantism became the basis for economic capitalism.

Wuthnow, Robert. 1988. The Restructuring of American Religion: Society and Faith Since WWII. Princeton, N.J.: Princeton University Press. A review of major trends in the United States. Wuthnow links trends in religion to other institutional changes in American society.

18

HEALTH AND MEDICINE

PROLOGUE

HAVE YOU EVER . . .

Thought about purposefully vomiting up your dinner in order to lose weight? If you have, you are probably either a wrestler or a young woman. Wrestlers go through all sorts of tortures to make weight limits: They sweat, they vomit, they dehydrate themselves. Young women who are fanatic about the quest for slimness may develop eating disorders such as anorexia (simply not eating) or bulimia (eating and then vomiting). On a slightly less damaging level, staying slim is the number one reason that young women give for smoking cigarettes.

Wrestlers and anorexics are taking chances with their health in order to meet socially prescribed standards. Many of the rest of us also take chances with our health in meeting norms for our age, sex, class, and social roles: We may drive too fast, drink too much, subject ourselves to too much stress and too long hours, use too many drugs, sleep irregularly, eat the wrong foods, or abuse steroids.

The sociology of health is really the sociology of life. To understand why some people are healthy and others are not, we need to understand age and gender roles, family and work roles, social class, race and ethnic inequalities, and cultural values. Although some of your health comes from your genes and some of it comes from the medical system, most of health comes from daily living. It reflects how you sleep, work, play, and eat. It is a *social product*, that reflects your social class and social roles.

Medical sociology is the largest single specialty within sociology and nearly one out of every 10 sociologists claims medical sociology as one of his or her primary interests ("Future Organizational Trends" 1989). The reason is obvious: Life and health are basic prerequisites to participation in society. The study of health is relevant to almost all branches of sociology. It is of interest to those who study inequalities by class, race, and sex and to those who study the elderly; to those concerned with the family and to those concerned with professions, as well as to those who study socialization and self-identity.

In this chapter, we address the social structuring of health and medicine. We begin at the micro level, by taking a symbolic interaction approach to understanding the meaning of health and illness. Then, we move toward the macro level by examining how health and health care are affected by class, gender, and race and how American health care is organized and paid for. For the most part, we will focus on physical rather than mental health.

THE SOCIAL CONSTRUCTION OF HEALTH AND SICKNESS

Mental and physical health can be viewed as achieved, even socially constructed, statuses. Rather than having them simply bestowed on us by social structure, we work toward them. We negotiate them, just as we negotiate the rest of our social identity. In this section, we use the symbolic interaction perspective to examine how individuals negotiate the health aspect of their self-concept.

CONCEIVING THE PHYSICAL SELF

In the dramaturgical perspective developed by Goffman (1959), all the world is a stage, and each of us chooses props and scripts suitable to support the roles we choose to play. One of the most central of these accessories is our physical body, and health can have an important effect on the kinds of roles we can play successfully.

Obviously, crippling conditions such as paralysis or cerebral palsy place physical limitations on the roles we can play successfully. More important than purely physical limitations, however, are the symbolic meanings that we (and others) attach to physical conditions. Losing a breast to cancer, losing the use of one's legs, or developing arthritis can be the signal to redefine oneself as ugly, sickly, infirm, or old. Yet others with the same conditions will be able to sustain a very positive self image (Olesen et al. 1990). The symbolic meanings attached to physical conditions are dependent on the relationships and social structures in which an individual finds himself or herself.

Most of us, of course, do not have to negotiate our self-identity around such dramatic incidents of ill health. Instead, we must cope with more mundane concerns about our physical self: being too short, being overweight and out of shape, and growing older. For all of us, however, our feelings about our bodies and our health have consequences for how we interact with the social world—whether we embrace new roles or hide from them.

TAKING THE SICK ROLE

Under normal conditions, self-esteem is enhanced by negotiating the healthiest self-concept possible. Under some conditions, however, we want to negotiate a sick identity.

Sociologist Peggy Thoits has illustrated the reasons why this occurs in the case of mental illness. Thoits points out that the majority of people who seek treatment for mental illness have voluntarily adopted the label "mentally ill;" they are self labeled (1986b). Why would they do this? They adopt this label, Thoits argues, as a way to negotiate a positive self image. These are people who keep getting into trouble of some sort or other— they cannot hold a job, keep friends, or stay sober. In order to explain their failures to others and themselves, they adopt the label "mentally ill" to explain their situation. A similar logic explains why some people embrace the role of being physically sick. Their bad back or mononucleosis are used to excuse or explain failures to meet society's expectations. If others agree that the person is indeed sick, then self-esteem may be protected.

In 1951, Talcott Parsons suggested that we could conceive of sickness as a role, a role that brings both responsibilities and rights. According to Parsons, the rights and responsibilities of the **sick role** are:

The **sick role** consists of the rights and obligations that accompany the social label *sick*.

1. *Sick people are exempt from normal social roles.* They can stay home from school and from work and not clean their homes, all without incurring censure from others. The sick are excused from fulfilling normal obligations.
2. *Sick people are not responsible for their condition.* When people are granted the sick role, they are absolved from any blame over their condition. We agree that it is not their fault that they are sick, and we do not believe that they could get well if they wanted to.
3. *Sick people should try to get well.* Although it is not their fault that they are sick, it is their obligation to follow instructions and to wish to be well.
4. *Sick people should seek technically competent help and cooperate with physicians.* Not only should they abstain from behaviors that will extend the sickness but they should also actively seek to get better.

In order to keep the rights of the sick role, the sick individual must follow instructions, seek competent help, and wish to be well.

Whether people are granted the sick role depends on many factors. The visibility of the problem and the degree to which the patient is thought to have brought it on himself or herself are two important factors. For example, if a student claims the rights of the sick role as an excuse for not taking a midterm, the claim is more likely to be honored if the student has a broken leg than a headache, has the flu instead of a hangover, or has been to the medical center. Even the broken leg may not be excused if it resulted from some deliberately risky behavior.

LABELING THEORY

The concept of the sick role emphasizes the individual actor's participation in negotiating a sickly or a healthy identity. This negotiation is not entirely an individual process, however, and society also plays a role in deciding who will be considered sick. Labeling theory (which was applied to deviance in Chapter 8) is used to explain how individual characteristics (such as sex, age, and social class) and socio-historical circumstances affect how the label "sick" is applied.

The Medicalization of Deviance.   Labeling theory is particularly helpful in understanding current debates about whether some forms of deviance may actually be better understood as diseases. Alcoholism is a prime example. In the 1970s, efforts were made to relabel alcoholism from "deviance" to "sickness." These efforts have been remarkably successful: Recent polls suggest that 60 percent of the public now believes that alcoholism is an illness (Public Opinion 1989b). As a result of this *medicalization of deviance,* alcoholics are now granted the sick role: Their condition is judged to be beyond their control, it is not their fault. Instead of being thrown in jail, alcoholics are put in hospitals; physicians and counselors rather than sheriffs and wardens take care of them.

Many other forms of behavior that were formerly considered deviance are now being considered forms of mental illness. Although some murderers and rapists are still judged to be deviants who should go to jail, others are labeled sick and sent to mental hospitals (Link 1987; Rosecrance 1985). There is no clear agreement on this issue among experts or the public, and this labeling process is still very much in flux.

A classic example of how both deviance and illness are socially constructed is our society's attitude toward homosexuality. For many decades, homosexuality was regarded as both deviant (actually criminal) and a form of mental illness. In 1976, however, the American Psychological Association took homosexuality off its list of mental illnesses. By simply taking a vote, they "de-medicalized" homosexuality. Although many Americans continue to regard homosexuality as deviant, there is also a growing movement to de-criminalize it.

A symbolic interactionist approach to health helps us recognize the relative quality of illness. What is regarded as illness in one time or place will not be regarded as illness in another; what is regarded as an illness for one age group will not be regarded as an illness in another. Obviously, however, there is more to health than symbolic meanings. Regardless of how positive a meaning you assign to it, a malignant tumor will threaten your life. The balance of this chapter examines differentials in physical health and reviews research on the health care system.

■

HEALTH AND SOCIAL STRUCTURE

Social epidemiology is the study of how social statuses relate to the distribution of illness and mortality.

Good health is not simply a matter of good luck and good genes. Although both elements play a part in health, we also find that good health is related to such social statuses as social class, gender, and ethnicity. The study of how social statuses relate to the distribution of illness and mortality in a population is called **social epidemiology** (Lin and Ensel 1989, 382). In this section, we review social epidemiology in the United States, and then look at the social structuring of healthy life-styles.

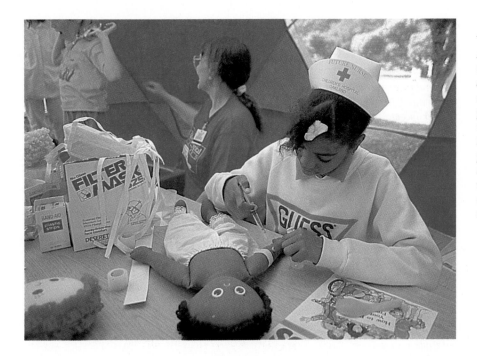

Medicine is one of our most familiar institutions. Nearly all children have enough experience with the medical institution to add playing doctor and playing nurse to their role-playing repertoire. Although playing doctor has some comical overtones, the popularity of doctor and nurse play sets and the large numbers of children who aspire to medical professions are indicators of how important medicine is to contemporary society.

SOCIAL EPIDEMIOLOGY

In the United States, the average newborn can look forward to 72 years of life. Although a few will die young, the average American now lives to be a senior citizen. This is a remarkable achievement given that life expectancy was less than 50 years at the beginning of this century. Not everyone benefited equally, however, and men and African Americans are significantly disadvantaged in terms of years of life as are people with lower socioeconomic status.

There is a great deal more to health, of course, than just avoiding death. The incidence of non-fatal conditions is at least as important as the distribution of mortality in evaluating a population's overall well-being (Verbrugge 1989a). Although only one out of every 100 people dies each year in the United States, well over half experience some sort of long-term or serious illness that affects the quality of their lives and their ability to hold a job or maintain social relationships. In the following sections we consider why gender, social class, and race are related to ill health and mortality.

Gender.   On the average, women live seven years longer than men (see Table 18.1). Some of this difference appears to be the result of a lifelong biological advantage: From conception to old age, females experience lower death rates than males. Ironically, however, women report significantly worse health than men: more high blood pressure, arthritis, asthma, diabetes, cataracts, corns, and hemorrhoids (U.S. Bureau of the Census 1989a).

Why do men have higher mortality despite apparently better health? Some of the answer may lie in biology, but social factors also play a very important and perhaps dominant role. Two aspects of the male gender role appear to put men at a disadvantage in terms of mortality.

■

TABLE 18.1

HEALTH AND LIFE EXPECTANCY BY SEX, RACE, AND FAMILY INCOME, UNITED STATES, 1987

Generally, people with higher status report better health: Men report better health than women, white Americans report better health than black Americans, and those with higher incomes report better health than those with lower incomes. For the most part, differentials in life expectancy parallel these differentials in health. The exception is sex: Despite their better health, men have lower life expectancy than women.

	LIFE EXPECTANCY AT BIRTH	PERCENT REPORTING EXCELLENT HEALTH
Total	74.9	27%
Sex		
Male	71.5	30
Female	78.3	25
Race		
White	75.5	29
Black	69.7	16
Family Income		
Under $10,000	NA	12
$10,000–19,000	NA	19
$20,000–34,999	NA	25
$35,000 and over	NA	38

SOURCE: United States National Center for Health Statistics 1988 and United States Bureau of the Census 1989a.

First, contemporary gender roles encourage males to be rowdy, aggressive, and risk taking. There is *normative* approval for higher rates of drinking, fighting, fast driving, and dangerous behavior for males. As a result, young men are three times more likely than young women to die in automobile accidents; by their 40s, men have twice the likelihood of dying of diseases associated with smoking and alcohol use.

Second, men appear to cope less well with stress than women do. Generally, studies find that men report lower levels of stress than women (Thoits 1987; Ulbrich, Warheit, and Zimmerman 1989) and that men are less likely than women to have high blood pressure. Nevertheless, men are more likely than women to die of stress-related diseases such as heart attack and stroke. Why is stress more deadly for men than women? Although there may be a biological difference in vulnerability to stress, different gender-role socialization plays an important part (Verbrugge 1989b). On the average, men do not take care of themselves as well as women do—men are less likely to go to the doctor when ill, to follow their doctor's recommendations, and to watch their diets. In addition, men are less likely to have a network of intimates in whom they can confide and from whom they can seek support (Nathanson 1984). Thus, men's stress is more likely than women's stress to develop into life-threatening proportions.

Social Class.   The higher one's social class, the longer one's life expectancy and the better one's health (see Table 18.1). A recent British study using five social class categories found that the death rates of men in the lowest class were nearly twice those of men in the highest class (Marmot, Kogevinas, and Elston 1987). In the United States, infants whose mothers failed to graduate from high school are two times more likely to die than infants whose mothers graduated from college (Bertoli et al. 1984).

The effects of social class are complex. Although they are partially attributable to the fact that poorer people cannot afford expensive medical care, the causes go far beyond simple access to health care (Rutter and Quine 1990). Figure 18.1 diagrams the paths through which low socioeconomic status affects health.

1. *Standard of living.* The lower your income, the more likely you are to live in substandard housing, have a poor diet, and receive inadequate health care. These purely economic consequences of low income have a direct effect on health.

2. *Stress.* Low-income people have less control over the world around them than do those who are better off. Among the kinds of stresses they encounter are not being able to pay their bills, evictions, unsatisfactory and demeaning jobs, and low self esteem. High levels of stress have a direct effect on health by increasing the incidence of high blood pressure, ulcers, and heart conditions. They also have an indirect effect on health by encouraging poor coping strategies—such as drinking, smoking, and risky behaviors.

3. *Low education.* Poorly educated people generally have less access to accurate information about health and health care. They are less likely to be

FIGURE 18.1
HOW POVERTY AND DISADVANTAGE CREATE ILL HEALTH

The relationship between poverty and poor health is complex. Not only do poor people have less access to health care but they are also more apt to get sick in the first place. Equalizing access to health care will not produce equal health as long as standards of living, stress, and education are unequally distributed.

SOURCE: Adapted from Rutter and Quine 1990.

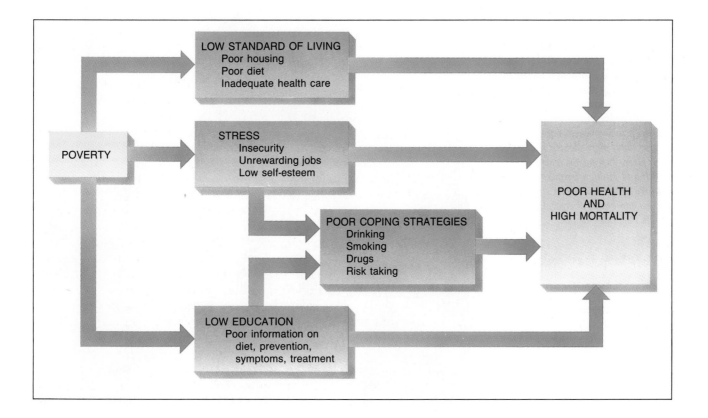

well informed about proper eating habits or appropriate responses to symptoms, and less likely to seek appropriate treatment. Watching one's cholesterol, joining a health club, and eating fiber are as closely related to education as is watching "Masterpiece Theater."

As long as social class differences in stress, education, and standard of living increase the likelihood that those with lower socioeconomic status will become sick in the first place, free medical care will not eliminate social class differences in health. In the 50 years since Britain instituted a free and universal system of national health care, the social class differentials in health have not narrowed perceptively (Marmot, Kogevinas, and Elston 1987).

Race. In the United States today, black infants are twice as likely as white infants to die in their first year of life. At every age after that, black American's mortality rates are substantially higher than those of white Americans. At ages 55 to 64, for example, black men are 50 percent more likely to die of cancer than are white men (U.S. Department of Health and Human Services 1988). As a result of this lifelong disadvantage in mortality rates, the average white male can expect to live seven years longer than the average black male; the difference is four years for females. Although this difference is far less than it was at the beginning of the century, in the late 1980s the United States recorded an alarming *decrease* in black life expectancy for two years in a row (Yared 1989). When asked to report about

For over 20 years, the U.S. Surgeon General's Office has been warning Americans that smoking causes cancer and emphysema. Although increased education has reduced smoking rates sharply for American men, there has been little reduction in the proportion of women who smoke. Among 20 to 24 year olds, more women smoke than men. Here, current Secretary of Health and Human Services, Louis Sullivan, models a t-shirt spoofing a well-known brand of cigarettes that targets American women.

their current health, black Americans are only half as likely as white Americans to report excellent health (see Table 18.1). What social factors lie behind these differentials?

Lower average income is obviously an important factor in the health disadvantage of black Americans. Because of lower incomes, black and Hispanic Americans are twice as likely as non-Hispanic whites to be without any health insurance (U.S. National Center for Health Statistics 1987). The most significant effects of low income, however, are those diagrammed in Figure 18.1: Because they have lower incomes, minority Americans are more likely to live in circumstances that make them sick in the first place.

Even after we control for income, however, black Americans have higher mortality rates than white Americans. Many observers attribute this non-economic disadvantage to the stress that accompanies minority-group status. Regardless of income, minority group members experience prejudice and discrimination that raise their risk of physical and psychological stress (Cooper et al. 1981; Ulbrich, Warheit, and Zimmerman 1989).

This pervasive pattern of disadvantage raises heart disease and cancer levels among older members of minority groups, and it also encourages risk-taking behaviors among young adults. Although most of the black/white differential in mortality is due to higher rates of heart attack, stroke, and cancer, it is notable that the cause of death demonstrating the single largest racial differential is homicide and legal intervention (deaths occurring during arrests and legal executions). Black Americans are six times more likely than white Americans to die from this cause, with the result that homicide is the fifth leading cause of death for black males (Yared 1989).

Healthy Life-styles and Social Structure

In the United States today, there is a lot of emphasis on the relationship between health and life-style. Magazine and newspaper articles proclaim your moral duty to take care of your health. These articles make the very good point that good health is more likely to be produced by good daily habits than it is by a miracle drug or regular checkups. Science can help solve some of your health problems, but it is easier and more effective if you can take good enough care of yourself that you don't get sick in the first place.

What is a healthy life-style? A long-term federal study uses seven personal health practices to assess healthy life-style. These risk factors are listed in Table 18.2. This list of bad habits doesn't look very awful: failing to eat breakfast doesn't match up to smoking crack as a way of ruining your health. Nevertheless, these health practices can make a big difference. One study found that 45-year-old men who had none of these bad habits could expect to live 11 years longer than men who had three or more (Belloc 1980)!

A central question for medical sociologists is whether life-style choices can explain the gender, race, and social class differences we observe in mortality and illness. The data in Table 18.2 suggest that life-style choices may go some way toward explaining the gender difference in mortality: On six of seven indicators, males have worse health practices than women. In terms of drinking, the difference is very substantial. Nevertheless, a

TABLE 18.2
PERSONAL HEALTH PRACTICES, BY SELECTED CHARACTERISTIC, 1985

The National Health Survey periodically collects data on seven bad health practices that are relatively widespread. Careful study of these data refutes the idea that health and mortality differentials are largely attributable to destructive health habits. Elderly respondents report the worst health but the best health practices, and the health practices of low income and low education respondents are not substantially worse than those of higher-status respondents. Although destructive habits can damage health, they do not explain very much of the race or social class differential in health or mortality.

CHARACTERISTIC	Sleeps 6 hours or less	Never eats breakfast	Snacks every day	Less physically active than contemporaries	Had 5 or more drinks on any one day[a]	Current smoker	30 percent or more above desirable weight[b]
All persons	**22.0%**	**24.3%**	**39.0%**	**16.4%**	**37.5%**	**30.1%**	**13.0%**
AGE							
18–29 years old	19.8	30.4	42.2	17.1	54.4	31.9	7.5
30–44 years old	24.3	30.1	41.4	18.3	39.0	34.5	13.6
45–64 years old	22.7	21.4	37.9	15.3	24.6	31.6	18.1
65 years old and over	20.4	7.5	30.7	13.5	12.2	16.0	13.2
65–74 years old	19.7	9.0	32.4	15.8	(NA)[c]	19.7	14.9
75 years old and over	21.5	5.1	27.8	9.8	(NA)	10.0	10.3
SEX							
Male	22.7	25.2	40.7	16.5	49.3	32.6	12.1
Female	21.4	23.6	37.5	16.3	23.3	27.8	13.7
RACE							
White	21.3	24.5	39.4	16.7	38.3	29.6	12.4
All other	26.6	23.2	36.3	14.3	29.9	33.1	16.4
Black	27.8	23.6	37.2	13.9	29.3	34.9	18.7
Other	21.4	21.5	32.6	16.5	33.3	24.8	6.7
EDUCATION LEVEL							
Less than 12 years	23.3	22.6	37.8	12.3	35.9	35.4	17.5
12 years	21.9	26.5	39.6	16.5	38.9	33.4	13.4
More than 12 years	21.2	23.3	39.2	19.1	36.8	23.1	9.4
FAMILY INCOME							
Less than $7,000	24.4	22.4	37.0	13.5	(NA)	31.1	16.1
$7,000 to $14,999	21.6	22.9	37.4	14.7	(NA)	33.4	15.3
$15,000 to $24,999	21.2	24.9	40.3	16.8	(NA)	32.2	13.4
$25,000 to $39,999	22.4	26.1	41.2	17.2	(NA)	30.0	12.1
$40,000 or more	21.8	25.4	39.9	19.4	(NA)	25.2	9.4

[a]Percent of drinkers who had five or more drinks on any one day in the past year.
[b]Based on 1960 Metropolitan Life Insurance Company standards. Data are self-reported.
[c]NA = Not available.
SOURCE: U.S. Bureau of the Census 1989a.

careful look at Table 18.2 tells us that bad health practices are not the chief explanation of race or social class differences in mortality. People with little education and low income are somewhat more likely to smoke, but there is little difference in alcohol consumption by education. Black Americans are *less* likely than white Americans to use alcohol and more likely to get physical exercise.

The trouble is that this list of health practices is very narrow. *From a sociological perspective, a healthy life-style is one that includes satisfying social roles, some control over one's social environment, and integration into one's community.* These aspects of a healthy life-style are closely correlated with social class and race. One cannot overcome a lifetime of disadvantage by eating one's vegetables.

Even if we are lucky, clean living, and well off, most of us get sick occasionally. At this point, our return to health may depend significantly on the health-care system and our access to it. We turn now to a detailed examination of health-care professions and the medical/industrial complex.

■

HEALTH-CARE PROFESSIONS

Medicine may be regarded as a social institution. It has a complex and enduring status network, and the relationships among actors are guided by shared norms or roles. Most of us occupy the status of patient in this institution. There are, however, dozens of other statuses. Over 7 million Americans are employed in health institutions. They include blood and X-ray technicians, orderlies, pharmacists, and hospital administrators. In this section, we focus on just two of these statuses: physicians and nurses.

PHYSICIANS

Less than 5 percent of the medical work force consists of physicians. Yet they are central to understanding the medical institution. Physicians are responsible both for defining ill health and for treating it. They define what is appropriate for those with the status of patient, and they play a crucial role in setting hospital standards and in directing the behavior of the nurses, technicians, and auxiliary personnel who provide direct care.

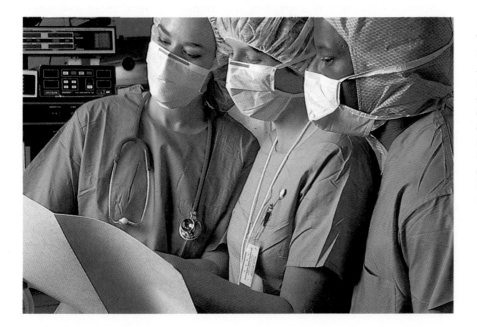

■

One of the most striking changes in American medicine is the growth in number of women physicians. Nearly one-third of the students currently enrolled in medical school are women, and it seems likely that sex will no longer be a good guide to which green-suited specialists are nurses and which are physicians. One consequence, however, is that there is a growing shortage of women entering nursing.

Physicians as Professionals.   The concept *profession* describes a special kind of occupation, one that demands specialized skills and creative freedom. No occupation fits this definition better than that of physician. Consider the six characteristics of a professional: (1) specialized knowledge, (2) a sense of obligation to one's field, (3) service to society, (4) a strong feeling of identity with others in one's field, (5) high personal involvement in one's work, and (6) an unstandardized product.

Until about 100 years ago, physicians neither possessed much specialized knowledge nor had a strong identity with others in the field. Almost anybody could claim the title of doctor; training and procedures were highly variable and mostly bad (Starr 1982). About the only professional characteristic of these early practitioners was that the product was highly unstandard!

In the United States, the professionalization of medicine began in 1848 with the establishment of the American Medical Association (AMA) and was virtually completed in 1910, when strict standards were set up for medical training. At the same time, state examinations began to be required before one could assume the title of physician and begin to practice medicine.

Learning the Physician Role.   Most people who enter the medical profession have high ideals about helping people. Studies of the medical school experience, however, suggest that the strenuous training schedule of student physicians deals a temporary blow to these ideals and makes daily endurance the chief objective. On crowded days, patients become defined as enemies who create unnecessary work. Thus, interns and residents learn to GROP (get rid of patients) by referring patients elsewhere, giving them the minimum amount of time, and discharging them as soon as possible (Mizrahi 1986). A patient who escapes GROP and actually engages the busy intern's attention usually has a really interesting condition, a curable disease, is intelligent, cooperative, and appreciative, and is not ill because of her or his own destructive life-style.

Medical education is a grueling experience. There is more and more technical information to learn, but the training period stays the same length. Recent reforms focus on developing skills of lifelong learning so that physicians will be prepared to keep up with new developments and on developing personal skills in working with patients and colleagues (Kendall and Reader 1988).

In many ways, the criticisms of medical education are the same as those of other major university programs. Teaching hospitals are primarily research centers: Professors are hired for their ability to do research rather than teach, and they are rewarded for their research productivity rather than for their ability to treat patients successfully or to teach medical students (Light 1988). After school too, the biggest rewards in medicine go to those who have the most technical and least personalized types of practices. Although many physicians renew their commitment to helping people once they survive the rigors of medical school, nowhere in the medical profession does the structure of rewards encourage personal care (Bloom 1988).

Understanding Physicians' Income and Prestige.   The medical profession provides a controversial case study of stratification theories.

Why are physicians predominantly male and nurses predominantly female? Why are physicians among the highest-paid and highest-status professionals in the United States? In 1986, the average physician earned $113,000 after paying for deductible professional expenses. The lowest average was $84,000 for pediatricians and the highest average was $204,000 for neurosurgeons (U.S. Bureau of the Census 1989a).

The structural-functional explanation of the status of physicians directly follows the Davis and Moore theory outlined in Chapter 9: There is a short supply of persons who have the talent and ability to become physicians and an even shorter supply of those who can be neurosurgeons. Moreover, physicians must undergo long and arduous periods of training. Consequently, high rewards must be offered to motivate the few who can do this work to devote themselves to it. The conflict perspective, on the other hand, argues that the high income and prestige accorded physicians have more to do with physicians' use of power to promote their self-interest than with what is best for society.

Central to the debate on whether physicians' privileges are deserved or are the result of calculated pursuit of self-interest is the American Medical Association (AMA). The AMA sets the standards for admitting physicians to practice, punishes physicians who violate AMA standards, and lobbies to protect physicians' interests in policy decisions. Although only about half of all physicians belong to the AMA, it has enormous power. One of the major objectives of the AMA is to ensure the continuance of the capitalist model of medical care, where the physician remains an independent provider of medical care on a fee-for-service basis. In pursuit of this objective, the AMA has consistently opposed all legislation designed to create national health insurance, including Medicare and Medicaid. It has also tried to ban or control a variety of alternative medical practices such as midwifery, osteopathy, and acupuncture. In 1987, the U.S. Supreme Court found that the American Medical Association was unfairly restraining trade by trying to drive osteopaths out of business. As a result of these apparent attempts to protect physicians' profits and independence rather than improve the nation's health care, the AMA has lost credibility among the public (Cockerham 1989).

The Changing Status of Physicians.   Thirty or forty years ago, the physician was an independent provider who had substantial freedom to determine the conditions of work and who was looked on as a nearly godlike source of knowledge and help by patients. Much of this is changing. Among the many signs of changes are the following (Light 1988):

1. There is a growing proportion of physicians who work in incorporated group practices, where fees, procedures, and working hours are determined by others. As a result, physicians have lost a significant amount of their independence. These bureaucratized structures are also more likely to have profit rather than service as a dominant goal.
2. The public has grown increasingly critical of physicians. Getting a second opinion is now general practice, and malpractice suits are about as common as unquestioning admiration. Patients are critical consumers of health care rather than passive recipients.

3. Fees and treatments are increasingly regulated by insurance companies and the government. The vast number of patients whose bills are paid by private or government insurance agencies allows these agencies' pay-out structures to determine what treatments will be given at what fee.

Being a physician is still a very good job, associated with high income and high prestige. It is also part of an increasingly regulated industry that is now receiving more critical scrutiny than ever before.

NURSES

Of the 7 million people employed in health care, the largest category includes the over 1 million who are registered nurses (Kahl and Clark 1986). Nurses play a critical role in health care, but they have relatively little independence. Although the nurse usually has much more contact with the patient than the physician, the nurse has no authority over patient care. Nurses are subordinate to physicians both in their day-to-day work and in their training. Physicians determine the training standards that nurses must meet, and they enforce these standards through licensing boards. On the job, physicians give instructions and supervise. Since the majority of physicians are male and the majority of nurses are female, the income and power differences between doctors and nurses parallel the gender differences in other institutions (see Table 18.3). This makes the hospital a major arena in the battle for gender equality.

In part women have fought the battle by joining them rather than beating them. Many women who would have previously become nurses are now raising their aspirations: Between 1975 and 1986, the number of female physicians increased twice as fast as the number of male physicians. Although women constitute only 20 percent of practicing physicians, they are nearly one-third of current medical students.

Within the field of nursing, training standards have risen and so have salaries. A decade ago, the standard credential in the field was the RN (registered nurse), which represented three years of classroom and practicum experience in a hospital training program. As nurses have attempted to raise their status in medical care, two new positions have developed. At the top of the nursing hierarchy is a relatively new status, the nurse

■

TABLE 18.3
PHYSICIANS AND REGISTERED NURSES: INCOME, SEX, AND RACE, 1987

Nurses earn less than a quarter as much as physicians. Critics wonder whether this reflects real differences in training and responsibility or whether it is another instance of traditional women's jobs being evaluated as less worthy than traditional men's jobs.

	PHYSICIANS	REGISTERED NURSES
Median Income	$112,800	$25,000
Percent Female	20%	95%
Percent Black	4%	8%

SOURCE: U.S. Bureau of the Census 1989a, 100, 388.

practitioner, who may provide direct patient care (for example, prescribing birth-control pills) with only very general supervision from a physician. Below her are the nurses with a BSN (bachelor of science in nursing) degree, who have the training of an RN plus a full bachelor's of science college degree. The BSN is becoming the new standard in nursing, and greater education is a lever nurses are using to demand higher wages and a greater role in health-care management.

Despite the higher wages, a serious nursing shortage is developing. Like teaching, nursing is a traditional women's occupation that is finding it difficult to attract members of the quality and in the quantity that they used to. Now that women have wider occupational opportunities, fewer choose a job that requires weekend and midnight shifts, makes severe emotional demands, includes relatively little independence, and has a short career ladder.

THE MEDICAL/INDUSTRIAL COMPLEX

HOSPITALS

The hospital was once idealized as the "temple of healing." Today it is more often part of a complex bureaucracy whose major concern is the bottom line—that is, money.

There are three types of hospitals in the United States: the for-profit or proprietary hospital, the nonprofit community or church hospital, and the state hospital. While only proprietary hospitals exist specifically to *make* money, non-profit hospitals are expected to break even, and government hospitals are expected to minimize their drain on the taxpayers' pockets. None of them can afford to neglect the dollars-and-cents aspect of medical care. Thus, each is concerned with attracting customers of the right sort (the sort who can pay their bills).

Hospitals are characterized by an awkward dual authority. The hospital is run by professional administrators who hire nurses and other staff and provide rooms, food, and equipment. Yet what goes on in the hospital is significantly determined by physicians, who are often not hospital employees. Nurses are the group most often caught in the middle: They get their orders from the physicians and their paychecks from the hospital (Cockerham 1989).

THE HIGH COST OF MEDICAL CARE: WHO PAYS?

Medical care is the fastest-rising part of the cost of living. Although the overall inflation rate between 1970 and 1985 was 100 percent, it was 400 percent for medical care. Doctors' services and hospital treatments that cost $300 in 1970 cost $1,300 in 1985 (U.S. Bureau of the Census 1989a).

Why is this so? With some risk of oversimplification, the reasons appear to be three: competition among providers, high consumer demand, and defensive medicine. All three factors are clearly illustrated in a case study of computerized axial tomography (CAT) scan equipment in a New England town as described by Ost and Antweiler (1986).

The practice of modern medicine is increasingly technical. Engineering and computer skills may be as valuable as a good bedside manner. Although this technology has increased our capacity to diagnose and cure illnesses, it has sharply increased the cost of medical care. The practice of defensive medicine—avoiding a malpractice suit by prescribing every possible test—has also played an important role in increasing costs.

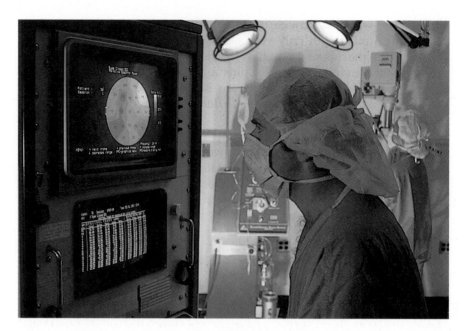

CAT Scans: A Case Study of Escalating Costs. CAT scans provide a sort of three-dimensional X-ray that illuminates soft tissues as well as bones. They are useful for diagnosing tumors and a variety of other conditions. Because such machines are incredibly expensive (the minimum installation fee is $1 million), it was initially intended that they be available only selectively in major research and public hospitals. Interhospital rivalries and high consumer demand soon scotched this idea.

Suppose that a community has two hospitals, General Hospital and Methodist Hospital, and that Methodist buys a scanner. Relatively shortly, physicians would start relying more and more on Methodist Hospital "because it has the best equipment." Naturally, General wants its own CAT scanner—even though Methodist can easily handle community demand.

The same scenario is played out over expensive cancer treatments, kidney dialysis, and so on. Each hospital must have the best in order to compete. As each hospital passes these costs along to patients, the cost of hospitalization spirals: The cost for a semi-private room rose faster than that of any other sort of medical service between 1970 and 1986 (U.S. Bureau of the Census 1989a, 95).

Another factor in rising health-care costs is higher consumer demand. It is one of the laws of economics that whenever demand is higher than the supply, costs go up. In the case of demand for medical services, there is apparently no upper limit. When consumers buy insurance or a computer, they engage in a cost/benefit analysis to see whether the expected gains are worth the cost. Such an analysis seems to be considered immoral in the case of medical care. Many members of the public believe that no cost is too great to save themselves or their loved ones, especially when the cost will be borne by their insurance company or the government.

The sharp increase in malpractice suits also plays a part in rising health-care costs. If 1,000 decisions to skip a CAT scan result in even one lawsuit over a tumor that could have been treated if detected earlier, the million-dollar lawsuit will cancel the savings from the 999 unnecessary tests. From the physicians' point of view, there is no contest: They pay for the malpractice insurance (or the damages), the insurance company or the government pays for the tests. Rational physicians cover themselves by ordering every possible test. This "defensive medicine" raises the cost of medical treatment substantially.

Who Pays the Bills?   Underlying many of the analyses of health care is one question: "Who pays?" There are three primary modes of financing health care in the United States: private payments, insurance, and government. The cost of health care is so high that only the very rich can rely on private payments. For the bulk of the population, private insurance or government programs must be relied on.

PRIVATE INSURANCE.   Approximately 75 percent of Americans are covered by a private health insurance plan. Almost all of these plans are available through place of employment, and insurance tends to be limited to those employed adults (and their families) who have a job in the corporate core. Many jobs in the periphery and most minimum-wage jobs do not include insurance benefits. Less than one-third of jobs in retail sales or food services (the fastest-growing sector of our economy) are covered by health insurance (Renner and Navarro 1989).

GOVERNMENT PROGRAMS.   The government has several programs that support medical care. The federal government provides some health care through its Veteran's Administration hospitals, but its two largest programs are Medicaid and Medicare. In addition, local governments provide medical care through public health agencies and public hospitals.

   Medicare is a government-sponsored health insurance policy for citizens over 65. Premiums are based on ability to pay and deducted from Social Security checks. Since many elderly persons have health problems that would make private insurance impossible or prohibitively expensive, the government-sponsored program is an essential means of providing insurance coverage for the elderly. The enactment of this program in 1965 did a great deal to improve the quality of health care for the elderly. Over 95 percent of the elderly are now covered by health insurance. This is not a cheap program, however, and in 1987, the government paid over $480 billion in Medicare benefits (U.S. Bureau of the Census 1989a).

   Technically a welfare program, *Medicaid* is a federal cost-sharing program that provides federal matching funds to states that provide medical services to the poor. Although the program was originally limited to people who were on welfare, in many states it is now available for poor children and pregnant women who are low income but not actually on welfare. The eligibility of individuals, however, and the services available are determined by states. As a result, some states offer much more generous medical care than others. Overall, only 2 percent of the U.S. population is believed to be covered by Medicaid. This is much smaller than the proportion who are below the poverty level. Nevertheless, this program cost $45 billion in 1987.

Senior citizens are the only group in the United States that is covered by a national health insurance plan. The introduction of Medicare in 1965 has guaranteed that virtually all citizens over the age of 65 have medical insurance. Because this insurance leaves many costs of nursing homes and catastrophic health problems uncovered, however, senior citizens remain concerned about health care costs.

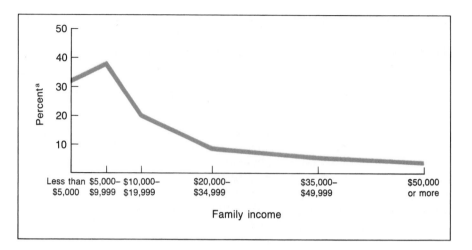

FIGURE 18.2
PERCENT OF PERSONS UNDER 65 WITHOUT HEALTH-CARE COVERAGE BY FAMILY INCOME

Approximately 14 percent of the U.S. population has no health insurance. These people, generally the unemployed and the working poor, are concentrated among those who are under 65 and have family incomes of less than $20,000. Ironically, those without health insurance have worse health than those with insurance.

SOURCE: U.S. National Center for Health Statistics 1987.

THE UNINSURED.   A significant portion of the American population—14 percent—has no medical coverage (Figure 18.2). Thanks to Medicare, nearly 100 percent of the elderly are insured; those who fall through the cracks are adults who are unemployed or the working poor. Ironically, those with poor health are nearly twice as likely to be uninsured as those with good health (19 percent versus 12 percent) (U.S. National Center for Health Statistics 1987).

The uninsured are not entirely without health care. Every county in the United States makes some provision for the so-called medically indigent. The care provided for these people is largely emergency treatment rather than prevention and diagnosis. Care is provided at clinics and emergency wards, where patients are often treated as unworthy, kept standing in long lines, and sometimes given second-rate treatment by overworked and underpaid staff members who aren't crazy about associating with the poor.

WHY DOESN'T THE U.S. HAVE NATIONAL HEALTH INSURANCE?

Health care in the United States is available on a fee-for-service basis. Like dry cleaning, you get what you can afford. If you cannot afford it, you might not get any.

This situation makes the United States unique among industrialized nations. We are "the only industrialized nation in the world that does not provide financial coverage for medical care of a majority of its citizens" (Cockerham, Kunz, and Lueschen 1988, 114). In the rest of the industrialized world, medical care is like education, regarded as a good that should be available to all regardless of ability to pay.

The advantages alleged for a national health insurance scheme are that it equalizes care to rich and poor and that it balances the costs and benefits of providing health care. The current combination of private insurance for the employed (healthier) and public insurance for the unemployed (less healthy) means that private companies get the profitable cases and government the expensive ones. A national health insurance scheme is seen as a way to benefit the taxpayer by letting government use the profits from insuring its healthy citizens to balance the costs of insuring its sick citizens.

Critics of such a scheme argue that government programs are less efficient and cost effective than private programs and that we need more diversity in health-care options than might be available under a single monolithic program.

Why is the United States alone among industrialized nations in having no national health insurance? Certainly the AMA has strongly opposed national health insurance, but that cannot be the whole reason. It opposed Medicaid and Medicare too, and those programs have been in place for 25 years. Nor is public opposition the reason. A recent poll showed that 71 percent of the American public believes that adequate medical care is a right to which a person is entitled as a citizen rather than a privilege that must be earned (Public Opinion 1988), and over half are willing to pay higher taxes to provide adequate health care to all who need it (Public Opinion 1989a). The reason that we have no national health insurance is suggested by a recent study showing that the quality of national health insurance across countries and the rapidity with which it was implemented vary directly with the political strength of the working class (Navarro 1989). If this is true, then the absence of national health insurance is linked directly to the absence of a working-class or socialist party in the United States (see Chapter 15).

■

STRATEGIES FOR IMPROVING AMERICA'S HEALTH

Health is a complex process. Good health depends on social roles and economic conditions, on genetic background and biological agents, on preventive health care and a healthy life-style, and on good medical care after illness develops. Efforts to improve the health of the population thus have to take a many-pronged approach. Generally, there are three strategies for improving America's health: encouraging healthy lifestyles, extending health care service, and reducing inequality. Each has its own political and economic price tag.

ENCOURAGING HEALTHY LIFE-STYLES

The first policy alternative, encouraging people to adopt healthy life-styles and educating them about the risks associated with life-style choices, is very attractive: It is inexpensive and politically safe. It assumes that the cause of poor health lies in individual bad habits and that the cure also lies in individual hands. Aspects of this plan include seat-belt legislation, anti-smoking campaigns, fitness programs, and the like. Although there are some people who believe that private behavior is not the government's business, there is relatively little opposition to this sort of program. Almost all of the programs outlined in the official U.S. health planning document are of this sort (Breslow 1987).

Conflict theorists generally see the emphasis on wellness and healthy life-styles as yet another instance of blaming the victim (Navarro 1986; Waitzkin 1983). They argue that the cause of disadvantage in health is the fundamental inequalities in our social structure, inequalities that cannot be alleviated by lectures about "just say no," "eat your vegetables," and "get plenty of exercise."

■

We receive continuous messages about how to lead a healthy life-style: low salt, low fat, low calories, more roughage, and lots of exercise. Although more Americans are paying attention to these messages, research shows that this message is most likely to be picked up by the well-educated and the well-off. Although anybody can do sit-ups at home, the people who are most likely to exercise are those who can afford memberships at health clubs or the Y.

PROVIDING MORE EQUITABLE HEALTH CARE

A second policy alternative is to extend health-care services to all citizens, rich and poor. Such a policy would provide better prenatal care, more vaccinations and inoculations, more screening and diagnostic tests, and more equitable distribution of treatment. This alternative is more expensive than encouraging healthy life-styles, but it is periodically on the national agenda. Although the United States remains alone among industrialized countries in not having a comprehensive health insurance scheme, Medicaid and Medicare have gone far to address some of the worst inequities in our system.

More universal availability of health care would decrease infant mortality and raise general life expectancy. A system of free, comprehensive health care, however, would not equalize mortality differences by social class. Studies in Britain demonstrate that although overall mortality dropped after socialized medicine was instituted, class differences in mortality have remained robust. Equal availability of treatment cannot erase the results of a lifetime of living under very different circumstances: worse neighborhoods, more dangerous jobs, less self-esteem and happiness, more unemployment, less control over one's life in general (Marmot, Kogevinas, and Elston 1987).

REDUCING CLASS AND RACE DISADVANTAGE

The most radical health-care policy would be to equalize life chances by reducing poverty, racism, unemployment, and other disadvantages that damage health and encourage poor health habits. Such a program would reduce the differentials in illness as well as the differentials in health care after becoming ill.

Because the racial differential in life expectancy is so embarrassingly large, the government has appointed several task forces to make recommendations about minority and low-income health problems. These task forces, however, have been "under strict orders . . . not to propose any remedies that would add to HHS [Department of Health and Human Services] spending" (cited in Greenberg 1989, 122). This unwillingness to spend money makes it seem very unlikely that any substantial progress will be made on the health deficit suffered by either minorities or the poor.

SUMMARY

Sociological analysis suggests that health and illness are socially structured. To paraphrase C. Wright Mills again, when one person dies too young from stress or bad habits or inadequate health care, that is a personal trouble, and for its remedy we properly look to the character of the individual. When whole classes, races, or sexes consistently suffer significant disadvantage in health and health care, then this is a social problem. The correct statement of the problem and the search for solutions require us to look beyond individuals to consider how social structures and institutions have fostered these patterns. The sociological imagination suggests that significant improvements in the nation's health will require changes in social institutions. Most of these changes will need to take place outside of the medical institution itself.

Improving Third World Health

Nearly every nation in the world has a policy objective of providing its citizens with longer, healthier lives. Many industrialized nations have already gone far toward meeting this goal, and the average citizen can expect to live to his or her mid 70s. Among the 41 poorest nations in the world, however, life expectancies are closer to 45, and more than one in 10 infants dies before its first birthday ("The World's Poorest" 1989). How are the world's poor countries, many with a GNP per capita of less than $300, to improve their people's health?

Obviously, they cannot rely on the same kinds of health-care institutions that exist in industrialized nations. In nations where 90 percent of the people live in poverty and in rural villages, many people will never see a physician in their life. Instead, two general strategies are being pursued: reducing risk of infection and providing primary health care (United Nations 1984).

Reducing Risk of Infection

In the less developed world, the majority of people are not dying from stress or from drinking too much or from old age; they are dying of infectious disease. Many infants die of diarrhea associated with parasitic infection (Goliber 1989). Relatively inexpensive strategies to reduce infectious disease include immunizing and vaccinating children, providing safe drinking water, providing for sewage disposal, and keeping down flies and mosquitoes.

On a somewhat more expensive level, the risk of infection can be re-

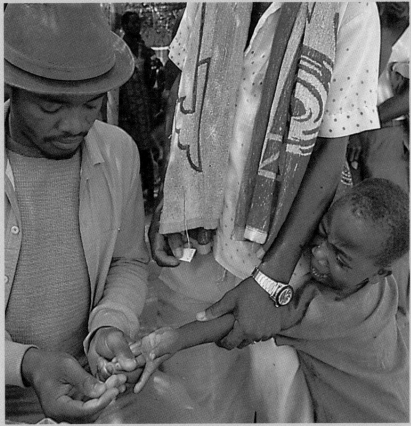

These health workers in the Ivory Coast are testing children for sleeping sickness. Studies show that a modest investment in training and vaccine can make a big dent in mortality in poor countries. Wide dispersion of primary health care workers is probably more effective at reducing Third World mortality than building high-tech hospitals.

duced by even modest improvements in standard of living—in particular, by better diets and better personal cleanliness. Cleanliness, of course, requires water—a commodity often in short supply. Better diets are also difficult to implement among impoverished peoples. One of the easiest and most effective ways to reduce infant vulnerability

to infection is to encourage mothers to breast-feed their children for a longer period.

Providing Primary Health Care

Primary health-care programs emphasize accessible caregivers over well-trained caregivers; they aim to get the largest amount of basic care to the most people. The best example of the primary health-care approach is China's "barefoot doctor" program. In the Chinese system, each neighborhood elects three individuals who will have part-time responsibility for health care: the barefoot doctor, the health aide, and the midwife. The barefoot doctor, who is given a three-month training course, is charged with basic health education and illness prevention, treatment of minor illnesses, vaccinations, and contraception. Since the barefoot doctor is responsible for only 100 to 200 people, he or she is expected to know them intimately and to be able to provide suggestions that will lead to a healthier life. The health aide's primary responsibility is sanitation—making sure that water and food supplies are clean. The midwife delivers babies. It is only in larger communities that physicians with Western-style training are available, and even these physicians have much shorter training periods than do U.S. physicians.

This system entails some loss in quality of care compared to what would be offered if Western-style physicians were available for everyone. A difficult birth is more likely to result in either infant or maternal mortality; it is likely to take longer before cancer is diagnosed. Nevertheless, this system allowed China, a nation whose 1990 GNP per capita was still only $330, to increase its life expectancy to 68 years and lower its infant mortality to 4 percent (Population Reference Bureau 1990).

Summary

Most people in the poorest, least developed nations have little access to modern health care (Goliber 1989). Happily, substantial increases in life expectancy can be realized even with few physicians, nurses, and hospitals. Aggressive use of infection reduction and primary care strategies may increase life expectancy to age 60 or 65 even without substantial increases in standard of living. According to the United Nations, however, closing the remaining gap in life expectancy depends on "the promotion of social justice, social mobility, and social development, and a more equitable distribution of income, land, social services, and amenities" (United Nations 1984, 45).

AIDS: A CASE STUDY IN THE SOCIOLOGY OF MEDICINE

In 1981, there were 185 AIDS cases in the United States; by 1991, projections suggest that there may be 250,000 to 300,000 cases. The U.S. experience is mirrored throughout the world. Although only a small portion of the population is currently infected by this disease, it already represents a severe burden on our health-care system and threatens to become a modern-day plague. In this section, we use the AIDS epidemic as a case study to illustrate the varieties of concern in the field of medical sociology.

AIDS: What Is It?

AIDS (Acquired Immunodeficiency Syndrome) was first recognized in 1981. At present, it has a 100 percent fatality rate, and of the 97,193 cases reported to the United States Centers of Disease Control by May 31, 1989, 56,468 people are already dead.

AIDS begins by exposure to a virus, HIV (human immunodeficiency virus). Present estimates suggest that somewhere between 500,000 and 3 million Americans carry the HIV virus ("1989 AIDS" 1989). Because we have recognized the illness only for a short time, we know little about how HIV is linked to AIDS. Current estimates suggest that 30 percent of HIV carriers will develop AIDS within seven years of becoming infected and that another 40 percent will develop AIDS-like symptoms (Allen and Curran 1988). Whether all those infected will eventually develop AIDS is simply not known.

THE SOCIAL EPIDEMIOLOGY OF AIDS

The social epidemiology of AIDS varies around the world. It can be spread by exchange of blood, but it is primarily a sexually transmitted disease (STD). Like all STDs, it is most characteristic of people who have multiple sexual partners.

Table 18.4 gives a breakdown of AIDS cases diagnosed in the United States according to sex, age, and risk factors. In the U.S., the primary risk factor leading to AIDS has been homosexual contact: Seventy-three percent of diagnosed cases are homosexual or bisexual males (65 percent without and 8 percent with intravenous drug use). The next largest category consists of intravenous (IV) drug users (17 percent). The fastest-growing categories of victims, however, are heterosexuals and children. Most of the children who have AIDS contracted it from their infected mothers during gestation. The rapidity with which AIDS may spread to the heterosexual population is indicated by a survey of blood donors in New York who were found to be HIV positive: Seventy percent of the homosexual males said they had had sexual intercourse with a woman in the last six months; nearly all of the intravenous drug users had had heterosexual relations.

AIDS is not a disease that anybody can get; it is not spread through casual contact. If you don't use drugs intravenously (or share needles when you do), if you are sexually inactive or your sexual activity is restricted to

■

TABLE 18.4

REPORTED AIDS CASES BY AGE, SEX, AND RISK FACTOR, UNITED STATES, 1988

The single largest category of AIDS victims consists of adult homosexual or bisexual males. The fastest-growing categories, however, are heterosexual intravenous drug users and their partners and children. Because taking precautions against AIDS is related to social class, it is expected that AIDS will bcome disproportionately a disease of the disadvantaged.

Total	100%
Sex	
Male	92%
Female	8
Age	
Adult	99
Children	1
Adults, by Risk Factor	
Homosexual/bisexual male	65
Homosexual/bisexual male AND intravenous drug user	8
Intravenous drug user only	17
Transfusion	3
Heterosexual contact with one of above	4
Other/undetermined	3
Children, by Risk Factor	
Parent IV drug user	56
Parent, other risk factor	21
Transfusion	18
Other/undetermined	5

SOURCE: United States Centers for Disease Control 1988, 18.

a single, faithful partner who is not infected, and if you don't admit unscreened blood into your system, you are not likely to get AIDS. For those who have multiple sexual partners, using a condom during intercourse reduces (but does not eliminate) the chances that one will contract AIDS. Who takes all of these precautions? The answer is the same kinds of people who watch their cholesterol and who exercise regularly.

Greater awareness of the risks of AIDS has reduced the number of AIDS cases among homosexual men—a group that spans the entire social class distribution of society. Intravenous drug users, however, are disproportionately drawn from lower social classes. They are a group that, by definition, is not particularly health conscious. As a result, it is expected that AIDS will become increasingly a disease of the poor and the disadvantaged. Already, blacks and Hispanics are two to five times more likely to contract AIDS than non-Hispanic whites with the same risk factors. Over 50 percent of children with AIDS are black (Selik, Castro, and Pappaioanou 1988).

AIDS AND THE NEGOTIATION OF IDENTITY

When AIDS was first identified in the United States, it was a disease associated with groups that were already stigmatized as deviant: gay men and IV drug users. The combination of a mysterious, fatal disease and stigmatized subgroups made AIDS doubly feared. Schools rejected children with AIDS, homes of AIDS victims were burned, and AIDS victims were discriminated against in transportation, housing, and employment.

Because AIDS is uniquely associated with life-style choices, AIDS victims were largely denied the sick role. The disease was thought to be their

The largest group of AIDS victims is gay or bisexual men, and this group continues to be disproportionately at risk of contacting AIDS. Nevertheless, the fastest growing group of AIDS victims is infants and children. These children's futures are short and their presents bleak. Because their parents also have AIDS, many are being reared in institutions. Here, volunteers help care for AIDS babies at the Birk Childcare Center in New York.

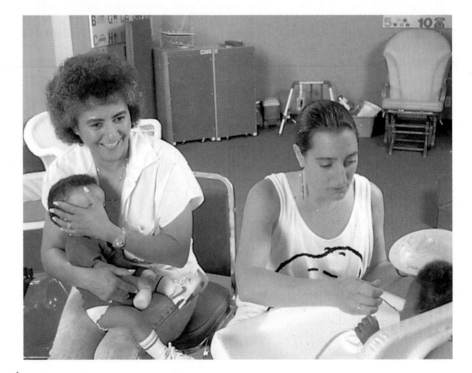

fault, something they could have avoided. The spread of AIDS into the heterosexual population and the growing number of children with AIDS have reduced the tendency to divide the victims into the innocent and the guilty and have increased the likelihood that AIDS victims will be granted the sick role. Increasingly, AIDS victims and HIV carriers are offered the same legal protection and health care available to people with other infectious diseases (Faden and Kass 1988).

All of us enter into a difficult negotiation when we face dying, a new role for which we are generally not well prepared (Lofland 1978). Whom do we tell? How should we act? Dying of AIDS is even more difficult than other terminal conditions. Some people dying of AIDS must deal with the first public acknowledgment of their homosexuality, bisexuality, or drug use. Nearly all AIDS victims find that some members of their communities respond to their condition with fear and hostility rather than sympathy. The stigma that AIDS patients face makes their maintenance of a positive identity especially difficult, and AIDS patients often experience great social distress in dealing with the social as well as the physical consequences of AIDS (Weitz 1989).

AIDS AND THE HEALTH-CARE SYSTEM

In 1988, it was estimated that the U.S. is spent $1.3 billion on the diagnosis and treatment of HIV and AIDS. As the disease gains momentum, it is likely to swamp our medical facilities and our capacities to pay for treatment. Already, in some central African nations, one out of every four hospital beds is occupied by an AIDS patient (Ankrah 1989). How are we to meet the demand? And how will our health-care workers cope with the risk of AIDS?

Doctors, nurses, and dentists deal with blood on a daily basis, which means that they are at risk if their patients have HIV. If HIV-infected blood touches an open sore on their hands or if they nick themselves with a needle just used on an AIDS patient, they risk getting the disease themselves. The risk is enough to drive a growing number of people out of the medical field and to make it increasingly difficult to recruit nurses.

The potential cost of AIDS treatment threatens to overwhelm current mechanisms of paying for health care. To focus on only one indicator of this cost, AZT (a drug that can control but not cure AIDS) costs $8,000 to $13,000 annually for one person. The cost of this drug is only a small part of the total cost of AIDS treatment from the patient's diagnosis to his or her death. As AIDS becomes more and more a disease of the disadvantaged, fewer AIDS patients will be covered by private health insurance, and the burden on federal, state, and local health agencies will be enormous.

WHAT CAN BE DONE?

Public policy on AIDS must advance on several fronts. First, we need to invest research efforts into learning how to prevent HIV from turning into AIDS and how to cure AIDS. We also need to reduce the transmission of HIV to uninfected populations. We have already virtually eliminated blood transfusions as a source of AIDS infection (Yankauer 1988); we need to move decisively on the other risk factors. Although one would not expect

IV drug users to be especially health conscious, programs encouraging needle sterilization have been effective (Becker and Joseph 1988). More generally, we need strong programs to prevent and treat intravenous drug abuse, which is a public health menace in and of itself (Ball et al. 1988).

Finally, we need to encourage safe-sex practices, primarily condom use and monogamy. Because sexual transmission plays such a major role in the disease, education about safe sex is a critical step. Studies in San Francisco show that fear of AIDS *can* scare people into using safer-sex practices and can actually reduce the rate at which new HIV cases are added to the population (Winkelstein et al. 1988). In areas where AIDS is less widespread, however, the attitude is more likely to be similar to that of one Phoenix resident who decided not to use safe-sex practices because "there's only nine people in Arizona who have it and four of them are dead and two of them live in Tucson. So what are your chances?" (Weitz 1989, 273). The man subsequently got AIDS.

Concern with AIDS ultimately brings us back to the same policy options that we confronted earlier in this chapter: promoting more healthful lifestyle choices, offering better health care, and reducing the social and economic inequities that damage health and encourage poor health practices. Educating people about their individual responsibility for their own health is important, but so, too, is changing the social structures that make some groups more vulnerable than others.

Rationing Health Care

Although we have been reluctant to admit it, there may be limits on the amount of health care that can be provided. The issue is clearest in the case of organ transplants: There are simply not enough donor organs to go around. There may also be limits on how much we, as a society, can reasonably spend on health care.

TRANSPLANTS: WHO SHOULD LIVE?

On any given day, there are approximately five to 10 people waiting for every donor organ that becomes available. Who will get these organs? In a free-market, capitalist health-care system, the answer would be that the price of the service could be raised so high that the market could allocate organs by income. Since most public and private health insurance policies now cover transplant costs, however, cost does not eliminate the overdemand. Furthermore, U.S. law forbids selling organs (Kutner 1987).

In cases of heart, liver, and kidney failure, all will die without treatment. How do we choose

who should live? One study of the British public asked respondents to choose which of two patients should be saved. When faced with such choices, there was strong support for saving a five-year-old over a 70-year-old, a 35-year-old over a 60-year-old, a married person over an unmarried person, a nonsmoker over a smoker, and a person with an inherited disease rather than a diet-related disease (Charny, Lewis, and Farrow 1989). This suggests that the public would use age, family responsibilities, and whether the disease was the result of a life-style choice in making its decisions.

Studies of medical administrators show that all or almost all used the following criteria: psychological stability (97 percent), probable length of survival after the procedure (96 percent), and quality of life after the procedure (97 percent) (Kilner 1988).

Few medical administrators or members of the public say that they would use race or class as an indicator of whose life is worth most. In fact, the study of the British public showed no significant preference for saving a company director over a

Laura Parker, playing here with her dad, is alive today because of a bone marrow transplant. Nearly everybody agrees that the expense of medical treatment is justified when the patient is a child such as Laura, but there is less consensus about how much public expense is justified for medical treatment at the other end of the life course.

dockworker. Studies suggest, however, that social class and race do play a role in these decisions. In the process of selecting patients who have the stable personal and family lives thought necessary to maximize their postsurgery care, social class and life-style factors enter in. There were many headlines in 1986 when a liver transplant was denied to an infant whose parents were not married on the grounds that they were unlikely to provide the sort of home life necessary to maximize the child's survival and long-term quality of life (Kutner 1987).

Is There a Limit?

Organ transplants, of which there is an absolute shortage, make the issue of health rationing starkly clear. Perhaps less clear is the more fundamental issue surrounding modern health care. Can we have it all? Is shortage of donor organs the only reason to ration medical care, or is there a limit on how much we should spend on medical care?

In 1970, the United States spent twice as much on education as we did on health care; in 1987, we spent equal amounts. The total bill for health care in 1987 was almost 11 percent of our gross national product (GNP) (Kutner 1987). The question for the future is whether we will spend growing proportions of our national income on health care at the expense of other social projects. This question will become increasingly pertinent because of the sharp growth expected in the aging population over the next 40 years.

In 1990, Oregon was the first state to consider publicly the issue of rationing health care. The criteria they are considering would give highest priority to programs that benefit the most people the most years. Generally, this means that preventive programs will receive priority over high-priced surgical interventions. Oregon's program, however, has not faced the critical issue posed by our aging population: It exempts Medicaid services from its prioritizing scheme.

The issue is a difficult one. Nobody wants to save money on medical care by cutting back treatments for himself or herself or for loved ones. Spending for health care and research is one of the only programs for which the public is willing to raise its taxes (Public Opinion 1989a). This suggests that, so far at least, the cost of health care has not surpassed the public's demand for more of it. Nevertheless, a realistic assessment of how health care fits into overall national goals may mandate some restrictions in medical treatment. One billion dollars will buy 500 people a liver transplant, pay for nine Stealth bombers, or fund the Arkansas public school system for a year. Can we have it all? Which should we choose? And if health care is to be rationed, what criteria should we use?

■
SUMMARY

1. Health and illness are negotiated statuses. If we can negotiate a sick role, we are excused from our normal obligations as long as we follow instructions and seek to get well. Whether a condition is labeled as sick, deviant, or perfectly normal is relative.

2. Three statuses are especially relevant to the social epidemiology of health in the U.S.: gender, social class, and race or ethnicity. Men, racial or ethnic minorities, and those with lower socioeconomic status have higher mortality.

3. The health disadvantage associated with lower socioeconomic status goes beyond a simple inability to afford health care. Lower social class is associated with lower standards of living, more stress, lower education, and poorer coping strategies, all of which increase the likelihood that individuals will be in need of health care.

4. From a sociological point of view, a healthy life-style is one that includes satisfying social roles, some control over one's social environment, and integration into one's community. Much more so than smoking, drinking, and eating one's vegetables, these aspects of healthy life-style are related to class and race.

5. Physicians are professionals; they have a high degree of control not only over their own work but also over all others in the medical institution. Structural functionalists argue that physicians earn so much because of scarce talents and abilities, but conflict theorists argue that high salaries are due to an effective union (the AMA). Physicians' independence is lower now than it used to be.

6. Nurses comprise the largest single occupation in the health-care industry. Nurses earn much less than physicians, have less prestige, take orders instead of give them, and are predominantly female. The hospital is a major arena in the battle for gender equality.

7. There are three kinds of hospitals: proprietary, nonprofit, and state hospitals. Hospital costs are driven up by competition to have the latest and best equipment, the practice of defensive medicine (in which physicians prescribe tests for everything), and consumer demand.

8. Most Americans (75 percent) are covered by private insurance. Medicare has covered most senior citizens successfully, but the poor are seriously underinsured: Fourteen percent have no insurance. The uninsured are less healthy than the insured.

9. The U.S. does not have national health insurance because we do not have a strong workers' party. We are one of the few nations in the Western world that does not make medical care available regardless of the patient's ability to pay.

10. There are three strategies for improving America's health: encouraging healthy life-styles, extending health-care service, and reducing inequality. The first is cheapest but may lead to blaming the victim. Better health care is important but will not deal with the fact that the poor and disadvantaged are more likely to have serious illnesses in the first place.

11. The two largest categories of AIDS victims are homosexual or bisexual men and intravenous drug users. Heterosexuals and children are the fastest-growing categories of victims. AIDS is likely to swamp our health-care system in the coming decade. Public policy must address its prevention and cure.

12. We may have to consider limits on health care. Not only is there a shortage of donor organs, but there may be limits on what we, as a society, can reasonably pay for health care. Setting unbiased criteria for the rationing of health care will be a difficult task.

SUGGESTED READINGS

Blank, Robert, 1988. Rationing Medicine. New York: Columbia University Press. Although concerned with rationing and the high-cost end of health-care delivery, this volume also covers more general issues, such as how health is related to life-style and how political culture affects health-care delivery.

Cockerham, William. 1989. Medical Sociology. (4th ed.) Englewood Cliffs, N.J.: Prentice-Hall. A textbook on medical sociology by an active researcher in the field, this volume provides a balanced presentation of theoretical views along with a detailed analysis of how medical institutions and professions operate.

Navarro, Vicente. 1986. Crisis, Health, and Medicine. New York: Tavistock. A conflict analysis of how inequalities in medical care and in health are produced by an unequal society.

Starr, Paul. 1982. The Social Transformation of American Medicine. New York: Bantam. Describes how disorganization and quackery in the 19th century gave way to a highly controlled profession. An important but controversial book that critics charge unfairly blames physicians for working in a capitalist economy.

United Nations. 1984. "Mortality and Health Policy." Population Studies 91:1–200. An evenhanded evaluation of health and health policy in both the developed and the less developed countries, this report covers causes of death and illness as well as policy recommendations.

CHANGE

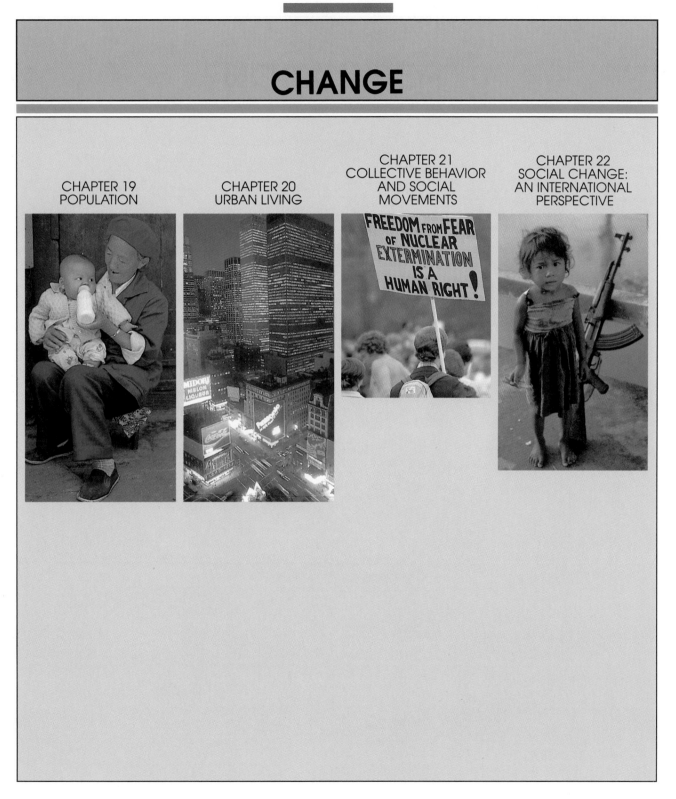

CHAPTER 19
POPULATION

CHAPTER 20
URBAN LIVING

CHAPTER 21
COLLECTIVE BEHAVIOR
AND SOCIAL
MOVEMENTS

CHAPTER 22
SOCIAL CHANGE:
AN INTERNATIONAL
PERSPECTIVE

FREEDOM FROM FEAR
OF NUCLEAR
EXTERMINATION
IS A
HUMAN RIGHT !

19

POPULATION

PROLOGUE

Have you ever . . .

Considered having a child? If you have given it any thought at all, you have probably come up with a list of pros and cons. For most people, the list of cons is a long one: Children are expensive, they tie you down, they interfere with school or work, and they give you a frightening level of responsibility. Yet, every year, about 70 out of every 1,000 American women ages 15 to 44 have a baby. Of course, some bumble into it by accident and some do it unthinkingly as part of the normal adult role, but others look over the list of pros and cons, gulp, and take the plunge. The amazing thing about fertility is that in spite of the diversity of motives on the individual level, the result on the societal level is very similar year after year.

Whether you have children and how many you have are likely to depend on your other goals. If you are committed to a career or to getting a graduate degree, the likelihood is that, male or female, you will postpone having children or even decide not to have any. Your decision will have ramifications far beyond your own life. For example, the age structure of the population is largely determined by fertility. If you and others of your generation look at the list of disadvantages and decide that childrearing isn't for you, the proportion of children in our population will go down. This would mean relatively few jobs in elementary education and relatively more jobs in social services for the elderly. In 40 years, your decision will translate into relatively few middle-aged people to support you in your old age! Having a child is one of the most intimate and private of experiences, yet perhaps nothing else we do has so much public impact.

This chapter explores the interrelationships of social structures and population. It takes a historical and cross-cultural perspective to illustrate how births and deaths relate to social institutions. Although studies of population are often highly technical and statistical, this chapter focuses on how population processes relate to social issues such as gender roles, family, and poverty.

THE DEMOGRAPHIC TRANSITION

THE CURRENT SITUATION

In 1990, the world population was 5.3 billion, give or take a couple hundred million. It is growing—rapidly. By the time current college students reach retirement age, the world population is likely to be 9 billion. This tremendous growth is totally alien to most human experience. Most societies before the industrial revolution grew either slowly or not at all (see Figure 19.1).

The world today has twice as many people in it as it did as recently as 1950. In part because of this growth, millions are poor, underfed, and undereducated. In part because of this growth, 15 to 20 percent of the world's species of plant and animal life may disappear by the end of this century. In part because of this growth, the world economic system is in danger of bankruptcy. Perhaps no other issue is so vitally connected to so

FIGURE 19.1
**THE GROWTH
OF WORLD POPULATION**

Until the last 100 years or so, world population grew very slowly or not at all. The population bomb is as much a child of the 20th century as is the atom bomb.

SOURCE: Van der Tak, Haub, and Murphy 1979.

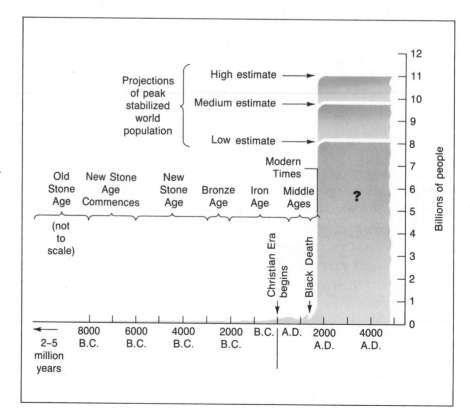

many of our era's crises. This section first describes the current world population and then the process by which it was reached.

Although population is concerned with such intimate human experiences as birth and death, the big picture of population growth and change can be understood only if we use statistical summaries of human experience. Four measures are especially important: the crude birthrate, the crude deathrate, the crude natural growth rate, and the doubling time.

$$\textbf{Crude birthrate (CBR)} = \frac{\text{Number of births in a year}}{\text{Estimated midyear population}} \times 1,000$$

$$\textbf{Crude deathrate (CDR)} = \frac{\text{Number of deaths in a year}}{\text{Estimated midyear population}} \times 1,000$$

$$\textbf{Crude natural growth rate} = \frac{\text{CBR} - \text{CDR}}{10}$$

$$\textbf{Doubling time (in years)} = \frac{70}{\text{Crude natural growth rate}}$$

Table 19.1 shows these rates in 1990. For the world as a whole, the crude birthrate in 1990 was 27 births per 1,000 population; the crude deathrate was a much lower 10 per 1,000. Because the number of births exceeded the number of deaths by 17 per 1,000, the crude natural growth rate of the world's population was 1.7 percent. If your savings were growing at the rate of 1.7 percent per year, you would undoubtedly think that the growth rate was very low. A growth rate of 1.7 percent in population, however, translates into a doubling time of 41 years. This means that *if* this growth rate continues, the population will double to 10.6 billion in just 41 years.

The frightening prospect of welcoming another 5.3 billion people in our lifetime is complicated by the fact that the growth is uneven. As Table 19.1

■

TABLE 19.1
THE WORLD POPULATION PICTURE, 1990

In 1990, the world population was 5.3 billion and growing at the rate of 1.7 percent per year. Growth was uneven, however; the less developed areas of the world were growing much more rapidly than the more developed areas. As a result, most of the additions to the world's population were in poor nations.

AREA	CRUDE BIRTH-RATE	CRUDE DEATH-RATE	CRUDE NATURAL GROWTH RATE	TOTAL POPULATION (in Millions)	DOUBLING TIME (in Years)
World	27	10	1.7%	5,321	41
Africa	44	15	2.9	661	24
Asia	27	9	1.8	3,116	39
Latin America	28	7	2.1	447	33
Soviet Union	19	10	0.9	291	78
North America	16	9	0.7	278	100
Europe	13	10	0.3	501	233

SOURCE: Population Reference Bureau 1990.

shows, growth rates are startlingly different across the areas of the world. Africa is the world's fastest-growing continent. At a growth rate of 2.9 percent per year, it will double its population size in only 24 years. In Europe, by contrast, births scarcely exceed deaths and population is barely growing.

These differentials in growth are of tremendous importance. Almost all the additions to world population in the next several decades will take place in the less developed nations. As a result, the world is likely to be proportionately poorer in 2030 than it is now. How did we get into this fix?

POPULATION IN PREINDUSTRIAL TIMES

Fertility is the incidence of childbearing.

Mortality is the incidence of death.

For most of human history, **fertility** (the incidence of childbearing) was barely able to keep up with **mortality** (the incidence of death), and the population grew little or not at all. Historical demographers estimate that in the long period before population growth exploded, both the birth- and deathrates hovered around 40 to 50 per 1,000.

Translated into human terms, a birthrate of 40 to 50 means that the average woman spends most of the years between ages 20 and 45 pregnant or nursing. If both she and her husband survive until they are 45, she will produce an average of six to 10 children. Estimates drawn from the first U.S. census in 1790 suggest that the average woman over 40 had borne eight children. Such high levels of childbearing have a powerful effect on the role of women. They virtually preclude any participation in social structures outside the home. Women will be tied close to home and excluded from participation in political, community, or economic affairs beyond the household. If women fail to keep up this level of childbearing, however, the deathrate exceeds the birthrate and the population begins to dwindle.

Life expectancy is the average number of years that a group of infants can expect to live.

On a personal level, a crude deathrate of 40 to 50 per 1,000 translates into a life expectancy of 25 to 30 years. **Life expectancy** is the average number of years a group of infants can expect to live. A simple example will show how high childhood mortality can bring down this average. Let us take a hypothetical group of 10 infants: Three die in infancy and therefore live zero years; two die at the age of 10; the other five live to 70. The total number of years lived by these 10 infants is 370:

$$3 \times 0 \text{ years} = 0$$
$$2 \times 10 \text{ years} = 20$$
$$5 \times 70 \text{ years} = \underline{350}$$
$$\text{Total} 370$$

The average number of years lived by this group of 10 infants—their life expectancy—is 37 (370 divided by 10). The example illustrates why preindustrial societies had such very low life expectancy: Although those who escaped the perils of childhood might manage to live to be elderly, as many as one-third of the population died before their first birthday.

When mortality is this high, death is a frequent visitor to most households. In the United States in 1900, life expectancy was approximately 45 to 50 years (Omram 1977). At this level of mortality, it is estimated that 62 percent of all parents experienced the childhood death of one of their children, and one quarter of all children experienced the death of a parent before they reached age 15 (Uhlenberg 1980).

THE TRANSITION IN THE WEST

The industrial revolution set in motion a whole series of events that revolutionized population in the West. First, mortality dropped; then, after a period of population growth, fertility declines followed. Because statistical studies of population are called **demography,** this process is called the **demographic transition.**

Demography is the study of population—its size, growth, and composition.

The **demographic transition** is the process of moving from the traditional balance of high birth- and deathrates to a new balance of low birth- and deathrates.

Decline in Mortality. General malnutrition was a major factor supporting high levels of mortality. Though few died of outright starvation, poor nutrition increased the susceptibility of the population to disease. Improvements in nutrition were the first major cause of the decline in mortality. New crop varieties from America (corn and potatoes especially), new agricultural methods and equipment, and increased communication all helped improve nutrition. Productivity increased, and greater trade reduced the consequences of localized crop failure. The second major cause of the decline in mortality was a general increase in the standard of living: better shelter and clothing . . . and soap. Changes in hygiene were vital in reducing communicable diseases, especially those affecting young children, such as typhoid fever and diarrhea (Razzell 1974). Because of these factors, the deathrate gradually declined between 1600 and 1850. Nevertheless, the life expectancy for women in the United States was only 40 years at the time of the Civil War.

In the late 19th century, public health engineering led to further reductions in communicable disease by providing clean drinking water and adequate sewage. Medical science did not have an appreciable effect on life expectancy until the 20th century, but its contributions have sparked a remarkable and continuing increase in life expectancy. During this century, the life expectancy of U.S. women has increased from 49 to 78 years. Thus, although mortality began a steady decline in about 1600, the fastest decreases have occurred in the 20th century. This decline reflects the almost total elimination of deaths from infectious disease and the steady progress in eliminating deaths caused by poor nutrition and an inadequate standard of living (McKeown and Record 1962; McKeown, Record, and Turner 1975).

Decline in Fertility. The industrial revolution also affected fertility, though much later and less directly. The reduction in fertility was not a response to the drop in mortality or even a direct response to industrialization itself. Rather, it appears to have been a response to changed values and aspirations triggered by the whole transformation of society (Coale 1973).

Industrialization meant increasing urbanization, greater education, the real possibility of getting ahead in an expanding economy, and, most important, a break with tradition—an awareness of the possibility of doing things differently than they had been done by previous generations. The idea of controlling family size to satisfy individual goals spread even to areas that had not experienced industrialization, and by the end of the 19th century, the idea of family limitation had gained widespread currency (van de Walle and Knodel 1980). In England and Wales, the average number of children per family fell from 6.2 to 2.8 between 1860 and 1910, the space of just two generations (Wrigley 1969).

The Calamitous Century

In the fifth decade of the 14th century, one-third of the world died. An international epidemic of the bubonic plague struck first in China, then followed the caravan routes to the Mediterranean and traveled by ship to Western Europe. In 1351, a ghost ship with a cargo of wool and a dead crew ran aground in Norway, and the disease spread to Scandinavia and Russia. In its first assault, perhaps one-third of the population of Europe and Asia died. The plague came back again and again throughout the century until the population of Europe was reduced to half of what it had been before.

Among those who caught the plague, death was both certain and quick. Stories were recorded of people who caught the plague in their sleep and died before they awoke. The deathrate was enormous; people died faster than they could be buried. Bodies piled up in the streets, and shallow mass graves were filled as fast as they could be dug.

The disaster was too large to comprehend in ordinary terms, and many believed that it meant the end of the world. This belief, plus the very realistic expectation of sudden death, meant that normal social relationships stopped. Crops went unharvested and fields unplowed; cathedrals being built were abandoned, never to be completed; livestock went untended and died almost as fast as their masters.

Overwhelming fear did not encourage human kindness. Each person was afraid to go near another, and the usual social ties were torn.

Parents abandoned children, and wives left husbands.

In yet a darker spirit, people looked for a scapegoat to blame for their misfortune. The answer in the 14th century, as it was in the 20th, was the Jews. Despite a papal statement that it was unreasonable to think that the Jews were poisoning the wells they too used, a flame of anti-Semitism swept Europe: Jews were burned to death in Maintz (Germany) on August 24, 1349; in Worms, York, Antwerp, and Brussels, entire Jewish communities were exterminated. The survivors moved eastward to Poland and Russia, and by 1350 there were few Jews left in Germany or the Low Countries.

In the long run, the 50 percent reduction in population had significant economic impact and may have hastened the end of feudalism. The 14th century was a preindustrial agricultural society. Without mechanical aids, the productivity of the soil was directly proportional to the amount of labor put into it. The

■

The plague came back again and again throughout the century until the population of Europe was reduced to half of what it had been before.

"La Peste de Tournai" (1348–1353) unknown artist.

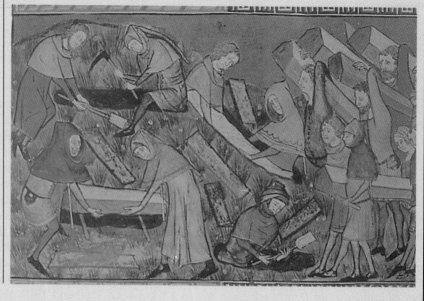

plague cut the amount of labor by half. The immediate consequence was an enormous fall in productivity. The very foundations of feudalism were shaken. Labor's bargaining power rose sharply, and wages for craftsmen and laborers doubled. Tenant farmers no longer had to stay with exploitive masters but could choose among manors competing for their services. Rents tumbled, and many tenant farms went empty; fields returned to the wild. Attempts were made to arrest this rapid change in economic relationships by legally restricting wage increases to 35 percent and by binding tenants to their land. In the face of severe competition for labor, however, these laws were ineffective and labor gained significant advantage.

A change in the supply and demand of labor did not revolutionize society. The people of the Middle Ages, both landlords and tenants, were still bound to one another by ties of custom. Nevertheless, the loss of half the population and the subsequent economic response deeply affected medieval society.

SOURCES: Tuchman 1978; McNeil 1976; and Hatcher 1977.

This decline in fertility took place without benefit of modern contraceptives. Toward the end of the decline, diaphragms and condoms were important, but much of the fertility decline in Europe was achieved through the ancient method of withdrawal—coitus interruptus.

The Transition to Low Growth.   In the West, mortality began to decline nearly 150 years before fertility started to drop. As a result, Europe and North America experienced a long period of unprecedented population growth (see Figure 19.2). Three factors reduced the problems associated with this century-long population boom: (1) technology grew even more rapidly than population so that the standard of living grew much faster than the population; (2) the population boom coincided with the colonization of North America and Australia so that the extra population simply moved overseas; and (3) growth rates were relatively modest because the decline in deathrates was so slow.

At the end of the 20th century, the demographic transition is nearly complete in the West. Fertility and mortality rates are once again close to equal, and the population has virtually ceased to grow. This new equilibrium is being reached at birth- and deathrates of 12 to 15 instead of 40 to 50 per 1,000.

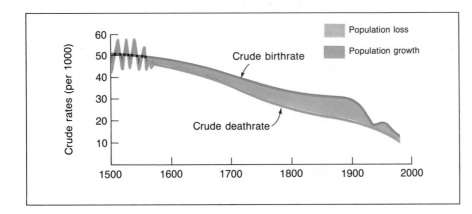

FIGURE 19.2
THE DEMOGRAPHIC TRANSITION IN THE WEST

Pre-industrial populations were characterized by fluctuating death rates and relatively stable birth rates. Mortality rates gradually stabilized and fell below the fertility rate. Because the decline in mortality was slow and because many of the excess people moved to North America or Australia, this growth did not cause dramatic problems for Europe.

FIGURE 19.3
THE DEMOGRAPHIC
TRANSITION IN THE THIRD WORLD

In the Third World, mortality rates fell suddenly while fertility continued at very high levels. The result was dramatic growth. Fertility rates have begun to decline but are still far higher than mortality rates.

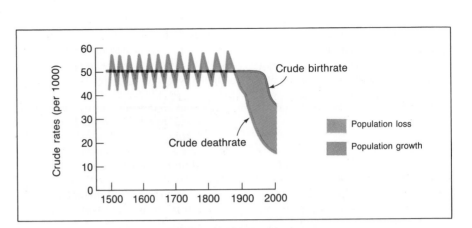

■

The importation of modern medicine from the West has reduced mortality significantly throughout the Third World. Vaccinations and basic education about nutrition and sanitation have reduced infant mortality to 6 percent in Papua-New Guinea. Nevertheless, life expectancy is only 54 years—substantially below the average for other Third World countries.

THE THIRD WORLD

In the Third World, the demographic transition is taking a very different course. Both birth- and deathrates remained at roughly preindustrial levels until World War II. Since then, mortality has fallen sharply, while fertility declines are just getting under way. In 1990, the birthrate in the Third World exceeds the deathrate by 21 per 1,000, implying a growth rate of 2.1 percent per year and a doubling time of 33 years. The result is rapid population growth (see Figure 19.3).

In the developing world today, life expectancy stands at about 61 years. This is a remarkable achievement in a short time. Much of the improvement in life expectancy has been the result of imported technology from the developed world: vaccinations and inoculations, insecticides to control malaria, and public health engineering to provide clean water in cities. This fall in mortality is unlike the mortality decline in the West in two ways: (1) It has been far more rapid, and (2) it has not been accompanied by rising standards of living.

Mortality is still unacceptably high in the Third World: Nearly one in 10 children die before their first birthdays. Although substantial improvements in mortality can be achieved through inexpensive preventative strategies (see Chapter 18), major improvements in mortality await increases in standard of living: better diets, better housing, better domestic sanitation.

Drops in fertility also depend on better standards of living. Experience tells us that fertility goes down when preindustrial social institutions—family, gender roles, and agricultural economies—are changed. In the following sections, we explore more deeply the link between social structures and fertility and mortality, and then we return to the question of how to bring both fertility and mortality down to acceptable levels.

■

FERTILITY, MORTALITY, AND SOCIAL STRUCTURE

THE EFFECTS OF SOCIAL STRUCTURE ON FERTILITY AND MORTALITY

Social Structure and Fertility.   In Kenya, the average woman has six or seven children; in Italy, the average woman has only one or two. These differences are not the result of biological differences; they are the product of values, roles, and statuses in very different societies. The average woman in Kenya wants six or seven children, and the average woman in Italy wants only one or two.

The level of fertility in a society is strongly related to the roles of women. Generally, fertility is higher where women marry at younger ages, where they have less access to education, and where their roles outside the household are limited. Fertility also reflects the development of society's institutions. When the family is the source of security, income, social interaction, and even salvation, fertility is high.

Social Structure and Mortality. The single most important social factor to affect mortality is standard of living—access to good nutrition, safe drinking water, economic security, protective housing, and decent medical care. Differences in standard of living account almost entirely for the fact that the average American can expect to live 25 years longer than the average Nigerian and that the average white American can expect to live four years longer than the average black American.

More subtly, social structure affects mortality through its structuring of social roles and life-style (see Chapter 18). Race, religion, and gender all affect exposure to dangerous life-styles. In 1988 in the United States, 19,000 young men died at the ages of 20 to 24, compared with 6,100 young women. Most died in automobiles, and the difference in number is a product of the different norms that structure the lives—and deaths—of men and women.

THE EFFECTS OF FERTILITY AND MORTALITY ON SOCIAL STRUCTURE

Fertility Effects. Fertility has powerful effects on the roles of women. The greater the number of children a woman has and the older she is at the time of the last birth, the less likely she is to have any involvement in social structures outside the family.

In the U.S. in 1990, the average woman has 2.0 children, with the first one born at age 26 and the second shortly thereafter. This means that she has plenty of time to finish her education and establish herself in a career before she starts childbearing. Both of her children will be in school before she is 35, and she still has 45 years of life expectancy to look forward to. Active childbearing and childrearing take only six to eight years of her life instead of 30 to 40. The difference has vast implications for women's social, economic, and political roles.

AGE STRUCTURE. In addition to affecting women's roles, fertility has a major impact on the age structure of the population: The higher the fertility, the younger the population. This is graphically shown in the population pyramids in Figure 19.4, which compares the age structure of the United States to that of Kenya. When fertility is low, the number of children is about the same as the number of adults; when fertility is high, there are many more children than adults and the age structure takes on a pyramidal shape.

One measure of a society's age structure is the **dependency ratio**—the number of people under 15 and over 65 divided by the population aged 15 to 65. This ratio is a rough measure of the number of dependents per productive adult. On a worldwide basis, it varies from 0.92 in Africa to

Although children impose burdens on parents, they also bring joy and entertainment. Moreover, children are one of the few sources of joy and reward equally available to rich and poor. As this photograph indicates, women and men with few economic rewards may still find pleasure in their children. Thus, poverty and children are not incompatible and poor people find it rational to have children.

The **dependency ratio** is the number of people under 15 and over 65 divided by the population 15 to 65.

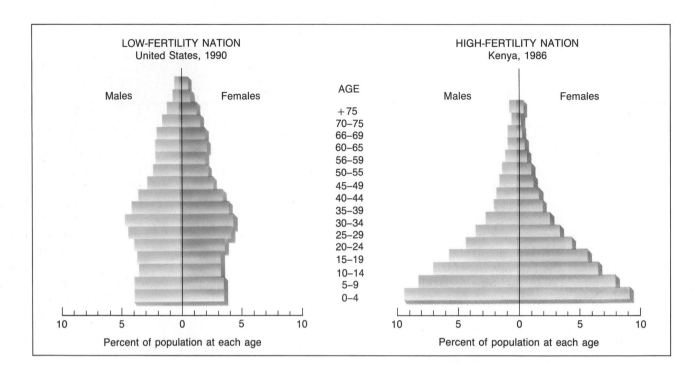

LOW-FERTILITY NATION
United States, 1990

Males   Females

HIGH-FERTILITY NATION
Kenya, 1986

Males   Females

AGE

+75
70–75
66–69
60–65
56–59
50–55
45–49
40–44
35–39
30–34
25–29
20–24
15–19
10–14
5–9
0–4

10   5   0   5   10
Percent of population at each age

10   5   0   5   10
Percent of population at each age

FIGURE 19.4

**A COMPARISON OF
AGE STRUCTURES IN
LOW- AND HIGH-FERTILITY SOCIETIES**

*When fertility is high, the number of
children tends to be much larger than
the number of parents. When this pattern is repeated for generations, the
result is a pyramidal age structure.
When fertility is low, however, each
generation has a similar size, and a
boxier age structure results.*

SOURCE: Derived from United Nations 1988 and
United States Bureau of the Census 1988.

0.49 in Europe. This means that in Africa there is nearly one dependent
for every producer and in the West there is one dependent for every two
producers (see Figure 19.5). On an individual level, this is the difference
between a family where one parent supports one child and a family where
two parents support one child. Obviously, the two-parent family is better
off. Not only is it better off now, but it is more likely to be able to set aside
some savings for the future, with the result that in the long run it will be
even better off.

Mortality Effects.   Like fertility, mortality has particularly strong effects
on the family. A popular myth about the preindustrial family is that it was
a multiple-generation household, what we call an extended family. A little
reflection will demonstrate how unlikely it is that many children lived with
their grandparents when life expectancy was only 25 to 30 years and when
fertility was seven to eight children per woman. Reconstructions tell us
that only a small percentage of all families could have been three-generational.
Even if the grandparents survived, they could live with only one of their
surviving children, leaving the other households without a grandparent.
And quite often, if the children lived with their grandparents, it was because their parents were dead. In short, the three-generation household
was impossible for many and affordable by few (Wrigley 1969). The household of a high-mortality society was probably as fractured, as full of step-
mothers, half-sisters, and stepbrothers, as is the current household of the
high-divorce society.

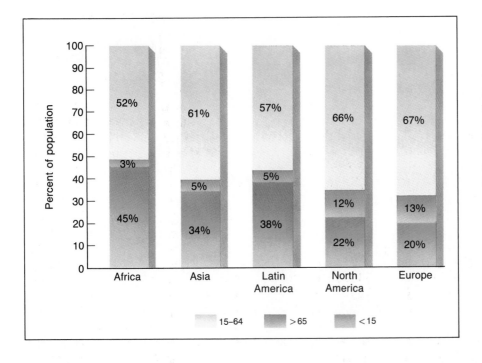

FIGURE 19.5
AGE COMPOSITION
AND DEPENDENCY

In the less developed nations of the world, high fertility means that children are a large proportion of the population. This means that much of current production has to go to feed new mouths.

SOURCE: Population Reference Bureau 1990.

POPULATION AND SOCIAL STRUCTURE: THREE EXAMPLES

KENYA: THE SEVEN-CHILD FAMILY

Kenya is an example of a society where traditional social structures encourage high fertility. It is also an example of a society where high fertility may ensure continuing traditionalism—and poverty.

The Effects of Social Roles on Fertility. Almost alone among the nations of the world, Kenya still has a crude birthrate of 46 per 1,000 population. Mortality, however, is down to 7 per 1,000. This means that the population of Kenya is growing at 3.9 percent per year. If that rate continues, the population will double in just 18 years. An aggressive family-planning program is unlikely to reduce this growth: The average woman in Kenya wants 6.2 children ("Survey Report" 1986).

The high value placed on fertility in Kenyan society is a reflection of several **pronatalist** (profertility) pressures. Among the pressures are tribal loyalties, women's roles, and the need for economic security (Mott and Mott 1980).

TRIBAL LOYALTIES. Kenya is a diverse nation in which there is jealous competition among tribal groups. Because the size of each tribe's population is an important factor in political power, large families are seen as politically advantageous. This is a common pronatalist pressure in any

Pronatalism refers to the social forces that encourage childbearing.

■

In Kenya, the family continues to be the center of economic and social relationships. Women and men find that having many children enhances their prestige, helps with their work, and provides them with economic security for their later years. Because there are few costs associated with having children, the average woman in Kenya desires six and has seven children.

diverse society. Earlier in this century, the French Canadians called it the revenge of the cradle.

WOMEN'S NEED FOR CHILDREN.   Regardless of the needs of their tribe or nation, most women give first consideration to how another child will affect them and their family. For the 80 percent of Kenyan women who are responsible for family farms, children are an asset. A substantial minority of Kenyan men work away from the family farm; even when they are there, their role is largely supervisory. Women bear the chief responsibility for planting, plowing, and harvesting and have full responsibility for cooking, drawing water, and finding firewood. As a result, three-quarters of Kenyan women list "help with work" as a reason for having children. In addition to helping with the work, children are an important, perhaps the only, source of esteem and power open to women. This is especially true of the 30 percent of Kenyan women who live in polygamous unions. The number of children, especially the number of sons, is an important determinant of a woman's position relative to that of other wives.

ECONOMIC SECURITY.   Children add to their parents' economic security in a number of ways. They are the only form of old-age insurance available. When they grow up and marry, they may also add to the family's economic and political security by their marriages. The greater the number of children, the greater the number of in-laws. A family that can bind itself to many other families has greater political power and more security.

In short, a family's income, status, and long-term security are all enhanced by its having many children. There are comparatively few rewards for having a small family. Children are virtually cost free—no expensive medical treatment is available, what schooling there is has no direct cost to the parents, and children's desires do not run to designer jeans or $75 tennis shoes. With a cost/benefit ratio of this sort, it is not surprising that Kenyans desire many children.

The Effect of Population Growth on Society. Although high fertility may appear to be in the best interests of individual women, it has negative consequences for the society. At current rates of fertility and mortality, Kenya's population is doubling every 18 years. As a result, development goals are shooting at a moving target. To double the proportion of children getting an elementary school education (from 45 to 92 percent), the government had to raise the dollars spent on education fourfold because the total number of children needing schooling doubled. Simply to maintain that level over the next 18 years, the Kenyan government would have to double again the dollars spent on education. Unfortunately, there are other demands on the budget—for defense, for highways, for development, for agriculture. All these areas face the same problem of escalating demand.

Thus, a decision that is rational on the individual level turns out to be irrational on the societal level. Occasionally, people in the West make remarks of the sort: "Can't they figure out they would be better off if they had fewer children?" Unfortunately for the argument, nations don't have children; women do. High fertility continues to be a rational choice for individual Kenyans.

Policy Response. Kenya was the first sub-Saharan African nation to establish an official family-planning program. The program has had some notable successes, and Kenya has recently relinquished the title of having the highest fertility in the world to its neighbor Rwanda. In the last 10 years, fertility has fallen from 8.4 to 6.7 children per woman, and the percentage of married women using contraception has more than doubled ("Kenya" 1989). Still, only 27 percent of married women use contraception. One reason for low contraceptive use is the desire for large families. When women *want* six to seven children, contraceptives aren't very relevant. For many women in Kenya and throughout the Third World, however, there is another element: Contraceptives are hard to use. They are available only at distant sites, they are expensive, and they are culturally alien and frightening.

So far, fertility declines and contraceptive improvements have been documented largely in urban areas among the minority of women who have some secondary education. These are the women who have experienced some change in social institutions *and* who find contraception more accessible and familiar. For the mass of the population that lives in rural areas, the pronatalism built into basic social institutions cannot be quickly eliminated just because official policy is **antinatalist.**

Antinatalism refers to social forces that discourage childbearing.

EUROPE: IS FERTILITY TOO LOW?

Many of the nations of Europe believe they have the opposite problem: Fertility is too low. Accordingly, many nations have official pronatalist policies to encourage larger families.

■

TABLE 19.2
FERTILITY AND POPULATION GROWTH IN EUROPE, 1990

Overall, births continue to exceed deaths in Europe, but the margin is increasingly slight and some nations are already experiencing population decline.

COUNTRY	CBR	CDR	CRUDE NATURAL GROWTH RATE	AVERAGE NUMBER OF CHILDREN PER WOMAN	POPULATION CHANGE, 1990 TO 2020
EUROPE, Total	13	10	+0.3%	1.7	+ 3%
Denmark	12	12	0	1.6	− 4
Austria	12	11	0.1	1.4	0
Italy	10	9	0.1	1.3	− 3
Romania	16	11	+0.5	2.3	+12
United Kingdom	14	12	+0.2	1.8	+ 6
Hungary	12	13	−0.1	1.8	− 2
U.S.S.R.	19	10	+0.9	2.5	+22

SOURCE: Population Reference Bureau 1990.

Levels of Fertility.   With modern levels of mortality, fertility must average 2.1 children per woman if the population is to replace itself: One child to replace the woman and her partner, plus a little extra to cover unavoidable losses of mortality. If fertility is less than this, the next generation will be smaller than the current one.

Currently in Europe, the average woman is having 1.7 children. This means that Europe as a whole will begin losing population over the next few generations. The problem is more severe in some nations than others (Table 19.2). In Austria and Italy, the average woman is having only 1.3 or 1.4 children. This means that the next generation will be only two-thirds the size of the current one. If this situation continues for several generations, the populations of these countries will be sharply reduced.

Why Is This a Problem?   Given the serious worldwide dilemmas posed by population growth and the very high density of many European nations, why should this be a problem? There are three broad areas of concern.

POPULATION SUICIDE.   One, of course, is anxiety about the disappearance of a nation and its culture. In 1984, French Prime Minister Chirac said, "[The prospect] is terrifying. In demographic terms, Europe is vanishing. Twenty years or so from now, our countries will be empty, and no matter what our technological strength, we shall be incapable of putting it to use" (Teitelbaum 1987).

TOO MANY OLD PEOPLE.   A very low-fertility society takes on an age structure that looks like an inverted pyramid. Because each generation is smaller than the preceding one, the older generation is larger than the younger generations on whom it relies for support. This age structure will cause a major dilemma for the old-age portions of many nations' social welfare programs—including that of the United States. As noted in Chapter 12, it

Il paraît que je suis
un phénomène socio-culturel.

LA FRANCE
A BESOIN
D'ENFANTS

CAMPAGNE RÉALISÉE PAR AVENIR.DAUPHIN GIRAUDY

Many countries in Europe have reduced fertility to levels below replacement and are now concerned about what this will mean for the future. Countries such as France are attempting to deal with this problem by actively encouraging fertility through billboard campaigns such as this one. In this picture, the infant portrays itself as a socio-cultural phenomenon!

will require heavy taxes on the working-age population, and the greater the fertility decline, the more serious will this problem become.

LABOR-FORCE SHORTAGES.   The decline in fertility has already caused labor-force shortages in many European nations. These shortages have been felt in industry and in the armed forces. The industrial shortages have, until recently, been made up by importing workers from the Middle East or the Mediterranean. Concern for cultural dilution, however, has caused many European nations to reduce the importation of workers and to urge their guest workers to return home.

Why Is Fertility So Low?   The major reasons for low fertility are changed gender roles and the reduced importance of the family (Kaa 1987). Almost all women in Europe are part of the paid labor force. This simultaneously reduces the uniqueness of childrearing as a source of a sense of achievement and accomplishment for women and increases the sense of overwork associated with childrearing. The pervasiveness of the welfare state is also a factor in Europe's low fertility: The family is simply not very essential for economic well-being. In a wealthy, urban society, the family is also less essential for an individual's social life. There is a lot to do and buy; fewer people are choosing to invest their time and money in a home and children, and more are choosing to invest in a career and an expensive stereo system (Westoff 1987). Children and families still provide social and emotional rewards, but increasingly people are finding that one child provides a reasonable balance of costs and rewards.

Policy Response.   In response to these concerns, many European nations have adopted wide-ranging incentives to encourage fertility. Among them are paid maternity leave, cash bonuses for extra children, longer vacations for mothers, and graduated family allowances. Czechoslovakia offers the most generous incentives. New mothers are eligible for six months of paid maternity leave, and many benefits (family allowances, housing subsidies, and even a lower age at retirement) are graded according to the number of children. Low-interest loans are available to newly married couples for buying and furnishing homes; and with each additional child, an increasing proportion of the loan is written off.

Studies suggest that these incentive plans have had modest effects. In some countries, birthrates jumped after the incentives were introduced, but subsequent analysis suggests that this was because some couples had their children earlier than they intended; the incentives did not prompt very many people to have third or fourth children (David 1982). The difficulty is that children are an expensive, intensive 50-year project. The incentives being offered—for example, Quebec offers a one-time payment of $3,000 for a third child ("Quebec" 1988)—are simply not enough to tempt a sensible person to plan another child. Quebec's payment works out to 50 cents a day for the child's first 18 years. Since current estimates suggest that it may cost as much as $100,000 to raise a middle-class child, any serious attempt to defray childrearing costs would be prohibitively expensive (Keyfitz 1987). As long as women and men have attractive alternatives outside the home, it is unlikely that governments can afford to bribe them into voluntarily taking on more than one or two children.

CHINA: MANDATORY LOW FERTILITY

In 1982, China conducted its first modern census. The results confirmed a population of slightly more than 1 billion people, one-fifth of the world's population. One billion is a lot of people to feed, educate, build roads for, and employ. It seems an especially daunting task in a nation with a per-capita GNP of $330. In order to meet its current needs and to implement ambitious plans for economic development, China feels that it needs to keep its population below 1.2 billion.

Policy Response.   In 1949, when the communists first came to power in China, they claimed that China had no population problem. "Of all things in the world, people are the most precious. Under the leadership of the Communist party, as long as there are people, every kind of miracle can be performed" (Mao Zedong, September 1949, cited in Aird 1972). After 20 years of poor harvests and near famine, however, this naïve approach was finally abandoned. During the 1970s, China experimented with a variety of policy options to reduce fertility, including exhortations to marry late and have few children and voluntary family-planning programs.

These programs had modest effects, but the population still grew alarmingly. In a last-ditch effort to try to contain the Chinese population to 1.2 billion by the end of this century, China launched its famous one-child policy in 1982. Incentives for a one-child family include supplementary food and housing, free health care, preferential treatment in schooling and jobs, larger farm allotments in rural areas, and higher pensions. Contraceptives and abortion are widely available, and sterilization is encouraged.

In many nations, family size is considered personal business. In China, fertility is everybody's business. At the height of the one-child program, whole communities were punished if more than 5 percent of their new babies were second or higher births. Women who had a second pregnancy were under intense community pressure to get an abortion. A third birth might cause the woman and her husband to lose their jobs and their home, be shunned by their families, left out of community affairs, and denied basic privileges.

Second Thoughts.   China's dramatic birth-control program was aided by the transformation of social institutions through the Communist revolution. Nevertheless, China remains a very poor, largely rural country, where many people still depend on their families for labor and security.

Officially, China's birthrate dropped from 33 per 1,000 in 1971 to 21 per 1,000 in 1990 and its growth rate went from 1.8 to 1.4 percent. The average number of children per woman fell dramatically, but the one-child family program has proved nearly impossible to reinforce. The average number of children per woman is 2.3, not 1. The policy has made lawbreakers out of the hundreds of millions of rural couples who still depend on their children for farm labor and their sons for old-age security. Recently, policy makers have admitted that insistence on a one-child policy would impose tremendous hardships on their people and would, in any case, be impossible to enforce (Tien 1989). Currently, couples whose first child is a girl are allowed to have a second child. Since this includes roughly half of all couples, the new policy might be called the one-and-a-half-child policy.

China has had the most aggressive family-planning program in the world, making it a top priority of government programs for a decade. This level of effort, coupled with the dramatic changes in social institutions, has allowed China's birthrates to tumble despite continuing poverty. Without a police officer in every household, however, it is doubtful that China can really achieve even a 1.5-child family until it has achieved greater economic development.

■

POPULATION GROWTH, ENVIRONMENT, AND POVERTY

Mention the world *population* and many people immediately think of *population problems*. Certainly the fact that the population is likely to grow to 9 to 10 billion in their lifetimes seems like a problem to most people. There are, however, many population problems: high mortality, illegal migration, low fertility in Europe, environmental devastation, starvation, and Third World poverty. In this section, we address two of these problems, the environment and poverty, and analyze the role of population growth in creating and resolving these problems.

ENVIRONMENTAL DEVASTATION: A POPULATION PROBLEM?

All around the world there are signs of enormous environmental destruction. In the developed world we have acid rain and oil spills; in South America, there is the destruction of the Amazon forest; in Africa, there is the rapid spread of desert environments through deforestation and over-

■

Even if you cannot read Chinese, the message on this billboard is unmistakable: One child is enough, even if that child is a girl. Although Chinese officials continue to press for a one-child family, they have relaxed their sanctions against people who have two children—especially when the first child is a girl. Strict enforcement of the one-child policy has been abandoned because of concerns about the age structure and because of widespread recognition that children continue to be valuable to rural families.

grazing. Although all of these pose serious threats to the natural order, only the last one is truly a population problem.

It is estimated that the U.S., which contains only 6 percent of the world's population, consumes one quarter of the world's resources. Our affluent, throw-away life-style requires large amounts of petroleum and other natural resources. This unceasing demand for more lies behind oil exploration of fragile lands and subsequent events such as the Exxon oil spill in Prince William Sound, Alaska in 1989. Our unwillingness to pay the price for emission controls lies behind the acid rain and smog that are killing our eastern forests and polluting lakes and rivers. Although these problems would be less severe if there were half as many of us (and hence half as many cars, factories, and Styrofoam cups), they are not really population problems. They stem from our way of life rather than our numbers.

The destruction of the Amazon forest is also not a population problem. It is a poverty problem (Durning 1989). Brazil needs export dollars to pay its foreign debt and to establish an industrial economy. To get these dollars, it sells what it has most of: trees. In addition, Brazil has encouraged settlement of the Amazon in order to postpone the demand for land redistribution among the landless poor. Reducing the number of Brazilians would not make a serious dent in problems of internal or international poverty.

In sub-Saharan Africa and on the Indian subcontinent, however, population pressure is a major culprit in environmental destruction. The typical scenario runs like this: Population pressure forces farmers to try to plow marginal land and to plant high-yielding crops in quick succession without soil-enhancing rotations or fallow periods. The marginal lands and the overworked soils produce less and less food, forcing farmers to push the land even harder. They cut down forests and windbreaks to free more land for production. Soon, water and wind erosion become so pervasive that the top soil is borne off entirely, and the tillable land is replaced by desert or barren rock.

This cycle of environmental destruction—which destroys forests, topsoil, and the plant and animal species that depend on them—is characteristic of high population growth *in combination with poverty*. These people are between a rock and a hard place. When one's children are starving, it is hard to make long-term decisions that will protect the environment for future generations.

Reducing population growth would reduce future pressure on natural resources, but it is no solution to the present problem. Immediate solutions include better management of existing resources, better crop varieties, better storage and less waste, and more scientifically managed crop rotation. Implementing these changes will require diverting investment dollars from cities to rural areas (Repetto 1987). This is a risky political strategy, however, since most governments depend for their support on urban settlements, not the rural hinterlands. If these governments raise rural incomes and the price of food, urban riots are possible.

Summary.   The world's environment is being destroyed at an alarming rate. Population growth has contributed to some of this problem, and sharply reduced population growth can keep the problems from accelerating. Unless we are willing to countenance mass mortality, however, population control cannot be the only or the most immediate solution. The

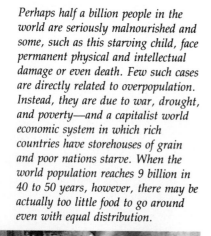

Perhaps half a billion people in the world are seriously malnourished and some, such as this starving child, face permanent physical and intellectual damage or even death. Few such cases are directly related to overpopulation. Instead, they are due to war, drought, and poverty—and a capitalist world economic system in which rich countries have storehouses of grain and poor nations starve. When the world population reaches 9 billion in 40 to 50 years, however, there may be actually too little food to go around even with equal distribution.

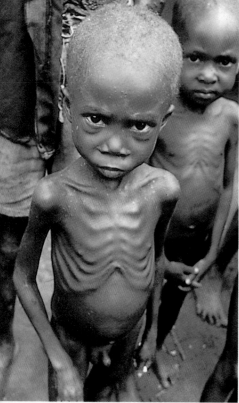

solution rests in an international moral and financial commitment to reducing rural poverty, improving farming practices, reducing Third World debt, and reducing our own wasteful and destructive practices.

THIRD WORLD POVERTY

There are over 5 billion people in the world. Three quarters of them live in less developed nations, where the gross national product (GNP) per capita is one-twentieth that of the developed world. Perhaps 500 million are seriously undernourished, and each year outbreaks of famine and starvation occur in Africa and Asia; a billion more are poorly nourished, poorly educated, and poorly sheltered ("How Many" 1985). These people live in the same nations that have high population growth.

There are some observers who blame Third World poverty on high fertility, thus neatly laying the entire fault at the victim's door. It is clear, however, that high fertility is not the only or even the primary cause of Third World poverty. The causes lie in the system of international stratification (described in detail in Chapter 22). Nigeria, for example, has become poorer because of the collapse of international oil prices in the 1980s, not because of its growing population. Ethiopians are dying of starvation because of war rather than because of high fertility.

Although fertility does not directly cause poverty, the two do go hand in hand. Poverty is synonymous with lack of development; it means that people lack education and that there is no system of old-age pensions, welfare, or insurance other than the family. Thus, fertility remains at its traditional high levels. Before fertility will fall, there must be some social or economic development that encourages people to change traditional ways of life. Studies show that one of the most critical aspects of development is education, especially for females. Education introduces young people to interests and ideas outside the family and reduces the number of children they want; it also makes it easier for them to seek and use modern contraceptives. Unfortunately, in many countries in Africa, as many as 75 percent of adult women are illiterate.

Summary.   Third World poverty and starvation are not the sole result of high fertility. Nevertheless, rapid population growth does provide a hurdle for developing nations. Short doubling times make it difficult to make any substantial progress in protecting the environment, increasing education, or raising the standard of living. As a result, "many—perhaps most—of these new lives will be miserable, malnourished, and brief" ("World Bank's" 1988).

PROGRAMS TO REDUCE FERTILITY

High fertility is not the primary cause of most of the problems that are often linked to population growth. Nor will reducing fertility by itself solve most of these problems. Nevertheless, fertility reduction programs are widely seen as desirable and even necessary. Lower growth rates will make it easier for governments to meet environmental and economic goals, will free parents to take better care of the children they have, and will prevent the birth of additonal children into impoverished circumstances. Programs to reduce fertility are of two general types: family-planning programs and economic development.

■

The level of fertility in any society is closely related to the roles women play. These women attending an open market near Nairobi (Kenya) are either choosing their family's groceries or marketing their farm's produce, tasks for which women are largely responsible. Neither activity is hampered by having many children. As long as women's roles remain centered around household activities, there is little incentive to have smaller families in societies like Kenya.

1. *Family-planning programs*. These programs attempt to make modern contraceptives and sterilization available inexpensively and conveniently. The programs are designed to help people plan their families; they do not attempt to alter the number of children individuals desire. There is a great need for these kinds of programs. A 1987 survey in Guatemala found that two-thirds of the women wanting no more children were not using contraception.

Easily available contraception will help women avoid unwanted births and, if it is easy enough to use, may even change their ideas about how many children they want. Between 1973 and 1987, an aggressive family-planning program doubled contraceptive use in Mexico and moved sterilization to the most popular form of birth control. The result is that the average number of children per woman dropped from 6.3 to 3.8 in just 15 years ("Survey Report" 1990). Mexico's success may be difficult to repeat in areas such as Kenya where income, education, and access to medical clinics are so much lower.

2. *Economic development*. Experience all over the world shows that a rise in education and other indices of development reduces fertility. For example, South Korea's fertility has plummeted from 5.5 children per woman in 1960 to only 1.6 in the wake of its dramatic economic development ("Dramatic" 1989). Since development is highly desired in its own right, this is an attractive policy for reducing fertility.

The most successful programs to reduce fertility have combined an aggressive family-planning program with a push toward economic development (Poston and Gu 1987). Thus, nations such as Indonesia, Mexico, and Colombia have reduced their fertility sharply within a matter of decades. Both family planning and development can have some effect on fertility by themselves, but the combination of easy access to contraception *and* a changed way of life is much more effective than either alone.

OUTLOOK: GOOD NEWS/BAD NEWS

Analysis of world population growth puts us in a good-news/bad-news situation. The good news is that fertility is declining. The decline is uneven, but it is visible in almost all corners of the world (see Table 19.3). Worldwide, fertility has declined by over 25 percent in the last 20 years.

The bad news is that the population of the world will double within 40 to 50 years anyway. The reason for this gloomy prediction lies in the current age structure. The next generation of mothers is already born—and there are a lot of them. As the pyramidal shape of Kenya's age structure in Figure 19.4 demonstrated, high-fertility nations have a population of children (future parents) that is much larger than the current generation of parents. This force for population growth is called *momentum*, and it is roughly measured by the ratio of girls aged zero to four to the number of women aged 25 to 29. In Kenya, the ratio is 3:1. This means that the next generation will have three times as many mothers as does this generation. The ratio for the United States is about 1:1.

Zero population growth (ZPG) means that the number of births is the same as the number of deaths, so the population does not grow.

Zero Population Growth.   In describing demographic goals, demographers distinguish two different ends: zero population growth and replacement. **Zero population growth (ZPG)** means that the number of births

■

TABLE 19.3
CHANGES IN AVERAGE FAMILY SIZE

In the last 20 years, there has been a 25 percent decrease worldwide in the average number of children being born per woman. This decrease has been noticeable in all parts of the world except Africa. Because mortality has fallen too, however, and because of the momentum of the age structure, population is still growing rapidly.

	AVERAGE NUMBER OF CHILDREN PER WOMAN		PERCENT CHANGE
	1968–1972	1990	
World	4.7	3.5	−25%
Africa	6.4	6.2	− 3
Asia	5.4	3.5	−35
Latin America	5.5	3.5	−36
Europe and North America	2.8	1.8	−36

SOURCE: Data for early years from Freyka 1973, T. 4-1; 1990 data from Population Reference Bureau 1990.

is the same as the number of deaths; no growth occurs. This goal is almost impossible when the age structure is pyramidal. When the population bearing children is much larger than the elderly population, it is likely that there will be many more births than deaths even when fertility is relatively low.

Replacement-Level Fertility.   A more modest reproductive goal is **replacement-level fertility.** This requires that each woman have approximately two children, one to replace herself and one to replace her husband. When this occurs, the next generation will be the same size as the current generation of parents. In the short run, replacing the large generation of current parents will mean relatively rapid population growth. In the long run, however, say four generations, the generation dying will be the same size as the one having children, and replacement-level fertility will create zero population growth.

Summary.   Neither zero population growth nor replacement is on the immediate horizon. There are only two possible ways to stop population growth *now:* massive mortality or forced sterilization and abortion programs that would restrict each woman to no more than one child. Since these solutions are widely regarded as worse than the problem, we must plan on a world population that will reach 9 to 10 billion in your lifetime.

Replacement-level fertility requires that each woman bear approximately two children, one to replace herself and one to replace her partner. When this occurs, the next generation will be the same size as the current generation of parents.

■

POPULATION IN THE UNITED STATES

The U.S. population picture is very much the same as that of Western Europe: low mortality and below-replacement fertility. In this section, we briefly describe fertility, mortality, growth, and immigration issues in the U.S.

■

Although a majority of American women continue to want children, there is growing variability in fertility behavior. Perhaps as many as 15 to 20 percent will decide to get a dog instead of having children. Among those who do have children, a growing proportion will stop at one; nearly one quarter will become mothers before they become wives.

FERTILITY

For nearly 20 years now, the number of children per woman in the U.S. has stood at 1.8 to 2.0—slightly less than the 2.1 necessary to replace the population. This low fertility has been accompanied by sharp reductions in social class, racial, and religious differences in fertility. Some women will have their children as teenagers and some when they are 30, but increasingly they will stop at two. The two most important changes in contemporary U.S. fertility are postponed childbearing and the increase in nonmarital births.

Postponed Childbearing.   In 1965, only 12 percent of the women who had ever been married were still childless at ages 25 to 29. In 25 years, this proportion more than doubled; by 1988, fully 34 percent of the ever-married women in the peak childbearing years were still childless. The majority of these childless women intend to have children, but it is likely that rates of permanent childlessness will rise at least moderately. Fifteen percent of American women were still childless at ages 40 to 44, in 1988 (U.S. Bureau of the Census 1989j).

Non-Marital Births.   Lower marriage rates have increased the number of unmarried women at the same time that changes in sexual behavior have increased their risk of pregnancy. As a result, an increasing proportion of U.S. babies are born to unmarried women: Twenty-five percent of the next generation will start life in a fatherless home. This is a major change in fertility patterns and family structure.

MORTALITY

Death is almost a stranger to U.S. families. The average age at death is now in the 70s, and people who survive to 65 can expect to live another 20 years. Parents can feel relatively secure that their infants will survive; young newlyweds, if they don't divorce, can safely plan on a golden wedding anniversary.

In the last 15 years, we have added four years to life expectancy. These increases are due to better diagnosis and treatment of the degenerative diseases (such as heart disease and cancer) that strike the elderly. In addition, increases in life expectancy have been made possible by reducing racial and social class differentials in mortality. At the time of World War II, black women lived a full 12 years less than white women; by 1988, the gap was down to four years.

THE FUTURE OF U.S. POPULATION

If American women continue to reproduce at less than replacement levels, it will not be long before the U.S. population ceases to grow *from natural increase*. Current projections (see Figure 19.6) suggest that the crude birthrate will dip below the crude deathrate around 2030. Within 40 years, the population could cease to grow and start to get smaller every year.

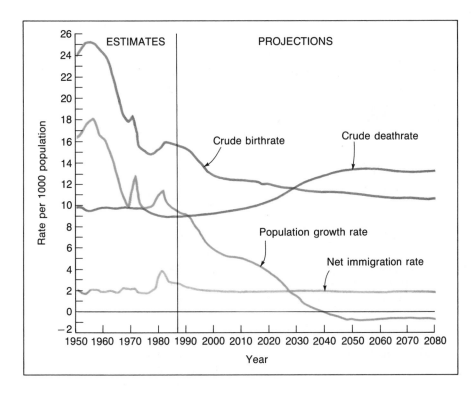

FIGURE 19.6
**THE FUTURE OF
U.S. POPULATION GROWTH**

By 2030, the natural population growth rate of the U.S. is predicted to dip below zero. Because of immigration, however, it does not seem likely that the U.S. population will actually decline.

SOURCE: U.S. Bureau of the Census 1988.

There are two alternatives to this shrinking population: increased fertility and immigration. Although any attempt to forecast the future is risky, it seems unlikely that fertility will rise substantially. In fact, European comparisons suggest that our fertility may fall still farther. Instead, the factor that is likely to forestall U.S. population reduction is **immigration**—the permanent movement of people across national borders.

At the present moment, immigration accounts for about one-third of U.S. population growth. By 2030, however, immigration will be the only source of growth, and whether our population grows or shrinks will depend on the levels of international immigration. In the Issues in Social Policy section, we take up U.S. immigration policy and its consequences for U.S. population growth and composition.

Immigration is the permanent movement of people into another country.

The New Immigrants—Aliens or Amigos?

Unlike fertility, mortality, and internal migration, immigration is seen as something that can be governmentally regulated in a free society. Beginning with the Chinese Exclusion Act of 1882, much of U.S. immigration policy has been frankly racist and ethnically biased. Since 1965, however, immigration policies have ceased to give preference to people from Northern and Western Europe; as a result, our population composition is changing.

CONCERNS ABOUT IMMIGRATION

Estimates suggest that as many as 1 million immigrants take up permanent residence in the United States each year. About half of these new residents are illegal aliens, 90 percent of whom are from Mexico or other countries in Latin America. Policy makers and the public are concerned about immigration for two primary reasons: one cultural and one economic.

Cultural

Almost all of the recent immigrants have come from Asia or Central America. A rough estimate suggests that nearly two-thirds are from Central America or Mexico, 25 percent are from Asia, and fewer than 10 percent from the rest of the world. If this mix of immigrants continues and if immigration continues at 1 million per year, the racial and ethnic composition of the United States will change substantially. In fact, by 2080, it is estimated that these trends will produce a U.S. population that is only 50 percent white and non-Hispanic, compared with an 80 percent share for that racial/ethnic group in 1980 (see Figure 19.7).

One need not be a racist to be uneasy about the expected changes in the ethnic mix of the United States' population. They signal potentially major changes in our culture and institutions. Since most of us have learned to value our culture and institutions, these changes provoke concern.

"The Coyote and His Prey" by Emmy Schoene

ISSUES IN SOCIAL POLICY continued

If the United States does grow to be a more pluralistic, perhaps even a bilingual society, without a majority population, we will have to redefine ourselves once more.

Economic

Little consensus exists about the economic consequences of legal or illegal immigration. There seem, however, to be three well-supported generalizations: (1) Immigrants are not taking jobs away from American citizens, but (2) the availability of low-wage illegals helps to keep wages low in some sectors of the economy, and (3) the ones hardest hit by this are Hispanic citizens and other minorities (Bouvier and Gardner 1986).

CURRENT POLICY ISSUES

Two legislative issues are currently on the national agenda: legal immigration ceilings and reducing the number of illegal aliens. Both are concerned with reducing immigration.

Legal Immigration Ceilings.

For over 20 years, there have been no numerical restrictions on immigration of relatives of U.S. citizens. This has led to a process of "chain migration," whereby one member of a family can move to the U.S., gain citizenship, and then bring in all of his or her family. This is the reason why legal immigration has generally been double the intended ceiling of 270,000. A recent proposal will change U.S. policy in two ways: First, it will set a firm limit of 590,000 legal immigrants (excepting refugees) per year, and second, it will give persons with English-language and occupational skills preference over members of U.S. citizens' extended families ("Now" 1988). Minor children, spouses, and parents of U.S. citizens will continue to get top priority. Such a policy will probably not reduce legal immigration significantly, but it will give fewer people the right to immigrate and give the U.S. government more control over whom and how many it admits.

Illegal Aliens

In 1986, Congress finally passed the long-discussed Immigration Reform and Control Act (IRCA). The three major provisions of this act (1) granted amnesty to all illegal aliens who had been in the United States before January 1, 1982, and opened the way for them to apply for resi-

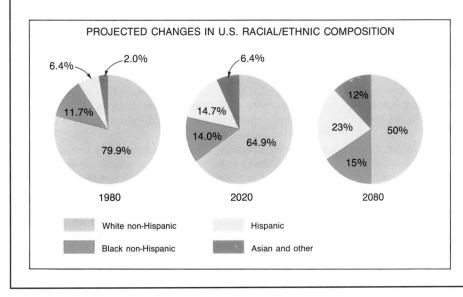

PROJECTED CHANGES IN U.S. RACIAL/ETHNIC COMPOSITION

6.4% 2.0%
11.7%
79.9%
1980

6.4%
14.7%
14.0% 64.9%
2020

12%
23% 50%
15%
2080

White non-Hispanic Hispanic
Black non-Hispanic Asian and other

FIGURE 19.7
CHANGING COMPOSITION OF U.S. POPULATION

If annual migration remains at 1 million and if fertility remains low, the racial and ethnic composition of the U.S. population will change substantially in the decades ahead. The most noticeable effect will be a sharp rise in the proportion who are Hispanic and a corresponding decrease in the proportion who are Anglo.

SOURCE: Bouvier and Gardner 1986; Davis, Haub, and Willette 1983 39.

ISSUES IN SOCIAL POLICY continued

dent alien status; (2) tried to reduce the demand for illegal immigration by imposing sanctions on employers who hired them; and (3) tried to reduce the supply of illegal immigrants through increased border patrols.

It is not clear that IRCA has had its intended effects. Although much more money has been put into border patrols, many immigration agents have been diverted into educating employers or catching drug smugglers. Critics say that reduced enforcement rather than reduced immigration accounts for the fact that half as many illegal aliens were apprehended in 1989 as in 1986 (Espenshade 1990). Supporters, however, claim that the new law has reduced the annual flow of immigrants across the Rio Grande by as much as one-third.

An especially controversial issue is whether the new law has increased discrimination against Hispanic workers. In 1990, the General Accounting Office reported the results of a study in which fictitious Hispanic and Anglo job applications with equal credentials were submitted to prospective employers. The study showed that Anglo appli-

cants were much more likely to be interviewed and eventually hired than were Hispanic applicants ("Hiring Discrimination" 1990). IRCA opponents argue that employer sanctions are to blame: It is easier for employers not to hire Hispanics at all than to verify their residence statuses. Although the study prompted some legislators to call for repealing IRCA, it is unclear how much of the hiring discrimination is due to IRCA and how much to simple discrimination.

It is unrealistic to think that we can totally eliminate illegal immigration. The bottom line is that a very rich nation shares a border with a poor one. If our economy continues to have employment opportunities for low-skill labor and if the economy of Mexico continues to deteriorate, there will be enormous incentives to escape the law. It is not surprising that a poll commissioned by the *Los Angeles Times* found that 22 percent of people living in Mexico said it was "very likely" or "fairly likely" that they would be living in the United States in the next year ("22 Percent" 1989).

SUMMARY

1. For most of human history, fertility was about equal to mortality, and the population grew slowly or not at all. Childbearing was a lifelong task for most women, and death was a frequent visitor to most households, claiming as many as one third of all infants in the first year of life.

2. The demographic transition in the West began with a decline in mortality. Major causes of the decreased mortality, in order of occurrence, were improved nutrition, an improved standard of living and hygiene, improved public sanitation, and modern medicine.

3. The decline of fertility in the West is attributable to the entire transformation of the social fabric that occurred as a result of industrialization, especially the changing roles of women and the family and a break with traditional values.

4. In the Third World, mortality declined very rapidly after World War II, while fertility has remained relatively unchanged. The result is rapid population growth, with a doubling time of 33 years. Future declines in fertility and mortality depend on economic development and improved standards of living.

5. Social structure, fertility, and mortality are interdependent; changes in one affect the others. Among the most important consequences of high fertility are restricted roles for women and a high dependency ratio.

6. The level of fertility in a society has much to do with the balance of costs and rewards associated with childbearing. In traditional societies, such as that of Kenya, most social structures (the economy, religion, and the family, for example) support high fertility. In many mod-

ern societies, such as those of Europe, and the United States, social structure imposes many costs on parents.

7. Population growth is not the only or even the primary cause of environmental devastation or Third World poverty, nor is it the primary solution. Continued population growth does contribute to these problems, however, and reducing growth will make it easier to seek solutions.

8. Fertility levels are declining all over the world. Nevertheless, the population of the world will reach at least 9 billion in the next 40 to 50 years. The age structure of the current population provides a momentum toward growth, and neither zero population growth nor replacement-level fertility will be achieved any time soon.

9. U.S. women are reproducing at less than replacement levels, and by 2030, it is estimated that the U.S. will dip below zero population growth. When this happens, immigration levels will determine whether our total population shrinks or grows.

10. There are approximately 1 million immigrants, legal and illegal, to the U.S. each year. Concerns include changing the ethnic/cultural mix of the population and the effect on citizens' economic prospects. Illegal immigration from Mexico will be difficult to control because the incentives to move north are so great and the border so long.

SUGGESTED READINGS

Bouvier, Leon and Gardner, Robert W. 1986. "Immigration to the U.S.: The Unfinished Story." Population Bulletin 41 (November): 1–50. A pamphlet that covers historical and contemporary migration with special emphasis on immigration policy.

Durning, Alan. 1989. Poverty and the Environment: Reversing the Downward Spiral. Worldwatch Paper 92. Washington, D.C.: Worldwatch Institute. A short pamphlet that probes the link between environmental degradation, Third World poverty, and the global economy.

Goliber, Thomas. 1989. "Africa's Expanding Population: Old Problems, New Policies." Population Bulletin 44 (3): 1–50. A contemporary look at the fastest-growing region in the world, this pamphlet examines all aspects of Africa's population-related problems: AIDS, infant mortality, the environment, and poverty.

Population Reference Bureau. 1982. "U.S. Population: Where We Are; Where We're Going." Population Bulletin 37 (2): 1–50. A pamphlet summarizing trends in fertility, mortality, and migration, with some projections about the future of the U.S. population.

Population Today. Washington, D.C.: Population Reference Bureau. This monthly publication is a digest of all important population news intended for an educated audience of nonprofessionals. It covers U.S. foreign policy and domestic population news and includes information about specific nations around the world.

Wrigley, E. A. 1969. Population and History. New York: McGraw-Hill. A detailed description of the demographic transition in Europe along with some lessons for today's developing world.

20

URBAN LIVING

HAVE YOU EVER . . .

Considered where you may be living in 10 years? Do you aspire to an apartment or condominium right downtown so that all you have to do is walk out your front door to be in the hustle and bustle of city life? Do you aspire to a three-bedroom ranch-style house in a suburb with room for kids, dogs, and a barbecue? Or do you perhaps aspire to live on a large number of acres so that you can have more horses than neighbors?

You will, of course, need to balance your druthers against your dollars. A conventional mortgage requires a 20 percent downpayment; this means that you need to save up $16,000 to buy an $80,000 house. Saving $16,000 is not easy (in fact, a lot of people borrow their first downpayment from their folks). Whether you can buy a house in your area for $80,000 is another question. In some parts of the country, notably California but also big cities on both coasts, an $80,000 house is a shack; in the South and Midwest, however, $80,000 buys a newish three-bedroom ranch-style house on a spacious suburban lot.

Generally, the farther you go from big cities and the coasts, the more house you can get for your money. Many people, however, prefer less house and more action. They are willing to live in an 800-square-foot apartment or on a tiny lot in exchange for easy access to cultural events, shopping, entertainment—and jobs. In this chapter, we consider the factors that shape the residential distribution of the population, and we look at the consequences of residential choices for individuals and society.

For most people in the contemporary United States, to speak of social life is to speak of urban life. More than 75 percent of this generation's college students were born and raised in metropolitan areas. Similarly, at least 75 percent of the mothers, lawyers, and junkies in the United States are urbanites. Thus, throughout this book, we have been examining largely urban experience. This chapter takes a self-conscious look at the settings of contemporary social activity. Among the questions it considers are the consequences of urban living for human social behavior, the changing balance among urban, suburban, and rural life, and the political economy of spatial distribution.

■

URBAN GROWTH AND CHANGE

Urban growth and change is largely a story of the last century. It has been estimated that as late as 1850 only 2 percent of the world's population lived in cities of 100,000 or more (Davis 1973). Today, nearly a quarter of the world's population and more than two-thirds of the U.S. population live in cities larger than 100,000. Paralleling this increasing urbanization of the world is an evolution in the character of the city. The modern city is very different from the city that developed in the second century—or even the 19th.

THE PREINDUSTRIAL CITY

The preindustrial economy is dominated by primary production. Whether it is farming, herding, mining, or forestry, economic activity is essentially rural activity. The cities that emerge under these conditions are largely trading and administrative centers.

The preindustrial city was a much smaller affair than the modern city and it was also very differently organized. Most people got from place to place by walking. The result was a great concentration of social life. Because transportation was difficult, people lived and worked in the same building. In the preindustrial city there was no central business district whose only occupants were men in three-piece togas. Instead, children, cooking odors, and laundry pervaded all parts of the city. Segregation was not between business and family but between kinds of businesses. People who needed to see one another in the course of business lived together in one quarter of the city. Craftsmen occupied one quarter, traders another, and officials yet another.

Then, as now, the city was a major force in the development of art, culture, and technology. It was also a crowded, filthy, and dangerous place. Human and animal waste turned streets and canals into open sewers, and the birthrate in cities could not keep up with the deathrate. The only way cities could maintain their populations was by constantly drawing new recruits from the countryside.

This description probably fit most of the world's cities until at least 1800. In 1790, Philadelphia, with a population of 44,000, was the largest U.S. city. Like Damascus or Cairo, early U.S. cities lacked sewers and safe drinking supplies. And far from offering bright lights, the absence of street-lights made the cities close down at nightfall.

■

This street scene in Morocco is typical of many of the ancient cities that grew up in preindustrial times. The narrow streets are built for pedestrians, not for automobiles. Many of the shops also include living quarters, and there is much less separation of residential and business areas.

THE INDUSTRIAL CITY

With the advent of the industrial revolution, production moved from the countryside to the urban factory, and industrial cities were born. These cities were mill towns, steel towns, shipbuilding towns, and, later, automobile-building towns; they were home to slaughterers, packagers, millers, processors, and fabricators. They were the product of new technologies, new forms of transportation, and vastly increased agricultural productivity that freed most workers from the land.

Fired by a tremendous growth in technology, the new industrial cities grew rapidly during the 19th century. In the United States, the urban population grew from 2 to 22 million in the half century between 1840 and 1890. In 1860, New York was the first U.S. city to reach 1 million. The industrial base that provided the impetus for city growth also gave the industrial city its character: tremendous density, a central business district, and a concentric zone pattern of land use.

Density.   A critical factor in explaining the character of the industrial city as it developed in the 19th century is that most people still walked to work—and everywhere else, for that matter. The result was dense crowding of working-class housing around manufacturing plants. Even in 1910, the average New Yorker commuted only two blocks to work. Thus, the industrial city saw much more crowding than either the preindustrial or post-industrial city. Entire families shared a single room; and in major cities such as New York and London, dozens of people crowded into a single cellar or attic. The crowded conditions, accompanied by a lack of sewage treatment and clean water, fostered tuberculosis, epidemic diseases, and generally high mortality. A glimpse of these conditions is provided by a letter that appeared in the London *Times* in 1849:

> Sur,—May we beg and beseach your proteckshion and power. We are Sur, as it may be, livin in a Wilderness, so far as the rest of London knows anything of us, or as the rich and great people care about. We live in muck and filth. We aint got no priviz, no dust bins, no drains, no water-splies, and no drain or suer in the hole place. The Suer Company, in Greek St., Soho Square, all great, rich powerfool men take no notice whasomdever of our complaints. The Stenche of a Gulley-hole is disguistin. We all of us suffer, and numbers are ill, and if the Cholera comes Lord help us.
>
> Some gentelmans comed yesterday. . . . They was much surprized to see the sellar in No. 12, Carrier St., in our lane, where a child was dying from fever, and would not believe that Sixty persons sleep in it every night. This here seller you couldent swing a cat in, and the rent is five shillings a week; but theare are great many sich deare sellers. . . .
>
> Praeye Sir com and see us, for we are living like piggs, and it aint faire we should be so ill treted (cited in Thomlinson 1976).

Central Business District (CBD).   The lack of transportation and communication facilities also contributed to another characteristic of the industrial city, the central business district (CBD). The CBD is a dense concentration of retail trade, banking and finance, and government offices, all clustered close together so messengers could run between offices and people could walk to meet one another. By 1880, most major cities had electric streetcars or railway systems to take traffic into and out of the city. Because

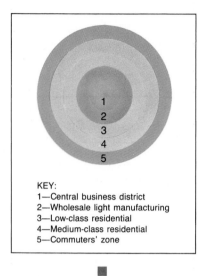

KEY:
1—Central business district
2—Wholesale light manufacturing
3—Low-class residential
4—Medium-class residential
5—Commuters' zone

■

FIGURE 20.1
CONCENTRIC ZONE MODEL
OF URBAN SPATIAL PATTERNS

The early industrial city developed a characteristic circular pattern. Because transportation was limited, business activity and working-class housing were densely concentrated toward the center. Only the more affluent could afford to live on the edges, away from the noise and pollution.

SOURCE: Harris and Ullman 1945.

most transit routes offered service only into and out of the CBD rather than providing crosstown routes, the earliest improvements over walking enhanced rather than decreased the importance of the CBD as the hub of the city.

Concentric Zone Pattern.   Spatial analysis of early industrial cities suggests that they often approximated a series of rings, or concentric zones (see Figure 20.1). Zone 1, the CBD, was characterized by dense building where land values were so high that only the most profitable commercial operations could afford to locate there. Residential use and large commercial operations were pushed to the periphery of the city. Meanwhile, high land values encouraged vertical growth, and eventually skyscrapers came to dominate the landscape of the CBD.

Zones 2 and 3 included the manufacturing plants and the families who worked in them. The working class was still largely dependent on walking to work; thus, most workers lived close to the plants. Noise, smoke, and pollution reduced the attractiveness of Zone 3 for residential use, thereby bringing housing prices into the reach of the working class. For the most part, Zone 3 housing consisted of tenements, apartment blocks, and row houses.

In the industrial city, everyone who could afford to live away from the noise and smoke and smell did so. The upper class could best afford a relatively long commute; consequently, it occupied the periphery of the city, Zone 5. The middle class occupied the intermediate area, Zone 4. Again, because of transportation problems—the middle class did not have access to automobiles until around 1920—all areas of the industrial city were densely packed. Even middle-class families more often lived in duplex and row houses than in single-family homes; as drives through older neighborhoods still indicate, single-family homes occupied small lots, with the houses almost touching each other.

THE POSTINDUSTRIAL CITY

The industrial city was a product of a manufacturing economy plus a relatively immobile labor force. Beginning about 1950, these conditions changed and a new type of city began to grow. Among the factors prominent in shaping the character of the late-industrial city are the change from secondary to tertiary production and greater ease of communication and transportation. These closely related changes have led to a much diminished role for the central business districts, a dispersion of retail, manufacturing, and residential areas, and a much lower urban density.

Change from Secondary to Tertiary Production.   As we noted in Chapter 16, the last decades have seen a tremendous expansion of jobs in tertiary production and the subsequent decline of jobs in secondary production. The manufacturing plants that shaped the industrial city are disappearing. Many of those that remain have moved to the suburbs where land is cheaper, taking working-class jobs, housing, and trade with them.

Instead of manufacturing, the contemporary central city is dominated by medical and educational complexes, information-processing industries, convention and entertainment centers, and administrative offices. These

■

During the 19th and early 20th century, many cities grew up around manufacturing plants. These industrial cities are characterized by high density. Since the working class walked to work (and everywhere else), working-class housing was crowded in the blocks immediately surrounding the plants. The middle and upper classes live in the suburbs. Although the plants are largely gone, this residential social-class pattern persists.

are the growth industries. They are also white-collar industries. These same industries, plus retail trade, also dominate the suburban economy.

Easier Communication and Transportation.   Development of telecommunications, the automobile, and good highways has greatly reduced the importance of physical location. The central business district of the industrial city was held together by the need for physical proximity. Once this need was eliminated, high land values and commuting costs led more and more businesses to locate on the periphery, where land was cheaper and housing more desirable.

Multiple Nuclei.   Spatial analysis of new cities suggests that they are no longer divided into concentric zones and are far less dominated by the central business district. The vertical growth so apparent before World War II has been partially replaced by horizontal growth in the form of urban sprawl. The general configuration of modern cities appears to conform to a multiple nuclei pattern (see Figure 20.2). No longer is the majority bound by subway and railway lines that go only back and forth to downtown. Retail trade is dominated by huge, climate-controlled, pedestrian-safe suburban malls. A great proportion of the retail and service labor force has also moved out to these suburban centers, and many of the people who live in the suburbs also work in them. The cities that have grown up in the last few decades have adapted rather easily to this new spatial pattern. Their central business districts are relatively small, housing primarily government offices, banking and commercial firms, and some professional offices. They have never been retail trade centers. In the cities that grew up before 1950, however, the development of the periphery has caused real problems, as the once-vital central business district is increasingly abandoned by business and shoppers, leaving behind empty buildings, unprofitable businesses, and a declining tax base.

■

FIGURE 20.2
THE MULTIPLE NUCLEI MODEL
OF URBAN SPATIAL PATTERNS

The automobile has given the late-industrial city a freedom of form that its predecessors did not have. Commercial and residential areas are spread throughout the city and the suburbs. The city center has declined in importance, and many smaller centers have developed.

SOURCE: Harris and Ullman 1945.

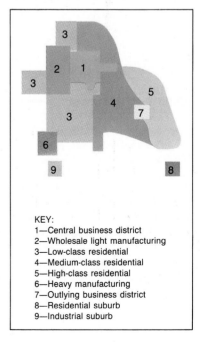

KEY:
1—Central business district
2—Wholesale light manufacturing
3—Low-class residential
4—Medium-class residential
5—High-class residential
6—Heavy manufacturing
7—Outlying business district
8—Residential suburb
9—Industrial suburb

URBANIZATION IN THE UNITED STATES

More than half of the U.S. population lives in metropolitan areas with more than 1 million population. Clearly, we are not just an urban nation but increasingly a nation of big-city dwellers. This section reviews some of the major patterns in American urban distribution.

What Is Metropolitan?   What is considered urban in one century or nation is often rural in another. To impose some consistency in usage, the U.S. Bureau of the Census has replaced the common words *urban* and *rural* with two technical terms: *metropolitan* and *nonmetropolitan*.

A **metropolitan area** is a county that has a city of 50,000 or more in it plus any neighboring counties that are significantly linked, economically or socially, with the core county. The Census Bureau refers to these units as MSAs (metropolitan statistical areas). Some MSAs have only one county; others, such as New York, San Francisco, or Detroit, include several neighboring counties. In each case, the metropolitan area goes beyond the city limits and includes what is frequently referred to as, for example, the Greater New York area. A **nonmetropolitan area** is a county that has no major city in it and is not closely tied to a county that does have such a city.

Figure 20.3 shows the current distribution of the U.S. population by type of residence. A total of 77 percent of the population lives in metropolitan areas. This metropolitan population is divided into those who live in the central city (within the actual city limits) and those who live in the balance of the county or counties, the suburban ring. More than half of the metropolitan population lives in the suburbs (and some even on farms) rather than in the central city itself. Although they are judged to have access to a metropolitan way of life, they may live as far as 30 or 50 miles from the city center.

The nonmetropolitan population of the United States has shrunk to 23 percent. Although there are nonmetropolitan counties in every state of the

A **metropolitan area** (MSA) is a county that has a city of 50,000 or more in it plus any neighboring counties that are significantly linked, economically or socially, with the core county.

A **nonmetropolitan area** is a county that has no major city in it and is not closely tied to a county that does have such a city.

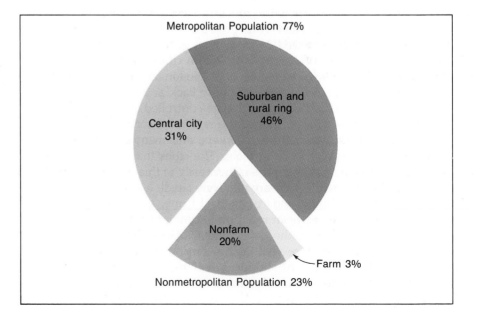

FIGURE 20.3.
THE URBANIZATION OF THE UNITED STATES POPULATION 1987

Three quarters of the U.S. population live in metropolitan areas, and nearly half lives in areas with more than 1 million people. Nevertheless, only one-third actually lives in central cities. The remainder lives in suburbs and small towns.

SOURCE: U.S. Bureau of the Census 1989i.

Metropolitan Population 77%

Suburban and rural ring 46%

Central city 31%

Nonfarm 20%

Farm 3%

Nonmetropolitan Population 23%

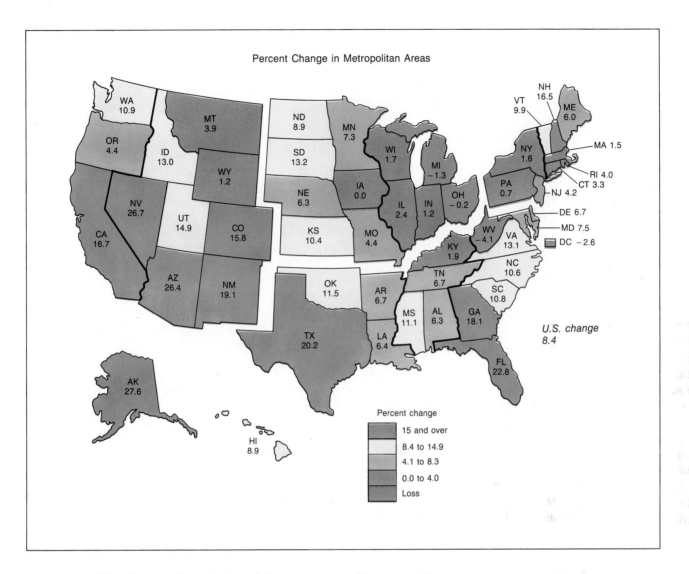

Percent Change in Metropolitan Areas

Percent change	
	15 and over
	8.4 to 14.9
	4.1 to 8.3
	0.0 to 4.0
	Loss

U.S. change 8.4

union except New Jersey, the majority of the nonmetropolitan population lives in either the Midwest or the South. Only a small proportion of these people live on farms; many live in small towns and cities of 10,000 or 30,000.

Changing Patterns. Until 1970, the story of U.S. population was one of progressive urbanization. Urban areas grew faster than rural areas, and the biggest urban areas grew the most. At the end of the 20th century, there are three major variations on this continuing pattern: shrinking central cities, Sunbelt growth, and nonmetropolitan resurgence.

SHRINKING CENTRAL CITIES. Central cities have grown much less rapidly than their suburban rings, and many of the largest central cities have actually lost population. Even Atlanta, whose metropolitan area grew by 28 percent between 1980 and 1988, lost population in its central city. The losses are greatest in midwestern and northern cities such as Detroit and Pittsburgh, but are notable even in the Sunbelt ("Central City" 1990).

■
FIGURE 20.4.
POPULATION CHANGE 1980–1987 BY STATE

Almost all of U.S. population growth—metropolitan and nonmetropolitan—has occurred in the West and to a lesser extent in the South. The North and Midwest have experienced little growth or actual losses in both metropolitan and nonmetropolitan populations.

SOURCE: U.S. Bureau of the Census 1989i, 7–8.

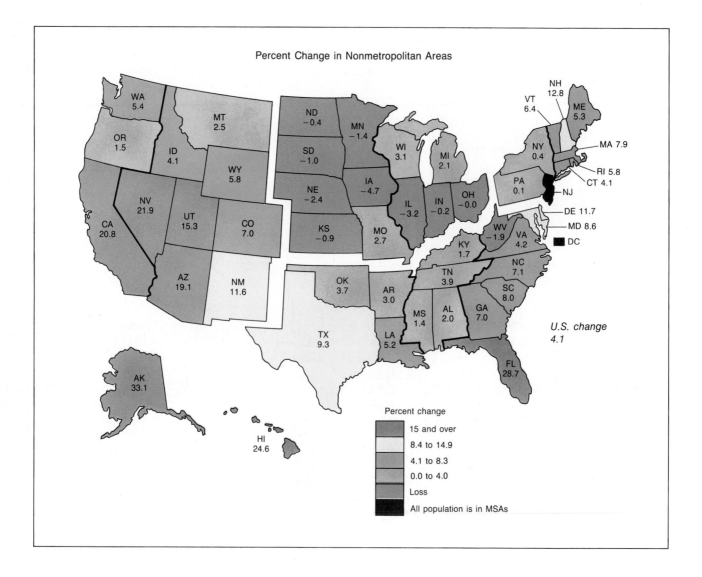

Percent Change in Nonmetropolitan Areas

SUNBELT GROWTH.   Almost all of the metropolitan growth in the last decade has been in the Sunbelt, and all of the 50 fastest-growing metropolitan areas are in the South or West ("U.S. Metro" 1986).

NONMETROPOLITAN RESURGENCE.   Since 1970, nonmetropolitan areas have stopped shrinking and have even begun to experience modest growth (Johnson 1989). Fewer people are moving away, and some areas are receiving in-migration. Although not growing as rapidly as metropolitan areas, small town and rural America are not disappearing either. Most of this growth reflects life-style choices: The people moving to nonmetropolitan areas are willing to give up urban amenities for outdoor recreation, lower taxes, and a slower pace of life. There is not a big boom in rural Iowa or Nebraska, though (see Figure 20.4). Most of the nonmetropolitan growth is in the South or the West, often in areas that are within a few hours' driving distance of a big city.

THIRD WORLD CITIES

Whereas the West has been predominantly urbanized since at least 1950, the less developed areas of the world—roughly Africa, Asia, and Latin American—are still predominantly rural. This is changing within our lifetime, however, on a scale that is difficult to grasp (see Figure 20.5).

The growth of large cities and an urban way of life has occurred everywhere very recently; in the Third World it is happening almost overnight. Mexico City, São Paulo, Bogotá, Seoul, Kinshasa, Karachi, Calcutta—these and other Third World cities are growing at 5 to 8 percent per year. This means that their populations will double in approximately a decade. The roads, the schools, and the sewers that used to be enough no longer are; neighborhoods triple their populations and change their character from year to year. These problems are similar to the problems that plagued Western societies at the onset of the industrial revolution, but they are on a much larger scale. Despite the obvious drawbacks, cities continue to attract new migrants. No matter how poor they are, the urban poor are better off than the rural poor (Berry and Kasarda 1977; Bradshaw and Fraser 1989). Most important, opportunity is in the city. In rural areas, the only means to wealth is land, and that means is static; its quantity never changes, and its ownership is seldom transferred. Thus, the possibility for self-improvement lies almost entirely in urban areas.

Third World urbanization differs from that of the developed world not only in pace but also in causal factors. First, more than half of the growth in Third World cities arises from a very high excess of births over deaths. Where overall population growth is 3 or even 4 percent annually, cities grow rapidly even without migration from the countryside. Second, many of the large and growing Third World cities have never been industrial cities. They are government, trade, and administrative centers. More than one-third of the regular full-time jobs in Mexico City are government jobs. These cities offer few working-class jobs, and the growing populations of unskilled men and women become part of a shadow labor force of the self-employed—artisans, peddlers, bicycle renters, laundry workers, and beggars.

■

URBAN LIFE IN THE UNITED STATES

Urbanization is the process of population concentration. Those who study it are concerned with the extent of urban growth and the forces that encourage the development of urban living. Although this is an important area of study, sociologists are mainly interested in **urbanism**—a distinctively urban mode of life that is developed in the city though not confined there (Wirth 1938). They are concerned with the extent to which social relations and the norms that govern them differ between rural and urban settlements.

THEORETICAL VIEWS

The Western world as a whole has an antiurban bias. Big cities are seen as haunts of iniquity and vice, corrupters of youth and health, and de-

■

This shanty town (or favela) in Rio de Janeiro is considered to be Rio's best. It is the shanty town to which Pope Paul was taken during his visit to Brazil. Such shanty towns abound in third-world cities. They have no streets, water, electricity, or garbage service, but they are the only homes available to the rural migrants who surge into the cities looking for employment opportunities that are, for the most part, nonexistent.

Urbanization is the process of population concentration in metropolitan areas.

Urbanism is a distinctively urban mode of life that is developed in the cities but not confined there.

■
FIGURE 20.5
**URBANIZATION TRENDS IN THE
DEVELOPED AND LESS DEVELOPED
WORLD, 1980 AND 2025**

Although the world is still more rural than urban, this is changing within our lifetime. Urbanization is growing particularly quickly in the less developed world. By the year 2025, three quarters of the world's urban population will live in less developed countries.

SOURCE: "Population Growth" 1985.

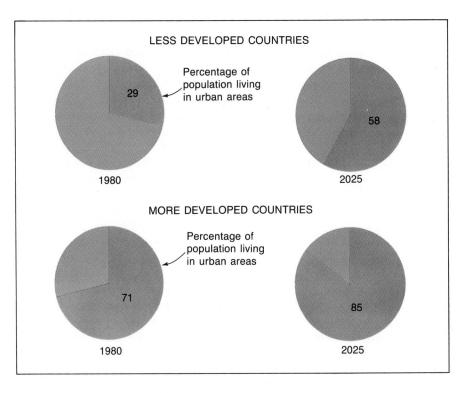

LESS DEVELOPED COUNTRIES

Percentage of population living in urban areas

29   58

1980   2025

MORE DEVELOPED COUNTRIES

Percentage of population living in urban areas

71   85

1980   2025

Gemeinschaft refers to society characterized by the personal and permanent ties associated with primary groups.

Gesellschaft refers to society characterized by the impersonal and instrumental ties associated with secondary groups.

stroyers of family and community ties. Cities are despised as artificial creations that compare poorly with creations of nature. City dwellers are characterized as sophisticated but artificial; rural people are characterized as possessing homegrown goodness and warmth.

This general antiurban bias (which has been around at least since the time of ancient Rome), coupled with the very real problems of the industrial city, had a great deal of influence on early sociologists. For the most part, Durkheim, Weber, and others believed that the quality of human social life was significantly worse in the cities. Only recently has evidence emerged that rural life is not as idyllic and city life is not as bleak as was supposed.

Early Writers.   Ferdinand Tönnies (1855–1930) offered one of the earliest sociological descriptions of the differences between urban and rural society. He argued that rural society was characterized by **gemeinschaft,** personal and permanent ties associated with primary groups. Urban society was characterized by **gesellschaft,** the impersonal and instrumental ties associated with secondary groups. Durkheim saw the essence of urbanization as a shift from social cohesion built on similarity (mechanical solidarity) to a cohesion built on a complex division of labor and high interdependence (organic solidarity). Weber spoke of a shift from tradition to rationalism as a guide to social activities.

These early writers were not blind to the drawbacks of rural society. They recognized that rural society was static and confining, that tradition bound individuals to a station in life and to ways of thinking that left little room for innovation or individualism. Their preference for rural life was based on the security it provided—the security of knowing exactly what was expected of you, what your place in the social order was and what

FOCUS ON ANOTHER CULTURE

Mexico City—26 Million?

Mexico City is the most dramatic example of Third World urbanization. At 18 million, it is currently the second largest city in the world (after Tokyo); by the year 2000, it is projected to be the largest city in the world, with a population of 26 million people. Mexico City is currently growing at about 4.0 percent each year—720,000 new inhabitants each year, 14,000 each week. Nearly two-thirds of this growth is due to natural increase, the excess of births over deaths. Only one-third is attributable to migration from the countryside ("Mexico's Population" 1987).

Tremendous size, rapid growth, and lack of job opportunity have resulted in multiple problems. Among the worst are dangerously high air pollution, severe overload on water and sewer systems, abject poverty, and a serious housing shortage.

Mexico is among the richest of the less developed countries. Nevertheless, the poverty is appalling by our standards. At least 4 million (25 percent) of Mexico City's inhabitants live in squatter housing outside the city. They lack water, sewers, public transportation, electricity, and employment. They live in tar-paper, scrap-lumber, or cardboard shacks. Because they lack legal title to their land, it does not pay them to invest either money or effort in improving their housing. And because of the relative impermanence of the housing, the government does not provide public services (Beier 1976).

In the mid 1960s, anthropologist Oscar Lewis drew a dramatic picture of life in these neighborhoods with a simple research technique: He went into a tenement and calculated the value of every possession owned by the people living there, from ashtrays to underwear. The tenement he studied was not the poorest of the poor, for the building was a permanent adobe structure with electrical service and a central water spigot. Nevertheless, 83 people lived in 14 one-room, dirt-floor apartments. On the average, these families owned $338 worth of material possessions; they had 23 beds for their 83 members. Almost all their goods had been purchased second-hand and would be pawned or sold off in times of economic emergency (Lewis 1969).

Like many other less developed countries faced with rapid urban growth, Mexico is trying to encourage decentralization. Growth in rural areas and smaller cities is being encouraged by the provision of electric power, transportation links, and low-interest loans for capital investment outside Mexico City. This strategy is unlikely to be very effective. In the first place, capital-intensive industries are not the ones likely to employ the unskilled urban poor or the rural migrants. In addition, part of Mexico's problem is overall population growth. With a 2.4 percent crude natural growth rate, the countryside, too, is over-

■

Mexico City is currently growing at about 4.0 percent each year—720,000 new inhabitants each year, 14,000 each week.

crowded. The best long-range strategy to slow the growth of Mexico City is to reduce fertility as fast as possible and to improve conditions in the countryside as a means of reducing migration flow. In the meantime, reforms that will help the city accommodate its vast new population, including legalizing the tenure of squatters and redirecting urban investment into poor neighborhoods, are desperately needed.

In 1990, many people in Mexico City continue to live in one-room apartments without electricity or running water. With 14,000 new residents each week, Mexico City cannot possibly provide decent housing for all its residents.

Big cities such as New York offer glamour, sophistication, and wonderful museums, music, and entertainment. Nevertheless, surveys show that the vast majority of Americans would rather visit big cities than live in them. Anxiety about crime is an important factor in this preference for suburban and small town living.

your neighbor's place was. In addition, the long-lasting personal relationships characteristic of rural society were thought to be essential to informal social control. Many were concerned that when people did not have to worry about what the neighbors would think, deviance would become commonplace and the social order would be threatened.

Wirth: Urban Determinism.   The classic statement of the negative consequences of urban life for the individual and for social order was made by Louis Wirth in 1938. In his influential work "Urbanism as a Way of Life," Wirth suggested that the greater size, heterogeneity, and density of urban living necessarily led to a breakdown of the normative and moral fabric of everyday life.

Greater size means that many members of the community will be strangers to us. Greater density means that we will be forced into close and frequent contact with these strangers. Wirth postulated that individuals would try to protect themselves from this crowd by developing a cool personal style that would allow them to ignore some people (including people who were physically close, such as in a crowded elevator) and to interact with others, such as salesclerks, in an impersonal style so that their personality would not be engaged. The Kitty Genovese incident, described in Chapter 2, is rightly cited as the kind of thing that is more apt to happen among strangers than among lifelong neighbors. Wirth did not suggest that urbanites had no friends or primary ties, but he did think that the city bred a personal style that was cold and calculating (Fischer 1976).

The heterogeneity of the city is also hypothesized to lead to an awareness of alternative normative frameworks or subcultures. Wirth suggested that this awareness would lead to normative confusion for the individual and lack of integration for the community. Faced with a welter of differing norms, Wirth thought, the dweller in a heterogeneous city was apt to conclude that anything goes. Such an attitude, coupled with the lack of informal social control brought on by size, would lead to greater crime and deviance and a greater emphasis on formal controls.

In sum, Wirth argued that city living brought negative consequences for individuals and society. That is, he believed that if a well-integrated, warm, and conforming person from the farm moved to the city, that person would change and become calculating, indifferent, and nonconforming.

The Compositional Model.   Later theorists have had a more benign view of the city. Compositional theorists suggest that individuals experience the city as a mosaic of small worlds that are manageable and knowable (Gans 1962). Thus, the person who lives in New York City does not have to cope with 9 million people and 500 square miles of city; rather the individual's private world is made up of family, a small neighborhood, and an immediate work group. Compositional theorists argue that the primary group lives on in cities and that the quality of interpersonal ties is not affected even though the number of impersonal contacts is much greater than in rural areas.

The compositional model does recognize that deviance, loneliness, and other problems are greater in cities than in rural areas. It suggests, however, that deviants, singles, people without children, the lonely, and the alien-

	CONCEPT SUMMARY		
	Comparing Three Theories of Urbanism		
	WIRTH'S URBAN DETERMINISM	COMPOSITIONAL THEORY	SUBCULTURAL THEORY
Essential aspects of urban living	Size, heterogeneity, density	Neighborhood; mosaic of manageable worlds	Critical mass
Consequences for the individual	Withdrawal; normative confusion	No consequences	Opportunity to develop subcultures
Societal consequences	Indifference; deviance	No consequences	More diversity
Why is crime higher in urban places?	Normative confusion; low social control	Nonconformists attracted to urban places	Deviant subcultures can develop that encourage crime

ated are attracted to the cities rather than created by them. Those with families and those willing to conform are attracted to the suburbs.

The Subcultural View.   In Wirth's view, the city has essentially negative effects; in the compositional view, urban environment has few direct consequences. The subcultural view straddles the two positions and presents a more moderate picture of the city. The essential idea of the subcultural view is that of critical mass. Special subcultures—intellectuals, radicals, gays—cannot develop until there are a relatively large number of people sharing some relatively uncommon set of norms or values. For example, one homosexual in a small community will be under constant pressure to conform to general standards; only when there are many others will it be possible to sustain a gay community with its own set of norms and values. Similarly, a symphony orchestra, a football team, and a synagogue all await the development of a critical mass of people who share the same interest. Once they identify one another, they will have group support for their identities and standards. In this way, the greater diversity and size of the city leads to development of subcultures with different, perhaps even deviant, norms and values. Wirth might interpret these subcultures as evidence of a lack of moral integration of the community, but they can also be seen as private worlds within which individuals find cohesion and primary group support.

EMPIRICAL CONSEQUENCES OF URBAN LIVING

One theory suggests that urban living has negative consequences, another that it has few consequences, and still another that it leads to the development of subcultures. This section reviews the evidence about the effects of urban living on social networks, neighborhood integration, and quality of life.

Social Networks.   The effects of urban living on social networks are rather small. Surveys asking about strong ties show that urban people have as many intimate ties as rural people. There is a slight tendency for urban people to name fewer kin and more friends than rural people, but the kin omitted from the urban lists are not parents, children, and siblings but more distant relatives. Thus, urban living may narrow the kin group and expand the number of nonkin who are listed as intimates (Fischer 1981). Overall, however, urban residents have the same number of intimate ties as do rural people and they see their intimates as often. There is no evidence that urban people are disproportionately lonely, alienated, or estranged from family and friends.

The Neighborhood.   Empirical research generally reveals the neighborhood to be a very weak group. Most city dwellers, whether central city or suburban, find that city living has freed them from the necessity of liking the people they live next to and has given them the opportunity to select intimates on a basis other than physical proximity; this freedom is something that people in rural areas do not have. There is growing consensus among urban researchers that physical proximity is no longer a primary basis of intimacy. Rather, people form intimate networks on the basis of kin, friendship, and work groups; and they keep in touch by telephone rather than relying solely on face-to-face communication. When in trouble, they call on their parents or their children for help (Wellman 1979). In short, urban people do have intimates, but they are unlikely to live in the same neighborhood with them.

Neighbors are seldom strangers, however, and there are instances in which being nearby is more important than being emotionally close. When we are locked out of our house, we need a teaspoon of vanilla, or we want someone to accept a United Parcels package, we still rely on our neighbors (Dono et al. 1979). Although we generally do not ask large favors of our neighbors and don't want them to rely heavily on us, most of us expect our neighbors to be good people who are willing to help in a pinch. This has much to do with the fact that neighborhoods are often segregated by social class and stage in the family life cycle. We know that our neighbors will be people pretty much like us.

Quality of Life.   Big cities are exciting places to live. People can choose from a wide variety of activities, 24 hours a day, seven days a week. The bigger the city, the more it offers in the way of entertainment, libraries, museums, zoos, parks, concerts, and galleries. The quality of medical services and police and fire protection also increases with city size. These advantages offer important incentives for big-city living.

On the other hand, there are also disadvantages: more noise, more crowds, more expensive housing, and more crime. The latter is a particularly important problem for many people. More than 50 percent of those living in cities over 1 million report that they would be afraid to walk alone at night in their neighborhood; only 29 percent of the rural population would be afraid. Data on crime rates (see Table 20.1) suggest this fear might be justified: Crime rates are strongly correlated with city size. This is especially true of the kind of crime that people fear most—violence against the person.

■

TABLE 20.1

CRIME AND THE FEAR OF CRIME BY CITY SIZE

One of the most outstanding differences in rural/urban quality of life is that big-city residents have a much greater fear of crime, apparently with good reason.

Is there any area around here—that is, within a mile—where you would be afraid to walk alone at night?

City Size	Yes
1,000,000+	56%
500,000–999,999	49
50,000–499,999	54
2,500–49,999	40
Rural	29

Rate of violent crimes reported per 100,000 population

City Size	Violent Crime Rate
250,000+	1,540
100,000–249,999	900
50,000–99,999	634
25,000–49,999	470
10,000–24,999	334
Less than 10,000	294
Rural	181

SOURCES: Public Opinion 1986a and U.S. Department of Justice 1989a.

Because of these disadvantages, many people would rather live close to a big city than actually in it. A 1989 survey asked a large national sample, "If you could live anywhere in the United States that you wanted to, would you prefer a city, suburban area, small town, or farm?" The results suggest that antiurban bias continues to be strong: Only 19 percent preferred the city, 24 percent the suburb, 34 percent the small town, and a full 22 percent said they would prefer to live on a farm (Gallup Reports 1989e). Some groups, however, prefer big-city living—in particular, childless people who work downtown. These people relish the entertainment and diversity that the city offers. Because of their affluence and childlessness, they can afford to dismiss many of the disadvantages of city living.

Are City Folks Cold?   From Tönnies' gemeinschaft/gesellschaft to Wirth's urban determinism, social theorists have assumed that urban dwellers tend to be cold and rational in their social relationships, whereas rural people are warm, open, and friendly. How much truth is there in these stereotypes?

Some research evidence suggests that urban people do develop a cool indifference to nonintimates. Research on the bystander effect and on helping behavior has consistently demonstrated that people in big cities are less apt to help a stranger in trouble than are people in rural areas. One research project looked at community size differentials in bystanders' response to a tearful child asking for help in finding his mother. The results show a substantially lower willingness to help in bigger cities than in small ones (Korte 1980; Milgram 1970). In big cities, many people ignored the child altogether or said something to the effect "Go away, I can't be bothered."

The suburbs are the fastest growing part of America, now encompassing nearly half of the entire American population. This suburb in Naperville, Illinois is characteristic: Each family has its own house, its own yard, and two cars. House structure, income, life-style, and values tend to be very similar within each development. Because of this, suburbs emphasize conformity.

THE OTHER AMERICAS

Sociological attention has been captured by cities such as Manhattan and San Francisco with their bright lights and ethnic diversity. Nevertheless, only a quarter of our population actually lives in these big-city centers. The rest live in suburbs and small towns. How does their experience differ?

SUBURBAN LIVING

The classic picture of a suburb is a development of very similar single-family detached homes on individual lots. This low-density housing pattern is the life-style to which a majority of Americans aspire; it provides room for dogs, children, and barbecues. This is the classic picture of suburbia. How has it changed?

The Changing Suburbs.   The suburbs are no longer bedroom communities that daily send all their adults elsewhere to work. They are increasingly major manufacturing and retail trade centers. Most people who live in the suburbs work in the suburbs. Thus, many of the close-in suburban areas have become densely populated and substantially interlaced with retail trade centers, highways, and manufacturing plants.

These changes have altered the character of the suburbs. Suburban lots have become smaller, and neighborhoods of townhouses, duplexes, and apartment buildings have begun to appear. Childless couples, singles, and retired couples are seen in greater numbers. Suburbia has become more crowded and less dominated by the station-wagon set.

With expansion, suburbia has become more diverse. Although each suburban neighborhood tends to have its own style, stemming in large part from the fact that each development includes houses of similar size and price, there are a wide variety of these styles. In addition to the neighborhoods of classic suburbia are spacious mini-estate suburbs where people have horses and riding lawn mowers, as well as dense suburbs of duplexes, townhouses, and apartment buildings. Some of the first suburbs are now 40 years old. Since people tend to age in place, these suburbs are more often characterized by retirees than young families (Fitzpatrick and Logan 1985). Many of the older suburbs are becoming rundown, and renting is more common than home owning.

Suburban Problems.   Many of the people who moved to suburbia did so to escape urban problems: They were looking for lower crime rates, less traffic, less crowding, and lower tax rates. The growth of the suburbs, however, has brought its own problems. Among the most important problems in the suburbs are the following (Baldassare 1986):

1. *Housing costs.* Increased demand for suburban housing has driven housing costs up to a level that is beyond the reach of people who could have afforded a home 10 or 15 years ago. As a result, more suburban housing consists of duplexes and other less expensive forms of housing.
2. *Fragmented governments.* Suburban governments are basically defensive organizations; they can protect their citizens' property from central-city taxes and their schools from central-city students. Beyond this, county governments and municipal governments of the small cities in the suburban ring are fragmented and relatively powerless. In many arenas, they are at the mercy of decisions made in the central city—where they cannot vote.
3. *Higher density.* The increased density of the suburbs recreates the urban problems of crowding, traffic congestion, and crime.
4. *Transportation.* Living in suburbia depends on access to automobiles, and there are few mass transit systems. People who don't have cars find it nearly impossible to work or shop. As a result, people who are poor in the suburbs find it harder to find work, buy groceries, or get social services (Burby and Rohe 1989).

SMALL-TOWN AND RURAL LIVING

Approximately 25 percent of the nation's population lives in small towns (populations of less than 2,500) or rural areas. Some of these rural and small-town people are included in the metropolitan population count because they live within the orbit of a major metro area, but most live in nonmetropolitan areas—in South Dakota and Alabama, but also in Vermont and Pennsylvania.

The nonmetropolitan population of the United States continues to grow. Although young people often leave to go to school or get jobs elsewhere, enough come back to keep populations growing. In addition, small-town growth is maintained by a small but steady stream of people seeking refuge from the problems of urban and suburban living.

People find small-town living attractive for a number of reasons: It offers lots of open space, low property taxes, affordable housing, and relative freedom from worry about crime. In addition, an important attraction for many people is the perceived opportunity for more neighboring and community involvement. Studies show that this perception is correct: Small-

A glance is enough to tell you that these guys don't live in Los Angeles. As this picture suggests, life-styles do differ depending on region and size of place. Although these Missouri farmers may be more conservative and less sophisticated than men of their same class and education in Los Angeles, rural/urban differences are smaller than they used to be. These fellows probably pick up David Letterman with their satellite dish.

town people do know more of their neighbors (Freudenburg 1986). This provides an important source of cohesion and social integration. It is not, however, an unalloyed blessing. Although the fact that everybody does indeed know everybody helps keep down the crime rate, some find that the lack of privacy and enforced conventionality are oppressive (Johansen and Fuguitt 1984).

Rubes and Hicks?   According to stereotype, rural people, especially farmers, are hicks, rednecks, and rubes. They use bad grammar and think that if it was good enough for Grandpa, it is good enough for me, that a woman's place is in the home, and that children should be seen and not heard. In contrast, the stereotype of the sophisticated city dweller suggests someone who is aware of current events, is innovative and upbeat.

These portraits are very much exaggerated. On most social issues, from churchgoing to support for welfare, there are little or no size-of-place differentials (Camasso and Moore 1985). One study found no size-of-place or metropolitan/nonmetropolitan differences on the importance people attached to any of the following values: working hard, achievement, personal freedom, helping others, salvation, or leisure (Christenson 1984). All but the remotest cabin dwellers have access to national culture via television, radio, movies, and news magazines. The automobile and a good highway system have also increased the access of rural people to urban culture.

Although they watch the same television shows and shop from the same catalogs as their urban counterparts, rural and urban life-styles do differ. The city continues to be the major source of innovation and change. New dress styles, music, educational philosophies, and technologies originate in the city and spread to the countryside. Thus, the rural/urban difference is constantly created anew and seems unlikely ever to be totally eliminated (Fischer 1979). Because the speed of cultural diffusion is now much more rapid than before, however, rural/urban differences are far less profound than they were in the past.

THE POLITICAL ECONOMY
OF SPATIAL DISTRIBUTION

If you asked the average citizen why people are leaving the central cities and moving to suburbia, you would get answers such as high housing costs and high crime rates. Your respondent might also note that a lot of jobs have moved to suburbia. These answers are correct, but they don't go quite far enough. *Why* is housing cheaper in suburbia? Why have the jobs left the central cities? Although some conservative scholars have suggested that these changes are the result of neutral economic forces, others have suggested that they are the result of political decisions. In this section, we want to consider the political economy of spatial distribution: Why are housing costs, segregation, and poverty correlated with place?

SPACE IS MONEY

For both Marxists and non-Marxists, land is a critical form of capital. Those who own land try to manipulate economic and political processes so as to maximize profit from their land or at least to protect its current value (Gottdiener and Feagin 1988). Who are these profit maximizers? Although some are bankers and developers, most are home owners. In contemporary capitalism, home ownership may be the critical class distinction (Paul 1989). For most of us, our home is our only tangible asset. In protecting this investment, we act like capitalists.

One of the most important tools that owners use to protect land values is *zoning*—restricting the use of land to certain purposes. Zoning ordinances are political decisions that are made by city councils and county commissioners. A typical zoning ordinance forbids multifamily dwellings or inexpensive housing in middle-class suburbs or forbids construction of convenience stores or other businesses in residential neighborhoods. Most zoning ordinances are designed to keep out people or properties that will cause property values to go down or cause taxes to go up (Burnell and Burnell 1989).

The Growth Machine?   City government, the chamber of commerce, bankers, and the average home owner all have an economic interest in growth: A growing city results in increased demand and increased property values. As a result, the city has been called a growth machine. Even the most avid pro-growth advocate, however, usually has pretty specific ideas about where growth should occur. Average home owners want a growing city, but they want to protect their own neighborhoods through zoning; they want growth elsewhere. Developers want growth where they own land, usually on the edge of town where they have been able to buy up large parcels of land cheaply. Both tendencies result in urban sprawl as developers and current home owners conspire to drive new housing outside of existing neighborhoods.

The heart of contemporary urban politics is the conflict about how much growth should take place and where to put it (Logan and Zhou 1989). Of course, not everybody wants growth. Some want to avoid the increased crime rates, crowding, environmental destruction, and increased cost of living associated with growth (Vogel and Swanson 1989). In relatively few communities in the U.S., however, are there enough people who care more about congestion and the environment than about property values. As a result, no-growth coalitions seldom win. Studies show that compromises— for example, requiring developers to set aside green space or to protect the environment—are seldom effective in slowing down growth. Because private interest groups are more organized than their opponents, they wield more political power. Regulatory agencies and planning commissions are often controlled by developers (Logan and Zhou 1989).

THE POLITICS OF HOUSING

Owning one's own home is a nearly universal American dream. It represents economic security and a modest kind of power—control over one's own space. It is a dream that has been realized by growing numbers in the last 50 years. In 1940, 60 percent of Americans between ages 35 and 65 were renters. Members of the working class and the lower-middle class could never save up enough money to buy their own home. In 1986, however, only 25 percent were still renting. During this period, the average age at which people bought their first home dropped from 41 to 29 (Chevan 1989).

This dramatic increase in home ownership has been associated with suburban growth and central-city decay. The decline of central-city housing in favor of the suburbs, however, is not a foregone conclusion. There are many advantages to living downtown, and some of the most elegant neighborhoods in America are in central cities. Scholars suggest that three kinds of political decisions structured this systematic shift in housing investment: redlining, federal loan programs, and federal housing projects.

Redlining. The housing market rests on two commodities: loans and insurance. Both are controlled by the biggest commercial firms in the United States. Before a family can obtain a mortgage loan, it must have insurance; the same thing is true for remodeling loans. A substantial body of research demonstrates that both home insurance and mortgage loans are more difficult to obtain in some parts of the city than in others. The process whereby these financial investments are systematically denied to one area of the city and diverted to other, more favored areas is called *redlining*. Typically, the areas discriminated against are heavily minority and low income, and the favored areas are suburban. Insurance companies, for example, charge rates for central-city areas that are much higher than is justified by the increased risk of fire or vandalism; they may also terminate policies in redlined areas or simply define such areas as outside their territory (Squires, Dewolfe, and Dewolfe 1979). The same process occurs in home mortgages (U.S. Department of Housing and Urban Development 1977).

These discriminatory practices are part of a systematic process of disinvestment in low-income and minority—that is, central-city—neighborhoods. Rather than being a natural cycle of aging, urban decay is the result of deliberate action. The lack of investment in a neighborhood means no construction jobs, no repairs, and deteriorating housing. Ultimately, it leads to simple abandonment, a critical and rapidly growing problem in

Although some of the most elegant neighborhoods in America are 100 years old, the average neighborhood slides into decay as it gets older. Middle-class neighborhoods that are close to downtown find it hard to fend off developers that can find more profitable uses for their land than single-family dwellings. Although some neighborhoods are able to use zoning restrictions to repel developers, many home owners are besieged by developers who want to bulldoze their homes and replace them with apartment buildings or convenience stores.

U.S. cities. Gaping windows and sagging doors provide targets for vandalism and havens for junkies, criminals, and rats; they also contribute to
further decline.

Federal Loan Programs.   Nearly half of all mortgage loans for home
purchases are guaranteed by the federal government through either the
Veteran's Administration (VA) or the Federal Housing Administration (FHA).
The federal guarantees remove the risk for local savings and loan associations and encourage them to offer loans to people whose ability to buy
is marginal, especially working-class and lower-middle-class people. These
federal programs give preference to new housing and thus have been used
almost exclusively to encourage suburban development rather than the
purchase and upkeep of established central-city neighborhoods. Because
loan guarantees are unavailable for older homes, renting becomes the rule
and the long decline begins. The lack of federal loan guarantees works in
parallel with redlining practices virtually to exclude central-city home
ownership.

Federal Housing Projects.   During the 1960s and 1970s, federal dollars
were funneled to local areas to build public housing projects for the urban
poor. The chief objective of these urban renewal projects was to replace
unsafe, rundown tenement housing with higher-quality housing. The result, however, was to drive away the working class, decrease the quality
of central city housing, and increase racial segregation and crime. This is
a remarkable record for a policy designed to improve housing.

Essentially, urban renewal bulldozed square miles of low-rise tenement
buildings and replaced them with modern high-rise apartment buildings.
The space saved was often used for freeways or public buildings. Despite
the fact that the apartments were superior to the destroyed housing, the
change had substantial negative consequences. First, unlike the destroyed
units, the new housing was public housing. Thus, the working poor were
displaced, and a dense aggregation of the poorest of the poor was created.
Second, dense high rises are poor places in which to raise children. Children who are playing 20 stories below their parents are effectively beyond
parental supervision. Finally, by eliminating the front porch as a neighborhood meeting ground, the physical basis for neighborhood cohesion
and integration was eliminated at the same time that increased density
vastly increased the possibilities of neighbors annoying one another. Furthermore, all the new projects were located in heavily minority areas, thus
contributing to the continuity of segregation.

The Consequences: Segregation and Poverty.   Over the past 40 to
50 years political decisions have been made that have resulted in systematic
disinvestment in central-city housing. The result is that the city is poorer
than it was before and more racially differentiated from the suburbs.

POVERTY.   In 1988, poverty was found less often in the suburbs than in
either central cities or nonmetropolitan areas: Eight percent of the suburban
population was below the poverty level, compared to 16–18 percent in
central-city and rural areas. The low rate of poverty in the suburbs is the

result of two trends: the exodus of jobs to the suburbs and the ability of suburban zoning regulations to exclude low-income housing (and thus low-income people).

RACIAL SEGREGATION.   Central cities have become increasingly populated by non-Anglos: Thirty-eight percent of the Anglo population lives in cities of over 1 million, but 51 percent of the African American, 60 percent of the Hispanic, and 50 percent of the Asian population lives in these largest urban areas ("Geographic Polarization" 1986). In several large American cities, racial and ethnic minorities are the numerical majority in a central city surrounded by largely Anglo suburbs.

Three trends have supported the development of racial segregation between cities and suburbs. From 1940 to 1980, there was a strong movement of rural blacks and Hispanics to the largest urban centers. During the same period, there was a trend toward suburbanization by Anglo Americans. Most recently, the large waves of Asian and Hispanic immigrants have settled largely in the biggest urban centers, thus contributing to the growth of the racial and minority population there (Waldinger 1989).

Suburbanization was a disproportionately Anglo phenomenon because Anglos were better able to afford new housing *and* because of racial discrimination. Studies during the 1970s and 1980s documented that race was more important than class in limiting black suburbanization and that middle-class blacks found it especially difficult to move into white suburbs (Farley 1977; Massey and Egger 1990). Thus, minority suburbanization frequently meant continued segregation. Racial and ethnic segregation is lower in the suburbs than in central cities, but it still remains very strong. African Americans who live in the suburbs are likely to find themselves living in suburbs largely populated by other African Americans (Massey and Denton 1988).

CITY LIMITS TO EQUALITY?

The average metropolitan county contains dozens of different governments (see Figure 20.6). The central-city government is ringed by the governments of half a dozen incorporated suburbs; the balance of the county is under the jurisdiction of the county government. Although all of the people in the county are linked together in a common economic network, their taxes and their social services depend on which jurisdiction they live in. The suburbs cannot be taxed to support central-city services; the school district of suburb A does not have to take children from the central city or from suburb B; each suburban government can develop zoning ordinances to keep undesirable city growth from spilling over into its boundaries. As one scholar has phrased it, this fragmented political control of space has put city limits on equality (James 1989). City and suburban political boundaries limit the sharing of social resources and isolate the well-off from the poor.

Independent political control of space contributes to many of the problems associated with today's urban areas, especially to school segregation and to central-city poverty. Central-city school districts, for example, may find that there are too few Anglo students in their district to create integrated schools. The Anglo students are inaccessible because they live in another school district. The growth of black and Hispanic suburbs also

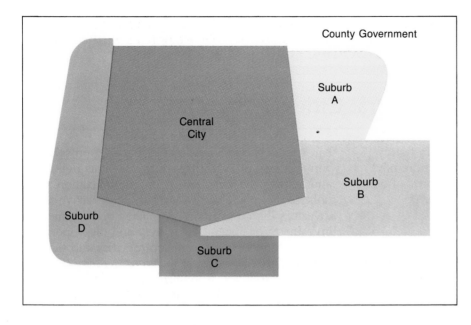

County Government

Suburb
A

Central
City

Suburb
B

Suburb
D

Suburb
C

■
FIGURE 20.6
**THE FRAGMENTED GOVERNMENT
OF A METROPOLITAN COUNTY**

The average metropolitan county is divided into half a dozen or more different governments. Despite the fact that they are all part of a common economic network, each jurisdiction controls its own taxes and expenditures. This system benefits affluent suburbs that can withdraw their resources from the common pool yet still share the amenities provided by other jurisdictions.

increases school segregation. The greater the proportion of blacks and Hispanics in a particular suburban school district, the lower will be its capacity for providing racial balance (James 1989).

Multiple government jurisdictions benefit those people in affluent neighborhoods that have been able to protect their space and tax dollars. These people can drive into town and enjoy museums, parks, shopping, and entertainment and not have to help foot the bill. One solution that is often mentioned is to move major taxing and spending decisions to the county level. In this way, suburban home owners could be taxed to support urban services (many of which they enjoy). Not surprisingly, however, surveys indicate that suburban residents oppose such a change by a two-to-one margin (Baldassare 1989).

ISSUES IN SOCIAL POLICY

Should Central Cities be Saved?

The problems of major central cities are tightly connected: fewer working-class jobs, more poverty, more segregation, less money. Parts of our central cities look like bombed-out Beirut.

THEORETICAL VIEWS

Some people, generally conservatives, treat the problem as if it were the outcome of neutral economic forces. They argue that people have voted with their feet. These critics see no point in trying to save big northern and midwestern cities. They urge migration as the answer to the poverty and joblessness of urban residents.

Observers from the liberal side are more likely to point to the political and economic decisions that have left the urban poor increasingly isolated: tax breaks to subsidize suburban rather than ur-

Nearly every major metropolitan area has neighborhoods that look like this. The obvious reason for the development of such neighborhoods is lack of money: Industry, jobs, and, subsequently, working-class families have left the area. The public policy dilemma is whether to try to encourage the redevelopment of such areas or simply bulldoze them.

ban housing, disproportionate spending on suburban and commuter transportation such as freeway and beltway systems, and zoning and taxation policies that made the suburbs more attractive to investors than the central city. They believe that investment has been deliberately and disproportionately aimed away from central cities and that the solution is to reinvest in the central city (Gottdiener 1985).

Among those who wish to salvage the central city, the major issue is urban revitalization. What is it and whom does it help?

URBAN REVITALIZATION

Urban revitalization involves massive upgrading of central-city neighborhoods. It occurs in two forms: municipal development and gentrification. Both are controversial.

Municipal Development

Government-sponsored revitalization has occurred in many big cities. The typical strategy is to replace low-income neighborhoods and decayed areas with parks, convention centers, and other facilities that bring in dollars and middle-class visitors. The city uses its right of eminent domain to acquire blocks of property and then uses tax breaks and other investment incentives to lure investors back to the downtown area. Under this planning, waterfronts and downtowns in many major cities have been transformed.

Gentrification

In the classic pattern of gentrification, a middle-class individual or couple buys a dilapidated older home at a bargain price and pours money and sweat into refurbishing it. After a second and a third house in the neighborhood is refurbished, the neighborhood begins to attract some attention

ISSUES IN SOCIAL POLICY continued

from people with perhaps more capital and less daring. When a sufficient core of restored houses develops, boutiques, antique shops, gourmet shops, and other trendy stores begin to replace bars, barbershops, and pawnshops. Scruffy apartment houses are refurbished and turned into condominiums.

Gentrification is to some extent a neutral economic process. The prices of suburban land and housing have become so high and the commuting distances grown so long that the city center once again appears to be a reasonable place to live. This is especially true for childless professionals who work and play downtown. On the other hand, the impetus for gentrification is often the very nice tax and loan breaks that are offered to encourage reinvestment in the downtown.

EVALUATION

How can this be controversial? In place of decayed housing, low tax base, and transient residents, we have top-quality housing, a high tax base, and stable residents. The question some ask, however, is whether the neighborhood has been revitalized or taken over. We may have saved the neighborhood, but what became of the neighbors?

Some observers argue that the long-time residents of a neighborhood benefit the most. Those "affected by decreasing property values in their neighborhood, deterioration, and increased crime—or the fear of increased crime—are the most likely beneficiaries, if they are able to remain in the neighborhood" (Schill and Nathan 1983). This is a big if. Evidence indicates that the previous residents can seldom afford to stay. The ones who aren't directly bought out find they cannot afford to shop in their own neighborhood, nor

can they afford the rapidly rising property taxes (Maher et al. 1985).

Two primary charges can be made against this breaking up of neighborhoods. One relies on a somewhat romantic notion of urban villages; it argues that the invasion of yuppies is destroying strong and vital neighborhoods (Palen and London 1984). For the most part, however, urban revitalization is not aimed at strong ethnic or subcultural neighborhoods, but at neighborhoods that have already disintegrated. The other charge has more substance: Municipal development and gentrification contribute to homelessness and reduce the stock of available housing for the poor (Adams 1986). Although empirical studies show that most of the displaced find other housing with little or no sacrifice (Schill and Nathan 1983), two groups stand out as exceptions to this generalization: the unemployed and the transient. Rental housing of any kind and especially the nightly and weekly rentals used by transients has almost disappeared from our nation's urban areas. The only alternatives are Salvation Army and city mission facilities, which have not expanded rapidly enough to take up the slack.

The issue has been posed by many observers: recovery for whom? for business? for the poor? (Porter and Sweet 1984). The urban revitalization movement has created two cities out of one: a more prosperous city for yuppies and tourists and another for the poor, who have progressively fewer housing or work opportunities (Ganz 1985). In the long run, the greater fiscal health of the central city brought about by urban revitalization may trickle down to the poor, but in the short term, urban investment decisions seem to have increased the disadvantages of central-city poor.

SUMMARY

1. The industrial city has three distinctive features: high density, a central business district, and a concentric spatial pattern.

2. The late-industrial city is characterized by low density and multiple nuclei. It is associated with the shift to tertiary production and the improvement of transportation and communication.

3. Three quarters of Americans live in metropolitan areas, but most of these live in the suburban ring rather than the central city. There have been three major changes in residence patterns: shrinking central cities, sunbelt growth, and nonmetropolitan resurgence.

4. Urbanization is exploding in the less developed world; many of its large cities will double in size in a decade. This urban growth is the result not of industrialization but of high urban fertility and the high rural density and poverty that drive peasants toward the city.

5. Three major theories of the consequences of urban living are Wirth's urban determinism, compositional theory, and subcultural theory. Urban determinism suggests negative effects of urban living, compositional theory suggests no effect, and subcultural theory says urban living encourages the development of subcultures.

6. Urban living is associated with less reliance on neighbors and kin and more reliance on friends, with greater fear of crime and less warmth toward strangers, but also with more diversity and entertainment.

7. Suburban living has become more diverse. Retail trade and manufacturing have moved to the suburbs, and the suburbs are now more densely populated, more congested, and less dominated by the station-wagon set.

8. Small-town and rural living is characterized by more emphasis on family and neighborliness, more social control, and less crowding. There are fewer cultural and lifestyle differences between rural and urban areas than there used to be.

9. The political economy of spatial distribution is concerned with political decisions that affect the allocation of people and dollars across space. This perspective suggests that home owners and elites both have a vested interest in growth and in increasing property values; they work together to keep lower-income people away from their neighborhoods and to segregate their tax dollars.

10. The decay of central-city housing and the growth of suburban housing reflect three processes: redlining, federal loan programs, and federal housing programs. The result is that central cities are poorer than they used to be and are racially segregated from their suburbs. There are city limits to equality.

11. Decaying central cities are being rebuilt through two processes of urban revitalization: municipal development and gentrification. Although these processes have improved the tax base of central cities, they raise questions about who benefits from revitalization.

SUGGESTED READINGS

Baldassare, Mark. 1986. Trouble in Paradise: The Suburban Transformation in America. New York: Columbia University Press. Documents the challenges to suburban quality of life created by increasing population pressure.

Fischer, Claude S. 1984. The Urban Experience. (2d ed.) San Diego: Harcourt Brace Jovanovich. A readable book that covers theoretical views of the city as well as contemporary research about urban problems and the quality of life in the city.

Johansen, Harley, and Fuguitt, Glenn. 1984. The Changing Rural Village in America: Demographic and Economic Trends Since 1950. Cambridge, Mass.: Ballinger. Through interviews with citizens and civic leaders, this book focuses on the quality of social and economic life in towns of less than 2,500. Demonstrates continuing vitality and growth of small-town America.

McGeary, Michael, and Lynn, Laurence (eds.). 1988. Urban Change and Poverty. National Research Council. Washington, D.C.: National Academy Press. A report from the National Committee on Urban Policy, this volume contains scholarly papers on the growth of poverty in urban areas and the committee's recommendations for federal policy change.

Riis, Jacob A. 1971. How the Other Half Lives. New York: Dover Publications. (Original work published 1901.) A liberally illustrated essay on conditions in U.S. urban slums at the turn of the century. Riis's early photographs provide ample documentation of the poverty and filth of the industrial city.

Smith, Michael Peter. 1988. City, State, and Market. New York: Basil Blackwell. A readable but scholarly statement of the political economy position, Smith talks about the reasons that politics matter in housing and spatial allocation and how local, national, and global economic issues affect urban policy.

■ PHOTO ESSAY: Information Technology: How Will It Change Society?

People in the academic community—students and teachers—have been prime beneficiaries of developments in information technology. Compared to 20 years ago, our ability to access and process information has been expanded enormously. Because today's hardware and software are both much better and much cheaper than that of ten years ago, a very large portion of all college students have access to personal computers and sophisticated word processing programs.

Consider the student in 1962 who is assigned the topic of writing a term paper on the consequences of parental divorce. She walks through the periodicals section until she stumbles on the *Journal of Marriage and the Family*, in which she eventually finds the five articles her professor requires. She takes notes on 3×5 cards (there are no photocopying machines) and goes home to draft her paper on her new electric typewriter. She cuts and tapes her draft copy until it looks good, checks words of dubious spelling in her dictionary, and then retypes a final copy. She uses carbon paper so she will have a copy for herself. When she makes a mistake, she erases it carefully and tries to type the correction in the original space.

■

The entire contents of the twenty-volume Oxford English Dictionary can be stored on one CD-ROM disk, a CD disk that looks just like the one you buy your favorite music on. It is now quite feasible to carry the Census, an encyclopedia, and, of course, the Oxford English Dictionary, in your pocket.

Compare this to the student in 1992. This student starts her paper by logging onto SOCIOFILE ©, an electronic bibliography of more than 100,000 sociology articles on a single CD ROM disk. When she enters the keywords 'divorce' and 'parental,' the program prints out full citations and a summary for 41 articles. After identifying and photocopying the 5 articles she wants, she drafts a report on her word processor, edits it to her satisfaction, runs it through her spellchecker, and spiffs up the vocabulary a bit by using the thesaurus built into her word processor. She also runs her report through her new grammar-checker, which will catch errors in punctuation, capitalization, and so forth. Finally, she sends the whole thing to her mother (who lives 2000 miles away) through electronic mail and asks her to read it for logic and organization. She receives the edited version back from her mother in an hour, prints two copies, and hands it in. If she is taking an off-campus course, she may send the paper to her instructor via electronic mail or she may FAX it.

Information technology—utilizing computers and telecommunication tools for storing, using, and sending information—has changed many aspects of our daily lives. Aside from enabling us to write better term papers with less hassle, how will information technology change our lives? Will it reduce or increase social class inequality? Make life safer and better, or make life more stressful and isolated?

The answer is likely to be some of both. In addition to the many blessings associated with

Joel Schatz travels all over the world in the course of his job. To keep in touch with his office, he simply hooks his portable computer up to any telephone and dials an electronic mailbox to check for messages.

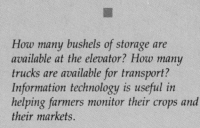

How many bushels of storage are available at the elevator? How many trucks are available for transport? Information technology is useful in helping farmers monitor their crops and their markets.

■ PHOTO ESSAY: Information Technology: How Will It Change Society?

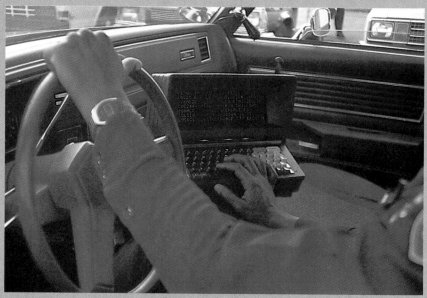

The development of portable equipment and easily accessible data banks adds a new dimension to law enforcement. An officer in a patrol car has instant access to information about individuals, cars, neighborhoods, and so on.

Clifford Stoll, a systems manager at California's Lawrence Berkeley Laboratory for defense research, discovered that someone was tapping into the lab's data banks. By planting a false data set, he eventually traced the unauthorized entry to a West German hacker.

information technology, there are new worries. For example, advances in information technology have introduced new forms of crime (hacking and electronic theft), new defense worries (breaches of our defense data system or faulty software programs that may inadvertently launch World War III), and new inefficiencies ("I'm sorry, the system is down"). We focus on three social implications of information technology: social integration, social control, and work.

On-Line to the Whole World

If you moved from Ohio to Oregon in 1850, chances are that your contacts with your family would be limited to one or two letters a year. It might take months for news of a major world event to reach you. How-

ever, today's information technology provides all of us access to far more information than ever before, faster than ever before. As a result of information technology, we are all linked to the rest of the world; we are linked to distant family and friends, to libraries and data banks, and to world events. Within hours of Iraq's takeover of Kuwait in 1990, gasoline prices went up at stations in almost every rural hamlet across America.

This improved communication has many ramifications for social institutions. Any new cultural invention—from fashion to software—will be introduced around the world very quickly, with the probable effect of reducing regional and international cultural differences. It *may* help reduce social isolation, encourage world peace and understanding, and help people make better decisions. Of course, information technology may also be used for less admirable purposes, such as allowing terrorists to monitor and sabotage air travel or economic markets. The development of advanced systems of information technology vastly increases the number of people to whom we are linked, but the content of our relationships with those people is still determined by social institutions.

Big Brother is Watching: Social Control

One of the most important consequences of information technologies is an increased ability to monitor and control. This includes the control of guided missiles, grocery store inventories, and the stock market (through, for example, programmed trading). It also includes a greater ability to monitor and control people—such as students, taxpayers, drivers, and employees.

When a police officer pulls you over, your license plate number and your driver's license number are entered into a computer. If your car has been stolen or if there are warrants out for your arrest or if you have unpaid citations from another state, the record will be there. Increasingly, your life will be an open book—available to bureaucratic surveillance at every step. Just over the horizon is the probability that your Social Security number will be encoded in a bar

Big brother is watching this steer. Food and water are luring this steer into a device where a computer will read his electronic ear tag and record his weight, temperature, water and food consumption.

code on a plastic card; you will present it whenever you make a transaction covered by government regulations, for example, when you buy or sell a car, get married, register a birth, get a traffic ticket, receive income, or pay taxes.

This increased control arouses concerns about potential invasions of privacy and loss of personal control (Rule and Attewell 1989). Even those people who have nothing to hide may not want their age, credit rating, marital history and so forth available to public scrutiny. There are two issues here. First,

can adequate safeguards be built into huge, interlinked data banks to ensure that no unauthorized persons use the information? Second, how will the authorities use the information? Will law enforcement agencies cross-check marriage and divorce records to identify bigamous marriages? Will authorities check marriage records to identify children who are falsely claimed to be born after a marriage when they were really born before it? Will local, state and federal tax officials use these records? The legal basis for controlling personal data banks is still evolving.

■ PHOTO ESSAY: Information Technology: How Will It Change Society?

Will information technology enable many of us to work at home in the future? Perhaps a more fundamental question is how many of us want to work at home. The "electronic cottage" is already technologically feasible for many jobs, but workers often find that the convenience of working at home is offset by conflicts between family and job and the absence of supportive colleagues.

Work: The Electronic Cottage

Some futurists have suggested that computers and telecommunications will allow us to return to a preindustrial social organization in which people can live in small communities and income-generating work can be carried out at home. The so-called "electronic cottage" will allow people to live in Dalton, Georgia, and work for a firm in New York City. The employee will receive and send work via electronic mail, keeping in daily, even hourly, touch with others (who may be scattered across the country and even the world). This scenario has many attractive features. It would enable people to live in smaller communities, a choice most say they prefer (Chapter 20); it would reduce the time and costs associated with commuting; it would eliminate the need and expense to dress for success; it would enable the worker to have more flexible working hours so that he or she could spend more time with the family and whip up cookies during the lunch hour. Is this glowing scenario likely?

The answer appears to be probably not. The reasons have more to do with people than with technology. Many people find electronic mail an inadequate substitute for coffee breaks with fellow employees (Forester, 1989). In addition, most people cannot work effectively with children underfoot. Working at home generally works well only for the single and childless or those whose children and spouse leave home for the day. Far from integrating the worker with family, working at home may create family stress. Another obstacle to telecommuting is that working at home requires a great deal more self-motivation and willpower than going to the office. Many people find that they get more work done, enjoy their work more, and experience more self-esteem from working at the office than working at home.

For the upper-level white-collar worker who wants the freedom to work at home occasionally or who wants to be able to write books while living in a cabin in the mountains, telecommuting is a clear blessing. As with many blessings, however, there may be a social class difference in its availability. Many observers believe that home work will be another means to oppress women, especially lower-level clerical workers. When routine clerical tasks such as data entry are done on a home-work basis, they are usually contracted out on a piecework—rather than salaried—basis. This means that employees rather than employers must buy and maintain the equipment; there are few or no benefits (no sick leave, vacation, or health insurance benefits). Labor unions are strongly opposed to home work, seeing it as a way to isolate workers and prevent solidarity. Many feminists oppose it because they see it as another tool to restrict women's lives to home and children.

For many of us, information technology simply provides convenience and speed. For the handicapped, new technologies mean the difference between social isolation and social participation, between silence and communication.

Summary

The effect of information technology on society will depend as much on social institutions as it does on the technological capacities of computers and telecommunications. Information technology offers us more freedom from drudgery and dangerous work, more freedom of residence, but we simultaneously receive some loss of privacy and autonomy. Whether the blessings or costs will predominate will depend on how these technologies are implemented in schools, workplaces, and government bureaucracies. To the extent that they affect relationships between work, class, neighborhood, and family, the new technologies are of vital interest to those concerned with social institutions.

This coach is entering baseball statistics into his portable computer so that he can instantly analyze player performance and find patterns in the opponent's game plan. As a result of the continuing explosion in information technology, all of us will be under more scrutiny.

21

COLLECTIVE BEHAVIOR AND SOCIAL MOVEMENTS

HAVE YOU EVER . . .

Run across a crowd or demonstration on campus? Almost every campus has several such events every term. These may range from five to six students carrying placards to hundreds of students demonstrating for or against abortion rights, gay rights, recycling, or just tuition hikes.

Most demonstrations or crowd gatherings come to a peaceful close. The TV cameras come and go, and the participants gradually fade away. Of course, not all demonstrations end peacefully. From New Jersey to Beijing, the gathering of a crowd sometimes leads to violence. When a crowd grows from 100 to 1,000 or even 100,000 a peaceful demonstration may end up in police confrontations, property destruction, and even death. Every crowd has a volatile character that makes outcomes unpredictable.

This chapter is concerned with those occasions in which people step outside of their usual school/work/play routines to take part in collective behavior and social movements. Who are the people that step forward, and what social processes govern the behavior of the groups that they form?

■ In June 1990, a triumphant crowd of Detroit Pistons fans pored into the streets after the Pistons won the National Basketball Association championship. Jubilant (and drunk) fans got so carried away that seven people died in the ensuing melee.

■ In June 1989, a month-long demonstration by 100,000 pro-democracy students in Tienanmen Square was violently squashed by the Chinese government. Several hundred students and soldiers died in the confrontation. The government followed its victory with a rigorous campaign against activists, and the shortrun effect was to reduce the likelihood of reform.

■ Every day in the United States, there are people picketing outside abortion clinics. In many places, these antiabortion activists have caused so much disruption that they are regularly hauled off to jail and saddled with large fines.

Collective behavior is nonroutine action by an emotionally aroused gathering of people who face an ambiguous situation.

Sociology divides these kinds of activities into two related but distinct topics: collective behavior and social movements. **Collective behavior** is nonroutine action by an emotionally aroused gathering of people who face an ambiguous situation (Lofland 1985, 29). It includes situations such as the impromtu celebration in Detroit. These are unplanned, relatively spontaneous actions, where individuals and groups improvise some joint response to an unusual or problematic situation (Zygmunt 1986).

A **social movement** is an ongoing, goal-directed effort to change social institutions from the outside.

On the other hand, a **social movement** is an ongoing, goal-directed effort to change social institutions from the outside. Examples include the antiabortion, gay rights, and civil rights movements. A social movement is extraordinarily complex. It may include sit-ins, demonstrations, and even riots, but it also includes meetings, fund-raisers, legislative lobbying, and letter-writing campaigns (Marwell and Oliver 1984).

Both collective behavior and social movements challenge the status quo. The primary distinction between them is that collective behavior is spontaneous and strictly confined to a particular place and time; a social movement is organized, broad based, and long term. Even a month-long demonstration in Beijing is an instance of collective behavior until and unless it develops into an organized attempted to change the political structure.

In this chapter, we examine the social structure of collective behavior and social movements; the circumstances under which people step outside the usual conventions; the processes through which some disorganized protests, riots, and outbreaks become organized, politicized social movements; and the responses of institutions and people who wish to maintain the status quo.

■

COLLECTIVE BEHAVIOR: CROWDS AND RIOTS

TYPES OF CROWDS

A **crowd** is a gathering of people who are reacting to a nonroutine event.

A **crowd** is a gathering of people who are reacting to a nonroutine event. This definition excludes most concert audiences, football spectators, and religious congregations, which are almost always pretty routine. In a small minority of cases, however, something happens to turn a passive audience into an aroused crowd. Winning the championship or clinching the division title can turn ordinary athletic spectators into an ecstatic crowd that revels in the streets. Similarly, people's behavior at rock concerts and revival meetings may change if the crowd becomes emotionally aroused.

Sociologist John Lofland (1981) has described six types of crowds that result from the combination of three dominant emotions in two organizational forms. The three dominant emotions are fear, hostility, and joy. These may appear in two organizational forms: crowd (confined to one time and place) and mass (repeated in other times and places). Looking at these two dimensions in combination yields the six types of collective behavior illustrated in Figure 21.1.

You may wonder how a mass behavior that occurs over and over again can still fit the definition of collective behavior. The case of mass hostility (followed by mass joy) can be illustrated by the waves of collective behavior that tumbled Communist governments across Eastern Europe in the fall of 1989. These mass uprisings were relatively spontaneous, unplanned events. Although repeated in nation after nation, they were not coordinated or the result of ongoing social movements. Similarly, the wave of race riots that swept U.S. cities in 1967 was not the result of a planned campaign but was the spontaneous response of aroused people to similar situations. It should be obvious, however, that there is a connection between collective behavior and social movements. Although one racial protest is an instance of collective behavior, a social movement is likely to emerge if the protests are repeated (Olzak 1989). Later in this chapter, we discuss the circumstances under which repeated but disorganized collective behavior is likely to turn into a social movement.

THEORIES OF CROWD BEHAVIOR

There are many types of crowds—happy crowds and hostile crowds and panic-stricken crowds. All crowds, however, have a volatile quality that

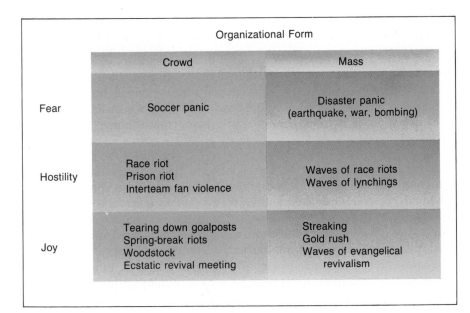

	Organizational Form	
	Crowd	**Mass**
Fear	Soccer panic	Disaster panic (earthquake, war, bombing)
Hostility	Race riot Prison riot Interteam fan violence	Waves of race riots Waves of lynchings
Joy	Tearing down goalposts Spring-break riots Woodstock Ecstatic revival meeting	Streaking Gold rush Waves of evangelical revivalism

FIGURE 21.1
TYPES OF COLLECTIVE BEHAVIOR

All episodes of collective behavior are characterized by strong emotional arousal. In this typology, episodes of collective behavior are categorized by whether this dominant emotion is fear, hostility, or joy. Even joyful crowds are extremely volatile and may become violent and destructive. An isolated episode is a crowd behavior, but collective behavior takes on a mass form if it appears repeatedly.

SOURCE: Adapted from Lofland 1981.

During the Spring of 1989, crowds of students and workers gathered in Tienanmen Square and throughout China to demand greater democracy. After weeks of uncertainty, authorities crushed the protests on June 4. The month-long demonstrations are a classic case of mass crowds, with the dominant emotion vacillating between jubilation and terror.

makes officials uneasy. Celebratory crowds can turn into violent riots. Why does this happen?

In ongoing groups, norms, roles, and sanctions set goals and structure conformity. In the absence of social structure, what accounts for crowd behavior? Three general theories have been offered: contagion theory, convergence theory, and emergent-norm theory.

Contagion Theory.   According to **contagion theory,** the crowd situation leads to the development of unanimous and intense feelings and behaviors that are at odds with the usual predispositions of the individual participants (Turner 1964). This theory attempts to explain only one kind of crowd behavior: the escalating response. It suggests that crowds are moved to extreme and irrational behaviors—lynchings, prison riots, mass suicide, religious frenzy—through a vicious circle of exchange. One person yells an obscenity, another throws a rock, and a third shoots a gun. Finally, the crowd is fired up to an emotional level that its members would not have reached if they had coolly considered the matter on their own. Many contagion theorists believe that this circular stimulation heightens and reinforces antisocial behavior, stripping away the effects of socialization so that crowd responses become irrational and instinctual (Blumer 1934; LeBon 1896).

Convergence Theory.   Whereas contagion theory argues that the crowd situation leads to escalating extremism among otherwise conforming individuals, **convergence theory** attempts to explain quiet as well as rowdy crowds. It contends that the cause, or triggering event, for crowd action selectively draws people who share a common set of predispositions. For example, street riots draw unattached, alienated, and angry young men. The convergence of many like-minded people provides the critical mass for their predispositions to be put into action. Similarly, crowds drawn by

Contagion theory suggests that the crowd situation leads to the development of unanimous and intense feelings and behaviors that are at odds with the usual predispositions of the individual participants.

Convergence theory contends that the cause, or triggering event, for crowd action selectively draws people who share a common set of predispositions.

In 1930, these two black men were lynched by a mob in Marion, Indiana. Despite this clear photograph, official reports recorded that the killers were "parties unknown." Between 1890 and 1930, there were over 1000 lynchings in the United States. Although lynching is often attributed to contagion that drives people to act differently than their better natures, the racial pattern of lynchings suggests that they were instead a product of shared values: racism.

a religious revival will have another set of predispositions. According to convergence theory, there is no process within crowds; nothing new develops. Thus, the lynch mob is not a group of well-meaning citizens whipped up into a frenzy by circular stimulation; it is instead a collection of racist killers.

Emergent-Norm Theory. **Emergent-norm theory** suggests that each crowd is governed by norms developed and validated by group processes within the crowd (Turner and Killian 1972). This theory views the crowd experience as an extension of the everyday processes by which we negotiate encounters. From this perspective, the major task of a crowd is to improvise a joint answer to the question, "What is going on here?" Once this answer is reached and the encounter framed, the crowd will be able to make sense of the encounter and decide what acts are appropriate. Is the police officer beating the defenseless woman, or is the police officer defending himself against a vicious and unprovoked assault? Whether right or wrong, the frame will evoke sets of norms about what the crowd *should* do.

Emergent-norm theory does not assume that the crowd is unanimous in the definition it reaches. It assumes that the crowd will be made up of leaders and followers, confused passersby, and curious spectators. As with the subject in Asch's experiment who didn't want to disagree publicly about which line was longest (see Chapter 5), many of these onlookers will keep silent despite disagreeing with views being expressed. They are not swept up by emotional contagion but merely doing what most of us do most of the time: maintaining an appearance of group conformity.

Emergent-norm theory suggests that each crowd is governed by norms developed and validated by group processes within the crowd.

CONCEPT SUMMARY
A Comparison of Theories About Crowd Behavior

	CONTAGION THEORY	CONVERGENCE THEORY	EMERGENT-NORM THEORY
Basic Assumptions	Through circular stimulation and reinforcement, irrational and extreme acts develop.	Crowds are characterized by like-minded people drawn together by common interest.	New norms emerge during crowd interaction that validate group actions.
Evaluation	Explains only the escalating response	Ignores the hetergeneity of most crowds; assumes that crowds cause no change in individual behavior	Explains quiet crowds as well as the escalating response

Most modern scholars prefer emergent-norm theory. It provides a broad framework that explains the behavior of the passive crowd as well as of the unruly mob. It suggests that the unruly crowd, far from representing a stripping away of normative inhibitions, actually develops new norms—for example, a shared conviction that looting is appropriate behavior in the situation—and internally validates them. Usually such convictions are rationalized by reference to widely shared values and symbols.

In addition, emergent-norm theory helps explain the cultural and historical differences in crowd behavior. The systematic variation in crowd targets and crowd behavior over time and place suggests that crowd behavior has a clear normative component. Like other cultural responses, crowd behavior is patterned. Whether mob violence is directed at Jews, women, blacks, Catholics, or AIDS victims depends on cultural norms.

The form of crowd behavior also changes over time. The witch hunt and the lynch mob have almost disappeared as forms of collective action; the demonstration and the sit-in, however, have gained in popularity. The fact that certain crowd behaviors remain characteristic of specific times and places suggests that each society has a repertoire of crowd behaviors from which to choose (Tilly 1979). This repertoire represents patterned responses to recurrent situations rather than any spontaneous or instinctive aspect of human nature.

Emergent-norm theory is our best general-purpose theory of collective behavior, but it cannot stand entirely alone. Both contagion and convergence theories are also relevant to explaining crowd behavior. The roles of all three theories in explaining specific instances of collective behavior are examined in the next section.

TWO CASE STUDIES OF COLLECTIVE BEHAVIOR

Theory is useful to the extent that it helps us understand past events and predict future ones. One way to evaluate the theories of collective behavior is to test them against actual experience. In this section, we describe two very different types of crowds—a panic crowd and a race riot. Both represent crowd rather than mass behavior, but the first is dominated by fear and the second by hostility.

The British Soccer Tragedy.   On April 16, 1989, over 180 people were seriously injured and 95 people were killed at a soccer match in Sheffield, England. The dead fans were accidentally crushed to death against a barrier fence by thousands of their own team's supporters.

Liverpool was scheduled to play Nottingham Forest in a stadium that could hold 54,000 fans. Because of inadequate guarding at the gates and perhaps the presence of broken barricades, more than a thousand unticketed Liverpool fans managed to overrun the entrances and get into the standing-room-only sections at the Liverpool end zone. Because of vast overcrowding and because illegal fans were pushing to get in quickly and then pushing to move to the front, the crowd panicked and pressed forward, crushing the fans in the front.

British soccer (which Britons call football) has been described as a "slum sport played in slum stadiums" ("Disaster" 1989). It draws its fans heavily from the working class in the most depressed industrial areas of England. Liverpool, for example, has suffered a 22 percent male unemployment rate in recent years. In the midst of this depressing environment, their often victorious football team has been a source of great pride. "They took our industries away and our jobs away. But they can't take our football away from us" was the comment of one fan ("There's Comfort" 1989).

Because of the frequent violence associated with interteam rivalries, British stadiums are very different from American stadiums. The fans are surrounded by mounted police in full riot gear; prisonlike fences separate the fans from the playing field and from the opposing team's fans. Going

Nearly 100 people died when panic stampeded a crowd of soccer fans in Sheffield, England in 1989. They were crushed against heavy fences designed to keep the fans off of the field. Almost a year later, over 1,400 Moslem pilgrims were crushed in a stampede in a Mecca tunnel. Such instances of short-lived panic are probably best explained by contagion theory.

to see a soccer game has all the drama of having a ringside ticket to a riot; it is not family entertainment but an activity that appeals to young people and especially young men.

A particular feature of British soccer stadiums is that the end zone is standing room only. There are broad steps or terraces in the end zones so that people standing farther back can see, but there is no equivalent to reserved seating. This means that whenever the situation is tense or exciting, the crowd tends to press toward the front barriers. The absence of designated seating also means that it is relatively easy for a few extra fans to sneak in without being noticed. These standing-room-only tickets are cheaper than the seated tickets, and they are naturally most often sold to those with the least money—the youngest and the poorest fans.

ANALYSIS.   The British soccer tragedy is a classic case of a panic crowd, and it is precisely the sort of event that contagion theory is designed to explain. People in the back pushed, and soon everyone was rushing forward in a blind panic. The whole thing took only a few minutes—too short a time for new norms to emerge or for any deliberate behavior.

At first glance, convergence theory appears to have merit for explaining this crowd: Violence resulted when crowd members of a particular sort were drawn together to watch rough play. A little reflection, however, suggests that convergence theory is not very plausible here. The killing of Liverpool fans by other Liverpool fans was an accident; although the fans were disproportionately young and male, they did not converge on the stadium to rough up other Liverpool fans. Under similar circumstances, a crowd of middle-aged, upper-class patrons of a sinking cruise ship could demonstrate the same panic reaction. This appears to be a simple instance of contagion.

The 1967 Newark Race Riot.   Racial tension in Newark, New Jersey, smoldered with increasing intensity throughout the early 1960s. Between 1960 and 1966, the city went from 65 percent white to 35 percent white; tax revenues sagged, schools were on double shifts, and poverty and discontent were rampant. In the summer of 1967, two issues heightened the tension. The first was the city's choice of secretary to the board of education. The black community's preference was for a black accountant with a master's degree; the mayor's candidate was a white man who had never attended college. Because more than 70 percent of the students in the public school system were black and because of their candidate's higher educational achievement, the black community believed that the appointment of the white would be a major injustice. The second and related issue was an attempt by the city planning commission to clear 150 square blocks of black housing in the central ward for urban renewal. The black community was opposed to the plan, seeing it as a political move designed to break up black neighborhoods and dilute black voting power.

Tension escalated throughout the summer, exacerbated by intense media coverage of race riots in other cities. On July 12, the triggering event occurred. A black cab driver was taken to jail for tailgating and harassing patrol cars. Residents of the high-rise housing project overlooking the police station saw the man being dragged into the station, and soon the story had spread that he had been beaten and was near death. Residents

This photograph shows a street scene during a Miami riot in 1984. Like most recent riots in America, it is a race riot in the sense that the incident that provoked the mayhem was racially charged. Although the spark for the riot is black rage against the white community, most of the damage from the riot occurred within the black community. Such riots are more common when there are large numbers of unemployed young men. When the disaffected and angry are working- or middle-class adults, they are more likely to form a social movement to address their concerns.

of the high rise formed a crowd outside the police station. Black leaders tried to channel the crowd into a peaceful march to city hall, but the march disintegrated when children began throwing rocks at the demonstrators and some demonstrators started throwing rocks back. Soon the rocks were aimed at police and at storefronts. A little looting and vandalism took place that night, but things were quiet by morning.

During the next 24 hours, inflammatory rumors circulated throughout the central ward, and a demonstration was scheduled for that evening. Again, rocks and other missiles thrown by isolated individuals caused both the police and the crowd to become violent and disorderly. The ensuing riot ebbed and flowed for several days. As it became clear that police had merely cordoned off the neighborhood rather than entering it, many residents were drawn into general looting. The next few days saw escalating responses as the police and the national guard tried to enter the central ward to restore order. Neither the police nor the national guard was trained to face such a situation, and their actions served to escalate rather than suppress the civil disobedience. For example, at 3:30 P.M. on July 14, three carloads of police officers opened fire on a group of looters. Bullets sprayed into nearby apartments, and one bullet struck a three-year-old girl. She survived, but she lost an eye and her hearing. In similar incidents, the national guard and police opened fire on looters and spectators alike, frightening and angering the black community. When the police and national guard were withdrawn on July 17, the riot was over (National Advisory Commission on Civil Disorders 1968).

ANALYSIS. This seems like a classic case of contagion on the part of both the rioters and the armed authorities. As rumor followed rumor and as rock throwing escalated into shooting and violence, both sides acted in ways that went far beyond their usual predispositions. The guardsmen were young and generally inexperienced; they had received no training for riot work. A firecracker was mistaken for a sniper's bullet, a volley of rifle fire was directed at the source of the noise, and the conflict thus escalated past what either side considered reasonable. Contagion certainly existed, but contagion theory is inadequate to describe fully the course of the riot. Frenzy and irrationality can explain neither the shifts in tempo and mood during the five-day riot nor the fact that most of the action took place during evenings and weekends, when people were finished with their regular jobs. Such scheduling hardly indicates frenzy.

Emergent-norm theory, however, helps explain why the black community first defined the riot as a protest and then redefined it as a police attack; it also helps explain why the police and national guard defined themselves as being in an us-against-them confrontation with a dangerous and hostile enemy. These definitions of the situation emerged during the course of the riot and helped guide the responses of participants.

SOCIAL MOVEMENTS

Collective behavior is by definition nonroutine and irregular. As such, it always challenges the established way of doing things. This challenge may be temporary or limited, such as a prison riot or a football melee, or it may be part of a repeated mass response to arousing conditions. In the latter case, collective behavior may be a prelude to a social movement—an organized attempt to change social structure or ideology that is carried on outside legitimate channels or that uses these channels in innovative ways (Ash 1972).

Social movements can best be understood as political processes (Tarrow 1988). The antinuclear movement, the environmental movement, and the civil rights movement have stepped outside the usual legislative process in their attempt to challenge the status quo; frequently they use demonstrations, sit-ins, graffiti, and other innovative tactics to affect public policy. Some social movements are very closely allied with traditional political groups such as parties; others seek to overthrow or radically change the state. Because all have the goal of affecting public policy decisions, however, they are a part of the political process. As a result, social movement members tend to be the same kinds of people that vote and write letters to their congressional representatives.

THEORIES OF SOCIAL MOVEMENTS

Most Americans have a relatively low interest in political processes. In Chapter 15 we documented that one-third of the American public cannot even be bothered to vote. What are the circumstances that prompt people to shake off this lethargy and try to change the system? Why do people step outside of their usual social roles and attempt to change the world?

Two major theories explain the circumstances in which social movements arise: relative-deprivation theory and resource mobilization theory. Both theories suggest that social movements arise out of inequalities and cleavages in society, but they offer somewhat different scenarios of how and why protest develops.

Relative-Deprivation Theory.   Poverty and injustice are universal phenomena. Why is it that they so seldom lead to social movements? According to **relative-deprivation theory,** social movements arise when people experience an intolerable gap between their rewards and what they believe they have a right to expect. This definition is prompted by comparing their own condition to that of some better-off group or to expectations based on past experience. It refers to deprivation relative to other groups or other times rather than to absolute deprivation—hence the label *relative*-deprivation theory.

Figure 21.2 diagrams three conditions for which relative-deprivation theory would predict the development of a social movement. In condition A, disaster or taxation suddenly reduces the absolute level of living. If there is no parallel drop in what people rightfully expect, then they will feel that their deprivation is illegitimate. In condition B, both expectations and real standard of living are improving, but expectations continue to rise even after the standard of living has leveled off. Consequently, people feel deprived relative to what they had anticipated. Finally, in condition C, expectations rise faster than the standard of living, again creating a gap between reality and expectations. Relative-deprivation theory has the merit of providing a plausible explanation of the fact that many social movements occur in times when objective conditions either are improving (condition C) or are at least a major improvement over the past (condition B). Because relative-deprivation theory relies ultimately on the disorganizing effects of social change, it is often referred to as *breakdown theory*.

CRITICISMS OF RELATIVE-DEPRIVATION THEORY.   There are two major criticisms of relative-deprivation theory. First, empirical evidence does not bear out the prediction that those who are most deprived, absolutely or relatively, will be the ones most likely to participate in a social movement. Often, social movement participants are the best off in their groups rather than the worst off. In many other situations, individuals participate in and lead social movements on behalf of groups to which they do not belong. An example is the anti-apartheid movement on American campuses. Second, the theory fails to specify the conditions under which relative deprivation will lead to social movements. Why do some relatively deprived groups form social movements and others do not? In general, empirical

Relative-deprivation theory argues that social movements arise when people experience an intolerable gap between their rewards and what they believe they have a right to expect; also known as breakdown theory.

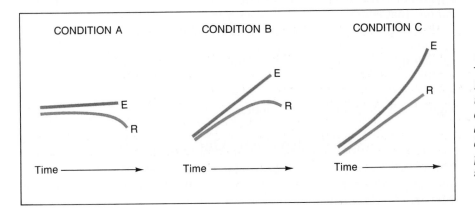

| CONDITION A | CONDITION B | CONDITION C |

Time   Time   Time

■
FIGURE 21.2
THE GAP BETWEEN
EXPECTATIONS AND REWARDS

Relative-deprivation theory suggests that whenever there is a gap between expectations (E) and rewards (R), relative deprivation is created. It may occur when conditions are stable or improving as well as when the real standard of living is declining.

studies suggest that relative deprivation by itself is not a good predictor of the development of social movements (Gurney and Tierney 1982).

Resource Mobilization Theory.   According to **resource mobilization theory,** social movements develop when organized groups are competing for scarce resources. This theory differs from relative-deprivation theory in two important ways. First, it argues that deprivation and competition are universal and thus relatively unimportant as predictors of social movements (Oberschall 1973). Second, it assumes that the spark for turning deprivation into a movement is not anger and resentment but rather organization.

Research shows that the most effective social movements emerge from groups that share two characteristics: relative homogeneity and many overlapping ties (Tilly 1978, 63). This implies that a black civil rights group that admitted whites would be less effective than one consisting only of blacks. Groups will be stronger if, in addition to homogeneity, their members share a strong network of ties—if they belong to the same clubs and organizations, if they work together, if they live in the same neighborhood.

Mobilization theory is often referred to as *solidarity theory* because it suggests that the building blocks of social movements are organized groups, not alienated, discontented individuals.

CRITICISMS OF RESOURCE MOBILIZATION THEORY.   The major criticism of resource mobilization theory is that it underestimates the importance of anger and spontaneity as triggers for social movements (Klandermas 1984; Zygmunt 1986). Although social movements may consist of rational conduct by organized groups, the triggering event may be an outbreak of collective behavior rather than the mobilization of integrated social networks.

Integration.   Recent research suggests that both theories have merit. Some social movements do develop out of a strongly felt sense of grievance; shared sentiment leads previously unacquainted people to join together to address their concern. Several of the protest groups that developed after the almost-disaster at the nuclear energy plant at Three Mile Island in 1980 were of this form (Cable, Walsh, and Warland 1988). On the other hand, some social movements have more to do with the strength of previously existing social networks than with the strength of their grievance. The League of Women Voters, for example, is one of the many civic organizations that adopts a new cause each year.

Resource mobilization theory is clearly the dominant theoretical perspective in contemporary accounts of social movements. If it is broadened to take into account the important role that spontaneous outbursts, triggering events, and emotionality play in occasioning and sustaining social movements, it provides a useful model of why social movements develop. Figure 21.3 compares the two models.

SOCIAL MOVEMENT ORGANIZATIONS

Many social movements include a wide spectrum of different groups, all pursuing, in their own way, the same general goal. For example, there are probably 50 different social movement organizations (SMOs) within the environmental movement. These range from the relatively conventional

---

Resource mobilization theory suggests that social movements develop when organized groups are competing for scarce resources; also known as solidarity theory.

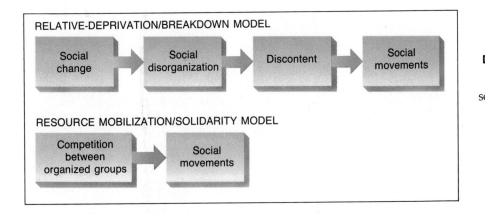

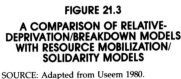

FIGURE 21.3
A COMPARISON OF RELATIVE-
DEPRIVATION/BREAKDOWN MODELS
WITH RESOURCE MOBILIZATION/
SOLIDARITY MODELS
SOURCE: Adapted from Useem 1980.

Audubon Society to the radical Greenpeace movement to the self-styled "eco-terrorists" of Earth First! As this example suggests, the SMOs within any given social movement may be highly divergent in tactics; some write letters and lobby their congressional representatives, while others disrupt nuclear power plants, chain themselves to trees, and blockade fishing grounds. The SMOs within a social movement usually reflect the racial, class, sex, age, and nationality schisms in the larger society (Benford 1989).

These divergent organizations are in some ways competitive: In the case of the environmental movement, for example, each is after the hearts and dollars of environmentally inclined citizens. Because this wide assortment of organizations provides avenues of participation for people with a variety of goals and styles, however, the existence of diverse SMOs is usually functional for the social movement. There is room for everybody.

SMOs can be organized in one of two basic ways: as professional or as volunteer organizations. On the one hand, we have organizations such as the Audubon Society or the Sierra Club that have offices in Washington, D.C., and a relatively large paid staff, many of whom are professional fund-raisers or lobbyists who develop an interest in the environment after being hired. At the other extreme is the SMO staffed on a volunteer basis by people who are personally involved—for example, neighbors who organize in the church basement in order to prevent a nuclear power plant from being built in their neighborhood. These two types of SMO are referred to, respectively, as the *professional* SMO and the *indigenous* SMO. Evidence suggests that the existence of both types of organizations facilitates a social movement's success. This is especially true for social movements that seek to help the disadvantaged.

The Professional SMO. The professional SMO provides three clear benefits to a social movement (Staggenborg 1988). First, it is usually better at soliciting resources from groups outside the disadvantaged group itself. It appeals to what is called a *conscience constituency*, people who are ideologically committed to the group's cause. For example, Jewish supporters of antidiscrimination laws have given generous support to professional black SMOs such as the NAACP. Because this is a respectable organization with accountants and lawyers, outsiders are more comfortable investing in it. Second, the professional SMO is better at building coalitions with related interest groups. Third, the professional SMO provides continuity

Mass demonstrations, such as this June, 1982 protest at Indian Point, New York, serve to gain publicity for social movements and to re-invigorate rank-and-file members. The real work of most social movements, however, goes on in committee meetings, at fundraisers, and other methodical tasks designed to mobilize resources and influence public opinion.

movement. While indigenous SMOs are likely to wax and wane with the urgency of the issues and the other demands on their leaders, professional SMOs provide long-term stability for the social movement. The paid staff maintains the movement when the demonstrators from the indigenous SMOs have gone back to work.

The Indigeneous SMO.   An effective social movement, however, also requires sustained indigenous organizations (Jenkins and Eckert 1986). Indigenous organizations perform two vital functions. By keeping the aggrieved group actively supportive of the social movement, they help to maintain the sense of urgency necessary for sustained effort. Second, anger and grievance propel indigenous organizations to more innovative, direct-action tactics (sit-ins, demonstrations, eco-terrorism, and the like) than are likely to be endorsed by professional organizations. This provides publicity for the movement and helps keep it on the national agenda. It also has the ironic effect of increasing support for the professional (more conservative) organizations, which begin to seem quite reasonable compared to the extremists.

The anti-apartheid movement is an excellent example of a social movement that combines both professional and indigeneous SMOs. The Americans and Europeans who are active in the battle against apartheid are members of conscience constituencies. Their sustained efforts have been critical in putting economic and political pressure on the South African government. Their efforts would be in vain, however, were it not for the continued direct action of black South Africans that makes racial conflict in South Africa a regular headline.

MOBILIZING THE MOVEMENT

Mobilization is the "process by which a unit gains significantly in the control of assets it previously did not control" (Etzioni 1968, 388). These assets may be weapons, technologies, goods, money, or members. The resources available to a social movement depend on two factors: the amount of resources controlled by group members and the proportion of their resources that the members are willing to contribute to the movement. Thus, mobilization can proceed by increasing the size of the membership, by increasing the proportion of assets that members are willing to give to the group, or by recruiting richer members.

The maximum state of mobilization, which Lofland (1979) has called white-hot mobilization, is reached when almost all members are fulltime and totally dedicated to the movement and when the movement's resources and number of members are expanding dramatically. Most movements, of course, never achieve this state. As Lofland notes, most social movements have only a few members who are especially dedicated, funding is slim, the program is timid and unacted on, and recruitment is haphazard and sparse.

Mobilization proceeds through two tactics: the recruitment of individual adherents (micromobilization) and the recruitment of supportive organizations (bloc mobilization). We discuss each of these in the following sections.

Micromobilization. The procedure through which SMOs attract individual new members has been called **frame alignment.** It is a process of convincing individuals that their interests, values, and beliefs are complementary to those of the social movement organization. According to Snow et al. (1986b), SMOs use four tactics for frame alignment:

1. *Frame bridging* targets people who have similar, though perhaps not identical interests and attempts to convince them that the similarities are great enough that they should support your organization, too. Thus, the Sierra Club may use computerized mailing lists to appeal to members of the National Wildlife Federation or the Audubon Society.
2. *Frame amplification* is equivalent to consciousness raising. This strategy gives structure to unfocused dissatisfaction by offering the SMO's frame as an explanation. It tries to convince people that their problems are caused by partiarchy or racism or whatever definition of the situation is used by the SMO.
3. *Frame extension* broadens the frame of the social movement so that more and more problems and concerns are included within its definition of the situation. For example, some peace movements have tried to attract more recruits by suggesting that the struggle for peace is also a struggle for social justice against racism, sexism, and poverty.
4. *Frame transformation* is equivalent to a religious conversion. It requires convincing individuals that the way they have seen things is entirely wrong. This is a strategy used by the Moonies, the Black Muslims, and radical feminists—groups that provide a radically different definition of a person's entire past and future and that frequently demand not just one evening a week but total, full-time dedication.

Who is most likely to be affected by these mobilization strategies? Studies of social movement activists show that, although ideology and grievances are important, the key factor is the strength of their personal ties

Frame alignment is a process by which social movement organizations attract individual new recruits; it seeks to convince individuals that their interests, values, and beliefs are complementary to those of the SMO.

The anti-nuclear movement, like most social movements, contains a variety of SMOs—some professional, some amateur, some radical, and some conservative. Although professional organizers provide many benefits, successful social movements also require the passion and commitment of those personally involved. These North Carolinians are protesting the location of a nuclear energy plant in their neighborhood.

with other movement activists. No matter how deeply committed they are ideologically to the movement, if they are not part of a network of others with similar convictions, they are unlikely to be more than token members (McAdam 1986).

Bloc Mobilization.   In addition to converting or mobilizing adherents one at a time through frame alignment processes, social movement organizations also use a strategy called **bloc mobilization** to recruit other organizations to support their cause. For example, the anti-pornography movement has asked for and received support from PTAs, fundamentalist churches, and feminist organizations.

Bloc mobilization is a very effective way to expand a movement's resources: It means access to other organizations' newsletters, members, and funds. It is, however, only suitable for social movements that make very low demands on their members. It would not be an effective means of recruiting members to a radical religious sect or to an extremist political group.

The Free-Rider Problem.   A serious problem that plagues all social movements is what is called the "free rider." The free rider is somebody who will benefit from the social movement but who declines to participate. The free rider sits back and lets others write the letters and do the demonstrating; he or she is glad that somebody is finally doing something about it but cannot be bothered to do more than sound supportive. For example, there are likely to be more than 1 million abortions this year; few of these women will participate in the prochoice movement. Similarly, only a tiny fraction of people who stand to benefit from a better environment participate in the environmental movement. How serious a problem are free riders?

Studies of social movement success document that, with equal resources and organization, a social movement that represents a larger group will be more effective (Oliver and Marwell 1988). Policy makers are more likely to listen if you represent the views of 100 million people than if you represent the interests of 300 people. Free riders can contribute to the social movement's success if polls show that the number of passive supporters of a movement is very large. The most successful movements, of course, are consistently "working their margins"—trying to convert free riders into active participants (Ennis and Schrauer 1987).

Networks and Mobilization.   According to resource mobilization theory, the likelihood that a grievance will be translated into an effective social movement is highly related to the existing linkages between aggrieved parties. This argument is illustrated in an example developed by Gerald Marwell and his associates (1988). Assume there are two cities, Alpha and Beta, each of which has passed a law saying that all city employees must live within the city limits. The law provides a one-year period during which city employees who live in the suburbs can either move into the city or look for other employment. This year also provides time for the suburban employees to organize a social movement to change the law.

In each city, there are 400 suburban employees that will be affected by the law. These people form a public or constituency for a social movement.

They can work with others to turn this constituency into an organized movement, or they can hope that somebody else will do it. Of course, if everybody falls into the free-rider category, nothing will get done, and all the suburban employees will lose their jobs. What is the likelihood that an effective social movement will develop?

Resource mobilization theory suggests that the answer depends on the degree of organization. Organization, in turn, depends significantly on the size and density of the social networks in Alpha and Beta. In Marwell and associates' example,

> Alpha is fairly isolated, and most of its affected employees live in a single suburb, Centauri. They attend Centauri's churches; their children attend Centauri's public schools; they belong to Centauri chapters of social and service clubs; they are all served by the same local telephone exchange. In contrast, Beta is part of an ethnically diverse two-state megalopolis, and its affected employees are scattered across a dozen different suburbs in two states and four counties. Thus, they rarely see one another after work. They go to different churches, send their children to different schools, read four or five different newspapers, and pay toll charges for telephone calls between many of the suburbs (Marwell, Oliver, and Prahl 1988, 505).

It doesn't take a Ph.D in sociology to guess that the employees in Alpha are much more likely to form an effective social movement. The network already exists; the employees need only mobilize it for the purpose of protecting their jobs. They do not need to form new mailing lists or write new newsletters; they can probably put free notices of their meetings in church bulletins or announce them at softball games.

Research confirms that dense social networks (where everyone is linked to everyone else) are important in promoting effective social movements. This high density reduces the cost of mobilization because every person can be reached quickly. High density also increases arousal: Each person can be reached through many network links, and this multiple-channel contact increases the likelihood that the individual will become involved in the movement.

FACTORS ASSOCIATED WITH MOVEMENT SUCCESS

Empirical analysis of social movements in the United States and around the world suggests that a number of factors are important to the success of a movement (G. Marx 1971):

1. The demands of the movement are seen to be consistent with the broader values of society. For example, the movement seeks to increase freedom or reduce injustice.

2. The movement has the support of influential third parties or can demonstrate that its demands will benefit other groups as well. For example, the abolitionist movement gained the support of the early feminist movement because women believed that extending suffrage to blacks would help women gain suffrage.

3. The movement's demands are concrete and focused. A protest against a specific urban renewal project is more likely to succeed than is a general protest against poor housing.

Whenever a social movement starts to get a lot of publicity and it appears that it may affect public policy, a countermovement tends to develop to support the status quo. These demonstrators marching in support of nuclear power are an example. Because countermovements generally support existing or traditional social arrangements, their members tend to be more conservative than the members of social movements. These are the same people who benefit from the current arrangements and thus want to maintain them.

4. The movement is able to exert pressure directly on the responsible party without harming uninvolved third parties. For example, a fruit boycott that hurts truckers as well as fruit growers will generate more opposition and less support.

5. The movement adopts techniques with which the authorities have had little experience. The nonviolent sit-in had tremendous impact when it was first employed during the early civil rights movement; in 1980, however, hundreds of protestors sitting in at the Seabrook Nuclear Plant were hauled away with little publicity and little effect. The police now know how to deal with the tactic, and the media no longer find it newsworthy.

6. Neutral third parties who have an interest in restoring harmony are present.

7. The movement's demands are negotiable rather than absolute.

8. The movement's demands involve a request for acceptance of social diversity, equal treatment, or inclusion, rather than a fundamental redistribution of income and power.

9. The movement seeks to veto proposed policies rather than implement new ones.

10. The movement is large enough to organize itself for conflict but not so large as to be perceived as a serious threat to the dominant group.

COUNTERMOVEMENTS

A **countermovement** seeks to reverse or resist change advocated by a social movement.

A major and growing category of social movements is the **countermovement,** which seeks to reverse or resist change advocated by a social movement (Lo 1982; Mottl 1980). Countermovements are almost always right wing in orientation. They seek to maintain traditional structures of status, power, and values.

Resource mobilization theory is particularly appropriate for understanding countermovements. Because they defend the status quo, they are often closely tied to vested-interest groups (Lo 1982; Mottl 1980), and bloc mobilization is a chief means of recruiting members and resources.

The anti-ERA movement is an excellent case study of a countermovement. The movement made heavy use of bloc mobilization strategies, tapping into the organizational resources of the anti-abortion movement, fundamentalist Protestant churches, the John Birch Society, and the American Farm Bureau. One of the most interesting features of the movement was the strategy used to portray its goals. As noted in the preceding section, successful movements claim to be supporting social values, not denying them. Thus, the anti-ERA movement could hardly campaign on the basis of being against equality. Instead, its rhetoric claimed to be supporting traditional values of family, motherhood, and womanhood, which were supposedly under attack by lesbians and other dissatisfied women (Marshall 1985).

A Case Study: The Gay Rights Movement

In recent Western thought, homosexuality has been considered a sin or a sickness. As a result, it has often been furtive and concealed. An active social movement now exists to change this situation. Like many social movements, it is diverse and fragmented, replete with competing SMOs and even a countermovement.

History of the Gay Rights Movement.   Homosexual acts are illegal in most states. Homosexuals are barred from service in the military and are dishonorably discharged if discovered; they are often barred from teaching in public schools; and they may be denied custody of their children and, in some cases, even visiting rights. Until a few years ago, they were barred from employment in the federal civil service and from immigration to the United States. In addition, they may be shunned by their family and co-workers, forced out of their jobs, and subjected to taunts and jeers.

As a result, most homosexuals have concealed their sexual preference. As long as they did so, there could be no social movement. For a movement to exist, there must be a group of people who acknowledge to themselves and to one another that they are members of the same group and share a common interest.

The beginning of the gay rights movement came when sufficient numbers of prominent individuals were willing to step forward and define themselves as homosexuals. This development began in Germany at the end of the 19th century. It was abruptly halted by Hitler, who included homosexuals among the undesirables of the world and who sent known homosexuals to concentration camps. In the United States, the gay rights movement began in the 1920s, when the Society for Human Rights was established to "protect the rights of people who by reasons of mental and physical abnormalities are abused and hindered in the legal pursuit of the happiness which is guaranteed by the Declaration of Independence" (cited in Altman 1983, 133). The organizers were quickly driven back into the closet by a police raid, and it was not until after World War II that the two founding SMOs of the gay rights movement—the Mattachine Society for male homosexuals and the Daughters of Bilitis for female homosexuals—were founded.

The early gay rights movement, as indicated in the preceding quote, seemed to accept society's view of its members as handicapped and abnormal. During the 1960s and 1970s, this view changed radically. Gay activists began to demand not just tolerance, not just the absence of persecution, but acceptance. They wanted homosexuality to be recognized simply as a variation of sexual orientation—not viewed as sin or sickness.

The Current Movement.   The gay rights movement is not unified. It is divided by sex, class, race, and political ideology. Broadly, however, the movement seeks to do five things (Altman 1983, 122):

1. *To define a gay community and a gay identity.* The movement seeks to help gay individuals realize they are not alone. As C. Wright Mills might have put it, movement members want homosexuals to recognize that their problems are not merely personal troubles but are shared by others.
2. *To establish the legitimacy of a gay identity.* The movement seeks to reduce the shame and internalized self-hatred that some homosexuals, who were socialized to believe they were wicked and sick, experience.
3. *To achieve civil rights for homosexuals.* The movement seeks to decriminalize homosexual acts and to establish antidiscrimination laws to protect homosexuals.
4. *To challenge the general ascription of gender roles in society.* The movement seeks to give people the right to choose roles rather than being forced to act out a role thrust on them by reason of their sex.
5. *To secure family rights.* The most recent goal of the movement is to allow gay couples the same legal rights as those of other couples, such as health insurance or survivor's benefits for a partner.

Conflict Within the Movement.   There are several major schisms within the gay rights movement. The most important is that between men and

Public demonstrations by the Gay Rights movement are designed to bring homosexuality out of the closet, to make it seem a less deviant and dangerous practice. By publicly acknowledging their sexual preference, men such as the ones in this parade, force society to acknowledge that there are relatively large numbers of people—many of them apparently normal and decent people—who are homosexuals. Thus, the public demonstration is a particularly important weapon in the social movement for homosexual rights.

women. Homosexual men (gays) and women (lesbians) have some goals in common—in particular, civil rights goals. However, lesbians face a situation of double jeopardy. They may be discriminated against on the basis of sex as well as sexual preference. Lesbian women often believe that they will make more progress working with straight women than with gay men; they believe that improvements in the status of women (especially in economic terms) will be more beneficial than will general improvements for homosexuals. As a result, there is relatively little cooperation among male and female homosexual groups.

A second schism is of class and politics. On the one side are the middle-class professionals who wear gender-appropriate suits and insist that homosexuals are respectable, decent people—good parents, good credit risks, good neighbors. On the other side are people who insist that gay rights means the freedom to wear lavender and leather and who wish to dismantle the entire system of gender roles and status politics. These are, respectively, the people who want to tinker with the system—to extend the basic rights package just a little further—and the people who think that the whole system is a sham and want to overthrow it.

Successes, Failures, and Prospects. The gay rights movement has seen some notable successes. The American Psychological Association voted in 1974 to declare that homosexuality is not a sickness; Wisconsin and Massachusetts have passed laws making discrimination on the basis of sexual orientation illegal; and acknowledged homosexuals have been elected to public office, including that of U.S. senator. Public opinion polls show substantial increases in support for homosexual rights: Between 1987 and 1989, the proportion who said that job discrimination against homosexuals should be illegal jumped from 59 to 71 percent ("The Future" 1990). In offices and families around the country, it is becoming possible to be open about one's homosexuality without losing the respect of others.

There are still many homes, offices, and neighborhoods, however, where the position of an acknowledged homosexual would be awkward at best. The military remains adamantly opposed to having homosexuals in the armed forces, and in 24 states homosexual acts are still a crime. In addition to these assaults on their dignity, homosexuals also have a high risk of incurring physical assaults. "Gay bashing" is a relatively frequent recreational activity of young toughs, and homosexual activists claim that gays are seven times more likely than straights to be assaulted ("The Future" 1990).

Recently, the male homosexual community has been galvanized by the spectre of AIDS (acquired immundeficiency syndrome), an apparently incurable blood disease that by mid 1989 had killed 100,000 Americans. Although the disease is not confined to homosexuals, 73 percent of the AIDS sufferers are homosexual or bisexual men. Many gays believe that mandatory AIDS testing would be another form of discrimination. This new basis for stigmatizing gays, as well as their own often realistic health concerns, has given an impetus to organization. AIDS hotlines and information meetings have triggered homosexual networks that cut across class, race, and political cleavages. By increasing the solidarity of the group, these new networks may increase the effectiveness of the gay rights movement.

THE ROLE OF THE MASS MEDIA

THE MASS MEDIA AND COLLECTIVE BEHAVIOR

The mass media contribute to nonroutine collective behavior in three ways: (1) by publicizing the triggering event, (2) by demonstrating collective action techniques, and (3) by providing rationales for collective behavior.

Publicizing Events.   Obviously, the media are an important means of quickly spreading the news. If a police officer shoots a minority youth, it will be on radio and television within minutes and in the newspapers within hours. The media reach the isolated as well as the integrated, the passive as well as the active. The mass media publicize triggering events faster and more thoroughly than rumor can.

Demonstrating Techniques.   As Tilly (1979) has noted, each culture has a repertoire of possible collective actions. One of the ways this repertoire is now learned is by watching the evening news. Publicity surrounding one sit-in, riot, or crowd may stimulate a rash of similar events in other communities.

Providing Rationales.   Nonroutine collective actions are typically spontaneous reactions to nonroutine events. Although norms may emerge to justify the actions, they are not well thought out. Many would not stand up under careful consideration at a later time. The media's attempt to explain events to the public may provide better-developed rationales. Following the Sheffield soccer disaster, for example, many commentators explained how unemployment and government policy had made the disaster inevitable. As one liberal member of Parliament put it, these fans were "treated like dirt inside and outside of the stadium" ("Disaster" 1989).

THE MASS MEDIA AND SOCIAL MOVEMENTS

A social movement is a deliberate attempt to create change. To do so, it must reach the public and try to get public opinion on its side. The relationship between the media and social movements is one of mutual need. The movements need publicity, and the media need material. Sometimes both needs can be met satisfactorily. In this mutual exchange, however, most of the power belongs to the media. The media can affect a social movement's success by giving or withholding publicity and by slanting the story positively or negatively. What the media choose to cover "not only affects the success of the movement but also shapes its leadership and its meaning to the general public and to its own adherents—in short, what the movement actually is" (Molotch 1979, 81).

Media coverage is a vital mechanism through which resource-poor organizations can generate public debate over their grievance. What does an organization have to do to get news coverage? Empirical studies show that four factors are critical (Kielbowicz and Scherer 1986).

FOCUS ON YESTERDAY

A Dirty, Filthy Book

The practice of birth control became a trend in 18th-century France. Without the aid of any organized social movement, it spread from the urban bourgeoisie to the rural and poorer classes. It was in England and the United States that birth control became an organized social movement. A number of liberal reformers seized on excessive population as the chief cause of poverty and other social problems. These reformers suggested that the use of birth control by the poor would reduce welfare costs and, by decreasing the numbers of the poor, increase the demand for their labor and cause wages to rise.

In this period, a U.S. physician, Charles Knowlton, produced a book entitled *The Fruits of Philosophy: The Private Companion of Young Married People*. In it, he discussed coitus interruptus (withdrawal), but he favored postcoital douching; he stated that he was "quite confident that a liberal use of pretty cold water would be a never-failing preventative" (Himes 1936, 227). (In fact, douching is almost totally ineffective as a contraceptive.)

The advocates of birth control created their first SMO in 1860, with the formation of the Malthusian League. The movement did not take off, however, until 1877, when the British government prosecuted Annie Besant and Charles Bradlaugh for distributing Knowlton's book in England. The charge was distributing obscene material, and the resulting publicity was exactly what the new movement needed. The trial was widely reported in the only mass media of the day, the newspapers, which included the prosecutor's accusation that "this is a dirty, filthy book, and the test of it is that no human being would allow that book on his table, no decently educated English husband would allow even his wife to have it" (cited in Chandrasekhar 1981, 1). The methods and morals of birth control were given detailed discussion in the popular press, and sales of Knowlton's book went from only 1,000 a year to more than 200,000. In a groundswell of free publicity, Malthusian Leagues were formed in almost every Western nation. Among the reasons produced for using birth control were that it would reduce both the misery and numbers of the poor, make early marriage possible and thus eliminate prostitution, and even lead to world peace. The birth control movement was an idealistic social movement that hoped to improve society by reforming individuals. (In succeeding generations, the Women's Christian Temperance Union—WCTU—sought to achieve the same goals by getting everyone to give up alcohol.)

The first birth control clinic in the United States was opened by Margaret Sanger in 1916. Throughout New York City, she distributed 5,000 leaflets in Yiddish, Italian, and English. They began: "Mothers! Can you afford to have a large family? Do you want any more children? If not, why do you have them? DO NOT KILL DO NOT TAKE LIFE, BUT PREVENT." After her clinic had been open 10 days, the police closed it and arrested her on a charge of "maintaining a public nuisance." She was held overnight and released on bail; she immediately reopened the clinic and was rearrested and sentenced to 30 days in jail. After several more convictions, she established the first permanent clinic, in 1923.

The birth control movement challenged many cherished values. It was opposed by physicians on the ground that the practice was injurious to health, by moralists on the ground that it encouraged pleasure seeking without concern for the consequences, by traditionalists on the ground that it altered women's natural functions, by nationalists on the ground that there would be too few soldiers, and by legal authorities on

"This is a dirty, filthy book, and the test of it is that no human being would allow that book on his table, no decently educated English husband would allow even his wife to have it."

the ground that it was obscene. The birth control movement was ultimately successful and is now a part of the institutional structure rather than an attacker of it. In fact, the government itself is now the chief provider of contraceptives to the poor.

1. *Dramatic, visible events.* This is particularly important for television. Sit-ins and demonstrations are more newsworthy than news conferences, and both are more newsworthy than a pamphlet.

2. *Authoritative sources.* Journalists want to save time and gain credibility by going straight to the horse's mouth. This means they tend to rely on established leaders who have public recognition.

3. *Timing.* News is published or aired according to regular deadlines. If you want to be on the evening news, your action should be scheduled (so that the news cameras can be there) before three in the afternoon (so it can be edited before the news hour) on a day when not much else is going on.

4. *News nets.* Most reporters have a beat, a particular area of the news they cover. If your movement falls in the cracks, you are less likely to get coverage.

Because they rely on the media, social movements find themselves changing to maximize news coverage. The link between action and newsworthiness encourages direct action rather than more quiet forms of activity such as lobbying or letter writing. And, since the public gets tired of watching demonstrators hauled off, the degree of extremism necessary to get news coverage may escalate. This may lead to inflamed rhetoric, greater conflict within the movement, and disproportionate attention to publicity rather than to other movement goals. Of course, if the alternative is no publicity at all, then it may be a price the movement has to pay. Without free publicity, the cost to a social movement of spreading its message is greatly increased.

Trees, Owls, and the Environmental Movement

Being in favor of protecting the environment sounds like an innocuous position to take. After all, who is in favor of dirty air, dirty water, and disappearing species? By default, nearly all of us.

Ruining our environment is part of the status quo; it is part of our accepted way of life, of manufacturing and packaging merchandise, and of dealing with garbage. The average American produces 35 pounds of garbage each week, only a tiny fraction of which is recycled. Environmental protectionism will entail costs: higher-priced goods, more bother over recycling, more regulation, and fewer consumer goods. It is also likely to result in the loss of some jobs.

THE BATTLE FOR TREES AND OWLS.

The battle over environmental policy is being fought on many fronts—over nuclear power, hazardous wastes, forests, and habitat. One of the

most contentious in recent years has been the battle over protecting old-growth forests. These forests provide a unique habitat, and some species—notably the spotted owl—do not live anywhere else. Recently the lumber companies won the right to clear-cut 130,000 acres of old-growth forests in the Pacific Northwest. To environmentalists this is a tragic loss, but for loggers it creates much-needed jobs. A bumper sticker distributed during this highly acrimonious controversy said, "Save a logger. Kill an owl."

Radical environmentalists refer to lumber companies and developers as "eco-thugs." Environmentalists have not been much more complimentary about the government, which frequently finds itself caught in the middle. The U.S. Forest Service is a classic case. The service was set up to administer the logging and lumbering of U.S. forest land. Its major reason for being was to grow and protect forests and to create and maintain logging

Dave Foreman, cofounder of Earth First!, is arrested at a demonstration against logging old growth forests in Oregon State. Earth First! is one of the most radical of the SMOs within the environmental movement. It performs a useful function for the movement in making all the other environmental organizations seem pretty reasonable by comparison. Recently Foreman himself declared that there were too many hippies and leftists in Earth First! and began developing an alternative SMO.

roads *so that loggers could cut down the trees*. The forest service and the loggers were colleagues, not opponents.

In recent years, the environmental movement has challenged the U.S. Forest Service to protect the forests *from* the loggers, not *for* the loggers. This effort to affect public policy has been joined on two fronts: in the courts and legislatures and literally in the trees. The professional SMOs of the environmental movement—the Sierra Club, the National Audubon Society, and the Wilderness Society—pursue the first strategy. They write letters to congressional representatives to urge support for clean-air laws or to lobby against dam projects; they throw a battery of lawyers into the effort to get court injunctions against development projects.

The militants despise the professionals for selling out, for being willing to negotiate and compromise. Among their tactics are sit-ins and demonstrations (mostly legal) and "monkey wrenching" or sabotage (mostly very illegal). For example, they have cut power lines, spiked trees to prevent their being logged, and damaged bulldozers. The forest service refers to these people as the "violent fringe," but supporters claim that their only crime is "to protect 4 billion years of evolution [and] I'm proud to be associated with that sort of criminal element" ("Trying" 1990, 25).

Although militants have done much to publicize and galvanize the environmental movement, they cannot succeed by themselves. Throwing one's body in front of the bulldozers will buy a few days or weeks, but permanent victory involves court orders and legal battles. Thus, both professional and indigenous, both conservative and radical SMOs are helpful in pushing forward the movement.

Increasingly the movement has infiltrated government organizations. To the great dismay of its former allies, the forest service has expanded its mission to include providing recreation and protecting wildlife. This new mission puts the forest service in the middle of two angry groups, neither of which is willing to accept compromise. As a result, one forest service ranger jokes about being a "combat biologist" ("Oregon's" 1989). With the militants nipping at their heels, mainstream groups are likely to continue to take even stronger positions on the environment.

THE ENVIRONMENTAL MOVEMENT ASSESSED

One reason that federal agencies have changed their policies on trees is the absolute size of the environmental constituency. The last decade has witnessed a strong growth in concern for the environment, with large majorities saying they are willing to pay more taxes to clean up the environment. Not all of today's activists are left over hippies. Many of those involved in campaigns against hazardous waste and nuclear power, for example, are "just moms and dads who are willing to protect their children at any cost" ("Trying" 1990, 24).

The environmental movement has had some notable successes, and it is in a fair way to becoming partially institutionalized. Afraid of being buried in their own waste, many communities in the United States are experimenting with mandatory recycling. Nevertheless, there are many controversial issues left to be negotiated. It is estimated that two percent of the world's species will disappear every year. If every one of them produces battles the size of that now being fought over the spotted owl in the Pacific Northwest, we are in for a long and bloody war. As environmental protectionism starts to threaten the life-styles and livelihoods of people other than isolated loggers, we are likely to see more controversy rather than less.

Summary

1. Collective behavior and social movements, although related, are distinct activities. Collective behavior is spontaneous and strictly confined to a particular place and time; a social movement is organized, broad based, and long term.

2. Three theories explain crowd behavior: contagion theory, convergence theory, and emergent-norm theory. Emergent-norm theory is the dominant theoretical perspective today.

3. Although sporadic, episodic, and often outside the law, crowd behavior is not random. Each society has a repertoire of collective actions from which to choose. In contemporary society, the mass media are an important source of information about this repertoire.

4. Relative-deprivation and resource mobilization theories offer two different scenarios for why inequalities and cleavages result in social movements. Relative-deprivation theory stresses the eruption of anger over a sense of deprivation; resource mobilization theory stresses the coincidence of competition over scarce resources with organizational solidarity as a precondition for a social movement.

5. An integration of the two theories suggests that both a sense of grievance and organizational resources are important for an effective social movement to develop.

6. Each social movement contains a variety of social movement organizations (SMOs). Some are professional SMOs and some are indigenous SMOs. The variety of SMOs tends to enhance the movement's ability to mobilize resources.

7. Mobilization occurs at two levels: the recruitment of individual adherents (micromobilization) and the recruitment of sympathetic organizations (bloc mobilization). Bloc mobilization is faster but is less likely to attract committed activists.

8. Movements are more successful if their demands are consistent with a society's larger values, if they have an innovative and attention-getting strategy, and if they can gain the support of, or at least not harm, third-party organizations.

9. When a social movement threatens to be at least partially successful, a countermovement often develops to defend the status quo. Countermovements depend highly on bloc mobilization.

10. The mass media play an important and growing role in collective behavior and social movements. By publicizing incidents of collective behavior, the media increase the likelihood that these incidents will be known and repeated. Because resource-poor social movements depend on free publicity, they are often forced to become more extremist to continue attracting media coverage.

11. The environmental movement uses a variety of tactics in its effort to affect public policy, ranging from courtroom battles to ecoterrorism. Among the reasons for the movement's growing successes are the wide variety of SMOs within the movement and the size of its public constituency.

Suggested Readings

Ash, Roberta. 1972. Social Movements in America. Chicago: Markham Publishing. A general introduction to the study of social movements, followed by detailed histories of the most prominent social movements in the United States. The material on the temperance movement is particularly interesting.

Lofland, John. 1985. Protest: Studies of Collective Behavior and Social Movements. New Brunswick, N.J.: Transaction. This collection of essays covers a wide variety of collective behaviors and social movements from the 1960s until the present, but it gives special attention to the Unification Church (the Moonies).

Rubenstein, Richard. 1987. Alchemists of Revolution: Terrorism in the Modern World. New York: Basic Books. Although not discussed in this chapter, terrorism is one strategy that social movements use to affect public policy. Rubenstein's purpose is to show that terrorists are not necessarily crazier than the rest of us but that they choose terrorism as a strategy when there are no alternatives.

Sperling, Susan. 1988. Animal Liberators: Research and Morality. Berkeley: University of California Press. Reviews the issues behind the animal rights movement, including an analysis of the links between the animal rights movement and the feminist and environmental movements.

Walsh, Edward. 1988. Democracy in the Shadows: Citizen Mobilization in the Wake of the Accident at Three Mile Island. Westport, Conn.: Greenwood Press. An impassioned analysis of how citizens in New York state organized in response to a near meltdown at the Three Mile Island nuclear plant.

22

Have you ever ...

Considered what the future holds? Your most immediate concern is probably whether you can live through this semester, pay your bills, and keep your car running. Even those most hassled by personal problems, however, recognize that their own future is intimately tied with the future of the world and the nation. Will Gorbachev be able to reform the Soviet Union and still hold the nation together? How will the United States resolve its dependence on oil from the Middle East? Will the Amazon forest be destroyed and the holes in the ozone enlarged? How on earth will we cope with a world population of 10 billion people?

Although social change has brought many wonderful developments in the last decades—from the destruction of the Berlin Wall to the VCR, from the eradication of smallpox to the development of the computer—most of us have reason to be profoundly ambivalent about social change. Balanced against the many changes that have made life longer, better, and more convenient have been other less positive changes. The scourge of AIDS, the proliferation of nuclear weapons to the Third World, drug wars in Colombia, guerrilla warfare throughout Africa and Latin America, and the doubling of the world population all give reason for anxiety about the future.

This last chapter takes an international perspective on the same sorts of issues that we have considered in earlier parts of this book. Here we look at inequality, competition, capitalism, and democracy on an international rather than a national scale and consider what they portend for the future.

This chapter focuses on the political economy of the international system. The nations of the world are bound together by economic ties, by joint dependency on the oceans and the air, and by a common fear of the bomb. We are also united by the universal pursuit of higher standards of living. Because the prosperity and peace of each nation depend in part on the larger international context, we give detailed consideration to issues of world stratification and competition. We begin by introducing two theories of development. The body of the chapter consists of a series of case studies illustrating the dilemmas that four societies—China, Nicaragua, the Soviet Union, and the United States—face as they attempt to maximize their own interests in a changing international context.

INEQUALITY AND DEVELOPMENT

The central fact in the international political economy is the vast inequality that exists in today's world. In 1990, the average United States citizen produced $19,780 worth of goods and services; the average Kenyan citizen produced only $360 worth. The average American would live to age 74 compared to age 63 for the Kenyan (Population Reference Bureau 1990). The massive disparities that exist not only in wealth and health but also in security and justice are the driving mechanism of current international relationships.

Because massive inequality leads to political instability and unjustifiable disparities in health and happiness, nearly every nation—both more and less developed—thinks that reductions in international inequality are desirable. The most accepted way to do this is through development—that is, by raising the standard of living of the less developed nations.

What is development? First, development is *not* the same as Westernization. It does not necessarily entail monogamy, three-piece suits, or any other cultural practices associated with the Western world. **Development** refers to the process of increasing the productivity and raising the standard of living of a society, leading to longer life expectancies, better diets, more education, better housing, and more consumer goods.

Development refers to the process of increasing the productivity and standard of living of a society—longer life expectancies, more adequate diets, better education, better housing, and more consumer goods.

THREE WORLDS

Almost all societies in the world have development as a major goal: They want more education, higher standards of living, better health, and more productivity. Their prospects and strategies are shaped by unique historical circumstances and by their place in the international system.

In discussing international development, we use a common typology that classifies countries on the basis of their position in the international political economy. The **First World** consists of those rich nations that have relatively high degrees of economic and political autonomy: the United States, the Western European nations, Japan, Canada, Australia, and New Zealand. Taken together, these nations make up roughly 16 percent of the world's population, produce between 55 to 60 percent of the gross world product, and consume approximately 54 percent of the world's energy

The **First World** consists of those rich nations that have relatively high degrees of economic and political autonomy: the United States, Western Europe, Canada, Japan, Australia, and New Zealand.

(Chirot 1986). Politically, economically, scientifically, and technologically, they dominate the international political economy.

The **Second World** is comprised of the Soviet Union and the former Communist bloc nations in Eastern Europe. Its chief distinguishing characteristic is the degree to which it was barricaded behind the Iron Curtain and isolated from the world economy for 40 years. The Second World holds an intermediate position in the world political economy. It is richer than the Third World but has far lower standards of living than the First World. The crumbling of the Iron Curtain may make economic intermediacy the most compelling characteristic of Second World nations. In 1990, these nations represented roughly 9 percent of the world's population, produced between 22 and 25 percent of the gross world product, and consumed nearly one-fourth of its energy.

The remaining 75 percent of the world's population lives in the **Third World**—the less developed nations that are characterized by poverty and political weakness. Although these nations vary in their populations, political ideologies, and resources, they are all considerably behind the First and Second World in every measure of development. They produce only 20 percent of the world's gross product and consume approximately the same amount of the world's energy (see Figure 22.1).

Although many of the differences between nations are matters of culture, there is general consensus that rich is better than poor, security is better than insecurity, and health is better than sickness. No nation wants to be a Third World nation. What are the causes of current inequalities and what are the prospects for their relief? We examine two general theories of development—modernization and world system theory—and discuss their implications for resolving Third World disadvantage.

The **Second World** includes the Soviet Union and the nations of the former Communist bloc.

The **Third World** consists of the less developed nations that share a peripheral or marginal status in the world capitalist system.

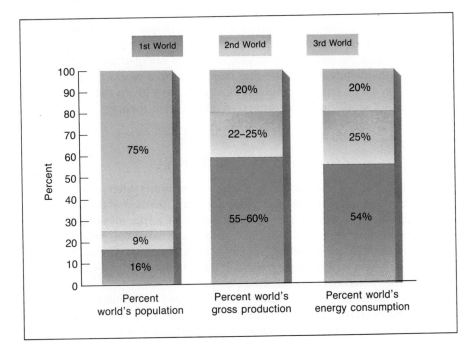

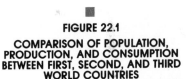

FIGURE 22.1

COMPARISON OF POPULATION, PRODUCTION, AND CONSUMPTION BETWEEN FIRST, SECOND, AND THIRD WORLD COUNTRIES

Modernization theory see development as the natural unfolding of an evolutionary process in which societies go from simple to complex institutional structures and from primary to secondary and tertiary production.

■

Despite the rapidity with which new ideas and new technologies can be diffused throughout the world, a very large share of the world's population does not share in the increased standard of living that development makes possible. Throughout much of the world, rickshaws, bicycles, mules, and good old feet are more common modes of transportation than are automobiles. In China there is only one car for every 1,374 people.

MODERNIZATION THEORY

Modernization theory sees development as the natural unfolding of an evolutionary process in which societies go from simple to complex institutional structures and from primary to secondary and tertiary production. This is a structural-functional theory based on the premise that adaptation is the chief determinant of social structures. According to this perspective, developed nations are merely ahead of the developing nations in a natural evolutionary process. Given time, the developing nations will catch up.

Modernization theory was very popular in the 1950s and 1960s. It implied that developing nations would follow pretty much the same path as the developed nations. Greater productivity through industrialization would lead to greater surpluses, which could be used to improve health and education and technology. Initial expansion of industrialization would lead to a spiral of ever-increasing productivity and a high standard of living. These theorists believed this process would occur more rapidly in the Third World than it had in Europe because of the direct introduction of Western-style education, health care, and technology (Chodak, 1973).

From today's vantage point, modernization theory seems naïve. The less developed countries have not caught up with the developed world. In many cases, the poor have become poorer, while the rich have become richer.

Why haven't the less developed nations followed in our footsteps to modernization? The primary reason is that they face an entirely different context: Population, environment, and world social organization are all vastly different now than they were in the 17th and 18th centuries. England, for example, was able to rely on surpluses extracted from her colonies in order to fuel industrialization. When improving conditions caused an overpopulation problem in the 19th century, the excess population was able to migrate to America and Australia.

The developing nations of the late 20th century face many obstacles not faced by earlier developers: population pressures of much greater magnitude and with no escape valve, environments ravaged by early colonialists, plus the disadvantage of being latecomers to a world market that is already carved up. These formidable obstacles have given rise to an alternative view of world modernization—world system theory.

WORLD SYSTEM THEORY

The entire world may be viewed as a single economic system that has been dominated by capitalism for the past 200 years. Nation-states and large multinational corporations are the chief actors in a free market system in which goods, services, and labor are organized to maximize profits (Chirot 1986; Turner and Musick 1985). This organization includes an international division of labor where some nations extract raw materials and others fabricate raw materials into finished products.

Nation-states can pursue a variety of strategies to maximize their profits on the world market. They can capture markets forcibly through invasion, they can try to manipulate markets through treaties or other special arrangements, or they can simply do the international equivalent of building

This combine in the American middle west will help reap a bountiful harvest of wheat. This bounty may not do anybody much good though. Because the people who need it most cannot afford to pay for it, the farmers will make little money and people will go hungry. The world economic system is capitalistic: goods and services are distributed on a for-profit basis.

a better mousetrap. The Japanese auto industry (indeed, all of Japanese industry) is a successful example of the latter strategy.

On a global basis, capitalism operates with less restraint than it does within any single nation. There is no organized equivalent of welfare or Medicaid to take care of indigent nations. In the absence of a world political structure, economic activity is regulated only by market forces such as supply and demand (Turner and Musick 1985).

World system theory is a conflict analysis of the economic relationships between developed and developing countries. It looks at this economic system with a distinctly Marxist eye. Developed countries are the bourgeoisie of the world capitalist system, and underdeveloped and developing countries are the proletariat. The division of labor between them is supported by a prevailing ideology (capitalism) and kept in place by an exploitive ruling class (rich countries and multinationals), which seeks to maximize its benefits at the expense of the working class (underdeveloped and developing countries).

World system theory distinguishes two classes of nations: core societies and peripheral societies. **Core societies** are rich, powerful nations that are economically diversified and relatively free of outside control. They arrive at their position of dominance, in part, through exploiting the periphery. On an international level, they are very similar to the industrial core of the United State's dual economy (Chapter 16).

Peripheral societies, by contrast, are poor and weak, with highly specialized economies over which they have relatively little control (Chirot 1977). Like the small-business sector in the U.S. dual economy, peripheral societies are vulnerable to change and little able to control their environment. Some of the poorest countries rely heavily on a single cash crop for their export revenue. For example, 91 percent of the export earnings in Chad come from raw cotton; 97 percent of Uganda's total export is coffee; and Bangladesh, the most densely populated country in the world, pro-

World system theory is a conflict perspective of the economic relationships between developed and developing countries, the core and peripheral societies.

Core societies are rich, powerful nations that are economically diversified and relatively free of outside control.

Peripheral societies are poor and weak, with highly specialized economies over which they have relatively little control.

FOCUS ON MEASUREMENT

The Human Suffering Index

The differences among the world's nations are glaringly obvious: Developed countries are more politically stable and their people are healthier, more educated, and richer. How important are these differences? How do they affect the average person's day-to-day quality of life and hope for the future?

One approach to answering questions like these is to select variables that have been measured for each nation and compare the differences: illiteracy, unemployment, children in the work force, or physicians per capita. Analysts who use this approach are often restricted in the choice of variables. The variables used must meet at least three essential criteria. Comparable information must exist for all nations, the measures selected must be quantified in a similar way so that comparisons are valid, and the measures for each nation must be judged to be reliable and accurate. These standards mean that some comparisons simply cannot be made.

Analysts on the Population Crisis Committee have combined 10 measures that meet these criteria into a human suffering index (HSI) (Camp and Speidel 1987). The 10 criteria used to assess human suffering on a global basis are GNP per capita, inflation, growth of the labor force, urban population pressures, infant mortality, per-capita calorie supply, access to clean drinking water, per-capita energy consumption, adult literacy rate, and personal freedom. Each nation is ranked from 0 to 10 on each indicator. For example, Japan, with the lowest infant mortality in the world (fewer than 1 percent of Japanese infants die before their first birthday) gets a zero on this indicator; Ethiopia, where 15 percent of the infants die, gets a 10. The human suffering index adds the values on each of the 10 measures to obtain a single figure, ranging from 0 to 100, for each country.

More than two-thirds of the world's population live in countries with extreme or high measures of human suffering.

Scores on this index range from a low of 4 for Switzerland to scores of 91 and 95 for Angola and Mozambique. According to this index, more than two-thirds of the world's population live in countries with extreme or high measures of human suffering (Table 22.1). These countries are disproportionately located in Africa, Asia, and Latin America—Third World countries. By contrast, the nations with the lowest human suffering are either in Western Europe or North America.

The human suffering index can be criticized on a number of technical and conceptual grounds (Ahlburg 1988). An obvious problem is that it treats each of the 10 measures as equally important. For example, it treats physicians per capita as if this measure were as important as the infant mortality rate. Most of us, however, would agree that the infant mortality rate is a far more important indicator and that, if a nation can achieve a low infant mortality rate without doctors, this is fine. Another problem is that

TABLE 22.1

DISTRIBUTION OF WORLD POPULATION ON THE HUMAN SUFFERING INDEX, 1987

Nearly two-thirds of the world's population—all of Africa and large portions of Asia and South America—are classified as being high in human suffering. These people are increasingly aware of their disadvantaged conditions, and pressures for immediate change are growing. These pressures may destabilize political and economic patterns in the world system.

SCORE	HUMAN SUFFERING CATEGORY	PERCENTAGE OF WORLD POPULATION
0–24	Minimal	21%
25–49	Moderate	10
50–74	High	58
75–100	Extreme	11

SOURCE: Camp and Speidel 1987.

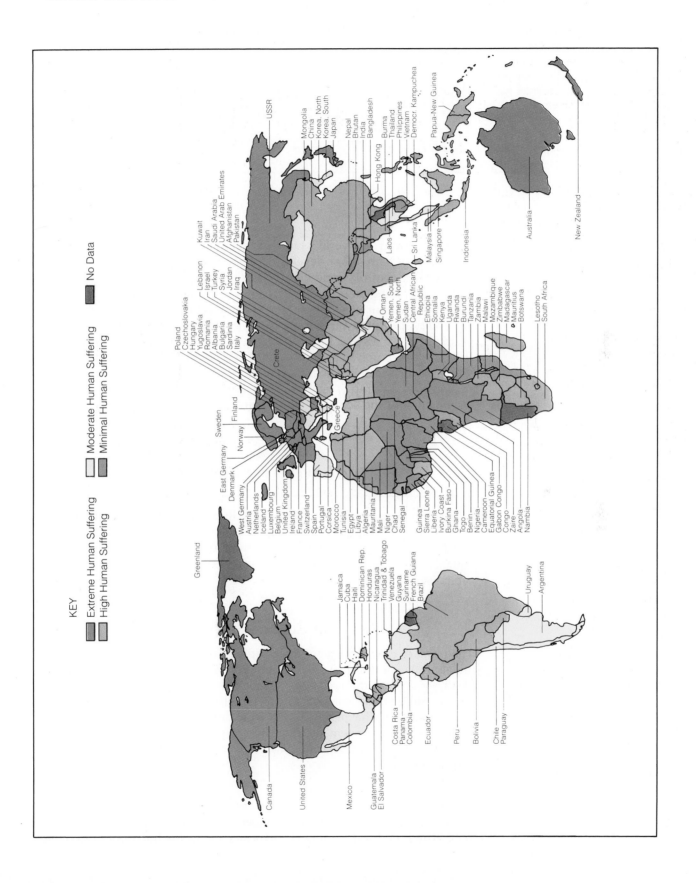

KEY

Extreme Human Suffering

High Human Suffering

Moderate Human Suffering

Minimal Human Suffering

No Data

some of the items included in the index—for example, growth in the labor force and growth in the population—are not in themselves good or bad. Certainly we would be reluctant to conclude that the fastest-growing U.S. states (California, Texas, and Florida) were experienc- ing "human suffering" on that account.

Despite these valid criticisms, the human suffering index developed by the Population Crisis Committee gives us a rough but generally accurate picture of where suffering occurs across the world. As Figure 22.2 so graphically demonstrates, this suffering is concentrated in the Southern Hemisphere. In the coming decades, it seems that the competition between East and West will be overshadowed by that between North and South.

vides 90 percent the world's jute (Europa Yearbook 1989). The economies of these and many other developing nations are vulnerable to conditions beyond their control: world demand, crop damage from infestation, flooding, drought, and so on.

A key element of world system theory is the connectedness between First World prosperity and Third World poverty. The message is clear: *Our prosperity is their poverty.* In other words, our inexpensive shoes, transistors, bananas, and so on depend on someone in a Third World nation getting low wages. Were their wages to rise, our prices would rise and our standard of living would drop. Testing the implications of this hypothesis requires examination of the actual forms of Third World dependency.

■

THIRD WORLD DEPENDENCY

Most contemporary scholars use some form of world system theory to understand development. Although many would reject the Marxist implications of the theory, there is general agreement that international inequality is the result of conflict and competition within an international capitalist economic framework.

FORMS OF ECONOMIC DEPENDENCY

The primary characteristic of the periphery is that these nations have relatively little control over their economies: They are dependent. In many cases, these dependent relationships represent a triple alliance among three actors: multinational corporations (generally based in the First World), the governments of the peripheral societies, and local elites. Scholars who study the world system identify three types of dependency (Bradshaw 1988): the classic "banana republic," industrial dependency, and foreign-capital dependency.

The Banana Republic.   The classic case of dependency occurs in a Third World nation whose economy is dependent on the export of raw materials—bananas, fruit, or minerals. African nations, the Indian subcontinent,

■

TABLE 22.2
COLOMBIA'S INTERNATIONAL TRADE

Colombia's international trade situation demonstrates the classic "banana republic" form of Third World dependency. Colombia's major exports are primary goods. Profits from primary goods are small and depend on low wages. Instead of gradually developing a modern economy, Colombia remains dependent on imports for industrial products.

Goods	Value (In Millions of U.S. dollars)
IMPORTS	
Mechanical and electrical equipment	$1,543
Chemical products	1,016
Transport equipment	729
Metals	563
Plastic and rubber goods	335
Vegetables and vegetable products	260
Paper and paper products	207
Mineral products	171
Food and drink	142
Textiles	137
TOTAL (incl. miscellaneous)	5,466
EXPORTS	
Raw coffee	$1,675
Fuel oil	331
Bananas	223
Cotton	112
Precious stones	60
Meat	31
Sugar	18
TOTAL (incl. miscellaneous)	3,878
NET BALANCE OF TRADE	−$1,588

SOURCE: Adapted from Europa Yearbook 1989, 749.

and Latin American countries have all fallen into this situation; many of the world's peripheral nations are still in it.

Colombia's economy provides an excellent example of a nation that still operates under the "banana republic" form of dependency. Table 22.2 provides a breakdown of the imports and exports from Colombia. This table illustrates the classic case of Third World dependency: Colombia exports raw materials and imports manufactured goods. Of course, the table omits one of Colombia's most profitable raw-material exports: cocaine.

Since bananas are cheaper than cars and printing presses, Colombia experiences a substantial trade deficit. In order to pay its debts, it must try to produce more and more export crops. This emphasis on production of export crops such as coffee and sugar reduces the nation's ability to feed itself and retards the development of economic diversity.

Industrial Dependency. Increasingly, multinational corporations are making use of one of the other major assets of less developed countries: cheap labor. Multinational corporations are setting up industrial assembly

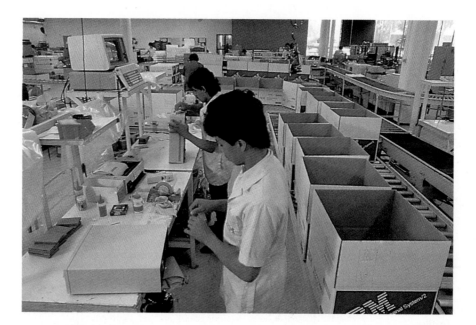

These workers in Guadalajara, Mexico are assembling IBM computers for the giant U.S. firm. By locating assembly plants in Third World nations, multinational firms realize huge savings in labor costs and U.S. consumers get cheaper products. Among the undesirable side effects, however, are loss of jobs for U.S. workers and the growth of inequality in Third World nations.

plants throughout the Third World. Third World assembly reduces labor costs dramatically (say from $10 an hour to $3 a day) and also reduces transportation costs for goods that will be sold in the Third World.

Many observers have hoped that investment in Third World industrial plants would provide jobs, spur development of indigenous subsidiary industries, and generally galvanize local economies. Empirical studies demonstrate that these good effects are seldom realized.

Consider, for example, the case of an international manufacturer of sewing machines who would like to build an assembly plant in sub-Saharan Africa (Bradshaw 1988). The plant will provide 1,000 jobs at wages that, while pitiful to North Americans, are attractive to local labor. The plant will use local material and labor to build its factory; its money will be funneled through local banks.

The assembly plant appears to be a plum worth having, and many nations are competing for it. This puts the manufacturing company in a position to bargain, and it is thus able to impose a variety of conditions on the government. These conditions usually include that the government provide guarantees on two points:

1. *No unionization:* The government must agree to outlaw unionization in general or otherwise to stop union movements in foreign plants. By guaranteeing that wages will remain low, the government becomes a party to the exploitation of its own people.
2. *No tax on corporate profits:* The multinational company that invests in a Third World country wants to take its money and run. It wants to take the profits back to the First World and distribute them among its stockholders. Thus, corporations try to negotiate sweetheart deals that will either excuse them from all tax on profits or provide them with a more favorable rate than that imposed on local companies.

What government would negotiate this kind of deal? The answer, of course, is only the poorest and most desperate. Nations with strong states and better indigenous economies are able to negotiate much better deals.

Foreign-Capital Dependency.   When there is a relatively strong indigenous elite, dependency may take the form of dependency on loans and investment (Wimberly 1990). In this case, the firms will be owned and operated by locals, rather than by foreign corporations. In theory, this should encourage development by providing additional capital.

Instead, the extension of loans to Third World nations has resulted in a dramatic debt crisis. Because of high inflation and worldwide recession in the early 1980s, many Third World countries suffered the double whammy of spiraling interest rates along with sharply reduced demands for their products. In order to meet their debt payments, Third Word nations had to reduce investment in their own economy and squeeze their own people even harder (Wimberly 1990).

THE CONSEQUENCES OF DEPENDENCY

By definition, dependency is a bad thing. It means that you do not have control—over your economy and perhaps over your government. Although ties to richer, stronger economies may theoretically be expected to benefit less developed nations, research does not bear out these sanguine expectations. Scholars have documented four primary consequences of foreign-capital penetration (Bradshaw 1988; Stokes and Anderson 1990; Wimberly 1990).

1. *Sectoral inequality:* The effort to develop the industrial infrastructure in order to attract foreign capital usually results in excessive investment in industrial and urban sectors and undesirably low investment in agricultural and rural sectors. Because the majority of the nation's population is likely to live in rural areas, this means that the many are ignored for the benefit of the few. Long-term consequences include reduced per-capita food production, increased investment in urban roads and airports at the expense of human welfare programs, and the growth of elephantine cities resulting from people's flight from the land. This is one reason for high rates of international migration, such as that from Mexico to the United States (Sassen 1988).

2. *Income inequality:* It is not surprising to learn that income inequality is one outcome of foreign-capital penetration: Low wages are what attract foreign capital in the first place. Agreements to keep wages low and prevent labor organization maintain and aggravate this condition. Low industrial wages, in turn, depress agricultural wages. (If urban wages were high, agricultural workers would need to be paid more to keep them on the farm.) There *are*, however, people who benefit from foreign-capital penetration. Generally, these are urban elites and the small urban middle class. These are the people who make the deals and manage the workers. Because these people are making more money while the workers are not, inequality grows.

World system theory argues that international capitalism is an important reason that Third World nations have not succeeded in reaching desired standards of living. Because profit making and competition drive international relationships, especially when the actors are multinational corporations, weak nations fall further and further behind. One consequence, according to this theory, is greater regime repressiveness and more conflict.

3. *Growing authoritarianism:* In order to entice foreign investors, governments are frequently forced to agree to keep wages low. This means that they must prevent unionization and many efforts at democratic reform. Certainly this may be done with the best of intentions, but it usually results in an antidemocratic regime that cooperates in the oppression of its own people.

4. *Conflict increases:* The end result of foreign-capital penetration is that a small local elite and the state ally themselves with foreign capital against their own people. Both the local elites and the foreigners are likely to invest their profits in American or European banks rather than in indigenous industries. Thus, investment in the nation may actually decrease. Certainly, anger and inequality grow. As a result, multinational penetration has been shown to increase the risk of political violence (London and Robinson 1989).

A substantial amount of research documents the undesirable consequences of foreign-capital penetration of Third World economies. (The implications of the word *penetrate* alone hint at these consequences.) Not only does it not bring prosperity but it often exacerbates poverty, inequality, and political instability.

CASE STUDIES: THE THIRD WORLD

To look more closely at the Third World, we will use two case studies: China and Nicaragua. One is a gigantic Asian nation that has tried to divorce itself from the world economy; the other is a small nation in the Western hemisphere with a history of "banana republic" dependency. Although both have very low incomes (see Table 22.3), they have very different problems and development strategies.

TABLE 22.3
COMPARISON OF FOUR NATIONS

In general, the more productive a nation is, the better the quality of life for its people. The correlation is far from perfect, however, as a comparison of China with Nicaragua and the Soviet Union will show. Despite very low income, China's life expectancy is substantially higher than Nicaragua's and nearly as high as the Soviet Union's.

	CHINA	NICARAGUA	SOVIET UNION	UNITED STATES
Human suffering index	50	67	19	8
Life expectancy	68	62	69	74
GNP per capita	$330	$830	$7,400	$19,780
Percentage of labor force in agriculture	61	42	17	3
Military expenditures per capita	$ 23	$215	$ 956	$ 1,077
People per car	1,374	unknown	24	2

SOURCES: Population Reference Bureau 1990; U.S. Bureau of the Census 1989a; Camp and Speidel 1987; Europa Yearbook 1989.

The People's Republic of China

On the surface, China is one of the poorest nations in the world; its people produce only $330 worth of goods and services per capita. Because of a commitment to equal distribution within the nation, however, China has a level of human welfare far higher than its gross national product would indicate. Life expectancy in China is 68 years, and its infant mortality rate is only 3.7 percent. Nearly all children attend primary and secondary school. On the other hand, with 1.1 billion people, one-fifth of the world's population, China faces a herculean task in increasing the productivity of its society and increasing its people's standard of living.

Background. Approximately 2,200 years ago, China was established as a united empire. Despite a succession of dynasties and invasions, the form of Chinese government and society remained remarkably constant over the ensuing millennia. Large masses of illiterate peasants supported small classes of merchants and imperial bureaucrats.

At the end of the 19th and beginning of the 20th century, many changes weakened this imperial structure. Foreign missionaries and trade, Japanese invasion, commercial competition, the sale of opium, and colonialism all attacked the legitimacy of traditional Chinese customs and institutions. Finally, in 1911, the empire was toppled in a revolution led by Sun Yat-sen. The republic he founded, however, had little institutional support and many external difficulties. By 1919, China had fallen into a civil war that was to last a full 30 years, through the Japanese occupation of World War II. Finally, in 1949, Communist forces under Mao Ze-dong won a definitive victory, and China experienced relative peace for the first time since the revolution. From that time to the present, China has been an authoritarian state governed by the Chinese Communist Party (CCP).

Nearly 80 percent of China's population still lives in rural areas. Because China is one of the poorest nations in the world, it cannot afford expensive equipment or fertilizers. As a result, Chinese agriculture is still very labor intensive. Recent reforms have sharply increased the productivity of Chinese agriculture, however, and China has been able to feed its one billion people without foreign assistance.

China After the Revolution.   In 1949, the CCP claimed leadership of a country that was disorganized, half starved, and exhausted. Civil wars, natural disasters, and foreign invasion had left China in shambles. The most immediate objective of the CCP was the rehabilitation of the national economy through gaining control over key industries (banking, trade, railways, steel) and securing agricultural land. Major investments were made in heavy industry, and market forces were initially allowed to determine the prices and allocation of agricultural resources. Gradually, the economy was nationalized, beginning with the establishment of agricultural collectives.

In further efforts to enhance economic development, promote egalitarianism, and consolidate political power, the CCP introduced numerous reforms between 1956 and the present. The most important of these reforms are the Great Leap Forward, the Cultural Revolution, and the Four Modernizations (Coye, Livingston, and Highland 1984).

THE GREAT LEAP FORWARD (1958–66).   Impatient with the slow pace of development, Mao initiated the Great Leap Forward (GLF) program to speed up China's progress toward socialism and higher productivity. The key to this program was decentralization. By reducing the central government's role in planning, Mao hoped to eliminate the stifling effects of bureaucracy. He hoped that encouragement of local initiative would make workers more creative, intensive, and dedicated. Greater efficiency was expected to result from each community devising solutions to and technologies for their unique problems. In the short run, however, the major outcome was that each community was thrown on its own resources without direction or help from the central government.

By a terrible coincidence, the GLF overlapped with a severe and sustained drought. This period also coincided with the withdrawal of Soviet aid to China, including technical experts in agriculture and industry. The combined effects of disorganization due to the GLF, drought, and withdrawal of Soviet aid caused grain production to fall 20 percent between 1957 and 1961. Between 1958 and 1961, China experienced the worst famine in human history: Recent estimates indicate that 30 million people may have died from starvation and malnutrition during this period ("China's Demographic" 1985).

The coincidence of the GLF with drought and Soviet withdrawal makes it difficult to assess the GLF. Some of the decline in agricultural production may have been due to the GLF program itself: Problems in higher-level communal organization, misinformation about collective production, lack of incentives to farmers, and rapid urbanization have been noted. It is also possible, however, that the collective organizations fostered by the GLF helped to soften the consequences of drought-induced food shortage by encouraging more equitable distribution of food and medical supplies (Fitzgerald 1984).

THE GREAT PROLETARIAN CULTURAL REVOLUTION (1966–76).   In the early 1960s, Mao became increasingly concerned about the danger that the Chinese Communist Party would become a new ruling class. To prevent this, in 1966 he launched a push for radical egalitarianism that has been called the Great Proletarian Cultural Revolution, or, more commonly, simply the Cultural Revolution.

For more than 30 years after the revolution, China withdrew from the world economic system, seeking neither foreign investment nor foreign trade. Within the last few years, however, China's leaders have decided that cooperation with foreign firms may help them develop more quickly. This woman is assembling American Motors' jeeps at a plant in Beijing.

Radical egalitarianism was to be achieved by purging the culture of the remnants of Imperial China and capitalism, transforming the schools into political training grounds, teaching urbanites humility by sending them to work with the peasants in the countryside, reducing economic centralization, and eliminating all market forces.

A principle mechanism for carrying out the Cultural Revolution was the Red Guard, a movement of militant youth who ransacked libraries, museums, and temples, destroying historical treasures, cultural artifacts, and symbols of intellectual elitism and capitalism. The consumers and producers of these materials (scholars, writers, poets, and artists), as well as some of the party's old-guard leadership, were publicly shamed and denounced. The result was chaos and destruction; schools and universities were abandoned and the economy stagnated. Eventually, the army was used to quell the Red Guard. After a decade of disruption, the Central Committee of the CCP in 1978 officially denounced Mao's Cultural Revolution as a major setback for China (Bonavia 1984).

THE FOUR MODERNIZATIONS (1975–PRESENT).   After Mao's death in 1976, his successor, Deng Xiaoping, promoted a new economic policy aimed at reducing the control of the central government and reintroducing market mechanisms into the economy. Four areas are targeted for modernization: agriculture, industry, defense, and science and technology (Sidel and Sidel 1984). Since 1978, the Four Modernizations has become a national campaign slogan throughout China.

A major thrust of the new policy is ridding society of the low productivity associated with the "iron rice bowl" system, where workers were guaranteed an income and lifetime employment regardless of productivity. Deng's modernization program replaced the iron rice bowl with an "individual responsibility" system based on production incentives. Although incentives vary in scope, they include capitalist-style practices such as promotion based on merit and a system of bonuses and penalties in factories. Agricultural production has been reorganized on a for-profit basis through a system of long-term leases to individuals and families. Deng also endorsed an open-door policy with the West to encourage educational exchanges, foreign trade, and foreign investments in banking and industry. Since the late 1970s, China's authoritarian political structure has also become less centralized.

These reforms are revolutionary. They are speeding up development, but they are also changing the ideological basis of modern China. The Four Modernizations actively encourage inequality (Chirot 1986). Whether Deng's policies will result in a permanent shift toward capitalism cannot be predicted. The most recent evidence, however, signals important changes in the direction of free enterprise, economic development, and government decentralization.

Current Concerns and Future Directions.   In regard to world system theory, one of the most unique characteristics of China's recent history is that, from 1949 to 1986, China rejected all foreign investment (Soviet aid during the 1950s is an important exception). In effect, China opted out of the world system (Walder 1989), and this may have something to do with its continued agricultural self-sufficiency as well as its accomplishments in terms of human welfare. In 1986, however, China announced its open-door policy. Limited foreign investment would be allowed in "special economic zones" along the coast. With a market of over 1 billion people and cheap labor, this was attractive for multinationals. Unlike many Third World nations, however, China has a very strong state that is able to negotiate terms favorable to itself and its people. China and the Chinese people are much more likely to share in the benefits of foreign-capital penetration than are the people of Central America.

Of most concern is China's political future. China stands virtually alone in the world now in its endorsement of strict Marxist-Leninism. China has experimented with limited capitalism, with the result that productivity and standards of living have risen. The massacre at Tienanmen Square in June 1989, however, indicates that China's government is not yet willing to relax its authoritarian political system. Whether China can continue to stand alone is unclear. The fact that Chinese dissidents have managed to fax their stories to confederates in other countries and that the massacre was recorded on personal camcorders to be passed around through a dissident underground suggests that maintaining an authoritarian regime is not as easy as it once was.

NICARAGUA

Nicaragua, a Third World country located in Central America, has a predominantly agricultural economy. Approximately 45 percent of the total labor force engages in farming, and roughly 88 percent of all export earnings come from cotton, coffee, sugar, bananas, and meat (Europa Yearbook 1989). Nicaragua has the largest land area in Central America, with a population of 3.9 million and an annual growth rate of 3.3 percent. Quality of life, as measured on the human suffering index (see the "Focus on Measurement" section in this chapter), is low. Despite a per-capita productivity figure nearly three times that of China ($830), life expectancy is only 62 years and the human suffering index score is 67.

Background.   For most of the 20th century, Nicaragua's political, economic, and social structures have been strongly affected by foreign investment and intervention. In the early 1900s, foreign companies (mostly from the United States) invested heavily in timber, bananas, and mining, extracting raw resources for export to international markets. These international firms and the local elites who worked with them controlled Nicaragua's political and economic life for their own benefit.

From the beginning, this external economic control caused dissension and conflict. Because political unrest threatened U.S. economic interests, the U.S. Marines occupied Nicaragua from 1912 to 1933. During this period, opposition to the U.S. military presence was led by Augusto César Sandino. The opposition was not successful, however, and U.S. forces did not withdraw until a pro-U.S. military government was established under General Anastasio Somoza García. Shortly thereafter, opposition leader Sandino was assassinated, reputedly by Somoza's agents.

The Somoza Dictatorship.   The Somoza family established a dictatorship in Nicaragua that was to last for 43 years. In cooperation with foreign investors, the Somoza family and a small ruling elite amassed fortunes, acquiring ownership of approximately 20 percent of the arable land. Class differences between this small ruling elite and the large peasant population grew, as did significant environmental problems (erosion, pesticide pollution, deforestation, and so on). All of these problems were rooted in the

By most international standards, Nicaragua is a poor nation. Its GNP per capita is only about 5 percent of that in the United States. Nicaragua's problems are exacerbated by sharp inequality, by an economy that has been too heavily dependent on foreign trade, and by a civil war that served as a surrogate war for the superpowers.

pillage of natural resources by local elites and foreign corporations (Karliner, Faber, and Rice 1986; Spalding 1987).

During the Somoza dictatorship, the opposition—called Sandinistas in honor of slain opposition leader Sandino—continued. Civil war erupted in the late 1950s, and the dictatorship became more authoritarian in an attempt to control dissent. As conditions worsened, the opposition broadened to include leaders from business and the Roman Catholic church. By 1979, the FSLN (Sandinista National Liberation Front) had gained enough support in the cities, towns, and countryside to cause a revolution overthrowing the Somoza dictatorship.

Socialist Democracy.   The revolution set up a provisional government, restored some civil rights lost under martial law, and drafted a new constitution. It aimed to create a mixed economy, with many socialized and cooperative enterprises mixed with a free-market economy. The new government strategy for development called for independence from foreign investment. Instead of selling raw materials, Nicaragua aimed to develop secondary industries that would manufacture raw materials into export goods (Wheelock 1986). During its first five years in power, there were substantial improvements in health care, education, and agricultural productivity (Garfield and Taboada 1986; Rosset and Vandermeer 1986).

In 1984, the military government was succeeded by a more-or-less civilian government when Daniel Ortega, former leader of the Sandinista People's Army, was elected president. The United States government, however, refused to recognize the election as valid and declared its intention to remove the Sandinistas from office. In 1985, the U.S. imposed a trade embargo on Nicaraguan goods. Because the U.S. had been receiving two times more Nicaraguan goods than any other trading partner, the embargo had the temporary effect of reducing Nicaragua's income substantially. The U.S. also attacked the Sandinista government directly by providing arms and technical assistance for regime opponents, the Contras. In 1986, the International Court of Justice in Geneva ruled that the U.S. had violated international law in trying to overthrow Nicaragua's elected government (Europa Yearbook 1989).

To a significant extent because of continued U.S. support for the Contras, Nicaragua was embroiled in a civil war from 1985 to 1989. During this time, incomes and productivity fell and infant mortality rose. The civil war ended in 1989. In March 1990 a second presidential election resulted in Daniel Ortega losing to U.S.-backed candidate Violeta Chamorro. Although Ortega's willingness to step down suggests that Nicaragua is more of a democracy than the U.S. government had thought, many problems remain. Nicaragua is a poorer country now than it was five years ago, and the people are bitter. Much remains to be worked out before Nicaragua can become a politically stable or economically prosperous nation.

Nicaragua remains very much a dependent Third World nation. If it is to develop successfully, it will need resources from abroad. Research suggests, however, that only if those resources take the form of foreign aid (gifts) will the new resources help Nicaragua on the road to development (Wimberly 1990). Foreign investment and loans are likely to help only the regime in power and its supporters.

CASE STUDIES: SECOND AND FIRST WORLDS

THE SECOND WORLD: THE SOVIET UNION

For 40 years, the Soviet Union dominated the Second World economically and politically. Geographically, the Soviet Union is the largest country in the world, having more than two times the land mass of Canada, the second largest country. A population of 291 million yields a relatively low population density (roughly 33 persons per square mile), although much of the population is concentrated in the west. The Soviet Union is a technologically advanced society that has used its resources to maintain a large military and police force at the expense of other economic developments. A bureaucratic, authoritarian government, backed by strong military and police force, has functioned to repress individual freedoms. In 1990, much of this is changing.

Background. In 1917, the Russian Empire was an authoritarian state badly weakened by massive losses from World War I. Disgruntled civilians and soldiers joined forces to topple the monarchy of Czar Nicholas II. After a period of political uncertainty and civil war, the Bolshevik wing of the Communist party gained control of the government, and the Soviet Union became the first nation to follow Marx's revolutionary path to socialism and economic development.

The goal of Marxism is to bring about a modern, efficient, egalitarian society based on collective rather than private ownership of the means of production. As interpreted by Lenin, however, communism included an additional and important non-Marxist element: the indefinite dictatorship of the party elite. Lenin believed that advancement toward an egalitarian state required the economy to be controlled by the state (through its agent, the Communist party) and that the state was justified in using force to regulate the daily lives of society's members to ensure progress (Acton 1986; Chirot 1986). Leninism, then, differs from Marxism in that it approves of the full use of state power, especially the military and police. Stalin, who gained control of the Communist party in 1928 following Lenin's death in 1924, expanded the role of the state police yet further.

A major priority after the 1917 revolution was reconstruction. To promote rapid economic growth, investments in heavy industry were given precedence over agriculture. Peasants were forced to become industrial laborers in urban centers, agriculture was collectivized, and personal consumption was restricted to divert additional resources into industry.

Although these policies and practices tripled industrial production during the 1930s, they were costly in terms of human lives and freedom. Massive forced internal migrations, deportations, arrests, jailings, and murder were common. Peasants protested forced collectivization in agriculture in the 1930s by burning crops, slaughtering livestock, and hiding grain, actions that triggered famine and starvation. As a result of Stalin's policies, it is estimated that between 1929 and 1949, 25 percent of the entire population had either died or been imprisoned. The total number of deaths resulting from these policies is estimated to be as high as 26 million (Chirot 1986, 149–54).

■

Seventy years after the communist revolution, the Soviet Union has been unable to deliver on its promises of a better standard of living for the Soviet people. Consumer goods such as food and socks are in very short supply, and shoppers have to wait in long lines for almost all of the basic staples. The necessity of devoting more resources to its internal productivity is one reason why the Soviet Union has reduced its militaristic posture.

The Soviet Union: 1945–1988.   During the long postwar era, the Soviets invested in defense, heavy industry, and foreign military aid at the expense of consumer goods. By the mid 1980s, the Soviets were spending between 12 and 15 percent of their total GNP on defense and another 2.5 percent for foreign aid to subsidize Eastern European allies and other dependent countries (such as Cuba and Vietnam).

Incapable of capturing markets through economic power, the Soviet Union relied on military domination to turn Eastern European nations into captive trading partners. In the Third World, the Soviet Union presented itself as a champion of the proletariat in the international class war. It urged developing nations to reject relationships with exploitive multinationals and First World nations and instead to ally themselves with the Communist bloc. The Soviets endorsed the right of subject peoples to employ force as a means of change, and they helped to underwrite the costs of revolution in Afghanistan, Vietnam, Angola, and Korea. In Soviet foreign policy, however, "liberation" meant liberation from capitalism rather than achievement of independence. Consequently, Soviet foreign policy sought to draw nations into its own network in an alignment against capitalism (McFarlane 1985).

Except for arms sales, the Soviet Union has not been a serious economic competitor in the world capitalist system. In a free market, neither its buying power nor its products have made it a major force. The Soviet commitment to a strong military, however, enabled it to control the economies of nearly 20 percent of the world's population and to have a powerful influence on world political events (Black 1986; Chirot 1986).

The cost of this strategy has been enormous. Although the Soviet Union has a low score on the human suffering index, it lags far behind the First World in productivity and standard of living. By the end of the 1980s, the

Soviet Union decided to admit the failure of its previous policies of central planning, domestic authoritarianism, and international militarism.

Prospects for the Future.   The Soviet Union's dynamic leader, Mikhail Gorbachev, has ambitious plans to restructure the Soviet government and economy and to carve out a new niche for the Soviet Union in the world economy. Two key elements are *glasnost* (political openness) and *perestroika* (reforming the economy by reducing central planning and making it more responsive to the market). So far, glasnost has had much more spectacular results than perestroika. Glasnost lies behind the crumbling of the Eastern bloc, the repudiation of the Communist party throughout Eastern Europe, and the move toward democracy within the Soviet Union.

Two serious problems plague Gorbachev's reform strategy. First, glasnost may lead not simply to the collapse of the empire but also to the collapse of the Soviet Union itself. At least seven of its republics (which are equivalent to U.S. states) are clamoring for independence. Second, economic restructuring has been halting and incomplete, and freedom has not been accompanied by productivity. If anything, productivity has fallen. Shelves are bare and people cannot get basic staples such as bread, soap, or socks. Economically, the Soviet Union now has much of the appearance of a Third World nation (Lipset 1990).

In terms of the Third World, the Soviet Union has admitted that its previous militaristic strategies have failed. Its military adventures have been costly, and they have not translated into political or economic gains (Kanet 1989). In fact, Soviet adventures in nations such as Afghanistan and Cambodia have drained domestic resources and alienated some of the Soviet Union's largest and most powerful neighbors, India and China. Thus, the new Soviet foreign policy calls for reduced military investment and increased economic ties with capitalist as well as socialist nations. The key to the success of this new policy will be an increase in Soviet productivity. For decades, the major Soviet export has been weapons. Whether the Soviets can beat their swords into plowshares is a formidable question. Until the Soviet economy has been restructured internally, it seems unlikely that their goods can compete in a free world market.

The First World: The United States

The United States is "the world's leading economic power" (Europa Yearbook 1989, 2,795). It has an extremely diversified economy and is in most respects self-sufficient, with the result that it has a great deal of economic independence. Although not the wealthiest nation in the world (that honor goes to Switzerland), the U.S. is very close to the top of the heap in every indicator of development. Productivity, life expectancy, education, and standard of living are all high.

Background.   The United States developed in a unique social and physical environment. Rich natural resources and a sparse population encouraged replacement of human labor with innovative technology. Commitment to mass education, the absence of military invasion, and exploitation of resources in undeveloped parts of the world (for example, Nicaragua)

The distribution of American soy meal in India, Ethiopia, and other troubled Third World countries serves many purposes: helping those in need, supporting U.S. farm prices, and furthering U.S. foreign policy objectives. The interdependence of the global food market is a potent symbol of the growing importance of the world political economy.

are additional reasons for the emergence of the United States as a dominant economic force (Turner and Musick 1986).

Still, it was not until the decade following World War II that the United States experienced unheralded prosperity. At the close of the war, the United States was the only core country not left in shambles. Industrial rearmament during the war provided jobs, fueled the economy, and boosted the nation out of its worst depression ever. While the industries of Europe and Asia had been demolished during the war, the industrial sector in the United States remained intact and in full swing. Thus, by the late 1940s, 60 percent of the world's total manufacturing output came from the United States (Chirot 1986).

Threats to Preeminence.   In the aftermath of the war, American assistance to countries in Western Europe and Asia (especially Japan) was instrumental in rebuilding cities and industries destroyed by the war. Foreign aid and credits were made available under the Marshall Plan in 1947, and in 1957 the core countries of Europe consolidated under the European Economic Community (EEC), also known as the Common Market. Both reconstruction and consolidation of the old core proved effective, causing the United States to lose some of its competitive advantage to other core countries in the world system.

Since World War II, the economy of the United States has shifted toward increased foreign investment and trade. Rather than invest profits in new equipment and technology in the United States, many U.S. corporations diversified into international markets for short-term profits. As a result, the productive capacities of U.S. factories and plants lost ground to core nations committed to maximizing long-term profit and modernizing their facilities. Since the 1960s, investments in secondary production (manufactured goods) have given way to a growing service economy (Chapter 16), which is consumption rather than production based. The overall effect of these changes is that America's share of manufactured products for world export has shrunk.

Future Prospects.   Although it is one of the most economically independent of all nations (unlike Japan and Germany, it does not depend heavily on imported energy), the prosperity and security of the U.S. are very much bound up in the international economy. Many of the goods we use in our everyday life have been made possible by the cheap labor of people in less developed countries.

The U.S. faces four challenges in the world economy. First, like Columbia and Nicaragua, we import more than we export. Many of our goods are not competitive on the international market. Second, the Third World debt crisis has resulted in a lot of bad debts for U.S. banks. This particular form of multinational capital penetration makes U.S. and other First World bankers very interested parties to foreign policy decisions. Third, we must decide how generous to be. After World War II, the Marshall Plan was essential in the redevelopment of Western Europe and Japan. There are now requests for a similar sort of investment in Eastern Europe. If this occurs, the Third World might lose out once again as U.S. and European nations look east rather than south. Finally, we must decide whether to intervene militarily in order to maintain access to international markets and resources on which the U.S. economy depends. The 1990 invasion of Kuwait by Iraq gave this question enormous urgency. Whatever the resolution, the issue reminds us of a lesson we learned in Chapter 9: Power is the most important determinant of the distribution of scare resource, internationally as well as locally.

War and Peace

In Chapter 1, we discussed the appropriate role of sociologists in studying social issues. Should sociologists be value free, or should they take a stand? The issues of war and peace bring this question into sharp focus. Although most sociologists continue to go about their business as if sociology were unrelated to issues of global war and peace, an increasingly vocal minority argues that it may be shortsighted to restrict our focus to racial integration, educational equity, or divorce when the world might end any day. These people state that sociologists can and should be actively involved in issues of war and peace. We conclude this text with a short analysis of world security and the role that sociologists can play.

THE COLD WAR

The Cold War began when East and West faced off in 1945 over the body of a defeated Germany. Neither Soviet nor U.S. troops withdrew from Germany for over 45 years after the end of the war. Both sides possessed vast arsenals of nuclear weapons and pursued a strategy dubbed, appropriately enough, MAD (mutual assured destruction). Since both sides had enough nuclear weapons to ensure the other's demise in case of an attack, the nuclear arsenal served as a deterrent to a hot war.

The Cold War put a strain on the budgets of both the Soviet Union and the United States. Because the Soviet economy is much less productive than that of the U.S., the Soviets had to devote a much larger share of their total GNP (15 to 17 percent) to defense than did the United States (5 to 7 percent) (Treverton 1990). In both nations, the arms race consumed not only money that could have been well spent elsewhere but also the best efforts of some of the nations' most talented engineers and scientists. No one can say that we would have cured cancer if the money and training had been spent on medical research rather

than on defense, but certainly the Cold War used up many resources.

THE COLD WAR FIZZLES

President Ronald Reagan presided over a massive peacetime arms buildup during the early 1980s, as the U.S. invested in half a dozen expensive and

SEEK AFTER PEACE
AND PURSUE IT
St. Bened

Rockport chapter

Children's Campaign for Nuclear Disarmament

ISSUES IN SOCIAL POLICY continued

---

experimental defense systems, such as the Strategic Defense Initiative (SDI or, more familiarly, Star Wars) and the B-2 bomber (Treverton 1990). Beginning in about 1985, however, the Cold War began to fizzle. The initiative was taken by the Soviet Union, and throughout the last half of the 1980s treaty talks were punctuated by periodic unilateral reductions of conventional forces and nuclear arsenals on both sides.

The Cold War didn't fizzle because we scared each other to death or because Gorbachev is a nicer guy than his predecessors. The Cold War fizzled largely because the Soviet Union couldn't afford it anymore (Bundy 1990). The Soviet Union's deepening economic crisis caused it to cast off the ideal of global Communist hegemony *and* to cut its defense budget. It has decided that it may be cheaper and more effective to trade with Eastern Europe than to occupy it, more profitable to trade with the U.S. than to threaten it.

NEW THREATS TO PEACE

Given the Soviet Union's precarious internal affairs, few observers recommend that the West cease to provide for its own defense. Nevertheless, many observers believe that the Third World may be a more legitimate source of peril. Nearly half a dozen Third World nations—Argentina, Brazil, India, Iraq, Pakistan, and South Africa—now have nuclear capacities. Moreover, we have less faith in our ability to scare these countries into not using their nuclear weapons. This suggests that we need to pay more attention to guerrilla wars and regional skirmishes.

Although it is possible that we can convince ourselves that Iraq or Libya is an "evil empire" (a title formerly reserved for the Soviet Union), it seems likely that we will have to look beyond the search for evil to understand new threats to world

peace. Issues such as inequality are likely to loom much larger than they have in the past.

WHAT CAN SOCIOLOGISTS DO?

What can sociologists contribute to protecting world peace? A few of the areas that can be pursued include the following:

1. *The study of conflict resolution.* A growing number of universities have special courses or programs on conflict resolution. These courses are concerned with the development of techniques for handling disputes and negotiating peaceful settlements (Katz 1989). Sociological research on topics such as small group decision making and organizational culture are relevant here.

2. *Developing social justice perspectives.* Sociological research can help us document the extent and causes of inequality and help us understand the role of inequality in promoting conflict.

3. *Developing practical development strategies.* Sociological research may help us understand which kinds of programs most effectively lead to improved well-being for Third World people. For example, we can evaluate the relative impacts of multinational investment, foreign aid, and investment loans.

The involvement of sociologists in issues of war and peace is not likely to be the crucial link in bringing about peace. We can be sure, however, that scholarly negligence of these issues is both shortsighted and immoral. To the extent that knowledge of the principles of human social behavior bears on issues of war and peace, we have an obligation—as scholars and citizens—to apply our knowledge to what is clearly one of the most critical policy issues of our century.

SUMMARY

1. Inequality is the key fact in the international political economy. Reductions of this disparity through development of less developed countries is a common international goal. Development is not the same as Westernization; it means increasing productivity and raising the standard of living.

2. Analysis of the world political economy often divides the world's nations into three categories. The First World consists of the rich, diversified, independent nations of the capitalist core. The Second World consists of the Soviet Union and the former Communist bloc countries. The Third World refers to those economically disadvantaged nations that have a peripheral status in the world economic system.

3. Modernization theory, a functionalist perspective of social change, rests on the assumption that less developed countries will evolve toward industrialization by adopting the technologies and social institutions used by the developed countries.

4. World system theory, a conflict perspective, views the world as a single economic system in which the already-industrialized countries control world resources and wealth at the expense of the less developed countries. The processes of economic exchange favor the developed countries so that the gap between rich and poor countries is increasing.

5. Third World dependency can take one of three forms: "banana-republic" dependency on the export of raw materials; industrial dependency on assembly projects for First World firms; and dependency on international capital. All entail a triple alliance among multinational (First World) firms, local elites, and the local state.

6. Empirical studies document that multinational penetration has four types of negative consequences for Third World nations: It increases sectoral inequality, income inequality, authoritarianism, and conflict.

7. Nicaragua and the People's Republic of China are examples of Third World nations that have pursued very different strategies for development. Nicaragua's involvement in the world system has led to revolution and civil war as well as lower levels of health and welfare. Although China has a lower income than Nicaragua, its withdrawal from the world system has produced greater equality and higher human welfare.

8. The Soviet Union and the rest of the former Communist bloc are industrialized but much poorer than nations in the First World. Until recently, they restricted trade to one another, and arms have been their major trade good on the world market.

9. The U.S. exemplifies a nation from the capitalist core. Its own economy is productive, diverse, and independent, and its multinational corporations have been very active in turning the cheap goods and cheap labor of the Third World to their economic advantage.

10. With the collapse of the Communist "evil empire," threats of war are increasingly likely to stem from Third World troubles—and this means that understanding and reducing inequality among and within nations will become more critical. Sociological studies of conflict resolution, social justice, and economic development can contribute to the prevention of war.

SUGGESTED READINGS

Chirot, Daniel. 1986. Social Change in the Modern Era. New York: Harcourt Brace Jovanovich. A historical and comparative approach to understanding social changes in the world. Excellent introduction to a complex area.

Coye, Molly Joel, Livingston, John, and Highland, Jean (eds.). 1984. China Yesterday and Today. New York: Bantam Books. Contains a variety of articles from officials, journalists, historians, and others that provides an excellent background for understanding China today. Very readable.

Kurtz, Lester with Dillard, John, and Benford, Robert. 1988. The Nuclear Cage: A Sociology of the Arms Race. Englewood Cliffs, N.J.: Prentice-Hall. This book offers a primer on the nuclear arms race and a recipe for its resolution. This is an explicitly sociological account that gives special attention to the symbolic meanings that fuel conflict and impede resolution.

Robinson, Kathryn. 1986. Stepchildren of Progress: The Political Economy of Development in an Indonesian Mining Town. Albany: SUNY Press. Based on two years of fieldwork in an Indonesian village, this monograph is an indictment of multinational investment. It is an enormously readable book, more like a horror story than a scholarly compendium.

Glossary

Absolute poverty is the inability to provide the minimum requirements of life.

Accommodation occurs when two groups coexist as separate cultures in the same society.

Acculturation occurs when the minority group adopts the culture of the majority group.

An **achieved status** is optional, one that a person can obtain in a lifetime.

Achievement motivation is the continual drive to match oneself against standards of excellence.

Ageism is the belief that chronological age determines the presence or absence of socially relevant characteristics and that age therefore legitimates unequal treatment.

An **aggregate** is people who are temporarily clustered together in the same location.

Alienation occurs when workers have no control over the work process or the product of their labor; they are estranged from their work.

Anglo conformity is the process of acculturation in which new immigrant groups adopt the English language and English customs.

Anomie is a situation where the norms of society are unclear or no longer applicable to current conditions.

Anticipatory socialization is role learning that prepares us for roles we are likely to assume in the future.

Antinatalism refers to social forces that discourage childbearing.

An **ascribed status** is fixed by birth and inheritance and is unalterable in a person's lifetime.

Assimilation is the full integration of the minority group into the institutions of society and the end of its identity as a subordinate group.

Authoritarian systems are political systems in which the leadership is not selected by the people and legally cannot be changed by them.

Authoritarianism is the tendency to be submissive to those in authority coupled with an aggressive and negative attitude toward those lower in status.

Authority is power supported by norms and values that legitimate its use.

Bloc mobilization is a strategy whereby social movement organizations recruit other organizations to support their cause rather than trying to recruit single individuals.

The **bourgeoisie** is the class that owns the tools and materials for their work—the means of production.

Bureaucracy is a special type of complex organization characterized by explicit rules and a hierarchical authority structure, all designed to maximize efficiency.

Capitalism is the economic system in which most wealth (land, capital, and labor) is private property, to be used by its owners to maximize their own gain; this economic system is based on competition.

Caste systems rely largely on ascribed statuses as the basis for distributing scarce resources.

A **category** is a collection of people who share a common characteristic.

Charisma refers to extraordinary personal qualities that set the individual apart from ordinary mortals.

Charismatic authority is the right to make decisions that is based on perceived extraordinary personal characteristics.

Churches are religious organizations that have become institutionalized. They have endured for generations, are supported by society's norms and values, and have become an active part of society.

Civil religion is the set of institutionalized rituals, beliefs, and symbols sacred to the nation.

Class refers to a person's relationship to the means of production.

Class consciousness occurs when people are aware of their relationship to the means of production and recognize their true class identity.

Class systems rely largely on achieved statuses as the basis for distributing scarce resources.

Coercion is the exercise of power through force or the threat of force.

Cohabitation occurs when couples live together without legal marriage.

Cohesion refers to the degree of attraction members feel to the group.

A **cohort** is a category of individuals who share a particular experience at the same point in time—for example, all of those who were born in 1930 or who married in 1990.

Collective behavior is nonroutine action by an emotionally aroused gathering of people who face an ambiguous situation.

Competition is a struggle over scarce resources that is regulated by shared rules.

Conflict is a struggle over scarce resources that is not regulated by shared rules; it may include attempts to destroy or neutralize one's rivals.

Conflict theory addresses the points of stress and conflict in society and the ways in which they contribute to social change.

Contagion theory suggests that the crowd situation leads to the development of unanimous and intense feelings and behaviors that are at odds with the usual predispositions of the individual participants.

A **control group** is the group in an experiment that does not receive the independent variable.

Control variables are measures of the background factors that may be confounding the true relationship between our study variables.

Convergence theory contends that the cause, or triggering event, for crowd action selectively draws people who share a common set of predispositions.

Cooperation is interaction that occurs when people work together to achieve shared goals.

Core societies are rich, powerful nations that are economically diversified and relatively free of outside control.

Correlation occurs when there is an empirical relationship between two variables.

Countercultures are groups having values, interests, beliefs, and life-styles that are opposed to those of the larger culture.

A **countermovement** seeks to reverse or resist change advocated by a social movement.

Credentialism is the use of educational credentials to measure social origins and social status.

Crimes are acts that are subject to legal or civil penalties.

A **cross-sectional design** uses a sample (or cross section) of the population at a single point in time.

A **crowd** is a gathering of people who are reacting to a nonroutine event.

The **crude birthrate** (CBR) is the number of births divided by the total midyear population and then multiplied by 1,000; it is read as births per thousand.

The **crude deathrate** (CDR) is the number of deaths divided by the total midyear population and then multiplied by 1,000; it is read as deaths per thousand.

The **crude natural growth rate** is the crude birthrate minus the crude deathrate and then divided by 10; it is read as the percentage growth rate.

A **cult** is a sectlike religious organization that is independent of the religious traditions of society.

Cultural capital refers to social assets such as familiarity and identification with elite culture.

Cultural relativity requires that each cultural trait be evaluated in the context of its own culture.

Culture is the total way of life shared by members of a society. It includes not only language, values, and symbolic meanings but also technology and material objects.

The **culture of poverty** is a set of values that emphasizes living for the moment rather than thrift, investment in the future, or hard work.

Deduction is the process of moving from theory to data by testing hypotheses drawn from theory.

Democracy is a political system that provides regular, constitutional opportunities for a change in leadership according to the will of the majority.

The **demographic transition** is the process of moving from the traditional balance of high birth- and deathrates to a new balance of low birth- and deathrates.

Demography is the statistical study of population—its size, growth, and composition.

Denominations are churchlike religious organizations that have accommodated to society and to other religions.

The **dependency ratio** is the number of people under 15 and over 65 divided by the population 15 to 65.

The **dependent variable** is the effect in cause-and-effect relationships. It is dependent on the actions of the independent variable.

Deterrence theories suggest that deviance results when social sanctions, formal and informal, provide insufficient rewards for conformity.

Development refers to the process of increasing the productivity and standard of living of a society—longer life expectancies, more adequate diets, better education, better housing, and more consumer goods.

Deviance refers to norm violations that exceed the tolerance level of the community and result in negative sanctions.

Dialectic philosophy views change as a product of contradictions and conflict between the parts of society.

Differential association theory argues that people learn to be deviant when more of their associates favor deviance than favor conformity.

Differentials are differences in the incidence of a phenomenon across subcategories of the population.

Discrimination is the unequal treatment of individuals on the basis of their membership in categories.

Disengagement theory, a functionalist theory of aging, argues that the aged voluntarily disengage themselves from active social participation.

The **divorce rate** is calculated as the number of divorces each year per 1,000 married women.

Double or triple jeopardy means having low status on two or three different dimensions of stratification.

Dramaturgy is a version of symbolic interaction that views social situations as scenes manipulated by the actors to convey the desired impression to the audience.

A **dual economy** consists of the complex giants of the industrial core and the small, competitive organizations that form the periphery.

Dysfunctions are consequences of social structures that have negative effects on the stability of society.

An **ecclesia** is a churchlike religious organization that automatically includes every member of a society.

Economic determinism means that economic relationships provide the foundation on which all other social and political arrangements are built.

Economic institutions are social structures concerned with the production and distribution of goods and services.

The **educational institution** is the social structure concerned with the formal transmission of knowledge.

Egalitarianism emphasizes equality in decision making, control of family resources, and childrearing.

Emergent-norm theory suggests that each crowd is governed by norms developed and validated by group processes within the crowd.

An **established sect** is a sect that has adapted to its institutional environment.

An **ethnic group** is a category whose members are thought to share a common origin and to share important elements of a common culture.

Ethnocentrism is the tendency to view the norms and values of our own culture as standards against which to judge the practices of other cultures.

Ethnomethodology is the study of the everyday strategies that individuals use to study and organize their world.

Exchange is voluntary interaction in which the parties trade tangible or intangible benefits.

Expectation states theory argues that status characteristics create expectation states in others about probable abilities and social status. When people act on the basis of these expectations, the expectations are confirmed.

The **experiment** is a method in which the researcher manipulates independent variables to test theories of cause and effect.

An **experimental group** is the group in an experiment that experiences the independent variable. Results for this group are compared with those for the control group.

Expressive describes activities or roles that provide integration and emotional support.

An **extended family** exists when the wife-husband pair and their children live with other kin and share economic and childrearing responsibilities with them.

Extrinsic rewards are tangible benefits such as income and security.

False consciousness is a lack of awareness of one's real position in the class structure.

The **family** is a relatively permanent group of persons linked together by ties of blood, marriage, or adoption, who live together and cooperate economically and in the rearing of the children.

Fertility is the incidence of childbearing.

The **First World** consists of those rich nations that have relatively high degrees of economic and political autonomy: the United States, Western Europe, Canada, Japan, Australia, and New Zealand.

Folkways are norms that are customary, normal, habitual ways a group does things.

Formal social controls are administrative sanctions such as fines, expulsion, and imprisonment.

A **frame** is an answer to the question, what is going on here? It is roughly identical to a definition of the situation.

Frame alignment is a process by which social movement organizations attract individual new recruits; it seeks to convince individuals that their interests, values, and beliefs are complementary to those of the SMO.

Functions are consequences of social structures that have positive effects on the stability of society.

Gemeinschaft refers to society characterized by the personal and permanent ties associated with primary groups.

Gender refers to the expected dispositions and behaviors that cultures assign to each sex.

Gender roles refer to the rights and obligations that are normative for men and women in a particular culture.

The **generalized other** is the composite expectations of all the other role players with whom we interact; it is Mead's term for our awareness of social norms.

Gesellschaft refers to society characterized by the impersonal and instrumental ties associated with secondary groups.

A **group** is two or more people who interact on the basis of shared social structure and who recognize mutual dependency.

The **guinea-pig effect** occurs when subjects' knowledge that they are participating in an experiment affects their response to the independent variable.

The **hidden curriculum** of schools socializes young people into obedience and conformity.

Homogamy is the tendency to choose a mate similar to oneself.

Hypotheses are statements about relationships that we expect to find if our theory is correct.

The **I** is the spontaneous, creative part of the self.

Identity salience hierarchy is a ranking of an individual's various role identities in order of their importance to him or her.

An **ideology** is a set of norms and values that rationalizes the existing social structure.

Immigration is the permanent movement of people into another country.

Incidence is the frequency with which an attitude or behavior occurs.

The **independent variable** is the variable that does the causing in cause-and-effect relationships.

The **indirect inheritance model** argues that children have occupations of a status similar to that of their parents because the family status and income determine children's aspirations and opportunities.

Induction is the process of moving from data to theory by devising theories that account for empirically observed patterns.

Influence is the ability to affect others' decisions through persuasion and personal appeals.

The **informal economy** is that part of the economy that escapes the record keeping and regulation of the state.

Informal social control is self-restraint exercised because of fear of what others will think.

Institutionalized racism occurs when the normal operation of apparently neutral processes systematically produces unequal results for majority and minority groups.

Institutions are enduring and complex social structures that meet basic human needs.

Instrumental describes activities or roles that are task oriented.

The **interaction school of symbolic interaction** focuses on the active role of the individual in creating the self and self-concept.

An **interest group** is a group or organization that seeks to influence political decisions.

Intergenerational mobility is the change in social class from one generation to the next.

Internalization occurs when individuals accept the norms and values of their group and make conformity to these norms part of their self-concept.

Intragenerational mobility is the change in social class within an individual's own career.

Intrinsic rewards are rewards that arise from the process of work; they include enjoying the people you work with and taking pride in your creativity and accomplishments.

The **iron law of oligarchy** is the tendency for an elite to dominate an organization.

A **kin group** is the set of relatives who interact on the basis of shared social structure.

Labeling theory is concerned with the processes by which labels such as *deviant* come to be attached to specific people and specific behaviors.

Latent functions or dysfunctions are consequences of social structures that are neither intended nor recognized.

Laws are rules that are enforced and sanctioned by the authority of government. They may or may not be norms.

Life course refers to the age-related transitions that are socially created, socially recognized, and shared.

Life expectancy is the average number of years that a group of infants can expect to live.

Lifetime divorce probability is the estimated probability that a marriage will ever end in divorce.

Linguistic relativity hypothesis argues that the grammar, structure, and categories embodied in each language affect how its speakers see reality.

The **looking-glass self** is the process of learning to view ourselves as we think others view us.

Macrosociology focuses on social structures and organizations and the relationships between them.

A **majority group** is a group that is culturally, economically, and politically dominant.

Manifest functions or dysfunctions are consequences of social structures that are intended and recognized.

Marriage is an institutionalized social structure that provides an enduring framework for regulating sexual behavior and childbearing.

Matriarchal authority is normatively approved female dominance.

Matrilocal residence occurs when norms of residence require newly married couples to take up residence with the wife's kin.

The **me** represents the self as social object.

A **metropolitan area** (MSA) is a county that has a city of 50,000 or more in it plus any neighboring counties that are significantly linked, economically or socially, with the core county.

Microsociology focuses on interactions among individuals.

A **minority group** is a group that is culturally, economically, and politically subordinate.

Modernization theory see development as the natural unfolding of an evolutionary process in which societies go from simple to complex institutional structures and from primary to secondary and tertiary production.

Modernization theory of aging argues that the elderly have low status in modern societies because the value of their traditional resources has eroded.

Monogamy is marriage in which there is only one wife and one husband.

Mores are norms associated with fairly strong ideas of right or wrong; they carry a moral connotation.

Mortality is the incidence of death.

Multinationals are large corporations that operate internationally.

Neolocal residence occurs when norms of residence require that a newly married couple take up residence away from their relatives.

A **nonmetropolitan area** is a county that has no major city in it and is not closely tied to a county that does have such a city.

The **norm of reciprocity** is the expectation that people will return favors and strive to maintain a balance of obligation in social relationships.

Norms are shared rules of conduct that specify how people ought to think and act.

A **nuclear family** consists of a husband, a wife, and their dependent children.

Operational definitions describe the exact procedures by which a variable is measured.

The **panel design** follows a sample over a period of time.

Participant observation includes a variety of research strategies—participating, interviewing, observing—that examine the context and meanings of human behavior.

Patriarchal authority is normatively approved male dominance.

Patrilocal residence occurs when norms of residence require a newly married couple to take up residence with the husband's kin.

Peripheral societies are poor and weak, with highly specialized economies over which they have relatively little control.

The **petit bourgeois** are those who use their own modest capital to establish small enterprises in which they and their family provide the primary labor.

Political alienation is a belief that voting is a useless exercise and that individual citizens have no influence on decision making.

Political institutions are institutions concerned with the social structure of power; the most prominent political institution is the state.

A **political party** is an association specifically organized to win elections and secure power over the personnel and policies of the state.

Polyandry is a form of marriage in which one woman may have more than one husband at a time.

Polygamy is any form of marriage in which a person may have more than one spouse at a time.

Polygyny is a form of marriage in which one man may have more than one wife at a time.

Positivism is the belief that the social world can be studied with the same scientific accuracy and assurance as the natural world.

Power is the ability to direct others' behavior, even against their wishes.

The **power elite** consists of the people who occupy the top positions in three bureaucracies—the military, industry, and the executive branch of government—and who are thought to act together to run the United States in their own interests.

Prejudice is irrationally based negative attitudes toward categories of people.

Primary groups are groups characterized by intimate, face-to-face interaction.

Primary production consists of extracting raw materials from the environment.

Primary socialization is personality development and role learning that occurs during early childhood.

The **profane** represents all that is routine and taken for granted in the everyday world, things that are known and familiar and that we can control, understand, and manipulate.

Professions are occupations that demand specialized skills and creative freedom.

The **proletariat** is the class that does not own the means of production. Members of this class must support themselves by selling their labor to those who own the means of production.

Pronatalism refers to the social forces that encourage childbearing.

Propinquity is spatial nearness.

A **public** is a category of citizens who are thought to share a common political agenda.

A **race** is a category of people whom we treat as distinct on account of physical characteristics to which we have assigned *social* importance.

Racism is a belief that inherited physical characteristics determine the presence or absence of socially relevant abilities and characteristics and that such differences provide a legitimate basis for unequal treatment.

Rational-legal authority is the right to make decisions that is based on rationally established rules.

Relative-deprivation theory argues that social movements arise when people experience an intolerable gap between their rewards and what they believe they have a right to expect; also known as breakdown theory.

Relative poverty is the inability to maintain what your society regards as a decent standard of living.

Religion is a system of beliefs and practices related to sacred things that unites believers into a moral community.

Replacement-level fertility requires that each woman bear approximately two children, one to replace herself and one to replace her partner. When this occurs, the next generation will be the same size as the current generation of parents.

Replication is repeating empirical studies with another investigator or a different sample to see if the same results occur.

Resocialization occurs when we abandon our self-concept and way of life for a radically different one.

Resource mobilization theory suggests that social movements develop when organized groups are competing for scarce resources; also known as solidarity theory.

Rites of passage are formal rituals that mark the end of one status and the beginning of another.

A **role** is a set of norms specifying the rights and obligations associated with a status.

Role conflict is caused by incompatibility between the roles of two or more statuses held by an individual.

Role identity is the image we have of ourself in a specific social role.

Role strain is caused by incompatible role demands within a single status.

Role taking involves imagining ourselves in the role of the other in order to determine the criteria the other will use to judge our behavior.

The **sacred** consists of events and things that we hold in awe and reverence—what we can neither understand nor control.

A **sample** is a systematic selection of representative cases from the larger population.

Sanctions are rewards for conformity and punishments for nonconformity.

Scapegoating occurs when people or groups who are blocked in their own goal attainment blame others for their failures.

Science is a way of knowing based on empirical evidence.

The **Second World** includes the Soviet Union and the nations of the former Communist bloc.

Secondary groups are groups that are formal, large, and impersonal.

Secondary production consists of the processing of raw materials.

Sects are religious organizations that reject the social environment in which they exist.

Secularization is the process of transferring things, ideas, or events from the sacred realm to the profane.

The **segmented labor market** parallels the dual economy. Hiring, advancement, and benefits vary systematically between the industrial core and the periphery.

Segregation refers to the physical separation of minority and majority group members.

The **self** is a complex whole that includes unique attributes and normative responses. In sociology, these two parts are called the I and the me.

The **self-concept** is the self we are aware of. It is our thoughts and feelings about our personality and social roles.

Self-esteem is the evaluative component of the self-concept; it is our judgment about our worth compared with others.

The **self-fulfilling prophecy** occurs when acting on the belief that a situation exists causes it to become real.

A **semicaste structure** is a hierarchical ordering of social classes within racial categories that are also hierarchically ordered.

Sex is a biological characteristic, male or female.

Sexism is a belief that men and women have biologically

different capacities and that these form a legitimate basis for unequal treatment.

Sexual harassment consists of unwelcome sexual advances, requests for sexual favors, or other verbal or physical conduct of a sexual nature.

The **sick role** consists of the rights and obligations that accompany the social label *sick*.

Significant others are the role players with whom we have close personal relationships.

Situated identity is the role identity used in a particular situation. It implies that our identity will depend on the situation.

Social choice theory (or exchange theory) argues that individual decisions are based on cost/benefit calculations.

Social class is a category of people who share roughly the same class, status, and power and who have a sense of identification with each other.

Social control consists of the forces and processes that encourage conformity, including self-control, informal control, and formal control.

Social-desirability bias is the tendency of people to color the truth so that they sound nicer, richer, and more desirable than they really are.

Social distance is the degree of intimacy in relationships between two groups.

Social epidemiology is the study of how social statuses relate to the distribution of illness and mortality.

Social mobility is the process of changing one's social class.

A **social movement** is an ongoing, goal-directed effort to change social institutions from the outside.

A **social network** is an individual's total set of relationships.

Social processes are the forms of interaction through which people relate to one another; they are the dynamic aspects of society.

A **social structure** is a recurrent pattern of relationships.

Socialism is an economic structure in which the group (or its representative, the state) owns the means of production and in which production and distribution are managed for the group's welfare rather than private profit; this economic system is based on cooperation.

Socialization is the process of learning the roles, statuses, and values necessary for participation in social institutions.

A **society** is the population that shares the same territory and is bound together by economic and political ties.

Sociobiology is the study of the biological basis of all forms of human behavior.

Socioeconomic status (SES) is a measure of social class that ranks individuals on income, education, occupation, or some combination.

The **sociological imagination** is the ability to see the intimate realities of our own lives in the context of common social structures; it is the ability to see personal troubles as public issues.

Sociology is the systematic study of human social interaction.

The **sociology of everyday life** focuses on the social processes that structure our experience in ordinary face-to-face situations.

The **state** is the social structure that successfully claims a monopoly on the legitimate use of coercion and physical force within a territory.

A **status** is a specialized position within a group.

Status is social honor, expressed in life-style.

Strain theory suggests that deviance occurs when culturally approved goals cannot be reached by culturally approved means.

Stratification is an institutionalized pattern of inequality in which social statuses are ranked on the basis of their access to scarce resources.

Street-level justice consists of the decisions the police make in the initial stages of an investigation.

Strong ties are relationships characterized by intimacy, emotional intensity, and sharing.

Structural-functional theory addresses the question of social organization and how it is maintained; it is also known as consensus theory.

The **structural school of symbolic interaction** focuses on the self as a product of social roles.

Subcultures are groups that share in the overall culture of society but also maintain a distinctive set of values, norms, life-styles, and even language.

Survey research is a method that involves asking a relatively large number of people the same set of standardized questions.

Symbolic interaction theory addresses the subjective meanings of human acts and the processes through which people come to develop and communicate shared meanings.

Tertiary production consists of the production of services.

Theory is an interrelated set of assumptions that explains observed patterns.

The **Third World** consists of the less developed nations that share a peripheral or marginal status in the world capitalist system.

Total institutions are facilities in which all aspects of life are strictly controlled for the purpose of radical resocialization.

Tracking occurs when evaluations relatively early in a child's career determine the educational programs the child will be encouraged to follow.

Traditional authority is the right to make decisions for others that is based on the sanctity of time-honored routines.

Trends are changes in phenomena over time.

The **underclass** is the group that is unemployed and unemployable, a miserable substratum that is alienated from American institutions.

Urbanism is a distinctively urban mode of life that is developed in the cities but not confined there.

Urbanization is the process of population concentration in metropolitan areas.

Value-free sociology concerns itself with establishing what is, not what ought to be.

Values are shared ideas about desirable goals.

Variables are measured characteristics that vary from one individual or group to the next.

Victimless crimes such as drug use, prostitution, gambling, and pornography are voluntary exchanges between persons who desire goods or services from each other.

Voluntary associations are nonprofit organizations designed to allow individuals an opportunity to pursue their shared interests collectively.

Weak ties are relationships with friends, acquaintances, and kin that are characterized by low intensity and intimacy.

White-collar crime is crime committed by respectable people of high status in the course of their occupation.

World system theory is a conflict perspective of the economic relationships between developed and developing countries, the core and peripheral societies.

Zero population growth (ZPG) means that the number of births is the same as the number of deaths, so the population does not grow.

References

Achenbaum, W. Andrew. 1985. "Societal Perceptions of Aging and the Aged." In Robert Binstock and Ethel Shanas (eds.), Handbook of Aging and the Social Sciences. (2nd ed.) New York: Van Nostrand Reinhold.

Acock, Alan, and Kiecolt, Jill. 1989. "Is It Family Structure or Socioeconomic Status? Family Structure During Adolescence and Adult Adjustment." Social Forces 68:553–71.

Acton, Edward. 1986. Russia. New York: Longman.

Adams, Bert N. 1971. The American Family: A Sociological Interpretation. Chicago: Markham.

Adams, Bert N. 1979. "Mate Selection in the United States: A Theoretical Summarization." In W. R. Burr, Reuben Hill, F. Ivan Nye, and Ira L. Reiss (eds.), Contemporary Theories About the Family. Vol. 1. New York: Free Press.

Adams, Bert N. 1985. "The Family: Problems and Solutions." Journal of Marriage and the Family 47 (August): 525–29.

Adams, Carolyn Teich. 1986. "Homelessness in the Postindustrial City: Views from London and Philadelphia." Urban Affairs Quarterly 21 (June): 527–49.

Affleck, Marilyn, Morgan, Carolyn, and Hayes, Maggie. 1989. "The Influence of Gender-Role Attitudes on Life Expectations of College Students." Youth and Society 20:307–19.

Agnew, Robert, and Petersen, David. 1989. "Leisure and Delinquency." Social Problems 36:322–50.

Ahlburg, Dennis. 1988. "An Analysis of the Population Crisis Committee's International Human Suffering Index." Unpublished manuscript. Minneapolis: University of Minnesota Center for Population Analysis and Policy.

Aird, John S. 1972. Population Policy and Demographic Prospects in the People's Republic of China. U.S. Department of Health, Education and Welfare. Washington, D.C.: U.S. Government Printing Office.

Akers, Ronald. 1968. "Problems in the Sociology of Deviance: Social Definitions and Behavior." Social Forces 46:455–65.

Alba, Richard D. 1985. "The Twilight of Ethnicity Among Americans of European Ancestry: The Case of Italians." In Richard Alba (ed.), Ethnicity and Race in the U.S.A.: Toward the Twenty-First Century. Boston: Routledge & Kegan Paul.

Albas, Daniel, and Albas, Cheryl. 1988. "Aces and Bombers: The Postexam Impression Management Strategies of Students." Symbolic Interaction 11:289–302.

Alexander, Karl, Entwisle, Doris, Cadigan, Doris, and Pallas, Aaron. 1987. "Getting Ready for First Grade: Standards of Deportment in Home and School." Social Forces 66:57–84.

Alexander, Karl L., Entwisle, Doris, and Thompson, Maxine. 1987. "School Performance, Status Relations, and the Structure of Sentiment: Bringing the Teacher Back In." American Sociological Review 52:665–82.

Alexander, Karl L., Natriello, Gary, and Pallas, Aaron M. 1985. "For Whom the School Bell Tolls: The Impact of Dropping out on Cognitive Performance." American Sociological Review 50 (June): 409–20.

Allan, Emilie, and Steffensmeier, Darrell. 1989. "Youth Unemployment and Property Crime." American Sociological Review 54: 107–23.

Allen, James R., and Curran, James W. 1988. "Prevention of AIDS and HIV Infection: Needs and Priorities for Epidemiologic Research." American Journal of Public Health 78:380–86.

Allen, Katherine. 1989. Single Women/Family Ties. Newbury Park, Calif.: Sage.

Allen, Walter R., and Farley, Reynolds. 1986. "The Shifting Social and Economic Tides of Black America, 1950–1980." Annual Review of Sociology 12:277–306.

Altman, Dennis. 1983. The Homosexualization of America. Boston: Beacon Press. (Original published 1982.)

Amato, Paul, and Keith, Bruce. Forthcoming. "Parental Divorce and Adult Well-Being: A Meta-Analysis." Journal of Marriage and the Family 53 (February).

Ambrose, Thomas. 1989. "The Official Language Movement in the United States: Contexts, Issues, and Activities." Language Problems and Language Planning 13:264–79.

"American Black Male in Crisis." 1989. Lincoln Star, December 31, p. 6B.

American Council on Education. 1990. Personal Communication, April.

American Sociological Association. 1988. Proposed Code of Ethics, December 1988. Washington, D.C.: American Sociological Association.

Andersson, Bengt-Erik. 1989. "Effects of Public Day Care: A Longitudinal Study." Child Development 60:857–66.

Aneshensel, Carol S., Fielder, Eve, and Becerra, Rosina. 1989. "Fertility and Fertility-Related Behavior Among Mexican American and Non-Hispanic White Female Adolescents." Journal of Health and Social Behavior 30:56–76.

Ankrah, E. 1989. "AIDS: Methodological Problems in Studying Its Prevention and Spread." Social Science and Medicine 29:267–76.

"Another Winter for the Homeless." 1989. Population Today 17 (February): 3–4.

Archer, Dane. 1985. "Social Deviance." In Gardner Lindzey and Elliot Aronson (eds.), The Handbook of Social Psychology Vol. 2. (3rd ed.) New York: Random House.

Aries, Philippe. 1962. Centuries of Childhood: A Social History of Family Life. New York: Knopf.

Asch, Solomon E. 1955. "Opinions and Social Pressure." Scientific American 193 (November): 31–35.

Ash, Roberta. 1972. Social Movements in America. Chicago: Markham.

Astin, Alexander, and Associates. 1989. The American

Freshman: National Norms for Fall 1989. Los Angeles: Graduate School of Education, University of California.

Atchley, Robert C. 1982. "Retirement as a Social Institution." American Review of Sociology 8:263–287.

Austrom, D., and Hanel, N. 1985. "Psychological Issues of Single Life in Canada: An Exploratory Study." International Journal of Women's Studies 8:12–23.

Babbie, Earl R. 1986. The Practice of Social Research. (4th ed.) Belmont, Calif.: Wadsworth.

Baldassare, Mark. 1986. Trouble in Paradise: The Suburban Transformation in America. New York: Columbia University Press.

Baldassare, Mark. 1989. "Citizen Support for Regional Government in the New Suburbia." Urban Affairs Quarterly 24:460–69.

Ball, John, Lange, W. Robert, Myers, C. Patrick, and Friedman, Samuel. 1988. "Reducing the Risk of AIDS Through Methadone Maintenance Treatment." Journal of Health and Social Behavior 29: 299–314.

Barker, Eileen. 1986. "Religious Movements: Cult and Anticult Since Jonestown." Annual Review of Sociology 12:329–46.

Baron, James. 1984. "Organizational Perspectives on Stratification." Annual Review of Sociology 10:37–69.

Baron, James N., and Bielby, William T. 1984. "The Organization of a Segmented Economy." American Sociological Review 49 (August): 454–73.

Baron, James N., and Reiss, Peter C. 1985a. "Same Time, Next Year: Aggregate Analysis of the Mass Media and Violent Behavior." American Sociological Review 50 (June): 347–63.

Baron, James N., and Reiss, Peter C. 1985b. "Reply to Phillips and Bollen." American Sociological Review 50 (June): 372–76.

Baron, Stephen. 1989. "Resistance and Its Consequences: The Street Culture of Punks." Youth and Society 21:207–37.

Barone, Michael, and Ujifusa, Grant. 1989. The Almanac of American Politics, 1990. Washington, D.C.: National Journal.

Bechhofer, F., and Elliott, B. 1985. "The Petite Bourgeoisie in Late Capitalism." Annual Review of Sociology 11:181–207.

Becker, Howard S. 1963. Outsiders: Studies in the Sociology of Deviance. New York: Free Press.

Becker, Marshall, and Joseph, Jill. 1988. "AIDS and Behavioral Change to Reduce Risk: A Review." American Journal of Public Health 78:394–411.

Beckwith, Carol. 1983. "Niger's Wodaabe: 'People of the Taboo.' " National Geographic 164 (October): 482–509.

Beegley, Leonard. 1989. The Structure of Stratification in the United States. Newton, Mass.: Allyn & Bacon.

Beier, George J. 1976. "Can Third World Cities Cope?" Population Bulletin 31 (December): 1–34.

Bell, Wendell, and Robinson, Robert V. 1978. "An Index of Evaluated Equality: Measuring Conceptions of Social Justice in England and the United States." In Richard F. Tomasson (ed), Comparative Studies in Sociology. Vol. 1. Greenwich, Conn.: JAI Press.

Bellah, Robert N. 1974. "Civil Religion in America." In Russel B. Richey and Donald G. Jones (eds.), American Civil Religion. New York: Harper & Row.

Bellah, Robert N., and Associates. 1985. Habits of the Heart: Individualism and Commitment in American Life. Berkeley: University of California Press.

Belloc, N. 1980. "Personal Behavior Affecting Mortality." In S. Preston (ed.), Biological and Social Aspects of Mortality and Length of Life. Liège, Belgium: International Union for the Scientific Study of Population.

Benbow, C. P., and Stanley, J. C. 1983. "Sex Differences in Mathematical Reasoning: More Facts." Science 222:1029–31.

Benford, Robert D. 1989. "Review." American Journal of Sociology 94:1451–53.

Bengston, Vern, Cutler, Neal, Mangen, David J., and Marshall, Victor W. 1985. "Generations, Cohorts, and Relations Between Age Groups." In Robert Binstock and Ethel Shanas (eds.), Handbook of Aging and the Social Sciences. 2nd ed.) New York: Van Nostrand Reinhold.

Bensman, Joseph, and Lilienfeld, Robert. 1979. Between Public and Private: The Lost Boundaries of Self. New York: Free Press.

Berger, Bennet M. 1981. The Survival of a Counterculture. Berkeley: University of California Press.

Berger, John, Rosenholtz, S. J., and Zelditch, M. 1980. "Status Organizing Process." Annual Review of Sociology 6:479–508.

Berger, Peter L. 1963. Invitation to Sociology: A Humanistic Perspective. New York: Doubleday.

Berk, Laura. 1989. Child Development. Newton, Mass: Allyn & Bacon.

Berry, Brian, and Kasarda, John. 1977. Contemporary Urban Ecology. New York: Macmillan.

Bertoli, Fernando, and Associates. 1984. "Infant Mortality by Socioeconomic Status for Blacks, Indians, and Whites: A Longitudinal Analysis of North Carolina, 1868–1977." Sociology and Social Research 68:364–77.

Biddle, B. J. 1986. "Recent Developments in Role Theory." Annual Review of Sociology 12:67–92.

Bielby, William T., and Baron, James N. 1986. "Men and Women at Work: Sex Segregation and Statistical Discrimination." American Journal of Sociology 91 (January): 759–98.

Bielby, William, and Bielby, Denise. 1989. "Family Ties: Balancing Commitments to Work and Family in Dual-Earner Households." American Sociological Review 54:776–89.

Billingsley, Andrew. 1989. "The Black Family." Address

given at the 1989 meetings of the National Council on Family Relations, New Orleans, November.

Black, Cyril E. 1986. Understanding Soviet Politics. Boulder, Colo.: Westview Press.

Black, Donald. 1976. The Behavior of Law. New York: Academic Press.

"Black-White Gap Persisting." 1989. Population Today 17 (October): 4.

Blakely, Edward, and Shapira, Philip. 1984. "Industrial Restructuring: Public Policies for Investment in Advanced Industrial Societies." Annals of the American Academy of Political and Social Science 475:96–109.

Blau, F. D. 1977. Equal Pay in the Office. Lexington, Mass: Lexington Books.

Blau, Judith R. 1986. "The Elite Arts, More or Less de Rigueur: A Comparative Analysis of Metropolitan Culture." Social Forces 64 (June): 875–905.

Blau, Peter. (ed.) 1975. Approaches to the Study of Social Structure. New York: Free Press.

Blau, Peter M. 1987. "Contrasting Theoretical Perspectives." In J. Alexander, B. Giesen, R. Munch, and N. Smelser (eds.). The Micro-Macro Link. Berkeley: University of California Press.

Blau, Peter M., and Meyer, Marshall W. 1971. Bureaucracy in Modern Society. (2nd ed.) New York: Random House.

Blau, Peter M., and Schwartz, Joseph E. 1984. Cross-Cutting Social Circles. Orlando, Fla.: Academic Press.

Blee, Kathleen M., and Billings, Dwight B. 1986. "Reconstructing Daily Life in the Past: An Hermeneutical Approach to Ethnographic Data." Sociological Quarterly 27 (Winter): 443–62.

Bloom, Samuel. 1988. "Structure and Ideology in Medical Education: An Analysis of Resistance to Change." Journal of Health and Social Behavior 29:294–306.

Blumberg, Rae Lesser. 1978. Stratification: Socioeconomic and Sexual Inequality. Dubuque, Iowa: Brown.

Blumer, H. 1934. "Collective Behavior." In A. M. Lee (ed.), New Outlines of the Principles of Sociology. New York: Barnes & Noble.

Blumer, H. 1969. Symbolic Interactionism: Perspective and Method. Englewood Cliffs, N.J.: Prentice-Hall.

Blumstein, Phillip, and Schwartz, Pepper. 1983. American Couples. New York: William Morrow.

Bohland, James R. 1982. "Indian Residential Segregation in the Urban Southwest: 1970 and 1980." Social Science Quarterly 63 (December): 749–761.

Bohrnstedt, George W., and Fisher, Gene. 1986. "The Effects of Recalled Childhood and Adolescent Relationships Compared to Current Role Performances in Young Adults' Affective Functioning." Social Psychology Quarterly 49 (1): 19–32.

Boies, John. 1989. "Money, Business, and the State." American Sociological Review 54:821–33.

Bollier, David. 1982. Liberty and Justice for Some. New York: Frederick Ungar.

Bonacich, Edna. 1972. "A Theory of Ethnic Antagonism: The Split Labor Market." American Sociological Review 37 (October): 547–59.

Bonavia, David. 1984. "Reassessing Mao." In Molly Joel Coye, John Livingston and Jean Highland (eds.), China: Yesterday and Today. New York: Bantam Books.

Booth, Alan, and Johnson, David. 1988. "Premarital Cohabitation and Marital Success." Journal of Family Issues 9:255–72.

Booth, Alan, Johnson, David, White, Lynn, and Edwards, John. 1984. Marital Instability and the Life Course: Methodology Report. Lincoln: Bureau of Sociological Research.

Bose, Christine E., and Rossi, Peter H. 1983. "Gender and Jobs: Prestige Standings of Occupations as Affected by Gender." American Sociological Review 48 (June): 316–330.

Bourdieu, P. 1973. "Cultural Reproduction and Social Reproduction." In R. Brown (ed.), Knowledge, Education, and Cultural Change. London: Tavistock.

Bouvier, Leon F. 1980. "America's Baby Boom Generation: The Fateful Bulge." Population Bulletin 35 (1): 1–45.

Bouvier, Leon, and Gardner, Robert W. 1986. "Immigration to the U.S.: The Unfinished Story." Population Bulletin 41 (November): 1–50.

Bowen, Howard R. 1977. Investment in Learning. San Francisco: Jossey-Bass.

Bowles, Samuel, and Gintis, Herbert. 1976. Schooling in Capitalist America: Educational Reform and the Contradictions of Economic Life. New York: Basic Books.

Bowles, Samuel, and Gintis, Herbert. 1986. Democracy and Capitalism: Property, Community, and the Contradictions of Modern Social Thought. New York: Basic.

Bozett, Frederick (ed.). 1987. Gay and Lesbian Parents. New York: Praeger.

Bradshaw, York. 1988. "Reassessing Economic Dependency and Uneven Development: The Kenyan Experience." American Sociological Review 53:693–708.

Bradshaw, York, and Fraser, Elvis. 1989. "City Size, Economic Development, and Quality of Life in China." American Sociological Review 54:986–1003.

Braithwaite, John. 1981. "The Myth of Social Class and Criminality, Reconsidered." American Sociological Review 46 (February): 36–58.

Braithwaite, John. 1985. "White Collar Crime." Annual Review of Sociology 11:1–25.

Brake, Mike. 1980. The Sociology of Youth Culture and Youth Subcultures. Boston: Routledge & Kegan Paul.

Brake, Mike. 1985. Comparative Youth Culture: The Sociology of Youth Cultures and Youth Subcultures in America, Britain, and Canada. Boston: Routledge & Kegan Paul.

Braverman, Harry. 1974. Labor and Monopoly Capital. New York: Monthly Review Press.

Breslow, Lester. 1987. "Setting Objectives for Public Health." Annual Review of Public Health 8:289–307.

Brossi, Kathleen B. 1979. A Cross-City Comparison of Felony Case Processing. Washington, D.C.: U.S. Government Printing Office.

Brown, R. S., Moon, M., and Zoloth, B. S. 1980. "Incorporating Occupational Attainment in Studies of Male-Female Earnings Differentials." Journal of Human Resources 15:3–28.

Brownell, Arlene, and Shumaker, Sally A. 1984. "Social Support: An Introduction to a Complex Phenomenon." Journal of Social Issues 40 (4): 1–10.

Bryk, Anthony. 1988. "School Organization and Its Effects: Research Prepared for the Advisory Council on Education Statistics." Washington, D.C.: National Center for Education Statistics.

Bumpass, Larry. 1984. "Children and Marital Disruption: A Replication and Update." Demography 21 (February): 71–82.

Bumpass, Larry, and Sweet, James. 1989. "National Estimates of Cohabitation." Demography 26:615–25.

Bundy, McGeorge. 1990. "From Cold War to Lasting Peace." Foreign Affairs 69 (1): 197–212.

Burby, Raymond, and Rohe, William. 1989. "Deconcentration of Public Housing." Urban Affairs Quarterly 25:117–41.

Burke, Peter J. 1980. "The Self: Measurement Requirements from the Interactionist Perspective." Social Psychological Quarterly 43 (1): 18–29.

Burnell, Barbara, and Burnell, James. 1989. "Community Interaction and Suburban Zoning Policies." Urban Affairs Quarterly 24:470–82.

Cable, Sherry, Walsh, Edward, and Warland, Rex. 1988. "Differential Paths to Political Activism: Comparisons of Four Mobilization Processes After the Three Mile Island Accident." Social Forces 66:951–69.

Cahill, Spencer E. 1983. "Reexamining the Acquisition of Sex Roles: A Social Interactionist Perspective." Sex Roles 9 (January): 1–15.

Callero, Peter L. 1985. "Role Identity Salience." Social Psychology Quarterly 48 (3): 203–15.

Camasso, Michael J., and Moore, Dan E. 1985. "Rurality and the Residualist Social Welfare Response." Rural Sociology 50 (Fall): 397–408.

Camp, Sharon L., and Speidel, J. Joseph. 1987. "The International Human Suffering Index." Washington, D.C.: Population Crisis Committee.

Campbell, Ernest Q. 1969. "Adolescent Socialization." In David A. Goslin (ed.), Handbook of Socialization Theory and Research. New York: Russell Sage Foundation.

Caplow, Theodore, and Chadwick, Bruce. 1979. "Inequality and Life-Style in Middletown, 1920–1978." Social Science Quarterly 60 (December): 367–386.

"Career Statistics." 1990. Husker Newsletter, March 1990, p. 1.

"Central-City Populations Continue to Slip." 1990. Population Today 18 (1): 8.

Chafetz, Janet S. 1984. Sex and Advantage. Totawa, N. J.: Rowman and Allanheld.

Chambliss, William. 1978. "Toward a Political Economy of Crime." In Charles Reasons and Robert Rich (eds.), The Sociology of Law: A Conflict Perspective. Toronto: Butterworths.

Chandrasekhar, S. 1981. A Dirty, Filthy Book. Berkeley: University of California Press.

Chapman, Jane R., and Gates, Margaret (eds). 1978. The Victimization of Women. Sage.

Chapman, Nancy J., and Pancoast, Diane L. 1985. "Working with the Informal Helping Networks of the Elderly: The Experiences of Three Programs." Journal of Social Issues 41 (1): 47–64.

Chappell, Neena L., and Havens, Betty. 1980. "Old and Female: Testing the Double-Jeopardy Hypothesis." Sociological Quarterly 21 (Spring): 157–171.

Charny, M. C., Lewis, P. A., and Farrow, S. C. 1989. "Choosing Who Shall Not Be Treated." Social Science and Medicine 28:1331–38.

Cheal, David. 1988. The Gift Economy. Boston: Routledge & Kegan Paul.

Check., J. V. P. 1985. The Effects of Violent and Nonviolent Pornography, Report to the Department of Justice. Ottowa: Canada.

Cherlin, Andrew. 1981. Marriage, Divorce, Remarriage. Cambridge, Mass.: Harvard University Press.

Cherlin, Andrew. 1990. "Message from the Chair." Family Forum (Winter): 1–2.

Chevan, Albert. 1989. "The Growth of Home Ownership: 1940–1980." Demography 26:249–66.

"China's Demographic Disaster of 1958–1962." 1985. Population Today 13 (March): 7.

Chirot, Daniel. 1977. Social Change in the Twentieth Century. San Francisco, Calif.: Harcourt Brace Jovanovich.

Chirot, Daniel. 1986. Social Change in the Modern Era. San Diego, Calif.: Harcourt Brace Jovanovich.

Chodak, Symon. 1973. Societal Development: Five Approaches with Conclusions from Comparative Analysis. New York: Oxford University Press.

Christenson, James A. 1984. "Gemeinschaft and Gesellschaft: Testing the Spatial and Communal Hypothesis." Social Forces 63 (September): 160–68.

Cicourel, Aaron V. 1985. "Text and Discourse." Annual Review of Anthropology 14:159–85.

Clawson, Dan, and Neustadtl, Alan. 1989. "Interlocks, PACs, and Corporate Conservatism." American Journal of Sociology 94:749–73.

Clegg, Stewart, Boreham, Paul, and Dow, Geoff. 1986. Class, Politics, and the Economy. Boston: Routledge & Kegan Paul.

Coale, Ansley. 1973. Cited in M. Teitelbaum. 1975. "Relevance of Demographic Transition Theory to Developing Countries." Science 188 (May 2): 420–425.

Cobarrubias, Juan. 1983. "Ethical Issues in Status Planning." In Juan Cobarrubias and Joshua Fishman (eds.), Progress in Language Planning: International Perspectives. Berlin: Mouton.

Cobb, S. 1979. "Social Support and Health Through the Life Course." In M. W. Riley (ed.), Aging from Birth to Death. Boulder, Colo.: Westview Press.

Cockerham, William C. 1989. Medical Sociology. (4th ed.) Englewood Cliffs, N.J.: Prentice-Hall.

Cockerham, William, Kunz, Gerhard, and Lueschen, Guenther. 1988. "Social Stratification and Health Life-Styles in Two Systems of Health Care Delivery: A Comparison of the United States and West Germany." Journal of Health and Social Behavior 29:113–26.

Cohn, Richard M. 1982. "Economic Development and Status Change of the Aged." American Journal of Sociology 87 (5): 1150–61.

Cole, Michael, and Cole, Sheila. 1989. The Development of Children. New York: Scientific American Books.

Coleman, James. 1988. "Competition and the Structure of Industrial Society: Reply to Braithwaite." American Journal of Sociology 94:632–36.

Coleman, James, and Associates. 1966. Equality of Educational Opportunity. Washington, D.C.: U.S. Government Printing Office.

Coleman, James, and Hoffer, Thomas. 1987. Public and Private High Schools, New York: Basic Books.

Coleman, James, Hoffer, Thomas, and Kilgore, Sally. 1982. High School Achievement: Public, Catholic, and Private Schools Compared. New York: Basic Books.

Collins, Randall. 1979. The Credential Society. Orlando, Fla.: Academic Press.

Comstock, George S. 1977. "Types of Portrayal and Aggressive Behavior." Journal of Communication 27 (Summer): 189–198.

Conrad, John P. 1983. "Deterrence, the Death Penalty and the Data." In Ernest van den Haag and John P. Conrad (eds.), The Death Penalty: A Debate. New York: Plenum.

Cool, Linda, and McCabe, Justine. 1983. "The 'Scheming Hag' and the 'Dear Old Thing': The Anthropology of Aging Women." In Jay Sokolvsky (ed.), Growing Old in Different Cultures. Belmont, Calif.: Wadsworth.

Cooley, Charles Horton. 1902. Human Nature and the Social Order. New York: Scribner's.

Cooley, Charles Horton. 1967. "Primary Groups." In A. Paul Hare, Edgar F. Borgotta, and Robert F. Bales (eds.), Small Groups: Studies in Social Interaction. (Rev. ed. New York: Knopf. (Originally published 1909.)

Cooper, Richard, and Associates. 1981. "Racism, Society, and Diseases: An Exploration of the Social and Biological Mechanisms of Differential Mortality." Journal of Health Services 11:389–414.

Cornell, Claire, and Gelles, Richard. 1982. "Adolescent to Parent Violence." Urban Social Change Review 15 (Winter): 8–14.

Coser, Lewis A. 1956. The Functions of Social Conflict. New York: Free Press.

"Counting Trees as the Forest Burns." 1989. Newsweek, September 11, pp. 26, 28–29.

Cowgill, Donald O. 1974. "Aging and Modernization: A Revision of the Theory." In John Hendricks and C. Davis Hendricks (eds.), Dimensions of Aging: Readings. Cambridge, Mass.: Winthrop.

Coye, Molly Joel, Livingston, John, and Highland, Jean (eds.). 1984. China: Yesterday and Today. (3rd ed.) New York: Bantam Books.

Crèvecoeur, J. Hector. 1974. "What Is an American?" In Richard J. Meister (ed.), Race and Ethnicity in Modern America. Lexington, Mass.: Heath. (Originally published 1782.)

Crozier, Michael, and Friedberg, Erhard. 1980. Actors and Systems: The Politics of Collective Action. Chicago: University of Chicago Press.

Cummings, Scott. 1987. "Vulnerability to the Effects of Recession: Minority and Female Workers." Social Forces 65 (March): 834–57.

Currie, Elliott. 1989. "Confronting Crime: Looking Toward the 21st Century." Justice Quarterly 6:5–25.

Curtis, Richard F. 1986. "Household and Family in Theory on Inequality." American Sociological Review 51 (April): 168–83.

Dahl, Robert. 1961. Who Governs? New Haven, Conn.: Yale University Press.

Dahl, Robert. 1971. Polarchy. New Haven, Conn.: Yale University Press.

Dale, Roger, 1977. "Implications of the Rediscovery of the Hidden Curriculum of the Sociology of Teaching." In Denis Gleeson (ed.), Identity and Structure: Issues in the Sociology of Education. Driffield, England: Nafferton Books.

Daly, Martin, and Wilson, Margo. 1983. Sex, Evolution, and Behavior. (2nd ed.) Boston: Willard Grant.

Daniels, Roger, and Kitano, Harry H. L. 1970. American Racism: Exploration of the Nature of Prejudice. Englewood Cliffs, N.J.: Prentice–Hall.

David, Henry. 1982. "Eastern Europe: Pronatalist Policies and Private Behavior." Population Bulletin 36 (6): 1–50.

Davis, Cary. 1982. "The Future Racial Composition of the U.S." Intercom 8–10.

Davis, Cary, Haub, Carl, and Willette, JoAnne. 1983. "U.S. Hispanics: Changing the Face of America." Population Bulletin 33 (June): 1–43.

Davis, James Allan, and Smith, Tom W. 1986. General Social Surveys, 1972–1986. Chicago: National Opinion Research Center.

Davis, James, and Stasson, Mark. 1988. "Small-Group Performance: Past and Future Research Trends." Advances in Group Processes 5:245–77.

Davis, Kingsley. 1961. "Prostitution." In Robert K. Merton and Robert A. Nisbet (eds.), Contemporary Social Problems. San Francisco: Harcourt Brace Joranovich.

Davis, Kingsley. 1973. "Introduction." In Kingsley Davis (ed.), Cities. New York: W. H. Freeman.

Davis, Kingsley, and Moore, Wilbert E. 1945. "Some Principles of Stratification." American Sociological Review 10 (April): 242–249.

Davis, Mike. 1986. Prisoners of the American Dream: Politics and Economy in the History of the U.S. Working Class. London: Verso Books.

Deaux, Kay. 1985. "Sex and Gender." Annual Review of Psychology 36:49–81.

Deegan, Mary Jo. 1987. Jane Addams and the Men of the Chicago School, 1892–1918. New Brunswick, N.J.: Transaction.

Delgado, Richard. 1983. "Limits to Proselytizing." In D. Bromley and J. T. Richardson (eds.), The Brainwashing/Deprogramming Controversy. New York: Mellen.

Denzin, Norman K. 1984. "Toward a Phenomenology of Domestic, Family Violence." American Journal of Sociology 90 (November) 483–513.

Devine, Joel, Sheley, Joseph, and Smith, M. Dwayne. 1988. "Macroeconomic and Social Control Policy Influences in Crime Rate Changes, 1948–85." American Sociological Review 53:407–20.

DeWitt, J. L. 1943. Japanese in the United States, Final Report: Japanese Evacuation from the West Coast, p. 34. Cited in Paul E. Horton and Gerald R. Leslie. Social Problems 1955. East Norwalk, Conn.: Appleton-Century-Crofts.

DiMaggio, Paul, and Mohr, John. 1985. "Cultural Capital, Educational Attainment, and Marital Selection." American Journal of Sociology 90 (May): 1231–61.

DiMento, Joseph. 1989. "Can Social Science Explain Organizational Noncompliance with Environmental Law?" Journal of Social Issues 45:109–32.

"Disaster Throws the Spotlight." 1989. New York Times, April 17, p. 12.

DiTomaso, Nancy. 1987. "Symbolic Media and Social Solidarity: The Foundations of Corporate Culture." Sociology of Organizations 5:105–34.

Dobbelaere, Karel. 1981. "Secularization: A Multidimensional Concept." Current Sociology 29:1–21.

Dono, John E., et al. 1979. "Primary Groups in Old Age: Structure and Function." Research on Aging 1 (December): 403–433.

Dore, Ronald P. 1973. British Factory, Japanese Factory. Berkeley: University of California Press.

Dornbusch, Sanford. 1989. "The Sociology of Adolescence." Annual Review of Sociology 15:233–59.

Dougherty, Kevin. 1987. "The Effect of Community Colleges: Aid or Hindrance to Socioeconomic Attainment?" Sociology of Education 60:86–103.

Douglas, Jack D., and Waksler, Frances C. 1982. The Sociology of Deviance: An Introduction. Boston: Little, Brown.

Douglas, Tom. 1983. Groups: Understanding People Gathered Together. London: Tavistock.

"Dramatic Fertility Declines in Two Countries?" 1989. Population Today 17 (9): 4.

Duncan, Greg. 1984. Years of Poverty, Years of Plenty. Ann Arbor: Institute for Social Research.

Duncan, Otis Dudley, Featherman, David L., and Duncan, Beverly. 1972. Socioeconomic Background and Achievement. New York: Seminar Books.

Durkheim, Emile. 1938. The Rules of Sociological Method. New York: Free Press. (Originally published 1895).

Durkheim, Emile. 1951. Suicide: A Study in Sociology. New York: Free Press. (Originally published 1897.)

Durkheim, Emile. 1961. The Elementary Forms of the Religious Life. London: Allen & Unwin. (Originally published 1915.)

Durning, Alan. 1989. "Poverty and the Environment: Reversing the Downward Spiral." Worldwatch Paper 92. Washington, D.C.: Worldwatch Institute.

Dworkin, Andrea. 1981. Pornography: Men Possessing Women. New York: Putnam.

Dye, Thomas R. 1983. Who's Running America? The Reagan Years. (3rd ed.) Englewood Cliffs, N.J.: Prentice-Hall.

Dye, Thomas R. 1986. Who's Running America: The Conservative Years. 4th ed. Englewood Cliffs, N.J.: Prentice-Hall.

Ebenstein, William. Today's Isms. Englewood Cliffs, N.J.: Prentice-Hall.

Eblen, Jack E. 1974. "New Estimates of the Vital Rates of the United States Black Population During the 19th Century." Demography 11 (2): 301–20.

Edwards, Richard. 1979. Contested Terrain. New York: Basic Books.

Eglit, Howard. 1985. "Age and the Law." In Robert Binstock and Ethel Shanas (eds.), Handbook of Aging and the Social Sciences. (2nd ed.) New York: Van Nostrand Reinhold.

Eisenhower, M. 1969. Commission Statement on Violence in Television Entertainment Programs. National Commission on the Causes and Prevention of Violence. Washington, D.C.: U.S. Government Printing Office.

Eisenstadt, S. N. 1985. "Macrosocietal Analysis—Background, Development, and Indications." In S. N. Eisenstadt and H. J. Helle (eds.), Macrosociological Theory: Perspectives on Sociological Theory. Newbury Park, Calif: Sage.

Elder, G. H., Jr. 1969. "Appearance and Education in Marriage Mobility." American Sociological Review 34 (August): 519–33.

Elder, G. H., Jr. 1974. Children of the Great Depression. Chicago: University of Chicago Press.

Elliott, Delbert S., and Ageton, Suzanne S. 1980. "Reconciling Race and Class Differences in Self-Reported Official Estimates of Delinquency." American Sociological Review 45 (February): 95–110.

Emerson, Richard M. 1962. "Power-Dependence Relations." American Sociological Review 27 (February): 31–41.

Engels, Friedrich. 1965. "Socialism: Utopian and Scientific." In Arthur P. Mendel (ed.), The Essential Works of Marxism. New York: Bantam Books. (Originally published 1880.)

Engels, Friedrich. 1972. The Origins of the Family, Private Property, and the State. (Eleanor Burke Leacock, trans.). New York: International Publishers. (Originally published 1884.)

England, Paula, and Dunn, Dana. 1988. "Evaluating Work and Comparative Worth." Annual Review of Sociology 14:227–48.

Ennis, James, and Schrauer, Richard. 1987. "Mobilizing Weak Support for Social Movements: The Role of Grievance, Efficacy, and Cost." Social Forces 62:390–409.

Erickson, Kai. 1986. "On Work and Alienation." American Sociological Review 51 (February): 1–8.

Eron, L. D. 1980. "Prescription for Reduction of Aggression." American Psychologist 35 (March): 244–52.

Espenshade, Thomas. 1990. "A Short History of U.S. Policy Toward Illegal Immigration." Population Today 18 (2): 6–8.

Etzioni, Amitai. 1968. The Active Society. New York: Free Press.

The Europa Yearbook. 1989. A World Survey. England: Europa Publications.

Faden, Ruth, and Kass, Nancy. 1988. "Health Insurance and AIDS." American Journal of Public Health 78: 437–39.

Farley, Reynolds. 1985. "Three Steps Forward and Two Back? Recent Changes in the Social and Economic Status of Blacks." In Richard Alba (ed.), Ethnicity and Race in the U.S.A.: Toward the Twenty-First Century. Boston: Routleldge & Kegan Paul.

Felson, Richard B. 1985. "Reflected Appraisal and the Development of Self." Social Psychology Quarterly 48 (1): 71–78.

Ferraro, Kenneth. 1989. "Reexamining the Double Jeopardy Health Thesis." Journal of Gerontology 44:514–17.

Festinger, Leon, Schachter, Stanley, and Back, Kurt. 1950. Social Pressure in Informal Groups. New York: Harper & Row.

Figueira-McDonough, Josefina. 1985. "Gender Differences in Informal Processing: A Look at Charge Bargaining and Sentence Reduction in Washington, D.C." Journal of Research in Crime and Delinquency 22 (May): 101–33.

Fine, Gary Alan. 1984. "Negotiated Orders and Organizational Cultures." Annual Review of Sociology 10:239–62.

Firebaugh, Glenn, and Davis, Kenneth. 1988. "Trends in Anti-Black Prejudice, 1972–84: Region and Cohort Effects." American Journal of Sociology 94:251–70.

Fischer, Claude S. 1976. The Urban Experience. San Diego, Calif.: Harcourt Brace Jovanovich.

Fischer, Claude S. 1979. "Urban-to-Rural Diffusion of Opinion in Contemporary America." American Journal of Sociology 84 (July): 151–59.

Fischer, Claude S. 1981. "The Public and Private Worlds of City Life." American Sociological Review 46 (June): 306–17.

Fischer, Claude S. 1982. To Dwell Among Friends: Personal Networks in Town and City. Chicago: University of Chicago Press.

Fisher, A. D. 1987. "Alcoholism and Race: The Misapplication of Both Concepts to North American Indians. Canadian Sociological and Anthropological Review 24:80–95.

Fishman, Joshua. 1985a. "Macrosociolinguistics and the Sociology of Language in the Early Eighties." Annual Review of Sociology 11:113–27.

Fishman, Joshua. 1985b. The Rise and Fall of the Ethnic Revival: Perspectives on Language and Ethnicity. Berlin: Mouton.

Fishman, Pamela M. 1978. "Interaction: The Work Women Do. Social Problems 25:397–406.

Fitzgerald, C. P. 1984. "Accomplishments of the Great Leap Forward." In Molly Joel Coye, John Livingston, and Jean Highland (eds.), China: Yesterday and Today. New York: Bantam Books.

Fitzpatrick, Kevin M., and Logan, John. 1985. "The Aging of the Suburbs, 1960–1980." American Sociological Review 50 (February): 106–17.

"Fixing Social Security." 1990. Newsweek, May 7, pp. 54ff.

Flexner, Eleanor. 1972. Century of Struggle. New York: Atheneum.

"The Forbes Four Hundred." 1989. Forbes 144 (October 23): 145–290.

Forester, Tom. 1989. "The Myth of the Electronic Cottage." Computers and Society 19(2): 4–19.

Form, William. 1982. "Self-Employment Manual Workers: Petty Bourgeois or Working Class?" Social Forces 60 (June): 1050–70.

Form, William. 1985. Divided We Stand: Working Class Stratification in America. Urbana: University of Illinois Press.

Frankl, Razelle. 1984. "Television and Popular Religion: Changes in Church Offerings." In David Bromley and Anson Shupe (eds.), New Christian Politics. Macon, Ga.: Mercer University Press.

Freudenburg, William R. 1986. "The Density of Acquaintanceship: An Overlooked Variable in Community Research." American Journal of Sociology 92 (July): 27–63.

Freyka, Tomas. 1973. The Future of Population Growth: Alternative Paths to Equilibrium. New York: Wiley.

Friedsam, H. J. 1965. "Competition." In Julius Gould and William L. Kolb (eds.), A Dictionary of the Social Sciences. New York: Free Press.

"Funds to Be Denied for Obscene Art." 1989. Lincoln Star.

Funk, Richard, and Willits, Fern. 1987. "College Attendance and Attitudinal Change: A Panel Study, 1970–81." Sociology of Education 60:224–31.

Furstenberg, Frank F., Jr., Brooks-Gunn, J., and Morgan, S. Philip. 1987. Adolescent Mothers in Later Life. Cambridge, England: Cambridge University Press.

"The Future of Gay America." 1990. Newsweek, March 12, pp. 20ff.

"Future Organizational Trends of the ASA." 1989. Footnotes 17 (September): 1ff.

Gaes, Gerald G., and McGuire, William J. 1985. "Prison Violence: The Contribution of Crowding Versus Other Determinants of Prison Assault Rates." Journal of Research in Crime and Delinquency 22 (February): 41–65.

Gagnon, J. H. 1977. Human Sexualities. Glenview, Ill.: Scott, Foresman.

Gagnon, J. H., Roberts, E., and Greenblat, C. 1978. "Stability and Change in Rates of Marital Intercourse." Paper presented at the annual meetings of the International Academy of Sex Research, Toronto, Canada, August.

Gallup Report. 1984. Nos. 227/228.

Gallup Report. 1989a. Nos. 282/283.

Gallup Report. 1989b. No. 285.

Gallup Report. 1989c. No. 286.

Gallup Report. 1989d. No. 288.

Gallup Report. 1989e. No. 289.

Gamoran, Adam, and Mare, Robert. 1989. "Secondary School Tracking and Educational Inequality." American Journal of Sociology 94:1146–83.

Gans, Herbert J. 1962. The Urban Villagers. New York: Free Press.

Gans, Herbert. 1974. Popular Culture and High Culture. New York: Basic Books.

Gans, Herbert J. 1989. "Sociology in America: The Discipline and the Public." American Sociological Review 54:1–16.

Ganz, Alexander. 1985. "Where Has the Urban Crisis Gone? How Boston and Other Large Cities Have Stemmed Economic Decline." Urban Affairs Quarterly 20 (June): 449–68.

Gardner, Howard. 1983. Frames of Mind: The Theory of Multiple Intelligences. New York: Basic Books.

Gardner, L. I. 1972. "Deprivation Dwarfism." Scientific American 227 July: 76–82.

Gardner, LeGrande, and Shoemaker, Donald. 1989. "Social Bonds and Delinquency: A Comparative Analysis." Sociological Quarterly 30:481–500.

Gardner, Robert W., Robey, Bryant, and Smith, Peter C. 1985. "Asian Americans: Growth, Change, and Diversity." Population Bulletin 40 (October): 5–8.

Garfield, Richard M., and Taboada, Eugenio. 1986. "Health Services Reforms in Revolutionary Nicaragua." In Peter Rossett and John Vandermeer (eds.), Nicaragua: Unfinished Revolution. New York: Grove Press.

Garfinkel, H. 1963. "A Conception of, and Experiments with, 'Trust' as a Condition of Stable Concerted Actions." In O. J. Harvery (ed.), Motivation and Social Interaction. New York: Ronald Press.

Garfinkel, H. 1967. Studies in Ethnomethodology. Englewood Cliffs, N.J.: Prentice-Hall.

Garrett, William. 1987. "Religion, Law, and the Human Condition." Sociological Analysis 47 (Supplement): 1–34.

Gecas, Viktor. 1981. "Contents of Socialization." In Morris Rosenberg and Ralph H. Turner (eds.), Social Psychology: Sociological Perspectives. New York: Basic Books.

Gecas, Viktor. 1989. "The Social Psychology of Self-Efficiency." Annual Review of Sociology 15:291–316.

Gecas, Victor, and Schwalbe, Michael. 1983. "Beyond the Looking-Glass Self: Social Structure and Efficacy-Based Self-Esteem." Social Psychological Quarterly 46 (2): 77–88.

Geertz, Clifford. 1973. "Thick Description: Toward an Interpretive Theory of Culture." In Clifford Geertz, The Interpretation of Cultures: Selected Essays. New York: Basic Books.

Gelles, Richard J., and Cornell, Claire. 1985. Intimate Violence in Families. Newbury Park, Calif.: Sage.

Gelles, Richard J., and Straus, Murray. 1988. Intimate Violence. New York: Simon & Schuster.

Genovese, Frank. 1988. "An Examination of Proposals for a U.S. Industrial Policy." American Journal of Economics and Sociology 47: 441–53.

"Geographic Polarization of Whites and Minorities in Large U.S. Cities: 1960–1980." 1986. Population Today 14 (March): 6–7.

Gerth, H. H., and Mills, C. Wright (eds. and trans.). 1970. From Max Weber: Essays in Sociology. New York: Oxford University Press. (Originally published 1946.)

Gerzon, Mark. 1982. A Choice of Heroes: The Changing Faces of American Manhood. Boston: Houghton Mifflin.

Giddens, Anthony. 1984. The Constitution of Society. Cambridge, England: Polity Press.

Gill, Colen. 1985. Work, Unemployment, and the New Technology. Cambridge, England: Polity Press.

Ginsberg, Benjamin, and Weissburg, Robert. 1978. "Elections and the Mobilization of Popular Support." American Journal of Political Science 22: 31–55.

Girdner, Audrie, and Loftis, Anne. 1969. The Great Betrayal. London: Macmillan.

Glassner, Barry. 1989. "Fitness and the Postmodern Self." Journal of Health and Social Behavior 30:180–91.

Glenn, Norval. 1990. "Research on Marital Quality During the 1980s: A Critical Review." Journal of Marriage and the Family 52 (November).

Glenn, Norval D., and Supancic, Michael. 1984. "Social and Demographic Correlates of Divorce and Separation in the United States: An Updated Reconsideration." Journal of Marriage and the Family 46 (August): 563–75.

Glick, Paul C. 1984. "American Household Structure in Transition." Family Planning Perspectives 16 (5): 205–11.

Goffman, Erving. 1959. The Presentation of Self in Everyday Life. New York: Doubleday.

Goffman, Erving. 1961a. Asylums: Essays on the Social Situation of Mental Patients and Other Inmates. New York: Doubleday.

Goffman, Erving. 1961b. Encounters: Two Studies in the Sociology of Interaction. Indianapolis, Ind.: Bobbs-Merrill.

Goffman, Erving. 1963a. Behavior in Public Places: Notes on the Social Organization of Gatherings. New York: Free Press.

Goffman, Erving. 1963b. Stigmas: Notes on the Management of Spoiled Identity. Englewood Cliffs, N.J.: Prentice-Hall.

Goffman, Erving. 1967. Interaction Ritual: Essays on Face-to-Face Behavior. New York: Doubleday.

Goffman, Erving. 1971. "The Insanity of Place." In Erving Goffman, Relations in Public. New York: Harper & Row.

Goffman, Erving. 1974a. Gender Advertisements. New York: Harper & Row.

Goffman, Erving. 1974b. Frame Analysis: An Essay on the Organization of Experience. New York: Harper & Row.

Goffman, Erving. 1983. "The Interaction Order." American Sociological Review 48 (February): 1–17.

Goldscheider, Frances, and Goldscheider, Calvin. 1989. "Family Structure and Conflict: Nest-Leaving Expectations of Young Adults and Their Parents." Journal of Marriage and the Family 51:87–97.

Goliber, Thomas. 1989. "Africa's Expanding Population: Old Problems, New Policies." Population Bulletin 44 (3): 1–50.

Goode, Erich. 1989. Drugs in American Society. New York: Knopf.

Goode, William. 1959. "The Theoretical Importance of Love." American Sociological Review 24:37–48.

Gottdiener, Mark. 1985. "Whatever Happened to the Urban Crisis." Urban Affairs Quarterly 20 (June): 421–27.

Gottdiener, Mark, and Feagin, Joe. 1988. "The Paradigm Shift in Urban Sociology." Urban Affairs Quarterly 24:163–87.

Gottlieb, Benjamin H. 1981. "Social Networks and Social Support in Community Mental Health." In B. H. Gottlieb (ed.), Social Networks and Social Support. Vol. 4. Sage Series in Community Mental Health. Newbury Park, Calif.: Sage.

Goudy, Willis J., Powers, Edward A., Keith, Patricia, and Reger, Richard A. 1980. "Changes in Attitude Toward Retirement: Evidence from a Panel Study of Older Males." Journal of Gerontology 35:942–48.

Gouldner, Alvin. 1960. "The Norm of Reciprocity." American Sociological Review 25 (February): 161–178.

Gove, Walter, Ortega, Suzanne, and Style, Carolyn. 1989. "The Maturational and Role Perspectives on Aging and Self Through the Adult Years: An Empirical Evaluation." American Journal of Sociology 94:1117–45.

Granovetter, Mark. 1973. "The Strength of Weak Ties." American Journal of Sociology 78 (May): 1360–80.

Greeley, Andrew M. 1979. "Ethnic Variations in Religious Commitment." In Robert Wuthnow (ed.), The Religious Dimension: New Directions in Quantitative Research. Orlando, Fla.: Academic Press.

Greenberg, David F. 1985. "Age, Crime, and Social Explanation." American Journal of Sociology, 91 (July): 1–21.

Greenberg, Michael R. 1989. "Black Male Cancer and American Urban Health Policy." Journal of Urban Affairs 11:113–30.

Greenblat, Cathy Stein. 1983. "The Salience of Sexuality in the Early Years of Marriage." Journal of Marriage and the Family 45 (May): 289–300.

Griffith, Jeanne, Frase, Mary, and Ralph, John. 1989. "American Education: The Challenge of Change." Population Bulletin 44:1–50.

Grimes, Michael D. 1989. "Class and Attitudes Toward Structural Inequalities: An Empirical Comparison of Key Variables in Neo- and Post-Marxist Scholarship." Sociological Quarterly 30:441–63.

Gross, Edward. 1958. Work and Society. New York: Crowell.

Guimond, Serge, Begin, Guy, and Palmer, Douglas. 1989. "Education and Causal Attributions: The Development of Person-Blame and System-Blame Ideology." Social Psychology Quarterly 52:126–40.

Gurney, Joan N., and Tierney, Kathleen J. 1982. "Relative Deprivation and Social Movements: A Critical Look at Twenty Years of Theory and Research." Sociological Quarterly 23 (Winter): 33–47.

Guterbock, Thomas M., and London, Bruce. 1983. "Race, Political Orientation, and Participation: An Empirical Test of Four Competing Theories. American Sociological Review 48 (August): 439–53.

Guy, Gregory. 1989. "International Perspectives on Linguistic Diversity and Language Rights." Language Problems and Language Planning 13:45–53.

Hagan, John, Gillis, A. R., and Simpson, John. 1985. "The Class Structure of Gender and Delinquency: Toward a Power-Control Theory of Common Delinquent Behavior." American Journal of Sociology 90 (May): 1151–78.

Hagestad, Gunhild O., and Neugarten, Bernice L. 1985. "Age and the Life Course." In Robert Binstock and Ethel Shanas (eds.), Handbook of Aging and the Social Sciences, (2nd ed.) New York: Van Nostrand Reinhold.

Halaby Charles N. 1986. "Worker Attachment and Workplace Authority." American Sociological Review 51 (October): 634–49.

Hall, E. 1969. The Hidden Dimension. New York: Doubleday.

Hall, John R. 1987. Gone from the Promised Land: Jonestown in American Cultural History. New Brunswick, N.J.: Transaction.

Halle, David. 1984. America's Working Man: Work, Home, and Politics Among Blue-Collar Property Owners. Chicago: University of Chicago Press.

Hallinan, M. 1988. "Equality of Educational Opportunity." Annual Review of Sociology 14:249–68.

Hallinan, Maureen T., and Sorenson, Aage B. 1986. "Student Characteristics and Assignment to Ability Groups:

Two Conceptual Formulations." Sociological Quarterly 27 (1): 1–13.

Hanks, Michael. 1981. "Youth, Voluntary Associations and Political Socialization." Social Forces 60 (September): 211–23.

Hardin, Clifford. 1968. "The Tragedy of the Commons." Science 162:1243–48.

Harlow, H. F., and Harlow, M. K. 1966. "Learning to Live." Scientific American pp. 244–72.

Harris, Chauncey D., and Ullman, Edward L. 1945. "The Nature of Cities." Annals of the American Association of Political and Social Science 242 (November): 7–17.

Harris, Louis, and Associates. 1975. The Myth and Reality of Aging in America. Washington, D.C.: National Council on Aging.

Harris Survey. 1989a. April 9.

Harris Survey. 1989b. October 29.

Hartman, Heidi. 1981. "The Family as the Locus of Gender, Class and Political Struggles: The Example of Housework." Signs 6 (3): 366–94.

Hatcher, John. 1977. Plagues, Population, and the English Economy, 1348–1530. London: Macmillan.

Haugen, Steven, and Mellor, Earl. 1990. "Estimating the Number of Minimum Wage Workers." Monthly Labor Review, January, pp. 70–72.

Hayward, Mark, Grady, William, Hardy, Melissa, and Sommers, David. 1989. "Occupational Influences on Retirement, Disability, and Death." Demography 26:393–409.

Hayward, Mark, Grady, William, and McLaughlin, Steven. 1988. "Changes in the Retirement Process Among Older Men in the United States: 1972–1980." Demography 25:371–86.

Hechter, Michael. 1987. Principles of Group Solidarity. Berkeley: University of California Press.

Heidensohn, Frances. 1985. Women and Crime: The Life of the Female Offender. New York: New York University Press.

Hendricks, Jon, and Hendricks, C. Davis. 1981. Aging in Mass Society: Myths and Realities. (2nd ed.) Cambridge. Mass.: Winthrop.

Henley, Nancy M. 1977. Body Politics: Power, Sex and Nonverbal Communication. Englewood Cliffs. N.J.: Prentice-Hall.

Hess, Beth. 1985. "Aging Policies and Old Women: The Hidden Agenda." In Alice Rossi (ed.), Gender and the Life Course. Hawthorne, New York: Aldine.

Heyl, Barbara. 1979. The Madam as Entrepreneur: Career Management in House Prostitution. New Brunswick, N.J.: Transaction.

Heyns, Barbara. 1978. Summer Learning and the Effects of Schooling. Orlando, Fla.: Academic Press.

Hickok, Kathleen. 1981. "The Spinster in Victorian England: Changing Attitudes in Popular Poetry." Journal of Popular Culture 15 (3): 118–31.

Himes, Norman E. 1936. The Medical History of Contraception. Baltimore, Md.: Johns Hopkins University Press.

Hindelang, Michael J., Hirschi, Travis, and Weis, Joseph. 1981. Measuring Delinquency. Newbury Park, Calif.: Sage.

"Hiring Discrimination Blamed on Immigration Reform Law." 1990. Lincoln Star, p. 3.

Hirsch, Arnold R. 1983. Making the Second Ghetto: Race and Housing in Chicago, 1940–1960. New York: Cambridge University Press.

Hirschi, Travis. 1969. Causes of Delinquency. Berkeley and Los Angeles: University of California Press.

Hirschi, Travis, and Gottfredson, Michael. 1983. "Age and the Explanation of Crime." American Journal of Sociology 89 (November): 552–84.

Hochschild, Arlie R. 1985. The Managed Heart: The Commercialization of Human Feeling. Berkeley: University of California Press.

Hochschild, Jennifer. 1981. What's Fair? American Beliefs About Distributive Justice. Cambridge, Mass.: Harvard University Press.

Hodge, Robert W., Siegel, Paul, and Rossi, Peter. 1964. "Occupational Prestige in the United States, 1925–63." American Journal of Sociology 70 (November): 286–302.

Hodge, Robert W., Treiman, Donald J., and Rossi, Peter. 1966. "A Comparative Study of Occupational Prestige." In Reinhard Bendix and Seymour Martin Lipset (eds.), Class, Status, and Power. (2nd ed.) New York: Free Press.

Hoffman, Saul, and Duncan, Greg. 1988. "What Are the Economic Consequences of Divorce?" Demography 25:641–45.

Hogan, D. P. 1981. Transitions and Social Change: The Early Lives of American Men. Orlando, Fla.: Academic Press.

Hogan, Dennis P., and Astone, Nan Marie. 1986. "The Transition to Adulthood." Annual Review of Sociology 12:109–30.

Holden, Karen, Burkhauser, Richard, and Feaster, Daniel. 1988. "The Timing of Falls into Poverty After Retirement and Widowhood." Demography 25:405–14.

Homans, George. 1950. The Human Group. San Diego, Calif.: Harcourt Brace Jovanovich.

Hooks, Gregory. 1984. "The Policy Response to Factory Closings: A Comparison of the United States, Sweden, and France." Annals of the American Academy of Political and Social Science 475:110–24.

Horwitz, Allan V. 1984. "The Economy and Social Pathology." Annual Review of Sociology 10:95–119.

Hostetler, John. 1963. Amish Society. Baltimore, Md.: Johns Hopkins University Press.

Houston, Jeanne Wakatsuke, and Houston, James D. 1973. Farewell to Manzanar. Boston: Houghton Mifflin.

"How Many People Can the World Feed?" 1985. Population Today 13 (January): 1, 8.

Howery, Carla. 1983. "Sociologists Shaping Public Policy: Two Profiles." Footnotes 11 (August): 12.

Hoyt, Danny, and Babchuk, Nicholas. 1983. "Adult Kinship Networks: The Selective Formation of Intimate Ties." Social Forces 62 (September): 84–101.

Huber, Joan, and Form, William H. 1973. Income and Ideology: An Analysis of the American Political Formula. New York: Free Press.

Huber, Joan, and Spitze, Glenna. 1983. Sex Stratification: Children, Housework, and Jobs. Orlando, Fla.: Academic Press.

Hudson, Robert B., and Strate, John. 1985. "Aging and Political Systems." In Robert H. Binstock and Ethel Shanas (eds.). Handbook of Aging and the Social Sciences (2nd ed.) New York: Van Nostrand Reinhold.

Huff-Corzine, Lin, Corzine, Jay, and Moore, David. 1986. "Southern Exposure: Deciphering the South's Influence on Homicide Rates." Social Forces 64:906–24.

Humpreys, Laud. 1970. Tearoom Trade: Impersonal Sex in Public Places. Hawthorne, N.Y.: Aldine.

Hurlbert, Jeanne S. 1989. "The Southern Region: A Test of the Hypothesis of Cultural Distinctiveness." Sociological Quarterly 30:245–66.

Inkeles, Alex, and Smith, David H. 1974. Becoming Modern: Individual Change in Six Developing Countries. Cambridge, Mass.: Harvard University Press.

Invararity, James, and McCarthy, Daniel. 1988. "Punishment and Social Structure Revisited: Unemployment and Imprisonment in the United States." Sociological Quarterly 29:263–79.

Jacobs, Jerry. 1989. "Long-Term Trends in Occupational Segregation." American Journal of Sociology 95:160–73.

James, David R. 1989. "City Limits on Racial Equality." American Sociological Review 54:963–85.

Janis, Irving. 1982. Groupthink: Psychological Studies of Policy Decisions and Fiascoes. Boston: Houghton Mifflin.

Jeffe, Douglas, and Jeffe, Sherry. 1989. "Gun Control: A Silent Majority Raises Its Voice." Public Opinion, May/June, p. 9ff.

Jencks, Christopher, Smith, M., Acland, H., Bane, J. J., Cohen D., Gintis, H., Heyns, B., and Michelson, S. 1972. Inequality: A Reassessment of the Effect of Family and Schooling in America. New York: Basic Books.

Jenkins, J. Craig, and Brent, Barbara. 1989. "Social Protest, Hegemonic Competition, and Social Reform." American Sociological Review 54:891–909.

Jenkins, J. Craig, and Eckert, Craig M. 1986. "Channeling Black Insurgency: Elite Patronage and Professional Social Movement Organizations in the Development of the Black Movement." American Sociological Review 51 (December): 812–29.

Jessor, R., and Jessor, S. 1977. Problem Behavior and Psychosocial Development: A Longitudinal Study of Youth. Orlando, Fla.: Academic Press.

Jiobu, Robert. 1988. "Ethnic Hegemony and the Japanese of California." American Sociological Review 53:353–67.

Johansen, Harley, and Fuguitt, Glenn. 1984. The Changing Rural Village in America: Demographic and Economic Trends Since 1950. Cambridge, Mass.: Ballinger.

Johnson, Benton. 1957. "A Critical Appraisal of the Church Sect Typology." American Sociological Review 22 (1): 88–92.

Johnson, Kenneth. 1989. "Recent Population Redistribution Trends in Nonmetropolitan America." Rural Sociology 54:301–26.

Johnson, Richard E. 1980. "Social Class and Delinquent Behavior: A New Test." Criminology 18 (1): 86–93.

Jones, James H. 1981. Bad Blood: The Tuskegee Syphilis Experiment. New York: Free Press.

Kaa, Dirk. 1987. "Europe's Second Demographic Transition." Population Bulletin 42 (March): 1–50.

Kahl, Anne, and Clark, Donald. 1986. "Employment in Health Services." Monthly Labor Review 109 (8): 17–37.

Kalab, Kathleen. 1987. "Student Vocabularies of Motive: Accounts for Absence." Symbolic Interaction 10:71–83.

Kanet, Roger. 1989. "New Thinking and New Foreign Policy Under Gorbachev." Political Science and Politics 22:215–24.

Kanter, Rosabeth Moss. 1977. Men and Women of the Corporation. New York: Basic Books.

Kaplan, Howard. 1989. "Methodological Problems in the Study of Psychosocial Influences on the AIDS Process." Social Science and Medicine 29:277–92.

Kaplan, Howard B., Martin, Steven S., and Johnson, Robert J. 1986. "Self-Rejection and the Explanation of Deviance: Specification of the Structure Among Latent Constructs." American Journal of Sociology 92 (September): 384–411.

Karliner, Joshua, Faber, Daniel, and Rice, Robert. 1986. "An Environmental Perspective." In Peter Rosset and John Vandermeer (eds.), Nicaragua: Unfinished Revolution. New York: Grove Press.

Katz, Michael. 1987. Reconstructing American Education. Cambridge, Mass.: Harvard University Press.

Katz, Neil. 1989. "Conflict Resolution and Peace Studies." The Annals 504 (July): 14–21.

Kendall, Patricia, and Reader, George. 1988. "Innovations in Medical Education of the 1950s Contrasted with Those of the 1970s and 1980s." Journal of Health and Social Behavior 29:279–93.

Kennan, George. 1989. "After the Cold War." New York Times Magazine, February 5, 1989, pp. 32ff.

"Kenya." 1989. Population Today 17 (10): 5.

Kephart, William M. 1983 and 1987. Extraordinary Groups: The Sociology of Unconventional Life-Styles. (2nd and 3rd ed.) New York: St. Martin's Press.

Kerckhoff, Alan C., and Davis, Keith E. 1962. "Value Consensus and Need Complementarity in Mate Selection." American Sociological Review 27 (June): 295–303.

Kessler, Ronald C., and McLeod, Jane. 1984. "Sex Differences in Vulnerability to Undesirable Life Events." American Sociological Review 49 (October): 620–31.

Kessler, Ronald C., Turner, J. Blake, and House, James. 1989. "Unemployment, Reemployment, and Emotional Functioning in a Community Sample." American Sociological Review 54:648–57.

Keyfitz, Nathan. 1987. "The Family that Does not Reproduce Itself." In Kingsley Davis, Mikhail Bernstam, and Rita Ricardo-Campbell, (eds.), Below Replacement Fertility in Industrial Societies: Causes, Consequences, Policies. Cambridge, England: Cambridge University Press.

Kielbowicz, Richard B., and Scherer, Clifford. 1986. "The Role of the Press in the Dynamics of Social Movements." Research in Social Movements, Conflicts, and Change 9:71–96.

Kilner, John. 1988. "Selecting Patients When Resources Are Limited: A Study of U.S. Medical Directors of Kidney Dialysis and Transplantation Facilities." American Journal of Public Health 78 (2): 144–47.

Kinsey, A. C. 1948. Sexual Behavior in the Human Male. Philadelphia: Saunders.

Kinsey, A. C. 1953. Sexual Behavior in the Human Female. Philadelphia: Saunders.

Kitson, Gay, and Sussman, Marvin. 1982. "Marital Complaints, Demographic Characteristics, and Symptoms of Mental Distress in Divorce." Journal of Marriage and the Family 44:87–101.

Klandermas, Bert. 1984. "Mobilization and Participation: Social-Pyschological Expansion of Resource Mobilization Theory." American Sociological Review 49 (October): 583–600.

Kleck, Gary. 1981. "Racial Discrimination in Criminal Sentencing: A Critical Evaluation of the Evidence with Additional Evidence on the Death Penalty." American Sociological Review 46 (December): 783–805.

Kleck, Gary. 1982. "On the Use of Self-Report Data to Determine the Class Distribution of Criminal and Delinquent Behavior." American Sociological Review 47 (June): 427–33.

Klepper, Steven, and Nagin, Daniel. 1989. "The Deterrent Effect of Perceived Certainty and Severity of Punishment Revisited." Criminology 27:721–46.

Kluegel, James R., and Smith, Eliot R. 1983. "Affirmative Action Attitudes: Effects of Self-Interest, Racial Affect, and Stratification Beliefs on Whites' Views." Social Forces 61 (March): 170–81.

Knoke, David. 1981. "Commitment and Detachment in Voluntary Associations." American Sociological Review 46 (2): 141–58.

Kogamawa, Joy. 1981. Obason. Toronto: Lester and Orpen Dennys.

Kohn, Melvin, and Schooler, Carmi, and Associates. 1983. Work and Personality: An Inquiry into the Impact of Social Stratification. Norwood, N.J.: Ablex.

Kohn, Robert L. 1972. "The Meaning of Work: Interpretation and Proposals for Measurement." In A. Campbell and P. Converse (eds.), The Human Meaning of Social Change. New York: Basic Books.

Kollock, Peter, Blumstein, Philip, and Schwartz, Pepper. 1985. "Sex and Power in Interaction: Conversational Privileges and Duties." American Sociological Review 50 (February): 34–46.

Konig, René. 1968. "Auguste Comte." In David J. Sills (ed.), International Encyclopedia of the Social Sciences. Vol. 3. New York: Macmillan and Free Press.

Korpi, Walter. 1989. "Power, Politics, and State Autonomy in the Development of Social Citizenship." American Sociological Review 54: 309–28.

Korte, C. 1980. "Urban-Nonurban Differences in Social Behavior: Social Psychological Models of Urban Impact." Journal of Social Issues 36 (1): 29–51.

Krohn, Marvin D., Akers, Ronald L., Radosevich, Marcia J., and Lanza-Kaduce, Lonn. 1980. "Social Status and Deviance." Criminology 18:303–18.

Kutner, Nancy. 1987. "Issues in the Application of High-Cost Medical Technology: The Case of Organ Transplantation." Journal of Health and Social Behavior 28:23–36.

Langton, John. 1984. "The Ecological Theory of Bureaucracy: The Case of Josiah Wedgwood and the British Pottery Industry." Administrative Science Quarterly 29: 330–54.

Lareau, Annette, 1987. "Social Class Differences in Family-School Relationships: The Impact of Cultural Capital." Sociology of Education 60:73–85.

LaRossa, Ralph. 1988. "Fatherhood and Social Change." Family Relations 37:451–57.

Larson, Reed. 1978. "Thirty Years of Research on the Subjective Well-Being of Older Americans." Journal of Gerontology 33 (January): 109–25.

Lavee, Yoar, McCubbin, Hamilton I., and Patterson, Joan M. 1985. "The Double ABCX Model of Family Stress and Adaptation: An Empirical Test by Analysis of Structural Equations with Latent Variables." Journal of Marriage and the Family 47 (November): 811–25.

Lebergott, Stanley. 1975. Wealth and Want. Princeton, N.J.: Princeton University Press.

LeBon, Gustav. 1896. The Crowd: A Study of the Popular Mind. London: Ernest Benn.

Lee, Gary R., and Stone, Loren Hemphill. 1980. "Mate-Selection Systems and Criteria: Variation According to Family Structure." Journal of Marriage and the Family 42 (May): 319–26.

Lee, Valerie, and Bryk, Anthony. 1989. "A Multilevel Model of the Social Distribution of High School Achievement." Sociology of Education 62:172–92.

Lehman, Edward. 1988. "The Theory of the State Versus the State of Theory." American Sociological Review 53:807–23.

Lemert, Edwin. 1981. "Issues in the Study of Deviance."

Sociological Quarterly 22 (Spring): 285–305.

Lenski, Gerhard. 1966. Power and Privilege: A Theory of Social Stratification. New York: McGraw-Hill.

Lerner, Robert, Rothman, Stanley, and Lichter, S. Robert. 1989. "Christian Religious Elites." Public Opinion 11 (March/April): 54–59.

"Lessons from Bigotry 101." 1989. Newsweek, September 25, pp. 48–50.

Levin, William. 1988. "Age Stereotyping: College Student Evaluations." Research on Aging 10:134–48.

Levinger, George. 1986. "The Editor's Page." Journal of Social Issues 43 (3): x.

Lewis, Oscar. 1969. "The Culture of Poverty." In Daniel P. Moynihan (ed.), On Understanding Poverty. New York: Basic Books.

Lichter, Daniel T. 1989. "Race, Employment Hardship, and Inequality in the American Nonmetropolitan South." American Sociological Review 54:436–46.

Lieberson, Stanley. 1980. A Piece of the Pie: Blacks and White Immigrants Since 1880. Berkeley: University of California Press.

Lieberson, Stanley. 1985. "Unhyphenated Whites in the United States." In Richard Alba (ed.), Ethnicity and Race in the U.S.A.: Toward the Twenty-First Century. Boston: Routledge & Kegan Paul.

Lieberson, Stanley, and Waters, Mary. 1988. From Many Strands: Ethnic and Racial Groups in Contemporary America. New York: Russell Sage Foundation.

Liebow, Elliot. 1967. Tally's Corner. Boston: Little, Brown.

Light, Donald W. 1988. "Toward a New Sociology of Medical Education." Journal of Health and Social Behavior 29:307–22.

Lin, Nan, and Ensel, Walter. 1989. "Life Stress and Health Stressors and Resources." American Sociological Review 54:382–99.

Lincoln, James R., and McBride, Kerry. 1987. "Japanese Industrial Organization in Comparative Perspective." Annual Review of Sociology 13:289–312.

Lincoln, Yvonna, and Guba, Egan. 1985. Naturalistic Inquiry. Newbury Park, Calif.: Sage.

Link, Bruce. 1987. "Understanding Labeling Effects in the Area of Mental Disorders: An Assessment of the Effects of Expectations of Rejection." American Sociological Review 52 (February): 96–112.

Linz, D., Penrod, S., and Donnerstein, E. 1986. "Media Violence and Antisocial Behavior: Alternative Legal Policies." Journal of Social Issues 42 (3).

Lipset, Seymour. 1990. "Politics and Society in the U.S.S.R." Political Science and Politics 23 (March): 20–8.

Liska, Allen E., Chamlin, Mitchell B., and Reed, Mark. 1985. "Testing the Economic Production and Conflict Models of Crime Control." Social Forces 64 (September): 119–38.

Litwak, Eugene. 1961. "Voluntary Association and Neighborhood Cohesion." American Sociological Review 26 (April): 266–71.

Lo, Clarence Y. H. 1982. "Countermovements and Conservative Movements in the Contemporary U.S." Annual Review of Sociology 8:10–34.

Lofland, John. 1979. "White-Hot Mobilization." In M. Zald and J. McCarthy (eds.), the Dynamics of Social Movements. Boston: Little, Brown.

Lofland, John. 1981. "Collective Behavior: The Elementary Forms." In M. Rosenberg and Ralph Turner (eds.), Social Psychology: Sociological Perspectives. New York: Basic Books.

Lofland, John. 1985. Protest: Studies of Collective Behavior and Social Movements. New Brunswick, N.J.: Transaction.

Lofland, Lyn H. 1978. The Craft of Dying: The Modern Face of Death. Newbury Park, Calif.: Sage.

Logan, John, and Zhou, Min. 1989. "Do Suburban Growth Controls Control Growth?" American Sociological Review 54:461–71.

London, Bruce, and Robinson, Thomas. 1989. "The Effect of International Dependence on Income Inequality and Political Violence." American Sociological Review 54:305–08.

Love, Douglas, and Torrence, William. 1989. "The Impact of Worker Age on Unemployment and Earnings After Plant Closings." Journal of Gerontology 44:S190–5.

Lurigio, Arthur. 1990. "Introduction." Crime and Delinquency 36:3–5.

Lynch. J. J. 1979. The Broken Heart: The Medical Consequences of Loneliness. New York: Basic Books.

McAdam, Doug. 1986. "Recruitment to High-Risk Activism." American Journal of Sociology 92 (July): 64–90.

McConnell, Harvey. 1977. "The Indian War on Alcohol." Social Resources Series, Alcohol I 76:72–81.

McDill, Edward L., Natriello, Gary, and Pallas, Aaron. 1986. "A Population at Risk: Potential Consequences of Tougher School Standards for School Dropouts." American Journal of Education 94 (February): 135–81.

McFarlane, S. Neil. 1985. Superpower Rivalry and Third World Radicalism: The Idea of National Liberation. London: Croom Helm.

McGhee, Jerrie L. 1985. "The Effect of Siblings on the Life Satisfaction of the Rural Elderly." Journal of Marriage and the Family 47 (February): 85–90.

McGuigan, Patrick. 1989. "Loose Cannons: Self-Inflicted Wounds at the National Rifle Association." Policy Review 49 (Summer): 54–6.

McKeown, T., and Record, R. G. 1962. "Reasons for the Decline of Mortality in England and Wales During the Nineteenth Century." Population Studies 16 (March): 94–122.

McKeown, T., Record, R. G., and Turner, R. D. 1975. "An Interpretation of the Decline of Mortality in England and Wales During the Twentieth Century." Population Studies 29 (November): 390–421.

McLanahan, Sara. 1985. "Family Structure and the Reproduction of Poverty." American Journal of Sociology 90 (January): 873–901.

McLanahan, Sara. 1988. "Family Structure and Dependency: Early Transitions to Female Household Headship." Demography 25:1–16.

McLanahan, Sara, and Booth, Karen. 1989. "Mother-Only Families: Problems, Prospects, and Policies." Journal of Marriage and the Family 51:557–80.

McLanahan, Sara, Garfinkel, Irwin, and Watson, Dorothy. 1986. "Family Structure, Poverty, and the Underclass." Paper presented at the Workshop on Contemporary Urban Conditions sponsored by the Committee on National Urban Policy of the National Research Council, July.

McLaughlin, Steven, and Associates. 1988. The Changing Lives of American Women. Chapel Hill: University of North Carolina Press.

McNeil, William H. 1976. Peoples and Plagues. Garden City, New York: Anchor Press.

McPherson, J. Miller, and Smith-Lovin, Lynn. 1986. "Sex Segregation in Voluntary Associations." American Sociological Review 51 (February): 61–79.

McPherson, Miller. 1983. "The Size of Voluntary Organizations." Social Forces 61:1044–64.

McQueen, 1982. Gone Tomorrow. Melbourne, Australia: Angus & Robertson.

MacLeod, Jay. 1987. Ain't No Making It: Leveled Aspiratons in a Low-Income Neighborhood. Boulder, Colo.: Westview.

Maher, Timothy, Haas, Ain, Levine, Betty, and Liell, John. 1985. "Whose Neighborhood? The Role of Established Residents in Historical Preservation Areas." Urban Affairs Quarterly 21 (December): 267–81.

Malamuth, Neil, and Donnerstein, Edward (eds.). 1984. Pornography and Sexual Aggression. Orlando, Fla.: Academic Press.

Mannheim, Karl. 1929. Ideology and Utopia: An Introduction to the Sociology of Knowledge. San Diego, Calif.: Harcourt Brace Jovanovich.

Manski, Charles, and Wise, David. (eds.) 1983. College Choice in America. Cambridge: Harvard University Press.

Marini, Margaret. 1989. "Sex Differences in Earnings in the United States." Annual Review of Sociology 15:343–80.

Marini, Margaret Mooney. 1984. "Age and Sequencing Norms in the Transition to Adulthood." Social Forces 63 (September): 229–44.

Marmot, M. G., Kogevinas, M., and Elston, M. 1987. "Social/Economic Status and Disease." Annual Review of Public Health 8:111–35.

Marsden, Peter V. 1987. "Core Discussion Networks of Americans." American Sociological Review 52 (February): 122–131.

Marsh, Robert M., and Mannari, Hiroshi. 1976. Modernization and the Japanese Factory. Princeton, N.J.: Princeton University Press.

Marshall, Susan E. 1985. "Ladies Against Women: Mobilization Dilemmas of Antifeminist Movements." Social Problems 32 (April): 348–62.

Martin, Teresa, and Bumpass, Larry. 1989. "Recent Trends in Marital Disruption." Demography 26:37–51.

Martz, Larry. 1987. "God and Money." Newsweek, April 6, 16–22.

Marwell, Gerald, and Oliver, Pamela. 1984. "Collective Action Theory and Social Movement Research." Research in Social Movements, Conflicts, and Change 7:1–27.

Marwell, Gerald, Oliver, Pamela, and Prahl, Ralph. 1988. "Social Networks and Collective Action: A Theory of the Critical Mass III." American Journal of Sociology 94:502–34.

Marx, Gary T. (ed.). 1971. Racial Conflict. Boston: Little, Brown.

Marx, Karl, and Engels, Friedrich. 1965. "The Communist Manifesto." In Arthur Mendel (ed.), Essential Works of Marxism. New York: Bantam Books. (Originally published 1848.)

Masatsugu, Mitsuyuki. 1982. The Modern Samurai Society: Duty and Dependence in Contemporary Japan. New York: American Management Association.

Massey, Douglas, and Denton, Nancy. 1988. "Suburbanization and Segregation in U.S. Metropolitan Areas." American Journal of Sociology 94:592–626.

Massey, Douglas S., and Bitterman, Brooks. 1985. "Explaining the Paradox of Puerto Rican Segregation." Social Forces 64 (December): 306–31.

Massey, Douglas S., and Mullan, Brendan P. 1984. "Processes of Hispanic and Black Spatial Assimilation." American Journal of Sociology 89 (January): 836–73.

Matsueda, Ross, and Heimer, Karen. 1987. "Race, Family Structure, and Delinquency: A Test of Differential Association and Social Control Theories." American Sociological Review 52:826–40.

Mead, George Herbert. 1934. Mind, Self, and Society: From the Standpoint of a Social Behaviorist. (Charles W. Morris, ed.) Chicago: University of Chicago Press.

Medley, Morris. 1976. "Satisfaction with Life Among Persons Sixty-Five Years and Older." Journal of Gerontology 32 (July): 448–55.

Merton, Robert. 1949. "Discrimination and the American Creed." In Robert MacIver (ed.), Discrimination and National Welfare. New York: Harper & Row.

Merton, Robert. 1957. Social Theory and Social Structure. (2nd ed.) New York: Free Press.

Messenger, John C. 1969. Inis Beag: Isle of Ireland. New York: Holt, Rinehart & Winston.

Messner, Steven F. 1989. "Economic Discrimination and Societal Homicide Rates: Further Evidence on the Cost of Inequality." American Sociological Review 54:597–611.

"Mexico's Population: A Profile." 1987. Population Education Interchange 16 (May): 1–4.

Michels, R. 1962. Political Parties. New York: Free Press.

Michener, H. Andrew, DeLamater, John D., and Schwartz, Shalom H. 1986. Social Psychology. San Diego, Calif.: Harcourt Brace Jovanovich.

Miles, Ian, Rush, Howard, Turner, Kevin, and Bessant,

John. 1988. Information Horizons: The Long-Term Social Implications of New Information Technologies. Aldershot, England: Elgar.

Milgram, Stanley. 1970. "The Experience of Living in Cities." Science 167 (March): 461–68.

Miller, Karen, Kohn, Melvin, and Schooler, Carmi. 1986. "Educational Self-direction and Personality." American Sociological Review 51:372–90.

Miller, Karen A., Kohn, Melvin L., and Schooler, Carmi. 1985. "Educational Self-Direction and the Cognitive Functioning of Students." Social Forces 63 (June): 923–44.

Mills, C. Wright. 1940. "Situated Actions and Vocabularies of Motives." American Sociological Review 5:904–13.

Mills, C. Wright. 1956. The Power Elite. New York: Oxford University Press.

Mills, C. Wright. 1959. The Sociological Imagination. Oxford, England: Oxford University Press.

Mizrahi, Terry. 1986. Getting Rid of Patients: Contradictions in the Socialization of Physicians. New Brunswick, N.J.: Rutgers University Press.

Mizruchi, Mark. 1989. "Similarity of Political Behavior Among Large American Corporations." American Journal of Sociology 95:401–24.

Moen, Phyllis, Dempster-McClain, Donna, and Williams, Robin. 1989. "Social Integration and Longevity: An Event-History Analysis of Women's Roles and Resilience." American Sociological Review 54:635–47.

Molotch, Harvy. 1979. "Media and Movements." In M. Zald and J. McCarthy (eds.), The Dynamics of Social Movements. Cambridge, Mass.: Winthrop.

Moore, Charles, and Hoban-Moore, Patricia. 1990. "Some Lessons from Reagan's HUD: Housing Policy and Public Service." Political Science and Politics 23 (March): 13–17.

Moore, Helen A., and Whitt, Hugh P. 1986. "Multiple Dimensions of the Moral Majority Platform: Shifting Interest Group Coalitions." The Sociological Quarterly 27 (3): 423–39.

Moorman, Jeanne, and Hernandez, Donald. 1989. "Married-Couple Families with Step-, Adopted, and Biological Children." Demography 26:267–77.

Mortimer, Jeyland T. 1979. Changing Attitudes Toward Work. Scarsdale, N.Y.: Work in America Institute.

Mortimer, Jeyland T., and Simmons, R. G. 1978. "Adult Socialization." Annual Review of Sociology 4:421–54.

Mott, Frank, and Mott, Susan. 1980. "Kenya's Record Population Growth: A Dilemma of Development." Population Bulletin 35 (3): 1–45.

Mottl, Tahi L. 1980. "The Analysis of Countermovements." Social Problems 27 (June): 620–35.

Mukerji, Chandra, and Schudson, Michael. 1986. "Popular Culture." Annual Review of Sociology 12:47–66.

Muller, Edward. 1988. "Democracy, Economic Development, and Income Inequality." American Sociological Review 53:50–68.

Munch, Richard, and Smelser, Neil J. 1987. "Relating the Micro and Macro." In J. Alexander, B. Giesen, R. Munch, and N. Smelser (eds.), The Micro-Macro Link. Berkeley: University of California Press.

Murdock, George Peter. 1949. Social Structure. New York: Free Press.

Murdock, George Peter. 1957. "World Ethnographic Sample." American Anthropologist 59 (August): 664–97.

Mushane, Michael, Palumbo, Dennis, Maynard-Moody, Steven, and Levine, James. 1989. "Community Correctional Innovation: What Works and Why?" Journal of Research on Crime and Delinquency 26: 136–67.

Mutran, Elizabeth, and Reitzes, Donald C. 1984. "Intergenerational Support Activities and Well-Being Among the Elderly: A Convergence of Exchange and Symbolic Interaction Perspectives." American Sociological Review 49 (February): 117–30.

Myrdal, Gunnar. 1962. Challenge to Affluence. New York: Random House.

Nakanishi, Don. 1989. "A Quota on Excellence?" Change, November–December. pp. 38–47.

Naoi, Atsushi, and Schooler, Carmi. 1986. "Occupational Conditions and Psychological Functioning in Japan." American Journal of Sociology 90 (4): 729–52.

Nasaw, David. 1985. Children of the City: At Work and At Play. New York: Oxford University Press.

Nathanson, C. A. 1984. "Sex Differences in Mortality." Annual Review of Sociology 10:191–213.

National Advisory Commission on Civil Disorder. 1968. Report of the National Advisory Commission on Civil Disorders. New York: Bantam Books.

Navarro, Vicente. 1986. Crisis, Health, and Medicine. New York: Tavistock.

Navarro, Vicente. 1989. "Why Some Countries Have National Health Insurance, Others Have National Health Service, and the U.S. Has Neither." Social Science and Medicine 28:887–98.

Nee, Viktor. 1989. "A Theory of Market Transition: From Redistribution to Markets in State Socialism." American Sociological Review 54:663–81.

Neidert, Lisa. J., and Farley, Reynolds. 1985. "Assimilation in the United States: An Analysis of Ethnic and Generation Differences in Status and Achievement." American Sociological Review 50 (December): 840–50.

Nemeth, Charlan J. 1985. "Dissent, Group Process, and Creativity: The Contribution of Minority Influence." Advances in Group Processes 2:57–75.

Neugarten, Bernice. 1968. "The Awareness of Middle Age." In Bernice Neugarten (ed.), Middle Age and Aging. Chicago: University of Chicago Press.

Neugarten, Bernice L., and Neugarten, Dail A. 1986. "Changing Meanings of Age in the Aging Society." In Alan Pifer and Lydia Bronte (eds.), Our Aging Society: Paradox and Promise. New York: Norton.

Neuhauser, Kevin. 1989. "The Radicalization of the Brazilian Catholic Church in Comparative Perspective." American Sociological Review 54:233–44.

Neustadtl, Alan, and Clawson, Dan. 1988. "Corporate Political Groupings: Does Ideology Unify Business Political Behavior?" American Sociological Review 53:172–90.

Niebuhr, H. Richard. 1957. The Social Sources of Denominationalism. New York: Holt, Rinehart & Winston. (Originally published 1929.)

Nielsen, Frances. 1985. "Toward a Theory of Ethnic Solidarity in Modern Societies." American Sociological Review 50 (April): 133–49.

"1989 AIDS." 1989. Newsweek, July 3, p. 57.

Norman, Jane, and Harris, Myron. 1981. The Private Life of the American Teenager. New York: Rawson, Wade.

"Now It's Bush's War." 1989. Newsweek, September 18, p. 22.

"Now, Legal Immigration Reform?" 1988. Population Today 6 (September): 3.

Noyes, John Humphrey. 1961. History of American Socialism. New York: Hillary House. (Originally published 1869.)

Oakes, Jeannie. 1985. Keeping Track: How Schools Structure Inequality. New Haven: Yale University Press.

Oberschall, A. 1973. Social Conflict and Social Movements. Englewood Cliffs, N.J.: Prentice-Hall.

Oberschall, Anthony, and Leifer, Eric J. 1986. "Efficiency and Social Institutions: Uses and Misuses of Economic Reasoning in Sociology." Annual Review of Sociology 12:233–53.

"Observing." 1990. Footnotes 18 (January): 1 ff.

O'Dea, Thomas F. 1966. The Sociology of Religion. Englewood Cliffs, N.J.: Prentice-Hall.

O'Hare, William. 1989. "Hispanic Americans in the 1980s." Population Today 17 (July–August): 6–8.

Olesen, Virginia, Schatzman, Nellie, Hatton, Diane, and Chico, Nan. 1990. "The Mundane Ailment and the Physical Self." Social Science and Medicine 30:449–55.

Oliver, Pamela, and Marwell, Gerald. 1988. "The Paradox of Group Size in Collective Action: A Theory of the Critical Mass II." American Sociological Review 53:1–8.

Olzak, Susan. 1989. "Analysis of Events in the Study of Collective Action." Annual Review of Sociology 15:119–41.

Omram, Abdul. 1977. "Epidemiological Transition in the U.S." Population Bulletin 32 (2): 1–45.

Oppenheimer, Martin. 1985. White-Collar Politics. New York: Monthly Review Press.

"Oregon's Not-So-Sweet Home." 1989. Newsweek, December 12, p. 55.

Orum, Anthony. 1987. "In Defense of Domhoff: A Comment on Manning's Review of Who Rules America Now." American Journal of Sociology 92 (January): 975–77.

Osgood, D. Wayne, and Wilson, Janet. 1989. "Role Transitions and Mundane Activities in Late Adolescence and Early Adulthood." Paper read at the 1989 meetings of the Midwest Sociological Society, St. Louis.

Ost, John, and Antweiler, Phillip. 1986. "The Social Impact of High-Cost Medical Technology: Issues and Conflicts Surrounding the Decision to Adopt CAT Scanners." Research in the Sociology of Health Care 4:33–92.

Ouchi, William G., and Wilkins, Alan L. 1985. "Organizational Culture." Annual Review of Sociology 11:457–83.

Palen, J. John, and London, Bruce (eds.). 1984. Gentrification, Displacement, and Neighborhood Revitalization. Albany: State University of New York Press.

Pampel, Fred C., and Williamson, John B. 1985. "Age Structure, Politics, and Cross-National Patterns of Public Pension Expenditures." American Sociological Review 50 (December): 782–99.

Parelius, Robert, and Parelius, Ann. 1987. The Sociology of Education. (2nd ed.) Englewood Cliffs: Prentice-Hall.

Parsons, Talcott. 1951. The Social System. New York: Free Press.

Parsons, Talcott. 1964. "The School Class as a Social System: Some of Its Functions in American Society." In Talcott Parsons (ed.), Social Structure and Personality. New York: Free Press.

Paternoster, Raymond. 1989. "Absolute and Restrictive Deterrence in a Panel of Youth: Explaining the Onset, Persistence/Desistance, and Frequency of Delinquent Offending." Social Problems 36:289–309.

Paul, R. E. 1989. "Is the Emperor Naked? Some Questions on the Adequacy of Sociological Theory in Urban and Regional Research." International Journal of Urban and Regional Research 13:709–20.

Pearlin, Lenard I. 1982. "Discontinuities in the Study of Aging." In Tamara K. Hareven and Kathleen J. Adams (eds.), Aging and Life Course Transition: An Interdisciplinary Perspective. New York: Guilford Press.

Pebley, Anne R., and Westoff, Charles F. 1982. "Women's Sex Preferences in the United States: 1970 to 1975." Demography 19 (2): 177–90.

Perrow, Charles. 1986. Complex Organizations: A Critical Essay. (3rd ed.) New York: Random House.

Peterson, Richard. 1989. "Firm Size, Occupational Segregation, and the Effects of Family Status on Women's Wages." Social Forces 68:397–414.

Peterson, Ruth. 1988. "Youthful Offender Designations and Sentencing in the New York Criminal Courts." Social Problems 35:111–30.

Peterson, William. 1978. "Chinese Americans and Japanese Americans." In Thomas Sowell (ed.), American Ethnic Groups. Washington, D.C.: Urban Institute.

Petersen, William. 1988. "Politics and the Measurement of Ethnicity." In William Alonso and Paul Starr (eds.), The Politics of Numbers. New York: Russell Sage Foundation.

Pettigrew, Thomas F. 1982. "Prejudice." In Thomas F. Pettigrew, George M. Fredrickson, Dale T. Knobel, Nathan Glazer, and Reed Ueda (eds.), Prejudice: Dimensions of Ethnicity. Cambridge, Mass.: Harvard University Press.

Pettigrew, Thomas F. 1985. "New Black-White Patterns: How Best to Conceptualize Them?" Annual Review of Sociology 11:329–46.

Phares, Ross. 1964. Bible in Pocket, Gun in Hand. Lincoln: University of Nebraska Press.

Phillips, David P. 1983. "The Impact of Mass Media Violence on U.S. Homocides." American Sociological Review 48 (August): 560–68.

Phillips, David P., and Bollen, Kenneth A. 1985. "Same Time, Last Year: Selective Data Dredging for Negative Findings." American Sociological Review 50 (June): 364–71.

Piliavin, Irving, Gartner, Rosemary, Thornton, Craig, and Matsueda, Ross. 1986. "Crime, Deterrence, and Rational Choice." American Sociological Review 51:101–19.

Pitts, Jesse R. 1964. "The Structural-Functional Approach." In Harold T. Christensen (ed.), Handbook of Marriage and the Family. Skokie, Ill.: Rand McNally.

Podolsky, Doug. 1986–1987. "NIAAA Minority Research Activities." Alcohol Health and Research World 11 (2): 4–7.

Pollock, Philip H., III. 1982. "Organizations and Alienation: The Mediation Hypothesis Revisited." The Sociological Quarterly 23 (Spring): 143–55.

"Population Growth to Create New Array of LDC Mega-Cities." 1985. Population Today 13 (June): 3.

Population Reference Bureau. 1990. World Population Data Sheet. Washington, D.C.: Population Reference Bureau.

Porter, Paul, and Sweet, David. 1984. Rebuilding American's Cities: Roads to Recovery. New Brunswick, N.J.: Center for Urban Policy Research.

Portes, Alejandro, and Sassen-Koob, Saskia. 1987. "Making It Underground: Comparative Material on the Informal Sector in Western Market Economies." American Journal of Sociology 93:30–61.

Portes, Alejandro, and Truelove, Cynthia. 1987. "Making Sense of Diversity: Recent Research on Hispanic Minorities in the United States." Annual Review of Sociology 13:359–85.

Poston, Dudley, and Gu, Baochang. 1987. "Socioeconomic Development, Family Planning, and Fertility in China." Demography 24:531–51.

Pratt, William. 1984. "Understanding U.S. Fertility: Findings from the National Survey of Family Growth Cycle III." Population Bulletin 39 (1): 1–50.

Presser, Harriet. 1988. "Shift Work and Child Care Among Young Dual-Earner American Parents." Journal of Marriage and the Family 50:133–48.

Presser, Harriet. 1989. "Can We Make Time for Children?" Demography 26:523–43.

Preston, Samuel H. 1976. Mortality Patterns in National Populations with Special Reference to Recorded Causes of Death. Orlando, Fla.: Academic Press.

Preston, Samuel H. 1984. "Children and the Elderly: Divergent Paths for America's Dependents." Demography 21 (November): 435–58.

Provence, Sally, and Lipton, Rose. 1962. Infants in Institutions: A Comparison of Their Development with Family-Reared Infants During the First Year of Life. New York: International Universities Press.

Przeworski, Adam. 1985. Capitalism and Social Democracy. Cambridge, England: Cambridge University Press.

Public Opinion. 1986a. Vol. 9, no. 1.

Public Opinion. 1986b. Vol. 9, no. 6.

Public Opinion. 1989a. March–April, p. 21.

Public Opinion. 1989b. May–June, p. 33.

Quadagno, Jill. 1990. "Race, Class, and Gender in the U.S. Welfare State: Nixon's Failed Family Assistance Plan." American Sociological Review 55:11–28.

"Quebec Encouraging Births with New Baby Bonuses." 1988. Population Today 16 (July–August): 8.

Quinn, Naomi. 1977. "Anthropological Studies of Women's Status." Annual Review of Anthropology 6:181–225.

Quinney, Richard. 1980. Class, State, and Crime. (2nd ed.) New York: Longman.

Rawlings, Stephen. 1978. "Perspectives on American Husbands and Wives." Current Population Reports, Special Studies Series P-23 No. 77. U.S. Department of Commerce, Bureau of the Census. Washington, D.C.: U.S. Government Printing Office.

Razzell, P. 1974. "An Interpretation of the Modern Rise of Population in Europe: A Critique." Population Studies 28 (March): 5–15.

Reichman, Nancy. 1989. "Breaking Confidences: Organizational Influences on Insider Trading." Sociological Quarterly 30:185–204.

Reid, Robert. 1986. Land of Lost Content: The Luddite Revolt, 1812. London: Heinemann.

Reiss, Ira L. 1980. Family Systems in America. (3rd ed.) New York: Holt, Rinehart & Winston.

Reiterman, Tim. 1982. Raven: The Untold Story of the Rev. Jim Jones and His People. New York: Dutton.

Renner, Craig, and Navarto, Vicente. 1989. "Why Is Our Population of Uninsured and Underinsured Persons Growing? The Consequences of the Deindustrialization of America." Annual Review of Public Health 10:85–94.

Repetto, Robert. 1987. "Population, Resources, Environment: An Uncertain Future." Population Bulletin 42 (2): 1–50.

Reskin, Barbara. 1989. "Women Taking 'Male' Jobs Because Men Leave Them." IlliniWeek, July 20, p. 7.

Reskin, Barbara, and Hartmann, Heidi (eds.). 1986. Women's Work, Men's Work: Sex Segregation on the Job. Washington, D.C.: National Academy Press.

Retherford, R. D. 1975. The Changing Sex Differential in Mortality. Westport/London: Greenwood.

Rich, Robert. 1977. The Sociology of Law. Washington, D.C.: University Press of America.

Richardson, James T. 1988. "Changing Times: Religion, Economics, and the Law in Contemporary America." Sociological Analysis 49 (S): 1–14.

Richardson, John G. 1980. "Variation in Date of Enactment of Compulsory School Attendance Laws." Sociology of Education 53:153–63.

Ridgeway, Cecilia L., Berger, Joseph, and Smith, LeRoy. 1985. "Nonverbal Cues and Status: An Expectation States Approach." American Journal of Sociology 90 (March): 955–78.

Riedmann, Agnes. 1987. "Ex-Wife at the Funeral: Keyed Antistructure." Free Inquiry in Sociology 16: 123–29.

"The Rise of Black Mayors." 1989. Parade Magazine, December, Robbins, Thomas. 1986. "Review." Sociological Analysis 47:83–4.

Robertson, Roland. 1970. The Sociological Interpretation of Religion. Oxford, England: Blackwell.

Robinson, J. Gregg, and McIlwee, Judith. 1989. "Women in Engineering: A Promise Unfulfilled." Social Problems 36:455–72.

Rogers, Everett M. 1960. Social Change in Rural Society: A Textbook in Rural Sociology. East Norwalk, Conn.: Appleton-Century-Crofts.

Ronan, Laura, and Reichman, Walter. 1987. "Back to Work." Alcohol Health and Research World 11:34.

Roof, Wade Clark. 1989. "Multiple Religious Switching: A Research Note." Journal for the Scientific Study of Religion 28:530–35.

Roof, Wade Clark, and Hoge, Dean R. 1980. "Church Involvement in America: Social Factors Affecting Membership and Participation." Review of Religious Research 21 (4): 405–26.

Rook, Karen S., and Dooley, David. 1985. "Applying Social Support Research: Theoretical Problems and Future Directions." Journal of Social Issues 41 (1): 5–28.

Rose, Peter. 1981. They and We: Racial and Ethnic Relations in the United States. (3rd ed.) New York: Random House.

Rosecrance, John. 1985. "Compulsive Gambling and the Medicalization of Deviance." Social Problems 32 (February): 273–84.

Rosenbaum, James, and Kariya, Takehiko. 1989. "From High School to Work: Market and Institutional Mechanisms in Japan." American Journal of Sociology 94:1334–65.

Rosenberg, Morris. 1965. Society and the Adolescent Self-Image: Princeton, N.J.: Princeton University Press.

Rosenberg, Morris, 1979. Conceiving the Self. New York: Basic Books.

Rosenberg, Morris, Schooler, Carmi, and Schoenbach, Carrie. 1989. "Self-Esteem and Adolescent Problems: Modeling Reciprocal Effects." American Sociological Review 54:1004–18.

Rosenthal. A. M. 1964. Thirty-Eight Witnesses. New York: McGraw-Hill.

Rosenthal, Carolyn J. 1985. "Kinkeeping in the Familial Division of Labor." Journal of Marriage and the Family 47 (Nov.): 965–74.

Roscow, Irving. 1974. Socialization to Old Age. Berkeley: University of California Press.

Rosset, Peter, and Vandermeer, John (eds.). 1986. Nicaragua: Unfinished Revolution. New York: Grove Press.

Rossi, Alice. 1984. "Gender and Parenthood." American Sociological Review 49 (February): 1–19.

Rothschild, Joyce. 1986. "Alternatives to Bureaucracy: Democratic Participation in the Economy." Annual Review of Sociology 12:307–28.

Rothschild-Whitt, Joyce. 1979. "The Collectivistic Organization: An Alternative to Rational Bureaucratic Models." American Sociological Review 44 (4): 509–27.

Roy, William, and Bonacich, Philip. 1988. "Interlocking Directorates and Communities of Interest Among American Railroad Companies, 1905." American Sociological Review 53:368–79.

Roy, William G. 1984. "Class Conflict and Social Change in Historical Perspective." Annual Review of Sociology 10:483–506.

Rubel, Maxmilien. 1968. "Karl Marx." In David Sills (ed.), International Encyclopedia of the Social Sciences. Vol. 10. New York: Macmillan and Free Press.

Rule, James, and Attewell, Paul. 1989. "What Do Computers Do?" Social Problems 36:225–41.

Rutter, D. R., and Quine, Lyn. 1990. "Inequalities in Pregnancy Outcome: A Review of Psychosocial and Behavioral Mediators." Social Science and Medicine 30:553–68.

Ryan, William. 1981. Equality. New York: Pantheon Books.

Saigo, Roy. 1989. "The Barriers of Racism." Change, November–December, pp. 8, 10, 69.

Sampson, Robert. 1987. "Urban Black Violence: The Effect of Male Joblessness and Family Disruption." American Journal of Sociology 93:348–82.

Sampson, Robert. 1988. "Local Friendship Ties and Community Attachment in Mass Society: A Multilevel Systemic Model." American Sociological Review 53:766–79.

Sampson, Robert, and Groves, W. Byron. 1989. "Community Structure and Crime: Testing Social-Disorganization Theory." American Journal of Sociology 94:774–802.

Sandefur, Gary D., and Sakamoto, Arthur. 1988. "American Indian Household Structure and Income." Demography 25:71–80.

San Miguel, Guadalupe, Jr. 1987. Let Them All Take Heed. Austin: University of Texas Press.

Sapiro, Virginia. 1986. Women in American Society. Palo Alto, Calif.: Mayfield.

Saraceno, Chiara. 1984. "The Social Construction of Childhood: Child Care and Education Policies in Italy and the United States." Social Problems 3 (February): 351–63.

Sarkitov, Nikolay. 1987. "From 'Hard Rock' to 'Heavy Metal':

The Stupefaction Effect." Sotsiologicheskie-Issledovaniya. 14 (July–August): 93–4.

Sassen, Saskia. 1988. The Mobility of Capital and Labor: A Study in International Investment and Labor Flow. Cambridge, England: Cambridge University Press.

Scanzoni, John. 1989. "Alternative Images for Public Policy: Family Structure Versus Families Struggling." Policy Studies Review 8:610–21.

Scheff, Thomas J. 1988. "Shame and Conformity: The Deference-Emotion System." American Sociological Review 53:395–406.

Schervish, Paul. 1983. The Structural Determinants of Unemployment: Vulnerability and Power in Market Relations. Orlando, Fla.: Academic Press.

Schill, Michael H., and Nathan, Richard P. 1983. Revitalizing America's Cities: Neighborhood Reinvestment and Displacement. Albany: State University of New York Press.

Schlafly, Phyllis. 1977. The Power of the Positive Woman. New Rochelle, N.Y.: Arlington House.

Schlesinger, Arthur, Jr. 1965. A Thousand Days. Boston: Houghton Mifflin.

Schneider, David J. 1981. "Tactical Self-Presentations: Toward a Broader Conceptualization." In J. T. Tedeschi (ed.), Impression Management Theory and Social Psychological Research. Orlando, Fla.: Academic Press.

Schoen, Robert, and Kluegel, James. 1988. "The Widening Gap in Black and White Marriage Rates." American Sociological Review 53:895–907.

Schuman, Howard, and Scott, Jacqueline. 1989. "Generations and Collective Memories." American Sociological Review 54:359–81.

Schur, Edwin M. 1979. Interpreting Deviance: A Sociological Introduction. New York: Harper & Row.

Schwartz, Barry. 1983. "George Washington and the Whig Conception of Heroic Leadership." American Sociological Review 48 (February): 18–33.

Schwartz, Shalom H., and Gottlieb, Avi. 1980. "Bystander Anonymity and Reaction to Emergencies." Journal of Personality and Social Psychology 39 (3): 418–40.

Scott, Marvin B., and Lyman, Stanford M. 1968. "Accounts." American Sociological Review 33 (December): 46–62.

Seaman, Barbara. 1972. Free and Female. New York: Fawcett.

Seligman, Clive. 1989. "Environmental Ethics." Journal of Social Issues 45: 169–84.

Selik, Richard, Castro, Kenneth, and Pappaioanou, Marguerite. 1988. "Distribution of AIDS Cases by Racial/Ethnic Group and Exposure Category, United States, June 1, 1981–July 4, 1988." Morbidity and Mortality Weekly Report 37 (July): 1–10.

Serpe, Richard. 1987. "Stability and Change in Self: A Structural Symbolic Interactionist Explanation." Social Psychology Quarterly 50 (1): 44–55.

Shafer, John. 1989. "Theories of Alcohol Abuse: What Do Native Americans Think?" Unpublished manuscript, Department of Sociology, University of Nebraska–Lincoln.

Shalin, Dmitri, 1986. "Pragmatism and Social Interaction." American Sociological Review 51 (February): 9–29.

Shamir, Boas. 1986. "Self-Esteem and the Psychological Impact of Unemployment." Social Psychology Quarterly 49 (1): 61–72.

Shavit, Yossi. 1984. "Tracking and Ethnicity in Israeli Secondary Education." American Sociological Review 49 (April): 210–20.

Shepard, William. 1985. To Secure the Blessings of Liberty. Chico, Calif.: Scholars Press and Crossroads.

Sherif, Muzafer. 1936. The Psychology of Social Norms. New York: Harper & Row.

Shkilnyk, Anastasia M. 1985. A Poison Stronger Than Love: The Destruction of an Ojibwa Community. New Haven: Yale University Press.

Shupe, Anson, and Stacy, William A. 1982. Born-Again Politics and the Moral Majority: What Social Surveys Really Show. New York: Mellen Press.

Sidel, Ruth, and Sidel, Victor. 1984. "Health Care from Liberation to the Cultural Revolution." In Molly Joel Coye, John Livingston, and Jean Highland (eds.), China: Yesterday and Today. New York: Bantam Books.

Silvestri, George, and Lukosiewicz, John. 1989. "Projections of Occupational Employment 1988–2000." Monthly Labor Review 122 (November): 42–66.

Simmel, Georg. 1950. The Sociology of Georg Simmel. (Kurt Wolff, ed. and trans.) New York: Free Press. (Originally published 1908.)

Simmel, Georg. 1955. Conflict. (Kurt H. Wolf, trans.) New York: Free Press.

Simmons, Roberta, Bureson, R., Carlton-Ford, S., and Blyth, D. 1987. "The Impact of Cumulative Change in Early Adolescence." Child Development 58:1220–34.

Simon, Rita, and Landis, Jean. 1989. "Poll Report: A Woman's Place and Role." Public Opinion Quarterly 53:265–76.

Simons, Ronald, and Gray, Phyllis. 1989. "Perceived Blocked Opportunity as an Explanation of Delinquency Among Lower-Class Black Males." Journal of Research on Crime and Delinquency 26:90–101.

Simpson, Richard L. 1985. "Social Control of Occupations and Work." Annual Review of Sociology 11:415–36.

Sjoberg, Gideon. 1960. The Preindustrial City. New York: Free Press.

Sloan, Irving. 1981. Youth and the Law. Dobbs Ferry, N.Y.: Oceana.

Smith, Douglas. 1987. "Police Response to Interpersonal Violence: Defining the Parameters of Legal Control." Social Forces 65 (March): 767–82.

Smith, Douglas A., and Visher, Christy A. 1981. "Street-Level Justice: Situational Determinants of Police Arrest Decisions." Social Problems 29 (2): 167–77.

Smith, Kevin, and Stone, Lorence. 1989. "Rags, Riches, and Bootstraps." Sociological Quarterly 30: 93–107.

Smith-Lovin, Lynn, and Brady, Charles. 1989. "Interruptions in Group Discussions: The Effect of Gender and Group Composition." American Sociological Review 54:424–35.

Snow, David, Baker, Susan, and Anderson, Leon. 1988. "On the Precariousness of Measuring Insanity in Insane Contexts." Social Problems 35: 192–96.

Snow, David, Baker, Susan, Anderson, Leon, and Martin, Michael. 1986. "The Myth of Pervasive Mental Illness Among the Homeless." Social Problems 33: 407–23.

Snow, David A., and Anderson, Leon. 1987. "Identity Work Among the Homeless: The Verbal Construction and Avowal of Personal Identities." American Journal of Sociology 92 (May): 1336–71.

Snow, David A., Rochford, E. Burke, Jr., Worden, Steven K., and Benford, Robert D. 1986. "Frame Alignment Processes, Micromobilization, and Movement Participation." American Sociological Review 51 (August): 464–81.

Sokolovsky, Jay, and Cohen, Carl. 1981. "Being Old in the Inner City: Support Systems of the SRO Aged." In Christine Fry (ed.), Dimensions: Aging, Culture, and Health. New York: Praeger.

Soldo, Beth. 1981. "The Living Arrangements of the Elderly in the Near Future." In Sara B. Kiesler, James N. Morgan, and Valerie Kincade Oppenheimer (eds.), Aging, Social Change. Orlando, Fla.: Academic Press.

Sombart, Werner. 1974. "Why Is There No Socialism in the U.S.?" Excerpted in John Laslett and S. M. Lipset (eds.), Failure of a Dream: Essays in the History of American Socialism. New York: Doubleday Anchor Books. (Originally published 1906.)

Sone, Monica. 1953. Nisei Daughter. Boston: Little, Brown.

Sorokin, Pitirim, and Lundin, Walter. 1959. Power and Morality. Boston: Sargent.

Sowell, Thomas. 1981. Ethnic America: A History. New York: Basic Books.

Spalding, Rose J. (ed.). 1987. The Political Economy of Revolutionary Nicaragua. London: Allen & Unwin.

Spilka, Bernard, Shaver, Phillip, and Kirkpatrick, Lee A. 1985. "A General Attribution Theory for the Psychology of Religion." The Journal for the Scientific Study of Religion 24 (1): 1–20.

Spiro, Melford E. 1956. Kibbutz: Venture in Utopia. Cambridge, Mass.: Harvard University Press.

Spitz, René. 1945. "Hospitalism: An Inquiry into the Genesis of Psychiatric Conditions in Early Childhood." In Anna Freud, Heinz Hartman, and Ernst Kris (eds.), The Psychoanalytic Study of the Child. Vol 1. New York: International Universities Press.

Spitze, Glenna. 1986. "The Division of Task Responsibility in U.S. Households: Longitudinal Adjustments to Change." Social Forces 64 (March): 689–701.

Squires, Gregory, DeWolfe, Ruthanne, and DeWolfe, Alan. 1979. "Urban Decline or Disinvestment." Social Problems 27: 79–95.

Staggenborg, Susan. 1988. "The Consequences of Professionalization and Formalization in the Pro-Choice Movement." American Sociological Review 53:585–606.

Stark, Rodney, and Bainbridge, William S. 1985. The Future of Religion. Berkeley: University of California Press.

Stark, Rodney, and Bainbridge, William Sims. 1979. "Of Churches, Sects, and Cults: Preliminary Concepts for a Theory of Religious Movements." Journal for the Scientific Study of Religion 18 (2): 117–33.

Stark, Rodney, and Bainbridge, William Sims. 1981. "American-Born Sects: Initial Findings." Journal for the Scientific Study of Religion 20 (2): 130–49.

Stark, Rodney, and Finke, Roger. 1988. "American Religion in 1976: A Statistical Portrait." Sociological Analysis 49 (1): 39–51.

Starr, Paul. 1982. The Social Transformation of American Medicine. New York: Basic Books.

Stearn, Peter N. 1976 "The Evolution of Traditional Culture Toward Aging." In Jon Hendricks and C. Davis Hendricks (eds.), Dimensions of Aging: Readings. Cambridge, Mass.: Winthrop.

Steffensmeier, Darrel J., Allan, Emilie, Harer, Miles, and Streifel, Cathy. 1989. "Age and the Distribution of Crime." American Journal of Sociology 94:803–31.

Steinberg, L., Blinde, P. L., and Chan, K. S. 1984. "Dropping Out Among Language Minority Youth." Review of Educational Research 54:113–32.

Steinmetz, George, and Wright, Erik. 1989. "The Fall and Rise of the Petty Bourgeoisie." American Journal of Sociology 94:973–1018.

Stephens, John D. 1980. The Transition from Capitalism to Socialism. Atlantic Highlands. N.J.: Humanities Press.

Stokes, Randall, and Anderson, Andy. 1990. "Disarticulation and Human Welfare in Less Developed Countries." American Sociological Review 55:63–74.

Stokes, Randall, and Hewitt, John. P. 1976. "Aligning Actions." American Sociological Review 41:839–49.

Stolte, John F. 1983. "The Legitimation of Structural Inequality." American Sociological Review 48 (June): 331–42.

Stone, John. 1985. Racial Conflict in Contemporary Society. Cambridge, Mass.: Harvard University Press.

Strain, Charles R., and Goldberg, Steven. 1987. "Introduction: Modern Technology and the Humanities." In Steven Goldberg and Charles Strain (eds.), Technological Change and the Transformation of America. Carbondale: Southern Illinois University Press.

Straus, Murray, and Gelles, Richard. 1986. "Societal Change and Change in Family Violence from 1975 to 1985 as Revealed by Two National Surveys." Journal of Marriage and the Family 48:465–79.

Streib, Gordon. 1985. "Social Stratification and Aging." In Robert Binstock and Ethel Shanas (eds.), Handbook of Aging and the Social Sciences. (2nd ed.) New York: Van Nostrand Reinhold.

Stroebe, Margaret S., and Stroebe, Wolfgang. 1983. "Who Suffers More? Sex Differences in Health Risks of the Widowed." Psychological Bulletin 93:279–301.

Stryker, Sheldon. 1981. "Symbolic Interactionism: Themes and Variations." In Morris Rosenberg and Ralph H. Turner (eds.), Social Psychology: Sociological Perspectives. New York: Basic Books.

Summers, Gene. 1984. "Preface." Annals of the American Academy of Political and Social Science 475:9–14.

Suomi, S. J., Harlow, H. H., and McKinney, W. T. 1972. "Monkey Psychiatrists." American Journal of Psychiatry 128 (February): 927–32.

"Survey Report, Kenya." 1986. Population Today 14 (June): 5.

"Survey Report, Mexico." 1990. Population Today 18 (February): 5.

Sutherland, Edwin H. 1961. White-Collar Crime. New York: Holt, Rinehart & Winston.

Suzuki, Bob. 1989. "Asian Americans as the Model Minority." Change, November–December, pp. 12–20.

Swidler, Ann. 1986. "Culture in Action: Symbols and Strategies." American Sociological Review 51 (April): 273–86.

Switzer, Arlene. 1989. "Interview." Human Resources Management 188 (February 8): 20.

Tamir, Lois M. 1982. Men in Their Forties: The Transition to Middle Age. New York: Springer.

Tannenbaum, Frank. 1979. "The Survival of the Fittest." In George Modelski (ed.), Transnational Corporations and the World Order. New York: W. H. Freeman. (Originally published 1968.)

Tarrow, Sidney. 1988. "National Politics and Collective Action: Recent Theory and Research in Western Europe and the United States." Annual Review of Sociology 14:421–40.

Taylor, Robert. 1986. "Receipt of Support from Family Among Black Americans: Demographic and Familial Differences." Journal of Marriage and the Family 48:67–77.

Teachman, Jay. 1987. "Family Background, Educational Resources, and Educational Attainment." American Sociological Review 52:548–57.

Tedeschi, James T., and Riess, Marc. 1981. "Identities, the Phenomenal Self, and Laboratory Research." In J. T. Tedeschi (ed.), Impression Management Theory and Social Psychological Research. Orlando, Fla.: Academic Press.

Teitelbaum, Michael S. 1987. "The Fear of Population Decline." Population Today 15 (March) 6–8.

"There's Comfort in Loving." 1989. New York Times, April 22, p. 4.

Thoits, Peggy. 1986a. "Multiple Identities: Examining Gender and Marital Status Differences in Distress." American Sociological Review 51:259–72.

Thoits, Peggy. 1986b. "Self-Labeling Processes in Mental Illness: The Role of Emotional Deviance." American Journal of Sociology 91:221–49.

Thoits, Peggy. 1987. "Gender and Marital Status Differences in Control and Distress: Common Stress Versus Unique Stress Explanations." Journal of Health and Social Behavior 28:7–22.

Thomas, W. I., and Thomas, Dorothy. 1928. The Child in America: Behavior Problems and Programs. New York: Knopf.

Thomis, Malcolm I. 1970. The Luddites: Machine-Breaking in Regency England. Hamden, Conn.: Archon Books.

Thomlinson, Ralph. 1976. Population Dynamics: Causes and Consequences of World Demographic Change. (2nd ed.) New York: Random House.

Thompson, Anthony P. 1983. "Extramarital Sex: A Review of the Research Literature." Journal of Sex Research, February 1–21.

Thompson, Kevin. 1989. "Gender and Adolescent Drinking Problems: The Effects of Occupational Structure." Social Problems 36:30–47.

Thompson, Linda, and Walker, Alexis. 1989. "Gender in Families." Journal of Marriage and the Family 51:845–71.

Thornberry, Terence P., and Farnworth, Margaret. 1982. "Social Correlates of Criminal Involvement: Further Evidence on the Relationship Between Social Status and Criminal Behavior." American Sociological Review 47 (August): 505–18.

Thornton, Arland, Alwin, Duane, and Camburn, Donald. 1983. "Causes and Consequences of Sex-Role Attitudes and Attitude Change." American Sociological Review 48 (April): 211–27.

Tien, H. Yuan. 1989. "Second Thoughts on the Second Child." Population Today 17 (4): 6–8.

Tilly, Charles. 1978. From Mobilization to Revolution. Reading, Mass.: Addison-Wesley.

Tilly, Charles. 1979. "Repertoires of Contention in America and Britain, 1750–1830." In M. Zald and J. McCarthy (eds.), The Dynamics of Social Movements. Cambridge, Mass.: Winthrop.

Tittle, Charles R., Villemez, Wayne, and Smith, Douglas. 1978. "The Myth of Social Class and Criminality: An Empirical Assessment of the Empirical Evidence." American Sociological Review 43 (October): 643–56.

Tomeh, Aida K. 1973. "Formal Voluntary Organizations: Participation, Correlates, and Interrelationships." Sociological Inquiry 43 (3–4): 89–122.

Torres-Gil, Fernando. 1986. "Hispanics: A Special Challenge." In Alan Pifer and Lydia Bronte (eds.), Our Aging Society: Paradox and Promise. New York: Norton.

Treverton, Gregory. 1990. "The Defense Debate." Foreign Affairs 69 (1): 183–96.

"The Triumph of the Alkali Lake Indian Band." 1987. Alcohol Health and Research World 12 (1): 57.

Troeltsch, Ernst. 1931. The Social Teaching of the Christian Churches. New York: Macmillan.

"Trying to Take Back the Planet." 1990. Newsweek, February 5, pp. 24ff.

Tuchman, Barbara. 1978. A Distant Mirror: The Calamitous Fourteenth Century. New York: Knopf.

Tucker, M. Belinda, and Taylor, Robert. 1989. "Demographic Correlates of Relationship Status Among Black Americans." Journal of Marriage and the Family 51:655–65.

Turner, Jonathan, and Musick, David. 1985. American Dilemmas. New York: Columbia University Press.

Turner, Jonathan H. 1972. Patterns of Social Organization. New York: McGraw-Hill.

Turner, Jonathan H. 1982. The Structure of Sociological Theory. (3rd ed.) Homewood, Ill.: Dorsey Press.

Turner, Ralph, and Killian, Lewis. 1972. Collective Behavior. (2nd ed.) Englewood Cliffs, N.J.: Prentice-Hall.

Turner, Ralph H. 1964. "Collective Behavior." In R. E. L. Faris (ed.), Handbook of Modern Sociology. Skokie, Ill.: Rand-McNally.

Turner, Ralph H. 1985. "Unanswered Questions in the Convergence Between Structuralist and Interactionist Role Theories." In S. N. Eisenstadt and H. J. Helle (eds.), Microsociological Theory: Perspectives on Sociological Theory. Vol. 2. Newbury Park, Calif.: Sage.

"22 Percent of Mexico Moving North?" 1989. Population Today 17 (November): 4.

Udry, J. Richard. 1988. "Biological Predispositions and Social Control in Adolescent Sexual Behavior." American Sociological Review 53:709–22.

Uhlenberg, Peter. 1980. "Death and the Family." Journal of Family History 5:313–20.

Ulbrich, Patricia, Warheit, George, and Zimmerman, Rick. 1989. "Race, Socioeconomic Status, and Psychological Distress: An Examination of Differential Vulnerability." Journal of Health and Social Behavior 30:131–46.

Unger, Donald G., and Wandersman, Lois P. 1985. "Social Support and Adolescent Mothers: Action Research Contributions to Theory and Applications." Journal of Social Issues. 41 (1): 29–46.

United Nations. 1984. "Mortality and Health Policy." Population Studies, no. 91. New York: United Nations.

United Nations. 1988. 1986 Demographic Yearbook. New York: United Nations.

United Nations. 1989. 1987 Demographic Yearbook. New York: United Nations.

U.S. Bureau of the Census. 1986. "Fertility of American Women: June 1985." Current Population Reports, Series P-20, no. 406. Washington, D.C.: U.S. Government Printing Office.

U.S. Bureau of the Census. 1988. "Projections of the Population of the United States by Age, Sex, and Race: 1988 to 2080." Current Population Reports, Series P-25, no. 1018. Washington, D.C.: U.S. Government Printing Office.

U.S. Bureau of the Census. 1989a. Statistical Abstract of the United States: 1989. Washington, D.C.: U.S. Government Printing Office.

U.S. Bureau of the Census. 1989b. "The Black Population of the United States: March 1988." Current Population Reports, Series P-20, no. 442. Washington, D.C.: U.S. Government Printing Office.

U.S. Bureau of the Census. 1989c. "The Hispanic Population of the United States: March 1988." Current Population Reports, Series P-20, no. 438. Washington, D.C.: U.S. Government Printing Office.

U.S. Bureau of the Census. 1989d. "Household and Family Characteristics: March 1988." Current Population Reports, Series P-20, no. 437. Washington, D.C.: U.S. Government Printing Office.

U.S. Bureau of the Census. 1989e. "Marital Status and Living Arrangements: March 1988." Current Population Reports, Series P-20, no. 433. Washington, D.C.: U.S. Government Printing Office.

U.S. Bureau of the Census. 1989f. "Money Income of Households, Families, and Persons in the United States: 1987." Current Population Reports, Series P-60, no. 162. Washington, D.C.: U.S. Government Printing Office.

U.S. Bureau of the Census. 1989g. "Money Income and Poverty Status in the United States: 1988." Current Population Reports, Series P-60, no. 166. Washington, D.C.: U.S. Government Printing Office.

U.S. Bureau of the Census. 1989h. "Patterns of Metropolitan Area and County Population Growth: 1980 to 1987." Current Population Reports, Series P-25, no. 1039. Washington, D.C.: U.S. Government Printing Office.

U.S. Bureau of the Census. 1989i. "Population Profile of the United States: 1989." Current Population Reports, Series P-23, no. 159. Washington, D.C.: U.S. Government Printing Office.

U.S. Bureau of the Census. 1989j. "Fertility of American Women: June 1988." Current Population Reports, Series P-20, no. 436. Washington, D.C.: U.S. Government Printing Office.

U.S. Bureau of the Census. 1989k. "Voting and Registration in the Election of November 1988 (Advance Report)." Current Population Reports, Series P-20, no. 435. Washington, D.C.: U.S. Government Printing Office.

U.S. Centers for Disease Control. 1988. Morbidity and Mortality Weekly Report 37 (May 13).

U.S. Department of Education. 1985. The Condition of Education, 1985. Washington, D.C.: Government Printing Office.

U.S. Department of Education. 1989. "Projections of Education Statistics to 2000." Washington, D.C.: U.S. Government Printing Office.

U.S. Department of Health and Human Services. 1988. Vital Statistics of the United States 1986, Volume II—Mortality, Part A. Public Health Service, Washington, D.C.: U.S. Government Printing Office.

U.S. Department of Housing and Urban Development. 1977. Redlining and Disinvestment as Discriminatory Practices in Residential Mortgage Loans. Washington, D.C.: U.S. Government Printing Office.

U.S. Department of Justice. 1989a. Uniform Crime Reports, 1988. Bureau of Justice Statistics. Washington, D.C.: U.S. Government Printing Office.

U.S. Department of Justice. 1989b. "Prisoners in 1988." Bureau of Justice Statistics Bulletin. Washington, D.C.: Bureau of Justice Statistics.

U.S. Department of Justice. 1989c. Sourcebook of Criminal Justice Statistics: 1988. Bureau of Justice Statistics. Washington, D.C.: U.S. Government Printing Office.

U.S. Department of Labor. 1985. The Impact of Technology on Labor in Four Industries. Bulletin 2263. Washington, D.C.: U.S. Government Printing Office.

U.S. Department of Labor. 1986a. Employment Projections for 1995: Data and Methods. Bureau of Labor Statistics Bulletin 2253. Washington, D.C.: U.S. Government Printing Office.

U.S. Department of Labor. 1986b. The Impact of Technology on Labor in Four Industries. Bulletin 2263. Washington, D.C.: U.S. Government Printing Office.

U.S. Department of Labor. 1990. Employment and Earnings: March 1990. Washington, D.C.: U.S. Government Printing Office.

"U.S. Metro Areas on the March Again." 1986. Population Today 14 (January): 12.

U.S. National Center for Health Statistics. 1987. "Health Care Coverage by Sociodemographic and Health Characteristics, U.S.: 1984." Series 10, no. 162. Washington D.C.: U.S. Government Printing Office.

U.S. National Center for Health Statistics. 1988. "Current Estimates from the National Health Interview Survey, United States: 1987." Series 10, no. 166. Washington, D.C.: U.S. Government Printing Office.

"U.S. to Face Population Decline?" 1989. Population Today 17 (March): 3.

Unnever, James D., Frazier, Charles E., and Henretta, John C. 1980. "Race Differences in Criminal Sentencing." Sociological Quarterly 21 (Spring): 197–205.

Useem, Bert. 1980. "Solidarity Model, Breakdown Model, and the Boston Anti-Busing Movement." American Sociological Review 45 (June): 357–69.

Vago, Steven. 1989. Law and Society. (2nd ed.) Englewood Cliffs, N.J.: Prentice-Hall.

Valdivieso, Rafael, and Davis, Cary. 1988. "U.S. Hispanics: Challenging Issues for the 1990s." Population Reference Bureau, Population Trends and Public Policy no. 17, December, pp. 1–16.

Vallas, Steven P., and Yarrow, Michael. 1987. "Advanced Technology and Worker Alienation." Working and Occupations 14 (February): 126–42.

van de Walle, Etienne, and Knodel, John. 1980. "Europe's Fertility Transition." Population Bulletin 34 (6): 1–43.

van den Berghe, Pierre L. 1978. Man in Society. New York: Elsevier North-Holland.

van der Tak, Jean, Haub, Carl, and Murphy, Elaine. 1979. "Our Population Predicament: A New Look." Population Bulletin 34 (5): 1–49.

Vanfossen, Beth, Jones, James, and Spade, Joan. 1987. "Curriculum Tracking and Status Maintenance." Sociology of Education 60:104–22.

Vaughn, Brian, Gove, Frederick, and Egeland, Byron. 1980. "The Relationship Between Out-of-Home Care and the Quality of Infant-Mother Attachment in an Economically Disadvantaged Population." Child Development 51:1203–14.

Vedlitz, Arnold, and Johnson, Charles A. 1982. "Community Racial Segregation, Electoral Structure, and Minority Representation." Social Science Quarterly 63 (December): 729–36.

Verbrugge, Lois. 1989a. "Recent, Present, and Future Health of American Adults." Annual Review of Public Health 10:333–61.

Verbrugge, Lois. 1989b. "The Twain Meet: Empirical Explanations of Sex Differences in Health and Mortality. Journal of Health and Social Behavior 30:282–304.

Villemez, Wayne, and Bridges, William. 1988. "When Bigger Is Better: Differences in the Individual-Level Effect of Firm and Establishment Size." American Sociological Review 53:237–55.

Vogel, Ronald, and Swanson, Bert. 1989. "The Growth Machine Versus the Antigrowth Coalition: The Battle for Our Communities." Urban Affairs Quarterly 25:63–85.

Wagner, David G., Ford, Rebecca S., and Ford, Thomas W. 1986. "Can Gender Inequalities Be Reduced." American Sociological Review 51 (February): 47–61.

Waitzkin, Howard. 1983. The Second Sickness. New York: Free Press.

Waitzkin, Howard. 1989. "A Critical Theory of Medical Discourse: Ideology, Social Control, and the Processing of Social Context in Medical Encounters." Journal of Health and Social Behavior 30:220–39.

Wald, Kenneth D. 1987. Religion and Politics in the United States. New York: St. Martin's Press.

Walder, Andrew. 1989. "Social Change in Post-Revolution China." Annual Review of Sociology 15:405–24.

Waldinger, Roger. 1989. "Immigration and Urban Change." Annual Review of Sociology 15:211–32.

Waldron, Ingrid. 1983. "Sex Differences in Human Mortality: The Role of Genetic Factors." Social Science and Medicine 17 (6): 321–33.

Wallace, Walter. 1969. Sociological Theory. Hawthorne, N.Y.: Aldine.

Wallerstein, J., and Kelly, J. 1980. Surviving the Breakup. New York: Basic.

Walster, Elaine, Arenson, V., Abrahams, D., and Rottman, L. 1966. "Importance of Physical Attractiveness in Dating Behavior." Journal of Personality and Social Psychology 4 (November): 508–16.

Warr, Mark. 1985. "Fear of Rape Among Urban Women." Social Problems 32 (February): 238–50.

Weber, Max. 1954. Law in Economy and Society. (Max Rheinstein, ed.; Edward Shils and Max Reinstein, trans.) Cambridge, Mass.: Harvard University Press.

Weber, Max. 1958. The Protestant Ethic and the Spirit of Capitalism. (Talcott Parsons, trans.) New York: Scribner's. (Originally published 1904–5.)

Weber, Max. 1970a. "Bureaucracy." In H. H. Gerth and C. Wright Mills (trans.), From Max Weber: Essays in Sociology. New York: Oxford University Press. (Originally published 1910.)

Weber, Max. 1970b. "Class, Status, and Party." In H. H. Gerth and C. Wright Mills (trans.), From Max Weber: Essays in Sociology. New York: Oxford University Press. (Originally published 1910.)

Weber, Max. 1970c. "Religion." In H. H. Gerth and C. Wright Mills (trans.), From Max Weber: Essays in Sociology. New York: Oxford University Press. (Originally published 1922.)

Weber, Max. 1970e. "The Sociology of Charismatic Authority." In H. H. Gerth and C. Wright Mills (trans.), From Max Weber: Essays in Sociology. New York: Oxford University Press. (Originally published 1910.)

Wechsler, David. 1958. The Measurement and Appraisal of Adult Intelligence. (4th ed.) Baltimore, Md.: Williams & Wilkins.

Weibel-Orlando, Joan. 1986–1987. "Drinking Patterns of Urban and Rural American Indians." Alcohol Health and Research World 11 (2): 8–12,54.

Weil, Frederick. 1989. "The Sources and Structure of Legitimation in Western Democracies." American Sociological Review 54:682–706.

Weil, Frederick. 1985. "The Variable Effects of Education on Liberal Attitudes." American Sociological Review 50:458–74.

Weitz, Rose. 1989. "Uncertainty and the Lives of Persons with AIDS." Journal of Health and Social Behavior 30:270–81.

Weitzman, Lenore. 1985. The Divorce Revolution: The Unexpected Social and Economic Consequences for Women and Children in America. New York: Free Press.

"Weitzman's Research Plays Key Role in New Legislation." 1985. Footnotes 13 (8): 1, 9.

Welch, Charles, E., III, and Glick, Paul C. 1981. "The Incidence of Polygamy in Contemporary Africa: A Research Note." Journal of Marriage and the Family 43 (February): 191–4.

Welch, Susan, Gruhl, John, Steinman. Michael, and Comer, John. 1990. American Government. (3rd ed.) St. Paul, Minn.: West.

Wellman, Barry. 1979. "The Community Question: The Intimate Networks of East Yorkers." American Journal of Sociology 84 (March): 1201–31.

Wellman, Barry, and Berkowitz, S. D. (eds.). 1988. Social Structures: A Network Approach. New York: Cambridge University Press.

West, Candace. 1984. Routine Complications: Troubles with Talk Between Doctors and Patients. Bloomington: Indiana University Press.

Westoff, Charles. 1987. "Perspective on Nuptiality and Fertility." In Kingsley Davis, Mikhail Bernstam, and Rita Ricardo-Campbell (eds.), Below Replacement Fertility in Industrial Societies: Causes, Consequences, Policies. Cambridge, England: Cambridge University Press.

Wheelock, Jaime. 1986. "A Strategy for Development: The Agroindustrial Axis." In Peter Rosset and John Vandermeer (eds.), Nicaragua: Unfinished Revolution. New York: Grove Press.

"When Taxes Pay for Art." 1989. Newsweek, July 3, p. 68.

White, Lynn. 1990. "Determinants of Divorce: A Review of Research in the Eighties." Journal of Marriage and the Family 52 (November).

White, Lynn K., and Booth, Alan. 1985. "The Quality and Stability of Remarriage: The Role of Stepchildren." American Sociological Review 50 (October): 689–98.

White, Lynn, and Edwards, John. 1990. "Emptying the Nest and Parental Well-Being." American Sociological Review 55:235–42.

Whitt, J. Allen. 1979. "Toward a Class-Dialectical Model of Power." American Sociological Review 44 (February): 81–99.

Whitworth, John M. 1975. God's Blueprints: A Sociological Study of Three Utopian Sects. Boston: Routledge & Kegan Paul.

Whorf, Benjamin L. 1956. Language, Thought, and Reality. Cambridge, Mass.: MIT Press.

Wiesenfeld, A. R., and Weiss, H. M. 1979. "Hairdressers and Helping: Influencing the Behavior of Informal Caregivers." Professional Psychology 7:786–92.

Williams, Kirk, and Drake, Susan. 1980. "Social Structure, Crime, and Criminalization: An Empirical Examination of the Conflict Perspective." Sociological Quarterly 21 (Autumn): 563–75.

Williams, Kirk, and Flewelling, Robert. 1988. "The Social Production of Criminal Homicide: A Comparative Study of Disaggregated Rates in American Cities." American Sociological Review 53:421–31.

Williams, Robin M., Jr. 1970. American Society: A Sociological Interpretation. (3rd ed.) New York: Knopf.

Wilson, Edward O. 1978. "Introduction: What Is Sociobiology?" In Michael S. Gregory, Anita Silvers, and Diane Sutch (eds.), Sociobiology and Human Nature. San Francisco: Jossey-Bass.

Wilson, Thomas C. 1986. "Interregional Migration and Racial Attitudes." Social Forces 65 (September): 177–86.

Wilson, William J. 1978. The Declining Significance of Race. Chicago: University of Chicago Press.

Wilson, William J. 1987. The Truly Disadvantaged. Chicago: University of Chicago Press.

Wilson, William J. (ed.). 1988. The Ghetto Underclass. Annals 501.

Wimberly, Dale. 1990. "Investment Dependence and Alternative Explanations of Third World Mortality: A Cross-National Study." American Sociological Review 55:75–91.

Winkelstein, Warren, and Associates. 1988. "The San Francisco Men's Health Study: Continued Decline in HIV Seroconversion Rates Among Homosexual/Bisexual Men." American Journal of Public Health 78:1472–4.

Wirth, Louis. 1938. "Urbanism as a Way of Life." American Journal of Sociology 44 (1): 1–24.

Wojthiewicz, Roger, McLanahan, Sara, and Garfinkel, Irwin. 1990. "The Growth of Families Headed by Women: 1950–1980." Demography 27:19–30.

"Woman Loses Custody of Kids Because of Punishment, Cultism." 1990. Lincoln Star, February 1, pp. 1ff.

Woodrum, Eric, and Bell, Arnold. 1989. "Race, Politics, and Civil Religion Among Blacks." Sociological Analysis 49:353–67. Lerner, Robert, Rothman, Stanely, and Lichter, S. Robert. 1989.

"World Bank's Conable Voices Concern over Population Growth Effects." 1988. Population Today 16 (11): 4.

"The World's Poorest 370 Million People." 1989. Population Today 17 (April): 4.

Wright, Erik O. 1985. Classes. London: Verso.

Wright, Gavin. 1978. The Political Economy of the Cotton South. New York: Norton.

Wright, James. 1988a. "The Mentally Ill Homeless: What Is Myth and What Is Fact?" Social Problems 35:182–91.

Wright, James, and Lam, Julie. 1987. "Homelessness and the Low-Income Housing Supply." Social Policy 17:48–53.

Wright, James D. 1988b. "Second Thoughts About Gun Control." Public Interest 91 (Spring): 23–39.

Wrigley, E. A. 1969. Population in History. New York: McGraw-Hill.

Wrong, Dennis. 1961. "The Oversocialized Conception of Man in Modern Sociology." American Sociological Review 26 (April): 183–93.

Wrong, Dennis. 1979. Power. New York: Harper & Row.

Wuthnow, Robert. 1988. "Government Activity and Civil Privatism." Journal for the Scientific Study of Religion 27: 157–74.

Wuthnow, Robert, and Witten, Marsha. 1988. "New Directions in the Sociology of Culture." Annual Review of Sociology 8:49–67.

Wylie, Ruth. 1979. The Self-Concept: Theory and Research on Selected Topics. Vol. 2. (Rev. ed.) Lincoln: University of Nebraska Press.

Yankauer, Alfred. 1988. "AIDS and Public Health." American Journal of Public Health 78:364–5.

Yared, Roberta. 1989. "U.S. Black Life Expectancy Falls for Second Straight Year." Population Today 17 (1): 3–4.

Yinger, J. Milton. 1957. Religion, Society, and the Individual. New York: Macmillan.

Yinger, J. Milton. 1985. "Ethnicity." Annual Review of Sociology 11:151–80.

"York Woman Appeals Custody Ruling." 1990. Lincoln Star, February 1, p. 1, 4.

Young, Kimball. 1954. Isn't One Wife Enough? New York: Holt, Rinhart & Winston.

Zillman, D., and Bryant, J. 1982. "Pornography, Sexual Callousness and the Trivialization of Rape." Journal of Communication 32 (4): 10–21.

Zipp, John F., Landerman, Richard, and Luebke, Paul. 1982. "Political Parties and Political Participation: A Reexamination of the Standard Socioeconomic Model." Social Forces 60 (June): 1140–53.

Zurcher, Louis. 1983. Social Roles: Conformity, Conflict, and Creativity. Newbury Park, Calif.: Sage.

Zygmunt, Joseph E. 1986. "Collective Behavior as a Phase of Societal Life: Blumer's Emergent Views and Their Implications." Research in Social Movements, Conflicts, and Change 9:25–46.

Name Index

Subject Index

677